INTERACTIVE CASEBOOK SERIES[SM]

PROFESSIONAL RESPONSIBILITY

A Contemporary Approach

FOURTH EDITION

Renee Knake Jefferson

LARRY AND JOANNE DOHERTY CHAIR IN LEGAL ETHICS
PROFESSOR OF LAW, UNIVERSITY OF HOUSTON LAW CENTER

Russell G. Pearce

EDWARD & MARILYN BELLET CHAIR IN LEGAL ETHICS, MORALITY & RELIGION
PROFESSOR OF LAW, FORDHAM UNIVERSITY SCHOOL OF LAW

Bruce A. Green

LOUIS STEIN CHAIR, PROFESSOR OF LAW
FORDHAM UNIVERSITY SCHOOL OF LAW

Peter A. Joy

HENRY HITCHCOCK CHAIR IN LAW, PROFESSOR OF LAW
WASHINGTON UNIVERSITY SCHOOL OF LAW

Sung Hui Kim

PROFESSOR OF LAW
UNIVERSITY OF CALIFORNIA, LOS ANGELES

M. Ellen Murphy

ASSOCIATE DEAN, STRATEGIC INITIATIVES
PROFESSOR OF PRACTICE, WAKE FOREST UNIVERSITY SCHOOL OF LAW

Laurel S. Terry

H. LADDIE MONTAGUE JR. CHAIR IN LAW, PROFESSOR OF LAW
THE PENNSYLVANIA STATE UNIVERSITY, DICKINSON LAW

Lonnie T. Brown, Jr.

A. GUS CLEVELAND DISTINGUISHED CHAIR OF LEGAL ETHICS & PROFESSIONALISM,
JOSIAH MEIGS DISTINGUISHED TEACHING PROFESSOR
UNIVERSITY OF GEORGIA SCHOOL OF LAW

WEST
ACADEMIC
PUBLISHING

Interactive Casebook Series is a servicemark registered in the U.S. Patent and Trademark Office.

© 2011 Thomson Reuters
© 2014, 2017 LEG, Inc. d/b/a West Academic
© 2020 LEG, Inc. d/b/a West Academic
    444 Cedar Street, Suite 700
    St. Paul, MN 55101
    1-877-888-1330

Printed in the United States of America

ISBN: 978-1-64242-285-6

To Grace & James
R.K.J.

To Michele, Jacob & Seth
R.P.

To Nancy, Anna & Isaac
B.G.

To Rebecca
P.J.

To Jerry & Taera
S.H.K.

To The Whole Gang
E.M.

To Howard & Devon
L.S.T.

To Kim, Sophie & Olivia
L.T.B.

Preface to the Fourth Edition

We believe that Professional Responsibility is the most important course in law school. It teaches you the rules and laws you must follow when you practice law and provides a framework for exploring questions of role and professionalism that are central to finding meaning in your life as a lawyer.

To achieve these goals, we have written a Casebook that is comprehensive, challenging and engaging. It is both an innovative paper text and the foundation for a computer interactive pedagogy that features thought-provoking internet links.

The Casebook's features include:

- Coverage of the topics you will need to practice as an ethical lawyer and to pass the Multistate Professional Responsibility exam.

- In-depth examination of professionalism and the lawyer's role that will enable you to shape your own understanding of how to become an outstanding lawyer.

- Learning outcomes that explain the teaching goals for each Chapter.

- Problems presented in a multiple-choice format, and online self-assessment in CasebookPlus, that provide formative assessment opportunities for you consistent with ABA formative assessment requirements. You can find the answers to the problems, with explanations, on CasebookPlus™. Although you can sign in to CasebookPlus online separately, you will also find a "Test Your Knowledge" box at the end of each Chapter that will allow you to link to CasebookPlus for answers to the problems earlier in that Chapter.

- Thought-provoking internet features, including short audio lectures on difficult topics, as well as videos that illustrate and develop issues of ethics and professionalism.

- Global Perspectives Boxes that provide wide-ranging international and comparative coverage.

We owe a great debt to West and, in particular, to Editor-in-Chief Louis Higgins for his vision for the interactive casebook series, as well as his constant and unflagging confidence and encouragement. Thanks to the whole West team. We recognize that producing an interactive casebook requires more work and therefore want to give special thanks to Lead Publishing Specialist Laura Holle and editor Jon Harkness for their skill, wisdom, and hard work.

This book would not have been possible without the extraordinary contributions of the team of law students, law graduates, and others who helped us.

RENEE KNAKE JEFFERSON

RUSSELL G. PEARCE

BRUCE A. GREEN

PETER A. JOY

SUNG HUI KIM

M. ELLEN MURPHY

LAUREL S. TERRY

LONNIE T. BROWN, JR.

January 2020

A Note on Sources

When quoting the ethical rules that govern lawyer conduct, this casebook uses the word "Rule" to refer to rules from various jurisdictions that are substantially similar to those in the American Bar Association (ABA) Model Rules of Professional Conduct. Generally, we will refer to the Delaware Rules of Professional Conduct, unless they differ from the ABA Model Rules, in which case we cite to another jurisdiction's rule. In Chapter 7, we will also introduce the ABA Model Code of Judicial Conduct with digital hyperlinks to jurisdictions that have adopted substantially similar language. The language of official state rules governing the conduct of lawyers and judges is in the public domain.

Features of This Casebook

Throughout the book you will find various text boxes on either side of the page. These boxes provide information that will help you to understand a case or cause you to think more deeply about an issue.

 For More Information These boxes point you to resources to consult for more information on a subject.

 Food for Thought These boxes pose questions that prompt you to think about issues raised by the material.

 What's That? These boxes explain the meaning of special legal terms that appear in the main text.

 See It These boxes point you to visual information that is relevant to the material in the text.

 Take Note Here you will be prompted to take special notice of something that deserves further thought or attention.

 FYI A self-explanatory category that shares useful or simply interesting information relevant to material in the text.

 Practice Pointer Here you will find advice relevant to legal practice typically inspired by the actions (or inactions) of legal counsel in the cases or simply prompted by an important issue being discussed.

 Global Perspective Notes and material to help you understand the commonalities and differences of law and lawyering elsewhere in the world.

 It's Latin to Me The law is fond of Latin terms and phrases; when you encounter these for the first time, this box will explain their meaning.

 Go Online If there are relevant online resources that are worth consulting in relation to any matter being discussed, these boxes will direct you to them.

Hear from the Authors These boxes direct you to audio clips in which the authors expand on important legal concepts contained in the case or other related text.

 Test Your Knowledge These boxes contain hyperlinks to online assessment questions that will help you test your understanding of the material in each chapter.

 Make the Connection When concepts or discussions that pertain to information covered in other law school courses appear in a case or elsewhere in this text, often you will find this text box to indicate the course in which you can study those topics. Here you may also be prompted to connect information in the current case to material that you have covered elsewhere in this course.

Acknowledgments

We gratefully acknowledge receiving permission to reprint excerpts from the following materials:

Richard Abel, *Transnational Law Practice*, 44 Case W. Res. L. Rev. 737 (1994).

Azizah al-Hibri, *On Being a Muslim Corporate Lawyer*, 27 Tex. Tech. L. Rev. 946 (1996).

Joseph Allegretti, *Christ and the Code: The Dilemma of the Christian Attorney*, 34 Cath. Law. 131 (1991).

Larry Bodine, Writing your Personal Marketing Plan, L. Prac. Today, Feb. 2007.

Eduardo Capulong, *Client Activism in Progressive Lawyering Theory*, 16 Clinical L. Rev. 109 (2009).

Lenore Carpenter, *Getting Queer Priorities Straight: How Direct Legal Services Can Democratize Issue Prioritization in the LGBT Rights Movement*, 17 U. Penn. J.L. & Social Change 107 (2014).

Renwei Chung, *Implicit Bias: The Silent Killer of Diversity in the Legal Profession*, Above the Law (2015).

Stacy Clark, *Networking: If Done Right, It Really Works, Law Practice Today*, ABA LPM (2009).

Ashley E. Compton, Note, *Shifting the Blame: The Dilemma of Fee-Shifting Statutes and Fee-Waiver Settlements*, 22 Geo J. Legal Ethics 761 (2009). Reprinted with permission of the publisher, Georgetown Journal of Legal Ethics® 2009.

Kristen M. Dama, Comment, *Redefining a Final Act: The Fourteenth Amendment and States' Obligation to Prevent Death Row Inmates from Volunteering To Be Put to Death*, 9 U. Pa. J. Const. L. 1083 (2007).

Suzanne Darrow-Kleinhaus, *Response to the Society of American Law Teachers Statement on the Bar Exam*, 54 J. Legal Educ. 442 (2004).

John S. Dzienkowski & Robert J. Peroni, *The Decline in Lawyer Independence: Lawyer Equity Investments in Clients*, 81 Tex. L. Rev. 405 (2002).

John S. Dzienkowski & Robert J. Peroni, *Multidisciplinary Practice and the American Legal Profession: A Market Approach to Regulating the Delivery of Legal Services in the Twenty-First Century*, 69 Fordham L. Rev. 83 (2000).

Timothy W. Floyd & John Gallagher, *Legal Ethics, Narrative, and Professional Identity: The Story of David Spaulding*, 59 Mercer L. Rev. 941 (2008).

Posting of Monroe H. Freedman, *On Teaching and Testing in Law School*, to Legal Ethics Forum: The Purpose of Law School Classes?, http://www.legalethicsforum.com/blog/2006/10/the_purpose_of_.html (Oct. 11, 2006).

Jim Gallagher, *Drugs, Alcohol, Mental Health, and the Vermont Lawyer*, Vt. Bar. J&L Dig. Spring 2006, at 5.

Stephen Gillers, *"Eat Your Spinach?,"* 51 St. Louis U. L.J. 1215 (2007). Reprinted with permission of the Saint Louis University Law Journal © 2007. St. Louis University School of Law, St. Louis, Missouri.

Neil Graffin, Emma Jones, Mathijs Lucassen and Rajvinder Samra, *The legal profession has a mental health problem—which is an issue for everyone,* The Conversation, April 18, 2019.

Bruce A. Green & Russell G. Pearce, *"Public Service Must Begin At Home": The Lawyer as Civics Teacher in Everyday Practice*, 50 Wm. & Mary L. Rev. 1207 (2009).

Mark I. Harrison and Timothy K. McPike, *The True Story on Lawyer Discipline*, 70 A.B.A. J. 3 (1984).

Jim Hawkins & Renee Knake, *The Behavioral Economics of Lawyer Advertising: An Empirical Assessment*, 2019 Illinois L. Rev. 1005 (2019).

Geoffrey C. Hazard, Jr., Russell G. Pearce & Jeffrey W. Stempel, *Why Lawyers Should Be Allowed to Advertise: A Market Analysis of Legal Services*, 58 N.Y.U. L. Rev. 1084, 1094–1100 (1983).

Silvia Hodges, *I Didn't Go to Law School to Become a Salesperson—The Development of Marketing in Law Firms*, 26 Geo. J. of Legal Ethics 225 (2013).

Stephanie Kimbro, *Virtual Law Practice: How to Deliver Legal Services Online*, ABA LPM Publishing (2010).

Renee Newman Knake, *Why Law Students Should Be Thinking About Entrepreneurship and Innovation in Legal Services,* Bloomberg Law, December 2012.

Renee Knake, How Big Data Analytics Is Changing Legal Ethics, Bloomberg Law, August 10, 2016.

Nicole Lancia, Note, *New Rule, New York: A Bifocal Approach to Discipline and Discrimination*, 22 Geo. J. Legal Ethics 949 (2009). Reprinted with permission of the publisher, Georgetown Journal of Legal Ethics® 2009.

Gerald P. Lopez, *Living and Lawyering Rebelliously*, 73 Fordham L. Rev. 2041 (2005).

David Luban, *Lawyers and Justice: An Ethical Study*, Princeton University Press (1988).

Heather MacDonald, *What Good is Pro Bono?*, 10 City J., Spring 2000, at 14.

Maryland State Bar Association Committee on Ethics, Ethics Docket No. 2001-18 (2001). Reprinted with permission of the Maryland State Bar Association.

Therese Maynard, *Ethics for Business Lawyers Representing Start-Up Companies*, 11 Wake Forest J. Bus. & Intell. Prop. L. 401 (2011).

Carrie Menkel-Meadow, *Portia in a Different Voice: Speculations on a Women's Lawyering Process*, 1 Berkeley Women's L.J. 39 (1985). © 1985 by the Regents of the University of California. Reprinted from the Berkeley Women's Law Journal, Vol. 1, No. 1, by permission of the Regents of the University of California.

New York City Bar, Committee on Professional Ethics, Formal Opinion 2018-2: Prosecutor's post-conviction duties regarding potential wrongful convictions. Reprinted with permission of the New York City Bar Association.

Bill Ong Hing, *The Great Opportunity in Law*, 15 UCLA Asian Pacific American L. J. 30 (2009–2010).

Richard Painter, *Rules Lawyers Play By*, 76 N.Y.U. L. Rev. 665 (2001).

Russell G. Pearce, *The Jewish Lawyer's Question*, 27 Tex. Tech. L. Rev. 1259 (1996).

Russell G. Pearce, *Teaching Ethics Seriously, Legal Ethics as the Most Important Subject in Law School*, 29 Loy. U. Chi. L.J. 719 (1998).

Russell G. Pearce, Brian Danitz & Romelia S. Leach, *Revitalizing the Lawyer-Poet: What Lawyers Can Learn From Rock and Roll*, 14 Widener L.J. 907 (2005).

Russell G. Pearce, *The Legal Profession as a Blue State: Reflections on Public Philosophy, Jurisprudence, and Legal Ethics*, 75 Fordham L. Rev. 1339 (2006).

Andrew M. Perlman, *Towards the Law of Legal Services*, 37 Cardozo L. Rev. 88 (2015).

Deborah L. Rhode, *Cultures of Commitment: Pro Bono for Lawyers and Law Students*, 67 Fordham L. Rev. 2415 (1999).

Deborah L. Rhode, *Moral Character as a Professional Credential*, 94 Yale L.J. 491 (1985). Reprinted with permission of the Yale Law Journal Company, Inc.

William G. Ross, *The Ethics of Hourly Billing by Attorneys*, 44 Rutgers L. Rev. 1 (1991).

Tanina Rostain, *Ethics Lost: Limitations of Current Approaches to Lawyer Regulation*, 71 S. Cal. L. Rev. 1273 (1997–1998).

William B. Rubenstein, On What A "Private Attorney General" Is—and Why It Matters, 57 Vand. L. Rev. 2129 (2004).

Anthony Sebok, *Litigation Investment and Legal Ethics: What are the Real Issues?*, 55 Canadian Bus. L. J. 111 (2014).

Vijay Sekhon, *Over-Education of American Lawyers: An Economic and Ethical Analysis of the Requirements for Practicing Law in the United States*, 14 Geo. Mason L. Rev. 769 (2007).

William H. Simon, *Ethical Discretion in Lawyering*, 101 Harv. L. Rev. 1083 (1988). Reprinted with permission of the Harvard Law Review Association.

Society of American Law Teachers Statement on the Bar Exam, 52 J. Legal Educ. 446 (2002).

Jean R. Sternlight and Jennifer K. Robbnnolt, *Behavioral Legal Ethics*, 45 Ariz. St. L. J. 1107 (2013), first published by Arizona State Law Journal, Volume 45, Issue 3.

Marcy Strauss, *Toward a Revised Model of Attorney-Client Relationship: The Argument for Autonomy*, 65 N.C. L. Rev. 315 (1987). Reprinted with permission of the North Carolina Law Review, Vol. 65, pp. 324–25.

Jeffrey D. Swett, Comment, *Determining A Reasonable Percentage in Establishing a Contingency Fee: A New Tool to Remedy an Old Problem*, 77 Tenn. L. Rev. 653 (2010). The full text of this article was published originally at 77 Tenn. L. Rev. 653 (2010) and the portion is reprinted here by permission of the author and the Tennessee Law Review Association, Inc.

Akshat Tewary, *Legal Ethics as a Means to Address the Problem of Elite Law Firm Non-Diversity*, 12 Asian L.J. 1 (2005).

Robert K. Vischer, *Heretics in the Temple of the Law: The Promise and Peril of the Religious Lawyering Movement*, 19 J.L. & Religion 427 (2004).

Eli Wald and Russell G. Pearce, *Being Good Lawyers: A Relational Approach to Law Practice*, 29 Geo. J. Legal Ethics 601, 602–03, 639–41 (2016).

Michael Waterstone, *A New Vision of Public Enforcement*, 92 Minn. L. Rev. 434 (2007).

W. Bradley Wendel, *Are There Ethical Pitfalls in the Use of Third-Party Litigation Financing?*, 80 The Advocate (Texas) 51 (2017).

David B. Wilkins, *Identities and Roles: Race, Recognition, and Professional Responsibility*, 57 Md. L. Rev. 1502 (1998).

Table of Contents

Table of Cases

The principal cases are in bold type.

PROFESSIONAL RESPONSIBILITY

A Contemporary Approach

FOURTH EDITION

CHAPTER 1

Introducing Professionalism and Legal Ethics

Learning Outcomes

At the end of this Course, you will be able to:

*   Identify and apply the fundamental rules and laws regulating lawyers' conduct

*   Reflect upon how to integrate conceptions of professionalism and the lawyers' role into your career

*   Recognize the trends that will influence the future of lawyers' work

*   Master the material you need to know for the Multistate Professional Responsibility Exam ("MPRE")

At the end of this Chapter, you will be able to:

*   Determine how to gain admission to the bar

*   Describe the framework for the rules and laws that regulate lawyers' conduct

*   Differentiate professionalism and the dominant conception of the lawyer's role

*   Reflect on the connection between personal and professional values

*   Articulate your expectations for this course

Topic Outline for Chapter 1

	TOPIC	RELEVANT AUTHORITY	CHAPTER QUESTIONS
I.	How Do You Become a Lawyer?	Rule 8.1	1-1
II.	The Legal Definition of Professional Responsibility	ABA Model Rules, Restatement of the Law Governing Lawyers	1-2 to 1-4
III.	This Professional Responsibility Course Is About You		--

My practice experience tells me that [legal ethics is] the most important class a law student can take. Sure, sure. I anticipate the objections: What about constitutional law? What about corporations? What about contracts? And, anyway, nearly everyone thinks that his or her class is the most important. True, but only one of us is right. My reason is simple. Legal ethics is the only class in the law school curriculum whose content is relevant to the daily professional life of all graduates who practice law, which is nearly everyone. Bankruptcy is important to bankruptcy lawyers, but most lawyers do not need to know much, if any, bankruptcy law. The same point can be made about criminal law and securities and civil procedure. And so on. But all lawyers "practice" legal ethics just by going to work.

The common denominator does not stop there. All lawyers also have clients, at least one, often hundreds or thousands across a career. Indirectly, the class is for clients too. Or to put it another way: How can a law school conscientiously certify graduates as competent professionals without making an earnest effort to ensure that they understand the responsibilities of their profession to clients? And the class is for the courts, adversaries, and the public as well, because every law graduate who practices law has obligations to each group. There's more. Many students will go on to run government law offices, corporate law departments, private law firms, and public interest organizations. In these roles and others, they will make choices that define the culture of their offices. Some students will be active in bar associations or become judges. In these roles, they will influence or decide the content of rules governing the profession. In short, no other law school subject will have as much importance across the population of each graduating class.

—Professor Stephen Gillers[1]

Professor Gillers uses the term Legal Ethics. We prefer the term Professional Responsibility. But whatever the term, we all refer to the same constellation of concepts—not only to the legal ethics rules but also to laws relevant to lawyer practice and to professional values. We agree that Professional Responsibility is the most important course you will take in law school but recognize that many of you will be skeptical of this claim. As Professor Gillers notes, Professional Responsibility is the only course that applies to the work of every practicing lawyer. Moreover, it will help you understand the importance of the work of lawyers generally, as well as of your own career as a lawyer. As a result, the American Bar Association requires law schools to teach students "competency in . . . the [e]xercise of proper professional and ethical responsibilities to clients and the legal system;" as well as in "[o]ther professional skills needed for competent

---

1   Stephen Gillers, "Eat Your Spinach?," 51 St. Louis U. L.J. 1215, 1220–21 (2007).

and ethical participation as a member of the legal profession."[2] Moreover, in almost every jurisdiction, you must pass the Multistate Professional Responsibility Exam (MPRE) in order to gain admission to the bar.

This Chapter will briefly introduce you to the topics of ethics and professionalism, including the controversies regarding whether law is a business or a profession and whether professional responsibility is an important course. It begins with a short overview of the sources of applicable law. When discussing the ethical rules that govern lawyer conduct, the Casebook uses the word "Rule" to refer to rules from various jurisdictions that are substantially similar to those in the American Bar Association (ABA) Model Rules of Professional conduct. Generally, we will refer to the Delaware Rules of Professional Conduct, unless they differ from the ABA Rules, in which case we cite to another jurisdiction's rule. From time to time, we will identify significant variations among jurisdictions. In Chapter 7, we will also introduce the ABA Model Code of Judicial Conduct with citations to jurisdictions that have adopted the same language.

I.   How Do You Become a Lawyer?

[Question 1-1]

Identify a website that describes the requirements for bar admission in the jurisdiction or jurisdictions where you plan to seek admission to practice law.

The rules and cases you will study this semester govern the conduct of lawyers. But how do you become a lawyer? The United States uses a lawyer licensing framework where you must apply for a license to the relevant authority in each jurisdiction where you want to practice law, including states, the District of Columbia, Puerto Rico, and United States territories. If you want to learn how to gain admission in the jurisdictions where you are considering practicing law, you can consult the webpage of the National Conference of Bar Examiners, which identifies the relevant agencies in each jurisdiction and summarizes the requirements for bar admission.

Most jurisdictions generally require that applicants have graduated from an accredited law school and have passed both the jurisdiction's bar examination and the MPRE. The MPRE covers the ABA's rules for lawyers and for judges, as well as "controlling constitutional decisions and generally accepted principles established in leading federal and state cases and in procedural and evidentiary rules."[3] This casebook includes these topics. To do so, it will cite to jurisdictions that have provisions that are the same as those of the ABA Model Rules of Professional Conduct and the ABA Model Code of Judicial Conduct, and will introduce you to the fundamental legal doctrines governing lawyers.

---

2   https://www.americanbar.org/content/dam/aba/publications/misc/legal_education/Standards/2018-2019ABAStandardsforApprovalofLawSchools/2018-2019-aba-standards-chapter3.pdf.

3   Subject Matter, *Preparing for the MPRE*, National Conference of Bar Examiners (January 2017).

(handwritten note in margin: Come back to this)

In addition, most jurisdictions require applicants to satisfy character and fitness standards. The issues that are most likely to cause concern in this area are dishonesty on the bar application, recent criminal conduct, and fraud or other financial misdeeds. Indeed, Rule 8.1 prohibits an individual who submits "an application for admission to the bar" from "knowingly mak[ing] a false statement of material fact" or "fail[ing] to disclose a fact necessary to correct a misapprehension . . . or knowingly fail[ing] to respond to a lawful demand for information from an admissions or disciplinary authority."

Global Perspective

Many foreign-educated applicants apply to sit for a U.S. bar examination. For example, more than twenty-five percent of those who have taken the New York bar examination in recent years have been foreign educated applicants. While New York may be alone in the number of foreign-educated applicants who sit for its bar exam, in recent years, foreign-educated applicants have taken bar examinations in more than one-half of U.S. jurisdictions. Unlike the regulators in Canadian provinces and territories, who have delegated to the National Committee on Accreditation certain decisions about foreign-educated applicants, admissions authorities in the United States do not have a central authority to which they can turn in order to learn about the lawyer admissions processes elsewhere in the world. Luckily, this situation is starting to change. For example, "admissions" was one of the topics at the 2016 International Conference of Legal Regulators.

If you want to be licensed in more than one jurisdiction, you can take multiple bar examinations or—in many jurisdictions—you can now take the Uniform Bar Examination. Once you have practice experience, in many jurisdictions you can apply for "Admission on Motion," which does not require that you take a bar exam but usually requires a certain number of years in practice. The particular requirements vary by jurisdiction. Note that for admission to federal courts, you must apply separately to each court in which you want to practice, but you will not have to take another bar exam. Rather, you generally must obtain a sponsor admitted in the jurisdiction and establish that you are in good standing in your state of admission. In addition, if you are appearing in a trial in a state or federal court in which you are not licensed to practice, you can apply for admission *pro hac vice* (for this occasion only), the rules for which vary by jurisdiction.

II. The Legal Definition of Professional Responsibility

Read the questions first and then find the answers in the text that follows.

[Question 1-2]

The ABA Model Rules of Professional Conduct are:

(A) Binding on attorneys in all jurisdictions.

(B) Models which jurisdictions can accept, reject, or modify.

(C) Binding only on members of the ABA.

(D) The only legal standards governing lawyer conduct.

[Question 1-3]

In the United States, the predominant, although not exclusive, authority for lawyer regulation is:

    (A)   The legislature.

    (B)   The executive.

    (C)   The judiciary.

    (D)   The state bar association.

[Question 1-4]

Which, if any, of the following sources of authority is not binding on lawyers?

    (A)   Restatement of the Law Governing Lawyers.

    (B)   Case law on malpractice.

    (C)   Criminal law.

    (D)   The Sarbanes-Oxley regulations on practice before the SEC.

The basic resources for exploring lawyers' legal obligations are the ethics rules, bar association opinions, the Restatement of the Law Governing Lawyers (the "Restatement"), case law, and statutes.

The ABA Model Rules of Professional Conduct (the "Rules") are the basic source of rules governing the conduct of lawyers. The American Bar Association promulgates the Rules as the standard guide to lawyer regulation. The Rules are not binding on governmental jurisdictions, but every jurisdiction has adopted their own version of the Rules. In each jurisdiction, the Courts promulgate the ethics rules, with the exception of California where the legislature has a major role. Restatement § 1(c) explains that "[t]he highest courts in most states have ruled as a matter of state constitutional law that their power to regulate lawyers is inherent in the judicial function. . . . The power is said to derive from the historical role of courts in the United States in regulating lawyers through admission and disbarment and from the traditional practice of courts in England." The federal courts establish their own ethics rules for lawyers appearing before them, but they often adopt the rules of their local jurisdiction.

Practice Pointer

Because every jurisdiction is free to adopt its own version of the Rules, make sure to consult the applicable Rules in the jurisdiction where you are admitted or are practicing.

Global Perspective

Although the United States primarily uses a system of state-based judicial regulation of lawyers, jurisdictions differ with respect to their lawyer regulatory systems and the question of *"who regulates lawyers?"*:

> [There are a] number of high-profile examples of movement away from self-regulation and toward co-regulation [of lawyers]. For example, Australia, the United Kingdom, and Scotland have all adopted a co-regulatory approach. In each jurisdiction, oversight authority is placed in an alternate body. In the United Kingdom and Scotland, a regulatory board with a nonlawyer majority and a nonlawyer chair maintains oversight. In Australia, regulatory oversight is largely placed with statutory bodies such as Commissions or Boards. As Australia moves closer toward establishing a national regulatory system, oversight will be solidified by the creation of a proposed national legal services board that would include nonlawyer members and a National Legal Services Commissioner who may or may not be a lawyer.

Laurel S. Terry, Steve Mark, Tahlia Gordon, *Trends and Challenges in Lawyer Regulation: The Impact of Globalization and Technology,* 80 Fordham L. Rev. 2661, 2669 (2012). For further discussion of the changes in the United Kingdom, see the Global Perspectives Box in Chapter 9.

The Rules are the ABA's third codification of legal ethics. The first was the Canons of Professional Ethics, promulgated in 1908. The Canons were hortatory but courts and bar associations would nonetheless apply them to govern lawyers' conduct. The second was the Model Code of Professional Responsibility, adopted in 1970. The Code consisted of aspirational Ethical Considerations, as well as binding Disciplinary Rules. In 1983, the ABA enacted the Rules, most of which require compliance. Since 1983, the ABA has amended the Rules from time to time. Some of the most recent amendments introduce an explicit anti-bias requirement, as well as responses to changes in law practice resulting from technological developments and the globalization of legal practice.

In addition to the Rules, the ABA promulgated the Canons of Judicial Ethics in 1924 and in 1990 the Model Code of Judicial Conduct, which has been amended since that time.

To provide you with relevant language from the ABA Model Rules of Professional Conduct and Model Code of Judicial Conduct, the casebook will quote from jurisdictions that have adopted provisions that are the same or substantially similar to those of the ABA models.

As noted above, courts in most jurisdictions promulgate ethics rules. Courts also interpret those rules through their review of discipline for violation of the rules, as well as in court matters, such as motions to disqualify, where courts apply the rules. Depending on the jurisdiction, another role of courts is to promulgate procedural and evidentiary rules that regulate lawyers, such as Rule 11 of the Federal Rules of Civil Procedure or the attorney-client evidentiary privilege.

Bar associations also play an important role in interpreting the rules. Many bar associations establish ethics committees to advise lawyers on whether their proposed conduct conforms to the Rules. This advice can take the form of informal, telephone advice in urgent situations or systematic, written opinions. Bar opinions typically are not binding on courts either in disciplinary or other matters. Nonetheless, courts generally tend to treat bar opinions with some deference and compliance with a bar opinion can help mitigate discipline even where the court disagrees with the bar committee's substantive determination of the relevant ethical question. Both courts and bar associations rely on the American Law Institute's Restatement of the Law Governing Lawyers. The Restatement is not binding but has proven very influential.

Practice Pointer

Note that the ABA is a voluntary trade organization. Lawyers are not required to be members and ABA ethics opinions, while persuasive authority, are not binding on practicing lawyers in any jurisdiction. A majority of United States jurisdictions make membership in that jurisdiction's bar association mandatory. These are unified bar associations. In other jurisdictions, bar associations are voluntary trade organizations. Whether bar associations are unified or voluntary, bar opinions remain persuasive, but not binding, authority.

Beyond the Rules, common law and statutes also regulate lawyer conduct. The most familiar common law regulation of lawyers is the law of malpractice, but other common law doctrines, such as fraud, also apply to lawyers. In addition, legislatures regulate lawyers directly, such as the Sarbanes-Oxley provisions governing lawyers who practice before the Securities and Exchange Commission or the Bankruptcy Reform Act that applies to bankruptcy lawyers, as well as through laws of general application, such as criminal law.

III. This Professional Responsibility Course Is About You

Food for Thought

Why did you come to law school? Have your goals, values, or self-conception changed at law school? What are your career goals? How do you plan to find meaning in your work? Do you believe lawyers can make money, do good, and have fun, all at the same time?

Professional Responsibility is about the rules and values you will encounter in law practice. In other courses, you study law and policy concerning clients. In this course, you also study law and policy concerning yourself, your friends, your colleagues, and your adversaries. As you begin this course, take a few minutes to reflect on your aspirations and expectations for your legal career. This will help you establish a starting point for evaluating and applying what you will learn in the course.

IV. Professional Responsibility Is About the Legal Profession

Professionalism requires lawyers to satisfy high ethical standards. Of course, the exact meaning of professionalism—or of high ethical standards—is often subject to debate. This section will provide you with a basic introduction to professionalism, professional responsibility, and the lawyer's role. The questions below are, of course, quite important to your career and how you will find meaning in your work as a lawyer. Please review the following readings before answering the questions. Questions 1-6, 1-7, and 1-9 have objective answers. The other questions require a personal response that may change throughout this course and indeed throughout your career.

[Question 1-5]

Your college has invited you to meet with undergraduates to describe a career in law. In no more than 30 seconds, how would you describe the meaning of professionalism?

[Question 1-6]

All of the following are traditional elements of professionalism except:

(A) **Representing clients as zealously as possible within the bounds of the law.**

(B) **Expertise that is inaccessible to nonlawyers.**

(C) **Putting the public good above self-interest.**

(D) **Significant autonomy from government and market regulation.**

[Question 1-7]

The dichotomy between a business and a profession:

(A) **Described law as a business.**

(B) **Viewed consumers as capable of making informed purchases of legal services.**

(C) **Justified the exclusive right of lawyers to practice law.**

(D) **Rejected the idea that lawyers are America's governing class.**

[Question 1-8]

In your view, legal practice is:

(A) **A business.**

(B) **A profession.**

(C) **Both a business and a profession.**

[Question 1-9]

The perspectives on professionalism in the readings reflect all of the following views EXCEPT:

(A) **Only the business-profession dichotomy explains lawyers' high ethical standards.**

(B) **The business-profession dichotomy is no longer persuasive.**

(C) **Most lawyers continue to believe in the business-profession dichotomy.**

(D) The business-profession dichotomy is not necessary to high ethical standards.

[Question 1-10]

In your view, lawyers should have high ethical standards because:

(A) Law is a profession.

(B) Lawyers' work has the potential to have a major impact on individuals, businesses and society.

(C) All people should have high ethical standards.

[Question 1-11]

All of the following are elements of the dominant conception of the lawyer's role EXCEPT:

(A) Role morality.

(B) The public good.

(C) Extreme partisanship.

(D) Moral non-accountability.

AMERICAN BAR ASSOCIATION COMMISSION ON PROFESSIONALISM, ". . . IN THE SPIRIT OF PUBLIC SERVICE:" A BLUEPRINT FOR THE REKINDLING OF LAWYER PROFESSIONALISM

112 F.R.D. 243, 261–62 (1986)

'Professionalism' is an elastic concept the meaning and application of which are hard to pin down. That is perhaps as it should be. The term has a rich, long-standing heritage, and any single definition runs the risk of being too confining.

Yet the term is so important to lawyers that at least a working definition seems essential. Lawyers are proud of being part of one of the 'historic' or 'learned' professions, along with medicine and the clergy, which have been seen as professions through many centuries.

When he was asked to define a profession, Dean Roscoe Pound of Harvard Law School said:

> The term refers to a group . . . pursuing a learned art as a common calling in the spirit of public service-no less a public service because it may incidentally be a means of livelihood. Pursuit of the learned art in the spirit of a public service is the primary purpose.

The rhetoric may be dated, but the Commission believes the spirit of Dean Pound's definition stands the test of time. The practice of law 'in the spirit of a public service' can and ought to be the hallmark of the legal profession.

More recently, others have identified some common elements which distinguish a profession from other occupations. Commission member Professor Eliot Freidson of New York University defines our profession as:

An occupation whose members have special privileges, such as exclusive licensing, that are justified by the following assumptions:

    1.   That its practice requires substantial intellectual training and the use of complex judgments.

    2.   That since clients cannot adequately evaluate the quality of the service, they must trust those they consult.

    3.   That the client's trust presupposes that the practitioner's self-interest is over-balanced by devotion to serving both the client's interest and the public good, and

    4.   That the occupation is self-regulating—that is, organized in such a way as to assure the public and the courts that its members are competent, do not violate their client's trust, and transcend their own self-interest.

Russell G. Pearce, Brian Danitz & Romelia S. Leach, *Revitalizing the Lawyer-Poet: What Lawyers Can Learn From Rock and Roll*

14 Widener L.J. 907, 907–22 (2005)

Lawyer professionalism is all about the dichotomy between a business and a profession.

- Business people work to make money.
- Lawyers work primarily to promote the public good.
- Consumers are capable of evaluating business goods and services.
- Consumers are not capable of evaluating the expertise of lawyers.

Market competition makes business goods and services available for the best quality at the lowest price with government intervention when market failures occur. In contrast, the inaccessible expertise and unique altruism of lawyers require significant limits on market competition and government regulation. Only lawyers are allowed to provide legal services. Nonlawyers cannot compete with them. Lawyers by and large regulate themselves—deciding who has the privilege to practice law, creating the rules governing lawyers, and controlling the enforcement of those rules. The public can trust the legal profession to regulate itself because lawyers work primarily to promote the public good and not their own

Food for Thought

In 2016, the ABA for the first time adopted Model Regulatory Objectives for Legal Services. Compare the ABA's Model Regulatory Objectives with the traditional elements of professionalism. In what ways are they different? Similar?

self-interest. This commitment to the public good also makes lawyers the governing class in American democracy. Among the formal institutions of government, lawyers play a key role in the executive and legislature and a dominant role in the judiciary. Equally—or more— important, lawyers are the key to informal governance. On a daily basis, they serve as the primary intermediaries between the law and the people. As Erwin Smigel described in his famous study of Wall Street Lawyers, lawyers remind people and businesses of their obligations to the spirit of the law and the public good, and not just the minimal requirements of the letter of the law. No wonder that Alexis de Tocqueville had described lawyers as the aristocracy of the United States.

Food for Thought

You might enjoy the 15 minute film version of this article, "Revitalizing the Lawyer-Poet: What Lawyers Can Learn From Rock and Roll," directed by Sundance-featured documentary filmmaker Brian Danitz. It includes appearances by numerous lawyers and rock musicians, including Richard Nixon and Jimi Hendrix. The DVD should be available in your law school library. If not, the library can obtain it free from lawyersrock@law.fordham.edu. Before you watch the film, you may find it helpful to review the thought-provoking questions raised in the Teacher's Guide.

ELI WALD AND RUSSELL G. PEARCE, *BEING GOOD LAWYERS: A RELATIONAL APPROACH TO LAW PRACTICE*

29 Georgetown Journal of Legal Ethics 601, 602–03, 639–41 (2016)

The practice of law is great work. In a liberal democracy, the law shapes how people live their personal lives and participate in business and in civil society. In the United States, lawyers perform much, but not all, of law work. Yet, for more than a generation, bar leaders and scholars have bemoaned the decline, betrayal, or death of the legal profession. [These critiques arose from a perception that lawyers have failed to live up to] the traditional lawyer professionalism paradigm, which historically had provided the dominant, although not universal, guide to the lawyer's vocation. That historical paradigm—the business-profession dichotomy—held that in contrast to businesspeople who sought to maximize profit, lawyers worked primarily for the public good in their representation of clients and their civic leadership. Under this paradigm, lawyers combined zealous representation with a responsibility to counsel their clients on the spirit, as well as the letter of the law, and the public good. And zealous representation did not permit lawyers to be uncivil or to subvert the legal system.

While the trend in the 1990s was to bemoan business conduct by lawyers [in an unsuccessful effort to revive commitment to the business-profession dichotomy], the trend in the twenty-first century has been different, with leading scholars acknowledging that law has always been to some extent a business and rejecting traditional professionalism's contention that professional lawyers should have the exclusive privilege to practice law. Tom Morgan, for example, long a leading professional responsibility scholar, has observed that "very good people have tried to make something of the professional rhetoric, but we are a long way from [those] grandiose claims . . . . In my view, professionalism in the sense developed by the A.B.A. during the twentieth century is—and should be seen as—dead." But Morgan sees opportunity in this transformation. He asserts that "[l]awyers, like all citizens, have a moral obligation to devote their best efforts to using their skills in ways that contribute to the public interest" and observes that "consumers of legal services are likely to reward providers" who adopt the business ethic of "deliver[ing] services more efficiently and at lower costs." According to Morgan, this will increase access to justice and will not undermine lawyer's values. Morgan notes that "[t]hose values have not and will not go out of date . . . . The lives of practitioners using legal training, whatever their number or the nature of their individual training and practice, will be the best instruments of justice." To Morgan, whether lawyers or not, legal services providers can serve the public good. Morgan is only one of a number of distinguished scholars who have argued—contrary to the business-profession dichotomy—that increased competition would lower the price and improve the quality of services and thereby increase access to justice.

Dana Remus and Rebecca Roiphe also reject the business-profession dichotomy, but in a way that differs from Morgan. Whereas Morgan seeks to replace the business-profession dichotomy with a business, or market, ideology which has inherent guarantees of the public interest, Remus and Roiphe seek to "redefine" and "reconstruct" professionalism in ways that reject the business-profession dichotomy, but oppose a largely market driven approach to delivering legal services as well. Remus asserts that the tension between commercialism and professionalism cannot be resolved through an embrace of market forces any more than it can be hidden behind traditional rhetoric of professionalism and commitment to the public interest. Rather, it must be continually mediated and managed through professional structures and ethical rules that harness market forces in productive rather than protective ways. Roiphe, in turn, argues that professional "independence is an aspect of professional identity rather than a condition that results from the isolation of lawyers from businessmen and others[.]" Roiphe asserts that the danger to professional independence arises not "from innovative markets, sources of funding, or new law firm structures" but rather from "proposals to segment the profession in ways that might erode a common identity" that "has consistently provided a language for debating the nature of the lawyer's role in a democracy."

In rejecting the business-profession dichotomy, these varied perspectives share an understanding that law work is relational and that law workers are both business people and professionals at the same time.

———————

———————

4   *Facing the Challenge of a New Age*, Address delivered at the First Annual Institute on Nonviolence and Social Change (December 3, 1956), in 3 Papers Of Martin Luther King, Jr. 457 (Clayborne Carson et al. eds., 1992).

Food for Thought

Some thinkers argue that all people, whatever their occupation, have the highest ethical obligations in their work. Martin Luther King, Jr., for example, famously wrote that:

> Whatever your life's work is, do it well. Even if it does not fall in the category of one of the so-called big professions, do it well. . . . If it falls your lot to be a street sweeper, sweep streets like Michelangelo painted pictures, like Shakespeare wrote poetry, like Beethoven composed music; sweep streets so well that all the host of Heaven and earth will have to pause and say, "Here lived a great street sweeper, who swept his job well."[4]

Click here to listen to Martin Luther King, Jr.

In addition to professionalism, the conception of the lawyer's role provides an important source for constructing a lawyer's professional responsibility. In Chapter 8, you will encounter a wide range of perspectives on the lawyer's role. Among those perspectives, one has been described by commentators as the dominant or standard approach—a role variously identified as the neutral partisan or hired gun. David Luban has described the elements of this conception and how it serves as a role morality:

> The theory of role morality takes off from a distinction between universal moral duties that binds us all because we are all moral agents and special duties that go with various roles or "stations in life." . . . This notion, at the level of general ethical theory, explains how people in certain social roles may be morally required to do things that seem immoral.

> [T]he standard conception of the lawyer's role [consists] of (1) a role obligation (the "principle of partisanship") that identifies professionalism with extreme partisan zeal on behalf of the client and (2) the "principle of nonaccountability," which insists that the lawyer bears no moral responsibility for the client's goals or the means.[5]

Food for Thought

Your law school has decided that each first-year student must swear to a professionalism oath on the first day of first year orientation. In light of what you have learned in this Chapter, as well as your own personal and professional values, draft a one or two paragraph oath.

V. Can Professional Responsibility Be Taught?

The readings earlier in this Chapter explain why the profession believes that teaching professional responsibility is important. After the questions below, you will find readings discussing

---

5   David Luban, *Lawyers And Justice: An Ethical Study* xx (1986).

how law students and professors view the course. Use all the texts to answer the following questions. Only Question 1-12 has an objective answer. Remember that your views on the subjective questions may very well change as the course proceeds.

[Question 1-12]

Which of the following is true?

- (A) Leading legal ethics experts have not always believed that legal ethics could be taught.
- (B) Research finds that law students' altruism increases during law school.
- (C) Bar associations have always required law schools to provide training in legal ethics.
- (D) Research indicates that moral development ends after adolescence.

[Question 1-13]

I expect this Professional Responsibility course to be:

- (A) Fun.
- (B) Challenging.
- (C) Both fun and challenging.
- (D) Neither fun nor challenging.

[Question 1-14]

I want the following from my Professional Responsibility course:

- (A) Knowledge of the law and rules governing lawyers.
- (B) Development of my professional identity.
- (C) Development of my capacity for moral reasoning.
- (D) A & B.
- (E) A, B & C.

[Question 1-15]

I believe that my Professional Responsibility course is:

- (A) The most important course in law school.
- (B) The second most important course in law school.
- (C) Less important than my first year subject matter classes.
- (D) Relatively unimportant.

RUSSELL G. PEARCE, *TEACHING ETHICS SERIOUSLY: LEGAL ETHICS AS THE MOST IMPORTANT SUBJECT IN LAW SCHOOL*

29 Loy. U. Chi. L.J. 719, 722–35 (1998)

The modern era of teaching legal ethics began in 1974. The notorious conduct of lawyers implicated in the Watergate scandal undermined "public confidence in the legal profession." In order to restore public confidence and bolster the integrity of lawyers, the ABA House of Delegates "mandat[ed] the teaching of professional responsibility in all ABA-accredited law schools." A late 1970s *Doonesbury* cartoon summarized law schools' response to this requirement. Discussing whether a legal ethics course would make a difference, a law student responds "nah—all that ethics stuff is just more Watergate fallout! Trendy lip service to our better selves." Law schools resented the "ABA's assertion of curricular authority." Although these schools may have complied with the letter of the ABA requirement, the course offerings were largely "second class."

Law students got the message. A 1975–76 American Bar Foundation ("ABF") study found that law students "perceived [professional responsibility courses] as "requiring less time, as substantially easier, as less well taught, and as a less valuable use of class time." The courses had "a low status in the latent curriculum hierarchy" because they were more likely to be taught by the discussion method rather than the socratic method and were less intellectually challenging due to the lack of doctrinal complexity. Ronald Pipkin, author of the ABF study, concluded "that the prevailing mode of [professional responsibility] instruction in fact socializes students into the belief that legal ethics are *not* important."

Since the undertaking of the Pipkin study, however, significant change has occurred. As observed by Roger Cramton and Susan Koniak, "the volume and complexity of case law dealing with the responsibilities of lawyers has exploded; new and more challenging textbooks have been published on the subject; and the subject we refer to as 'the law and ethics of lawyering' has become a half-way respectable field of academic scholarship." Deborah Rhode has provided an excellent text for making pervasive ethics a reality. Further, schools like Fordham University have developed advanced and contextual ethics courses, and a number of commentators have offered proposals for innovations in teaching ethics. Teaching ethics in a clinical setting has received more focus, and some schools have included ethics as a first year course.

Many law faculty believe that law schools cannot improve the moral conduct of students through the teaching of legal ethics. They assert that students' values have been fully formed prior to law school and are not likely to change. This view, that the ethical capacity of adults is relatively static, appears to be a survival of the feudal concept of status wherein one's character and place in society was dictated by birth and family status. If birth and family circumstances dictate character, education in ethics can make little or no difference.

Global Perspective

In other jurisdictions in the world, legal ethics is not a required course and often is not even available as part of a university's legal education curriculum. To the extent that formal legal ethics instruction is available, it may be taught by practicing lawyers, rather than academics, and included as part of an apprenticeship or training program. One explanation for this different approach is that in many countries, legal education is an undergraduate program and many graduates may not go on to become practicing lawyers. Legal ethics is viewed as a "practical" course that need not be included in the undergraduate academic education. Second, many countries lack the academic materials that were developed in the U.S. One of the purposes of the International Association of Legal Ethics (IAOLE), which was established in 2010, is to make it easier for legal ethics academics (and others active in the field of legal ethics) around the world to share information. IALOE sponsors the biennial International Legal Ethics Conferences.

This view reflects two major manifestations. The first is the historical proposition that legal education and admission to practice should be limited to the "right kind of people." As one critic of required legal ethics education stated in 1930, the " 'right kind' of law student already knows what constitutes moral and ethical conduct, and . . . a formal course in Legal Ethics will not supply the proper sort of character training for students who are not the 'right kind'." Henry Drinker, perhaps the most prominent legal ethicist of the mid-twentieth century, reflected this view when he observed that "Russian Jew boys" were disproportionately "guilty of professional abuses" because their family background and education did not inculcate them in American ideals.

The second manifestation of this view, common in legal academia today, incorporates Drinker's view that family and environmental influences prior to law school determine law students' and lawyers' ethics. Rather than associate unethical conduct with particular groups, it relies on the notion that a person's capacity for moral development maximizes once a person reaches adulthood.

By their own terms, these perspectives are unpersuasive. Even if a student's moral development was generally complete before law school, that student would still have to apply this moral framework to the pursuit of law. John Mixon and Robert Schuwerk observe that "while law students have well-formed personal values stemming from family, church, and society, they nonetheless have relatively unsophisticated and unformed ideas of what it means to be a 'good lawyer'."

Research demonstrating that values are malleable in adulthood renders these perspectives even less persuasive. Psychologists have shown that adulthood, like childhood, is a time of personal growth and development. Not surprisingly, studies reveal that moral development continues "after the age of 18." As the Committee on Professionalism of the ABA Section of Legal Education and Admissions concluded, "[t]he once widely held view that ethical precepts are fully formed before law school has been proven to be untrue."

Food for Thought

The notion that a Professional Responsibility course teaches the basics of the law and ethics of lawyering is uncontroversial. You need to know this material in order to practice law and gain admission to the bar. The Carnegie Foundation's influential report, *Educating Lawyers: Preparation for the Profession of the Law*, argues that:

> Law schools fail to complement the focus on skill in legal analyses with effective support for developing ethical and social skills. Students need opportunities to learn about, reflect on and practice the responsibilities of legal professionals. Despite progress in making legal ethics a part of the curriculum, law schools rarely pay consistent attention to the social and cultural contexts of legal institutions and the varied forms of legal practice. To engage the moral imagination of students as they move toward professional practice, seminaries and medical, business and engineering schools employ well-elaborated case studies of professional work. Law schools, which pioneered the use of case teaching, only occasionally do so.[6]

What has been your experience? Does professionalism require that a Professional Responsibility course go beyond the law and ethics of lawyering? What is your view on whether professional values should also be included in a Professional Responsibility course?

Research further confirms that law school in particular is a time when students' values change. For example, political scientist Robert Stover documented the law school experience and its effect on students as making them less altruistic and less willing to work in a public interest job. Further underscoring the dramatic impact of a law school on a law student's personal development is an American Bar Foundation study reporting that law students' rate of significant mental health problems begins at an average rate but rises to as much as four times the average by graduation. Other studies support the specific proposition that ethics can be taught. Deborah Rhode notes that "[m]ore than a hundred studies evaluating moral education courses find that well-designed curricula can significantly improve capacities of moral reasoning . . . ."

The literature on legal ethics education, however, is less definitive. Some commentators have found ethics education to be significant, while others have not. Despite these mixed findings, Deborah Rhode observes that "[t]here is . . . more evidence on the effectiveness of professional responsibility instruction than there is on the effectiveness of most professional education."

---

6   *Educating Lawyers: Preparation for the Practice of Law 6* (William Sullivan, et al., eds. 2007).

Food for Thought

You are now familiar with professionalism and the neutral partisan role. How would you apply these perspectives to the following situation? Matthew Hale, a white supremacist, applied for admission to the Illinois bar. He argued that his white supremacist views would not interfere with his following the law. The character and fitness committee rejected his application on the ground that:

> The Bar and our courts stand committed to these fundamental truths: All persons are possessed of individual dignity. As a result, every person is to be judged on the basis of his or her own individuality and conduct, not by reference to skin color, race, ethnicity, religion or national origin. The enforcement and application of these timeless values to specific cases have, by history and constitutional development, been entrusted to our courts and its officers—the lawyers—a trust that lies at the heart of our system of government. Therefore, the guardians of that trust—the judges and lawyers, or one or more of them—cannot have as their mission in life the incitement of racial hatred in order to destroy those values.

In the Matter of the Application for Admission to the Bar of Matthew Hale, Decision of Inquiry Panel of the Committee on Character and Fitness of the Supreme Court of Illinois for the Third Appellate District of the Supreme Court of Illinois (Dec. 16, 1998). For a longer excerpt from this opinion, see Chapter 9. What are the perspectives on professionalism and lawyers' role that underly this approach? In contrast, most state bars appear to take a contrary view that being a white supremacist is neither a bar to admission nor a ground for discipline. Jessica Schulberg, Should White Supremacists Be Allowed to Practice Law?, Huffington Post, December 26, 2017. What is your view and why?

Test Your Knowledge

To assess your understanding of the material in this Chapter, click here to take a quiz.

CHAPTER 2

The Basic Elements of Law Practice

Learning Outcomes

At the end of Units I and II, you will be able to:

- Evaluate when lawyers may share fees with nonlawyers and participate in law-related businesses

- Analyze whether a nonlawyer is engaged in activities traditionally considered the unauthorized practice of law

- Determine whether a lawyer is engaged in one of the activities that constitutes a "safe harbor" to the unauthorized practice of law

- Articulate the arguments for and against a finding of unauthorized practice of law in nontraditional settings such as technology-assisted legal services

At the end of Unit III, you will be able to:

- Recognize the importance of establishing a lawyer-client relationship

- Evaluate whether a lawyer-client relationship exists

- Identify when a lawyer has a duty to accept or reject representation

At the end of Unit IV, you will be able to:

- Determine when a lawyer is required, permitted, or not permitted, to withdraw from representation

- Recognize the actions a lawyer must take before withdrawing from representation

At the end of Unit V, you will be able to:

- Distinguish the goals of the disciplinary system, the malpractice liability system, and the ineffective assistance of counsel doctrine

- Apply to any given fact pattern the elements that would subject a lawyer to discipline for lack of competence, the elements that would subject a lawyer to malpractice liability, and the elements needed to support a finding of ineffective assistance of counsel

- Comply with the rules that govern a lawyer's ability to limit malpractice liability

At the end of Unit VI, you will be able to:

- Evaluate whether a decision is the type of decision that clearly is allocated to clients rather than lawyers

- Apply the appropriate allocation principles for those decisions that are not clearly allocated to clients

- Evaluate whether the attorney's representation of a client implicates other principles governing the lawyer-client relationship, including rules about clients with diminished capacity and limits on the services a lawyer may provide

Topic Outline for Chapter 2

TOPIC		RELEVANT AUTHORITY	CHAPTER QUESTIONS
I.	Introduction		
II.	Defining the Practice of Law		
	A. The Prohibition		
	B. Limits on Nonlawyers Providing Low Cost Legal Assistance [Brumbaugh]		
	1. Debates Regarding Unauthorized Practice Restrictions		
	2. Legal Advice Books [Dacey]		
	3. Legal Software [UPL C'ee v. Parsons Technology; Legal Zoom]		
	C. Lawyers Working with Nonlawyers and Lawyers Providing Ancillary Nonlegal Services		
	1. Working with Non-lawyers	5.3, 5.4, 5.5	2-1 to 2-2
	2. Ancillary Businesses	5.7, *see also* 1.8(a)	2-3
	D. Unauthorized Practice of Law by Lawyers [Birbrower]	5.5, 8.5	2-4 to 2-6
III.	Creating the Lawyer-Client Relationship		
	A. General Principles [Morris, Westinghouse]	Restatement § 14, 1.13(a) & (f-g)	2-7

I. Introduction

> Just after I had entered the practice at my firm . . . one of my senior partners, perhaps sensing my frustration, approached me with a few words. He pointed out that . . . in our vocation there are three basic relationships with which we must be concerned. First and foremost, of course, is how we relate with our clients—the returned phone call, the short note providing an update, the unhurried time just to listen and a sense of loyalty and efficiency in handling our clients' business.[1]

Most lawyers represent clients, whether in private practice, public service, public interest, or in-house for a business. The representation of clients is therefore the core of the legal and ethical governance of the legal profession.

This chapter examines the building blocks of the lawyer-client relationship. Section II begins by noting that lawyers provide legal services to clients. While this idea sounds simple, Section II

---

1   C. Wendell Manning, *Words of Encouragement to New Admittees*, 44 La. Bar J. 374 (1996).

explores the increasingly complex issue of whether lawyers are the *only* ones that can lawfully provide legal services to clients. Technology and other developments have led to a rise in the number of websites, software, and apps that offer what looks a lot like "legal services." How are these regulated? This section of the chapter also addresses *whether* and *how* lawyers can work with others to provide services to clients and the rules about *where* lawyers can provide their services.

FYI

You might want to look at the numbers of lawyers in particular types of jobs or sizes at law firms, including numbers by gender. Clara N. Carson, *The Lawyer Statistical Report: The U.S. Legal Profession in 2000* (The American Bar Foundation). The National Association for Law Placement also has useful <u>data here</u>.

Section III examines how the lawyer-client relationship is created and explores obligations that may exist even in the absence of a lawyer-client relationship. Once begun, how does the lawyer-client relationship end? Section IV explains the rules lawyers must follow. These sections are critically important because the lawyer-client relationship is the framework that establishes many obligations.

Sections V and VI set forth the basic ground rules for the attorney-client relationship. First, the services lawyers provide must be competent. Questions of competence arise in the contexts of ethics, malpractice, and the constitutional right to counsel. Second, who makes what decisions in the lawyer-client relationship? Many lawyers and members of the public think the client is in charge, but the chapter explains that some decisions belong

Take Note

For this Chapter and the entire casebook, when the text refers to a Rule, remember to read the entire Rule and Comment even though the text only includes excerpts.

to the client and others to the lawyer. Determining which is which is not always easy. Section VI also covers some additional rules about the lawyer-client relationship.

II. Defining the Practice of Law

For More Information

If you want to read more about the history of the unauthorized practice restrictions, two excellent articles are Deborah L. Rhode, *Policing the Professional Monopoly: A Constitutional and Empirical Analysis of Unauthorized Practice Prohibitions*, <u>34 Stan. L. Rev. 1 (1981)</u> and Bruce A. Green, *The Disciplinary Restrictions on Multidisciplinary Practice: Their Derivation, Their Development, and Some Implications for the Core Values Debate*, <u>84 Minn. L. Rev. 1115 (2000)</u>.

Lawyers belong to one of the oldest professions in the world. In most countries, those who are licensed or qualified as lawyers have the exclusive right to provide certain services. The size and scope of this monopoly may vary from country to country and from time to time, but there are generally certain activities that are "reserved" for lawyers.

In the United States, the scope of the legal profession's monopoly has varied over time. The courts have generally determined the qualification of those who were able to appear in court as litigators.

Until the twentieth century, however, businesses or not-for-profit organizations controlled by nonlawyers often provided transactional and litigation services, employing lawyers when necessary to appear in court on behalf of the organization or its customers. Today, most states broadly define what is meant by the phrase "the practice of law" and thus the scope of the lawyer's monopoly. Although some countries limit the lawyer's monopoly to courtroom work, in the U.S. today, it is commonly understood that the "practice of law" includes certain kinds of transactional, litigation, and regulatory work. Most, if not all, states prohibit the "practice of law" by nonlawyers, as well as lawyers who are not licensed in that state. Some exceptions exist by custom or law. For example, generally speaking, nonlawyers may represent themselves in court, accountants may provide tax advice, and nonlawyers may represent social security disability claimants. Despite some clear exceptions, however, it can be difficult to define what is included within the phrase "the practice of law" and the scope of activities exclusively reserved for lawyers. Moreover, even when the meaning of the phrase is clear, there have been debates about whether the restrictions are appropriate. The sections that follow show the framework that has been used to address these issues and debates.

A. The Prohibition

Similar to the rules in other states and the ABA Model Rules of Professional Conduct, Delaware Rule of Professional Conduct 5.5(a) provides that a lawyer "shall not practice law in a jurisdiction in violation of the regulation of the legal profession in that jurisdiction, or assist another in doing so." Comment [2] to Rule 5.5 explains that "[t]he defi-

What About Your State?

Click here for information on each state's definition of the practice of law.

nition of the practice of law is established by law and varies from one jurisdiction to another."

States differ not only with respect to their definitions of "the practice of law" (and thus the unauthorized practice of law or "UPL"), but also with respect to where the definition of the "practice of law" or UPL is found. For example, in some jurisdictions, the definition is found in a statute, whereas in other jurisdictions the definition is found in caselaw. At least one state—Colorado—specifies in its Rules of Professional Conduct those activities that may not be conducted by a disbarred lawyer. A jurisdiction may also choose to elaborate upon its UPL definition in a handbook or policy manual.

For example, Section 6126(a) of the California Business and Professions Code provides that:

> Any person advertising or holding himself or herself out as practicing or entitled to practice law or otherwise practicing law who is not an active member of the State Bar, or otherwise authorized pursuant to statute or court rule to practice law in this state at the time of doing so, is guilty of a misdemeanor punishable by up to one year in a county jail or by a fine of up to one thousand dollars ($1,000), or by both that fine and imprisonment.

The Los Angeles County Office of the District Attorney's Unauthorized Practice of Law Manual for Prosecutors 6 (2004) adds:

* * *

California today defines law practice as providing *"legal advice and legal instrument and contract preparation, whether or not these subjects were rendered in the course of litigation." Birb[r]ower, Montalban, Condo & Frank, P.C. v Superior Court. . . .* Providing legal advice or service is a violation of the State Bar Act if done by an unlicensed person, even if the advice or service does not relate to any matter pending before a court.

Make the Connection

You can find an excerpt from the *Birbrower* case in Part II.D., *infra*.

As a general matter, the state Attorney General, local District Attorney, or bar association enforces a state's unauthorized practice laws through "criminal prosecutions, civil injunctions, restitution, disbarment, [and] contempt of court."[2] A private cause of action is a more recent development that is available only in some states.

B. Limits on Nonlawyers Providing Low Cost Legal Assistance

Many of the leading UPL cases have arisen in the context of nonlawyers who attempt to provide low cost assistance to clients. This section begins with some of the early UPL cases so that you understand how the law in this area has evolved. The cases included in sections B(1–3) examine whether nonlawyers were violating UPL provisions when engaged in the following activities:

1) selling hard-copy legal forms;

2) typing in blanks on a legal form for a customer;

3) advising customers in person on how to complete a legal form; and

4) publishing a book that advises people on how to complete legal forms.

These cases should help you understand the justifications offered in favor of UPL provisions and the critiques. This section also provides an opportunity to examine whether and how this traditional UPL framework is involved in contemporary cases that involve more sophisticated technology than blank legal forms or hard-copy books.

---

2   Susan D. Hoppock, *Current Developments: Enforcing Unauthorized Practice of Law Prohibitions: The Emergence of the Private Cause of Action and Its Impact on Effective Enforcement*, 20 Geo. J. Legal Ethics 719, 730 (2007).

Florida Bar v. Brumbaugh

355 So. 2d 1186 (Fla. 1978)

PER CURIAM.

The Florida Bar has filed a petition charging Marilyn Brumbaugh with engaging in the unauthorized practice of law, and seeking a permanent injunction prohibiting her from further engaging in these allegedly unlawful acts. Respondent, Marilyn Brumbaugh, is not and has never been a member of the Florida Bar, and is, therefore, not licensed to practice law within this state. She has advertised in various local newspapers as "Marilyn's Secretarial Service" offering to perform typing services for "Do-It-Yourself" divorces, wills, resumes, and bankruptcies. The Florida Bar charges that she performed unauthorized legal services by preparing for her customers those legal documents necessary in an uncontested dissolution of marriage proceeding and by advising her customers as to the costs involved and the procedures which should be followed in order to obtain a dissolution of marriage. For this service, Ms. Brumbaugh charges a fee of $50.

* * * In State v. Sperry, 140 So. 2d 587, 595 (Fla.1962), we noted:

> The reason for prohibiting the practice of law by those who have not been examined and found qualified to practice is frequently misunderstood. It is not done to aid or protect the members of the legal profession either in creating or maintaining a monopoly or closed shop. It is done to protect the public from being advised and represented in legal matters by unqualified persons over whom the judicial department can exercise little, if any, control in the matter of infractions of the code of conduct which, in the public interest, lawyers are bound to observe.

The Florida Bar as an agent of this Court, plays a large role in the enforcement of court policies and rules and has been active in regulating and disciplining unethical conduct by its members. Because of the natural tendency of all professions to act in their own self interest, however, this Court must closely scrutinize all regulations tending to limit competition in the delivery of legal services to the public, and determine whether or not such regulations are truly in the public interest.

With regard to the charges made against Marilyn Brumbaugh, this Court appointed a referee to receive evidence and to make findings of fact, conclusions of law, and recommendations as to the disposition of the case. The referee found that respondent, under the guise of a "secretarial" or "typing" service prepares, for a fee, all papers deemed by her to be needed for the pleading, filing, and securing of a dissolution of marriage, as well as detailed instructions as to how the suit should be filed, notice served, hearings set, trial conducted, and the final decree secured. The referee also found that in one instance, respondent prepared a quit claim deed in reference to the marital property of the parties. The referee determined that respondent's contention that she merely operates a typing service is rebutted by numerous facts in evidence. Ms. Brumbaugh has no blank forms either to sell or to fill out. Rather, she types up the documents for her customers after they have asked her to prepare a petition or an entire set of dissolution of marriage papers. Prior to typing up the papers, respondent asks her customers whether custody, child support, or alimony is involved. Respondent has four sets of dissolution of marriage papers, and she chooses which set is appropriate for the particular customer. She then types out those papers, filling in the blank spaces with the appropriate information. Respondent instructs her customers how the papers are to be signed, where they are to be filed, and how the customer should arrange for a final hearing.

Marilyn Brumbaugh, who is representing herself in proceedings before this Court * * * argues that she has never held herself out as an attorney, and has never professed to have legal skills. She does not give advice, but acts merely as a secretary. She is a licensed counselor, and asserts the right to talk to people and to let her customers make decisions for themselves.

This case does not arise out of a complaint by any of Ms. Brumbaugh's customers as to improper advice or unethical conduct. It has been initiated by members of The Florida Bar who believe her to be practicing law without a license. The evidence introduced at the hearing below shows that none of respondent's customers believed that she was an attorney, or that she was acting as an attorney in their behalf. Respondent's advertisements clearly addressed themselves to people who wish to do their own divorces. These customers knew that they had to have "some type of papers" to file in order to obtain their dissolution of marriage. Respondent never handled contested divorces. During the past two years respondent has assisted several hundred customers in obtaining their own divorces. The record shows that while some of her customers told respondent exactly what they wanted, generally respondent would ask her customers for the necessary information needed to fill out the divorce papers, such as the names and addresses of the parties, the place and duration of residency in this state, whether there was any property settlement to be resolved, or any determination as to custody and support of children. Finally, each petition contained the bare allegation that the marriage was irretrievably broken. Respondent would then inform the parties as to which documents needed to be signed, by whom, how many copies of each paper should be filed, where and when they should be filed, the costs involved, and what witness testimony is necessary at the court hearing. Apparently, Ms. Brumbaugh no longer informs the parties verbally as to the proper procedures for the filing of the papers, but offers to let them copy papers described as "suggested procedural education."

The Florida Bar argues that the above activities of respondent violate the rulings of this Court in *The Florida Bar v. American Legal and Business Forms, Inc.*, 274 So. 2d 225 (Fla. 1973), and *The Florida Bar v. Stupica*, 300 So. 2d 683 (Fla. 1974). In those decisions we held that it is lawful to sell to the public printed legal forms, provided they do not carry with them what purports to be instructions on how to fill out such forms or how to use them. We stated that legal advice is inextricably involved in the filling out and advice as to how to use such legal forms, and therein lies the danger of injury or damage to the public if not properly performed in accordance with law. In *Stupica, supra*, this Court rejected the rationale of the New York courts in *New York County Lawyers' Ass'n v. Dacey*, 28 A.D.2d 161, 283 N.Y.S.2d 984, *rev'd and dissenting opinion adopted* 21 N.Y.2d 694, 287 N.Y.S.2d 422, 234 N.E.2d 459 (N.Y. 1967), which held that the publication of forms and instructions on their use does not constitute the unauthorized practice of law if these instructions are addressed to the public in general rather than to a specific individual legal problem. The Court in *Dacey* stated that the possibility that the principles or rules set forth in the text may be accepted by a particular reader as solution to his problem, does not mean that the publisher is practicing law. Other states have adopted the principle of law set forth in *Dacey*, holding that the sale of legal forms with instructions for their use does not constitute unauthorized practice of law. However, these courts have prohibited all personal contact between the service providing such forms and the customer, in the nature of consultation, explanation, recommendation, advice, or other assistance in selecting particular forms, in filling out any part of the forms, suggesting or advising how the forms should be used in solving the particular problems.

Although persons not licensed as attorneys are prohibited from practicing law within this state, it is somewhat difficult to define exactly what constitutes the practice of law in all instances. This Court has previously stated that:

> . . . if the giving of such advice and performance of such services affect important rights of a person under the law, and if the reasonable protection of the rights and property of those advised and served requires that the persons giving such advice possess legal skill and a knowledge of the law greater than that possessed by the average citizen, then the giving of such advice and the performance of such services by one for another as a course of conduct constitute the practice of law.

This definition is broad and is given content by this Court only as it applies to specific circumstances of each case. We agree that "any attempt to formulate a lasting, all encompassing definition of 'practice of law' is doomed to failure 'for the reason that under our system of jurisprudence such practice must necessarily change with the ever-changing business and social order.' "

The policy of this Court should continue to be one of encouraging persons who are unsure of their legal rights and remedies to seek legal assistance from persons licensed by us to practice law in this state. However, in order to make an intelligent decision as whether or not to engage the assistance of an attorney, a citizen must be allowed access to information which will help determine the complexity of the legal problem.

Present dissolution procedures in uncontested situations involve a very simplified method of asserting certain facts required by statute, notice to the other parties affected, and a simple hearing where the trial court may hear proof and make inquiries as to the facts asserted in those pleadings.

The legal forms necessary to obtain such an uncontested dissolution of marriage are susceptible of standardization. This Court has allowed the sale of legal forms on this and other subjects, provided that they do not carry with them what purports to be instructions on how to fill out such forms or how they are to be used. *The Florida Bar v. American Legal and Business Forms, Inc., supra; The Florida Bar v. Stupica, supra.* These decisions should be reevaluated in light of those recent decisions in other states which have held that the sale of forms necessary to obtain a divorce, together with any related textual instructions directed towards the general public, does not constitute the practice of law. * * *

Although there is a danger that some published material might give false or misleading information, that is not a sufficient reason to justify its total ban. We must assume that our citizens will generally use such publications for what they are worth in the preparation of their cases, and further assume that most persons will not rely on these materials in the same way they would rely on the advice of an attorney or other persons holding themselves out as having expertise in the area. The tendency of persons seeking legal assistance to place their trust in the individual purporting to have expertise in the area necessitates this Court's regulation of such attorney-client relationships, so as to require that persons giving such advice have at least a minimal amount of legal training and experience. Although Marilyn Brumbaugh never held herself out as an attorney, it is clear that her clients placed some reliance upon her to properly prepare the necessary legal forms for their dissolution proceedings. To this extent we believe that Ms. Brumbaugh overstepped proper bounds and engaged in the unauthorized practice of law. We hold that Ms. Brumbaugh, and others in similar situations, may sell printed material purporting to explain legal practice and procedure to the public in general and she may sell sample legal forms. To this extent we limit our prior holdings in *Stupica* and *American Legal and Business Forms, Inc.* Further, we hold that it is not improper for Marilyn Brumbaugh to engage in a secretarial service, typing such forms for her clients, provided that she only copy the information given to her in writing by her clients. In addition, Ms. Brumbaugh may advertise her business activities of providing secretarial and notary services and selling legal forms and general printed information. However, Marilyn Brumbaugh must not, in conjunction with her business, engage in advising clients as to the various remedies available to them, or otherwise assist them in preparing those forms necessary for a dissolution proceeding. More specifically, Marilyn Brumbaugh may not make inquiries nor answer questions from her clients as to the particular forms which might be necessary, how best to fill out such forms, where to properly file such forms, and how to present necessary evidence at the court hearings. Our specific holding with regard to the dissolution of marriage also applies to other unauthorized legal assistance such as the preparation of wills or real estate transaction documents. While Marilyn Brumbaugh may legally sell forms in these areas, and type up instruments which have been completed by clients, she must not engage in personal legal assistance in conjunction with her business activities, including the correction of errors and omissions.

Food for Thought

May a nonlawyer help a "sick friend" from church prepare papers in a worker's compensation case? Does the answer depend on whether the particular jurisdiction is one of those that allows nonlawyer advocates to represent clients in worker compensation cases? *See* Kate Howard, *Defiant Jacksonville Retiree Charged With Practicing Law Without A License*, jacksonville.com, June 16, 2010.

Accordingly, having defined the limits within which Ms. Brumbaugh and those engaged in similar activities may conduct their business without engaging in the unauthorized practice of law, the rule to show cause is dissolved.

It is so ordered.

1. Debates Regarding Unauthorized Practice Restrictions

The Rules of Professional Conduct share the *Brumbaugh* Court's view of the purpose of the restrictions on nonlawyer practice. The Comment to Rule 5.5 explains that the rationale for the prohibition on nonlawyer practice is to "protect[] the public against rendition of legal services by unqualified persons." However, the unauthorized practice restrictions have prominent critics. Professor Deborah L. Rhode has challenged the bar's stated rationale:

> Almost from conception, the unauthorized practice movement has been dominated by the wrong people asking the wrong questions. Enforcement of sweeping prohibitions has rested with those least capable of disinterested action. Judicial involvement has been infrequent and generally unedifying. Invoking standards that are conclusory, circular, or both, courts have typically inquired only whether challenged activity calls for "legal" skills, not whether lay practitioners in fact possess them. At every level of enforcement, the consumer's need for protection has been proclaimed rather than proven. * * *

> Particularly at a time when lawyers are justifiably concerned about their public image, the bar itself has much to gain from abdicating its role as self-appointed guardian of the professional monopoly. Given mounting popular skepticism about unauthorized practice enforcement, prudential as well as policy considerations argue for greater consumer choice. Absent evidence of significant injuries resulting from lay assistance, individuals should be entitled to determine the cost and quality of legal services that best meet their needs. Where there are demonstrable grounds for paternalism, it should emanate from institutions other than the organized bar. A profession strongly committed to maintaining both the fact and appearance of impartiality in other contexts should recognize the value of more dispassionate decisionmaking in unauthorized practice enforcement. If, as bar spokesmen repeatedly insist, the "fight to stop [lay practice] is the public's fight," it is time for the profession to relinquish the barricades.[3]

Which view do you find more persuasive?

2. Legal Advice Books

As the *Brumbaugh* Court notes, most jurisdictions permit the publication of books that aid people in representing themselves. In the pathbreaking case of *New York County Lawyers' Ass'n. v. Dacey*, 234 N.E.2d 459 (N.Y. 1967), the New York Court of Appeals, which is New York's highest court, endorsed the dissenting opinion of the lower court and held that by writing the book *How to Avoid Probate!*, Norman Dacey was simply providing information about law and

---

3   Deborah L. Rhode, *Policing the Professional Monopoly: A Constitutional and Empirical Analysis of Unauthorized Practice Prohibitions*, 34 Stan. L. Rev. 1, 98–99 (1981). For an update to this article, see Deborah L. Rhode and Lucy Buford Ricca, *Protecting the Profession or the Public? Rethinking Unauthorized-Practice Enforcement*, 82 Fordham L. Rev. 2587 (2014).

not actually practicing law. In the dissent of *New York County Lawyers' Ass'n v. Dacey*, Justice Stevens wrote:

> Stripped of the arguments and the contentions of the various parties, the question may be briefly and baldly expressed: Does the writing, publication, advertising, sale and distribution of "How To Avoid Probate!" constitute the unauthorized practice of law * * *? It cannot be claimed that the publication of a legal text which purports to say what the law is amounts to legal practice. And the mere fact that the principles or rules stated in the text may be accepted by a particular reader as a solution to his problem does not affect this. Courts and lawyers continuously use and cite texts for this very purpose. So also with forms. The publication of a multitude of forms for all manner of legal situations is a commonplace activity and their use by the Bar and the public is general. In fact, many statutes and court rules contain the forms to be used in connection with them. Apparently it is urged that the conjoining of these two, that is, the text and the forms, with advice as to how the forms should be filled out, constitutes the unlawful practice of law. But that is the situation with many approved and accepted texts.
>
> Dacey's book is sold to the public at large. There is no personal contact or relationship with a particular individual. Nor does there exist that relation of confidence and trust so necessary to the status of attorney and client. This is the essential of legal practice—the representation and the advising of a particular person in a particular situation. The lectures of a law school professor are not legal practice for the very reason that the principles enunciated or the procedures advised do not refer to any activity in immediate contemplation though they are intended and conceived to direct the activities of the students in situations which may arise.
>
> * * *
>
> At most the book assumes to offer general advice on common problems, and does not purport to give personal advice on a specific problem peculiar to a designated or readily identified person.
>
> "How To Avoid Probate!" may be purchased by anyone willing to pay the purchase price. One is free to purchase or not as he wills. There is no personal reliance upon the selection and judgment of Dacey in the discretionary choice of a form adapted to the customer's needs.

See It

Today, one of the major publishers of legal self-help books is Nolo Press. To see the extensive list of legal books that Nolo Press publishes, click here.

> "How To Avoid Probate!" has been published and freely sold for more than one year. There is no showing in this record that this book has exploited the public or led its members astray improperly or incorrectly. In fact there is no factual evidence submitted as to the effect of the publication and sale of the book. In order to sustain petitioner's position one has to conclude

that the book by its very nature comprises the unauthorized practice of law. "How To Avoid Probate!" is, in one sense, a do-it-yourself kit. To that extent it could encroach upon the preserves of lawyers, though the present record does not give evidence of that fact. Every individual has a right to represent himself if he chooses to do so, and to assume the risks attendant upon what could prove a precarious undertaking. Those of sufficient substance to require trusts or wills for the most part are persons of some common sense and, normally, would hardly be expected to rely completely and unquestioningly upon a mass-printed form, even with accompanying instructions. However, they have a right to do so.

3. Legal Software

Today, as a result of technological advances, the question of unauthorized practice is more complex than it was in the 1960s and 1970s when the *Brumbaugh* and *Dacey* cases were decided. Many consumers now use computer software, web sites, or apps. One of the first cases to apply UPL principles to legal software was *Unauthorized Practice of Law Committee v. Parsons Technology, Inc.*, 1999 WL 47235 (N.D. Tex. 1999). In *Parsons,* the District Court enjoined the sale of Quicken Family Lawyer software, finding it constituted unauthorized practice of law under Texas UPL law:

> * * * QFL offers over 100 different legal forms (such as employment agreements, real estate leases, premarital agreements, and seven different will forms) along with instructions on how to fill out these forms. QFL's packaging . . . indicates that QFL will have the user "answer a few questions to determine which estate planning and health care documents best meet [the user's] needs;" and that QFL will "interview you in a logical order, tailoring documents to your situation." Finally, the packaging reassures the user that "[h]andy hints and comprehensive legal help topics are always available."
>
> * * *

Go Online

Click here to see an advertisement for wills from LegalZoom.

QFL goes beyond merely instructing someone how to fill in a blank form. While no single one of QFL's acts, in and of itself, may constitute the practice of law, taken as a whole Parsons, through QFL, has gone beyond publishing a sample form book with instructions, and has ventured into the unauthorized practice of law.

The Texas legislature responded swiftly to the *Parsons* case, amending state law in response to the court's ruling. As a result, the Fifth Circuit Court of Appeals vacated the District Court's injunction:

> [T]he . . . Legislature enacted an amendment to § 81.101 providing that "the 'practice of law' does not include the design, creation, publication, distribution, display, or sale . . . [of] computer software, or similar products if the products clearly and conspicuously state that the products are not a substitute for the advice of an attorney," effective immediately. H.B. 1507, 76th Leg., Reg. Sess. (Tex. 1999). We therefore VACATE the injunction. . . .

Unauthorized Practice of Law Committee v. Parsons Tech., Inc., 179 F.3d 956 (5th Cir. 1999).

The *Parsons* case, which involved the Quicken Family Lawyer software and subsequent remedial legislation, happened in 1999. Since that time, technology has continued to evolve. The 2016 Final Report of the ABA Commission on the Future of Legal Services included the finding that "new providers of legal services are proliferating and creating additional choices for consumers and lawyers." The Report noted that in 2009, fifteen legal startups appeared on AngelList, which is a website for startup companies and their "angel" investors, whereas in 2016, there were more than 400 legal startups (and perhaps as many as 1,000).

Online providers such as LegalZoom and Rocket Lawyer have become major forces in the legal services market. For example, when LegalZoom was contemplating selling shares as a publicly traded company, it filed an SEC disclosure document that stated that "20 percent of new California limited liability companies were formed using our online legal platform in 2011."

Another development is the rise of artificial intelligence and legal-oriented apps, which have become much more common since Apple launched its App Store in July 2008. For example, in 2016, a nineteen-year-old college student created a robot lawyer or "bot" that successfully challenged more than 160,000 parking tickets in less than two years. Another 2016 development was the announcement by a leading U.S. law firm that it had retained IBM's ROSS, which is an artificial intelligence "attorney," for its bankruptcy practice. Scholars have written about the dramatic changes in legal practice that are likely to come from advances in artificial intelligence.

For More Information

If you want to read more about ways in which nonlawyers have helped customers prepare legal documents through software or the internet, *see* Catherine J. Lanctot, *Scriveners in Cyberspace: Online Document Preparation and the Unauthorized Practice of Law*, 30 Hofstra L. Rev. 811 (2002); ABA Resolution 10A (August 2019) (adopting the ABA Best Practice Guidelines for Online Legal Document Providers dated August 2019).

Courts and regulators have been grappling with the issue of how to respond to developments such as these and whether and how they fit into the UPL framework previously developed. For example, Missouri and North Carolina, among other jurisdictions, have asserted that LegalZoom is engaged in the unauthorized practice of law. In 2012, LegalZoom filed a lawsuit against The North Carolina State Bar alleging, *inter alia*, that the State Bar exceeded its statutory powers when it communicated to the public that LegalZoom was prohibited from offering its services in North Carolina and when it refused to register LegalZoom's prepaid legal services plans. LegalZoom also sought a declaration that it was not engaged in the unauthorized practice of law. The State Bar filed a counterclaim against LegalZoom that sought an injunction against LegalZoom on the grounds of UPL.

After LegalZoom filed its lawsuit against the North Carolina State Bar seeking injunctive relief and the North Carolina State Bar filed its counterclaim, the judge considered cross motions, including the State Bar's motion for judgment on the pleadings regarding its UPL counterclaim. In *LegalZoom, Inc. v. North Carolina State Bar,* 2014 N.C. B. C. 9, the trial court denied the State Bar's request for judgment on the pleadings, finding in paragraph 51 that "a more developed record is appropriate. . . ." The court stated that it found the "self-representation" exception to UPL inapplicable, but that it was unclear whether LegalZoom should be able to rely on the "scrivener's exception," which allows unlicensed individuals to "record information that another provides without engaging in UPL as long as they do not also provide advice or express legal judgments." In other words, the court was unsure whether principles reminiscent of those used in the *Brumbaugh* case were appropriate in the LegalZoom case. The trial court posed the following questions in its order and opinion denying the motions for judgment on the pleadings:

> [65] In some instances, LegalZoom's software operations may comfortably remain within the permissible boundaries of these cases, such as where a legal form closely tracks a state agency form, the information a customer supplies is routine, and no significant part of the form is added or omitted based on customer responses. There are other aspects of the LegalZoom program that may not comfortably fit the scrivener exception, such as instances where LegalZoom may, either by itself or in association with another, go beyond recording information, for example, in obtaining or approving legal descriptions for deeds, reviewing and assessing potentially interfering trademarks, or taking actions to finalize incorporation.

> [66] The court is not yet comfortable that it understands the overall process of preparing more complex documents, and hopes to develop a greater understanding of how the branching software process is implemented in preparing such documents, including whether and how a customer's answer to one question effects what further parts of the template are offered and what further choices the customer is asked to make. Questions include, for example, if a customer makes one choice presented to him by the branching software, are there portions of the template that are then never shown to the customer? If so, what is the reasoning behind and the legal significance of the software's determination not to present that portion of the form? If *Pledger* teaches that an unlicensed individual has the right to "practice law" on his own behalf, . . . does its premise require that only the unlicensed individual make choices in drafting a legal document, and that the choice or risk of an incorrect choice about which portions of a form to include must belong exclusively to the individual? Is there then a legally significant difference between how one engaging in self-representation uses a form book versus LegalZoom's interactive branching software? A form book presents the customer with the entire form, often

accompanied by opinions or directions on how to use the form, but any choice and its implications are solely the customer's. Does the LegalZoom software effectively make choices for its customer? Do responses depend in any part on the effects of statements embodied in the software, either those that promote the program or those that disclaim legal advice being given?

[67] The court does not by any means suggest these are the controlling or only relevant questions or that they have certain answers. Rather, they are examples of questions the court is not comfortable answering based on the current record alone.

In 2015, the parties signed a consent judgment in which they agreed that the definition of the "practice of law" as set forth in North Carolina's UPL statute did not "encompass LegalZoom's operation of a website that offers consumers access to interactive software that generates a legal document based on the consumer's answers to questions presented by the software so long as LegalZoom complies with [the six items listed in Paragraph 2]." As you review this Consent Judgment, which appears below, consider how the traditional UPL framework reflected by cases such as *Brumbaugh*, *Dacey*, and *Parsons Technology* likely shaped the settlement of this case.

LegalZoom.com, Inc. v. N.C. State Bar

2015 N.C. Bus. Crt. 96

THIS MATTER is before the Court on the parties' joint request for entry of a consent judgment. The Complaint in this action was filed by the Plaintiff LegalZoom.com, Inc. (LegalZoom) against the Defendant The North Carolina State Bar (the State Bar) asserting the right to provide its internet-based document services to consumers in North Carolina. The State Bar filed a Counterclaim asserting that LegalZoom's document services constitute the practice of law as defined in Chapter 84 of the North Carolina General Statutes. LegalZoom and the State Bar desire to settle all claims and issues raised in this action and, for that purpose, agree to the continuing jurisdiction of this Court over them and over the subject matter of this action, and waive the entry of findings of fact and conclusions of law. As evidenced by the signatures below of counsel of record, the parties have settled the dispute and have agreed to the disposition of this action by entry of this agreed Consent Judgment and to comply with the following terms:

1.   The parties agree that the definition of the "practice of law" as set forth in N.C.G.S. § 84-2.1 does not encompass LegalZoom's operation of a website that offers consumers access to interactive software that generates a legal document based on the consumer's answers to questions presented by the software so long as LegalZoom complies with the provisions of Paragraph 2 below.

2.   LegalZoom agrees that it must continue to ensure, for the shorter of a period of two (2) years after the entry of this Consent Judgment or the enactment of

legislation in North Carolina revising the statutory definition of the "practice of law," that:

(a)　LegalZoom shall provide to any consumer purchasing a North Carolina product (a North Carolina Consumer) a means to see the blank template or the final, completed document before finalizing a purchase of that document;

(b)　An attorney licensed to practice law in the State of North Carolina has reviewed each blank template offered to North Carolina Consumers, including each and every potential part thereof that may appear in the completed document. The name and address of each reviewing attorney must be kept on file by LegalZoom and provided to the North Carolina Consumer upon written request;

(c)　LegalZoom must communicate to the North Carolina Consumer that the forms or templates are not a substitute for the advice or services of an attorney;

(d)　LegalZoom discloses its legal name and physical location and address to the North Carolina Consumer;

(e)　LegalZoom does not disclaim any warranties or liability and does not limit the recovery of damages or other remedies by the North Carolina Consumer; and

(f)　LegalZoom does not require any North Carolina Consumer to agree to jurisdiction or venue in any state other than North Carolina for the resolution of disputes between LegalZoom and the North Carolina Consumer.

3.　The parties have agreed to mutually support and use best efforts to obtain passage by the North Carolina General Assembly of HB 436 in the form currently pending before the House Judiciary Committee.

4.　The Court will retain jurisdiction over this action for the purpose of ensuring compliance and enforcing the provisions of this Consent Judgment for two (2) years from this date. The parties may choose to extend the terms of this Consent Judgment by mutual agreement. The Court's jurisdiction may be terminated earlier upon joint notification by the parties that the General Assembly has passed legislation which covers the matters addressed herein. If no such legislation is passed, and if the parties do not jointly request that the terms of this Consent Judgment be extended, the terms of this Consent Judgment shall terminate two (2) years from this date and the parties will no longer be bound by any of the terms of this Consent Judgment. Upon such termination of this Consent Judgment at the end of the two year period, the parties shall be deemed to have preserved each of its claims and defenses in the present case and shall not be deemed to have waived any of its arguments under the statute defining the practice of law.

5.   Upon entry of this Consent Judgment, LegalZoom may request registration of its modified pre-paid legal services plans submitted to the State Bar for registration without additional filing or registration fees. Upon registration of the modified plans by the State Bar, LegalZoom shall, within ten (10) business days, file a Notice of Dismissal of the pending Federal Court case, *LegalZoom.com, Inc. v. North Carolina State Bar, et al.*, (No. 1:15-CV-439, M.D.N.C.), without prejudice as to the State Bar and as to "official capacity" claims against the individual defendants, and with prejudice as to "individual capacity" claims against the individual defendants. The Notice of Dismissal shall reflect that each party bears its own attorneys' fees and costs. Also, within ten (10) business days of entry of this Consent Judgment, LegalZoom shall file a voluntary dismissal without prejudice in *LegalZoom.com, Inc. v. North Carolina State Bar* (No. 13 CVS 13755, Wake County).

6.   Nothing in this Consent Judgment is intended or may be construed as an admission by either party or constitute a finding or judgment by the Court that either party has violated any statute, regulation, common law, or other legal obligation.

7.   The parties must provide notice and a thirty-day cure period and negotiate in good faith to resolve any dispute relating to the interpretation or implementation of this Consent Judgment before bringing any matter to the Court's attention for resolution, including but not limited to any claim that the other party has violated or failed to comply with any term of this Consent Judgment.

8.   The parties to this action and no one else shall have standing to seek construction or enforcement of this Consent Judgment. At the request of either party, after providing the parties with notice and hearing, and upon entering written findings after hearing, the Court may grant declaratory and all other relief necessary to construe or enforce this Consent Judgment.

9.   This Consent Judgment embodies in full the terms of the agreement and understanding between the parties related to the subject matter of this action and this Consent Judgment.

10.   The parties shall bear their own costs and expenses in this matter, including attorneys' fees.

[The Consent Judgment order was dated Oct. 22, 2015 and was signed by the attorneys for the parties and by the Chief Special Superior Court Judge for Complex Business Cases]

————————

While this Consent Judgment has resolved for the time being the UPL issue in North Carolina with respect to LegalZoom, it seems inevitable that state courts and regulators will continue to be faced with issues related to UPL and the question of whether and how UPL provisions should apply to new legal services technology and providers. The trial court order denying the State Bar's request for judgment on the pleadings illustrates the types of questions that are likely to be raised as regulators and others address the issue of how to apply traditional UPL doctrine to a changed world. Other recent decisions show the difficulty that courts have had in determining what constitutes the practice of law. In *In re Serendipity Morales*, 2016 VT 85, the Vermont Supreme Court held that there was not probable cause to find that a "jailhouse lawyer" violated Vermont's UPL provisions by helping fellow inmates in their cases, including performing legal research and drafting motions. In *Lola v. Skadden, Arps, Slate, Meagher & Flom*, 620 F. App'x 37 (2d Cir. 2015), the Second Circuit refused to dismiss a complaint that alleged that plaintiff's document review was devoid of legal judgment, and, therefore, he was not engaged in the practice of law and was entitled to overtime pay. (The case was subsequently settled.) As these cases suggest, the courts continue to be asked to apply UPL provisions in a variety of circumstances that require the court to examine the goals and consequences of UPL provisions.

Another development that may be relevant to the enforcement of UPL provisions is the U.S. Supreme Court's 2015 decision entitled *North Carolina State Board of Dental Examiners v. Federal Trade Commission*. In that case, the Supreme Court held that the North Carolina State Board of Dental Examiners could not invoke the state action immunity defense in an antitrust suit that sought to enjoin a Dental Board rule that provided that only licensed dentists were entitled to perform teeth whitening. The Supreme Court found that because a number of the Dental Board's decision-makers were active market participants in the occupation the Board regulated, the Dental Board could invoke the state-action antitrust immunity only if it was subject to active supervision

For More Information

Are you interested in the impact of the Supreme Court's *Dental Board* case on lawyer regulation? Click here for a webpage with resources devoted to this topic. In November 2018, the Supreme Court of Washington established a Bar Structure Work Group and asked it to develop recommendations based on the *Dental Board* and other cases.

by the State. The Supreme Court found that the active supervision requirement was not met. The *Dental Board* case has had an impact on UPL regulation. For example, the Oregon State Bar, which is a unified bar association, added Article 20.2 to its Bylaws; the new Bylaw specified that no more than one-quarter of its UPL Committee members may be lawyers engaged in the private practice of law. The Virginia Supreme Court amended its UPL rules by requiring that all UPL Advisory Opinions or rules be submitted to the Court for its review and thereafter by eliminating the State Bar's UPL Committee. The *Dental Board* case has spawned at least one lawsuit that has challenged the UPL-related activities of state and local bar associations.

Changes in technology, an increased focus on access to legal services issues, and possible scrutiny from antitrust authorities may lead to changes in traditional UPL enforcement. For example, the 2016 Final Report of the ABA Commission on the Future of Legal Services contained findings about access to legal services gaps and recommended that courts "consider regulatory innovations in the area of legal services delivery." The Report noted that the ABA's Model Regulatory Objectives for the Provision of Legal Services "offer courts much-needed guidance as they consider how to regulate the practice of law in the 21st century." This section of the report was referring to a 2016 ABA resolution that adopted Model Regulatory Objectives for the Provision of Legal Services and that urged "each state's highest court, and those of each territory and tribe, be guided by [the regulatory objectives] when they assess the court's existing regulatory framework and any other regulations they may choose to develop concerning non-traditional legal service providers."

Regulatory objectives may provide a useful mechanism when jurisdictions evaluate whether and how to adapt their definition of the practice of law, and the rules that govern the conditions under which lawyers may work with nonlawyers, which is addressed in the next section. Regulatory objectives can provide a framework for policy debates about how the existing rules should apply to new technology developments and whether regulatory change is needed. For example, many U.S. jurisdictions likely would conclude that client protection is an appropriate regulatory objective, but preventing innovation in the delivery of legal services and protecting the legal profession from competition are not appropriate regulatory objectives. If a jurisdiction decides to include access to legal services as a regulatory objective, as Colorado has, it will then need to decide the same issues confronted by the *Brumbaugh*, *Dacey* and *Parsons Technology* courts—how to balance the objectives of client and public protection and the objective of access to legal services. The 2016 *Futures Report*, for example, included these findings: 1) most people living in poverty, and the majority of moderate-income individuals do not receive the legal help they need; 2) the public often does not obtain effective assistance with legal problems, either because of insufficient financial resources or a lack of knowledge about when legal problems exist that require resolution through legal representation; 3) the vast number of unrepresented parties in court adversely impacts all litigants, including those who have representation; 4) many lawyers, especially recent law graduates, are un- or under-employed despite the significant unmet need for legal services; and 5) the traditional law practice business model constrains innovations that would provide greater access to, and enhance the delivery of, legal services. Some commentators believe that some of the major regulatory questions of the next ten years will include whether and how to apply the UPL principles to nonlawyers and determining the degree to which lawyers may work with nonlawyers to develop new legal services delivery methods. Arizona, California, Illinois, and Utah are among the states that currently are or have considered issues related access, innovation, and UPL. This topic of the degree to which lawyers and nonlawyers may work together is addressed in the next section.

C. Lawyers Working with Nonlawyers

The last sentence of the ABA's 2016 Model Regulatory Objectives resolution stated that "nothing contained in this Resolution abrogates in any manner existing ABA policy prohibiting nonlawyer ownership of law firms or the core values adopted by the [ABA] House of Delegates." For those who are aware of lawyer regulatory history, this sentence reflects the fact that for more than thirty years, there have been debates about whether lawyers should be able to share an ownership interest with nonlawyers when providing legal services.

Lawyers have long had nonlawyer employees who help them deliver legal services. Lawyers have also worked with nonlawyers who have helped lawyers provide nonlegal services associated with legal services, such as title insurance connected to real estate transactions. Although these relationships are perfectly acceptable, all but a handful of U.S. jurisdictions prohibit lawyers from having nonlawyer partners if any of the activities of the partnership consist of the practice of law. These jurisdictions also prohibit lawyers from splitting their legal fees with nonlawyers, except in very narrow circumstances. The jurisdictions that are exceptions are: (1) Washington, D.C., which, for more than twenty years, has had a rule that allows lawyers and nonlawyers to be partners and share fees when delivering legal services; and (2) states such as Washington and Utah, which have approved limited law licenses. These states allow lawyers to partner with, and share legal fees with, those holding these limited law licenses. (Washington calls these individuals *Limited License Legal Technicians* or LLLTs. For more information, see Stephen R. Crossland & Paula C. Littlewood, *Washington's Limited License Legal Technician Rule and Pathway to Expanded Access for Consumers,* 122 Dick. L. Rev. 859 (2018).)

Although virtually all states prohibit lawyers and nonlawyers from splitting legal fees or forming a partnership for the delivery of legal services, this issue has been the subject of debate since the ABA Model Rules of Professional Conduct were first adopted. The ABA Model Rules were developed by the Kutak Commission and adopted in 1983. The Kutak Commission proposed a version of Rule 5.4 that would have allowed partnerships among lawyers and nonlawyers so long as certain safeguards were employed. (The proposed safeguards were similar to the safeguards currently found in Rule 1.8(a).) During the debates before the ABA House of Delegates, someone asked "Does this mean Sears can open a law firm?" Professor Geoffrey Hazard, who was the Reporter for the Commission, answered "Yes," and the debate ended with a resounding defeat of the proposal.

The issue of lawyers working with nonlawyers resurfaced during the 1990s in what has come to be called the multidisciplinary practice or "MDP" debates. Some of the discussion was driven by the fact that the "Big 5" accounting firms were hiring a large number of lawyers who offered services that some considered to be legal services, in violation of the rules that prohibited fee sharing and partnership among lawyers and nonlawyers. The ABA established a Commission on Multidisciplinary Practice that was active between 1998 and 2000. In advance of the August 1999 Annual Meeting, the Commission recommended that the ABA Model Rules be amended in order to permit MDPs. The ABA House of Delegates rejected the Commission's proposal and adopted a substitute motion that said that the ABA should "make no change, addition or amendment to the Model Rules of Professional Conduct which permits a lawyer to offer legal services through a multidisciplinary practice unless and until additional study demonstrates that such changes will further the public interest without sacrificing or compromising lawyer independence and the legal profession's tradition of loyalty to clients." The language about "further study" illustrates the fundamentally different views that proponents and opponents have had with respect to the allocation of the "burden of proof" on this issue.

> **For More Information**
>
> You can find an excellent summary of the MDP debates in Mary C. Daly, *What the MDP Debate Can Teach Us About Law Practice in the New Millennium and the Need for Curricular Reform,* 50 J. Legal Educ. 521 (2000).

The Commission returned a year later, in July 2000, and recommended that lawyers be "permitted to share fees and join with nonlawyer professionals in a practice that delivers both legal and nonlegal professional services provided that the lawyers have the control and authority necessary to assure lawyer independence in the rendering of legal services." The ABA House of Delegates once again rejected the Commission's proposed resolution and adopted a lengthy substitute resolution that said, among other things, that it was "in the public interest to preserve the core values of the legal profession." The resolution identified six core values which included undivided loyalty to the client; the duty to competently exercise independent legal judgment for the benefit of the client; the duty to hold client confidences inviolate; the duty to avoid conflicts of interest with the client; the duty to help maintain a single profession of law with responsibilities as a representative of clients, an officer of the legal system, and a public citizen having special responsibility for the quality of justice; and the duty to promote access to justice. Paragraph 7 of the successful substitute resolution stated that the "sharing of legal fees with nonlawyers and the ownership and control of the practice of law by nonlawyers are inconsistent with the core values of the legal profession." Paragraph 8 stated that the "law governing lawyers, that prohibits lawyers from sharing legal fees with nonlawyers and from directly or indirectly transferring to nonlawyers ownership or control over entities practicing law, should not be revised." The resolution called upon states to reaffirm their commitment to enforcing vigorously their respective law governing lawyers, to reevaluate and refine to the extent necessary the definition of the "practice of law," and to retain and enforce laws that generally bar the practice of law by entities other than law firms.

Two years later, and in the wake of the Enron scandal, Congress adopted the Sarbanes-Oxley Act of 2002. Sarbanes-Oxley (or SOX as it is sometimes called) limited the ability of auditors of publicly traded companies to offer other kinds of services, including legal services, to the companies they audited. Following the ABA's MDP vote and the passage of SOX, public discussion about nonlawyer ownership and partners largely disappeared.

Two global developments have contributed to a revival of discussions about lawyers partnering with nonlawyers. In 2007, the Australian personal injury law firm of Slater & Gordon became the first publicly traded law firm in the world when it issued shares on the Australian Stock Exchange. This development prompted significant discussion in the U.S. about whether it was important for law firms to be able to raise outside capital (and the risks that might be associated with this development). The second significant global development was the United Kingdom's adoption of a new legal services act. In addition to a number of other significant changes contained in the act, the 2007 UK Legal Services Act created a framework that allowed lawyers and nonlawyers to become partners and allowed outside investment in, and ownership of, law firms. In March 2012, the UK Solicitors Regulation Authority (SRA), which is the "front-line" regulator for solicitors in England and Wales, issued the first set of licenses to these "alternative business structure" or ABS firms. Three-and-one-half years later, the SRA had issued more than 400 ABS licenses to a variety of entities, including law firms, insurance company affiliates, the Coop, which is a large consumer cooperative with a diverse family of retail businesses in more than 4,500 locations, LegalZoomUK, a hedge fund, and others. U.S.

law firms, including Alston & Bird and Reed Smith, are among those who hold an ABS license for their UK offices. (You can search for ABS licenses here.)

The ABA Commission on Ethics 20/20 took note of the global developments described above. (The Commission was established in 2009 to review the ABA Model Rules of Professional Conduct and the U.S. system of lawyer regulation in the context of advances in technology and global legal practice developments.) In April 2011, the Commission circulated for comment an "Issues Paper Concerning Alternative Business Structures." In December 2011, following the submission of a number of comments, the Commission revised its approach and circulated for comment a discussion paper on "Alternative Law Practice Structures." (Note that the acronym had changed from ABS to ALPS.) The ALPS Discussion Paper sought comments on a "form of nonlawyer ownership that is similar to the form of nonlawyer ownership that the District of Columbia has permitted for 21 years." In April 2012, after receiving a number of comments, the 20/20 Commission issued a press release stating that it would not propose any changes to the ABA policy prohibiting nonlawyer ownership of law firms.

Despite this pronouncement, in less than three years, the ABA was once again examining issues related to the relationship between lawyers and nonlawyers. In 2014 the ABA created another commission entitled the "Commission on the Future of Legal Services." Its purpose statement noted that easy access to affordable legal services is critical in a society based on the rule of law, but the courts are seriously underfunded. This statement also noted that procedures are complex, and many who need legal advice cannot afford to hire a lawyer and are forced to represent themselves. The Commission's purpose statement also observed that technology, globalization, and other forces were transforming the ways in which legal services are accessed and delivered. It noted that the ABA was in a position to lead the effort to improve the delivery of, and access to, legal services in the United States and to inspire innovation, leverage technology, encourage new models for regulating legal services, and foster the development of financially viable models for delivering legal services that meet the public's needs. Among other things, the ABA Commission on the Future of Legal Services was asked to "propose new approaches that are not constrained by traditional models for delivering legal services and are rooted in the essential values of protecting the public, enhancing diversity and inclusion, and pursuing justice for all."

By the time the ABA Futures Commission disbanded in August 2016, it had issued a lengthy final report and two recommendations that were adopted by the ABA. Acting upon the recommendation of the Commission, the ABA voted to establish a Center for Innovation and adopted a resolution encouraging states to adopt its model regulatory objectives. As noted at the beginning of this section, the last paragraph of the regulatory objectives resolution stated that "nothing contained in this Resolution abrogates in any manner existing ABA policy prohibiting nonlawyer ownership of law firms or the core values adopted by the [ABA] House of Delegates." Despite the language in the February 2016 resolution, Recommendation 2.3 in the Commission's Final Report stated that "[c]ontinued exploration of alternative business structures (ABS) will be useful, and where ABS is allowed, evidence and data regarding the risks and benefits associated with these entities should be developed and assessed."

This lengthy background information has been included because the issue of lawyers working with nonlawyers continues to be relevant—and controversial. Most states have rules of professional conduct that limit the ways in which lawyers and nonlawyers can work together to deliver legal services. Recently, however, the documented gaps in access to legal services and the billions of dollars invested in the "legal services space" have given rise to initiatives to reconsider these rules. In 2019, the Utah Supreme Court unanimously voted to implement an August 2019 Report that recommended eliminating or substantially relaxing Rule 5.4. During the same year, an Arizona Supreme Court Task Force Report recommended eliminating Rule 5.4 and the State Bar of California circulated for public comment a set of recommendations from its *Task Force on Access Through Innovation of Legal Services* that included substantial changes to Rule 5.4. In February 2020, the ABA was scheduled to consider Resolution 115 that encourages U.S. jurisdictions to consider regulatory innovations that foster new ways to deliver legal services and that have the potential to improve the accessibility and affordability of those services, while recognizing the continued need for protection of the public. Regardless of what happens with these specific initiatives, they demonstrate continued interest in issues related to Rule 5.4 and lawyer-nonlawyer relationships. Thus, as you apply the rules set forth in the sections that follow, consider the policy arguments that may be offered in support of keeping the rules in their current form and the arguments that may be offered in support of changing these rules.

For More Information

As the Casebook explains, although the ABA has repeatedly declined to recommend significant changes to the lawyer-nonlawyer partnership provisions in Rule 5.4, there is significant state interest in this issue. One source of information to monitor these developments is the IAALS "Unlocking Regulation Knowledge Center," which is found here. For links to the ABA's prior initiatives, as well as other Rule 5.4 information and resources, see Laurel S. Terry, *Resources and URLs Related to ABA Model Rule of Professional Conduct 5.4* (2019) (prepared for the ABA's 2019 annual ethics conference).

1. Lawyers Working with Nonlawyers to Deliver Legal Services

Lawyers may employ or retain nonlawyers to assist them in providing legal services, but the lawyers must supervise the nonlawyers to ensure that they comply with the lawyer's ethical obligations. Rule 5.3 governs the lawyer's supervisory obligations toward nonlawyers. The first obligation is organizational. Rule 5.3(a) provides that both "a partner" and lawyers with "comparable managerial authority" must "make reasonable efforts to ensure that the firm has in effect measures giving reasonable assurance that the [nonlawyer's] conduct is compatible with professional obligations of the lawyer." Rule 5.3(b) focuses on the "lawyer having direct supervisory authority over the nonlawyer." That lawyer has an obligation to "make reasonable efforts to ensure that the [nonlawyer's] conduct is compatible with the professional obligations of the lawyer[.]" Rule 5.3(b) and Rule 5.5(a), which were cited in Section II(A), *supra*, mean that a lawyer has an obligation to supervise nonlawyer employees in order to avoid the unauthorized practice of law. (As you will recall, Rule 5.5(a) prohibits a lawyer from assisting another to engage in UPL.)

For More Information

The extent to which lawyers must supervise nonlawyer employees in order to avoid unauthorized practice is not always clear. Paul Tremblay observes that "[a] lawyer cannot know with confidence . . . whether the delegation of some tasks to a nonlawyer colleague might result in her assisting in the unauthorized practice of law, because the state of the law and the commentary about nonlawyer practice is so confused and incoherent. Some respected authority within the profession instructs the lawyer that she may only delegate preparatory matters and must prohibit the nonlawyer from either discussing legal matters with clients or negotiating on behalf of clients. Other authority suggests that the lawyer may delegate a wide array of tasks as long as the lawyer supervises the work of the nonlawyer and accepts responsibility for it." Paul R. Tremblay, *Shadow Lawyering: Nonlawyer Practice Within Law Firms*, 85 Ind. L.J. 653, 698 (2010).

Consider Rule 5.4(a), which governs the financial arrangements between lawyers and nonlawyers, when you analyze the question that follows. The threshold provision of the Rule 5.4(a) prohibition states that "[a] lawyer or law firm shall not share legal fees with a nonlawyer."

Rule 5.4 includes several exceptions, one of which states that "a lawyer or law firm may include nonlawyer employees in a compensation or retirement plan, even though the plan is based in whole or in part on profit-sharing arrangement[.]" Additional exceptions allow a lawyer to share legal fees pursuant to an agreement that provides for the payment of money, over a reasonable period of time after the lawyer's death, to the lawyer's estate or to one or more specified persons or pursuant to the sale of a law practice provisions of Rule 1.17. Another exception allows a lawyer to share "court-awarded legal fees with a nonprofit organization that employed, retained or recommended employment of the lawyer in the matter." While many states, such as Illinois, have adopted a version of Rule 5.4 that is the same as the ABA Model Rule version, other states, such as Colorado and Delaware, have included an additional exception to Rule 5.4 that provides an incentive to lawyers to complete the unfinished legal business of a deceased lawyer.

[Question 2-1]

An attorney is the managing partner at a small law firm. The attorney believes that technology will be increasingly important in the delivery of affordable legal services and hires a nonlawyer to manage the law office's technology services. This person is given the title of Chief Technology Strategist. The Chief Technology Strategist does not participate in any decisions involving legal judgment. The firm pays the Chief Technology Strategist a fixed salary that is larger than the salaries of some of the associate lawyers and larger than the salaries of all of the other nonlawyer staff. The Chief Technology Strategist is included as a participant in the firm's year-end profit-sharing plan along with the lawyers and other nonlegal staff who work at the firm.

Is the attorney subject to discipline?

(A) **Yes, because legal fees are used to fund the year-end profit-sharing plan.**

(B) **Yes, because the Chief Technology Strategist makes more money than some of the lawyers in the law firm.**

(C) **No, because the Chief Technology Strategist is included in the firm's year-end profit sharing arrangement.**

(D) **No, because the attorney reasonably believes that the year-end profit sharing plan is necessary in order to attract top talent and deliver competent services to clients.**

Rule 5.4 contains additional provisions that set the ground rules for lawyers' relationships with nonlawyers. Please review the remainder of Rule 5.4 and then apply its provisions to Question 2-2:

(b) A lawyer shall not form a partnership with a nonlawyer if any of the activities of the partnership consist of the practice of law.

(c) A lawyer shall not permit a person who recommends, employs, or pays the lawyer to render legal services for another to direct or regulate the lawyer's professional judgment in rendering such legal services.

(d) A lawyer shall not practice with or in the form of a professional corporation or association authorized to practice law for a profit, if:

> (1) a nonlawyer owns any interest therein, except that a fiduciary representative of the estate of a lawyer may hold the stock or interest of the lawyer for a reasonable time during administration;

> (2) a nonlawyer is a corporate director or officer thereof or occupies the position of similar responsibility in any form of association other than a corporation; or

> (3) a nonlawyer has the right to direct or control the professional judgment of a lawyer.

Food for Thought

In-house counsel work for organizations that have nonlawyer owners, officers, or directors. Why is that permitted? The rationale is that organizations may generally represent themselves and that in-house counsel are assisting in that effort, not representing an outside client as an employee of an organization. In addition, for constitutional and policy reasons, public interest organizations are permitted to represent outside clients in pursuit of their public interest objectives.

[Question 2-2]

An attorney, who is a certified elder law specialist, entered into a partnership with a certified financial planner. The partnership provided legal and other assistance to clients in connection with issues related to aging. The attorney did not allow the certified financial planner to interfere with the attorney's independent legal judgment. The financial planner performed only work that she was authorized to perform as a certified financial planner.

Is the attorney subject to discipline?

(A) **Yes, because the attorney formed a partnership with a certified financial planner and some of the activities of this partnership consisted of the practice of law.**

(B) **Yes, because the attorney's clients are subject to undue influence if they receive their legal services and financial planning at the same time.**

(C) **No, because it is in the best interests of the attorney's clients to receive coordinated advice about both legal services and financial planning.**

(D) **No, because the attorney did not allow the certified financial planner to interfere with the attorney's independent legal judgment.**

2. Ancillary Businesses

The topic of ancillary businesses, which are sometimes referred to as law-related businesses, is related to, but distinct from, the profit-sharing, joint ownership, and MDP and ABS issues implicated by Rule 5.4. The topic of ancillary businesses is covered by Rule 5.7 and assumes that a lawyer is involved in the delivery of services that are not legal services. Rule 5.7 determines whether the rules of [legal] professional conduct will apply to law-related services that are not legal services. The ABA MDP debates led to changes in Rule 5.7 in a number of states. (The MDP resolution adopted in 2000 had called on the ABA "to develop any necessary rule amendments related to strategic alliances and other contractual relationships with nonlegal professional service providers." The ABA did so and thereafter a number of states amended their version of Rule 5.7.)

After you review Rule 5.7 and Rule 1.8(a), which is cited in the Comment to Rule 5.7, analyze the fact pattern in Question 2-3.

Rule 5.7(b) defines law-related services as "services that might reasonably be performed in conjunction with and in substance are related to the provision of legal services, and that are not prohibited as unauthorized practice of law when provided by a nonlawyer." Rule 5.7(a) makes a lawyer:

> subject to the Rules of Professional Conduct with respect to the provision of law-related services * * * if the law-related services are provided:
>
> (1) by the lawyer in circumstances that are not distinct from the lawyer's provision of legal services to clients; or
>
> (2) in other circumstances by an entity controlled by the lawyer individually or with others if the lawyer fails to take reasonable measures to assure that a person obtaining the law-related services knows that the services are not legal services and that the protections of the client-lawyer relationship do not exist.

The Comment to <u>Rule 5.7</u> provides additional information:

[5] When a client-lawyer relationship exists with a person who is referred by a lawyer to a separate law-related service entity controlled by the lawyer, individually or with others, the lawyer must comply with Rule 1.8(a).

[6] In taking the reasonable measures referred to in paragraph (a)(2) to assure that a person using law-related services understands the practical effect or significance of the inapplicability of the Rules of Professional Conduct, the lawyer should communicate to the person receiving the law-related services, in a manner sufficient to assure that the person understands the significance of the fact, that the relationship of the person to the business entity will not be a client-lawyer relationship. The communication should be made before entering into an agreement for provision of or providing law-related services, and preferably should be in writing.

[7] The burden is upon the lawyer to show that the lawyer has taken reasonable measures under the circumstances to communicate the desired understanding. For instance, a sophisticated user of law-related services, such as a publicly held corporation, may require a lesser explanation than someone unaccustomed to making distinctions between legal services and law-related services, such as an individual seeking tax advice from a lawyer-accountant or investigative services in connection with a lawsuit.

[Question 2-3]

An attorney has a regulatory law practice and is also a part owner of a lobbying firm, which employs lawyers and nonlawyers to provide lobbying services. The lobbying firm's rates and policies are comparable to those of other local lobbying firms. Each week, the attorney spends time conducting lobbying activities from the lobbying firm offices, and time providing legal services from the attorney's law firm, which is located in a different building.

The attorney recently advised one of her legal services clients that the client might want to lobby the legislature to change the regulations that govern the client's conduct. The attorney advised the client that the attorney owned a lobbying firm. The attorney carefully explained that the services provided by the lobbying firm were not legal services and that the legal ethics rules did not apply to the lobbying firm or to the attorney while engaged in lobbying for the lobbying firm. The attorney told the client to feel free to consult other lobbyists and lawyers in order to decide who to hire, and that there was no obligation to hire the attorney's lobbying firm. Following these disclosures, the client retained the attorney's lobbying firm to lobby the legislature for a rule change.

In conducting lobbying activities for the client, must the attorney comply with the rules of professional conduct relating to client confidentiality?

(A) Yes, because the attorney's lobbying services for the client are law-related activities.

(B) **Yes, because the attorney's lobbying services are not distinct from the legal services the attorney provided to the client.**

(C) **No, because the attorney's provision of lobbying services was distinct from the attorney's provision of legal services to the client and the attorney took reasonable measures to make sure that the client knew that the lobbying services were not legal services and that the protections of the client-lawyer relationship would not exist with respect to the lobbying services.**

(D) **No, because the rates and policies of lobbying firm are comparable to those of other lobbying firms that are not subject to the Rules of Professional Conduct.**

It is important to remember that Rule 5.7 addresses the issue of what rules govern the provision of services that are law-related services but are not legal services. To state it differently, Rule 5.7 only applies to situations in which a client receives services that are law-related services but are not considered to be legal services. (If the services a client receives are legal services, then the rules of professional conduct clearly apply to the delivery of those services.)

Although Rule 5.7 tells a lawyer whether the lawyer must follow the rules of professional conduct with respect to services that are law-related services, but not legal services, Rule 5.7 is not the only rule with which a lawyer must be concerned when engaged in this type of ancillary business. Although many of the rules of professional conduct only apply in connection with a lawyer's representation of a client, some rules apply to lawyers 24/7. For example, under Rule 8.4(c), it is professional misconduct for a lawyer to engage in conduct involving dishonesty, fraud, deceit or misrepresentation even if that conduct does not occur in the course of representing a client. Thus, a lawyer providing a law-related or ancillary business is subject to Rule 8.4(c) with respect to those activities. Rule 1.8(a) is another rule with which a lawyer providing ancillary business services must comply. As you will see in Chapter 5, Rule 1.8(a) prohibits a lawyer from entering into a business transaction with a current client unless the three cumulative requirements in Rule 1.8(a) are satisfied. Lawyers who provide law-related services to a client must also comply with Rule 1.8(a).

D. Unauthorized Practice of Law by Lawyers

Although UPL provisions often are directed towards nonlawyers, lawyers can also violate UPL provisions if they engage in the practice of law in a jurisdiction in which they are not licensed or otherwise authorized. As you saw in Chapter 1, a lawyer who is not licensed in a jurisdiction may file a motion to appear *pro hac vice* ("for this time only") before a court in that jurisdiction. In other words, a lawyer who wants to appear on a temporary basis in another jurisdiction in order to litigate a particular case has a mechanism available to do so—the *pro hac vice* motion. Each U.S. jurisdiction has a *pro hac vice* rule and information about how to use this process is available online. In contrast to the procedures that have long been available to litigators, until recently, there was not a rule or mechanism that authorized a transactional lawyer to appear temporarily in a jurisdiction in which that lawyer was not licensed. Nor was there a rule that an out-of-state lawyer could use when representing a client in an arbitration matter, as opposed to representing a client before a court. The 1998 *Birbrower* case was a landmark decision that focused attention on the unauthorized practice of law by lawyers. It prompted significant changes. As the descriptive material after the case explains, after *Birbrower* was decided, the ABA and most U.S. states revised their versions of Rule 5.5 in order to allow transactional lawyers who were not licensed in their state to practice there on a temporary basis.

Birbrower, Montalbano, Condon & Frank, P.C. v. Superior Court

949 P.2d 1 (Cal. 1998), *cert. denied*, 525 U.S. 920 (1998)

Chin, J.

* * *

The facts with respect to the unauthorized practice of law question are essentially undisputed. [Birbrower, Montalbano, Condon & Frank, P.C. (Birbrower)] is a professional law corporation incorporated in New York * * *. During 1992 and 1993, Birbrower attorneys, defendants Kevin F. Hobbs and Thomas A. Condon (Hobbs and Condon), performed substantial work in California relating to the law firm's representation of [ESQ Business Services, Inc. (ESQ)]. Neither Hobbs nor Condon has ever been licensed to practice law in California. None of Birbrower's attorneys were licensed to practice law in California during Birbrower's ESQ representation.

ESQ is a California corporation * * *. In July 1992, the parties negotiated and executed the fee agreement in New York, providing that Birbrower would perform legal services for ESQ, including "All matters pertaining to the investigation of and prosecution of all claims and causes of action against Tandem Computers Incorporated [Tandem]." The "claims and causes of action" against Tandem, a Delaware corporation with its principal place of business in Santa Clara County, California, related to a software development and marketing contract between Tandem and ESQ dated March 16, 1990 (Tandem Agreement). The Tandem Agreement stated that "The internal laws of the State of California (irrespective of its choice of law principles) shall govern the validity of this Agreement, the construction of its terms, and the interpretation and enforcement of the rights and duties of the parties hereto." Birbrower asserts, and ESQ disputes, that ESQ knew Birbrower was not licensed to practice law in California.

While representing ESQ, Hobbs and Condon traveled to California on several occasions. In August 1992, they met in California with ESQ and its accountants. During these meetings, Hobbs and Condon discussed various matters related to ESQ's dispute with Tandem and strategy for resolving the dispute. They made recommendations and gave advice. During this California trip, Hobbs and Condon also met with Tandem representatives on four or five occasions during a two-day period. At the meetings, Hobbs and Condon spoke on ESQ's behalf. Hobbs demanded that Tandem pay ESQ $15 million. Condon told Tandem he believed that damages would exceed $15 million if the parties litigated the dispute.

Around March or April 1993, Hobbs, Condon, and another Birbrower attorney visited California to interview potential arbitrators and to meet again with ESQ and its accountants. Birbrower had previously filed a demand for arbitration against Tandem with the San Francisco offices of the American Arbitration Association (AAA). In August 1993, Hobbs returned to California to assist ESQ in settling the Tandem matter. While in California, Hobbs met with ESQ and its accountants to discuss a proposed settlement agreement Tandem authored. Hobbs also met with Tandem representatives to discuss possible changes in the proposed agreement. Hobbs gave ESQ legal advice during this trip, including his opinion that ESQ should not settle with Tandem on the terms proposed.

ESQ eventually settled the Tandem dispute, and the matter never went to arbitration. But before the settlement, ESQ and Birbrower modified the contingency fee agreement. The modification changed the fee arrangement from contingency to fixed fee, providing that ESQ would pay Birbrower over $1 million. The original contingency fee arrangement had called for Birbrower to receive "one-third (1/3) of all sums received for the benefit of the Clients . . . whether obtained through settlement, motion practice, hearing, arbitration, or trial by way of judgment, award, settlement, or otherwise . . . ."

In January 1994, ESQ sued Birbrower for legal malpractice and related claims in Santa Clara County Superior Court. * * * Birbrower * * * filed a counterclaim, which included a claim for attorney fees for the work it performed in both California and New York. * * * ESQ moved for summary judgment and/or adjudication * * * [arguing] that by practicing law without a license in California * * * Birbrower violated section 6125, rendering the fee agreement unenforceable. Based on these undisputed facts, the Santa Clara Superior Court granted ESQ's motion for summary adjudication. * * * The court concluded that: (1) Birbrower was "not admitted to the practice of law in California"; (2) Birbrower "did not associate California counsel"; (3) Birbrower "provided legal services in this state"; and (4) "The law is clear that no one may recover compensation for services as an attorney in this state unless he or she was a member of the state bar at the time those services were performed."

Although the trial court's order stated that the fee agreements were unenforceable, at the hearing on the summary adjudication motion, the trial court also observed: "It seems to me * * * if they aren't allowed to collect their attorney's fees here, I don't think that puts the attorneys in a position from being precluded from collecting all of their attorney's fees, only those fees probably that were generated by virtue of work that they performed in California and not that work that was performed in New York."

* * *

We granted review to determine whether Birbrower's actions and services performed while representing ESQ in California constituted the unauthorized practice of law under section 6125 and, if so, whether a section 6125 violation rendered the fee agreement wholly unenforceable.

II. DISCUSSION

A. The Unauthorized Practice of Law

The California Legislature enacted section 6125 in 1927 as part of the State Bar Act (the Act), a comprehensive scheme regulating the practice of law in the state. Since the Act's passage, the general rule has been that, although persons may represent themselves and their own interests regardless of State Bar membership, no one but an active member of the State Bar may practice law for another person in California. The prohibition against unauthorized law practice * * * is designed to ensure that those performing legal services do so competently.

Although the Act did not define the term "practice law," case law explained it as " 'the doing and performing services in a court of justice in any matter depending therein throughout its various stages and in conformity with the adopted rules of procedure.' " (*People ex rel. Lawyers' Institute of San Diego v. Merchants' Protective Corp.* (1922). 209 P. 363 (*Merchants*).) *Merchants* included in its definition legal advice and legal instrument and contract preparation, whether or not these subjects were rendered in the course of litigation. * * *

In addition to not defining the term "practice law," the Act also did not define the meaning of "in California." In today's legal practice, questions often arise concerning whether the phrase refers to the nature of the legal services, or restricts the Act's application to those out-of-state attorneys who are physically present in the state.

Section 6125 has generated numerous opinions on the meaning of "practice law" but none on the meaning of "in California." In our view, the practice of law "in California" entails sufficient contact with the California client to render the nature of the legal service a clear legal representation. In addition to a quantitative analysis, we must consider the nature of the unlicensed lawyer's activities in the state. Mere fortuitous or attenuated contacts will not sustain a finding that the unlicensed lawyer practiced law "in California." The primary inquiry is whether the unlicensed lawyer engaged in sufficient activities in the state, or created a continuing relationship with the California client that included legal duties and obligations.

Our definition does not necessarily depend on or require the unlicensed lawyer's physical presence in the state. Physical presence here is one factor we may consider in deciding whether the unlicensed lawyer has violated section 6125, but it is by no means exclusive. For example, one may practice law in the state in violation of section 6125 although not physically present here by advising a California client on California law in connection with a California legal dispute by telephone, fax, computer, or other modern technological means. Conversely, although we decline to provide a comprehensive list of what activities constitute sufficient contact with the state, we do reject the notion that a person automatically practices law "in California" whenever that person practices California law anywhere, or "virtually" enters the state by telephone, fax, email, or satellite. (*See, e.g., Baron v. City of Los Angeles*, 469 P.2d 353 (1970) ["practice law" does not encompass all professional activities].) * * *

This interpretation acknowledges the tension that exists between interjurisdictional practice and the need to have a state-regulated bar. As stated in the American Bar Association Model Code of Professional Responsibility, Ethical Consideration EC 3–9, "Regulation of the practice of law is accomplished principally by the respective states. Authority to engage in the practice of law conferred in any jurisdiction is not *per se* a grant of the right to practice elsewhere, and it is improper for a lawyer to engage in practice where he is not permitted by law or by court order to do so. However, the demands of business and the mobility of our society pose distinct problems in the regulation of the practice of law by the states. In furtherance of the public interest, the legal profession should discourage regulation that unreasonably imposes territorial limitations upon the right of a lawyer to handle the legal affairs of his client or upon the opportunity of a client to obtain the services of a lawyer of his choice in all matters including the presentation of a contested matter in a tribunal before which the lawyer is not permanently admitted to practice." *Baron* implicitly agrees with this canon.

Exceptions to section 6125 do exist, but are generally limited to allowing out-of-state attorneys to make brief appearances before a state court or tribunal. They are narrowly drawn and strictly interpreted. * * *

In addition, with the permission of the California court in which a particular cause is pending, out-of-state counsel may appear before a court as counsel *pro hac vice*. A court will approve a *pro hac vice* application only if the out-of-state attorney is a member in good standing of another state bar and is eligible to practice in any United States court or the highest court in another jurisdiction. The out-of-state attorney must also associate an active member of the California Bar as attorney of record and is subject to the Rules of Professional Conduct of the State Bar. * * *

> ## It's Latin to Me
>
> Black's Law Dictionary defines *pro hac vice* "[f]or this occasion or a particular purpose. The phrase [usually] refers to a lawyer who has not been admitted to practice in a particular jurisdiction but who is admitted there temporarily for the purpose of conducting a particular case."

B. The Present Case

The undisputed facts here show that neither *Baron's* definition nor our "sufficient contact" definition of "practice law in California" would excuse Birbrower's extensive practice in this state. Nor would any of the limited statutory exceptions to section 6125 apply to Birbrower's California practice. As the Court of Appeal observed, Birbrower engaged in unauthorized law practice in California on more than a limited basis, and no firm attorney engaged in that practice was an active member of the California State Bar. * * *

Birbrower contends, however, that section 6125 is not meant to apply to any out-of-state attorneys. Instead, it argues that the statute is intended solely to prevent non-attorneys from practicing law. This contention is without merit because it contravenes the plain language of the statute. Section 6125 clearly states that no person shall practice law in California unless that person is a member of the State Bar. The statute does not differentiate between attorneys or non-attorneys, nor does it excuse a person who is a member of another state bar. * * *

Birbrower next argues that we do not further the statute's intent and purpose-to protect California citizens from incompetent attorneys-by enforcing it against out-of-state attorneys. Birbrower argues that because out-of-state attorneys have been licensed to practice in other jurisdictions, they have already demonstrated sufficient competence to protect California clients. But Birbrower's argument overlooks the obvious fact that other states' laws may differ substantially from California law. Competence in one jurisdiction does not necessarily guarantee competence in another. By applying section 6125 to out-of-state attorneys who engage in the extensive practice of law in California without becoming licensed in our state, we serve the statute's goal of assuring the competence of all attorneys practicing law in this state. * * *

Assuming that section 6125 does apply to out-of-state attorneys not licensed here, Birbrower alternatively asks us to create an exception to section 6125 for work incidental to private arbitration or other alternative dispute resolution proceedings. Birbrower points to fundamental differences between private arbitration and legal proceedings, including procedural differences relating to discovery, rules of evidence, compulsory process, cross-examination of witnesses, and other areas. As Birbrower observes, in light of these differences, at least one court has decided that an out-of-state attorney could recover fees for services rendered in an arbitration proceeding. * * *

We decline Birbrower's invitation to craft an arbitration exception to section 6125's prohibition of the unlicensed practice of law in this state. Any exception for arbitration is best left to the Legislature, which has the authority to determine qualifications for admission to the State Bar and to decide what constitutes the practice of law. * * * In the face of the Legislature's silence, we will not create an arbitration exception under the facts presented. * * *

Finally, Birbrower urges us to adopt an exception to section 6125 based on the unique circumstances of this case. Birbrower notes that "Multi-state relationships are a common part of today's society and are to be dealt with in commonsense fashion." In many situations, strict adherence to rules prohibiting the unauthorized practice of law by out-of-state attorneys would be " 'grossly impractical and inefficient.' " * * *

Although * * * we recognize the need to acknowledge * * * the multistate nature of law practice, the facts here show that Birbrower's extensive activities within California amounted to considerably more than any of our state's recognized exceptions to section 6125 would allow. Accordingly, we reject Birbrower's suggestion that we except the firm from section 6125's rule under the circumstances here.

* * *

Because Birbrower violated section 6125 when it engaged in the unlawful practice of law in California, the Court of Appeal found its fee agreement with ESQ unenforceable in its entirety. Without crediting Birbrower for some services performed in New York, for which fees were generated under the fee agreement, the court reasoned that the agreement was void and unenforceable because it included payment for services rendered to a California client in the state by an unlicensed out-of-state lawyer. * * * We agree with the Court of Appeal to the extent it barred Birbrower from recovering fees generated under the fee agreement for the unauthorized legal services it performed in California. We disagree with the same court to the extent it implicitly barred Birbrower from recovering fees generated under the fee agreement for the limited legal services the firm performed in New York.

It is a general rule that an attorney is barred from recovering compensation for services rendered in another state where the attorney was not admitted to the bar. * * * The general rule, however, has some recognized exceptions.

* * * The [first] exception does not apply in this case; none of Birbrower's activities related to federal court practice.

A second exception on which Birbrower relies to enforce its entire fee agreement relates to "Services not involving courtroom appearance." * * * California has implicitly rejected this broad exception through its comprehensive definition of what it means to "practice law." Thus, the exception Birbrower seeks for all services performed outside the courtroom in our state is too broad under section 6125.

Some jurisdictions have adopted a third exception to the general rule of nonrecovery for in-state services, if an out-of-state attorney "makes a full disclosure to his client of his lack of local license and does not conceal or misrepresent the true facts." * * * In this case, Birbrower alleges that ESQ at all times knew that the firm was not licensed to practice law in California. Even assuming that is true, however, we reject the full disclosure exception for the same reasons we reject the argument that section 6125 is not meant to apply to non-attorneys. Recognizing these exceptions would contravene not only the plain language of section 6125 but the underlying policy of assuring the competence of those practicing law in California.

Therefore, as the Court of Appeal held, none of the exceptions to the general rule prohibiting recovery of fees generated by the unauthorized practice of law apply to Birbrower's activities in California. * * * Enforcing the fee agreement in its entirety would include payment for the unauthorized practice of law in California and would allow Birbrower to enforce an illegal contract.

Birbrower asserts that even if we agree with the Court of Appeal and find that none of the above exceptions allowing fees for unauthorized California services apply to the firm, it should be permitted to recover fees for those limited services it performed exclusively in New York under the agreement. In short, Birbrower seeks to recover under its contract for those services it performed for ESQ in New York that did not involve the practice of law in California, including fee contract negotiations and some corporate case research. Birbrower thus alternatively seeks reversal of the Court of Appeal's judgment to the extent it implicitly precluded the firm from seeking fees generated in New York under the fee agreement.

We agree with Birbrower that it may be able to recover fees under the fee agreement for the limited legal services it performed for ESQ in New York to the extent they did not constitute practicing law in California, even though those services were performed for a California client. Because section 6125 applies to the practice of law in California, it does not, in general, regulate law practice in other states. Thus, although the general rule against compensation to out-of-state attorneys precludes Birbrower's recovery under the fee agreement for its actions in California, the severability doctrine may allow it to receive its New York fees generated under the fee agreement, if we conclude the illegal portions of the agreement pertaining to the practice of law in California may be severed from those parts regarding services Birbrower performed in New York. * * *

In this case, the parties entered into a contingency fee agreement followed by a fixed fee agreement. ESQ was to pay money to Birbrower in exchange for Birbrower's legal services. The object of their agreement may not have been entirely illegal, assuming ESQ was to pay Birbrower compensation based in part on work Birbrower performed in New York that did not amount to the practice of law in California. The illegality arises, instead, out of the amount to be paid to Birbrower, which, if paid fully, would include payment for services rendered in California in violation of section 6125.

Therefore, we conclude the Court of Appeal erred in determining that the fee agreement between the parties was entirely unenforceable because Birbrower violated section 6125's prohibition against the unauthorized practice of law in California. Birbrower's statutory violation may require exclusion of the portion of the fee attributable to the substantial illegal services, but that violation does not necessarily entirely preclude its recovery under the fee agreement for the limited services it performed outside California.

Thus, the portion of the fee agreement between Birbrower and ESQ that includes payment for services rendered in New York may be enforceable to the extent that the illegal compensation can be severed from the rest of the agreement. * * *

III. Disposition

We conclude that Birbrower violated section 6125 by practicing law in California. To the extent the fee agreement allows payment for those illegal local services, it is void, and Birbrower is not entitled to recover fees under the agreement for those services. The fee agreement is enforceable, however, to the extent it is possible to sever the portions of the consideration attributable to Birbrower's services illegally rendered in California from those attributable to Birbrower's New York services. Accordingly, we affirm the Court of Appeal judgment to the extent it concluded that Birbrower's representation of ESQ in California violated section 6125, and that Birbrower is not entitled to recover fees under the fee agreement for its local services. We reverse the judgment to the extent the court did not allow Birbrower to argue in favor of a severance of the illegal portion of the consideration (for the California fees) from the rest of the fee agreement, and remand for further proceedings consistent with this decision.

———————

The Aftermath of Birbrower

Birbrower's ruling proved controversial and led policymakers and others to reconsider UPL issues. Following *Birbrower*, the California legislature modified its unauthorized practice statute to permit an out-of-state attorney to represent a party in an arbitration provided certain requirements were met. *See* California Code of Civil Procedure § 1282.4. The California legislature did not, however, adopt broad exceptions.

The influence of *Birbrower* extended well-beyond California. Because clients have legal needs that transcend state borders (and indeed national borders), it was common for lawyers throughout the country, not just the lawyers in the *Birbrower* case, to perform activities in states in which they were not licensed. This was true of lawyers who practiced in large law firms, lawyers who practiced in small law firms, and lawyers who practiced as in-house counsel. But, according to the *Birbrower* court, unauthorized out-of-state activity by lawyers in jurisdictions in which they were not licensed constituted the unauthorized practice of law. Moreover, unlike litigation lawyers, lawyers who were doing transactional work or arbitration did not have a rule or mechanism such as *pro hac vice* that they could use to obtain authorization to provide temporary legal services in a jurisdiction in which they were not licensed.

For More Information

For further discussion of the background of these rules, see Carol A. Needham, *Multijurisdictional Practice Regulations Governing Attorneys Conducting a Transactional Practice*, 2003 U. Ill. L. Rev. 1331; Cynthia L. Fountaine, *Have License, Will Travel: An Analysis of the New ABA Multijurisdictional Practice Rules*, 81 Wash. U. L.Q. 737 (2003).

The *Birbrower* case was one of the factors that led the ABA to establish the Commission on Multijurisdictional Practice. Although some commentators asked the Commission to recommend dramatic changes in the way lawyers are licensed in order to better reflect client needs and the national and global economy, the Commission's first resolution, which was adopted by the ABA House of Delegates in 2002, affirmed ABA support "for the principle of state judicial regulation of the practice of law." The Commission recommended, and the ABA adopted, a number of additional resolutions designed to balance "the interests of a state in protecting its residents and justice system, on the one hand; and the interests of clients in a national and international economy in the ability to employ or retain counsel of choice efficiently and economically." Some of the most important changes were the amendments to Rules 5.5 and 8.5. Among other changes, Rule 5.5 was amended to add a number of "safe harbor" provisions that would allow lawyers to practice in jurisdictions in which they were not licensed. The amendments to Rule 8.5 provided accountability by making lawyers subject to the ethics rules not only of the jurisdictions in which they were licensed, but jurisdictions in which they were engaged in the practice of law. Because this change meant that many lawyers would be subject to multiple—and perhaps conflicting—sets of ethics rules, the ABA modified the choice of law provision found in Rule 8.5(b). Many, but not all, jurisdictions followed the ABA's lead and amended their versions of Rules 5.5 and 8.5. Approximately one decade later, in 2013, the ABA added foreign in-house counsel to the safe-harbor provisions that appeared in Model Rule 5.5(d). In 2016, the ABA amended the foreign in-house counsel section of Rule 5.5(d) and added the definitions of foreign lawyers found in Model Rule 5.5(e). Many states have adopted the ABA's 2002 and 2013 changes to Rule 5.5, but few have adopted the ABA's 2016 changes. (The Food for Thought box, *infra*, has additional information about foreign lawyers' practice rights.)

For More Information

Should the regulation of lawyers be primarily a matter of state or federal concern? For arguments favoring federal regulation based largely on national policy considerations, *see* James W. Jones, Anthony E. Davis, Simon Chester & Caroline Hart, *Reforming Lawyer Mobility—Protecting Turf or Serving Clients?* 30 Geo. J. Legal Ethics 125 (2017) (proposing a new federal statute); Fred C. Zacharias, *Federalizing Legal Ethics,* 73 Tex. L. Rev. 335 (1994). Laurel Terry has explained that global considerations will further increase the pressure for more federal and international regulation of legal services. *See* Laurel S. Terry, *The Future Regulation of the Legal Profession: The Impact of Treating the Legal Profession as "Service Providers,"* 2008 J. Prof. Law. 189; *see also* Laurel S. Terry, *From GATS to APEC: The Impact of Trade Agreements on Legal Services,* 43 Akron L. Rev. 875 (2010).

Questions 2-4 through 2-6 will help you better understand the many subsections in Rule 5.5 and the scope of its safe-harbor provisions. Please review Delaware Rule 5.5[4], which appears below, and then answer these questions.

Rule 5.5. Unauthorized Practice of Law; Multijurisdictional Practice of Law

(a)　A lawyer shall not practice law in a jurisdiction in violation of the regulation of the legal profession in that jurisdiction, or assist another in doing so.

(b)　A lawyer who is not admitted to practice in this jurisdiction shall not:

(1)　except as authorized by these Rules or other law, establish an office or other systematic and continuous presence in this jurisdiction for the practice of law; or

(2)　hold out to the public or otherwise represent that the lawyer is admitted to practice law in this jurisdiction.

(c)　A lawyer admitted in another United States jurisdiction . . . and not disbarred or suspended from practice in any jurisdiction, may provide legal services on a temporary basis in this jurisdiction that:

(1)　are undertaken in association with a lawyer who is admitted to practice in this jurisdiction and who actively participates in the matter; [or]

(2)　are in or reasonably related to a pending or potential proceeding before a tribunal in this or another jurisdiction, if the lawyer, or a person the lawyer is assisting, is authorized by law or order to appear in such proceeding or reasonably expects to be so authorized; [or]

4　Delaware Rule 5.5 is different than ABA Model Rule of Professional Conduct 5.5 in a few respects. Delaware Rule 5.5(d)(1) requires in-house counsel to comply with Delaware's in-house counsel registration rule. (The ABA recognizes that some states might want to require registration and has adopted a Model Rule for Registration of In-House Counsel.) The second difference is that Delaware has not adopted the 2016 ABA amendments to Rule 5.5(d)(1) regarding foreign in-house counsel or the new definition of foreign lawyers found in ABA Model Rule 5.5(e).

(3)   are in or reasonably related to a pending or potential arbitration, mediation, or other alternative dispute resolution proceeding in this or another jurisdiction, if the services arise out of or are reasonably related to the lawyer's practice in a jurisdiction in which the lawyer is admitted to practice and are not services for which the forum requires *pro hac vice* admission; or

(4)   are not within paragraphs (c)(2) or (c)(3) and arise out of or are reasonably related to the lawyer's practice in a jurisdiction in which the lawyer is admitted to practice.

(d)   A lawyer admitted in another United States jurisdiction, or in a foreign jurisdiction, and not disbarred or suspended from practice in any jurisdiction, may provide legal services in this jurisdiction that:

(1)   are provided to the lawyer's employer or its organizational affiliates * * * and are not services for which the forum requires pro hac vice admission; or

(2)   are services that the lawyer is authorized to provide by federal law or other law of this jurisdiction.

[Question 2-4]

An attorney, who is admitted to practice only in State A, agrees to represent a client incorporated in State B in connection with the client's purchase of a State B company. The attorney from State A was retained to represent the State B client because the attorney had previously represented that client on a related matter and the client's parent corporation, which was a State A corporation. (Representing the parent and the subsidiary corporations did not create a conflict of interest for the attorney.) The attorney travels to State B from his State A office several times to negotiate the purchase of the company for the client.

Is the attorney subject to discipline?

(A)   Yes, because the attorney did not have a license to practice law in State B.

(B)   Yes, because the attorney did not associate with local counsel in State B.

(C)   No, because the attorney's representation of the client was reasonably related to the lawyer's practice in State A, where the lawyer is admitted to practice.

(D)   No, because the client asked the attorney to come to State B to handle the negotiations.

[Question 2-5]

An attorney is admitted in State A and works in the State A office of a law firm that has offices in States A and B. The law firm's office in State B does not have any litigators; the only firm lawyers who are licensed by State B are lawyers who handle complicated (and esoteric) regulatory issues.

On one occasion when a law firm client was sued for breach of contract in State B, the law firm asked the attorney to handle the State B litigation matter for the law firm client. The attorney filed a petition to appear pro hac vice in the State B case and expected the application to be granted. While the pro hac vice petition was still pending, the attorney traveled to State B where she interviewed trial witnesses and prepared documents to be used during the trial. As expected, the pro hac vice application was granted two weeks later.

Is the attorney subject to discipline?

> (A) Yes, because the attorney's presence in State B will be systematic and continuous during the lengthy trial.
>
> (B) Yes, because the attorney conducted work in State B before receiving permission to appear pro hac vice.
>
> (C) No, because the attorney's law firm has an office in State B.
>
> (D) No, because the attorney reasonably expected to be admitted pro hac vice by the State B court.

Question 2-5 involved a litigation matter. What if the attorney in Question 2-5 had been asked to handle an arbitration matter, rather than a litigation matter? Note that if the facts in Question 2-5 had involved an arbitration matter, a different section of Rule 5.5 would apply. The ultimate result, however, would be similar.

[Question 2-6]

An attorney is admitted in State A and works in the State A office of a personal injury law firm that has offices in States A and C. With the firm's permission, the attorney decides to relocate and practice full-time in the firm's office in State C. The attorney gives advice to clients, signs correspondence, and negotiates transactions on behalf of clients. The attorney is supervised by a State C-admitted partner who meets periodically with the attorney to review her work.

Is the attorney subject to discipline?

> (A) Yes, because the attorney has a systematic and continuous presence in State C, where she performs legal work.
>
> (B) Yes, because the attorney did not obtain informed consent from her clients before performing work in State C.
>
> (C) No, because the attorney's work is undertaken in association with a lawyer who is admitted to practice in State C who actively participates in the matter.
>
> (D) No, because the attorney's work is reasonably related to attorney's practice in State A.

This question requires that you consider the differences among the safe harbor provisions in Rule 5.5 (c) and the "federal law" and "in-house counsel" safe harbor provisions found in Rule 5.5(d). Note that Rule 5.5(d)'s provisions do not require the services to be offered on a temporary basis.

When considering Question 2-6, it is worth noting that in August 2012, the ABA adopted a Model Rule on Practice Pending Admission. If a state has adopted an admission rule that is similar to the provisions of the Model Rule on Practice Pending Admission, then a lawyer who moves to a state where he or she is not licensed might be able to practice pursuant to this admission rule, even if the practice is not permitted under the safe harbor provisions found in Rule 5.5(c) or (d).

Food for Thought
Foreign Lawyer Practice Rights in the United States and Rule 5.5

Under what circumstances, if any, should foreign lawyers who are not licensed in a U.S. state be authorized to practice there? This question is increasingly relevant because entity clients and individual clients have global interests and may occasionally or regularly need the assistance of a foreign lawyer. For example, in 2018, all U.S. states except Hawaii exported more than $1.25 billion of goods. Some of these sales undoubtedly required the assistance of foreign lawyers. Moreover, in an increasingly interconnected world, individuals, as well as entities may need the assistance of foreign lawyers to help them with legal issues such as inheritance, family law, or small business matters.

There are five methods by which foreign lawyers might actively practice law in a U.S. jurisdiction: 1) as a fully-licensed [normal] lawyer in that state; 2) as a foreign legal consultant (FLC), which is a limited license that authorizes the foreign lawyer to practice foreign law and perhaps international and third country law; 3) by appearing *pro hac vice* in a litigation matter or in an arbitration; 4) by conducting temporary transactional work; or 5) by working pursuant to an in-house counsel license, which is another type of limited license. Many states have rules that allow foreign lawyers to apply for permission to appear *pro hac vice* or to provide advice on the law of their home country as a licensed foreign legal consultant. Approximately sixty percent of U.S. states allow foreign lawyers to become fully licensed without requiring them to start over from scratch with their legal education. Many states have adopted a version of Rule 5.5(d) that creates a safe-harbor provision for foreign in-house counsel. A handful of states have an explicit rule that allows foreign lawyers to perform the type of temporary transactional work or arbitration work that is permitted by Rule 5.5 (c). Should all states have these kinds of rules? In 2015, the Conference of Chief Justices adopted Resolution 2 which "strongly encourages its members to adopt explicit policies that permit the following qualified activities by foreign lawyers as a means to increase available legal services and to facilitate movement of goods and services between the United States and foreign nations." The Resolution continued by listing, *inter alia*, policies that would address foreign lawyers' ability to perform temporary [transactional] practice; to apply for *pro hac vice* admission; to serve as an in-house counsel under Rule 5.5(d)(1); and to appear in an arbitration. (The Conference of Chief Justices is an organization that includes the chief judicial officer of the highest court in each U.S. jurisdiction.)

Choice of Law Issues

The amendments to Rule 5.5 expanded the UPL safe harbors for lawyers who are not licensed in a jurisdiction. Rule 8.5(a) was amended at the same time in order to provide a system of accountability for lawyers who practice in a jurisdiction but are not licensed in that jurisdiction. The current version of Rule 8.5(a) provides as follows:

Rule 8.5. Disciplinary Authority; Choice of Law

(a)   Disciplinary Authority: A lawyer admitted to practice in this jurisdiction is subject to the disciplinary authority of this jurisdiction, regardless of where the lawyer's conduct occurs. A lawyer not admitted in this jurisdiction is also subject to the disciplinary authority of this jurisdiction if the lawyer provides or offers to provide any legal services in this jurisdiction. A lawyer may be subject to the disciplinary authority of both this jurisdiction and another jurisdiction for the same conduct.

If lawyers are subject to the rules of professional conduct in all jurisdictions in which they are licensed and if they are also subject to the rules of professional conduct in all jurisdictions in which they are not licensed but provide legal services, then there is the potential for conflicts and contradictions among the professional rules that a lawyer must follow. Rule 8.5(b) addresses this potential dilemma. It provides as follows:

(b)   Choice of Law. In any exercise of the disciplinary authority of this jurisdiction, the rules of professional conduct to be applied shall be as follows:

(1)   for conduct in connection with a matter pending before a tribunal, the rules of the jurisdiction in which the tribunal sits, unless the rules of the tribunal provide otherwise; and

(2)   for any other conduct, the rules of the jurisdiction in which the lawyer's conduct occurred, or, if the predominant effect of the conduct is in a different jurisdiction, the rules of that jurisdiction shall be applied to the conduct. A lawyer shall not be subject to discipline if the lawyer's conduct conforms to the rules of a jurisdiction in which the lawyer reasonably believes the predominant effect of the lawyer's conduct will occur.

———————

The choice of law provisions in Rule 8.5(b) are important given the wide variation among rules of professional conduct. Each jurisdiction has made modifications to the ABA Model Rules of Professional Conduct when implementing them, some of which are relatively small changes and some of which are quite dramatic.

Many experts agree that Rule 8.5(b)(1) is more likely to provide a clearer answer to choice of law questions than Rule 8.5(b)(2), but interpretative questions arise even under Rule 8.5(b)(1). For example:

- Which jurisdiction's ethics rules should a lawyer use with respect to a lawyer's actions taken before a lawsuit is filed, but in anticipation of litigation? Rule 8.5(b)(1) applies when the matter is pending before a tribunal and Comment [4] makes it clear that Rule 8.5(b)(2) applies to some conduct that occurs in anticipation of a tribunal proceeding, but where is the dividing line? Jurisdictions differ, for example, with respect to the rules that apply to fee agreements for matters before a tribunal. Which provision of Rule 8.5(b) applies to this decision and whose rules should apply?

- Rule. 8.5(b)(1) applies to matters before a tribunal, which is defined to include arbitration but not mediation. If a lawyer participates in a required court-annexed mandatory mediation, which rules apply?

- Which ethics rules apply to appellate lawyers from different states who appear in a case in front of a U.S. Court of Appeals that has not specified the governing ethics rules? For example, until recently, the U.S. Court of Appeals for the Third Circuit did not specify the governing ethics rules.

See Rule 8.5. *See also* ABA Commission on Ethics 20/20, *Issues Paper: Choice of Law in Cross-Border Practice* (Jan. 18, 2011), available here, which highlighted some of the ambiguities in Rule 8.5 and asked questions about six different fact patterns. These examples show that choice of law issues can be difficult to resolve even under Rule 8.5(b) (1), which is viewed as the simpler of the two choice of law rules under Rule 8.5(b). In 2013, concerns over the difficulty in applying Rule 8.5(b)(2) led to the addition of this sentence to the Comment: "With respect to conflicts of interest, in determining a lawyer's reasonable belief under paragraph (b)(2), a written agreement between the lawyer and client that reasonably specifies a particular jurisdiction is within the scope of that paragraph may be considered if the agreement was obtained with the client's informed consent confirmed in the agreement."

III. Creating the Lawyer-Client Relationship

The key building block of law practice and lawyer regulation is the lawyer-client relationship. In the United States, the general rule is that a lawyer has full discretion to decide whether to represent a client, subject to very limited exceptions. These exceptions include the lawyer's obligation to accept a court appointment and to comply with any applicable anti-discrimination laws. Determining whether a lawyer-client relationship exists is critically important because many of the rules and principles you will study only apply if there is a lawyer-client relationship.

Hear from the Authors

To hear from the authors about Restatement § 14 and creating the lawyer-client relationship, click here.

A. General Principles

Practice Pointer

What steps, if any, would you recommend that a lawyer or law firm take in order to avoid the situation of unintended lawyer-client relationships?

Even though many of the rules of professional conduct only apply if there is a lawyer-client relationship, the rules of professional conduct do not themselves explain how a lawyer-client relationship is created. Instead, state substantive law provides the test(s) that will be used to determine whether a lawyer-client relationship exists. Although the substantive law of a particular jurisdiction will control, Restatement § 14 summarizes the principles that likely will be used to determine whether a lawyer-client relationship exists:

§14. Formation of a Client-Lawyer Relationship

A relationship of client and lawyer arises when:

> (1) a person manifests to a lawyer the person's intent that the lawyer provide legal services for the person; and either
>
>> (a) the lawyer manifests to the person consent to do so; or
>>
>> (b) the lawyer fails to manifest lack of consent to do so, and the lawyer knows or reasonably should know that the person reasonably relies on the lawyer to provide the services. * * *

The case that follows illustrates circumstances in which a lawyer and a client might have different views about whether a lawyer-client relationship exists. This case also illustrates the importance to a lawyer of being aware of both Restatement § 14(1)(a) and § 14(1)(b).

> In contrast to the US approach, English barristers have traditionally followed a "cab-rank" rule requiring that "irrespective of whether his client is paying privately or is publicly funded [a barrister must] accept any brief to appear before a Court in which he professes to practise . . . irrespective of (i) the party on whose behalf he is instructed (ii) the nature of the case and (iii) any belief or opinion which he may have formed as to the character reputation cause conduct guilt or innocence of that person." *See* Paragraph 602 of a previous Code of Conduct of the English Bar. One commentator explains that "[t]he 'cab-rank rule' generally requires barristers to accept any case given by a solicitor, thereby undertaking the representation of a particular client without passing judgment on the merits or public appeal. The cab-rank rule evokes a 'patrician sense of conducting a service,' and has been praised as 'a crucial pillar of British justice, ensuring that unpopular causes or clients never go without representation.' " William C. McMahon III, *Declining Professionalism in Court: A Comparative Look at the English Barrister*, 19 Geo. J. Legal Ethics 845, 851–52 (2006). In 2013, England and Wales considered whether it should make any changes to the cab-rank rule but retained a cab-rank rule.

Morris v. Margulis

718 N.E.2d 709 (Ill. App. Ct., 5th Dist. 1999), *rev'd on other grounds,* 754 N.E.2d 314 (Ill. 2001)

JUSTICE MAAG delivered the opinion of the court:

* * *

This action grows out of the failure of the former Germania Bank (Germania), a St. Louis, Missouri-based savings and loan. Various civil and criminal actions flowed from Germania's failure, including actions against some officers and directors of Germania. The plaintiff in this action, Morris, was sued civilly and prosecuted criminally. Morris was convicted of various criminal charges. His conviction was affirmed on appeal. In this action, Morris alleges an attorney-client relationship existed between himself and the defendants [who were Bryan Cave, LLP and four lawyers who worked for the Bryan Cave law firm.] Morris claims that the defendants breached the fiduciary duties owing from them to him and that he was damaged as a result. With this general background, we will now address the issues raised in this case.

* * *

II. Analysis

We will now discuss the issues raised in this appeal. Unless otherwise indicated, a reference to Bryan Cave also includes the individually named partners.

Bryan Cave claimed in the trial court that it was entitled to summary judgment on several grounds. In this court its position is similar. Bryan Cave claims that (1) no attorney-client relationship existed with Morris in regard to Germania matters and thus it owed him no fiduciary duties. * * * The trial court, without specifying the basis, stated in its judgment order that it accepted "the reasoning and conclusions" of the defendants and granted summary judgment in favor of all defendants. Morris appeals. * * *

A. The Attorney-Client Relationship

Because the issues raised on appeal turn in large part on the question of whether an attorney-client relationship existed between Edward Morris and Bryan Cave with respect to Germania matters, we begin with that issue. * * *

The existence of an attorney-client relationship between Bryan Cave and Morris with respect to estate planning, domestic relations matters, and other personal matters is not contested by Bryan Cave. Bryan Cave argues, however, that no attorney-client relationship existed between Bryan Cave and Morris regarding Germania. * * *

Bryan Cave points out that Morris was represented by other counsel with respect to Germania-related matters. Bryan Cave argues that no attorney-client relationship existed between Morris and Bryan Cave because Bryan Cave formally declined representation of Morris in Germania-related matters. Bryan Cave contends further that Morris did not confide in Bryan Cave attorneys regarding Germania matters. Bryan Cave claims that it never purported to represent Morris in relation to Germania matters.

The fact that Morris was represented by counsel other than Bryan Cave with relation to Germania matters, the S.E.C. investigation, and the criminal investigation does not preclude him from having an attorney-client relationship on the same matter with Bryan Cave. A client may form an attorney-client relationship with more than one attorney or law firm on the same legal matter. * * *

The *Herbes* court, in discussing the creation of the attorney-client relationship, stated:

> "Taken together, the cases teach that an attorney-client relationship need not be explicit or expressed and is not dependent on the amount of time the client spends

with the attorney, the payment of fees or execution of a contract, the consent of the attorney, or the actual employment of the attorney. * * * Rather, the relationship can come into being during the initial contact between the layperson and the professional and appears to hinge on "'the client's belief that he is consulting a lawyer in that capacity and his manifested intention to seek professional legal advice." '
* * * Like King, the Federal cases focus on the client's viewpoint rather than that of the attorney. If the client consults the attorney for the evident purpose of securing legal advice, an attorney-client relationship will probably be found regardless of the attorney's intent or the fact that a further relationship did not develop as a result of the primary consultation." * * *

ACTA NON VERBA! (Deeds not words!) Bryan Cave's denial of an attorney-client relationship with Morris conflicts with the admitted facts. By their own admission they aided in the preparation of a "Wells" submission. Bryan Cave admits that they met with Morris and discussed the Germania problem, and he asked them to represent him. In his deposition, Morris was asked the following question and gave the following answer.

"Q. No, sir. Here, so we get to the nub of this, I mean, you have made certain allegations here about a disclosure of confidential information, as I understand it, and the word 'confidential' is used in the lawsuit that you filed. So, I'm asking you now to give me your recollection as to what the confidential information was that you related to Bryan, Cave regarding your activities as an officer of Germania.

A. As far as I'm concerned, everything that I talked to Jack Goebel about, or other members of Bryan, Cave, with respect to Germania's activities, my activities, were [*sic*] all confidential, and those-those discussions were ongoing from the time Bryan, Cave represented the bank and Jack Goebel was a director, through, you know, we stopped talking."

It must be remembered that Morris had been represented previously by Bryan Cave on a variety of personal matters over a period of several years. Whom does a person consult on a legal problem when it arises? His attorney. Whom did Morris meet with to request representation on the Germania matter? Bryan Cave, of course.

The key to the creation of the relationship is not any belief on the part of Bryan Cave about whether an attorney-client relationship was formed. "Rather, the relationship can come into being during the initial contact," and its creation hinges on " 'the client's belief that he is consulting a lawyer in that capacity[.' "] * * * Even a brief meeting, resulting in no formal retainer or payment of fees, is sufficient to create the relationship. * * *

The record fails to show what took place when Morris and Goebel met and Morris asked for representation. If in seeking counsel Morris had substantive conversations with Goebel on the Germania matter, then as a matter of law an attorney-client relationship came into being. At the very least, based on the record before us, we cannot say that no attorney-client relationship was formed. Therefore, summary judgment should not have been granted on this basis. * * *

CONCLUSION

Accordingly, the order of the circuit court granting summary judgment in favor of Bryan Cave, LLP, John Goebel, Daniel O'Neill, J. Thomas Archer, and Alan J. Dixon is reversed, and the cause is remanded.

Reversed and remanded.

———————————

[Question 2-7]

An attorney represented a company on transactional matters. After the U.S. Securities and Exchange Commission (SEC) advised the company that it was the subject of an investigation, the company asked the attorney if the attorney would represent it in the SEC investigation. The attorney declined to do so and the company retained other counsel. Nonetheless, from time to time, the company's representatives asked the attorney legal questions about the SEC investigation and the attorney provided off-the-cuff answers.

Does the attorney have a lawyer-client relationship with the company for purposes of the SEC investigation?

(A) **Yes, because the attorney answered the company's legal questions when the attorney knew or reasonably should have known that the company would reasonably rely on the attorney's answers.**

(B) **Yes, because the attorney previously represented company in its transactional work.**

(C) **No, because the attorney declined to represent company in the SEC investigation.**

(D) **No, because the company did not pay the attorney to represent it in the SEC matter.**

Morris v. Margulis & Grant showed you how a lawyer and client might have different views about whether a relationship exists. The *Westinghouse* case, which is reprinted below and is a landmark case, also addressed the lawyer-client relationship. This case is approximately forty years old and predates the adoption of Rule 1.13(a). That rule states that "[a] lawyer employed or retained by an organization represents the organization acting through its duly authorized constituents." Rule 1.13's Comment explains that even when constituents of an organization communicate with the lawyer, "[t]his does not mean * * * that the constituents of an organizational client are the clients of the lawyer."

Although the general rule is that a lawyer who represents an organization does *not* represent its constituents, in any given fact pattern, the parties' conduct may lead to a different conclusion. Both Rule 1.13(f) and the conflict of interest rules (which are covered in Chapter 5) recognize that it is theoretically possible for a lawyer to represent more than one client. Thus, there may be circumstances in which a lawyer will represent an organization and will also represent one or more of its constituents. If the *Westinghouse* case were decided today and the court applied Rule 1.13 and the Restatement § 14 factors, do you think it would reach the same result?

Westinghouse Elec. Corp. v. Kerr-McGee Corp.

580 F.2d 1311 (7th Cir. 1978), *cert. denied*, 439 U.S. 955 (1978)

SPRECHER, CIRCUIT JUDGE.

The novel issues on this appeal are (1) whether an attorney-client relationship arises only when both parties consent to its formation or can it also occur when the lay party submits confidential information to the law party with reasonable belief that the latter is acting as the former's attorney. * * *

I

On September 8, 1975, Westinghouse, a major manufacturer of nuclear reactors, notified utility companies that 17 of its long-term uranium supply contracts had become "commercially impracticable" under § 2-615 of the Uniform Commercial Code. In response, the affected utilities filed 13 federal actions, one state action, and three foreign actions against Westinghouse, alleging breach of contract and challenging Westinghouse's invocation of § 2-615. * * *

As an outgrowth of its defense of these contract actions, Westinghouse on October 15, 1976, filed the present antitrust action against 12 foreign and 17 domestic corporations engaged in various aspects of the uranium industry.

Kirkland's representation of Westinghouse's uranium litigation has required the efforts of 8 to 14 of its attorneys and has generated some $2.5 million in legal fees.

Contemporaneously with its Westinghouse representation in the uranium cases, Kirkland represented [the American Petroleum Institute (API)], using six of its lawyers in that project.

In October, 1975, Congress was presented with legislative proposals to break up the oil companies, both vertically by separating their control over production, transportation, refining and marketing entities, and horizontally by prohibiting cross-ownership of alternative energy resources in addition to oil and gas. Since this proposed legislation threatened oil companies with a potential divestiture of millions of dollars of assets, in November, 1975, the API launched a Committee on Industrial Organization to lobby against the proposals. On December 10, 1975, API's president requested that each company designate one of its senior executives to facilitate coordination of the Committee's activities with the individual companies.

The Committee was organized into five task forces. The Legal Task Force was headed by L. Bates Lea, General Counsel of Standard Oil of Indiana, assisted by Stark Ritchie, API's General Counsel.

On February 25, 1976, Ritchie wrote to Frederick M. Rowe, a partner in Kirkland's Washington office, retaining the firm to review the divestiture hearings and "prepare arguments for use in opposition to this type of legislation." On May 4, 1976, Ritchie added that the Kirkland firm's work for API "should include the preparation of possible testimony, analyzing the probable legal consequences and antitrust considerations of the proposed legislation" and "you should make an objective survey and study of the probable effects of the pending legislation, specifically including probable effects on oil companies that would have to divest assets." Ritchie noted that "(a)s a part of this study, we will arrange for interviews by your firm with a cross-section of industry personnel." The May 4 letter to Rowe concluded with:

> Your firm will, of course, act as an independent expert counsel and hold any company information learned through these interviews in strict confidence, not to be disclosed to any other company, or even to API, except in aggregated or such other form as will preclude identifying the source company with its data.

On May 25, 1976, Ritchie sent to 59 API member companies a survey questionnaire seeking data to be used by Kirkland in connection with its engagement by API. In the introductory memorandum to the questionnaire, Ritchie advised the 59 companies that Kirkland had "ascertained that certain types of data pertinent to the pending anti-diversification legislation are not now publicly available" and the API "would appreciate your help in providing this information to Kirkland. . . ." The memorandum included the following:

> Kirkland, Ellis & Rowe is acting as an independent special counsel for API, and will hold any company information in strict confidence, *not to be disclosed to any other company, or even to API*, except in aggregated or such other form as will preclude identifying the source company with its data.

(Emphasis in original). The data sought was to assist Kirkland "in preparing positions, arguments and testimony in opposition to this type of legislative (divestiture)" and was not to be sent to API but rather to Kirkland.

Pursuant to the provision in Ritchie's May 4, 1976 letter to Rowe that interviews would be arranged with a cross-section of industry personnel, Nolan Clark, a Kirkland partner, interviewed representatives of eight oil companies between April 29 and June 15, 1976.

After going through several drafts, the final Kirkland report to API was released on October 15, 1976. The final report contains 230 pages of text and 82 pages of exhibits. References to uranium appear throughout the report and uranium is the primary subject of about 25 pages of text and 11 pages of exhibits. The report marshalls a large number of facts and arguments to show that oil company diversification does not threaten overall energy competition. In particular the report asserts that the relatively high concentration ratios in the uranium industry can be expected to decline, that current increases in uranium prices are a result of increasing demand, that oil company entry into uranium production has stimulated competition and diminished concentration, that oil companies have no incentive to act in concert to restrict coal or uranium production and that the historical record refutes any charge that oil companies have restricted uranium output. The report concludes that "the energy industries, both individually and collectively, are competitive today and are likely to remain so."

As noted at the outset of this opinion, the API report was issued on the same day as the present antitrust suit was filed against several defendants, including Gulf, Kerr-McGee and Getty.

The district court concluded that "(a) comparison of the two documents reveals a rather basic conflict in their contentions and underlying theories." The court also observed that "[p]erhaps in recognition of the diametrically opposing theories of the API report and the Westinghouse complaint, Kirkland does not attempt to rebut the oil companies' charges that it has simultaneously taken inconsistent positions on competition in the uranium industry."

Gulf, Kerr-McGee and Getty are substantial dues-paying members of API. Kerr-McGee and Getty are also represented on API's board of directors.

At Ritchie's request, the cross-section interviews were mainly arranged by Gerald Thurmond, Washington Counsel of Gulf Oil Company and a member of API's Antitrust Strategy Group. On May 11, 1976, Thurmond advised Gulf officials that Nolan Clark of Kirkland planned to visit them. Attached to Thurmond's letter were the questions "which will be covered" in the meeting.

The meeting was held on May 28, 1976 in Denver. Nolan Clark represented Kirkland. In attendance for Gulf were six vice presidents, a comptroller and a regional attorney. Also present was a Harvard professor who "also is working with API on the same subject." The meeting lasted more than two hours followed by lunch, during which discussions continued. After the meeting and in three letters from Gulf vice president Mingee to Clark dated August 10, 11 and 13, Gulf submitted specific information sought by Clark through the questionnaire and other written questions and in each letter Mingee stressed the confidential basis upon which the information was supplied.

Nolan Clark's interview with two Kerr-McGee vice presidents took place in Oklahoma City on June 9, 1976 and lasted about three hours. Clark was given considerable background information on Kerr-McGee's uranium industry, including mining locations, uranium conversion process, and pellet fabrication. On the subject of uranium marketing and pricing, one of the Kerr-McGee vice presidents described the escalating prices and tightening supplies in the current market, and the reasons behind the trends. Kerr-McGee sent its completed questionnaire to Clark on August 25, 1976.

Kirkland did not interview any Getty personnel. However, Getty received the confidential API questionnaire which requested it to estimate the value of its assets subject to proposed divestiture and its research and development outlays in alternative energy fields. Getty completed the questionnaire and mailed its data sheets to Nolan Clark on June 4, 1976, with the understanding that the data would be held in confidence. * * *

II

The crux of the district court's determination was based upon its view that an "attorney-client relationship is one of agency to which the general rules of agency apply" and "arises only when the parties have given their consent, either express or implied, to its formation." * * *

Mr. Chief Justice (then Judge) Burger said[:]

* * * The basic elements of the attorney-client relationship are not changed because the contract for services is expressed in a formal written contract. Indeed the very making of a formal contract and its performance impose a high duty on the attorney because he is dealing in an area in which he is expert and the client is not and as to which the client must necessarily rely on the attorney. . . . This is not to suggest that a formal contract is unimportant but rather that a formal long-term contract, superimposed on the normal attorney-client relationship, alters the relationship only by adding new dimensions of duties and obligations on the attorney.

For these reasons it is obvious why an attorney-client relationship does not arise only in the agency manner such as when the parties expressly or impliedly consent to its formation as the district court erroneously concluded.

The district court first determined that there existed no explicit or express attorney-client relationship in that no oil company representative requested Kirkland to act as its attorney orally or in writing and Kirkland did not accept such employment orally or in writing. The district court found that "Kirkland sent its legal bills to the API, and was compensated only by the API." A professional relationship is not dependent upon the payment of fees nor, as we have noted, upon the execution of a formal contract.

The court then purported to determine whether the professional relationship "may be implied from the conduct of the parties." First, it found no "indicia" such as "the preparation of a legally-binding document like a contract or a will, or the attorney's appearance in a judicial or quasi-judicial proceeding." Second, the court searched for evidence of three fundamental characteristics of an agency relationship: the power to affect the legal relations of the principal and others; a fiduciary who works on behalf of his principal and primarily for his benefit; and a principal who has the right to control the conduct of the agent. Using these tests, the court concluded that "[v]iewed in its totality, we believe that the evidence shows that no attorney-client relationship has existed between Kirkland and the oil companies." As we have indicated, to apply only the agency tests is too narrow an approach for determining whether a lawyer's fiduciary obligation has arisen. * * *

III

The client is no longer simply the person who walks into a law office. A lawyer employed by a corporation represents the entity but that principle does not of itself solve the potential conflicts existing between the entity and its individual participants.

Three district courts have held that each individual member of an Unincorporated association is a client of the association's lawyer. In *Halverson v. Convenient Food Mart, Inc.*, 458 F.2d 927, 930 (7th Cir. 1972), we held that a lawyer who had represented an informal group of 75 franchisees "[b]ecause . . . [he] in effect had represented and benefited every franchisee, . . . [they] could reasonably believe that each one of them was his client."

Here we are faced with neither an ordinary commercial corporation nor with an informal or unincorporated association, but instead with a nation-wide trade association with 350 corporate and 7,500 individual members and doing business as a non-profit corporation.

We need not make any generalized pronouncements of whether an attorney for such an organization represents every member because this case can and should be decided on a much more narrow ground.

There are several fairly common situations where, although there is no express attorney-client relationship, there exists nevertheless a fiduciary obligation or an implied professional relation:

(1)　The fiduciary relationship existing between lawyer and client extends to preliminary consultation by a prospective client with a view to retention of the lawyer, although actual employment does not result.

(2)　When information is exchanged between co-defendants and their attorneys in a criminal case, an attorney who is the recipient of such information breaches his fiduciary duty if he later, in his representation of another client, is able to use this information to the detriment of one of the co-defendants, even though that co-defendant is not the one which he represented in the criminal case.

(3)　When an insurer retains an attorney to investigate the circumstances of a claim and the insured, pursuant to a cooperation clause in the policy, cooperates with the attorney, the attorney may not thereafter represent a third party suing the insured nor indeed continue to represent the insurer once a conflict of interest surfaces.

(4)　In a recent case, where an auditor's regional counsel was instrumental in hiring a second law firm to represent some plaintiffs suing the auditor and where the second firm through such relationship was in a position to receive privileged information, the second law firm, although having no direct attorney-client relationship with the auditor, was disqualified from representing the plaintiffs.

(5)　In a recent case in this circuit, a law firm who represented for many years both the plaintiff in an action and also a corporation which owned 20% of the outstanding stock of the defendant corporation, was permitted to continue its representation of the plaintiff but was directed to disassociate itself from representing or advising the corporation owning 20% of defendant's stock.

In none of the above categories or situations did the disqualified or disadvantaged lawyer or law firm actually represent the "client" in the sense of a formal or even express attorney-client relation. In each of those categories either an implied relation was found or at least the lawyer was found to owe a fiduciary obligation to the laymen.

The professional relationship for purposes of the privilege for attorney-client communications "hinges upon the client's belief that he is consulting a lawyer in that capacity and his manifested intention to seek professional legal advice." The affidavits before the district court established that: the Washington counsel for Gulf "was given to believe that the Kirkland firm was representing both API and Gulf;" Kerr-McGee's vice president understood a Kirkland partner to explain that Kirkland was working on behalf of API and also its members such as Kerr-McGee; and Getty's vice president stated that in submitting data to Kirkland he "acted upon the belief and expectation that such submission was made in order to enable (Kirkland) to render legal service to Getty in furtherance of Getty's interests." * * *

[R]eversed and remanded.

Make the Connection

We will consider the *Westinghouse* case again in Chapter 5. To read more about similar situations, *see* Nancy J. Moore, *Expanding Duties of Attorneys to "Non-Clients": Reconceptualizing the Attorney-Client Relationship in Entity Representation and Other Inherently Ambiguous Situations*, 45 S.C. L. Rev. 659 (1994); John Leubsdorf, *Pluralizing the Client-Lawyer Relationship*, 77 Cornell L. Rev. 825 (1992).

Food for Thought
Lawyer Websites and the Lawyer-Client Relationship

Lawyers' use of the internet has resulted in new variations on issues relating to creation of a lawyer-client relationship.

Professor David Hricik writes:

> Has a lawyer who merely opens an unsolicited email done something to indicate to its sender that the lawyer assents to receive information in confidence or is open to representing that person? Should an email sent unilaterally by a prospective client through a law firm website be treated any differently than a phone call placed to a lawyer, or a meeting held between lawyer and prospective client? Is email different enough from these "old-world" forms of communications so that a different rule should apply, and so these advance waivers are unnecessary?

> The opinions so far conclude that by posting a website, a lawyer has manifested an intent to offer to form attorney-client relationships and to keep submitted information confidential. * * * Thus, disclaimers are necessary.

David Hricik, *The Speed of Normal: Conflicts, Competency, and Confidentiality in the Digital Age*, 10 Comp. L. Rev. & Tech. J. 73, 77–78 (2005).

B. Exceptions to the General Rule: The Duty to Accept Particular Cases

The prior material noted the general rule that a lawyer is not obligated to accept representation and explored the question of what facts are sufficient to establish a lawyer-client relationship. This section addresses a different question: whether a lawyer ever has a duty to accept representation.

[Question 2-8]

The court advises an attorney that the court plans to appoint the attorney to represent a teenage girl seeking court permission to obtain an abortion without the consent of her parents. The attorney believes that abortion is murder and asks the court not to appoint him to represent the teenage girl. The attorney advises the court that the attorney cannot do a competent job for the client given the attorney's personal beliefs.

Is the attorney subject to discipline?

    (A) Yes, because an attorney should not seek to avoid a court appointment.

    (B) Yes, because the attorney was required to set aside the attorney's personal beliefs.

    (C) No, because the attorney did not believe that the attorney could provide competent representation to the teenage girl.

    (D) No, because an attorney has no obligation to accept a court appointment.

In answering this question, consider Restatement § 14(2), Rule 6.2, and the ethics opinion that follows.

Restatement § 14(2) explains that a lawyer-client relationship arises when "a tribunal with power to do so appoints the lawyer to provide services." Rule 6.2 provides that a lawyer "shall not seek to avoid appointment * * * to represent a person except for good cause, such as:

    (a)   representing the client is likely to result in violation of the Rules of Professional Conduct or other law;

    (b)   representing the client is likely to result in an unreasonable financial burden on the lawyer; or

    (c)   the client or the cause is so repugnant to the lawyer as to be likely to impair the client-lawyer relationship or the lawyer's ability to represent the client."

Board of Professional Responsibility of the Supreme Court of Tennessee

Formal Ethics Op. No. 96-F-140

Inquiry is made as to several issues involving the ethical obligations of court-appointed counsel for minors who obtain abortions via judicial bypass of the parental consent for abortion provisions within Tennessee Code Annotated (T.C.A.) §§ 37–10–303 and 37–10–304.

The inquiring attorney routinely practices before the Juvenile Court in a particular county, and said attorney has been appointed to represent minors who have elected to petition the Juvenile Court for waivers of the parental consent requirement to obtain abortions. Several moral, ethical and constitutional law issues have been presented in the inquiry, [including the question of whether the attorney can] decline to accept the appointment for moral, religious or malpractice insurance reasons. * * *

[This] question is the most difficult to answer, given that legal and ethical issues are inextricably intertwined. Essentially, counsel asks whether he can ethically decline such appointments due to malpractice insurance reasons, and a deep-seated, sincere belief that appointments in such cases constitute state action violative of his free exercise of religion rights guaranteed by the First Amendment to the United States Constitution. DR 6-102(A) states that a lawyer should not attempt to exonerate himself from or limit his liability to his client for personal malpractice; thus, this reason does not appear to be a sufficient ground for declining such appointments. Counsel also alleges that he is a devout Catholic and cannot, under any circumstances, advocate a point of view ultimately resulting in what he considers to be the loss of human life. The religious beliefs are so compelling that counsel fears his own personal interests will subject him to conflicting interests and impair his independent professional judgment in violation of DR 5-101(A). In other words, counsel contends his status is akin to that of a conscientious objector, who is opposed to participation in abortion in any form.

Although counsel's religious and moral beliefs are clearly fervently held, EC 2-29 exhorts appointed counsel to refrain from withdrawal where a person is unable to retain counsel, except for compelling reasons. Compelling reasons as contemplated by this EC do not include such factors as:

> . . . the repugnance of the subject matter of the proceeding, the identity or position of a person involved in the case, the belief of the lawyer that the defendant in a criminal proceeding is guilty, or the belief of the lawyer regarding the merits of the civil case.

Several Tennessee cases addressing this issue from the perspective of contempt cast serious doubt on whether such an argument would prevail. * * * Reported federal cases are similarly pessimistic on whether one's free exercise rights are unconstitutionally burdened under analogous facts. * * * Ultimately, counsel should allow the juvenile court to determine as a matter of law the propriety of his withdrawal after motion and hearing to develop an adequate record. * * * Tennessee Formal Ethics Opinion 84-F-73 is also instructive on this issue, although this opinion specifically addresses ethical obligations of counsel in first degree murder cases. The Board opined, though, in cases involving conflicts between the moral and ethical beliefs of counsel and those of his client that:

> . . . [c]ounsel's moral beliefs and usually acceptable ethical standards and duties must yield to the moral beliefs and legal rights of the defendant . . . Counsel is ethically obligated to follow the law and to do nothing in opposition to the client's moral and legal choices. . . .

FYI

The client has a right "to reject appointed counsel and proceed *pro se.*" Restatement § 14, Reporter's Note to Comment g (citing *Faretta v. California*, 422 U.S. 806 (1975) (criminal); *Knox Leasing v. Turner*, 562 A.2d 168 (N.H. 1989) (civil)). Nonetheless, courts may appoint standby counsel, even where the client objects. *See, e.g., McKaskle v. Wiggins*, 465 U.S. 168 (1984). *See also* Section VI, *infra*, on allocation of decisionmaking authority.

Counsel should move the court to withdraw during the portion of the trial where the conflict is manifested. In the event the court fails to grant such motions, the attorney should seek an immediate review by the appellate court. . . .

* * *

This opinion is only intended to address the ethical obligations of counsel.

Approved and adopted by the Board

————————————

The Tennessee Board of Professional Responsibility opinion addresses the issue of a lawyer's duty to accept a case. The case that follows also addresses this issue.

Nathanson v. MCAD

16 Mass. L. Rptr. 761 (Mass. Super. 2003)

Elizabeth M. Fahey, Justice of the Superior Court.

The plaintiff, Attorney Judith Nathanson, ("Nathanson"), seeks judicial review of a decision and order rendered by a Commissioner of the Massachusetts Commission Against Discrimination ("MCAD"), which was subsequently adopted by the full Commission. The order required Nathanson to cease and desist her discriminatory practices in refusing to represent men in her [divorce] practice. For the reasons stated herein, the plaintiff's motion for judgment on the pleadings is denied and the MCAD decision is affirmed. * * *

III. Discussion

A. Whether the Commission Erred in Asserting Jurisdiction

Arguing that the Commission erred in asserting jurisdiction over Stropnicky's claims, Nathanson claims that issues pertaining to her behavior as an attorney are within the exclusive jurisdiction of the Supreme Judicial Court and the Board of Bar Overseers. * * * The Massachusetts Canons of Ethics and Disciplinary Rules, in effect at the time of the alleged discriminatory conduct, provide that "[t]he practice of law by members of the Massachusetts Bar shall be *regulated* by the Canons of Ethics and Disciplinary Rules attached hereto and incorporated by reference herein." S.J.C. Rule 3:07 (Introduction) (emphasis added). While the Supreme Judicial Court and Board of Bar Overseers do have jurisdiction over Nathanson's conduct as a member of the bar, this jurisdiction is not exclusive.

Nathanson makes the additional argument that, under the 1991 rules and under the rules in effect today, an attorney must represent her clients zealously, and Nathanson's commitment to representing women in divorce proceedings precludes her from advocating zealously on behalf of men. It is certainly true that Nathanson had a duty to represent her clients zealously at the time of the alleged discriminatory conduct. S.J.C. Rule 3:07, Canon 7 ("A Lawyer Should

Represent a Client Zealously Within the Bounds of the Law"). While an attorney's ability to advocate zealously for a client is a relevant consideration in determining whether an attorney is legally required to provide representation, it is not permissible for an attorney to assert a discriminatory agenda as grounds that she is unable to advocate zealously for a client. This is because an attorney is required to adhere to and follow the law. Nathanson's belief, that her advocacy on behalf of women in divorce would be undermined should she take on a male client, cannot be countenanced. Nathanson's claim that she was devoting her professional expertise to "the betterment of a disadvantaged protected class," "women in divorce proceedings" cannot be supported when the male she declines to represent is similarly situated to many of Nathanson's female clients. Nathanson's ethical obligations as an attorney licensed to practice law in this Commonwealth require that she uphold the law in her practice. As an officer of the court, she, as a lawyer, is prohibited from practicing discrimination such as the discrimination at issue in the instant case.

* * *

D. Whether Nathanson's First Amendment Rights Are Abridged by Application of the Statute

Nathanson's final argument against the MCAD's decision is that her exclusion of male clients in her divorce practice is constitutionally protected free speech and free association.

* * *

[A]ssuming *arguendo* that requiring Nathanson to represent Stropnicky infringes her rights to free association, these rights are subordinate to "regulations adopted to serve compelling state interests." Statutes enacted for purposes of abating discrimination, such as the Massachusetts Public Accommodation statute, serve compelling state interests. Accordingly, Nathanson's free association rights are not outweighed by society's interest in non-discrimination in this case.

2. Free Speech

An attorney may advocate for a client and concurrently engage in constitutionally protected free speech. Nevertheless, the right to free speech is not absolute and will be forfeited to a compelling state interest. * * *

The Commonwealth's compelling interest in abating gender discrimination outweighs Nathanson's constitutionally protected right to free speech in her capacity as a private attorney.

* * *

A private attorney, when representing a client, operates more as a conduit for the speech and expression of the client, rather than as a speaker for herself. In contrast to *Hurley*, the public accommodation at issue here is the client's access to legal rights and remedies, rather than use of Nathanson's speech and her law office as a vehicle for her own expression. As a practical matter, Nathanson's legal practice aims to elevate the status of divorced women by providing them access to their legal rights and remedies, and Stropnicky sought representation for that purpose (*i.e.*, because he wanted to have his rights vindicated). Nathanson rejected Stropnicky as a client specifically because he is a male, and not because his business would burden any particular message that her legal practice attempts to communicate. Compare *Hurley*, 515 U.S. at 573 (for homosexuals in parade, "participation as a unit in the parade was equally expressive" and the homosexual organization was "formed for the very purpose of marching in order to celebrate its members' identity as openly gay, lesbian and bisexual . . ."). The defendant MCAD has sufficiently demonstrated a compelling interest in the elimination of gender discrimination, including elimination of gender discrimination against the male Stropnicky. Even if the MCAD's interest does not rise to the level of a "compelling interest" because of Stropnicky's male gender, it is sufficient to overcome the interference with private attorney Nathanson's free expression.

For these reasons, any free speech activities that Nathanson engages in are subordinate to the state's compelling interest in eliminating discrimination on the basis of gender.

* * *

Accordingly, plaintiff's motion for Judgment on the Pleadings is *DENIED*, and the MCAD decision is *AFFIRMED*.

———————

The *Nathanson v. MCAD* decision was controversial. *See, e.g.,* Martha Minow, *Symposium: A Duty to Represent? Critical Reflections on Stropnicky v. Nathanson: Foreword: Of Legal Ethics, Taxis, and Doing the Right Thing,* 20 W. New Eng. L. Rev. 5 (1998).

C. The Duty to Reject Certain Cases

Section III (A) set forth the general principles that govern the establishment of a lawyer-client relationship. That section taught you that lawyers generally are not treated as "public utilities" who are required to accept each client that requests that lawyer's services. Section III (A) also discussed the Restatement § 14 test that is used to determine whether a lawyer-client relationship exists. Section III (B) examined exceptions to the general rule and explained when a lawyer might have a duty to accept a case. Section III (C) also addresses the topic of the establishment of the lawyer-client relationship. But unlike the prior sections, this section focuses on the issue of when a lawyer has a duty to reject representation of a client.

A lawyer's duty to reject representation is governed by Rule 1.16(a). As Section IV of this Chapter, *infra*, explains, Rule 1.16(a) governs the end of the lawyer-client relationship and sets forth three circumstances in which a lawyer has a mandatory duty to withdraw from representation that the lawyer already had undertaken. But, Rule 1.16(a) also governs the beginning of the lawyer-client relationship. Rule 1.16(a)(1) sets forth two circumstances in which a lawyer has a mandatory obligation to reject representation of a client. This obligation to reject representation is absolute; there are no exceptions:

Rule 1.16. Declining or Terminating Representation

(a) . . . [A] lawyer shall not represent a client . . . if:

(1)   the representation will result in violation of the rules of professional conduct or other law; [or]

(2)   the lawyer's physical or mental condition materially impairs the lawyer's ability to represent the client[.]

Although Rule 1.16(a)(1) incorporates by reference all of the Rules of Professional Conduct, there are several rules that are particularly likely to require a lawyer to reject representation of a potential client. The conflict of interest rules, which are found in Rules 1.7–1.12, are among the main reasons why a lawyer might be required to reject a client. As you will learn in Chapter 5, certain kinds of conflicts are "non-consentable" and require that a lawyer reject the proposed representation.

In addition to the conflicts of interest rules that might require a lawyer to reject a prospective client, if the potential representation involves litigation, Rule 3.1 might lead a lawyer to reject the case. This rule is similar to Federal Rule of Civil Procedure 11. Rule 3.1 provides that "[a] lawyer shall not bring or defend a proceeding, or assert or controvert an issue therein, unless there is a basis in law and fact for doing so that is not frivolous, which includes a good faith argument for an extension, modification or reversal of existing law."

Rule 1.2(d) might also require a lawyer to reject representation. This rule applies in all practice settings, including litigation, transactional, and regulatory practice settings. It states that a lawyer "shall not counsel a client to engage, or assist a client, in conduct that the lawyer knows is criminal or fraudulent." Rule 1.2(d) supplements Rule 1.16(a)(1), which says that a lawyer has a mandatory obligation to reject representation if it will result in a violation of "other law."

While it is beyond the scope of this casebook to address all of the "other law" that is incorporated by reference in Rule 1.16(a)(1), Question 2-9 introduces you to the "other law" that is the federal criminal money laundering statute.

[Question 2-9]

A client is a citizen of a foreign country known for corruption. The client asks an attorney with whom the client previously had no professional relationship to help the client purchase an expensive apartment with cash. During a meeting to discuss the details of this purchase, the client tells the attorney that the client would like to structure the purchase so that it is difficult if not impossible for someone to find out that the client purchased the property. When the attorney asks why, the client winks and says, "I need a place to stash some money that I don't want my government to know about or be able to trace back to me." The attorney agrees to accept the representation and says that the attorney will structure the transaction so that the client is the sole shareholder in a corporation which owns another corporation which will purchase the apartment with cash. The attorney tells the client that this corporate structure makes it extremely difficult for anyone to determine the client's identity as the purchaser of the property. The client had stolen the funds that the client plans to use to purchase the apartment.

Is the attorney subject to discipline?

(A) **Yes, because the attorney must reject the representation since the client is engaged in criminal moneylaundering activities.**

(B) **Yes, because an attorney may never represent a foreign citizen.**

(C) **No, because an attorney may assist a client to create multiple corporations, including shell corporations, even if the client's goal is to invest the proceeds of crime in a manner that makes it difficult to trace those proceeds.**

(D) **No, because an attorney only violates 18 U.S.C. § 1956 if the attorney conceals the proceeds of his own crime.**

In order to determine whether the lawyer in this question is subject to discipline, one must consider not only Rule 1.16(a) and Rule 1.2(d), but also the substantive crime of money laundering. One of the federal money laundering statutes is 18 U.S.C. § 1956. This statute makes it a felony for an individual "to conceal or disguise the nature, the location, the source, the ownership, or the control" of the proceeds of crime. In other words, under § 1956, action that might otherwise be legal—such as forming a Delaware corporation or series of corporations—is a felony if it is undertaken in order to conceal the source or location of the proceeds of a crime.

In order to comply with Rule 1.2(d) and Rule 1.16(a) and to avoid violating this federal money laundering statute, a lawyer needs to realize that conduct that may be perfectly legal in some situations—such as forming a Delaware corporation—may be illegal under 18 U.S.C. § 1956 if the client's motive is improper and if the client is using the proceeds of crime (even if the lawyer was not involved in the crime that generated the illegal proceeds). For example, in 2016, a lawyer in San Diego was sentenced to five years in prison for improper use of his client trust account. The plea agreement stated that the attorney "knew *or had reason to know* that the cash transactions described [therein] were proceeds of unlawful activity, or were intended to promote unlawful activity." (Emphasis added). This case illustrates the point that if a lawyer fails to inquire into the source of a client's funds and a client's motives, that lawyer may face criminal sanctions for performing legal work that is not—in itself—illegal. The ABA has produced or co-produced several documents that help lawyers identify "red flags" that might suggest that a client is asking a lawyer to help that client engage in illegal money laundering activity. These documents are available on the webpage of the ABA Task Force on Gatekeeper Regulation and the Profession. A two-page summary of these "red flag" indicators is available here. In July 2018, the New York City Bar has issued an ethics opinion on this topic. See Formal Opinion 2018-4: Duties When an Attorney Is Asked to Assist in a Suspicious Transaction, which is available here.

Because Rules 1.16(a) and 1.2(d) apply to all crimes, one might ask why a particular substantive crime—such as money laundering—should be singled out in a professional responsibility casebook. The answer is threefold. First, money laundering is one of the crimes or "other law" that *all lawyers* should know about, not just criminal law specialists. This is because money laundering is a significant societal problem and because those who launder money may seek out the services of a lawyer to help them purchase property or set up fictitious entities. It is important for lawyers to educate themselves so that they do not inadvertently or unknowingly help clients who are engaged in efforts to launder an estimated $300 billion in annual illicit proceeds. The second reason to highlight this particular "other law" is to reduce the chance that you will face, as the San Diego lawyer described above did, a felony charge that alleges that you "should have known" that your client was engaged in illegal money laundering activities. The third reason why it is important for U.S. lawyers to learn the substantive criminal law regarding money laundering is because a failure to be familiar with these provisions could lead to draconian federal legislation that would dramatically change the professional responsibility principles contained in this book.

The website of the ABA Task Force on Gatekeeper Regulation and the Profession includes a number of documents that explain why this issue could lead to a change in lawyer regulation. For example, it includes a link to the December 2016 4th Mutual Evaluation Report of the United States by the Financial Action Task Force (FATF). The 2016 U.S. Mutual Evaluation Report noted that U.S. lawyers were not part of the federal anti-moneylaundering (AML) scheme that requires "gatekeepers" like real estate agents and casinos (called DNFBPs) to undertake activities such as conducting due diligence when receiving money or transferring property, reporting suspicious transactions to the government, and avoiding "tipping off" the person reported. The 2016 FATF Report identified priority recommended actions and called on the U.S. to apply appropriate AML obligations, including "on the basis of a specific vulnerability analysis, to lawyers, accountants, trust and company service providers." Federal legislation that changes the nature of the lawyer-client relationship in the U.S. could be proposed if the U.S. legal profession is not able to convince the federal government and FATF countries that the U.S. legal profession adequately understands the crime of money laundering, that the profession is subject to both criminal and disciplinary provisions that forbid a lawyer from either personally committing or assisting a client engaged in money laundering activities, and that the profession is engaged in education efforts designed to ensure that lawyers do not inadvertently assist clients who are engaged in illegal money laundering activities. One commentator has argued that although the U.S. legal profession is not subject to the same type of strict AML national legislation that applies to lawyers in some other countries, the U.S. legal profession has the potential to have one of the most effective AML systems. U.S. lawyers have been global leaders in learning to recognize conflicts of interest and in rejecting representation because of those conflicts. If U.S. lawyers learn to internalize AML questions and to recognize money laundering fact patterns in the same way that U.S. lawyers recognize and respond to conflicts of interest issues, then Rule 1.16(a)(1) and its mandatory duty to reject clients will be a powerful AML tool. *See* Laurel S. Terry, *U.S. Legal Profession Efforts to Combat Money Laundering & Terrorist Financing*, 59 N. Y. L. Sch. L. Rev. 487, 502, 510, 514 (2014/15); Laurel S. Terry and José Carlos Llerena Robles, *The Relevance of FATF's Recommendations and Fourth Round of Mutual Evaluations to the Legal Profession*, 42 Fordham Int'l L. J. 627, 685–87, 715–18 (2018).

D. Other Issues Related to the Establishment of the Lawyer-Client Relationship

Before concluding this unit on Creating the Lawyer-Client Relationship, it is worth considering whether and how a client's views should be attributed to a lawyer. This issue arises regularly, although the contexts vary. Rule 1.2(b) is relevant to this issue. It states:

> A lawyer's representation of a client, including representation by appointment, does not constitute an endorsement of the client's political, economic, social or moral views or activities.

Go Online

For a provocative discussion of Rule 1.2(b), see Andre A Borgeas, *Note, Necessary Adherence to Model Rules 1.2(b): Attorneys Do Not Endorse the Acts or Views of Their Clients by Virtue of Representation*, 13 Geo.J. Legal Ethics 761 (2000).

Despite Rule 1.2(b), a number of people believe that lawyers should be accountable for the choices they make about whom to represent. Because the general rule is that a lawyer is not "a public utility" who must provide service to every client that requests it, a lawyer has great freedom in deciding which clients to represent. This fact may explain why there periodically are efforts to hold lawyers accountable for the choices they make.

For example, during the administration of President George W. Bush, government officials criticized several Wall Street law firms for their pro bono representation of Guantanamo detainees and urged the law firms' clients to boycott these firms. The American Bar Association and others strongly condemned these comments and cited the principles underlying Rule 1.2(b). In 2012, Harvard Law School students established a group called "Firmly Refuse" that urged Harvard students not to work at certain large law firms. The group's webpage identified by name law firms that had defended clients that allegedly were responsible for massive environmental disasters, torture, and mass discrimination. Another example is the Republican Governor's Association, which criticized a political candidate running for office by noting that as a criminal defense lawyer, the candidate had worked to let murderers go free. In evaluating this issue which recurs with regularity, commentators sometimes point to the Ethical Considerations (EC) found in the ABA Model Code of Professional Responsibility, which was the precursor to the ABA Model Rules of Professional Conduct. EC 2-27 stated, *inter alia*, that "Regardless of his personal feelings, a lawyer should not decline representation because a client or a cause is unpopular or community reaction is adverse." It also stated that the "personal preference of a lawyer to avoid adversary alignment against judges, other lawyers, public officials, or influential members of the community does not justify his rejection of tendered employment." Consider this hypothetical:

> An attorney defended a tobacco company in numerous suits brought by the survivors of those who allegedly died from second-hand smoke. The attorney argued on behalf of the company that second-hand smoke did not pose significant health risks for the plaintiffs in the cases. A law school classmate who learns about this representation calls up the attorney and chastises the attorney for endorsing the

tobacco company's view that second-hand smoke was not a significant health risk. The attorney responded that the classmate should not criticize the attorney for the arguments made in the course of this representation because the rules of professional conduct state that a client's views and conduct should not be ascribed to the client's lawyer.

The issues raised by this hypothetical arise on a regular basis. The reactions by the legal profession and the larger society sometimes vary depending on the circumstances in which the issues arise. It is clear that Rule 1.2(b) provides that a lawyer's representation of a client does not constitute an endorsement of the client's political, economic, social or moral views or activities. But it is also true that outside of the context of court appointments, lawyers in private practice have significant freedom to decide which clients they accept, and some people believe that lawyers should be accountable, on some level, for the choices they make when deciding whom to represent.

IV. Ending the Lawyer-Client Relationship

Having explored the creation of the lawyer-client relationship, we now turn to the special rules governing the termination of that relationship. Lawyers do not always have the freedom to unilaterally terminate the lawyer-client relationship. While both a lawyer and a client are able to terminate the lawyer-client relationship, a lawyer who does so must comply with the rules of professional conduct that govern the lawyer's conduct. As you review the questions and the material that follows, consider when a lawyer *must* withdraw, when a lawyer *may* withdraw, and *how* a lawyer should withdraw, that is, what steps, if any, a lawyer must take.

[Question 2-10]

An attorney represented a client in connection with the client's divorce. The attorney and the client had several disagreements about the tactics to use and the client stopped paying the attorney. After a few weeks, the client decided he would be better off with another lawyer and told the attorney he was fired. After giving the client sufficient notice to obtain replacement counsel, the attorney requested the court's permission to withdraw from the divorce litigation, but the court denied the request. The attorney continued representing the client.

Is the attorney subject to discipline?

(A) **Yes, because the attorney had a mandatory duty to cease the representation because he was discharged by the client.**

(B) **Yes, because the attorney's representation of the client will result in an unreasonable financial burden on the attorney.**

(C) **No, because the attorney was required to remain in the case after the court denied the attorney permission to withdraw.**

(D) No, because the attorney's withdrawal would have caused material prejudice to the client.

[Question 2-11]

An attorney had represented a client, who was a developer, for more than a year on a large complicated development project. The attorney recently became concerned about the adequacy of the disclosures that the client planned to make to regulatory agencies and to individuals who soon would be signing contracts with the client. The attorney advised the client that the attorney thought the client's disclosures might possibly be viewed as fraudulent and asked the client to issue supplemental disclosures. The client refused, saying that it did not think its disclosures were fraudulent and that it was a business risk that the client was willing to take. After thinking about this answer, the attorney decided that because of this fundamental disagreement, the attorney did not want to continue representing the client. Accordingly, the attorney notified the client that the attorney was resigning from the representation and that the client should hire another lawyer. The attorney agreed to work with the client's new lawyer to protect the client's interests. After receiving the attorney's letter, the client called the attorney and said that the client refused to accept the attorney's resignation. The client stated that the client would be materially prejudiced if the attorney resigned because the client would have to pay to educate another lawyer on everything that had happened to date and because the attorney's departure might put the development project at risk because people would wonder why the attorney had left. The attorney resigned anyway.

Is the attorney subject to discipline?

(A) Yes, because the resignation would have a material adverse effect on the interests of the client.

(B) Yes, because the attorney did not have actual knowledge that the client was engaged in criminal or fraudulent conduct.

(C) No, because the attorney did not need permission of a tribunal to resign from the representation.

(D) No, because the attorney and the client had a fundamental disagreement about how much disclosure was necessary.

Rule 1.16 governs the termination of the lawyer-client relationship. Rule 1.16(a) requires a lawyer to withdraw from representation if:

(1) the representation will result in violation of the rules of professional conduct or other law;

(2) the lawyer's physical or mental condition materially impairs the lawyer's ability to represent the client; or

(3) the lawyer is discharged.

Rule 1.16(b) permits a lawyer to withdraw from representation under the following circumstances:

(1) withdrawal can be accomplished without material adverse effect on the interests of the client;

(2) the client persists in a course of action involving the lawyer's services that the lawyer reasonably believes is criminal or fraudulent;

(3) the client has used the lawyer's services to perpetrate a crime or fraud;

(4) the client insists upon taking action that the lawyer considers repugnant or with which the lawyer has a fundamental disagreement;

(5) the client fails substantially to fulfill an obligation to the lawyer regarding the lawyer's services and has been given reasonable warning that the lawyer will withdraw unless the obligation is fulfilled;

(6) the representation will result in an unreasonable financial burden on the lawyer or has been rendered unreasonably difficult by the client; or

(7) other good cause for withdrawal exists.

Even where Rule 1.16(a) would require withdrawal or Rule 1.16(b) would permit withdrawal, Rule 1.16(c) provides that "[a] lawyer must comply with applicable law requiring notice to or permission of a tribunal when terminating a representation. When ordered to do so by a tribunal, a lawyer shall continue representation notwithstanding good cause for terminating the representation."

Where a lawyer satisfies the conditions for terminating the representation, Rule 1.16(d) further requires that "a lawyer shall take steps to the extent reasonably practicable to protect a client's interests, such as giving reasonable notice to the client, allowing time for employment of other counsel, surrendering papers and property to which the client is entitled and refunding any advance payment of fee or expense that has not been earned or incurred. The lawyer may retain papers relating to the client to the extent permitted by other law."

Hear from the Authors

To hear from the authors about Rule 1.16 and ending the lawyer-client relationship, click here.

The *Whiting v. Lacara* case that appears below is a 20th Century case that was decided using the principles of the older Code of Professional Responsibility, rather than Rule 1.16 of the Rules of Professional Conduct. Despite this, *Lacara* is a useful case to read because it vividly illustrates the fact that it is often much easier for a lawyer to create a lawyer-client relationship than it is to end a lawyer-client relationship.

In this case, it took an appeal to the Second Circuit before lawyer Lacara was allowed to withdraw from his representation of client Whiting. Moreover, the Second Circuit's opinion states that if it had relied solely on the papers filed with the court, it would have affirmed the trial court's order and would have found that the trial court did not abuse its discretion when it denied lawyer Lacara's motion to withdraw from representation. As you will see from the case, it was the comments that client Whiting made during the Second Circuit's oral argument that led the Second Circuit to reverse the trial court order denying Lacara permission to withdraw. Despite its age, *Whiting v. Lacara* is a case worth remembering.

Whiting v. Lacara

187 F.3d 317 (2d Cir. 1999)

PER CURIAM:

Garrett R. Lacara appeals from two orders of Judge Spatt denying Lacara's motions to withdraw as counsel for plaintiff-appellee Joseph M. Whiting. Although the record before Judge Spatt justified denial of the motions, amplification of Whiting's position at oral argument persuades us to reverse.

BACKGROUND

In July 1996, appellee, a former police officer, filed a civil rights action against Nassau County, the Incorporated Village of Old Brooksville, the Old Brooksville Police Department, other villages, and various individual defendants. The action was based on the termination of his employment as an officer. He sought $9,999,000 in damages. * * *

Whiting retained Lacara in December 1997. In June 1998, the district court partially granted defendants' summary judgment motion and dismissed plaintiff's due process claims. The court scheduled the remaining claims, one free speech claim and two equal protection claims, for a jury trial on August 18, 1998. * * *

On August 6, 1998, Lacara moved to be relieved as counsel. In support, he offered an affidavit asserting that appellee "[had] failed to follow legal advice," that appellee "[wa]s not focused on his legal rights," and that appellee "demand[ed] publicity against legal advice." Lacara also asserted that appellee had failed to keep adequate contact with his office, was "not sufficiently thinking clearly to be of assistance at the time of trial," and would "be of little or no help during trial." Furthermore, Lacara stated that appellee had "demand[ed] that [Lacara] argue collateral issues which would not be allowed in evidence," demanded that Lacara continue to argue a due process claim already dismissed by the court, and drafted a Rule 68 Offer without Lacara's consent and demanded that he serve it on defendants. Finally, Lacara asserted that on July 30, 1998, Whiting had entered his office and, without permission, had "commenced to riffle [Lacara's] 'in box.' " Lacara stated that he had to call 911 when Whiting had refused to leave the office. Lacara offered to provide further information to the court in camera. Whiting's responsive affidavit essentially denied Lacara's allegations. Whiting stated that he would not be opposed to an order relieving counsel upon the condition that Lacara's firm refund the legal fees paid by Whiting.

On August 13, Judge Spatt denied Lacara's motion to withdraw as counsel. * * *

On August 13, 1998, Lacara filed a notice of appeal and moved for an emergency stay of the district court's order and to be relieved as appellee's attorney. We granted Lacara's motion for an emergency stay pending appeal but denied his request for relief on the merits at that time. At a status conference on September 23, 1998, the district court entertained another motion from Lacara to withdraw as counsel, which Judge Spatt again denied. Lacara filed a timely appeal, which was consolidated with the earlier appeal.

DISCUSSION

* * *

We review a district court's denial of a motion to withdraw only for abuse of discretion. District courts are due considerable deference in decisions not to grant a motion for an attorney's withdrawal. The trial judge is closest to the parties and the facts, and we are very reluctant to interfere with district judges' management of their very busy dockets.

Judge Spatt denied Lacara's motion pursuant to Rule 1.4 of the Civil Rules of the United States District Court for the Southern and Eastern Districts of New York, which provides that

> [a]n attorney who has appeared as attorney of record for a party may be relieved or displaced only by order of the court and may not withdraw from a case without leave of the court granted by order. Such an order may be granted only upon a showing by affidavit or otherwise of satisfactory reasons for withdrawal or displacement and the posture of the case, including its position, if any, on the calendar.

In addressing motions to withdraw as counsel, district courts have typically considered whether "the prosecution of the suit is [likely to be] disrupted by the withdrawal of counsel."

Considerations of judicial economy weigh heavily in favor of our giving district judges wide latitude in these situations, but there are some instances in which an attorney representing a plaintiff in a civil case might have to withdraw even at the cost of significant interference with the trial court's management of its calendar. For example, the Code of Professional Responsibility might mandate withdrawal where "the client is bringing the legal action . . . merely for the purpose of harassing or maliciously injuring" the defendant. Model Code of Professional Responsibility ("Model Code") DR 2-110(B)(1). In such a situation, by denying a counsel's motion to withdraw, even on the eve of trial, a court would be forcing an attorney to violate ethical duties and possibly to be subject to sanctions.

Lacara does not claim that he faces mandatory withdrawal. Rather, he asserts three bases for "[p]ermissive withdrawal" under the Model Code: (i) Whiting "[i]nsists upon presenting a claim or defense that is not warranted under existing law and cannot be supported by good faith argument for an extension, modification, or reversal of existing law," Model Code DR

2-110(C)(1)(a); (ii) Whiting's "conduct [has] render[ed] it unreasonably difficult for [Lacara] to carry out employment effectively," DR 2-110(C)(1)(d); and (iii) Whiting has "[d]eliberately disregard[ed] an agreement or obligation to [Lacara] as to expenses or fees," DR 2-110(C)(1)(f). Although the Model Code "was drafted solely for its use in disciplinary proceedings and cannot by itself serve as a basis for granting a [m]otion to withdraw as counsel," we continue to believe that "the Model Code provides guidance for the court as to what constitutes 'good cause' to grant leave to withdraw as counsel." However, a district court has wide latitude to deny a counsel's motion to withdraw, as here, on the eve of trial, where the Model Code merely permits withdrawal.

In the instant matter, we would be prepared to affirm if the papers alone were our only guide. Although Lacara has alleged a nonpayment of certain disputed fees, he has not done so with sufficient particularity to satisfy us that withdrawal was justified on the eve of trial. Moreover, there is nothing in the district court record to suggest error in that court's finding that "Whiting has been very cooperative and desirous of assisting his attorney in this litigation." To be sure, we are concerned by Lacara's allegation that appellee trespassed in his office and that appellant had to call 911 to get Whiting to leave. However, Whiting disputes Lacara's description of these events. Moreover, we strongly agree with the district court that, as the third attorney in this case, Lacara had ample notice that appellee was a difficult client.

Nevertheless, we reverse the denial of appellant's motion for withdrawal under Model Code DR 2-110(C)(1)(a). Among Lacara's allegations are that Whiting insisted upon pressing claims already dismissed by the district court and calling witnesses Lacara deemed detrimental to his case. At oral argument, Whiting confirmed Lacara's contention that Whiting intends to dictate how his action is to be pursued. Whiting was asked by a member of the panel:

> Are you under the impression that if we affirm Judge Spatt's ruling, you will be able to tell Mr. Lacara to make the arguments you want made in this case? . . . [T]hat, if Mr. Lacara says, "That witness doesn't support your case," and you don't agree with that, are you under the impression that if we affirm Judge Spatt's ruling you'll be able to force him to call that witness?

To which Whiting replied, "Yes I am."

Moreover, in his statements at oral argument, Whiting made it clear that he was as interested in using the litigation to make public his allegations of corruption within the Brookville police department as in advancing his specific legal claims. For example, Whiting thought it relevant to inform us at oral argument that police officers in the department were guilty of "illegal drug use, acceptance of gratuities, [and] ongoing extramarital affairs while they were on duty." Appellee stated that he wanted to call an officer to testify that the officer could not "bring up anything criminal about the lieutenant, the two lieutenants, or the chief, which could get them in trouble or make the department look bad." Finally, Whiting made clear that he disagreed with Lacara about the handling of his case partly because Whiting suspects that Lacara wants to cover up corruption. Appellee stated: "For some strange reason, Mr. Lacara states that he doesn't want to put certain witnesses on the stand. . . . The bottom line is he does not want to make waves and expose all of the corruption that's going on within this community."

Also, at oral argument, appellee continued to bring up the already-dismissed due process claims. He asserted: "They found me guilty of something which was investigated by their department on two separate occasions and closed as unfounded on two separate occasions." We thus have good reason to conclude that Whiting will insist that Lacara pursue the already dismissed claims at trial.

Finally, appellee indicated that he might sue Lacara if not satisfied that Lacara provided representation as Whiting dictated. After admitting that he did not consider Lacara to be the "right attorney" for him in this case, Whiting asserted that he deemed Lacara "ineffective." The following exchange also occurred:

> *Question from Panel:* If you think that Mr. Lacara is ineffective in representing you as you stand here now, doesn't Mr. Lacara face the prospect of a . . . malpractice suit, by you, against him, if he continues in the case?
>
> *Appellee's Reply:* Yes, I believe he absolutely does.
>
> *Question from Panel:* Then, isn't that all the more reason to relieve him? So that what you say is ineffective and is in effect a distortion of the attorney-client relationship, doesn't continue?
>
> *Appellee's Reply:* I believe I do have grounds to sue Mr. Lacara for misrepresentation. . . .
>
> We believe that appellee's desire both to dictate legal strategies to his counsel and to sue counsel if those strategies are not followed places Lacara in *so impossible a situation that he must be permitted to withdraw.*

Make the Connection

For a discussion of the rules prohibiting lawyers from making frivolous arguments, *see* Chapter 6.

(emphasis added).

Model Code DR 2-110(C)(1)(a) limits the obligations of attorneys to follow their clients' dictates in how to conduct litigation. Attorneys have a duty to the court not to make "legal contentions . . . [un]warranted by existing law or by a nonfrivolous argument for the extension, modification, or reversal of existing law. . . ." Fed.R.Civ.P. 11(b)(2) * * * In this case, appellee's belief that he can dictate to Lacara how to handle his case and sue him if Lacara declines to follow those dictates leaves Lacara in a position amounting to a functional conflict of interest. If required to continue to represent Whiting, Lacara will have to choose between exposure to a malpractice action or to potential Rule 11 or other sanctions. To be sure, such a malpractice action would have no merit. However, we have no doubt it would be actively pursued, and even frivolous malpractice claims can have substantial collateral consequences.

As previously noted, the interest of the district court in preventing counsel from withdrawing on the eve of trial is substantial. Moreover, we would normally be loath to allow an attorney to withdraw on the eve of trial when the attorney had as much notice as did Lacara that he was taking on a difficult client. However, the functional conflict of interest developed at oral argument causes us to conclude that the motion to withdraw should be granted.

We therefore reverse and order the district court to grant appellant's motion to withdraw as counsel. We note that Lacara agreed in this court to waive all outstanding fees and to turn over all pertinent files to Whiting.

———————

Before you leave the unit on ending the lawyer-client relationship, think back to Chapter 1. According to Professor David Luban, the dominant conception "consist[s] of (1) a role obligation (the 'principle of partisanship') that identifies professionalism with extreme partisan zeal on behalf of the client and (2) the 'principle of nonaccountability,' which insists that the lawyer bears no moral responsibility for the client's goals or the means used to attain them."[5] Do you see anything in Rule 1.16 that is inconsistent with this view of the lawyer's role?

V. Competence

Section III focused on the creation of the lawyer-client relationship. But why do clients retain lawyers? It is useful for lawyers to remember that clients hire lawyers because they want their lawyers to help them achieve a goal or solve a problem. The client's goal may involve something that has happened in the past, in which case litigation may be involved, or something that the client would like to happen in the future, in which case the lawyer may be doing transactional or regulatory work for the client. But regardless of the type of legal practice that a lawyer has, a client who retains a lawyer seeks that lawyer's assistance. Thus, a bedrock obligation of the lawyer is to provide competent representation to the client. The very first rule in the Rules of Professional Conduct—Rule 1.1—states this obligation of competence. Closely related to competence are Rules 1.3 and 1.4 regarding diligence and communication.

Under Rule 8.4, a lawyer engages in misconduct, and is therefore subject to discipline, if the lawyer violates or attempts to violate the Rules of Professional Conduct, knowingly assists or induces another to do so, or does so through the acts of another. Reports from disciplinary authorities show that competence, diligence, and communication are among the most frequent complaints against lawyers. For example, the Attorney Registration & Disciplinary Commission of the Supreme Court of Illinois highlighted the following statistics in its 2014 Annual Report:

- •   5,921 grievances were docketed against 3,935 different attorneys, representing about 4% of all registered attorneys

———————

5   David Luban, *Lawyers and Justice: An Ethical Study* 20 (1988). See Murray L. Schwartz, *The Professionalism and Accountability of Lawyers*, 66 Cal. L. Rev. 669, 671–73 (1978); *see also* William H. Simon, THE PRACTICE OF JUSTICE: A THEORY OF LAWYERS' ETHICS (1998).

- 54% of all grievances involved issues of poor attorney-client relations: neglect of a client matter (39% of all grievances) or failure to communicate with a client (15% of all grievances)

- Top practice areas likely to attract a grievance include criminal law, domestic relations, real estate, and tort.

Lack of competence, lack of diligence, and lack of communication are common themes in the reports from disciplinary authorities. This summary is taken from a report summarizing 2012 lawyer discipline cases in Michigan:

> Conduct characterized by a lack of diligence, lack of competence, and or neglect of client matters was the largest category of professional misconduct in 2012, accounting for 27% of the discipline orders issued in 2012. . . . Thirty Michigan lawyers were publicly disciplined in 2012 as the result of a criminal conviction. These cases accounted for 26% of discipline orders in 2012. . . . The third largest category of misconduct, accounting for 17% of all discipline orders in 2012, involved a lawyer's improper handling of client funds in cases ranging from poor bookkeeping practices to intentional misappropriation of client funds. Other types of misconduct resulting in discipline in 2012 included a lawyer's failure to comply with a prior discipline order; conflicts of interest; misrepresentations to a tribunal; and failure to supervise non-lawyer employees.

Robert L. Agacinski & Robert E. Edick, *State of Michigan Attorney Discipline Board & Attorney Grievance Commission: 2012 Joint Annual Report 1, 5 (Jan. 1–Dec. 31, 2012).*

Food for Thought

How competent are lawyers? Chief Justice Burger famously asserted that "one-third to one-half of the lawyers who appear in serious cases are not really qualified to render fully adequate representation." Warren E. Burger, *The Special Skills of Advocacy: Are Specialized Training and Certification of Advocates Essential to Our System of Justice?*, 83 Fordham L. Rev. 1147 (2014) (reprinting the 1973 article). A Federal Judicial Center study found that judges described only 8.6% of trial performances as incompetent. Roger C. Cramton & Erik M. Jensen, *The State of Trial Advocacy and Legal Education: Three New Studies*, 30 J. Legal Educ. 253, 257 (1979). For a more recent study with a number of interesting statistics, see Richard A. Posner & Albert H. Yoon, *What Judges Think of the Quality of Legal Representation*, 63 Stanford L. Rev. 317 (2010). Scholars have suggested that competency requires mastery of a number of different skills. *See, e.g.*, Susan Swaim Daicoff, *Expanding the Lawyer's Toolkit of Skills and Competencies: Synthesizing Leadership, Professionalism, Emotional Intelligence, Conflict Resolution, and Comprehensive Law*, 52 Santa Clara L. Rev. 795 (2012).

As you read the materials in this section, consider the similarities and differences among the standards for competence under the Rules of Professional Conduct, malpractice law, and the Constitutional guarantee of effective assistance of counsel. You should also consider the goals of each of these tools, the different roles that each of these three tools can play in the effort to ensure competent delivery of legal services, and the role that other tools, such as market pressure, reputation, external rankings, and legal education might play in the efforts to ensure lawyer competence.

Finally, as you read these materials on competence, keep in mind the language of Rule 5.1 and Rule 5.3. These rules require law firm partners to make "reasonable efforts" to ensure that the firm has in place "measures" that will give reasonable assurance that the lawyers and nonlawyers in the firm comply with their professional obligations. What sorts of "measures" or "systems" would help lawyers deliver competent legal service to clients?

A. Discipline

[Question 2-12]

An inventor retained an attorney to help the client file a patent. The inventor told the attorney that time was of the essence because there were competitors with similar ideas. The attorney and the inventor signed a retainer agreement that set forth the attorney's hourly rate and agreed that the attorney would bill the inventor monthly. After spending significant time researching the inventor's potential patent, the attorney concluded that the inventor had a reasonable chance of success. The attorney sent a bill to the inventor, but through no fault of the inventor's, the bills were not delivered (and were not returned to the attorney). During the six months that the attorney was not paid, the attorney did no further work on the inventor's potential patent. In month seven, the inventor called the attorney and asked if the patent had been awarded. The attorney explained that the attorney had not worked on the patent during the past six months because the inventor's bill was outstanding. The inventor hand-delivered a check that same day. Upon receiving the inventor's check, the attorney resumed work on the patent. The attorney checked and saw that no one had filed a similar or identical patent during the past six months. The attorney filed the patent application and took the necessary steps so that the inventor could issue her invention with the label "patent pending."

Is the attorney subject to discipline?

    (A) **Yes, because the attorney did not work on the inventor's patent for six months.**

    (B) **Yes, because the attorney did not seek permission from a tribunal to withdraw from the representation.**

    (C) **No, because a client cannot compel an attorney to work without payment.**

    (D) **No, because the inventor did not sustain any harm as a result of the attorney's action.**

To answer this question, apply the standard of Rule 1.1. It requires a lawyer to "provide competent representation to a client. Competent representation requires the legal knowledge, skill, thoroughness, and preparation reasonably necessary for the representation." Note that a single incident can be the basis for discipline and that, unlike many rules, this rule does not include a client waiver provision. In 2012, the ABA House of Delegates amended Comment

[8] to Rule 1.1 to indicate that lawyers should keep abreast of the benefits and risks associated with relevant technology.

[Question 2-13]

An attorney is a certified specialist in family law and a partner in a law firm that practices family law exclusively. The attorney was working very late one night when she received a telephone call from one of her clients who had been arrested and was currently in jail. The client told the attorney that he was claustrophobic and begged the attorney to try to get him released on bail. The attorney advised the client that the attorney did not have any criminal law expertise and did not handle criminal cases. The client said that he had now used his one free phone call and pleaded with the attorney to come to the police station and see what the attorney could do to get him out on bail.

Because the attorney lived relatively close to the police station and the client was distraught, the attorney went to the police station to try to secure the client's release. As a result of the attorney's lack of experience, the attorney was unable to secure the client's release. The next morning, the attorney found an experienced criminal lawyer who obtained the client's release within one hour.

Global Perspective

Regulators from the U.S., Canada, and Australia have gotten together in recent years to discuss whether they might be able to regulate more proactively and help lawyers practice competently. One of the reasons for the interest in this topic was an empirical study from New South Wales, Australia that found a two-thirds reduction in client complaints after the regulator had certain kinds of firms perform a self-assessment. Some of the most interesting work in this area is currently being done by the regulator in Nova Scotia. For more information on proactive regulation, including the 2019 ABA Resolution on this topic, see this Nova Scotia webpage, https://perma.cc/Y9WN-MKL2; Laurel S. Terry, *When it Comes to Lawyers . . . Is an Ounce of Prevention Worth a Pound of Cure?*, JOTWELL (July 13, 2016); and the additional items cited in the Chapter 9 Global Perspective box.

Was the attorney's conduct proper?

    (A) Yes, because neither referral to another lawyer nor consultation with another lawyer was practical under the circumstances.

    (B) Yes, because the attorney did not charge the client for his services.

    (C) No, because the attorney did not have the legal knowledge and skill necessary to handle this criminal case.

    (D) No, because the attorney was not able to secure the client's release on bail.

The prior question and Question 2-14, *infra*, raise the issue of what circumstances would justify a lawyer working for a client when the lawyer is not familiar with the substantive law involved in the representation. If this were true, it would be extremely difficult for a new lawyer to practice law without violating Rule 1.1. A new lawyer might be limited to handling matters that involved subjects that a lawyer studied during law school. As you consider what Rule 1.1 requires, you should also consult the Comment:

> [1] . . . In determining whether a lawyer employs the requisite knowledge and skill in a particular matter, relevant factors include the relative complexity and specialized nature of the matter, the lawyer's general experience, the lawyer's training and experience in the field in question, the preparation and study the lawyer is able to give the matter and whether it is feasible to refer the matter to, or associate or consult with, a lawyer of established competence in the field in question. In many instances, the required proficiency is that of a general practitioner. Expertise in a particular field of law may be required in some circumstances.

> [2] A lawyer need not necessarily have special training or prior experience to handle legal problems of a type with which the lawyer is unfamiliar. A newly admitted lawyer can be as competent as a practitioner with long experience. Some important legal skills, such as the analysis of precedent, the evaluation of evidence and legal drafting, are required in all legal problems. Perhaps the most fundamental legal skill consists of determining what kind of legal problems a situation may involve, a skill that necessarily transcends any particular specialized knowledge. A lawyer can provide adequate representation in a wholly novel field through necessary study. Competent representation can also be provided through the association of a lawyer of established competence in the field in question.

> [3] In an emergency a lawyer may give advice or assistance in a matter in which the lawyer does not have the skill ordinarily required where referral to or consultation or association with another lawyer would be impractical. Even in an emergency, however, assistance should be limited to that reasonably necessary in the circumstances, for ill-considered action under emergency conditions can jeopardize the client's interest.

> [4] A lawyer may accept representation where the requisite level of competence can be achieved by reasonable preparation. * * *

Practice Pointer

During the 2009 and 2011 terms, the Supreme Court held that missed filing deadlines violated constitutional protections of death row inmates. In *Holland v. Florida*, 560 U.S. 631 (2010), an attorney ignored his client's repeated letters requesting an appeal. In *Maples v. Thomas*, 565 U.S. 266 (2012), a critical ruling never made it out of the mailroom because attorneys failed to notify the court that they had withdrawn from the case. What steps can lawyers and law firms take to avoid problems such as these?

[Question 2-14]

An attorney is a partner in a law firm that performs a variety of legal tasks for clients. This law firm recently hired an associate who had just graduated from law school, passed the bar exam and been admitted as a lawyer. Since joining the law firm, the associate has worked exclusively on trusts and estates matters under the supervision of a firm partner with expertise. After another lawyer unexpectedly left the law firm, the attorney told the associate that the firm was shorthanded and that associate would

have to try a case the following week. The associate protested, stating that she had never seen a trial, had not taken the evidence course or trial advocacy in law school, and did not feel prepared. The attorney told the associate that the "sink or swim" method of learning had worked just fine when the attorney was a young lawyer. The attorney told the associate that he would not ask for an extension because the client wanted to go to trial soon. The associate prepared diligently but many of her questions were in an improper form and the judge repeatedly sustained the evidentiary objections that the opposing counsel raised during the associate's direct examinations and cross-examinations. As a result, associate was not able to introduce key pieces of evidence. After a two-day trial, the jury returned a verdict in favor of the opposing party.

Is the attorney subject to discipline?

- (A) Yes, because the attorney should not have selected an associate from the trusts and estates department.

- (B) Yes, because the attorney did not make "reasonable efforts" to put in place measures that give reasonable assurance that all lawyers in the firm conformed to the duty of competence.

- (C) No, because it is impossible to know whether the associate's trial conduct caused the jury verdict in favor of the opposing party.

- (D) No, because the associate was able to telephone the attorney for advice during lunchtime and other breaks during the trial.

Before answering this question, review Rule 1.1, its Comment, and Rule 5.1. Rule 5.1(a) requires "[a] partner in a law firm, and a lawyer who individually or together with other lawyers possesses comparable managerial authority in a law firm, [to] make reasonable efforts to ensure that the firm has in effect measures giving reasonable assurance that all lawyers in the firm conform to the Rules of Professional Conduct." Rule 5.1(b) makes "[a] lawyer having direct supervisory authority over another lawyer" responsible for "reasonable efforts to ensure that the other lawyer conforms to the Rules of Professional Conduct." Last, Rule 5.1(c) makes a lawyer responsible for another lawyer's violation of the Rules of Professional Conduct if:

(1)   the lawyer orders or, with knowledge of the specific conduct, ratifies the conduct involved; or

(2)   the lawyer is a partner or has comparable managerial authority in the law firm in which the other lawyer practices, or has direct supervisory authority over the other lawyer, and knows of the conduct at a time when its consequences can be avoided or mitigated but fails to take reasonable remedial action.

Rule 5.3 contains analogous provisions that govern a lawyer's "responsibilities regarding nonlawyer assistance." As noted in the section on working with nonlawyers, Rule 5.3(a) provides that "a partner in a law firm, and a lawyer who individually or together with other lawyers possesses comparable managerial authority in a law firm, shall make reasonable efforts to ensure that the firm has in effect measures giving reasonable assurance that the person's conduct is compatible with the professional obligations of the lawyer." With regard to "a lawyer having direct supervisory authority over the nonlawyer," Rule 5.3(b) requires the lawyer to "make reasonable efforts to ensure that the person's conduct is compatible with the professional obligations of the lawyer[.]" Rule 5.3(c) makes a lawyer responsible for conduct of a nonlawyer if the conduct would be a violation of the Rules of Professional Conduct if engaged in by a lawyer and if:

> (1)　the lawyer orders or, with the knowledge of the specific conduct, ratifies the conduct involved; or

> (2)　the lawyer is a partner or has comparable managerial authority in the law firm in which the person is employed, or has direct supervisory authority over the person, and knows of the conduct at a time when its consequences can be avoided or mitigated but fails to take reasonable remedial action.

B.　Malpractice Liability

Global Perspective

At the time this casebook was written, Oregon and Idaho were the only U.S. states that required lawyers to carry malpractice insurance, although other states were considering this issue. *See* Susan Saab Fortney, *Mandatory Legal Malpractice Insurance: Exposing Lawyers' Blind Spots*, 9 St. Mary's J. Legal Malpractice & Ethics 190 (2019). The ABA adopted a Model Court Rule on Insurance *Disclosure* (rather than coverage) which has been adopted in whole or in part by a number of states, but even that rule is controversial among U.S. lawyers. In contrast to the U.S. situation, non-U.S. lawyers often are surprised to learn that U.S. lawyers are not required to carry malpractice insurance. In many jurisdictions elsewhere in the world, malpractice insurance is mandatory. Some of the insurance carriers, such as LawPro in Ontario, devote substantial resources toward preventing malpractice by lawyers.

General

A lawyer may be disciplined for violation of a rule of professional conduct even in the absence of harm to the client. If there is harm, discipline is not designed to remedy that harm. The remedy for harm is a civil lawsuit, such as a malpractice suit. State law determines malpractice liability. According to Restatement § 48, "a lawyer is civilly liable for professional negligence to a person to whom the lawyer owes a duty of care * * * if the lawyer fails to exercise care * * * and if that failure is a legal cause of injury[.]" Restatement § 52 defines the "standard of care" as "the competence and diligence normally exercised by lawyers in similar circumstances."

Standard of Care

In determining the relevant standard of care, courts look to the "practices and standards * * * of lawyers undertaking similar matters in the relevant jurisdiction (typically, a state)." Restatement § 52 Comment [b], *Competence*. In some legal areas, such as federal securities law or federal court litigation of federal legislation, "there exists a national practice with national standards." *Id.*

A lawyer may be held to a higher standard where a lawyer has a "special skill" or where a lawyer "represents to a client that the lawyer has greater competence or will exercise greater diligence than that normally demonstrated by lawyers * * * undertaking similar matters." Restatement § 52(d).

Violation of a Rule or Statute

As Restatement § 52 Comment f explains, "[a] rule or statute regulating the conduct of lawyers but not providing a damages remedy does not give rise to an implied cause of action for lack of care or fiduciary breach." Nevertheless, "the trier of fact may consider the content and construction of a relevant statute or rule, for example a statute or a rule of professional conduct * * * designed for the protection of persons in the position of the claimant. Such a provision is relevant to whether a lawyer has failed to exercise * * * competence and diligence [or] has violated a fiduciary duty[.]" *Id. See* also Scope [20] in the Rules: "Violation of a Rule should not itself give rise to a cause of action against a lawyer nor should it create any presumption in such a case that a legal duty has been breached. . . . Nevertheless, since the Rules do establish standards of conduct by lawyers, a lawyer's violation of a Rule may be evidence of breach of the applicable standard of care."

Nonclients

Restatement § 51 identifies three limited circumstances under which lawyers have a duty of care to nonclients. These are:

1. "[T]he lawyer or (with the lawyer's acquiescence) the lawyer's client invites the nonclient to rely on the lawyer's opinion or provision of other legal services, and the nonclient so relies; and * * * the nonclient is not, under applicable tort law, too remote from the lawyer to be entitled to protection[.]"

2. "[T]he lawyer knows that a client intends as one of the primary objectives of the representation that the lawyer's services benefit the nonclient; * * * such a duty would not significantly impair the lawyer's performance of obligations to the client; and * * * the absence of such a duty would make enforcement of those obligations to the client unlikely[.]"

3. "[T]he lawyer's client is a trustee, guardian, executor, or fiduciary acting primarily to perform similar functions for the nonclient; * * * the lawyer knows that appropriate action by the lawyer is necessary with respect to a matter within the scope of the representation to prevent or rectify the breach of a fiduciary duty owed by the client to the nonclient, where (i) the breach is a crime or fraud or (ii) the lawyer has assisted or is assisting the breach; * * * the nonclient is not reasonably able to protect its rights; and * * * such a duty would not significantly impair the performance of the lawyer's obligations to the client."

Contract or Tort?

Restatement § 48, Comment d explains that:

Ordinarily, a plaintiff may cast a legal-malpractice claim in the mold of tort or contract or both[.] * * * Whether the claim is considered in tort or in contract is usually of practical significance when it must be decided whether it is subject to a tort or a contract statute of limitations in a jurisdiction having a different limitations period for each. * * * Some jurisdictions assign all legal-malpractice claims to one category, while others treat some claims as in contract and others as in tort, depending on the facts alleged or the relief sought.

Hear from the Authors

To hear from the authors about legal malpractice, click here.

Law Firm Liability

A difference between malpractice and discipline is that, with exception of New York Rule 5.1(a) and New Jersey Rule 5.1(a), and N.J. Court Rule 1:20-1(a), law firms are generally not subject to discipline. With regard to malpractice, Restatement § 58(1) explains that "[a] law firm is subject to civil liability for injury legally caused to a person by any wrongful act or omission of any principal or employee of the firm who was acting in the ordinary course of the firm's business or with actual or apparent authority."

[Question 2-15]

A transactional attorney regularly advises closely-held corporations on tax and corporate issues. An acquaintance asked the attorney if they could meet to discuss a legal matter. The attorney agreed. During their 30 minute conversation, the acquaintance told the attorney that a relative had died and named the acquaintance the executor of the relative's estate. The acquaintance asked the attorney to represent him. The attorney advised the acquaintance that the attorney did not have experience and was too busy to do the work necessary to become competent. The attorney offered to refer the acquaintance to another lawyer who regularly practiced in the field and advised the acquaintance that he should see another lawyer promptly because there might be deadlines he should follow as the executor. The acquaintance did not contact another lawyer until eight months after meeting with the attorney. At that time, the acquaintance learned that his method of interacting with the estate's creditors had created a complicated, expensive situation for the estate, including a significant amount of money in legal fees to reverse the errors. If the acquaintance had received legal advice, the acquaintance would not have committed these expensive errors.

Is the attorney subject to civil liability?

    (A) Yes, because the attorney should not have agreed to meet with the acquaintance unless the attorney was prepared to accept his case.

(B) **Yes, because the attorney did not advise the acquaintance of a specific date by which he should consult a lawyer.**

(C) **No, because the attorney did not violate any duty owed to the acquaintance.**

(D) **No, because the acquaintance declined the attorney's offer to refer the acquaintance to a lawyer with expertise.**

Prospective Clients

In the prior question, there was no lawyer-client relationship under the test set forth in Restatement § 14 because the attorney chose not to represent the potential client and clearly communicated that fact. But does that mean that a lawyer cannot be liable to such a person? Restatement § 48 states that a lawyer is civilly liable for professional negligence to a person to whom the lawyer owes a duty of care. Restatement § 50 makes it clear that a lawyer owes a duty of care to his or her clients. But do lawyers ever owe a duty of care to those who are not clients, what are those duties, and what do we call these nonclients to whom any duties are owed? Restatement § 51 answers these questions. It identifies the situations in which a lawyer owes a duty of care to a nonclient. One of these situations is if the plaintiff is a "prospective client, as stated in [Restatement] § 15."

Both the Rules of Professional Conduct and the Restatement refer to a "rejected" client, such as the man in Question 2-15, as a "prospective client." This terminology can be confusing because "prospective client" sounds forward-looking, but this term is used to describe events and relationships that occurred in the past. Thus, in the context of malpractice and discipline, it is useful to remember that a "prospective client" is a "rejected client"—that is, someone with whom the lawyer did not establish a lawyer-client relationship but to whom the lawyer nevertheless owes certain duties. The rule of professional conduct that applies to prospective clients is Rule 1.18, which you will study in Chapters 4 and 5. The Restatement provision that applies to prospective clients is § 15. A lawyer must "use reasonable care to the extent the lawyer provides * * * legal services" to a prospective client. Restatement § 15(1)(c). What services might a lawyer provide to a prospective client? Restatement § 15 Comment e explains that:

> When a prospective client and a lawyer discuss the possibility of representation, the lawyer might comment on such matters as whether that person has a promising claim or defense, whether the lawyer is appropriate for the matter in question, whether conflicts of interest exist and if so how they might be dealt with, the time within which action must be taken and, if the representation does not proceed, what other lawyer might represent the prospective client. * * * The lawyer must also not harm a prospective client through unreasonable delay after indicating that the lawyer might undertake the representation.

In addition to asking "to whom is a duty owed?", in a malpractice suit, one must also consider what type of conduct can constitute a breach of the duty of care. *Ziegelheim v. Apollo* addresses this issue.

Ziegelheim v. Apollo

607 A.2d 1298 (N.J. 1992)

HANDLER, J.

In this case we must decide what duties an attorney owes a client when negotiating a settlement and whether a client's agreement to a negotiated settlement bars her from recovering from her attorney for the negligent handling of her case.

* * *

Like most professionals, lawyers owe a duty to their clients to provide their services with reasonable knowledge, skill, and diligence. We have consistently recited that command in rather broad terms, for lawyers' duties in specific cases vary with the circumstances presented. "What constitutes a reasonable degree of care is not to be considered in a vacuum but with reference to the type of service the attorney undertakes to perform." The lawyer must take "any steps necessary in the proper handling of the case." Those steps will include, among other things, a careful investigation of the facts of the matter, the formulation of a legal strategy, the filing of appropriate papers, and the maintenance of communication with the client.

In accepting a case, the lawyer agrees to pursue the goals of the client to the extent the law permits, even when the lawyer believes that the client's desires are unwise or ill-considered. At the same time, because the client's desires may be influenced in large measure by the advice the lawyer provides, the lawyer is obligated to give the client reasonable advice. As a legal matter progresses and circumstances change, the wishes of the client may change as well. Accordingly, the lawyer is obligated to keep the client informed of the status of the matter for which the lawyer has been retained, and is required to advise the client on the various legal and strategic issues that arise.

In this case, Mrs. Ziegelheim made several claims impugning Apollo's handling of her divorce, and the trial court dismissed all of them on Apollo's motion for summary judgment. As we explain, we believe that the trial court's rulings on several of her claims were erroneous.

In legal malpractice cases, as in other cases, summary disposition is appropriate only when there is no genuine dispute of material fact. A litigant has a right to proceed to trial "where there is the slightest doubt as to the facts." All inferences are drawn in favor of the party opposing the motion for summary judgment.

On Mrs. Ziegelheim's claim that Apollo negligently advised her with respect to her chances of winning a greater proportion of the marital estate if she proceeded to trial, we conclude, as did the Appellate Division, that there was a genuine dispute regarding the appropriate advice that an attorney should give in cases like hers. According to the expert retained by Mrs. Ziegelheim, women in her position—who are in relatively poor health, have little earning capacity, and have been wholly dependent on their husbands—often receive upwards of fifty percent of the marital estate. The expert said that Mrs. Ziegelheim's chances of winning such a large fraction of the estate had she gone to trial would have been especially good because the couple had enjoyed a high standard of living while they were together and because her husband's earning capacity was "tremendous" and would remain so for some time. Her expert's opinion was brought to the trial court's attention, as was the expert report of Mr. Ziegelheim. If plaintiff's expert's opinion were credited, as it should have been for purposes of summary judgment, then Apollo very well could have been found negligent in advising her that she could expect to win only ten to twenty percent of the marital estate.

Apollo urges us to adopt the rule enunciated by the Pennsylvania Supreme Court * * * that a dissatisfied litigant may not recover from his or her attorney for malpractice in negotiating a settlement that the litigant has accepted unless the litigant can prove actual fraud on the part of the attorney. Under that rule, no cause of action can be made based on negligence or contract principles against an attorney for malpractice in negotiating a settlement. The Pennsylvania Supreme Court rationalized its severe rule by explaining that it had a "longstanding public policy which encourages settlements."

New Jersey, too, has a longstanding policy that encourages settlements, but we reject the rule espoused by the Pennsylvania Supreme Court. Although we encourage settlements, we recognize that litigants rely heavily on the professional advice of counsel when they decide whether to accept or reject offers of settlement, and we insist that the lawyers of our state advise clients with respect to settlements with the same skill, knowledge, and diligence with which they pursue all other legal tasks. Attorneys are supposed to know the likelihood of success for the types of cases they handle and they are supposed to know the range of possible awards in those cases.

As we noted [previously:] "One who undertakes to render services in the practice of a profession or trade is required to exercise the skill and knowledge normally possessed by members of that profession in good standing in similar communities." * * * Lawyers are clearly included[.] * * * Like most courts, we see no reason to apply a more lenient rule to lawyers who negotiate settlements. After all, the negotiation of settlements is one of the most basic and most frequently undertaken tasks that lawyers perform. * * *

Although the Appellate Division reversed the trial court on Mrs. Ziegelheim's claim relating to Apollo's advice, it affirmed the trial court on all other claims. On the issue of Apollo's alleged failure to make a proper investigation into Mr. Ziegelheim's assets, the trial court ruled that litigation on that issue was precluded by the family court's determination that the settlement was fair and equitable. We conclude that the family court's determination should not have barred Mrs. Ziegelheim from litigating that claim. * * *

The fact that a party received a settlement that was "fair and equitable" does not mean necessarily that the party's attorney was competent or that the party would not have received a more favorable settlement had the party's incompetent attorney been competent. Thus, in this case, notwithstanding the family court's decision, Mrs. Ziegelheim still may proceed against Apollo in her negligence action.

Moreover, another aspect of the alleged professional incompetence that led to the improvident acceptance of the settlement was the attorney's own failure to discover hidden marital assets. When Mrs. Ziegelheim sought to reopen her divorce settlement, the family court denied her motion with the observation that "[a]mple opportunity existed for full discovery," and that "the parties had their own accountants as well as counsel." The court did not determine definitively that Mr. Ziegelheim had hidden no assets, but stated instead that it "suspected that everything to be known was known to the parties." The earlier ruling did not implicate the competence of counsel and, indeed, was premised on the presumptive competence of counsel. Hence, defendant cannot invoke that ruling now to bar a challenge to his competence. Mrs. Ziegelheim should have been allowed to prove that Apollo negligently failed to discover certain assets concealed by her former husband.

The Appellate Division also affirmed the trial court's dismissal of Mrs. Ziegelheim's claims that Apollo negligently delayed in finalizing the settlement and that the written settlement differed from the one recited by Mr. Ziegelheim's lawyer. Again we conclude that she should have been allowed to litigate those claims on the merits. To be sure, lawyers generally cannot be held liable for their failure to persuade opposing parties to agree to terms, but Mrs. Ziegelheim alleges here that the two sides had agreed to terms and that Apollo simply failed to see to it that the terms were put into writing. Apollo may be able to refute her factual account, but he should not have prevailed on summary judgment, for there were genuine disputes concerning the accuracy of the written version and the reason for the nine-month delay in finalizing it.

Mrs. Ziegelheim's final claim is that Apollo was negligent in not writing down the terms of the settlement prior to the hearing in which the settlement was recited and approved by her and Mr. Ziegelheim. She asserts that a competent attorney would have written them down so that she could review them and make an informed and reasoned assessment of their fairness. At trial she may be able to prove that she would not have accepted the settlement offer had it been presented to her in writing for her review. She may be able to demonstrate, for example, that Apollo's oral presentation of the settlement obscured the fact that it did not include the tax and insurance provisions she desired. We cannot determine the merits of those allegations and decline to speculate on defendant's possible refutation of them. We simply observe that on this record, her final claim, too, presents genuine issues of material fact and should not have been resolved on summary judgment.

In holding as we do today, we do not open the door to malpractice suits by any and every dissatisfied party to a settlement. Many such claims could be averted if settlements were explained as a matter of record in open court in proceedings reflecting the understanding and assent of the parties. Further, plaintiffs must allege particular facts in support of their claims of attorney incompetence and may not litigate complaints containing mere generalized assertions of malpractice. We are mindful that attorneys cannot be held liable simply because they are not successful in persuading an opposing party to accept certain terms. Similarly, we acknowledge that attorneys who pursue reasonable strategies in handling their cases and who render reasonable advice to their clients cannot be held liable for the failure of their strategies or for any unprofitable outcomes that result because their clients took their advice. The law demands that attorneys handle their cases with knowledge, skill, and diligence, but it does not demand that they be perfect or infallible, and it does not demand that they always secure optimum outcomes for their clients.

* * *

The judgment of the Appellate Division is affirmed in part and reversed in part and the matter is remanded in accordance with this opinion.

———————————————

Given human nature, a certain amount of lawyer malpractice is probably inevitable. Lawyers need to know that the Rules have provisions that tell lawyers how to handle malpractice before it arises and after it occurs. Questions 2-16 and 2-17, Rule 1.8(h), and the material that follows address these kinds of issues.

[Question 2-16]

An attorney has been asked to represent an inventor who wants to bring a multimillion dollar lawsuit for patent infringement. Although the attorney reasonably believes that he is capable of conducting the lawsuit competently, he does not have sufficient insurance coverage in the event of malpractice. The attorney asks the client to agree to an upper limit of $20 million on the attorney's potential malpractice liability. The attorney shows the client the proposed agreement and fully discusses the consequences of including such a provision in the retainer agreement. The attorney also recommends that the client consult independent counsel before signing the retainer agreement, but the client decides to sign the agreement without doing so, explaining that he did not want to pay the legal fees to have another lawyer review this agreement. The limitation of liability agreement is not prohibited by law in the client's jurisdiction.

Is the attorney's conduct proper?

(A) Yes, because the agreement is not prohibited by law in the client's jurisdiction.

(B) Yes, because the client gave informed consent, the agreement was in writing, and the client was told of the advisability of consulting independent counsel.

(C) No, because the client did not consult independent counsel before signing the agreement.

(D) No, because a lawyer may not make an agreement limiting malpractice liability to a client.

[Question 2-17]

An attorney represented a client who was injured in a car accident while driving a car. The attorney negotiated and the client signed a settlement agreement with the client's insurance company in which the client provided a general release of all of the client's "personal injury protection" or PIP benefits. After this settlement agreement was signed, the client received an additional medical bill that the insurance company normally would have had to pay as part of the client's PIP insurance benefits. The attorney concluded that she had been negligent in drafting the settlement agreement because a competent lawyer would not have had her client the driver sign a general release of PIP benefits, but would have listed the specific medical bills (PIP benefits) covered by the release. The attorney disclosed the negligence to the driver, and said that if the driver agreed to settle this malpractice claim, the attorney would reimburse the driver for the new medical bill and for any future medical bills. The attorney reasonably believed that this proposed settlement was fair to the driver. The attorney advised the driver, in writing, to seek independent representation before entering this settlement agreement and gave the driver time to retain independent counsel. The driver did not retain independent counsel, but did sign the settlement agreement.

Was the attorney's conduct proper?

    (A)   **Yes, because the attorney advised the driver in writing to seek independent representation before entering the settlement agreement and gave the driver time to retain independent counsel.**

    (B)   **Yes, because the attorney initiated the settlement discussions with the driver.**

    (C)   **No, because the attorney, rather than another lawyer, drafted the agreement that settled the driver's potential malpractice claim.**

    (D)   **No, because the driver was not independently represented when signing the settlement agreement with the attorney.**

Rule 1.8(h) provides that "a lawyer shall not:

(1) make an agreement prospectively limiting the lawyer's liability to a client for malpractice unless the client is independently represented in making the agreement; or

(2) settle a claim or potential claim for such liability with an unrepresented client or former client unless that person is advised in writing of the desirability of seeking and is given a reasonable opportunity to seek the advice of independent legal counsel in connection therewith."

Rule 1.8(h) specifies the conditions under which a lawyer may limit his or her malpractice liability. The materials that follow ask you to consider the circumstances under which a lawyer may limit the scope of representation and how this limitation might affect a lawyer's malpractice liability.

[Question 2-18]

An attorney is a specialist in the field of e-discovery. The plaintiff in a complex lawsuit retained the attorney to work with the plaintiff's trial counsel to frame e-discovery requests and responses. After being fully advised, the client signed the attorney's retainer agreement which specified that the attorney's representation would be limited to advice about e-discovery matters.

Is the attorney's conduct proper?

    (A)   **Yes, because the client initiated the request for limited representation.**

    (B)   **Yes, because a lawyer may limit the scope of the representation as long as the limitation is reasonable under the circumstances and the client gives informed consent.**

    (C)   **No, because the plaintiff was not independently represented in making the agreement.**

    (D)   **No, because the attorney was required to work directly with the plaintiff rather than working with the plaintiff's trial counsel.**

As you analyze this question, consider the *Lerner* case, which follows, and Rule 1.2(c). The *Lerner* case considers whether a limitation on the scope of representation will affect a lawyer's malpractice liability. Rule 1.2(c) tells you, as a discipline matter, when it is proper for a lawyer to enter into a limited scope relationship. It states that a lawyer may "limit the scope of the representation if the limitation is reasonable under the circumstances and the client gives informed consent." Comment [6] provides several examples:

> When a lawyer has been retained by an insurer to represent an insured, for example, the representation may be limited to matters related to the insurance coverage. A limited representation may be appropriate because the client has limited objectives for the representation. In addition, the terms upon which representation is undertaken may exclude specific means that might otherwise be used to accomplish the client's objectives. Such limitations may exclude actions that the client thinks are too costly or that the lawyer regards as repugnant or imprudent.

Comment [7] explains when a limited scope representation might not be reasonable:

> Although this Rule affords the lawyer and client substantial latitude to limit the representation, the limitation must be reasonable under the circumstances. If, for example, a client's objective is limited to securing general information about the law the client needs in order to handle a common and typically uncomplicated legal problem, the lawyer and client may agree that the lawyer's services will be limited to a brief telephone consultation. Such a limitation, however, would not be reasonable if the time allotted was not sufficient to yield advice upon which the client could rely. Although an agreement for a limited representation does not exempt a lawyer from the duty to provide competent representation, the limitation is a factor to be considered when determining the legal knowledge, skill, thoroughness and preparation reasonably necessary for the representation. *See* Rule 1.1.

Lerner v. Laufer

819 A.2d 471 (N.J. Super. App.Div. 2003)

WELLS, J.A.D.

We address in this appeal from a judgment dismissing a legal malpractice action, the issue of whether and to what extent, if any, an attorney may limit the scope of his representation of a matrimonial client in reviewing a mediated property settlement agreement (PSA).

The circumstances out of which the appeal arises are undisputed. The plaintiff, Lynne C. Lerner, was married to Michael H. Lerner in November 1969 and had been married to him 24 years when he filed an action for divorce in 1994. The couple had two children, a son and a daughter, born in 1974 and 1976. Michael contacted a New York lawyer, Brett Meyer, who represented him and his company in New York, but who also was a friend of the family and trusted by Lynne, to mediate a PSA. The couple had amassed a considerable fortune.

Meyer mediated over several sessions as the result of which a comprehensive, written PSA emerged. He then gave Lynne a list of New Jersey attorneys to consult prior to signing the agreement. That list, in turn, had been given to Meyer by James Andrews, a New Jersey attorney who would represent Michael in the divorce proceedings. While the record does not disclose whether Andrews alerted everyone on the list, he did alert the defendant, William Laufer, that Lynne might call, and on January 26, 1994, sent him a draft of the mediated PSA. Lynne selected Laufer of the firm of Courter, Kobert, Laufer, Purcell & Cohen, P.C. (CKLP & C) from the list. Laufer was an experienced matrimonial attorney and held himself out as a specialist in the field.

On January 28, 1994, Lynne and Laufer spoke by telephone. On February 2, 1994, the first time that Lynne and Laufer met in person, Laufer produced a two-page letter, dated that day, for Lynne to consider. While the letter is of some length, its importance to this case is such that we reproduce it in full:

> Dear Mrs. Lerner:
>
> This letter will confirm that you have retained my law firm for the purpose of reviewing a Property Settlement Agreement that was the product of divorce mediation conducted by Mr. Brett J. Meyer, an Attorney at Law of the State of New York.
>
> This letter will further confirm that I have not conducted any discovery in this matter on your behalf. I have not reviewed income tax returns or other financial documentation to confirm or verify your husband's income for the past several years. I have no information concerning the gross and net values of the properties in Summit, Belmar, Telluride, Colorado or Short Hills, New Jersey. I have seen no information concerning the value of the stock in Marisa Christina, Inc. or the other corporations referred to on Page 10 of the Property Settlement Agreement. In

addition, I have not had the opportunity to review any documentation concerning the respective incomes, assets, liabilities or other financial information in your case.

Based upon the fact that I have not had an opportunity to conduct full and complete discovery in this matter, including but not limited to appraisals of real estate and business interests, depositions and interrogatories, I am not in a position to advise you as to whether or not the Agreement is fair and equitable and whether or not you should execute the Agreement as prepared. Accordingly, it is difficult for me to make a recommendation as to whether you should accept the sum of $500,000.00 and 15% of the stock that the two of you have acquired during the marriage in consideration for waiving your right to 85% of the stock that was acquired during the marriage.

In sum, I am not in a position to make a recommendation or determination that the Property Settlement Agreement as prepared represents a fair and reasonable compromise of the issues concerning equitable distribution or whether the amount of alimony and/or child support that you will receive under the terms of the Agreement is an amount that would be awarded to you if, in fact, this matter proceeded to trial.

This letter will confirm that I have reviewed and suggested various modifications to the Property Settlement Agreement to the mediator. I have discussed the contents of the Agreement with you, and in your opinion you are satisfied that the Agreement represents a fair and reasonable compromise of all issues arising from the marital relationship. You have indicated to me that you are entering into the Agreement freely and voluntarily and that you have been satisfied with the services of the mediator in this matter. You have further indicated to me that the Agreement will be providing you with a substantial amount of assets in excess of Three Million Dollars, and that you will be receiving alimony payments as specifically set forth in Paragraph 5 of the Property Settlement Agreement.

After reviewing the Agreement with you and Mr. Meyer, I am satisfied that you understand the terms and conditions of the Agreement; that you feel that you are receiving a fair and equitable amount of the assets that were acquired during the marriage; and that the amount of support that is provided in the Agreement will, in fact, provide you with an income that will allow you to maintain a respectable lifestyle.

This letter will also confirm that you are accepting my services based upon the representations specifically set forth above and that under no circumstances will you now or in the future be asserting any claims against me or my firm arising from the negotiation or execution of your Property Settlement Agreement.

Thank you for the opportunity to be of service to you in this matter, and if I can be of any future assistance, please do not hesitate to contact me.

Lynne read and signed the letter. She and Laufer then conferenced for about an hour, during which time each term of the mediated PSA was read and discussed. In addition, they discussed the value of the couple's interest in Marisa Christina, a very valuable company doing business in New York. Thereupon, a four-way conference ensued between Lynne, Laufer, Michael and Andrews, and the PSA was executed.

Five days later, on February 7, 1994, a standard retainer agreement issued from Laufer's office to Lynne, which she signed and returned. It provided in part:

> The legal services which I anticipate will be rendered to you will involve legal research and factual investigation as to (i) assets which you owned at the time you were married, assets which were acquired over the course of the marriage; (ii) income and your ability/need for support; (iii) grounds for divorce; (iv) custody and visitation, and (v) payment of counsel fees and costs.

The retainer agreement also provided that the plaintiff: "will have the benefit of my [defendants'] advice and my prediction of the likely results if the matter were not settled, and were instead submitted for judicial resolution."

* * *

Practice Pointer

What did you think of the February 2 and February 9 letters sent by attorney William Laufer to his client? Which, if any, would you consider to be the letter(s) of engagement? What items do you think should be included in a lawyer's letter of engagement? How could attorney Laufer have better handled this situation?

The divorce was granted, and the PSA was incorporated into the final judgment dated May 6, 1994. We note that during the course of his representation of Lynne between January 28, 1994 and April 11, 1994, the date of the divorce hearing, Laufer suggested changes in the mediated PSA either to Meyer or to Andrews. Some of the changes were adopted and some were not. * * *

In September 1999, Lynne commenced the present malpractice action against Laufer through the office of Hilton Stein. * * *

I

Lynne argues that the judge * * * permitted Laufer to assume the role of a "potted plant" in representing her contrary to the general duty of a lawyer to act with reasonable knowledge, skill and diligence. She urges that Laufer had a duty to perform those duties reasonably and usually expected of a lawyer engaged by a matrimonial client, anything short of which constituted malpractice. She claims that the letter of February 2, 1994 does not constitute either a limitation on the scope of Laufer's representation or a waiver of her right to full representation.

* * * Lynne asserts that it makes no difference that she described the second amended PSA as fair and equitable in the 1999 divorce proceeding because had Laufer competently represented her at the outset, she would not have been burdened by the baggage of the mediated PSA. In the latter respect, she contends that because the judge did not vacate the mediated agreement along with the divorce, she was presented with the prospect that were she to go to trial in the second proceeding, the mediated agreement would be re-approved by the judge.

Laufer argues that Lynne ignores RPC 1.2(c), which permits an attorney to limit the scope of his representation "if the client consents after consultation." He urges that the letter of February 2, 1994 disclosed the limited purpose of his representation, the details of those services he would not perform, and that he "was not in a position to advise . . . as to whether or not the agreement is fair or equitable and whether or not [Lynne] should execute the Agreement as prepared." He urges that the letter is an effective consent to limit his representation under the RPC and constitutes a waiver of full representation.

Laufer also claims that Lynne is estopped to claim in this case that the PSA was unfair because she stated under oath in the 1999 divorce proceeding that she understood that she had a right to go to trial as to all issues raised in the second divorce proceeding.

II

At the heart of this case lies a clash over two significant values to the legal community. The first is the value more recently discerned and encouraged in resolving disputes by mediation. The second is the older, more established value perceived in the resolution of conflict in adversarial proceedings by parties represented by fully independent and empowered attorneys. In the former process, it is the clients, assisted by a mediator, who arrange the disposition of their own dispute. It is largely a self-help process only tangentially informed by what the law would allow or dictate. In the latter process, it is lawyers who seek to reach ends sought by their clients under laws and rules often little understood by those clients. It is a process whereby established rights and duties are sought to be vindicated.

* * *

When a PSA reached through the mediation process must be formally incorporated in a judgment of divorce, the participation of attorneys governed by the adversarial process gives rise to a question as to the nature and extent of the duty of care imposed upon the attorneys. A mediated divorce settlement may well look substantially different on the same facts than would such a settlement hammered out in adversarial proceedings. * * *

Yet the law has never foreclosed the right of competent, informed citizens to resolve their own disputes in whatever way may suit them. "Clients have the right to make the final decision as to whether, when, and how to settle their cases and as to economic and other positions to be taken with respect to issues in the case." * * * The courts approve hundreds of such settlements in all kinds of cases without once looking into their wisdom or the adequacy of the consideration that supports them. In divorce proceedings, the court daily approves settlements upon the express finding that it does not pass upon the fairness or merits of the agreement, so long as the parties acknowledge that the agreement was reached voluntarily and is for them, at least, fair and equitable.

RPC 1.2(c) expressly permits an attorney with the consent of the client after consultation to limit the scope of representation. In *Ziegelheim*, . . . the Court stated " 'what constitutes a reasonable degree of care is not to be considered in a vacuum but with reference to the type of service the attorney undertakes to perform.' To us that means if the service is limited by consent, then the degree of care is framed by the agreed service.' "* * *

We hold it is not a breach of the standard of care for an attorney under a signed precisely drafted consent agreement to limit the scope of representation to not perform such services in the course of representing a matrimonial client that he or she might otherwise perform absent such a consent. Except as we hereinafter note, we are satisfied that Laufer, with Lynne's consent after consultation, properly limited the scope of his representation of her under RPC 1.2(c), to a review of the terms of the mediated agreement without going outside its four corners. We acknowledge that the letter of February 2, 1994 does not quote or cite RPC 1.2(c) nor does it expressly describe itself as a "limit to the scope of representation." It, indeed, could have been more precise in those respects. Nevertheless, we reject the argument that the content failings of the letter deprive it of its intended efficacy to limit the scope of Laufer's duties as an attorney. We are satisfied that the letter is unmistakable in its import that Laufer did not and would not perform the named services, could not render an opinion on the fairness of the agreement, and could not advise Lynne whether or not to execute it.

Armed as he was with the letter of February 2, 1994, Laufer did not, therefore, breach a proved standard of care by performing no discovery or related investigatory services necessary to evaluate the merits in fact of the mediated PSA.

Food for Thought

Under what circumstances should a lawyer be permitted to provide legal assistance that does not meet the standard of competent representation? The legal profession is grappling with this question in responding to the reality that many low- and middle-income people cannot afford full legal services. One commentator has noted that "[t]he majority of litigants now proceed *pro se* in state courts." Alicia M. Farley, *An Important Piece of the Bundle: How Limited Appearances Can Provide An Ethically Sound Way to Increase Access to Justice for Pro Se Litigants*, 20 Geo. J. Legal Ethics 563, 564 (2007). In response, courts and bar leaders are seeking to permit unbundled legal services,

> a practice in which the lawyer and client agree that the lawyer will provide some, but not all, of the work involved in traditional full service representation. Clients choose the legal assistance according to their needs and perform the remaining tasks on their own. Unbundling has been described as ordering "a la carte," rather than from the "full-service menu." A client might hire a lawyer for trial representation, but not for court filings, discovery, and negotiations. Unbundled services can take many forms, including telephone, Internet, or in-person advice; assisting clients in negotiations and litigation; assistance with discovery; or limited court appearances. For many clients, these limited engagements make a lawyer's services affordable.

Fern Fisher-Brandveen & Rochelle Klempner, *Unbundled Legal Services: Untying the Bundle in New York State*, 29 Fordham Urb. L.J. 1107, 1108 (2002). See also Forrest S. Mosten, Julie Macfarlane & Elizabeth P. Scully, *Educating the New Lawyer: Teaching Lawyers to Offer Unbundled and Other Client-Centric Services*, 122 Dick. L. Rev. 801 (2018).

Furthermore, we reject the argument that by his conduct in suggesting modifications to the PSA, some of which were adopted, Laufer stepped from under the protection of his limited scope of representation and became fully liable as if no such limitation existed. First, we harken to Laufer's own testimony that his role was to see to it that the agreement was "clear and concise," to resolve interpretation problems in the text, and to clarify the agreement. Second, we discern no evidence that in performing his role Laufer's conduct actually altered Lynne's expectations of Laufer's duty or changed her demands for the kind of service she wished.

* * *

There are several aspects of what Laufer did, of which we expressly disapprove. We mention them in answer to Lynne's contentions that they have a bearing on the issue of Laufer's alleged malpractice. Our conclusion is that while these actions were improper, they do not alter our opinion that Laufer's overall representation of Lynne did not fall below any standard of care established by Lynne's proofs.

Laufer should not have included in his letter of February 2, 1994, an undertaking not to sue him. Such a limitation violated the express terms of RPC 1.8(h). Such a provision should not be included in a consent to limit the scope of representation presented to a client for consideration or signature. We note that in the course of these proceedings Laufer did not rely on that part of his letter as a defense. He acknowledged that the limitation was unenforceable.

Laufer should not have presented Lynne with a separate, standard form of retainer agreement. Whether or not the retainer was "boilerplate" as the motion judge thought, the point is that it conflicted with the letter of February 2, 1994. It is undisputed that that letter, not the standard retainer agreement, formed the basis of Laufer's representation. Lynne does not argue nor are there facts to support any contention that she reasonably believed the retainer supplanted the terms of the February 2 letter or that she expected from Laufer unlimited representation under the retainer. Consent to limit the scope of representation under RPC 1.2(c) should be included in a single, specifically tailored form of retainer agreement.

* * *

Affirmed.

C. Ineffective Assistance of Counsel

[Question 2-19]

An attorney represented a client who was convicted of murder. In preparing for the sentencing phase of the case, the attorney investigated potential mitigation evidence. The attorney spoke with the client and five of his family members who described the client's childhood and mental condition as normal. The attorney also consulted with mental health experts who did not offer helpful mitigation evidence. The attorney was aware that the prosecution was planning to introduce evidence of the client's previous convictions for a violent rape, as well as a juvenile record. The attorney did not examine the files of the earlier cases. If the attorney had done so, the attorney would have discovered

mitigating evidence of schizophrenia, organic brain damage, alcoholism, and serious childhood problems, and there is a reasonable probability that this evidence would have persuaded the jury to impose a life sentence. Instead, the client was sentenced to death. Afterward, the client filed a post-conviction motion claiming that the attorney provided ineffective assistance of counsel.

Should the client's verdict be overturned because he received ineffective assistance of counsel?

(A) Yes, because the attorney failed to provide zealous representation to the client.

(B) Yes, because the attorney's conduct was unreasonable and prejudiced the client.

(C) No, because the attorney's interviews with the client and the client's family members did not indicate the existence of mitigating evidence.

(D) No, because it is not certain that the additional evidence would have changed the jury's decision.

Rompilla v. Beard

545 U.S. 374 (2005)

JUSTICE SOUTER delivered the opinion of the Court.

This case calls for specific application of the standard of reasonable competence required on the part of defense counsel by the Sixth Amendment. We hold that even when a capital defendant's family members and the defendant himself have suggested that no mitigating evidence is available, his lawyer is bound to make reasonable efforts to obtain and review material that counsel knows the prosecution will probably rely on as evidence of aggravation at the sentencing phase of trial.

* * *

Ineffective assistance under *Strickland v. Washington*, 466 U.S. 668, 104 S.Ct. 2052, 80 L.Ed.2d 674 (1984) is deficient performance by counsel resulting in prejudice, with performance being measured against an "objective standard of reasonableness, * * * under prevailing professional norms." * * * This case, like some others recently, looks to norms of adequate investigation in preparing for the sentencing phase of a capital trial, when defense counsel's job is to counter the State's evidence of aggravated culpability with evidence in mitigation. In judging the defense's investigation, as in applying *Strickland* generally, hindsight is discounted by pegging adequacy to "counsel's perspective at the time" investigative decisions are made, and by giving a "heavy measure of deference to counsel's judgments." * * *

A

A standard of reasonableness applied as if one stood in counsel's shoes spawns few hard-edged rules, and the merits of a number of counsel's choices in this case are subject to fair debate. This is not a case in which defense counsel simply ignored their obligation to find mitigating evidence, and their workload as busy public defenders did not keep them from making a number of efforts, including interviews with Rompilla and some members of his family, and examinations of reports by three mental health experts who gave opinions at the guilt phase. None of the sources proved particularly helpful.

Rompilla's own contributions to any mitigation case were minimal. Counsel found him uninterested in helping, as on their visit to his prison to go over a proposed mitigation strategy, when Rompilla told them he was "bored being here listening" and returned to his cell. To questions about childhood and schooling, his answers indicated they had been normal, save for quitting school in the ninth grade. There were times when Rompilla was even actively obstructive by sending counsel off on false leads.

The lawyers also spoke with five members of Rompilla's family (his former wife, two brothers, a sister-in-law, and his son), and counsel testified that they developed a good relationship with the family in the course of their representation. The state post-conviction court found that counsel spoke to the relatives in a "detailed manner," attempting to unearth mitigating information, although the weight of this finding is qualified by the lawyers' concession that "the overwhelming response from the family was that they didn't really feel as though they knew him all that well since he had spent the majority of his adult years and some of his childhood years in custody[.]" Defense counsel also said that because the family was "coming from the position that [Rompilla] was innocent . . . they weren't looking for reasons for why he might have done this."

The third and final source tapped for mitigating material was the cadre of three mental health witnesses who were asked to look into Rompilla's mental state as of the time of the offense and his competency to stand trial. But their reports revealed "nothing useful" to Rompilla's case, and the lawyers consequently did not go to any other historical source that might have cast light on Rompilla's mental condition.

Take Note

Is it reasonable for a lawyer to exclude the mental health history of a death row inmate in sentencing? What if she does so for strategic reasons? What if she fails to do so because of her inexperience? The Court held that it is reasonable in *Wood v. Allen*, 558 U.S. 290 (2010), notwithstanding the lawyer's inexperience in handling death row appeals.

When new counsel entered the case to raise Rompilla's post-conviction claims, however, they identified a number of likely avenues the trial lawyers could fruitfully have followed in building a mitigation case. School records are one example, which trial counsel never examined in spite of the professed unfamiliarity of the several family members with Rompilla's childhood, and despite counsel's knowledge that Rompilla left school after the ninth grade. Other examples are records of Rompilla's juvenile and adult incarcerations, which counsel did not consult, although they were aware of their client's criminal record. And while counsel knew from police reports provided in pretrial discovery that Rompilla had been drinking heavily at the time of his offense, and although one of the mental health experts reported that Rompilla's troubles with alcohol merited further investigation, counsel did not look for evidence of a history of dependence on alcohol that might have extenuating significance.

Before us, trial counsel and the Commonwealth respond to these unexplored possibilities by emphasizing this Court's recognition that the duty to investigate does not force defense lawyers to scour the globe on the off chance something will turn up; reasonably diligent counsel may draw a line when they have good reason to think further investigation would be a waste. * * * The Commonwealth argues that the information trial counsel gathered from Rompilla and the other sources gave them sound reason to think it would have been pointless to spend time and money on the additional investigation espoused by post-conviction counsel, and we can say that there is room for debate about trial counsel's obligation to follow at least some of those potential lines of enquiry. There is no need to say more, however, for a further point is clear and dispositive: the lawyers were deficient in failing to examine the court file on Rompilla's prior conviction.

B

There is an obvious reason that the failure to examine Rompilla's prior conviction file fell below the level of reasonable performance. Counsel knew that the Commonwealth intended to seek the death penalty by proving Rompilla had a significant history of felony convictions indicating the use or threat of violence, an aggravator under state law. Counsel further knew that the Commonwealth would attempt to establish this history by proving Rompilla's prior conviction for rape and assault, and would emphasize his violent character by introducing a transcript of the rape victim's testimony given in that earlier trial. There is no question that defense counsel were on notice, since they acknowledge that a "plea letter," written by one of them four days prior to trial, mentioned the prosecutor's plans. It is also undisputed that the prior conviction file was a public document, readily available for the asking at the very courthouse where Rompilla was to be tried.

It is clear, however, that defense counsel did not look at any part of that file, including the transcript, until warned by the prosecution a second time. In a colloquy the day before the evidentiary sentencing phase began, the prosecutor again said he would present the transcript of the victim's testimony to establish the prior conviction.

* * * At the post-conviction evidentiary hearing, Rompilla's lawyer confirmed that she had not seen the transcript before the hearing in which this exchange took place, *id.*, at 506–507, and crucially, even after obtaining the transcript of the victim's testimony on the eve of the sentencing hearing, counsel apparently examined none of the other material in the file.

With every effort to view the facts as a defense lawyer would have done at the time, it is difficult to see how counsel could have failed to realize that without examining the readily available file they were seriously compromising their opportunity to respond to a case for aggravation. The prosecution was going to use the dramatic facts of a similar prior offense, and Rompilla's counsel had a duty to make all reasonable efforts to learn what they could about the offense. Reasonable efforts certainly included obtaining the Commonwealth's own readily available file on the prior conviction to learn what the Commonwealth knew about the crime, to discover any mitigating evidence the Commonwealth would downplay, and to anticipate the details of the aggravating evidence the Commonwealth would emphasize. Without making reasonable efforts to review the file, defense counsel could have had no hope of knowing whether the prosecution was quoting selectively from the transcript, or whether there were circumstances extenuating the behavior described by the victim. The obligation to get the file was particularly pressing here owing to the similarity of the violent prior offense to the crime charged and Rompilla's sentencing strategy stressing residual doubt. Without making efforts to learn the details and rebut the relevance of the earlier crime, a convincing argument for residual doubt was certainly beyond any hope.

Nor is there any merit to the United States's contention that further enquiry into the prior conviction file would have been fruitless because the sole reason the transcript was being introduced was to establish the aggravator that Rompilla had committed prior violent felonies. The Government maintains that because the transcript would incontrovertibly establish the fact that Rompilla had committed a violent felony, the defense could not have expected to rebut that aggravator through further investigation of the file. That analysis ignores the fact that the sentencing jury was required to weigh aggravating factors against mitigating factors. We may reasonably assume that the jury could give more relative weight to a prior violent felony aggravator where defense counsel missed an opportunity to argue that circumstances of the prior conviction were less damning than the prosecution's characterization of the conviction would suggest.

The notion that defense counsel must obtain information that the State has and will use against the defendant is not simply a matter of common sense. As the District Court points out, the American Bar Association Standards for Criminal Justice in circulation at the time of Rompilla's trial describes the obligation in terms no one could misunderstand in the circumstances of a case like this one:

> "It is the duty of the lawyer to conduct a prompt investigation of the circumstances of the case and to explore all avenues leading to facts relevant to the merits of the case and the penalty in the event of conviction. The investigation should always include efforts to secure information in the possession of the prosecution and law enforcement authorities. The duty to investigate exists regardless of the accused's admissions or statements to the lawyer of facts constituting guilt or the accused's stated desire to plead guilty."

1 *ABA Standards for Criminal Justice* 4-4.1 (2d ed. 1982 Supp.).

"[W]e long have referred [to these ABA Standards] as 'guides to determining what is reasonable.' " [Precedent] and the Commonwealth has come up with no reason to think the quoted standard impertinent here.

Later, and current, ABA Guidelines relating to death penalty defense are even more explicit:

"Counsel must . . . investigate prior convictions . . . that could be used as aggravating circumstances or otherwise come into evidence. If a prior conviction is legally flawed, counsel should seek to have it set aside. Counsel may also find extenuating circumstances that can be offered to lessen the weight of a conviction."

ABA Guidelines for the Appointment and Performance of Defense Counsel in Death Penalty Cases 10.7, comment. (rev. ed. 2003).

Our decision in *Wiggins* made precisely the same point in citing the earlier 1989 ABA Guidelines. ("The ABA Guidelines provide that investigations into mitigating evidence 'should comprise efforts to discover *all reasonably available* mitigating evidence and evidence to rebut any aggravating evidence that may be introduced by the prosecutor'" (quoting 1989 ABA Guideline 11.4.1.C; emphasis in original)). For reasons given in the text, no such further investigation was needed to point to the reasonable duty to look in the file in question here.

At argument the most that Pennsylvania (and the United States as *amicus*) could say was that defense counsel's efforts to find mitigating evidence by other means excused them from looking at the prior conviction file. And that, of course, is the position taken by the state post-conviction courts. Without specifically discussing the prior case file, they too found that defense counsel's efforts were enough to free them from any obligation to enquire further.

We think this conclusion of the state court fails to answer the considerations we have set out, to the point of being an objectively unreasonable conclusion. It flouts prudence to deny that a defense lawyer should try to look at a file he knows the prosecution will cull for aggravating evidence, let alone when the file is sitting in the trial courthouse, open for the asking. No reasonable lawyer would forgo examination of the file thinking he could do as well by asking the defendant or family relations whether they recalled anything helpful or damaging in the prior victim's testimony. Nor would a reasonable lawyer compare possible searches for school reports, juvenile records, and evidence of drinking habits to the opportunity to take a look at a file disclosing what the prosecutor knows and even plans to read from in his case. Questioning a few more family members and searching for old records can promise less than looking for a needle in a haystack, when a lawyer truly has reason to doubt there is any needle there. *E.g., Strickland, supra,* at 699, 104 S.Ct. 2052. But looking at a file the prosecution says it will use is a sure bet: whatever may be in that file is going to tell defense counsel something about what the prosecution can produce.

The dissent thinks this analysis creates a "rigid, *per se*" rule that requires defense counsel to do a complete review of the file on any prior conviction introduced, but that is a mistake. Counsel fell short here because they failed to make reasonable efforts to review the prior conviction file, despite knowing that the prosecution intended to introduce Rompilla's prior conviction not merely by entering a notice of conviction into evidence but by quoting damaging testimony of the rape victim in that case. The unreasonableness of attempting no more than they did was heightened by the easy availability of the file at the trial courthouse, and the great risk that testimony about a similar violent crime would hamstring counsel's chosen defense of residual doubt. It is owing to these circumstances that the state courts were objectively unreasonable in concluding that counsel could reasonably decline to make any effort to review the file. Other situations, where a defense lawyer is not charged with knowledge that the prosecutor intends to use a prior conviction in this way, might well warrant a different assessment.

C

Since counsel's failure to look at the file fell below the line of reasonable practice, there is a further question about prejudice, that is, whether "there is a reasonable probability that, but for counsel's unprofessional errors, the result of the proceeding would have been different." * * * Because the state courts found the representation adequate, they never reached the issue of prejudice, and so we examine this element of the *Strickland* claim *de novo*, * * * and agree with the dissent in the Court of Appeals. We think Rompilla has shown beyond any doubt that counsel's lapse was prejudicial; Pennsylvania, indeed, does not even contest the claim of prejudice.

If the defense lawyers had looked in the file on Rompilla's prior conviction, it is uncontested they would have found a range of mitigation leads that no other source had opened up. In the same file with the transcript of the prior trial were the records of Rompilla's imprisonment on the earlier conviction, which defense counsel testified she had never seen. * * * The prison files pictured Rompilla's childhood and mental health very differently from anything defense counsel had seen or heard. An evaluation by a corrections counselor states that Rompilla was "reared in the slum environment of Allentown, Pa. vicinity. He early came to [the] attention of juvenile authorities, quit school at 16, [and] started a series of incarcerations in and out Penna., often of assaultive nature and commonly related to over-indulgence in alcoholic beverages." The same file discloses test results that the defense's mental health experts would have viewed as pointing to schizophrenia and other disorders, and test scores showing a third grade level of cognition after nine years of schooling. The accumulated entries would have destroyed the benign conception of Rompilla's upbringing and mental capacity defense counsel had formed from talking with Rompilla himself and some of his family members, and from the reports of the mental health experts. With this information, counsel would have become skeptical of the impression given by the five family members and would unquestionably have gone further to build a mitigation case. Further effort would presumably have unearthed much of the material post-conviction counsel found, including testimony from several members of Rompilla's family, whom trial counsel did not interview. Judge Sloviter summarized this evidence:

> "Rompilla's parents were both severe alcoholics who drank constantly. His mother drank during her pregnancy with Rompilla, and he and his brothers eventually developed serious drinking problems. His father, who had a vicious temper, frequently beat Rompilla's mother, leaving her bruised and black-eyed, and bragged

about his cheating on her. His parents fought violently, and on at least one occasion his mother stabbed his father. He was abused by his father who beat him when he was young with his hands, fists, leather straps, belts and sticks. All of the children lived in terror. There were no expressions of parental love, affection or approval. Instead, he was subjected to yelling and verbal abuse. His father locked Rompilla and his brother Richard in a small wire mesh dog pen that was filthy and excrement filled. He had an isolated background, and was not allowed to visit other children or to speak to anyone on the phone. They had no indoor plumbing in the house, he slept in the attic with no heat, and the children were not given clothes and attended school in rags." * * *

The jury never heard any of this and neither did the mental health experts who examined Rompilla before trial. While they found "nothing helpful to [Rompilla's] case," their post-conviction counterparts, alerted by information from school, medical, and prison records that trial counsel never saw, found plenty of " 'red flags' " pointing up a need to test further. * * * When they tested, they found that Rompilla "suffers from organic brain damage, an extreme mental disturbance significantly impairing several of his cognitive functions." They also said that "Rompilla's problems relate back to his childhood, and were likely caused by fetal alcohol syndrome [and that] Rompilla's capacity to appreciate the criminality of his conduct or to conform his conduct to the law was substantially impaired at the time of the offense."

These findings in turn would probably have prompted a look at school and juvenile records, all of them easy to get, showing, for example, that when Rompilla was 16 his mother "was missing from home frequently for a period of one or several weeks at a time." * * * The same report noted that his mother "has been reported . . . frequently under the influence of alcoholic beverages, with the result that the children have always been poorly kept and on the filthy side which was also the condition of the home at all times." School records showed Rompilla's IQ was in the mentally retarded range.

This evidence adds up to a mitigation case that bears no relation to the few naked pleas for mercy actually put before the jury, and although we suppose it is possible that a jury could have heard it all and still have decided on the death penalty, that is not the test. It goes without saying that the undiscovered "mitigating evidence, taken as a whole, 'might well have influenced the jury's appraisal' of [Rompilla's] culpability," * * * and the likelihood of a different result if the evidence had gone in is "sufficient to undermine confidence in the outcome" actually reached at sentencing, *Strickland*, 466 U.S., at 694, 104 S.Ct. 2052.

The judgment of the Third Circuit is reversed, and Pennsylvania must either retry the case on penalty or stipulate to a life sentence.

It is so ordered.

———

Note on Malpractice Suits Arising from Criminal Cases

A convicted criminal defendant faces higher hurdles than other plaintiffs in malpractice actions. Restatement § 53(d) explains:

A convicted criminal defendant suing for malpractice must prove both that the lawyer failed to act properly and that, but for that failure, the result would have been different, for example because a double-jeopardy defense would have prevented conviction. Although most jurisdictions addressing the issue have stricter rules, under this Section it is not necessary to prove that the convicted defendant was in fact innocent.

FYI

> In recent years the Court repeatedly held that faulty advice during plea negotiations violated the constitutional rights of criminal defendants. In *Padilla v. Kentucky*, 559 U.S. 356 (2010), the lawyer incorrectly advised his client that a guilty plea would not result in deportation. The lawyer in *Missouri v. Frye*, 566 U.S. 133 (2012) neglected to inform his client about two deals offered by prosecutors before he pled guilty. The defendant in *Lafler v. Cooper*, 566 U.S. 156 (2012) was advised against taking a plea deal by his attorney only to be found guilty. Professor Renee Newman Knake explores the American Bar Association's advocacy role in the *Padilla* appeal and other cases in this Legal Ethics Forum Blog post.

VI. Principles That Govern the Relationship Between Lawyers and Clients

A. Allocating Decision-Making Between Lawyer and Client

The dominant understanding that lawyers serve as partisans for their clients would seem to translate into a rule that lawyers must follow client instructions within the bounds of the law. In fact, the law and rules are more complicated. In part, this complexity results from competing understandings of the lawyer's role. The Restatement explains that:

> Traditionally, some lawyers considered that a client put affairs in the lawyer's hands, who then managed them as the lawyer thought would best advance the client's interests. So conducting the relationship can subordinate the client to the lawyer. The lawyer might not fully understand the client's best interests or might consciously or unconsciously pursue the lawyer's own interests. An opposite view of the client-lawyer relationship treats the lawyer as a servant of the client, who must do whatever the client wants limited only by the requirements of the law. That view ignores the interest of the lawyer and of society that a lawyer practices responsibly and independently.

> A middle view is that the client defines the goals of the representation and the lawyer implements them, but that each consults with the other.[6]

---

6   Restatement (Third) of Law Governing Lawyers, Introductory Note: Topic 3. Authority to Make Decisions, (Am. Law. Inst. 2000) at 168–69.

This "middle view" is the approach used in the rules of professional conduct. <u>Rule 1.2(a)</u> governs allocation of decision-making authority between lawyer and client and provides that:

> Subject to paragraphs (c) and (d), a lawyer shall abide by a client's decisions concerning the objectives of representation and, as required by Rule 1.4, shall consult with the client as to the means by which they are to be pursued. A lawyer may take such action on behalf of the client as is impliedly authorized to carry out the representation. A lawyer shall abide by a client's decision whether to settle a matter. In a criminal case, the lawyer shall abide by the client's decision, after consultation with the lawyer, as to a plea to be entered, whether to waive jury trial and whether the client will testify.

The case that follows addresses the Constitutional issues implicated by the allocation of decision making authority.

Jones v. Barnes

<u>463 U.S. 745 (1983)</u>

CHIEF JUSTICE BURGER delivered the opinion of the Court.

We granted certiorari to consider whether defense counsel assigned to prosecute an appeal from a criminal conviction has a constitutional duty to raise every nonfrivolous issue requested by the defendant.

I

In 1976, Richard Butts was robbed at knifepoint by four men in the lobby of an apartment building; he was badly beaten and his watch and money were taken. Butts informed a Housing Authority Detective that he recognized one of his assailants as a person known to him as "Froggy," and gave a physical description of the person to the detective. The following day the detective arrested respondent David Barnes, who is known as "Froggy."

Respondent was charged with first and second degree robbery, second degree assault, and third degree larceny. The prosecution rested primarily upon Butts' testimony and his identification of respondent. During cross-examination, defense counsel asked Butts whether he had ever undergone psychiatric treatment; however, no offer of proof was made on the substance or relevance of the question after the trial judge *sua sponte* instructed Butts not to answer. At the close of trial, the trial judge declined to give an instruction on accessorial liability requested by the defense. The jury convicted respondent of first and second degree robbery and second degree assault.

It's Latin to Me

Black's Law Dictionary explains that the term *sua sponte* refers to a court acting "[w]ithout prompting or suggestion; on its own motion."

The Appellate Division of the Supreme Court of New York, Second Department, assigned Michael Melinger to represent respondent on appeal. Respondent sent Melinger a letter listing several claims that he felt should be raised. Included were claims that Butts' identification testimony should have been suppressed, that the trial judge improperly excluded psychiatric evidence, and that respondent's trial counsel was ineffective. Respondent also enclosed a copy of a *pro se* brief he had written.

In a return letter, Melinger accepted some but rejected most of the suggested claims, stating that they would not aid respondent in obtaining a new trial and that they could not be raised on appeal because they were not based on evidence in the record. * * * [After argument, the Appellate Division affirmed the decision below.]

> **It's Latin to Me**
>
> Black's Law Dictionary explains that the term *pro se* refers to acting "[f]or oneself; on one's own behalf; without a lawyer."

[O]n March 31, 1980, [Barnes] filed a petition in the New York Court of Appeals for reconsideration of that court's denial of leave to appeal. In that petition, respondent for the first time claimed that his appellate counsel, Melinger, had provided ineffective assistance. The New York Court of Appeals denied the application on April 16, 1980.

Respondent then returned to United States District Court * * * with a petition for habeas corpus based on the claim of ineffective assistance by appellate counsel. The District Court * * * dismissed the petition, holding that the record gave no support to the claim of ineffective assistance of appellate counsel on "any . . . standard which could reasonably be applied." The District Court concluded:

"It is not required that an attorney argue every conceivable issue on appeal, especially when some may be without merit. Indeed, it is his professional duty to choose among potential issues, according to his judgment as to their merit and his tactical approach."

A divided panel of the Court of Appeals reversed. Laying down a new standard, the majority held that when "the appellant requests that [his attorney] raise additional colorable points [on appeal], counsel must argue the additional points to the full extent of his professional ability." In the view of the majority, this conclusion followed from *Anders v. California*, 386 U.S. 738 (1967). In *Anders*, this Court held that an appointed attorney must advocate his client's cause vigorously and may not withdraw from a nonfrivolous appeal. The Court of Appeals majority held that, since *Anders* bars counsel from abandoning a nonfrivolous appeal, it also bars counsel from abandoning a nonfrivolous issue on appeal. * * *

The court concluded that Melinger had not met the above standard in that he had failed to press at least two nonfrivolous claims: the trial judge's failure to instruct on accessory liability and ineffective assistance of trial counsel. The fact that these issues had been raised in respondent's own *pro se* briefs did not cure the error, since "[a] *pro se* brief is no substitute for the advocacy of experienced counsel." The court reversed and remanded, with instructions to grant the writ of habeas corpus unless the State assigned new counsel and granted a new appeal.

* * * We granted certiorari, and we reverse.

II

* * *

Neither *Anders* nor any other decision of this Court suggests * * * that the indigent defendant has a constitutional right to compel appointed counsel to press nonfrivolous points requested by the client, if counsel, as a matter of professional judgment, decides not to present those points.

This Court, in holding that a State must provide counsel for an indigent appellant on his first appeal as of right, recognized the superior ability of trained counsel in the "examination into the record, research of the law, and marshalling of arguments on [the appellant's] behalf." * * * Yet by promulgating a *per se* rule that the client, not the professional advocate, must be allowed to decide what issues are to be pressed, the Court of Appeals seriously undermines the ability of counsel to present the client's case in accord with counsel's professional evaluation.

Take Note

Does a defendant have the right to reject appellate counsel in favor of self-representation as a way of circumventing the ruling in *Jones v. Barnes?* *See Martinez v. Court of Appeal of Cal., Fourth App. Dist.*, 528 U.S. 152 (2000) (holding that a convicted defendant does not have the right to a *pro se* appeal under either the Sixth Amendment or Due Process Clause). This ruling contrasts with the right to represent oneself *pro se* under the *Faretta* case that was cited in *Jones v. Barnes.*

Experienced advocates since time beyond memory have emphasized the importance of winnowing out weaker arguments on appeal and focusing on one central issue if possible, or at most on a few key issues. * * *

There can hardly be any question about the importance of having the appellate advocate examine the record with a view to selecting the most promising issues for review. This has assumed a greater importance in an era when oral argument is strictly limited in most courts—often to as little as 15 minutes—and when page limits on briefs are widely imposed. * * * Even in a court that imposes no time or page limits, however, the new *per se* rule laid down by the Court of Appeals is contrary to all experience and logic. A brief that raises every colorable issue runs the risk of burying good arguments—those that, in the words of the great advocate John W. Davis, "go for the jugular," in a verbal mound made up of strong and weak contentions. * * *

With the exception of these specified fundamental decisions, an attorney's duty is to take professional responsibility for the conduct of the case, after consulting with his client. * * *

Reversed.

* * *

JUSTICE BRENNAN, with whom JUSTICE MARSHALL joins, dissenting.

The Sixth Amendment provides that "[i]n all criminal prosecutions, the accused shall enjoy the right . . . to have the *Assistance* of counsel for his defence" (emphasis added). I find myself in fundamental disagreement with the Court over what a right to "the assistance of counsel" means. The import of words like "assistance" and "counsel" seems inconsistent with a regime under which counsel appointed by the State to represent a criminal defendant can refuse to raise issues with arguable merit on appeal when his client, after hearing his assessment of the case and his advice, has directed him to raise them. I would remand for a determination whether respondent did in fact insist that his lawyer brief the issues that the Court of Appeals found were not frivolous.

* * * What is at issue here is the relationship between lawyer and client-who has ultimate authority to decide which nonfrivolous issues should be presented on appeal? I believe the right to "the assistance of counsel" carries with it a right, personal to the defendant, to make that decision, against the advice of counsel if he chooses.

If all the Sixth Amendment protected was the State's interest in substantial justice, it would not include such a right. However, in *Faretta v. California*, 422 U.S. 806, 95 S.Ct. 2525, 45 L.Ed.2d 562 (1975), we decisively rejected that view of the Constitution[.] * * *

Faretta establishes that the right to counsel is more than a right to have one's case presented competently and effectively. It is predicated on the view that the function of counsel under the Sixth Amendment is to protect the dignity and autonomy of a person on trial by *assisting* him in making choices that are his to make, not to make choices for him, although counsel may be better able to decide which tactics will be most effective for the defendant. *Anders v. California* also reflects that view. Even when appointed counsel believes an appeal has no merit, he must furnish his client a brief covering all arguable grounds for appeal so that the client may "raise any points that he chooses." * * *

The right to counsel as *Faretta* and *Anders* conceive it is not an all-or-nothing right, under which a defendant must choose between forgoing the assistance of counsel altogether or relinquishing control over every aspect of his case beyond its most basic structure (*i.e.*, how to plead, whether to present a defense, whether to appeal). A defendant's interest in his case clearly extends to other matters. * * * He may want to press the argument that he is innocent, even if other stratagems are more likely to result in the dismissal of charges or in a reduction of punishment. He may want to insist on certain arguments for political reasons. He may want to protect third parties. This is just as true on appeal as at trial, and the proper role of counsel is to *assist* him in these efforts, insofar as that is possible consistent with the lawyer's conscience, the law, and his duties to the court.

* * *

It is no secret that indigent clients often mistrust the lawyers appointed to represent them. There are many reasons for this, some perhaps unavoidable even under perfect conditions—differences in education, disposition, and socio-economic class—and some that should (but may not always) be zealously avoided. A lawyer and his client do not always have the same interests. Even with paying clients, a lawyer may have a strong interest in having judges and prosecutors think well of him, and, if he is working for a flat fee—a common arrangement for criminal defense attorneys—or if his fees for court appointments are lower than he would receive for other work, he has an obvious financial incentive to conclude cases on his criminal docket swiftly. Good lawyers undoubtedly recognize these temptations and resist them, and they endeavor to convince their clients that they will. It would be naive, however, to suggest that they always succeed in either task. A constitutional rule that encourages lawyers to disregard their clients' wishes without compelling need can only exacerbate the clients' suspicion of their lawyers. As in *Faretta*, to force a lawyer's *decisions* on a defendant "can only lead him to believe that the law conspires against him." In the end, what the Court hopes to gain in effectiveness of appellate representation by the rule it imposes today may well be lost to decreased effectiveness in other areas of representation.

* * *

Finally, today's ruling denigrates the values of individual autonomy and dignity central to many constitutional rights, especially those Fifth and Sixth Amendment rights that come into play in the criminal process. * * * The role of the defense lawyer should be above all to function as the instrument and defender of the client's autonomy and dignity in all phases of the criminal process.

* * *

Food for Thought

Do you agree with the majority or dissent? Which best represents your view of the lawyer's role? For a more extensive discussion of perspectives on the lawyer's role, *see* Chapter 8, *infra*.

[The majority] subtly but unmistakably adopts a different conception of the defense lawyer's role- he need do nothing beyond what the State, not his client, considers most important. In many ways, having a lawyer becomes one of the many indignities visited upon someone who has the ill fortune to run afoul of the criminal justice system.

I cannot accept the notion that lawyers are one of the punishments a person receives merely for being accused of a crime. * * *

———

Although allocation of authority issues are particularly difficult in criminal cases, these issues also arise in civil cases. In some cases, resolution of the issue will be straightforward because the decision clearly rests with the client under Rule 1.2(a). In other cases, however, it will be much more difficult to determine how decision-making authority should be allocated.

[Question 2-20]

A client retained an attorney to recover for a personal injury. In the retainer agreement signed by the client and the attorney, the client agreed to cooperate fully and pay the attorney a contingent fee computed as a percentage of the amount of recovery after expenses: 25 percent if settled before trial, 30 percent if settled before verdict, 35 percent after verdict, and 40 percent after appeal.

Go Online

Click here to tinker with a personal injury calculator. For more on contingency fees, *see* Chapter 3, *infra*.

The attorney's representation of the client in the matter extended over a three-year period, during which time the attorney advanced a large amount for litigation expenses. After trial, the client obtained a jury verdict for an amount larger than either the attorney or the client had anticipated. However, the defendant appealed the client's favorable verdict based on questions of evidence and the measure of damages. Meanwhile, the defendant made an offer of settlement for approximately the amount the attorney had originally projected as reasonable to expect. The client, who was hard pressed financially, directed the attorney to accept the offer and settle. Confident that there was no reversible error in the trial and that the appeal was without merit, the attorney refused the settlement. The attorney reasonably believed that the appeal was filed solely to gain negotiating advantage in settlement negotiations.

Is the attorney subject to discipline?

> (A) **Yes, because the attorney's percentage under the fee contract increased after appeal.**
>
> (B) **Yes, because the attorney did not comply with the client's direction to accept the settlement offer.**
>
> (C) **No, because the decision whether to settle or defend an appeal is a tactical matter for the attorney to determine.**
>
> (D) **No, because evaluation of the merits of an appeal requires an attorney to exercise independent professional judgment.**

Before you answer this question, review Rule 1.2(a). Does it provide a clear answer?

While Rule 1.2(a) clearly allocates decision-making authority for a handful of decisions, most decisions are not specifically listed in the rule. Instead, lawyers and clients must determine whether a particular decision involves the "objectives of representation," in which case it is the client's decision to make, or a decision about "means," which often rests with the lawyer, but may require consultation with the client.

If a decision involves "means" rather than "objectives," the decision may implicate a number of other professional rules including Rules 1.3 (diligence), 3.1 (meritorious claims and contentions), 3.2 (expediting litigation), 3.3 (candor to the tribunal), 4.1 (truthfulness in statements to others), and 4.4 (respect for rights of third parties). Issues related to the allocation of decision-making authority can also have malpractice consequences, as well as disciplinary consequences. Consider Question 2-21 and the material that follows.

[Question 2-21]

An attorney represents a client in a divorce suit in which the client seeks primary custody of her children. The client instructs the attorney not to use evidence of her spouse's adultery. The attorney informs the client that evidence of adultery would be very helpful in gaining primary custody and avoiding joint custody. The client continues to insist that the attorney not introduce evidence of her spouse's adultery. The attorney followed

the client's instructions and did not introduce the evidence. The court denied the client primary custody and instead awarded the client joint custody. The client sued the attorney for malpractice based on the attorney's failure to introduce evidence of adultery.

Is the client likely to succeed?

(A) Yes, because the attorney breached a duty to the client when the attorney failed to introduce evidence that the attorney thought would be helpful.

(B) Yes, because the attorney was ethically required to follow all of the client's instructions.

(C) No, because the attorney explained the alternatives to the client and then followed the client's instructions.

(D) No, because the decision about which evidence to introduce is a "means" decision rather than an "objectives" decision.

Boyd v. Brett-Major

449 So. 2d 952 (Fla. Dist. Ct. App. 1984)

FERGUSON, JUDGE.

Appeal is taken by the plaintiffs below from a judgment entered on a jury verdict for an attorney and her insurer in a legal malpractice action. * * *

The salient facts are as follows. In May 1980, plaintiffs' son was required to post a criminal appearance bond in Palm Beach County. A bonding company agreed to post the $100,000 bond and in return plaintiffs signed a mortgage and promissory note encumbering their home. The bonding company failed to file an affidavit as required by Section 903.14, Florida Statutes (1983), thereby creating an absolute defense to any subsequent foreclosure action. When plaintiffs' son failed to appear in court, the bond was estreated. The bonding company unsuccessfully sought reimbursement from plaintiffs, and ultimately filed a mortgage foreclosure action.

Plaintiffs retained the defendant-attorney to represent them in the action. Plaintiffs claim on appeal that they wished to win the suit, and that the attorney assured them of success. Defendant-attorney contends, however, that because plaintiffs wished to maintain an ongoing relationship with the bonding company, they requested only that the action be delayed so that they could raise the funds to repay the debt. In any event, the attorney filed an answer in the foreclosure action, but failed to adequately plead Section 903.14 as an affirmative defense. A final summary judgment was entered against plaintiffs on the bonding company's motion. On appeal we affirmed the judgment.

Plaintiffs thereafter filed a legal malpractice action against the attorney and her insurer. Defendants alleged as an affirmative defense to the claim:

The Plaintiffs specifically instructed the Defendant, LIN BRETT-MAJOR, to protect their interests in an agreement which they had negotiated with all the bondsmen, including Frank McGoey, the bondsman for International Fidelity Insurance Company, and at all times, the Defendant, LIN BRETT-MAJOR, acted in accordance with the instructions given to her by the Plaintiffs, after having explained various potential defenses to the foreclosure actions brought by the bondsmen.

At the conclusion of the evidence, the jury was instructed:

The next issue for your consideration is that LIN BRETT-MAJOR was acting according to the specific instructions of her client and an attorney is duty bound to carry out the specific instructions of a client provided that criminal or fraudulent ends are not intended. If you find that LIN BRETT-MAJOR was carrying out the specific instructions of her client, then your verdict should be for the Defendant, LIN BRETT-MAJOR.

The proof at trial showed that the attorney was hired not to win the case but to delay the action (even though the bonding company's failure to file an affidavit created an absolute defense) because the clients intended to live up to their contractual obligation and wished to remain on good terms with the bondsman. Plaintiffs argue that to permit an affirmative defense such as that presented here, which is without legal precedence, would establish an untenable situation by which attorneys could avoid liability for their professional omissions simply by pleading that they followed a course of action desired by the client. We are not convinced that the door is opened to a parade of horribles unless we disapprove of, as a defense to a malpractice claim, that the course of action taken by counsel was at the direction of an otherwise well-advised client. The relevant inquiry is whether the attorney followed the explicit directions of his client, which presents a question of fact.

* * *

Affirmed.

———————————

As the *Boyd v. Brett-Major* case illustrates, the answer to the malpractice question posed in Question 2-21 is relatively straightforward. Accord Ronald E. Mallen, 1 Legal Malpractice § 8:30 (2019 ed.) ("if the attorney followed the client's instructions, there should be no liability if there was another course of action that might have been more beneficial and the lawyer explained that alternative to the client.").

The answer under the Rules of Professional Conduct, however, is more difficult. Comment [2] to Rule 1.2 contains the following observations:

[2] On occasion * * * a lawyer and a client may disagree about the means to be used to accomplish the client's objectives. Clients normally defer to the special knowledge and skill of their lawyer with respect to the means to be used to accomplish their objectives, particularly with respect to technical, legal and tactical matters.

Conversely, lawyers usually defer to the client regarding such questions as the expense to be incurred and concern for third persons who might be adversely affected. Because of the varied nature of the matters about which a lawyer and client might disagree and because the actions in question may implicate the interests of a tribunal or other persons, this Rule does not prescribe how such disagreements are to be resolved. Other law, however, may be applicable and should be consulted by the lawyer. The lawyer should also consult with the client and seek a mutually acceptable resolution of the disagreement. If such efforts are unavailing and the lawyer has a fundamental disagreement with the client, the lawyer may withdraw from the representation. *See* Rule 1.16(b)(4). Conversely, the client may resolve the disagreement by discharging the lawyer. *See* Rule 1.16(a)(3).

[3] At the outset of a representation, the client may authorize the lawyer to take specific action on the client's behalf without further consultation. Absent a material change in circumstances and subject to Rule 1.4, a lawyer may rely on such an advance authorization. The client may, however, revoke such authority at any time.

The Restatement also provides guidance to help a lawyer who may be struggling with the issue of whether to follow the client's directions:

Restatement § 21 Comment d

A lawyer is not required to carry out an instruction that the lawyer reasonably believes to be contrary to professional rules or other law or which the lawyer reasonably believes to be unethical or similarly objectionable.

Restatement § 23 Comment d

Lawyers * * * have inherent authority, not subject to alteration by contract with their clients, to act and decide for clients when the legal system requires an immediate decision without time for consultation. Whether a decision falls in that category depends on the requirements of procedural systems and orders of tribunals, as well as on such circumstances as the availability of the client for immediate consultation and the effect of interruption for consultation on the orderly and effective presentation of the client's matter. The lawyer must keep the client informed of the progress of the matter and must comply, when time permits, with the client's expressed wishes to be consulted about specified matters * * * A client may give advance instructions, which the lawyer must honor to the extent that court rules and professional obligations permit.

Having read this advice, consider how you would answer Question 2-21 if the call of the question had asked about the disciplinary issue rather than the malpractice issue. On the one hand, a decision not to use evidence of a spouse's adultery in a divorce could be viewed as a "means" question if evidence of adultery would be helpful in obtaining the client's objective of gaining primary custody. On the other hand, one might conclude that the client should make this decision because the client's objectives might also include avoiding, as much as possible, an acrimonious divorce.

Rule 1.2(c) can provide assistance to lawyers and clients who must decide whether an issue such as evidence of adultery is a "means" decision or an "objectives" decision. As you saw earlier in this chapter, under Rule 1.2(c), a lawyer and client may agree to "limit the scope of the representation if the limitation is reasonable under the circumstances and the client gives informed consent." If a lawyer and client limit the scope of the representation pursuant to Rule 1.2(c), the relevant issues will be whether the client gave informed consent and whether the "no adultery evidence" limitation is reasonable under the circumstances. A Rule 1.2(c) limitation makes it unnecessary for the lawyer to resolve whether a "no adultery evidence" decision, such as that in Question 2-21, is a "means" decision or an "objectives" decision.

The article that follows addresses the difficulties of applying the means/objective distinction.

MARCY STRAUSS, TOWARD A REVISED MODEL OF ATTORNEY-CLIENT RELATIONSHIP: THE ARGUMENT FOR AUTONOMY

65 N.C. L. Rev. 315, 324–25 (1987)

* * *The current allocation of decisionmaking authority assumes that it is possible to draw a workable distinction between means and ends. Absent a clear distinction, it is difficult to understand why the client gets "ends" decisions but not "means," and it is impossible to predict which decisions belong to the client and which to counsel.

The means-ends distinction rests on the assumption that there exists certain determinable decisions that can be classified as means or ends. Means are merely strategic decisions that are separate and independent from the ends, or the objectives, of the lawsuit. This assumed dichotomy between means and ends does not survive close analysis. In many cases what the attorney assumes to be mere means really are part of the client's ultimate objectives. Thus, "the client may want to win acquittal *by* asserting a certain right, because it vindicates him in a way that matters to him, or he may wish to obtain a settlement without using a certain tactic because he disapproves of the tactic." In other words, that which is often thought to be an end might really be a means; that which is assumed to be just a means could be an end to a particular client. For instance, "winning" is assumed to be an end of any lawsuit. As a result, criminal defendants are allowed to decide whether to plead guilty. But why assume that winning acquittal is the end? It could be that receiving the lightest possible sentence is the true end of many criminal defendants. From that perspective, pleading guilty is a means—a strategic decision—to the end of sentence reduction.

Perhaps this problem in the means—ends distinction can best be illustrated by a medical analogy. A woman diagnosed as having breast cancer obviously desires to be cured. That is the end result she wants. However, it would be difficult to accept that the only decision to be made by the woman is to choose life and that the means of a cure should be left to the discretion of others. The assumption that the woman has no legitimate interest in the type of treatment she receives—that the treatment is merely a tactical decision that can be viewed separately and independently from the end—would be repugnant to most of us.

Professor David Luban provides numerous hypothetical examples from law in which mere "tactical" decisions matter as much, if not more, to the client than the end result. In one hypothetical, which Luban calls the "Long Black Veil case," an innocent client, accused of murder, forbids his attorney from calling an alibi witness, even if it means losing the case. At the time of the murder defendant was in the arms of his best friend's wife, and his personal honor requires that this incident be kept secret. Despite the fact the client clearly views protecting his lover an "end" of the lawsuit, his attorney, under the current allocation of authority, may override the client and call the witness—in the client's own best interest. Such a decision is viewed as a means decision within the sole power of the attorney.

Food for Thought

What do you think about the means-ends distinction? Professor Strauss mentions that the law gives patient autonomy greater deference than client autonomy. Should it?

There are, of course, many less dramatic examples of means decisions that are difficult to distinguish from the ends. A client may not want his or her attorney to argue an insanity defense; the client's "pride" may be more important than succeeding on this argument. Or a client may not want any more continuances in a civil case because stress from the uncertainty outweighs the possible benefits of delay. Or a client may want a certain argument raised because it might establish a long sought after legal principle, even though the chance of success is low.

In sum, the line between means and ends is imprecise at best. At a minimum, clients have a legitimate, and at times, overriding interest in what many characterize as the "means" of the lawsuit. * * *

———————

The "Long Black Veil" hypothetical is based on a song sung by Johnny Cash, among others. The difficult "allocation of decision-making authority" issues it raises, however, have not been confined to hypothetical situations. In *Gilmore v. Utah*, which is reprinted below, the U.S. Supreme Court was asked whether to lift a stay of execution after convicted murderer Gary Gilmore waived his right to appeal his conviction.

Gilmore v. Utah

429 U.S. 1012 (1976)

[*Editor*: The first item in the *Gilmore v. Utah* case is an unsigned court order denying Bessie Gilmore's request for a stay of execution for her son Gary Gilmore. There were five opinions that followed the Court's order. In addition to the concurring opinion of Chief Justice Burger, excerpts of which are reprinted below, Justice Stevens filed a concurring opinion which Justice Rehnquist joined. Justice White filed a dissenting opinion, which Justices Brennan and Marshall joined. Justice Marshall dissented and filed an opinion and Justice Blackmun dissented and filed an opinion.]

ORDER

On October 7, 1976, Gary Mark Gilmore was convicted of murder and sentenced to death by a judgment entered after a jury trial in a Utah court. On December 3, 1976, this Court granted an application for a stay of execution of the judgment and sentence, pending the filing here by the State of Utah of a response to the application together with transcripts of various specified hearings in the Utah courts and Board of Pardons, and until "further action of the Court on the application for stay."

The State of Utah has now filed its response and has substantially complied with the Court's request for transcripts of the specified hearings. After carefully examining the materials submitted by the State of Utah, the Court is convinced that Gary Mark Gilmore made a knowing and intelligent waiver of any and all federal rights he might have asserted after the Utah trial court's sentence was imposed, and, specifically, that the State's determinations of his competence knowingly and intelligently to waive any and all such rights were firmly grounded.

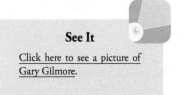

See It

Click here to see a picture of Gary Gilmore.

Accordingly, the stay of execution granted on December 3, 1976, is hereby terminated.

MR. CHIEF JUSTICE BURGER, with whom MR. JUSTICE POWELL, joins, concurring.

On December 2, 1976, Bessie Gilmore, claiming to act as "next friend" on behalf of her son, Gary Mark Gilmore, filed with this Court an application for stay of execution of the death sentence then scheduled for December 6, 1976. Since only a limited record was then before the Court, we granted a temporary stay of execution on December 3, 1976 in order to secure a response from the State of Utah. That response was received on December 7, 1976.[1] On December 8, 1976, a response was filed by Gary Mark Gilmore * * * challenging the standing of Bessie Gilmore to initiate any proceedings in his behalf.

For More Information

A little more than a year after the Court's decision, Gary Gilmore was executed by firing squad in Utah. For an exhaustive look into his life *see* Norman Mailer's Pulitzer Prize-winning novel, *The Executioner's Song*.

When the application for a stay was initially filed on December 2, a serious question was presented as to whether Bessie Gilmore had standing to seek the requested relief or any relief from this Court. Assuming the Court would otherwise have jurisdiction with respect to a "next friend" application, that jurisdiction would arise only if it were demonstrated that Gary Mark Gilmore is unable to seek relief in his own behalf. * * * However, in view

---

1   This case may be unique in the annals of the Court. Not only does Gary Mark Gilmore request no relief himself; on the contrary he has expressly and repeatedly stated since his conviction in the Utah courts that he had received a fair trial and had been well treated by the Utah authorities. Nor does he claim to be innocent of the crime for which he was convicted. Indeed, his only complaint against Utah or its judicial process . . . has been with respect to the delay on the part of the State in carrying out the sentence.

of Gary Mark Gilmore's response on December 8, 1976, it is now clear that the "next friend" concept is wholly inapplicable to this case. Since Gary Mark Gilmore has now filed a response and appeared in his own behalf, through his retained attorneys, any basis for the standing of Bessie Gilmore to seek relief in his behalf is necessarily eliminated. The only possible exception to this conclusion would be if the record suggested, despite the representations of Gary Mark Gilmore's attorneys, that he was incompetent to waive his right of appeal under state law and was at the present time incompetent to assert rights or to challenge Bessie Gilmore's standing to assert rights in his behalf as "next friend."

After examining with care the pertinent portions of the transcripts and reports of state proceedings, and the response of Gary Mark Gilmore filed on December 8, I am in complete agreement with the conclusion expressed in the Court's order that Gary Mark Gilmore knowingly and intelligently, with full knowledge of his right to seek an appeal in the Utah Supreme Court, has waived that right.[4] I further agree that the State's determinations of his competence to waive his rights knowingly and intelligently were firmly grounded. * * *

The U.S. Supreme Court's 2018 case of *McCoy v. Louisiana*, which is a 6–3 decision, reveals significant differences among the Justices with respect to issues related to the 6th Amendment and the allocation of decision-making authority.

4　At a hearing on November 1, 1976, on a motion for a new trial, Gilmore's attorneys informed the trial court that they had been told by Gilmore not to file an appeal and not to seek a stay of execution of sentence on his behalf. They also informed the trial court that they had advised Gilmore of his right to appeal; that they believed there were substantial grounds for appeal, that the constitutionality of the Utah death penalty statute had not yet been reviewed by either the Utah Supreme Court or the United States Supreme Court, and that in their view there was a chance that the statute would eventually be held unconstitutional. The trial court itself advised Gilmore that he had a right to appeal, that the constitutional issue had not yet been resolved, and that both counsel for the State and Gilmore's own counsel would attempt to expedite an appeal to avoid unnecessary delay. Gilmore stated that he did not "care to languish in prison for another day," that the decision was his own, and that he had not made the decision as a result of the influence of drugs or alcohol or as a result of the way he was treated in prison. On November 4, the state trial court concluded that Gilmore fully understood his right to appeal and the consequences of a decision not to appeal. On November 10, the Utah Supreme Court held a hearing on the Utah Attorney General's motion to vacate a stay of execution of sentence entered two days earlier by that Court. Gilmore was present, and, in response to questions from several Justices, stated that he thought he had received a fair trial and a proper sentence, that he opposed any appeal in the case, and that he wished to withdraw an appeal previously filed without his consent by appointed trial counsel. Finally, at a hearing before the trial court on December 1, Gilmore again informed the court that he opposed all appeals that had been filed. When the record establishing a knowing and intelligent waiver of Gary Mark Gilmore's right to seek appellate review is combined with the December 8 written response submitted to this Court, it is plain that the Court is without jurisdiction to entertain the "next friend" application filed by Bessie Gilmore. This Court has jurisdiction pursuant to Art. III of the Constitution only over "cases and controversies," and we can issue stays only in aid of our jurisdiction. There is no dispute, presently before us, between Gary Mark Gilmore and the State of Utah, and the application of Bessie Gilmore manifestly fails to meet the statutory requirements to invoke this Court's power to review the action of the Supreme Court of Utah. No authority to the contrary has been brought to our attention, and nothing suggested in dissent bears on the threshold question of jurisdiction. In his dissenting opinion, Mr. Justice WHITE suggests that Gary Mark Gilmore is "unable" as a matter of law to waive the right to state appellate review. Whatever may be said as to the merits of this suggestion, the question simply is not before us. Gilmore, duly found to be competent by the Utah courts, has had available meaningful access to this Court and has declined expressly to assert any claim here other than his explicit repudiation of Bessie Gilmore's effort to speak for him as next friend. It follows, therefore, that the Court is without jurisdiction to consider the question posed by the dissent.

McCoy v. Louisiana

138 S.Ct. 1500 (2018)

GINSBURG, J., delivered the opinion of the Court, in which ROBERTS, C.J., and KENNEDY, BREYER, SOTOMAYOR, and KAGAN, JJ., joined.

[*Editor*: The Defendant Robert McCoy was convicted of three counts of first-degree murder after the jury found that he murdered his estranged wife's mother, stepfather, and son. McCoy pleaded not guilty. Throughout the proceedings, McCoy insisted that he was out of state at the time of the killings and that corrupt police killed the victims when a drug deal went wrong. Before the trial, Defendant McCoy's public defender Larry English requested a sanity evaluation, which found Defendant McCoy competent to stand trial. Attorney English's trial strategy was to concede that McCoy committed the murders but argue that McCoy's mental state prevented him from forming the specific intent necessary for a first-degree murder conviction. Defendant McCoy, however, refused to concede his guilt and objected to his attorney's statements that he had committed the murders. Two days before trial, Defendant McCoy requested new counsel, but the trial court denied the motion. During the guilt phase of the trial, Defendant McCoy took the stand and testified that he was out of state at the time of the murders. In his Opening Statement and Closing Argument, however, McCoy's lawyer told the jury that McCoy had committed the murders. After he was convicted, Defendant McCoy obtained new counsel who moved for a new trial on Defendant's behalf. The motion was denied, and the denial was affirmed by the Louisiana Supreme Court. The Supreme Court granted certiorari to review that decision and then reversed and remanded for a new trial.]

* * * When a client expressly asserts that the objective of "his defence" is to maintain innocence of the charged criminal acts, his lawyer must abide by that objective and may not override it by conceding guilt. U.S. Const. Amdt. 6 (emphasis added); see ABA Model Rule of Professional Conduct 1.2(a) (2016) (a "lawyer shall abide by a client's decisions concerning the objectives of the representation"). * * *

In *Florida v. Nixon*, * * * this Court considered whether the Constitution bars defense counsel from conceding a capital defendant's guilt at trial "when [the] defendant, informed by counsel, neither consents nor objects" * * * In that case, defense counsel had several times explained to the defendant a proposed guilt-phase concession strategy, but the defendant was unresponsive. We held that when counsel confers with the defendant and the defendant remains silent, neither approving nor protesting counsel's proposed concession strategy, * * * "[no] blanket rule demand[s] the defendant's explicit consent" to implementation of that strategy, * * *.

In the case now before us, in contrast to *Nixon*, the defendant vociferously insisted that he did not engage in the charged acts and adamantly objected to any admission of guilt. App. 286–287, 505–506. Yet the trial court permitted counsel, at the guilt phase of a capital trial, to tell the jury the defendant "committed three murders. . . . [H]e's guilty." *Id.*, at 509, 510. We hold that a defendant has the right to insist that counsel refrain from admitting guilt, even when counsel's experienced-based view is that confessing guilt offers the defendant the best chance to avoid the death penalty. Guaranteeing a defendant the right "to have the *Assistance* of Counsel for *his* defence," the Sixth Amendment so demands. With individual liberty—and, in capital cases, life—at stake, it is the defendant's prerogative, not counsel's, to decide on the objective of his defense: to admit guilt in the hope of gaining mercy at the sentencing stage, or to maintain his innocence, leaving it to the State to prove his guilt beyond a reasonable doubt. * * *

Justice Alito, with whom Justice Thomas and Justice Gorsuch join, dissenting.

The Constitution gives us the authority to decide real cases and controversies; we do not have the right to simplify or otherwise change the facts of a case in order to make our work easier or to achieve a desired result. But that is exactly what the Court does in this case. The Court overturns petitioner's convictions for three counts of first-degree murder by attributing to his trial attorney, Larry English, something that English never did. The Court holds that English violated petitioner's constitutional rights by "admit[ting] h[is] client's guilt of a charged crime over the client's intransigent objection." Ante, at 1510–1511.1 But English did not admit that petitioner was guilty of first-degree murder. Instead, faced with overwhelming evidence that petitioner shot and killed the three victims, English admitted that petitioner committed one element of that offense, i.e., that he killed the victims. But English strenuously argued that petitioner was not guilty of first-degree murder because he lacked the intent (the mens rea) required for the offense. App. 508–512. So the Court's newly discovered fundamental right simply does not apply to the real facts of this case. * * * The real case is far more complex. Indeed, the real situation English faced at the beginning of petitioner's trial was the result of a freakish confluence of factors that is unlikely to recur. * * * So the fundamental right supposedly violated in this case comes down to the difference between the two statements set out below.

> Constitutional : "First-degree murder requires proof both that the accused killed the victim and that he acted with the intent to kill. I submit to you that my client did not have the intent required for conviction for that offense."

> Unconstitutional : "First-degree murder requires proof both that the accused killed the victim and that he acted with the intent to kill. I admit that my client shot and killed the victims, but I submit to you that he did not have the intent required for conviction for that offense."

The practical difference between these two statements is negligible. If English had conspicuously refrained from endorsing petitioner's story and had based his defense solely on petitioner's dubious mental condition, the jury would surely have gotten the message that English was essentially conceding that petitioner killed the victims. But according to petitioner's current attorney, the difference is fundamental. The first formulation, he admits, is perfectly fine. The latter, on the other hand, is a violation so egregious that the defendant's conviction must be reversed even if there is no chance that the misstep caused any harm. It is no wonder that the Court declines to embrace this argument and instead turns to an issue that the case at hand does not actually present. * * *

———————————

Even if the dissent is correct that *McCoy v. Louisiana* "was the result of a freakish confluence of factors that is unlikely to recur," it seems clear that in the criminal context, lawyers may face difficult allocation of decision-making issues. In 1998, the New Yorker magazine published a lengthy article about the "Unabomber" case that highlighted the issues facing lawyers for defendant Theodore Kaczynski. See William Finnegan, *Defending the Unabomber*, New Yorker 52 (March 16, 1998). More recently, a blog post discussed allocation of decision-making issues that the lawyers for the alleged Boston Marathon bomber might have had to confront:

> As you may be aware, the punishment phase of the [Boston Marathon bombing] case began today—the question is whether Tsarnaev will get the death penalty or life in prison. The hosts [of a radio show asked their guest, a criminal law professor] whether the defense would be able to argue, to mitigate the punishment and try to avoid the death penalty for their client, that the older brother, Tamerlan, who died in a police shootout * * * was the one truly behind the bombing — essentially that [the Defendant] was "under the influence" of his brother. The lawyer being interviewed was asked whether, if [the Defendant] doesn't want to use that defense, but rather considers his brother to be a hero in avenging US aggression overseas (comments he scrawled in ink and blood on the tarp covering the boat in which he hid before being arrested), could [the Defendant] deny his lawyers permission to use that defense theory. The lawyer said that it is clear that he could not forbid his lawyers from arguing that, and opined that these were merely "trial" tactics that are not in the client's control, but rather in the hands of the lawyers.

> I was frustrated that the radio show was not taking calls, as I was eager to dispute that conclusion, and to point out that this type of lawyering is far different from that which we in the clinical community practice as we guide our students through the principles of client-centered lawyering. It was anathema to me to hear the role of the client completely discounted.

Irene Scharf, *Best Practices in Counseling? Ethical Practices in Counseling?*, Best Practices in Legal Education Blog (April 22, 2015).

> ### Food for Thought
>
> In *Jones v. Barnes, supra*, Justice Brennan asserted that the Supreme Court had decided to view lawyers as protecting substantial justice rather than the autonomy of the client. In the death volunteer cases, such as *Gilmore v. Utah*, on the other hand, the Court has decided to protect the client's autonomy, without regard to the system's concern for substantive justice. What explains the Court's different approaches to these cases? Do you agree with the Court's decisions? For another perspective, see Kristen M. Dama, *Comment, Redefining A Final Act: The Fourteenth Amendment and States' Obligation to Prevent Death Row Inmates From Volunteering To Be Put To Death*, 9 U. Pa. J. Const. L. 1083, 1101–03 (2007).

B. Other Principles That Set the Parameters of the Lawyer-Client Relationship

Section VI(A) addressed the allocation of decision-making authority between lawyer and client. This section reviews a number of additional rules that set the parameters of the lawyer-client relationship. One of the most important of these rules is Rule 1.2(d), which says what a lawyer may—and may not—do for a client. Consider the following:

[Question 2-22]

A federal law requires most individuals who are in business for themselves to make estimated quarterly federal tax payments. The statute makes the willful failure to make estimated quarterly federal tax payments a misdemeanor that has significant penalties. Although a criminal misdemeanor charge is possible, it is significantly more common for the Internal Revenue Service to impose a civil penalty for a taxpayer's underpayment or failure to pay estimated taxes.

An attorney represents a small business owner client who finds it inconvenient to do the paperwork required to file estimated quarterly federal tax payments. When the client files an annual tax federal tax return, the client willingly pays the modest civil penalty that is imposed for the failure to pay estimated quarterly federal tax payments. The client recently telephoned the attorney and asked whether any taxpayers had been criminally prosecuted solely for failing to file their estimated quarterly tax payments. The client also asked the attorney if there was anything the client could do to minimize the risk of detection. The attorney accurately told the client that the attorney had not located any examples of taxpayers who had been criminally prosecuted for violating the federal statute where the only alleged misconduct was failing to file their estimated quarterly tax returns. The attorney also told the client that it would be improper for the attorney to advise the client about how to avoid detection. The client thanked the attorney for the information and hung up. Later that year, when the attorney prepared the client's taxes, the attorney noticed that the client had not made any estimated quarterly tax payments.

Is the attorney subject to discipline?

    (A) **Yes, because the attorney reasonably should have known that the information she gave the client would encourage the client to violate the law.**

    (B) **Yes, because the attorney did not discourage the client from breaking the law.**

    (C) **No, because the attorney provided the attorney's honest opinion about the consequences that were likely to result if the client violated the law.**

    (D) **No, because the attorney and the client are permitted to discuss methods to avoid detection.**

As you analyze this questions, consider the case that follows and Rule 1.2(d). This rule states:

(d)   A lawyer shall not counsel a client to engage, or assist a client, in conduct that the lawyer knows is criminal or fraudulent, but a lawyer may discuss the legal consequences of any proposed course of conduct with a client and may counsel or assist a client to make a good faith effort to determine the validity, scope, meaning or application of the law.

People v. Chappell

927 P.2d 829 (Colo. 1996)

PER CURIAM.

A hearing panel of the supreme court grievance committee approved the findings and the recommendation of a hearing board that the respondent in this lawyer discipline case be disbarred. The respondent has not excepted to the panel's action. We accept the hearing panel's recommendation.

I.

The respondent was admitted to practice law in Colorado in 1977. Because the respondent did not answer the complaint, a default was entered against her, and the allegations of fact contained in the complaint were deemed admitted. Based on the respondent's default and the evidence presented, the hearing board found that the following had been established by clear and convincing evidence.

A man and woman were married in April 1991, and their son was born later that year. On December 13, 1993, the husband filed a petition for dissolution of the marriage. The wife was then pregnant with their daughter who was born on June 13, 1994. The respondent represented the wife in the dissolution proceeding.

The husband vacated the family home in January 1994. A mutual restraining order prevented either party from removing the child from Colorado. The dissolution court granted temporary custody of the son and use of the family home to the respondent's client. The husband was ordered to pay child support and maintenance directly to the wife in the amount of $1,500 per month. A temporary orders hearing was scheduled for March 11, 1994.

Dr. Jean LaCrosse was appointed to do a custody evaluation for the court. Two days before the temporary orders hearing, the respondent and her client met with Dr. LaCrosse who advised them that she was recommending that the husband be granted sole custody of both the son and the unborn daughter.

Later, the respondent told her client that the court would probably accept Dr. LaCrosse's recommendations. The wife states that the respondent advised her as her attorney to stay, but as a mother to run. The respondent also informed her client about a network of safehouses for people in her situation, and helped her to liquidate her assets and empty her bank accounts. The respondent contacted a friend of her client and asked the friend to pack her client's belongings from the marital home and to put them into storage. The friend states that the respondent let her into the home with a key, and gave her money, provided to the respondent by her client, to pay for the moving and storage. The respondent kept the storage locker key according to the friend.

The respondent appeared for the temporary orders hearing on March 11, 1994 without her client. The respondent's request for a one week continuance was granted. Nevertheless, the court allowed the husband to testify concerning the temporary orders. The respondent argued against a change in the interim orders and stated that the child was doing well in his own home. When the trial judge questioned her as to the whereabouts of her client, the respondent replied that she was unable to answer because of the attorney-client privilege. The court then ordered an immediate change of custody to the husband, as well as continued support payments. The respondent asked the court to order the support payments to be made through the court's registry.

After the husband's lawyer requested it, the court rescinded the portion of the temporary restraining order that prohibited the husband from going onto the property where the child was located. The court asked the respondent to call the child's day care center and advise persons there of the change in the restraining order, and the respondent agreed to make the call. Following the hearing, the respondent notified her client of the change in the custody order.

When the husband went to the wife's residence, he discovered that she had moved. His lawyer then filed an emergency motion for custody and pick-up of the child, which was granted, and a petition for writ of habeas corpus, which was heard on March 16, 1994.

The respondent appeared in court on March 16, advised the court that she would assert the attorney-client privilege, and asked for time to hire a lawyer to represent her. The court also heard testimony from her client's friend concerning the events just prior to the March 11 hearing.

On March 21, 1994, the court ordered the return of the husband's property that was then in storage. In addition, the respondent, who was represented by counsel, testified regarding the attorney-client privilege and the exceptions to the privilege concerning a client's criminal or fraudulent acts or intentions. Upon order of the court, the respondent testified that she had notified her client of the March 11 revised custody order.

The respondent subsequently testified on March 25, 1994, that she and her client had been in contact five or six times since the March 11 hearing, and that her client was out of the state. The respondent also testified that her client had asked her to safeguard her property and that in compliance with that request, she had rented a storage facility for that purpose. The respondent then withdrew from the case.

The wife was out of Colorado for two weeks, and when she returned she and her child lived at a battered women's shelter. The husband gained physical custody of the child after the wife went to the hospital for a prenatal visit. She then retained another lawyer to represent her.

A few days after the birth of the daughter, the court entered temporary orders granting immediate custody of the infant to the husband. The court also found that the respondent had perpetrated a fraud on the court when she accepted the husband's offer to continue paying support and maintenance on March 11, despite the change in custody. The court stated that the respondent "was aware that her client was on the run with the child and yet accepted the offer of child support and maintenance." After terminating the support order, the court ordered that $1,500 held in the court's registry be returned to the husband.

A permanent orders hearing was held in March 1995. The wife testified that the respondent had explained "the underground" to her, had assisted in emptying her bank accounts, and had advised her on how to avoid being caught. The wife was charged with violation of a child custody order, contrary to section 18-3-304(2), 8B C.R.S. (1986), a class 5 felony. The wife pleaded guilty in exchange for a three-year deferred judgment.

The respondent's conduct violated R.P.C. 1.2(d) (a lawyer "shall not counsel a client to engage, or assist a client, in conduct that the lawyer knows is criminal or fraudulent"); R.P.C. 3.3(a)(2) (a lawyer shall not knowingly fail to disclose a material fact to a tribunal when disclosure is necessary to avoid assisting a criminal or fraudulent act by the client); R.P.C. 8.4(b) (it is professional misconduct for a lawyer to commit a criminal act by aiding the lawyer's client to commit a crime); and R.P.C. 8.4(c) (it is professional misconduct for a lawyer to engage in conduct involving dishonesty, fraud, deceit or misrepresentation).

II.

The hearing panel approved the board's recommendation that the respondent be disbarred, and the respondent has not excepted to that recommendation. * * *

In *People v. Bullock*, 882 P.2d 1390, 1391–92 (Colo.1994), we disbarred a lawyer following his conviction for aiding a client who was a fugitive from justice by arranging to supply the client with money. Given the seriousness of the respondent's conduct in aiding her client to violate the custody order resulting in the client being charged with a felony, the fact that the respondent has not been charged or convicted of an offense is not important for disciplinary purposes. * * *

The respondent used her license to violate the core ethical and professional standards of her profession. Disbarment is the only appropriate form of discipline. Accordingly, we accept the hearing panel's recommendation and order that the respondent be disbarred.

III.

It is hereby ordered that Lorraine A. Chappell be disbarred and that her name be stricken from the list of attorneys authorized to practice before this court, effective thirty days after the issuance of this opinion.

Rule 1.2(d) *limits* the type of advice that a lawyer may provide to a client. Rule 2.1, in contrast, requires a lawyer to exercise independent legal judgment and grants a lawyer permission to offer advice that is not strictly "legal advice." Rule 2.1 is relevant when answering the question that follows.

[Question 2-23]

An attorney represents a company that sells widgets. The client told the attorney that an unusually large number of customers had recently returned their widgets. The client asked the attorney to review the client's contractual agreement with its customers and advise the client whether it had to accept the customer returns and refund the customers their purchase price.

After reviewing the relevant contractual agreements and the law, the attorney advised the client that it only had to issue refunds to those customers who had returned their widgets within 14 days of purchase. The attorney recommended, however, that the client issue refunds to all customers who requested a refund, noting that it was in the client's long-term business interest to have fully satisfied customers.

Was the attorney's conduct proper?

    (A) Yes, because the attorney was required to give advice about relevant business considerations.

    (B) Yes, because the attorney was permitted to refer to relevant business considerations.

    (C) No, because the attorney was required to limit the attorney's advice to the relevant legal considerations.

    (D) No, because the attorney's advice was contrary to the client's short-term interests.

Rule 2.1 is relevant to this question. It states the following:

> In representing a client, a lawyer shall exercise independent professional judgment and render candid advice. In rendering advice, a lawyer may refer not only to law but to other considerations, such as moral, economic, social and political factors, that may be relevant to the client's situation.

While Rule 2.1 may seem like an obvious rule, it is not the only way one could look at this issue of non-legal advice. Consider the following ethics opinion, portions of which you read previously in Section III of this Chapter. The opinion relies on the Code of Professional Responsibility which predated the Rules of Professional Conduct. Do you think the Board would have reached the same result if it had applied the Rules of Professional Conduct? (Rule 1.1 regarding competence is the counterpart provision to the Code's "zealous representation" requirement.)

BOARD OF PROFESSIONAL RESPONSIBILITY OF THE SUPREME COURT OF TENNESSEE

Op. No. 96-F-140

[Section III(B) of this Chapter included the portion of this opinion that addressed a lawyer's obligations when appointed by a court to represent a teenage girl seeking court permission for an abortion without notifying her parents. The attorney also asked the Board of Professional Responsibility whether he could "advise the minor seeking an abortion about alternatives and/or advise her to speak with her parents or legal guardian about the potential abortion?" The Board responded that:]

> If the appointed attorney represents only the minor (as we believe), then counsel has a duty to "explain a matter to the extent reasonably necessary to permit the client to make informed decisions regarding the representation." * * * Whether informing the minor about alternatives to abortion and suggesting that she discuss the potential procedure with her parents or legal guardian is ethically appropriate may depend on a case-by-case analysis. If the minor is truly mature and well-informed enough to go forward and make the decision on her own, then counsel's hesitation and advice for the client to consult with others could possibly implicate a lack of zealous representation under DR 7-101(A)(4)(a) and (c) (a lawyer shall not intentionally fail to seek the client's lawful objectives, or prejudice or damage his client during the course of the professional relationship). Counsel also has a duty of undivided loyalty to his client, and should not allow any other persons or entities to regulate, direct, compromise, control or interfere with his professional judgment. * * * To the extent that counsel strongly recommends that his client discuss the potential abortion with her parents or with other individuals or entities which are known to oppose such a choice, compliance with Canon 5 [governing conflicts of interest] is called into question.

Rule 1.14 is another important rule that, if applicable, sets the parameters of the relationship between a lawyer and client. Rule 1.14 changes the rules that normally would apply to the lawyer-client relationship, including Rule 1.2(a) regarding the allocation of decision-making authority between a lawyer and client. Question 2-24 and the material that follows illustrate how this rule might operate.

[Question 2-24]

An attorney was asked by a partner in the law firm to work with a long-time client of the firm who had retained the firm to file a lawsuit against the client's landlord, alleging violation of the implied warranty of habitability. The partner told the attorney that because the partner was afraid that the statute of limitations was about to expire, the partner had filed a lawsuit on behalf of the client hurriedly last week. The only thing the

partner knew about the underlying situation was that the client said the landlord was violating a warranty of habitability.

When the attorney interviewed the client to get more details, the client told the attorney that the landlord was shooting invisible but dangerous gamma rays into the apartment. The client offered no scientific evidence for this contention. The client told the attorney that so long as there are gamma rays being shot into the apartment, the client will refuse to pay rent, even if it means being evicted and becoming homeless. The attorney tried to persuade the client that the client was mistaken and advised the client to pay rent. The client angrily rejected this suggestion. The attorney reasonably believes that the client has diminished capacity. The attorney took the following action: 1) asking the court's permission to withdraw from representing client in the implied warranty of habitability lawsuit; 2) consulting with the client's out-of-state daughter and sharing the information the attorney learned; and 3) preparing to file an action that seeks appointment of a guardian for the client in the event it is necessary.

Was the attorney's conduct proper?

  (A)   Yes, because the attorney was entitled to take the described action to protect a client with diminished capacity from foreseeable harm.

  (B)   Yes, because the attorney was worried that the statute of limitations was about to expire.

  (C)   No, because the proposed action would violate the duty of confidentiality that the attorney owes to the client.

  (D)   No, because the proposed action would violate the duty of loyalty that the attorney owes to the client.

In analyzing this question, you should examine not only Rules 1.2(a), 1.16(a), and 3.1, but also Rule 1.14, which changes the ordinary rules under which lawyers operate:

Rule 1.14. Client with Diminished Capacity

(a)   When a client's capacity to make adequately considered decisions in connection with a representation is diminished, whether because of minority, mental impairment or for some other reason, the lawyer shall, as far as reasonably possible, maintain a normal client-lawyer relationship with the client.

It's Latin to Me

Black's Law Dictionary defines *guardian ad litem* as "[a] guardian, [usually] a lawyer, appointed by the court to appear in a law situation on behalf of an incompetent or minor party."

(b) When the lawyer reasonably believes that the client has diminished capacity, is at risk of substantial physical, financial or other harm unless action is taken and cannot adequately act in the client's own interest, the lawyer may take reasonably necessary protective action, including consulting with individuals or entities that have the ability to take action to protect the client and, in appropriate cases, seeking the appointment of a *guardian ad litem*, conservator or guardian.

Rule 1.14's Comment includes the following additional information:

[1] The normal client-lawyer relationship is based on the assumption that the client, when properly advised and assisted, is capable of making decisions about important matters. When the client is a minor or suffers from a diminished mental capacity, however, maintaining the ordinary client-lawyer relationship may not be possible in all respects. In particular, a severely incapacitated person may have no power to make legally binding decisions. Nevertheless, a client with diminished capacity often has the ability to understand, deliberate upon, and reach conclusions about matters affecting the client's own well-being. * * *

[2] The fact that a client suffers a disability does not diminish the lawyer's obligation to treat the client with attention and respect. Even if the person has a legal representative, the lawyer should as far as possible accord the represented person the status of client, particularly in maintaining communication. * * *

[4] If a legal representative has already been appointed for the client, the lawyer should ordinarily look to the representative for decisions on behalf of the client. * * *

[5] If a lawyer reasonably believes that a client is at risk of substantial physical, financial or other harm unless action is taken, and that a normal client-lawyer relationship cannot be maintained as provided in paragraph (a) because the client lacks sufficient capacity to communicate or to make adequately considered decisions in connection with the representation, then paragraph (b) permits the lawyer to take protective measures deemed necessary. Such measures could include: consulting with family members, using a reconsideration period to permit clarification or improvement of circumstances, using voluntary surrogate decision making tools such as durable powers of attorney or consulting with support groups, professional services, adult-protective agencies or other individuals or entities that have the ability to protect the client. In taking any protective action, the lawyer should be guided by such factors as the wishes and values of the client to the extent known, the client's best interests and the goals of intruding into the client's decisionmaking autonomy to the least extent feasible, maximizing client capacities and respecting the client's family and social connections.

[6] In determining the extent of the client's diminished capacity, the lawyer should consider and balance such factors as: the client's ability to articulate reasoning leading to a decision, variability of state of mind and ability to appreciate consequences of a decision; the substantive fairness of a decision; and the consistency of a decision with the known long-term commitments and values of the client. In appropriate circumstances, the lawyer may seek guidance from an appropriate diagnostician.

[7] If a legal representative has not been appointed, the lawyer should consider whether appointment of a guardian ad litem, conservator or guardian is necessary

to protect the client's interests. * * * In many circumstances, however, appointment of a legal representative may be more expensive or traumatic for the client than circumstances in fact require. Evaluation of such circumstances is a matter entrusted to the professional judgment of the lawyer. In considering alternatives, however, the lawyer should be aware of any law that requires the lawyer to advocate the least restrictive action on behalf of the client. * * *

[8] Disclosure of the client's diminished capacity could adversely affect the client's interests. For example, raising the question of diminished capacity could, in some circumstances, lead to proceedings for involuntary commitment. Information relating to the representation is protected by Rule 1.6. Therefore, unless authorized to do so, the lawyer may not disclose such information. When taking protective action pursuant to paragraph (b), the lawyer is impliedly authorized to make the necessary disclosures, even when the client directs the lawyer to the contrary. Nevertheless, given the risks of disclosure, paragraph (c) limits what the lawyer may disclose in consulting with other individuals or entities or seeking the appointment of a legal representative. At the very least, the lawyer should determine whether it is likely that the person or entity consulted with will act adversely to the client's interests before discussing matters related to the client. The lawyer's position in such cases is an unavoidably difficult one.

———————————

Because the baby-boomer generation is aging, it is increasingly likely that lawyers will encounter situations such as the one in Question 2-24.

Go Online

The ABA, the Association of Professional Responsibility Lawyers, and the National Organization of Bar Counsel, which consists primarily of regulators, have collaborated to address the issue of aging lawyers. The 2014 Final Report of the Second Joint Committee on Aging Lawyers is available here.

Rule 1.14 is not limited, however, to older clients who suffer from diminished capacity.

Clients of all ages may have diminished capacity. Comment [1] to Rule 1.14 includes this reference to children:

> For example, children as young as five or six years of age, and certainly those of ten or twelve, are regarded as having opinions that are entitled to weight in legal proceedings concerning their custody. * * *

This statement is the only reference to children in Rule 1.14. Thus, lawyers who represent children may face difficult issues that include who can speak for the client/child and how the lawyer-client relationship should be managed. The answers to these questions may vary depending on the circumstances. For information about the extensive debates about how the representation of children should be handled, see Jonathan O. Hafen, *Children's Rights and*

Legal Representation—The Proper Roles of Children, Parents, and Attorneys, 7 Notre Dame J.L. Ethics & Pub. Pol'y 423 (1993).

The take-away lesson from Rule 1.14 and these examples is that it is important for lawyers to realize that while the principles set forth in this chapter and later chapters govern most lawyer-client relationships, there are exceptional situations.

This chapter has set forth the basic elements of law practice. The rules and concepts addressed in this chapter are the foundation for the material that follows.

Test Your Knowledge

To assess your understanding of the material in this chapter, click here to take a quiz.

CHAPTER 3

The Business, Technology, and Marketing of Legal Services

Learning Outcomes

At the end of Units I and II, you will be able to:

- Recognize ways in which lawyers are advertising with new media and technologies and analyze whether those efforts comport with the ethics rules

- Analyze whether a lawyer solicitation or advertisement complies with the ethics rules

- Identify the states' interest in regulating lawyer advertising as commercial speech

- Understand the distinction between solicitation and advertising

At the end of Unit III, you will be able to:

- Analyze whether a lawyer's fee is reasonable under the ethics rules

- Identify what funds or property a lawyer must maintain separately from the lawyer's property, and recognize the manner in which this must be accomplished

- Recognize the distinction between the types of fees a lawyer may charge

Topic Outline for Chapter 3

	TOPIC	RELEVANT AUTHORITY	CHAPTER QUESTIONS
I.	Introduction		
II.	Finding Clients		
	A. An Overview Of Marketing Legal Services	1.1	
	B. Solicitation [Ohralik; Primus]	7.3	3-1 to 3-2
	C. Advertising [Zang]	7.1 to 7.5	3-3 to 3-5
III.	Fees and Billing	1.4(b) 1.5, 7.1	
	A. The Hourly Billing Controversy	1.5, 1.8(i)	3-6 to 3-7

I. Introduction

To succeed in private practice, a lawyer needs to find clients and needs to get paid by those clients. Different types of lawyers will approach these tasks differently, depending in significant part on the types of legal services they provide and the size and geographic location of their practice. Whatever these differences, though, lawyers are subject to the same ethical framework. First, the ethics rules seek to protect clients and the public as consumers. Second, they seek to protect the professional identity of lawyers. Critics of the legal profession have questioned the sincerity of these rationales and have argued that the rules instead protect lawyers from competition and from stricter regulation. Challenges to these rules have resulted in significant court decisions regarding the constitutional limitations of lawyer regulation.

While lawyers recognize the vital importance of these topics to maintaining a successful practice, they sometimes find them challenging, especially in an increasingly online, digital and technology-driven world. The traditional understanding of professionalism relies on the distinction between the behavior of professionals and the behavior of business people.

Food for Thought

Professors Geoffrey Hazard, Russell Pearce, and Jeffrey Stempel have offered the following explanation for why many lawyers traditionally find the subject of lawyer advertising distasteful. Does their analysis apply more generally to the subject of finding and billing clients?

Perhaps the underlying anxiety about advertising stems from its tendency to portray legal services as a 'business' rather than a 'profession.' Of course, the practice of law manifestly is both a profession and a business, and a highly competitive business at that. Why the passion to deny its character as a business? The answer derives from the notion, basic to our legal ideals, that justice cannot be sold. This notion is central to the ideology of the bar. A group for which that notion is so important inevitably would find it difficult to recognize that access to justice is in any sense a question of buying and selling. Nevertheless, lawyers differ in skill, knowledge, and the time they can devote to a case, and individuals with more resources are usually able to purchase both a superior lawyer and more of his time. Therefore, justice—actual outcomes in the legal system—is related to the quality of lawyering that a client can afford; justice at the margin can often be bought.

The legal profession is understandably reticent to acknowledge this tension between ideal and reality. One means of avoiding the unpleasant implications of this tension is to minimize overt participation by lawyers in activities, such as advertising, that suggest that effective legal assistance is bought and sold. Opposition to legal advertising, in other words, is a consequence of the inconsistency between providing legal services through the free market and realizing equal justice before the law.

Geoffrey C. Hazard, Jr., Russell G. Pearce & Jeffrey W. Stempel, *Why Lawyers Should Be Allowed to Advertise: A Market Analysis of Legal Services*, 58 N.Y.U. L. Rev. 1084, 1112–13 (1983).

The tasks of finding and billing clients are examples of professionals engaging in business behavior—behavior that blurs the dichotomy between a business and a profession. Finding and billing clients are also two elements of law practice increasingly impacted by advances in technology. Keep in mind that a lawyer's duty of competence includes staying current on "the benefits and risks associated with relevant technology." Rule 1.1, Comment 8. As of early 2020, 38 states have adopted this provision as part of lawyer competence.

II. Finding Clients

A. An Overview of Marketing Legal Services

As a law student, you are not likely to have had much experience with marketing legal services. The materials in this section will provide you with samples from the voluminous literature on this topic. They will introduce you to the way lawyers discuss marketing and help provide the context for your evaluation of the relevant ethical rules.

LARRY BODINE, *WRITING YOUR PERSONAL MARKETING PLAN*

L. Prac. Today, Feb. 2007

* * *

If you really want to boost the revenue you bring in to your firm * * * you must have a *written* [sales] plan to devote 100 to 200 hours per year to business development. 100 hours a year is only 2 hours a week, and any lawyer can find that time in meeting a referral source for coffee, taking a client for lunch, or attending a trade association meeting after work.

Your aim is to develop or deepen relationships, because new business comes *in person*. Your plan should be filled with *face-to-face* meetings with clients and targets. The firm's Web site, brochure, articles, newsletters, public relations, direct mail marketing, announcements and press releases will *generate leads* for your sales effort, but you have to go out and *make the sale*.

Keep several things in mind:

- A sales call is not a pitch. No one wants to hear about your credentials. A sales call is an *interview* where you are asking questions to learn about the client's business.

- Don't make any cold calls because they rarely succeed. Focus on people you already know.

- Build on your strengths. If you like to speak in front of a crowd, find a meeting of clients and do so. If instead you are more comfortable one-on-one, then plan dinner parties and private get-togethers where you can talk. Mix business development into your outside activities, hobbies, club memberships and events you enjoy.

- By making the effort, you have already succeeded. * * * Closing a sale takes months of time spent in advance. The more people you know and the more activities you undertake, the better you'll do over the long run.

* * *

STEPHANIE KIMBRO, *VIRTUAL LAW PRACTICE: HOW TO DELIVER LEGAL SERVICES ONLINE*

ABA Publishing (2010)

What is a Virtual Law Practice?

A virtual law practice is a professional law practice that exists online through a secure portal and is accessible to both the client and the lawyer anywhere the parties may access the Internet. Legal services are delivered online using this method. The lawyers and their clients have the ability to securely discuss matters online, download and upload documents for review, create legal documents, and handle other business transactions related to the delivery of legal services in a secure digital environment. A virtual law practice has been referred to in the following ways: virtual law office (VLO), virtual law firm, Web-based law practice, or online law practice.

With future innovations in technology, additional * * * capabilities will evolve to expand the concept of virtual law practice and the delivery of online legal services.

SILVIA HODGES, *I DIDN'T GO TO LAW SCHOOL TO BECOME A SALESPERSON—THE DEVELOPMENT OF MARKETING IN LAW FIRMS*

26 Geo. J. of Legal Ethics 225 (2013)

If you asked them, the majority of lawyers would probably answer that they do not "do" marketing—at least until recently. And most law school students would likely say that they did not go to law school to become salespeople. After all, marketing is for toothpaste, cars, or soft drinks, but is inappropriate for the legal profession. While the most recent recession may have influenced some to be more positive about marketing, the legal profession has long resisted the idea of marketing its services. A normal and accepted discipline in the corporate world, only the last three decades have seen the advent of marketing in the profession.

What has happened? The legal sector has undergone greater transformations during the last three decades than in the prior two centuries. Deregulation and liberalization, increasing consumer expectations, new information technology, generational differences, and globalization have resulted in an increasingly competitive marketplace. The recent recession has further intensified the competition among law firms. Many services that were once considered to be highly specialized are being treated today more and more like commodities. A once elite and learned profession is now operating in a competitive, cutthroat business environment, much like any other profession. Lawyers no longer have the luxury of waiting for business to come to them.

Law schools teach students how to think like lawyers, but in today's highly competitive world, it is imperative to bring more to the table. Technical legal competence alone is not a guarantee of success in winning new business or keeping existing clients. Traditional conduct and approaches no longer ensure success or even survival. Consequently law firms are forced to compete in new ways. It's more than possible—it's extremely common—for law students to graduate into the real world in immaculate innocence of any exposure to economics or to how for-profit businesses actually run.

* * *

There is general recognition in academia and practice that marketing addresses the increased need to compete for business. Marketing is important since organizations need to be aware of their competition and aim to satisfy their customers in order to be successful. This is particularly true for service industries due to the direct interaction they have with their customers. While the rationale for marketing might be unquestionable, professional services firms, in particular law firms, traditionally resisted the diffusion of the marketing concept or market(ing) orientation. Little marketing used to occur in the legal profession, and lawyers began to adopt marketing "unenthusiastically" or not at all.

* * *

It has been argued that, from a microeconomic point of view, a law firm is essentially a service business like any other: it renders services to clients from whom it receives payment. Like any other business, a law firm combines resources in order to produce services and adheres to the basic principles of economics—profitability and financial liquidity, to ensure continuity. The "growth in the size of the profession, the size of firms, and the volume of the market, has led . . . [to] lawyers having to treat the practice of law as a business." Access to justice requires not only that the legal advice given be sound, but also "the presence of the business skills necessary to provide a cost-effective service in a consumer-friendly way." Customers are the lifeblood of any commercial organization. Without them, a business has no revenues, no profits, and therefore no market value. In fact, the basis of a business is its ability to create and keep a customer.

* * *

Technology is argued to be at the root of market orientation since it enabled efficient production, shifted the focus away from manufacturing and paved the way for marketing. The Internet-driven information revolution is widely perceived as having transformed the way businesses and consumers operate. Therefore, some law firms have already started modifying their traditional approach to legal advice. It is likely that it has not reached its full potential in the legal services sector. However, advances in information technology can so profoundly affect the practice of law as to cause a "shift in paradigm", transforming both supply and demand side. Technology has revolutionized lawyer's communication and information-seeking habits and created greater efficiency and lower costs. "[I]f you took away a firm's accounting, knowledge management, billing and word processing systems, the firm 'would die within a day.'"

In professional services, and legal services in particular, the Internet was viewed primarily as an information resource rather than a distribution channel. Websites allow law firms to provide information online and promote their services and can grant clients the opportunity for immediate access to the firms' resources. The widespread use of the Internet fundamentally changed the way in which clients interact and communicate with their legal services providers through emailing, instant messaging, and other wireless communication. While in 1987 two-thirds of the profession did not use computers, less than forty percent had Word processors and just over four percent a fax, by the turn of the millennium, the Internet had firmly established itself as the main form of communication between lawyers and their clients, and by 2004, every partner and large firm associate had a BlackBerry to ensure availability. Today, constant availability is the norm for most rather than the exception. "You're never off-duty now, never off-call." Technology therefore provides lawyers with new ways to better serve their clients and has driven marketing into firms.

Technology also potentially enhances client relationship management through sophisticated systems that enable lawyers to leverage relationships held by other lawyers in the firm and to monitor the satisfaction of key accounts and leverage the firm's knowledge about its client relationships. However, changing lawyer attitudes about sharing contact information is critical. Given that a law firm's business is essentially concerned with the retrieval and dissemination of information, technology offers an opportunity to improve service delivery. A number of large firms have launched extranets for their clients with online "deal rooms," where lawyers from both sides of a deal can exchange and manage documents and conduct secure, private conferences, in particular, in major merger and acquisition and corporate finance matters. Most large U.S. law firms, such as Davis Polk & Wardwell LLP, and all U.K. Magic Circle firms have established such extranets.

"Virtual lawyers" or legal advice systems of modern websites claim to contain the knowledge of lawyers that enable clients to receive legal information without consulting a lawyer directly. Larger firms typically are more advanced in integrating new technologies and working methods than smaller firms. An example is UK Magic Circle firm Linklaters that utilizes the Internet by offering standardized legal services. The firm introduced a second brand, Blue Flag®, to avoid confusion with the main brand. The firm promotes scope, quality, consistency, low(er) costs, and efficiency. Such offers are likely to be attractive to companies as well and pose significant competition to other law firms and may therefore drive marketing.

Also e-commerce or "e-lawyering" has the potential to fundamentally change the way in which lawyers operate and compete, and how they deliver their services. The information available online, like articles, "do-it-yourself" books, and "legal kits" as well as the scope for interaction (e.g. virtual discussion forums and consumer communities) have impacted former informational asymmetries, and empowered clients by increasing their knowledge. Online legal advice such as LegalZoom® or Rocket Lawyer® target the same clients as small private practice firms and reduce or even eliminate the client's need to pay for the same information or services from a law firm. Online technology is therefore likely to drive marketing activity by law firms, perhaps through emphasizing the added value of tailor-made solutions and individual care.

Technology that enables firms to export their services has had divergent effects on law firms. While some firms send aspects of their legal work (e.g. due diligence) to lawyers overseas, large companies also increasingly outsource legal services to low-cost providers in India, the Philippines, or similar locations. Mayson hence cautioned that lawyers should reflect on how much of their work is or could be conducted through a screen and a telephone, as technology has the potential to substitute for people and places. The increased use of technology can also lead to a substitution of capital for labor, thus potentially increasing the output of each lawyer, which again might raise the level of competition. On the other hand, IT platforms might bring efficiencies to firms that could enable these new players to significantly out-perform the market as transactions now run at unimaginable speeds and complexity compared with twenty years ago.

* * *

There appears to be a paradox that merits investigation, namely that professionals appeared to be better markerters when not intending to market, but poorer markerters when consciously deciding to use marketing as a way to operate in increasingly competitive markets. However, in order to market effectively, firms need to aspire to have marketing embedded in their firm culture, independent of whether the firm is a professional partnership or a managed professional business. This requires top management support, good marketing professionals, education, and a marketing structure within the firm. In addition, it also requires a measure of behavior modification: for marketing to succeed in a professional firm, every professional must participate and understand the competitive advantages of participating. Effective measurement processes need to be in place to help drive behavioral change. "What gets measured gets done" and "what gets measured and rewarded gets done even more," particularly when the measures are directly related to the firm's strategy. A challenge for the years to come is to link specific outcomes to specific marketing activity and demonstrate the return on investment of marketing.

GEOFFREY C. HAZARD, JR., RUSSELL G. PEARCE & JEFFREY W. STEMPEL, *WHY LAWYERS SHOULD BE ALLOWED TO ADVERTISE: A MARKET ANALYSIS OF LEGAL SERVICES*

58 N.Y.U. L. Rev. 1084, 1094–1100 (1983)

Advertising has advantages and disadvantages for producers as well. Before deciding to advertise, any individual producer must carefully weigh these costs and benefits. Advertising's primary advantage is that it enables the producer to reach and recruit a large number of consumers and thereby to increase revenue; the increased volume may permit the reduction of production costs through economies of scale and thereby generate further increases in profits. Advertising, however, also has drawbacks for the producer. Its chief drawback is its high cost; moreover, efficacy normally requires repetition. Advertising also incurs the costs associated with mass marketing, such as those of preparing for levels of production sufficient to meet the demand generated by advertising promotion. This increased demand may also require some form of standardized production, both to absorb marketing costs and to increase output, and standardized production entails start-up costs such as expenditures for research and development. * * *

Because advertising may fail to alter consumer choice, the producer who advertises is subject to considerable entrepreneurial risk. If he spends a great deal of money and fails to gain the consumers' attention, he has lost much. More importantly, * * * [t]he producer who advertises runs this risk of extraordinary loss because of the general effect that advertising has on consumer behavior. Advertising tends to cause consumers to seek information about the producer's reputation and about other consumers' direct experience with him. Moreover, advertising often better enables consumers to evaluate reputation information. If reputation and experience information are unfavorable, advertising can have the ironic effect of informing a much larger group of consumers about the poor quality of the producer's goods or services. * * *

JIM HAWKINS & RENEE KNAKE, *THE BEHAVIORAL ECONOMICS OF LAWYER ADVERTISING: AN EMPRICAL ASSESSMENT*

2019 Illinois L. Rev. 1005 (2019)

Lawyer advertising—what's the first thought that comes to mind? Likely it is the late-night television commercial for a failed medical device or a mass tort. Images of sledgehammers, swiveling gavels, flames, or even aliens appear with a voiceover asking: "Have you or someone you know been injured? If so, call now!" Selling lawyers is a big business, projected to soon reach almost a billion dollars.

The main source individuals use to actually find an attorney when in need, however, is not that late-night television commercial but increasingly websites. According to recent studies, an Internet search is a primary route to finding legal representation, even over asking family or friends for a recommendation. For most consumers of legal services, a website profile often will be the first encounter with the attorney they hire (or decline to hire).

Online websites with live-chat features and blogs surely are not what the United States Supreme Court had in mind when it struck down the nation-wide ban on lawyer advertising in *Bates v. Arizona State Bar*. Instead, the Court envisioned straightforward, easy to understand print ads like that published by newly-licensed attorneys John Bates and Van O'Steen in 1976. Their legal clinic advertisement listed routine services such as an uncontested divorce or a name change and the corresponding flat fee. The opening text read: "Do you need a lawyer? Legal services at very reasonable fees." The only graphic in the black and white ad was a scale, and it directed potential clients to the address of the Legal Clinic of Bates and O'Steen. The ad's clarity and simplicity is refreshing, easily understandable to all.

The Court justified its holding in *Bates*, at least in part, on a hypothesis that advertising would expand access to legal services for some 70% of the American public that could not afford an attorney or lacked information about legal rights and entitlements. In analyzing the market impact, the Court noted that advertising bans make it difficult, if not impossible, for consumers to find "the lowest cost seller of acceptable ability." Protecting attorneys from competition, wrote Justice Blackmun in the 5–4 majority opinion, decreases the "incentive to price competitively" but "where consumers have the benefit of price advertising, retail prices often are dramatically lower than they would be without advertising."

In an important *NYU Law Review* article published soon after the *Bates* decision [excerpted above in this casebook], scholars similarly speculated about the potentially positive impact of advertising on supply and demand in the legal services market. Yet, nearly a half-century later, the *Bates* Court's promise has gone unrealized. Studies show that at any given time as many as 85% of American households face two to three legal problems without assistance from a lawyer. Lack of information is the primary reason, followed by cost, according to a 2015 study by the American Bar Foundation—the very concerns the Supreme Court aimed to address.

More, not less, of the American public now goes without legal help even after decades of advertising. This incongruity between *Bates*'s aspirations and modern realities raises the question: was the Supreme Court's market analysis about the impact of lawyer advertising flawed?

Some suggest yes and argue for a return to the advertising ban. For example, with the aftermath of advertising like those notorious late night commercials that thrive post-*Bates*, Justice O'Connor declared that the Court should have gone the other way and upheld the ban. Her concern, however, is grounded in notions of professionalism rather than an economic market analysis.

Others contend that the complexity of restrictions currently placed on lawyer advertising by state regulatory authorities effectively compromises the market for legal services in the same way as a wholesale ban.[1] In other words, it may be that we have yet to see the full impact of advertising because lawyers are so restricted in the content and timing of the information they share. If lawyers were subject to fewer restrictions, advertising would be less costly and the public would have greater knowledge about legal options.

We offer a different explanation here, deploying a novel research method that uses advertisements to diagnose behavioral market failure in the legal services market. By performing an empirical content analysis of attorney advertisements, we detect ways in which consumers make irrational or suboptimal decisions in the current market for legal services because of their behavioral biases. Our study is the only comprehensive empirical examination of website advertisements for attorneys specializing in DWI/DUI (driving while intoxicated/driving under intoxication) and personal injury work. We use this analysis as a basis for recommending advertising reforms that will create advertisements that better achieve the objectives articulated in *Bates*.

---

1   *See, e.g.*, Gillian K. Hadfield, *Legal Barriers to Innovation: The Growing Economic Cost of Professional Control over Corporate Legal Markets*, 60 STAN. L. REV. 1689, 1692 (1980); Renee Newman Knake, *Legal Information, the Consumer Law Market, and the First Amendment*, 82 FORDHAM L. REV. 2843, 2844 (2014).

Time after time, regulatory bodies have implemented advertising regulations for lawyers without any empirical studies. Our research here provides empirical justification for regulatory intervention. Our argument is not that *Bates* should be reversed even though we challenge the Court's reliance on traditional economics in making the decision to overturn the advertising ban. Instead, we propose mechanisms to more fully realize the benefits of advertising in the legal services market espoused by *Bates*.

* * *

Advertising creates and influences markets. The market for legal services, for many years, went without advertising precisely because of this influence. Regulators of the legal profession feared advertising might manipulate the public to pursue unnecessary litigation or otherwise cause harm.

A Brief History of Lawyer Advertising

Lawyer advertising was not prohibited in the early years of the United States. Abraham Lincoln, for example, famously posted information about his services in Illinois newspapers during the 1830s. When the American Bar Association adopted its Canons of Professional Responsibility in 1908, however, among the restrictions was a complete bar on lawyer advertising and solicitation. The most a lawyer could do was to communicate via family, friends, or existing clients about their services, and list a phone number in a directory. Anything more was considered unprofessional and unethical. When the ABA revised the canons and adopted the Code of Professional Responsibility in 1969, the ban was reaffirmed.

The nationwide ban endured nearly seventy years until the Supreme Court struck down the State Bar of Arizona's prohibition on lawyer advertising because it violated the First Amendment. Chief among the Court's justifications for doing so was a concern about "the right of the public as consumers and citizens to know about the activities of the legal profession." The Court believed that advertising could address market inefficiencies caused by the lack of information about legal services. The particular advertisement at issue in the case is instructive.

Two newly licensed attorneys, John Bates and Van O'Steen, established a legal aid clinic targeting what is now known as the "consumer law market," *i.e.* those who do not qualify for legal aid but cannot afford a lawyer at six-figures-per-hour for multiple hours. In short, they aimed to fill a justice gap, a phenomenon that still persists today. In an effort to reach their target market, they placed a simple newspaper advertisement listing the cost of basic legal services including uncontested divorce, adoption, personal bankruptcy, and name change. The Arizona State Bar disciplined them, contending that all advertising compromised professionalism and might cause clients to have unjustified expectations or to sue when they otherwise would not do so, stirring up unnecessary litigation.

The Supreme Court sided with Bates and O'Steen. The Court criticized the advertising ban as the State Bar of Arizona's "failure to reach out and serve the community." Justice Blackmun, authoring the majority, opinion wrote: "Although advertising might increase the use of the judicial machinery, we cannot accept the notion that it is always better for a person to suffer a wrong silently than to redress it by legal action. As the bar acknowledges, the middle 70% of our population is not being reached or served adequately by the legal profession. Among the reasons for this underutilization is fear of the cost, and an inability to locate a suitable lawyer. Advertising can help to solve this acknowledged problem: Advertising is the traditional mechanism in a free-market economy for a supplier to inform a potential purchaser of the availability and terms of exchange. The disciplinary rule at issue likely has served to burden access to legal services, particularly for the not-quite-poor and the unknowledgeable. A rule allowing restrained advertising would be in accord with the bar's obligation to facilitate the process of intelligent selection of lawyers, and to assist in making legal services fully available." The Court acknowledged that "[a]dvertising does not provide a complete foundation on which to select an attorney," but went on to observe that "it seems peculiar to deny the consumer . . . at least some of the relevant information needed to reach an informed decision."

In the years that followed *Bates*, the Supreme Court continued to take up a variety of cases involving questions about state regulations of lawyer advertising. The Court struck down a rule constraining the American Civil Liberties Union from in-person solicitation, but upheld a rule banning ambulance chasers. A categorical ban on direct mailings to potential clients was struck, but a thirty day waiting period for sending such mailings upheld. The Court held that mandatory disclosures did not violate the First Amendment, but that some restrictions on the content of advertising might. Lower courts and disciplinary authorities continually grapple with questions about lawyer advertising, often reaching inconsistent results.

A state-by-state patchwork of advertising restrictions currently exists throughout the country. Although no jurisdiction bans lawyer advertising completely, many place significant restrictions on the content and the timing. At one end of the spectrum, some jurisdictions merely prohibit false or misleading advertising. At the other end, some jurisdictions impose heavy burdens, such as mandatory disclaimers, waiting periods, and pre-approval of advertising content by the regulatory authority. The American Bar Association, for its part, adopted Model Rules of Professional Conduct in 1983 to govern advertising and solicitation. While the Model Rules are simply that—models—most jurisdictions are heavily influenced by them. Model Rule 7.2 expressly authorizes lawyer advertising "subject to the requirements of Rules 7.1 and 7.3 . . . through public media, such as a telephone directory, legal directory, newspaper or other period-ical, outdoor advertising, radio or television, or through written or recorded communication." Rule 7.1 provides that "[a] lawyer shall not make a false or misleading communication about the lawyer or the lawyer's services." Rule 7.3 lays out the parameters for in-person or written solicitation of prospective clients. States subsequently adopted regulatory provisions based upon the ABA Model Rules, though they vary wildly in their specific requirements.

Even with these burdensome restrictions, advertising plays a significant role in the legal services markets. Lawyers spend millions of dollars annually on legal advertising, close to $800 million in 2016. While much of this goes to television commercials, increasingly lawyers invest in Internet advertising such as individual websites, pop-up ads, and search engine optimization Indeed, legal terms dominate Google's keyword search terms purchases, with "nine out of the top 10 and 23 of the top 25" terms being legal terms in 2015. The most expensive phrase is "San Antonio car wreck attorney," which cost $670.

* * *

The results of our empirical study lead us to several recommendations for regulatory interventions and related efforts to enhance consumer understanding about legal services.

First, we propose that policy-makers require certain disclosures or disclaimers to address consumer irrationality and biases. Some jurisdictions already require these sorts of statements[2] but the rules may be under-enforced. For example, New York requires a specific disclaimer when lawyers advertise about past success, though our study revealed that not all websites are in compliance. We recommend the requirement of disclaimers for statements about past success and client testimonials. While the effectiveness of disclosures is questioned in some contexts, for example the consumer credit literature, the unique circumstances of legal representation support their use. In other contexts, people have strongly criticized disclosures as a remedy for market failure. People argue that consumers ignore disclosures, that they cannot understand disclosures,[3] and that they cannot use disclosures in complex markets. While we are sympathetic to these critiques of traditional disclosure regimes, we do not think they are fatal to our suggestion here. At a minimum, disclosures are a signaling and, at best, they are informative. One model that might be adopted is the Federal Trade Commission's adequate substantiation standard, which requires that an "advertiser should possess and rely upon adequate substantiation" when making representations containing endorsements.

Second, we encourage lawyers to consider the images and readability of their websites. Studies show that individuals are more likely to engage with and trust professionals who reflect their own identities and personal characteristics. Readability is important for helping individuals address their legal issues, whether or not the ultimately hire an attorney, but it also may increase the likelihood that an individual will do so. Lawyers wanting to expand their client base would be especially wise to heed the findings of our study.

Third, we call on bar associations and legal education institutions use advertising to engage in education campaigns in order to remedy market failure. As the *Bates* Court observed: "it is the bar's role to assure that the populace is sufficiently informed [about legal services] as to enable it to place advertising in its proper perspective." We echo this observation, and expand it to law schools. One of us previously called for "democratizing legal education" with law schools "banding together to conduct a wide-spread public information campaign to encourage access to legal services." Our study here reinforces the need for this sort of education.

---

2   *See, e.g.*, Zauderer v. Office of Disciplinary Counsel, 471 U.S. 626, 627 (1985) (holding that mandated disclosure regarding payment of costs in lawyer advertisement does not violate the first amendment); Milavetz, Gallop & Milavetz, P.A. v. United States, 559 U.S. 229, 252–53 (2010) (applying *Zauderer* to uphold mandated disclosure in advertising by lawyers for bankruptcy-related services).

3   Debra Pogrund Star & Jessica M. Choplin, *A Cognitive and Social Psychological Analysis of Disclosure Laws and Call for Mortgage Counseling to Prevent Predatory Lending*, 16 PSYCHOL. PUB. POL'Y & L. 85, 98 (2010).

Nearly a half century after the U.S. Supreme Court liberalized lawyer advertising rules to increase public information about and access to legal services, the same access to justice gap endures. Our pioneering advertising study of lawyer websites and Avvo profiles helps explain the persisting market failure. We found that advertising is not aimed at rational consumers like *Bates* envisioned but instead that some advertising exploits systematic poor decision-making. Also, far from Blackmun's vision of advertising reaching the marginalized, current advertisements focus on pictures of white men and contain text that is inaccessible to many people with legal needs. New avenues of regulation are needed to cultivate advertising that enhances the efficiency of the legal services market, in particular expanding access to information about legal representation for those in need. Lawyer advertising should include disclaimers about prior successes and testimonials; lawyers should consider advertising images and readability; and bar associations as well as law schools should work together supporting public information campaigns. *Bates*'s vision for expanded access to legal services has been unrealized, but it does not have to be. Our study offers empirical evidence of the causes for advertising's failure and of potential solutions to makes *Bates*'s goals a reality.

RENEE NEWMAN KNAKE, *WHY LAW STUDENTS SHOULD BE THINKING ABOUT ENTREPRENEURSHIP AND INNOVATION IN LEGAL SERVICES*

Bloomberg Law, December 2012

Legal expertise no longer is sufficient to cultivate a rewarding and meaningful career in the law. All the legal knowledge in the world is of little value if clients cannot access it.

One of the most pressing issues facing the profession in the 21st century is the "justice gap": millions of people who need legal representation cannot afford or access a lawyer. The overwhelming majority of this country goes without much-needed legal help because they simply cannot afford to pay a lawyer three-figures-per-hour for multiple hours, but they also do not qualify for the limited legal aid programs available. The legal profession faces a delivery problem—we have failed to develop viable models for delivering legal services that are affordable, accessible and, importantly, adopted by clients who utilize them on a regular, long-term basis.

Meanwhile, thousands of lawyers are unemployed, and law schools continue to graduate new attorneys at record levels. For these attorneys, individuals in the gap represent an opportunity— an enormous untapped market. Thus the legal profession also faces a matching problem—we struggle to pair appropriately qualified lawyers with clients who need them.

These delivery and matching problems are not new, but they have become particularly acute given the recent convergence of economic pressures, global competition, and technological advances. Law schools excel at producing legal experts, but the delivery and matching problems faced by the profession largely go ignored by legal education. Students are left to their own resources. The luckiest come to law school with a background in innovation and entrepreneurship and others might obtain a joint degree that exposes them to these ideas. But this is not the case for most.

Our challenge is to create better delivery models that match appropriately qualified lawyers with the clients who need them. To find a solution, we need fuel to entrepreneurship and innovation in legal services.

A handful of other law schools also are beginning to recognize the importance of these sorts of classes within the curriculum. For students not at these schools, however, there are ways to be exposed to entrepreneurship and law practice innovation beyond the classroom. Here are a few ideas:

Read. According to Reid Hoffman, the founder of LinkedIn, everyone was born an entrepreneur. Even if you have no interest in starting your own business, knowledge of entrepreneurial skills can help you navigate toward a more rewarding and meaningful career. Pick up a copy of Hoffman's *The Start-up of You: Adapt to the Future, Invest in Yourself, and Transform Your Career*. Another recommended read for nurturing the inner-entrepreneur is Daniel Pink's *A Whole New Mind: Why Right-Brainers Will Rule the Future*. Although Pink predicts that the future for left-brained, analytical lawyers looks rather bleak, he offers encouraging guidance on how we left-brainers can embrace and capitalize on what he calls the coming "Conceptual Age."

Follow. A number of blogs track innovation and technology development in legal services. Follow them regularly, and you'll quickly become well-versed in the leading issues. LegalFutures covers the United Kingdom's incredible boom of "alternative business structures" in the wake of regulatory liberalization under the Legal Services Act. Law21 focuses heavily on innovation in law practice, with thoughtful posts forecasting the future for lawyers and providing the latest news on all things related to law, technology, and new legal services markets. The eLawyering Blog addresses all elements of virtual law practice, including law startups, marketing online legal services, and offering legal advice online. Computational Legal Studies blog curates an array of resources to inform and inspire on law, computational and complex systems, and beyond.

Explore. Take a look at some of the newest innovators and entrepreneurs on the legal services scene. LegalZoom and RocketLawyer offer online forms and services. LawGives, LawPivot, and LawZam aim to solve the matching problem in unique ways by connecting lawyers with those who need them. Docracy, a recent startup that emerged from a NYC TechCrunch Disrupt Hackathon, allows users to locate, edit, and execute electronic, crowd-sourced legal documents—for free. If you happen to be in Santa Monica, California, grab a cup of coffee at Legal Grind, where you will find lawyers in a community café setting. Chicago's Legal Café provides a similar service. LegalForce is opening a Palo Alto store, selling computer tablets and connecting customers to legal services. In the United Kingdom, businesses like Legal365 and Riverview Law are trying to meet the legal needs of those in the gap by offering free and low cost services online. Other British companies are focused on personal delivery. For example, you can connect

Global Perspective

Regulators in the United States have had to decide how their ethics codes apply to social media use by lawyers and judges. For a global perspective on the social media issue, you can consult this International Bar Association webpage.

with a lawyer while picking up a newspaper at the WHSmith through a QualitySolicitors kiosk, or while shopping and banking with the Co-operative.

Learn. Learning new technology is a great way to foster one's entrepreneurial and innovative nature. Want to build your own website? Visit Codecademy, which makes learning to code simple, fun, and interactive. Or search YouTube for instruction on WordPress, website hosting, and basic HTML coding.

* * *

Pitch. Spend a weekend inventing new models for legal services delivery and pitch the business plan to competition judges at a Startup Weekend, where winners leave with their startup launched. Startup Weekends have been held in over 600 cities around the world, and more than 300 are planned for the coming months. Or crowd-source seed money for your imaginative legal services idea at Kickstarter, an online platform for funding creative projects.

The time has come for legal services to be affordable, accessible, and adopted widely. The market for law and technology has been described as an "unpopulated multi-billion dollar industry." The question for today's law students is whether they will be left behind as others fill the gap, or whether they will seize the opportunity for innovation and entrepreneurship, pioneer new legal services delivery models, and help find a solution.

* * *

Hear from the Authors

Lawyer marketing and advertising changes rapidly with technology advances, and often the Rules do not cover these innovations. To hear more from the authors on examples of these changes, click here.

Legal Ethics for Big Data Analytics

RENEE KNAKE, *HOW BIG DATA ANALYTICS IS CHANGING LEGAL ETHICS*

Bloomberg Law, August 10, 2016

Big data analytics is changing how lawyers find clients, conduct legal research and discovery, draft contracts and court papers, manage billing and performance, predict the outcome of a matter, select juries, and more. Ninety percent of corporate legal departments, law firms, and government lawyers note that data analytics are applied in their organizations, albeit in limited ways, according to a 2015 survey. The Legal Services Corporation, the largest funder of civil legal aid for low-income individuals in the United States, recommended in 2012 that all states collect and assess data on case progress/outcomes to improve the delivery of legal services. Lawyers across all sectors of the market increasingly recognize how big data tools can enhance their work.

A growing literature advocates for businesses and governmental bodies to adopt data ethics policies, and many have done so. It is not uncommon to find data-use policies prominently displayed on company or government websites, or required a part of a click-through consent before gaining access to a mobile app or webpage. Data ethics guidelines can help avoid controversies, especially when analytics are used in potentially manipulative or exploitive ways. Consider, for example, Target's data analytics that uncovered a teen's pregnancy before her father did, or Orbitz's data analytics offered pricier hotels to Mac users. These are just two of numerous examples in recent years where companies faced criticism for how they used data analytics.

While some law firms and legal services organizations follow data-use policies or codes of conduct, many do not. Perhaps this is because the legal profession was not transformed as early or rapidly as other industries, or because until now, big data in legal was largely limited to e-discovery, where the data use is confined to the litigation and is subject to judicial oversight. Another reason may be that lawyers believe their rules of professional conduct provide sufficient guidance and protection. Unlike other industries, lawyers are governed by a special code of ethical obligations to clients, the justice system, and the public. In most states, this code is based in part upon the American Bar Association (ABA) Model Rules of Professional Conduct, though rules often vary from jurisdiction to jurisdiction. Several of the Model Rules are relevant to big data use. That said, the Model Rules are insufficient for addressing a number of fundamental ethical concerns.

At the moment, legal ethics for big data analytics is at best an incomplete mix of professional conduct rules and informal policies adopted by some, but not all law practices. Given the increasing prevalence of data analytics in legal services, lawyers and law students should be familiar not only with the relevant professional conduct rules, but also the ethical questions left unanswered. Listed below is a brief summary of both, followed by a proposed legal ethics agenda for data analytics.

Lawyer Ethics Rules Relevant to Big Data Analytics

[Relevant lawyer ethics rules include the duty of communication, the duty of competence, the duty of confidentiality, the duty to maintain, preserve, and return client records, restrictions on advertising and solicitation, and supervision of nonlawyer assistants.]

Questions Unanswered by Lawyer Ethics Rules

Access/Ownership. Who owns the original data—the individual source or the holder of the pooled information? Who owns the insights drawn from its analysis? Who should receive access to the data compilation and the results?

Anonymity/Identity. Should all personally identifiable or sensitive information be removed from the data? What protections are necessary to respect individual autonomy? How should individuals be able to control and shape their electronic identity?

Consent. Should individuals affirmatively consent to use of their personal data? Or is it sufficient to provide notice, perhaps with an opt-out provision?

Privacy/Security. Should privacy be protected beyond the professional obligation of client confidentiality? How should data be secured? The ABA called upon private and public sector lawyers to implement cyber-security policies, including data use, in a 2012 resolution and produced a cyber-security handbook in 2013.

Process. How involved should lawyers be in the process of data collection and analysis? In the context of e-discovery, for example, a lawyer is expected to understand how documents are collected, produced, and preserved, or to work with a specialist. Should a similar level of knowledge be required for all forms of data analytics use?

Purpose. Why was the data first collected from individuals? What is the purpose for the current use? Is there a significant divergence between the original and secondary purposes? If so, is it necessary for the individuals to consent to the secondary purpose? How will unintended consequences be addressed?

Source. What is the source of the data? Did the lawyer collect it directly from clients, or is the lawyer relying upon a third-party source? Client-based data is, of course, subject to the lawyer's professional conduct rules. Data from any source should be trustworthy, reasonable, timely, complete, and verifiable.

A Legal Ethics Agenda for Big Data Analytics

The legal profession has an important role to play not only in how it uses data analytics to better serve clients and the public, but also in how society establishes data-use rules, standards, and norms throughout all aspects of daily life. Bar associations should consider adopting uniform rules or promulgating model, best-practice policies on legal ethics for big data. Similarly, all lawyers should develop and implement data-use policies to address the relevant professional conduct rules as well as the broader ethical concerns highlighted here.

B. Solicitation

In popular usage, advertising is often understood as a form of solicitation. In the field of legal ethics, however, the word "solicitation" is generally used as a term of art that refers to a targeted communication initiated by a lawyer directed to a specific person. *See* Delaware Rule 7.3. It is important to note that in 2018, the ABA amended Model Rules 7.1-7.3, and deleted Rules 7.4 and 7.5, moving much of their content to Rules 7.2 and 7.1, respectively. Presently, only Connecticut has adopted the ABA's amendments (effective, January 2020), and references in this section to the content of these revisions will be made to the amended Connecticut rules. Because other jurisdictions have yet to adopt the ABA's amendments, and because Rules 7.1-7.5 vary widely in content from jurisdiction to jurisdiction, this section will also quote and reference the pertinent ABA Model Rules as they existed pre-amendment by citing primarily to Delaware's Rules of Professional Conduct.

With regard to revised Rule 7.3 it is significant that, unlike the pre-2018 version, it alters the definition of "solicitation" by requiring that the person being solicited is known or reasonably believed to be in need of legal services in the particular matter. *See* Connecticut Rule 7.3(a) (based on post-2018 Model Rule 7.3(a)). Although marketing literature suggests that direct contact is the most effective way to obtain business, the ethics rules and cases reveal that solicitation also creates the greatest threat of harm to consumers. This Part will familiarize you with the rules you will need to follow when engaged in targeted communication with prospective clients.

Take Note

The ABA Standing Committee on Ethics and Professional Responsibility explained that the primary objective of the 2018 revisions was "to streamline the rules by placing similar concepts in the same rule, while adhering to both the constitutional limitations on restricting commercial speech and the public policy concerns of protecting the public from misleading information regarding legal services." *See Ad It Up: Model Rule 7.1-7.5* (June 26, 2018). The full ABA article can be accessed here. While Connecticut is the only jurisdiction, to date, that has adopted these recent amendments, it seems safe to predict that given the general purpose of the amendments, many others will choose to follow the ABA's lead. To review Connecticut's revised rules (effective, January 2020), which are substantially the same as those enacted by the ABA, click here.

[Question 3-1]

A criminal defense attorney used publicly available police report data to contact arrested persons whom the attorney had represented in the past and who might need legal representation again. The attorney sent the following text message to the former clients, using cell phone numbers obtained from the police records:

> *Do you need a lawyer? Police records show you were arrested last night. I have represented you before, and I am available to help you. Reply to this text 24/7 for more information.*

Is the attorney subject to discipline?

 (A) Yes, because the attorney solicited legal business from persons known to be in need of legal services.

 (B) Yes, because the attorney solicited legal business from persons who were not current clients.

 (C) No, because lawyers are always permitted to solicit prospective clients by text.

 (D) No, because the attorney solicited former clients.

Ohralik v. Ohio State Bar Association

<u>436 U.S. 447 (1978)</u>

POWELL, J., delivered the opinion of the Court

* * *

Appellant, a member of the Ohio Bar, lives in Montville, Ohio. * * * On February 13, 1974, while picking up his mail at the Montville Post Office, appellant learned from the postmaster's brother about an automobile accident that had taken place on February 2 in which Carol McClintock, a young woman with whom appellant was casually acquainted, had been injured. Appellant made a telephone call to Ms. McClintock's parents, who informed him that their daughter was in the hospital. Appellant suggested that he might visit Carol in the hospital. Mrs. McClintock assented to the idea, but requested that appellant first stop by at her home.

During appellant's visit with the McClintocks, they explained that their daughter had been driving the family automobile on a local road when she was hit by an uninsured motorist. Both Carol and her passenger, Wanda Lou Holbert, were injured and hospitalized. In response to the McClintocks' expression of apprehension that they might be sued by Holbert, appellant explained that Ohio's guest statute would preclude such a suit. When appellant suggested to the McClintocks that they hire a lawyer, Mrs. McClintock retorted that such a decision would be up to Carol, who was 18 years old and would be the beneficiary of a successful claim.

Appellant proceeded to the hospital, where he found Carol lying in traction in her room. After a brief conversation about her condition, appellant told Carol he would represent her and asked her to sign an agreement. Carol said she would have to discuss the matter with her parents. She did not sign the agreement, but asked appellant to have her parents come to see her. Appellant also attempted to see Wanda Lou Holbert, but learned that she had just been released from the hospital. * * * He then departed for another visit with the McClintocks.

On his way, appellant detoured to the scene of the accident, where he took a set of photographs. He also picked up a tape recorder, which he concealed under his raincoat before arriving at the McClintocks' residence. Once there, he re-examined their automobile insurance policy, discussed with them the law applicable to passengers, and explained the consequences of the fact that the driver who struck Carol's car was an uninsured motorist. Appellant discovered that the McClintocks' insurance policy would provide benefits of up to $12,500 each for Carol and Wanda Lou under an uninsured-motorist clause. Mrs. McClintock acknowledged that both Carol and Wanda Lou could sue for their injuries, but recounted to appellant that "Wanda swore up and down she would not do it." * * * The McClintocks also told appellant that Carol had phoned to say that appellant could "go ahead" with her representation. Two days later appellant returned to Carol's hospital room to have her sign a contract, which provided that he would receive one-third of her recovery.

In the meantime, appellant * * * visited Wanda Lou at her home, without having been invited. He again concealed his tape recorder and recorded most of the conversation with Wanda Lou. After a brief, unproductive inquiry about the facts of the accident, appellant told Wanda Lou that he was representing Carol and that he had a "little tip" for Wanda Lou: the McClintocks' insurance policy contained an uninsured-motorist clause which might provide her with a recovery of up to $12,500. The young woman, who was 18 years of age and not a high school graduate at the time, replied to appellant's query about whether she was going to file a claim by stating that she really did not understand what was going on. Appellant offered to represent her, also, for a contingent fee of one-third of any recovery, and Wanda Lou stated "O. K."

Wanda's mother attempted to repudiate her daughter's oral assent the following day, when appellant called on the telephone to speak to Wanda. Mrs. Holbert informed appellant that she and her daughter did not want to sue anyone or to have appellant represent them, and that if they decided to sue they would consult their own lawyer. Appellant insisted that Wanda had entered into a binding agreement. A month later Wanda confirmed in writing that she wanted neither to sue nor to be represented by appellant. She requested that appellant notify the insurance company that he was not her lawyer, as the company would not release a check to her until he did so. Carol also eventually discharged appellant. * * *

Both Carol McClintock and Wanda Lou Holbert filed [grievances against appellant with the County Bar Association. Ultimately, the Supreme Court of Ohio affirmed a disciplinary board's finding that appellant had violated DR 2-103(A) and DR 2-104(A) of the Ohio Code of Professional Responsibility.]

* * * We now affirm the judgment of the Supreme Court of Ohio.

II

FYI

In *Bates v. State Bar of Arizona*, 433 U.S. 350 (1977), the Court held that the ban on lawyer advertising—then in effect throughout the US—violated the First Amendment. In the wake of Bates, the Court decided a number of cases involving lawyer advertising and solicitation.

The solicitation of business by a lawyer through direct, in-person communication with the prospective client has long been viewed as inconsistent with the profession's ideal of the attorney-client relationship and as posing a significant potential for harm to the prospective client. It has been proscribed by the organized Bar for many years. Last Term the Court ruled that the justifications for prohibiting truthful, "restrained" advertising concerning "the availability and terms of routine legal services" are insufficient to override society's interest, safeguarded by the First and Fourteenth Amendments, in assuring the free flow of commercial information. * * * The balance struck in *Bates* [*v. State Bar of Arizona*, 433 U.S. 350 (1977)] does not predetermine the outcome in this case. The entitlement of in-person solicitation of clients to the protection of the First Amendment differs from that of the kind of advertising approved in *Bates*, as does the strength of the State's countervailing interest in prohibition.

A

Appellant contends that his solicitation of the two young women as clients is indistinguishable, for purposes of constitutional analysis, from the advertisement in *Bates*. Like that advertisement, his meetings with the prospective clients apprised them of their legal rights and of the availability of a lawyer to pursue their claims. According to appellant, such conduct is "presumptively an exercise of his free speech rights" which cannot be curtailed in the absence of proof that it actually caused a specific harm that the State has a compelling interest in preventing. But in-person solicitation of professional employment by a lawyer does not stand on a par with truthful advertising about the availability and terms of routine legal services, let alone with forms of speech more traditionally within the concern of the First Amendment.

* * *

In-person solicitation by a lawyer of remunerative employment is a business transaction in which speech is an essential but subordinate component. While this does not remove the speech from the protection of the First Amendment, as was held in *Bates* and *Virginia Pharmacy*, it lowers the level of appropriate judicial scrutiny.

As applied in this case, the Disciplinary Rules are said to have limited the communication of two kinds of information. First, appellant's solicitation imparted to Carol McClintock and Wanda Lou Holbert certain information about his availability and the terms of his proposed legal services. In this respect, in-person solicitation serves much the same function as the advertisement at issue in *Bates*. But there are significant differences as well. Unlike a public advertisement, which simply provides information and leaves the recipient free to act upon it or not, in-person solicitation may exert pressure and often demands an immediate response, without providing an opportunity for comparison or reflection. The aim and effect of in-person solicitation may be to provide a one-sided presentation and to encourage speedy and perhaps uninformed decisionmaking; there is no opportunity for intervention or counter-education by agencies of the Bar, supervisory authorities, or persons close to the solicited individual. The admonition that "the fitting remedy for evil counsels is good ones" is of little value when the circumstances provide no opportunity for any remedy at all. In-person solicitation is as likely as not to discourage persons needing counsel from engaging in a critical comparison of the "availability, nature, and prices" of legal services, it actually may disserve the individual and societal interest, identified in *Bates*, in facilitating "informed and reliable decisionmaking."

* * *

B

The state interests implicated in this case are particularly strong. In addition to its general interest in protecting consumers and regulating commercial transactions, the State bears a special responsibility for maintaining standards among members of the licensed professions. "The interest of the States in regulating lawyers is especially great since lawyers are essential to the primary governmental function of administering justice, and have historically been 'officers of the courts.' " While lawyers act in part as "self-employed businessmen," they also act "as trusted agents of their clients, and as assistants to the court in search of a just solution to disputes."

As is true with respect to advertising, it appears that the ban on solicitation by lawyers originated as a rule of professional etiquette rather than as a strictly ethical rule. "[T]he rules are based in part on deeply ingrained feelings of tradition, honor and service. Lawyers have for centuries emphasized that the promotion of justice, rather than the earning of fees, is the goal of the profession." But the fact that the original motivation behind the ban on solicitation today might be considered an insufficient justification for its perpetuation does not detract from the force of the other interests the ban continues to serve. While the Court in *Bates* determined that truthful, restrained advertising of the prices of "routine" legal services would not have an adverse effect on the professionalism of lawyers, this was only because it found "the postulated connection between advertising and the erosion of true professionalism to be severely strained." The *Bates* Court did not question a State's interest in maintaining high standards among licensed professionals. Indeed, to the extent that the ethical standards of lawyers are linked to the service and protection of clients, they do further the goals of "true professionalism."

The substantive evils of solicitation have been stated over the years in sweeping terms: stirring up litigation, assertion of fraudulent claims, debasing the legal profession, and potential harm to the solicited client in the form of overreaching, overcharging, underrepresentation, and misrepresentation. The American Bar Association, as amicus curiae, defends the rule against solicitation primarily on three broad grounds: It is said that the prohibitions embodied in DR2-103(A) and 2-104(A) serve to reduce the likelihood of overreaching and the exertion of undue influence on lay persons, to protect the privacy of individuals, and to avoid situations where the lawyer's exercise of judgment on behalf of the client will be clouded by his own pecuniary self-interest.

We need not discuss or evaluate each of these interests in detail as appellant has conceded that the State has a legitimate and indeed "compelling" interest in preventing those aspects of solicitation that involve fraud, undue influence, intimidation, overreaching, and other forms of "vexatious conduct." We agree that protection of the public from these aspects of solicitation is a legitimate and important state interest.

III

Appellant's concession that strong state interests justify regulation to prevent the evils he enumerates would end this case but for his insistence that none of those evils was found to be present in his acts of solicitation.

* * *

Appellant's argument misconceives the nature of the State's interest. The Rules prohibiting solicitation are prophylactic measures whose objective is the prevention of harm before it occurs. The Rules were applied in this case to discipline a lawyer for soliciting employment for pecuniary gain under circumstances likely to result in the adverse consequences the State seeks to avert. In such a situation, which is inherently conducive to overreaching and other forms of misconduct, the State has a strong interest in adopting and enforcing rules of conduct designed to protect the public from harmful solicitation by lawyers whom it has licensed.

The State's perception of the potential for harm in circumstances such as those presented in this case is well founded. The detrimental aspects of face-to-face selling even of ordinary consumer products have been recognized and addressed by the Federal Trade Commission, and it hardly need be said that the potential for overreaching is significantly greater when a lawyer, a professional trained in the art of persuasion, personally solicits an unsophisticated, injured, or distressed lay person. Such an individual may place his trust in a lawyer, regardless of the latter's qualifications or the individual's actual need for legal representation, simply in response to persuasion under circumstances conducive to uninformed acquiescence. Although it is argued that personal solicitation is valuable because it may apprise a victim of misfortune of his legal rights, the very plight of that person not only makes him more vulnerable to influence but also may make advice all the more intrusive. Thus, under these adverse conditions the overtures of an uninvited lawyer may distress the solicited individual simply because of their obtrusiveness and the invasion of the individual's privacy, even when no other harm materializes. Under such circumstances, it is not unreasonable for the State to presume that in-person solicitation by lawyers more often than not will be injurious to the person solicited.

The efficacy of the State's effort to prevent such harm to prospective clients would be substantially diminished if, having proved a solicitation in circumstances like those of this case, the State were required in addition to prove actual injury. Unlike the advertising in *Bates*, in-person solicitation is not visible or otherwise open to public scrutiny. Often there is no witness other than the lawyer and the lay person whom he has solicited, rendering it difficult or impossible to obtain reliable proof of what actually took place. This would be especially true if the lay person were so distressed at the time of the solicitation that he could not recall specific details at a later date. If appellant's view were sustained, in-person solicitation would be virtually immune to effective oversight and regulation by the State or by the legal profession, in contravention of the State's strong interest in regulating members of the Bar in an effective, objective, and self-enforcing manner. It therefore is not unreasonable, or violative of the Constitution, for a State to respond with what in effect is a prophylactic rule.

* * *

We hold that the application of DR2-103(A) and 2-104(A) to appellant does not offend the Constitution.

Accordingly, the judgment of the Supreme Court of Ohio is

Affirmed.

Delaware Rule 7.3 Solicitation of Clients (based on pre-2018 Model Rule 7.3)

(a)   A lawyer shall not by in-person, live telephone or real-time electronic contact solicit professional employment when a significant motive for the lawyer's doing so is the lawyer's pecuniary gain, unless the person contacted:

(1)   is a lawyer; or

(2)   has a family, close personal, or prior professional relationship with the lawyer.

(b)   A lawyer should not solicit professional employment by written, recorded or electronic communication or by in-person, telephone or real-time electronic contact even when not otherwise prohibited by paragraph (a), if:

(1)   the target of the solicitation has made known to the lawyer a desire not to be solicited by the lawyer; or

(2)   the solicitation involves coercion, duress or harassment.

Take Note

The version of Rule 7.3 quoted was substantially revised by the ABA in August 2018. As already noted, Connecticut is the only jurisdiction, at present, that has adopted Rule 7.3, as amended by the ABA. Connecticut's revised Rule 7.3 can be accessed here. Be sure to note the differences between this version and the Delaware version. One difference of particular significance is the addition of an exemption from the rule's "person-to-person" solicitation prohibition, namely contact "[w]ith a person who routinely uses for business purposes the type of legal services offered by the lawyer." Connecticut Rule 7.3(b)(4) (which is essentially the same as Model Rule 7.3(b)(3), as amended). It is now permissible under the amended rule for lawyers to directly solicit professional employment from such persons.

[Question 3-2]

An attorney, working pro bono, solicited plaintiffs for a potential lawsuit challenging a requirement that pregnant mothers be sterilized in order to continue receiving government financial assistance. The attorney knew that all of the individuals he solicited were pregnant mothers who would be affected by the requirement. Is the attorney subject to discipline?

(A)   No, because the attorney was working pro bono.

(B)   No, because the attorney solicited plaintiffs before he filed the lawsuit.

(C)   Yes, because the attorney knew that the individuals he solicited were in need of legal services.

(D)   Yes, because lawyers may never solicit prospective clients.

With Delaware Rule 7.3 (based on pre-2018 Model Rule 7.3) in mind, consider the following case, decided on the same day as *Ohralik*. Also, consider whether the outcome would have been different under Connecticut Rule 7.3 (based on post-2018 Model Rule 7.3).

In re Primus

436 U.S. 412 (1978)

MR. JUSTICE POWELL delivered the opinion of the Court.

We consider on this appeal whether a State may punish a member of its Bar who, seeking to further political and ideological goals through associational activity, including litigation, advises a lay person of her legal rights and discloses in a subsequent letter that free legal assistance is available from a nonprofit organization with which the lawyer and her associates are affiliated. Appellant, a member of the Bar of South Carolina, received a public reprimand for writing such a letter. The appeal is opposed by the State Attorney General, on behalf of the Board of Commissioners on Grievances and Discipline of the Supreme Court of South Carolina. As this appeal presents a substantial question under the First and Fourteenth Amendments, as interpreted in *NAACP v. Button*, we noted probable jurisdiction.

I

Appellant, Edna Smith Primus, is a lawyer practicing in Columbia, S.C. During the period in question, she was associated with the "Carolina Community Law Firm," and was an officer of and cooperating lawyer with the Columbia branch of the American Civil Liberties Union (ACLU). She received no compensation for her work on behalf of the ACLU, but was paid a retainer as a legal consultant for the South Carolina Council on Human Relations (Council), a nonprofit organization with offices in Columbia.

During the summer of 1973, local and national newspapers reported that pregnant mothers on public assistance in Aiken County, S.C., were being sterilized or threatened with sterilization as a condition of the continued receipt of medical assistance under the Medicaid program. Concerned by this development, Gary Allen, an Aiken businessman and officer of a local organization serving indigents, called the Council requesting that one of its representatives come to Aiken to address some of the women who had been sterilized. At the Council's behest, appellant, who had not known Allen previously, called him and arranged a meeting in his office in July 1973. Among those attending was Mary Etta Williams, who had been sterilized by Dr. Clovis H. Pierce after the birth of her third child. Williams and her grandmother attended the meeting because Allen, an old family friend, had invited them and because Williams wanted "[t]o see what it was all about. . . ." At the meeting, appellant advised those present, including Williams and the other women who had been sterilized by Dr. Pierce, of their legal rights and suggested the possibility of a lawsuit.

Early in August 1973 the ACLU informed appellant that it was willing to provide representation for Aiken mothers who had been sterilized. Appellant testified that after being advised by Allen that Williams wished to institute suit against Dr. Pierce, she decided to inform Williams of the ACLU's offer of free legal representation. Shortly after receiving appellant's letter, dated August 30, 1973 the centerpiece of this litigation—Williams visited Dr. Pierce to discuss the progress of her third child who was ill. At the doctor's office, she encountered his lawyer and at the latter's request signed a release of liability in the doctor's favor. Williams showed appellant's letter to the doctor and his lawyer, and they retained a copy. She then called appellant from the doctor's office and announced her intention not to sue. There was no further communication between appellant and Williams.

On October 9, 1974, the Secretary of the Board of Commissioners on Grievances and Discipline of the Supreme Court of South Carolina (Board) filed a formal complaint with the Board, charging that appellant had engaged in "solicitation in violation of the Canons of Ethics" by sending the August 30, 1973, letter to Williams. Appellant denied any unethical solicitation and asserted, *inter alia*, that her conduct was protected by the First and Fourteenth Amendments and by Canon 2 of the Code of Professional Responsibility of the American Bar Association (ABA). The complaint was heard by a panel of the Board on March 20, 1975. The State's evidence consisted of the letter, the testimony of Williams, and a copy of the summons and complaint in the action instituted against Dr. Pierce and various state officials[.] Following denial of appellant's motion to dismiss, she testified in her own behalf and called Allen, a number of ACLU representatives, and several character witnesses.

The panel filed a report recommending that appellant be found guilty of soliciting a client on behalf of the ACLU, in violation of Disciplinary Rules (DR) 2-103(D)(5)(a) and (c) and 2-104(A)(5) of the Supreme Court of South Carolina, and that a private reprimand be issued. It noted that "[t]he evidence is inconclusive as to whether [appellant] solicited Mrs. Williams on her own behalf, but she did solicit Mrs. Williams on behalf of the ACLU, which would benefit financially in the event of successful prosecution of the suit for money damages." The panel determined that appellant violated DR 2-103(D)(5) "by attempting to solicit a client for a non-profit organization which, as its primary purpose, renders legal services, where respondent's associate is a staff counsel for the non-profit organization." Appellant also was found to have violated DR 2-104(A)(5) because she solicited Williams, after providing unsolicited legal advice, to join in a prospective class action for damages and other relief that was to be brought by the ACLU.

After a hearing on January 9, 1976, the full Board approved the panel report and administered a private reprimand. On March 17, 1977, the Supreme Court of South Carolina entered an order which adopted verbatim the findings and conclusions of the panel report and increased the sanction, *sua sponte*, to a public reprimand.

On July 9, 1977, appellant filed a jurisdictional statement and this appeal was docketed. * * * We now reverse.

II

This appeal concerns the tension between contending values of considerable moment to the legal profession and to society. Relying upon *NAACP v. Button*, and its progeny, appellant maintains that her activity involved constitutionally protected expression and association. In her view, South Carolina has not shown that the discipline meted out to her advances a subordinating state interest in a manner that avoids unnecessary abridgment of First Amendment freedoms. Appellee counters that appellant's letter to Williams falls outside of the protection of *Button*, and that South Carolina acted lawfully in punishing a member of its Bar for solicitation.

The States enjoy broad power to regulate "the practice of professions within their boundaries," and "[t]he interest of the States in regulating lawyers is especially great since lawyers are essential to the primary governmental function of administering justice, and have historically been 'officers of the courts.' " *Goldfarb v. Virginia State Bar*, 421 U.S. 773, 792. For example, we decide today in *Ohralik v. Ohio State Bar Assn.* that the States may vindicate legitimate regulatory interests through proscription, in certain circumstances, of in-person solicitation by lawyers who seek to communicate purely commercial offers of legal assistance to lay persons.

Unlike the situation in *Ohralik*, however, appellant's act of solicitation took the form of a letter to a woman with whom appellant had discussed the possibility of seeking redress for an allegedly unconstitutional sterilization. This was not in-person solicitation for pecuniary gain. Appellant was communicating an offer of free assistance by attorneys associated with the ACLU, not an offer predicated on entitlement to a share of any monetary recovery. And her actions were undertaken to express personal political beliefs and to advance the civil-liberties objectives of the ACLU, rather than to derive financial gain. The question presented in this case is whether, in light of the values protected by the First and Fourteenth Amendments, these differences materially affect the scope of state regulation of the conduct of lawyers.

III

In *Button, supra*, the Supreme Court of Appeals of Virginia had held that the activities of members and staff attorneys of the National Association for the Advancement of Colored People (NAACP) and its affiliate, the Virginia State Conference of NAACP Branches (Conference), constituted "solicitation of legal business" in violation of state law. Although the NAACP representatives and staff attorneys had "a right to peaceably assemble with the members of the branches and other groups to discuss with them and advise them relative to their legal rights in matters concerning racial segregation," the court found no constitutional protection for efforts to "solicit prospective litigants to authorize the filing of suits" by NAACP-compensated attorneys.

This Court reversed: "We hold that the activities of the NAACP, its affiliates and legal staff shown on this record are modes of expression and association protected by the First and Fourteenth Amendments which Virginia may not prohibit, under its power to regulate the legal profession, as improper solicitation of legal business violative of [state law] and the Canons of Professional Ethics." The solicitation of prospective litigants, many of whom were not members of the NAACP or the Conference, for the purpose of furthering the civil-rights objectives of the organization and its members was held to come within the right " 'to engage in association for the advancement of beliefs and ideas.' "

Since the Virginia statute sought to regulate expressive and associational conduct at the core of the First Amendment's protective ambit, the *Button* Court insisted that "government may regulate in the area only with narrow specificity." * * * The Court concluded that "although the [NAACP] has amply shown that its activities fall within the First Amendment's protections, the State has failed to advance any substantial regulatory interest in the form of substantive evils flowing from [the NAACP's] activities, which can justify the broad prohibitions which it has imposed."

Subsequent decisions have interpreted *Button* as establishing the principle that "collective activity undertaken to obtain meaningful access to the courts is a fundamental right within the protection of the First Amendment." The Court has held that the First and Fourteenth Amendments prevent state proscription of a range of solicitation activities by labor unions seeking to provide low-cost, effective legal representation to their members.

IV

We turn now to the question whether appellant's conduct implicates interests of free expression and association sufficient to justify the level of protection recognized in *Button* and subsequent cases. The Supreme Court of South Carolina found appellant to have engaged in unethical conduct because she " 'solicit[ed] a client for a non-profit organization, which, as its primary purpose, renders legal services, where respondent's associate is a staff counsel for the non-profit organization.' " It rejected appellant's First Amendment defenses by distinguishing *Button* from the case before it. Whereas the NAACP in that case was primarily a " 'political' " organization that used " 'litigation as an adjunct to the overriding political aims of the organization,' " the ACLU " 'has as one of its primary purposes the rendition of legal services.' " The court also intimated that the ACLU's policy of requesting an award of counsel fees indicated that the organization might " 'benefit financially in the event of successful prosecution of the suit for money damages.' "

Although the disciplinary panel did not permit full factual development of the aims and practices of the ACLU, the record does not support the state court's effort to draw a meaningful distinction between the ACLU and the NAACP. From all that appears, the ACLU and its local chapters, much like the NAACP and its local affiliates in *Button*, "[engage] in extensive educational and lobbying activities" and "also [devote] much of [their] funds and energies to an extensive program of assisting certain kinds of litigation on behalf of [their] declared purposes." * * * The court below acknowledged that " 'the ACLU has only entered cases in which substantial civil liberties questions are involved . . . ' " It has engaged in the defense of unpopular causes and unpopular defendants and has represented individuals in litigation that has defined the scope of constitutional protection in areas such as political dissent, juvenile rights, prisoners' rights, military law, amnesty, and privacy. * * * For the ACLU, as for the NAACP, "litigation is not a technique of resolving private differences"; it is "a form of political expression" and "political association." * * *

We find equally unpersuasive any suggestion that the level of constitutional scrutiny in this case should be lowered because of a possible benefit to the ACLU. The discipline administered to appellant was premised solely on the possibility of financial benefit to the organization, rather than any possibility of pecuniary gain to herself, her associates, or the lawyers representing the plaintiffs in the *Walker v. Pierce* litigation. It is conceded that appellant received no compensation for any of the activities in question. It is also undisputed that neither the ACLU nor any lawyer associated with it would have shared in any monetary recovery by the plaintiffs in *Walker v. Pierce*. If Williams had elected to bring suit, and had been represented by staff lawyers for the ACLU, the situation would have been similar to that in *Button*, where the lawyers for the NAACP were "organized as a staff and paid by" that organization.

Contrary to appellee's suggestion, the ACLU's policy of requesting an award of counsel fees does not take this case outside the protection of *Button*. Although the Court in *Button* did not consider whether the NAACP seeks counsel fees, such requests are often made both by that organization, * * * and by the NAACP Legal Defense Fund, Inc. * * * In any event, in a case of this kind there are differences between counsel fees awarded by a court and traditional fee-paying arrangements which militate against a presumption that ACLU sponsorship of litigation is motivated by considerations of pecuniary gain rather than by its widely recognized goal of vindicating civil liberties. Counsel fees are awarded in the discretion of the court; awards are not drawn from the plaintiff's recovery, and are usually premised on a successful outcome; and the amounts awarded often may not correspond to fees generally obtainable in private litigation. Moreover, under prevailing law during the events in question, an award of counsel fees in federal litigation was available only in limited circumstances. And even if there had been an award during the period in question, it would have gone to the central fund of the ACLU. Although such benefit to the organization may increase with the maintenance of successful litigation, the same situation obtains with voluntary contributions and foundation support, which also may rise with ACLU victories in important areas of the law. That possibility, standing alone, offers no basis for equating the work of lawyers associated with the ACLU or the NAACP with that of a group that exists for the primary purpose of financial gain through the recovery of counsel fees.

Appellant's letter of August 30, 1973, to Mrs. Williams thus comes within the generous zone of First Amendment protection reserved for associational freedoms. The ACLU engages in litigation as a vehicle for effective political expression and association, as well as a means of communicating useful information to the public. * * * As *Button* indicates, and as appellant offered to prove at the disciplinary hearing, * * * the efficacy of litigation as a means of advancing the cause of civil liberties often depends on the ability to make legal assistance available to suitable litigants. " 'Free trade in ideas' means free trade in the opportunity to persuade to action, not merely to describe facts." * * * The First and Fourteenth Amendments require a measure of protection for "advocating lawful means of vindicating legal rights," including "advis[ing] another that his legal rights have been infringed and refer[ring] him to a particular attorney or group of attorneys . . . for assistance[.]"

V

South Carolina's action in punishing appellant for soliciting a prospective litigant by mail, on behalf of the ACLU, must withstand the "exacting scrutiny applicable to limitations on core

First Amendment rights . . . ." South Carolina must demonstrate "a subordinating interest which is compelling," and that the means employed in furtherance of that interest are "closely drawn to avoid unnecessary abridgment of associational freedoms."

Appellee contends that the disciplinary action taken in this case is part of a regulatory program aimed at the prevention of undue influence, overreaching, misrepresentation, invasion of privacy, conflict of interest, lay interference, and other evils that are thought to inhere generally in solicitation by lawyers of prospective clients, and to be present on the record before us. * * * We do not dispute the importance of these interests. This Court's decision in *Button* makes clear, however, that "[b]road prophylactic rules in the area of free expression are suspect," and that "[p]recision of regulation must be the touchstone in an area so closely touching our most precious freedoms." Because of the danger of censorship through selective enforcement of broad prohibitions, and "[b]ecause First Amendment freedoms need breathing space to survive, government may regulate in [this] area only with narrow specificity."

A

The Disciplinary Rules in question sweep broadly. Under DR 2-103(D)(5), a lawyer employed by the ACLU or a similar organization may never give unsolicited advice to a lay person that he retain the organization's free services, and it would seem that one who merely assists or maintains a cooperative relationship with the organization also must suppress the giving of such advice if he or anyone associated with the organization will be involved in the ultimate litigation. * * *

B

Even if we ignore the breadth of the Disciplinary Rules and the absence of findings in the decision below that support the justifications advanced by appellee in this Court, we think it clear from the record—which appellee does not suggest is inadequately developed—that findings compatible with the First Amendment could not have been made in this case. As in *New York Times Co. v. Sullivan*, 376 U.S. 254, 284–285, "considerations of effective judicial administration require us to review the evidence in the present record to determine whether it could constitutionally support a judgment [against appellant]. This Court's duty is not limited to the elaboration of constitutional principles; we must also in proper cases review the evidence to make certain that those principles [can be] constitutionally applied." * * *

Where political expression or association is at issue, this Court has not tolerated the degree of imprecision that often characterizes government regulation of the conduct of commercial affairs. The approach we adopt today in *Ohralik*, 436 U.S. 447, that the State may proscribe in-person solicitation for pecuniary gain under circumstances likely to result in adverse consequences, cannot be applied to appellant's activity on behalf of the ACLU. Although a showing of potential danger may suffice in the former context, appellant may not be disciplined unless her activity in fact involved the type of misconduct at which South Carolina's broad prohibition is said to be directed.

The record does not support appellee's contention that undue influence, overreaching, misrepresentation, or invasion of privacy actually occurred in this case. Appellant's letter of August 30, 1973, followed up the earlier meeting—one concededly protected by the First and Fourteenth Amendments—by notifying Williams that the ACLU would be interested in supporting possible litigation. The letter imparted additional information material to making an informed decision about whether to authorize litigation, and permitted Williams an opportunity, which she exercised, for arriving at a deliberate decision. The letter was not facially misleading; indeed, it offered "to explain what is involved so you can understand what is going on." The transmittal of this letter-as contrasted with in-person solicitation-involved no appreciable invasion of privacy; nor did it afford any significant opportunity for overreaching or coercion. Moreover, the fact that there was a written communication lessens substantially the difficulty of policing solicitation practices that do offend valid rules of professional conduct. *See Ohralik*, 436 U.S., at 466–467. The manner of solicitation in this case certainly was no more likely to cause harmful consequences than the activity considered in *Button*. * * *

Nor does the record permit a finding of a serious likelihood of conflict of interest or injurious lay interference with the attorney-client relationship. Admittedly, there is some potential for such conflict or interference whenever a lay organization supports any litigation. That potential was present in *Button*, in the NAACP's solicitation of nonmembers and its disavowal of any relief short of full integration. But the Court found that potential insufficient in the absence of proof of a "serious danger" of conflict of interest, or of organizational interference with the actual conduct of the litigation. As in *Button*, "[n]othing that this record shows as to the nature and purpose of [ACLU] activities permits an inference of any injurious intervention in or control of litigation which would constitutionally authorize the application" of the Disciplinary Rules to appellant's activity. A "very distant possibility of harm," cannot justify proscription of the activity of appellant revealed by this record.

The State's interests in preventing the "stirring up" of frivolous or vexatious litigation and minimizing commercialization of the legal profession offer no further justification for the discipline administered in this case. The *Button* Court declined to accept the proffered analogy to the common-law offenses of maintenance, champerty, and barratry, where the record would not support a finding that the litigant was solicited for a malicious purpose or "for private gain, serving no public interest[.]" The same result follows from the facts of this case. And considerations of undue commercialization of the legal profession are of marginal force where, as here, a nonprofit organization offers its services free of charge to individuals who may be in need of legal assistance and may lack the financial means and sophistication necessary to tap alternative sources of such aid.

At bottom, the case against appellant rests on the proposition that a State may regulate in a prophylactic fashion all solicitation activities of lawyers because there may be some potential for overreaching, conflict of interest, or other substantive evils whenever a lawyer gives unsolicited advice and communicates an offer of representation to a layman. Under certain circumstances, that approach is appropriate in the case of speech that simply "propose[s] a commercial transaction[.]" In the context of political expression and association, however, a State must regulate with significantly greater precision.

VI

The State is free to fashion reasonable restrictions with respect to the time, place, and manner of solicitation by members of its Bar. The State's special interest in regulating members whose profession it licenses, and who serve as officers of its courts, amply justifies the application of narrowly drawn rules to proscribe solicitation that in fact is misleading, overbearing, or involves other features of deception or improper influence. As we decide today in *Ohralik*, a State also may forbid in-person solicitation for pecuniary gain under circumstances likely to result in these evils. And a State may insist that lawyers not solicit on behalf of lay organizations that exert control over the actual conduct of any ensuing litigation. Accordingly, nothing in this opinion should be read to foreclose carefully tailored regulation that does not abridge unnecessarily the associational freedom of nonprofit organizations, or their members, having characteristics like those of the NAACP or the ACLU.

We conclude that South Carolina's application of its DR2-103(D)(5)(a) and (c) and 2-104(A)(5) to appellant's solicitation by letter on behalf of the ACLU violates the First and Fourteenth Amendments. The judgment of the Supreme Court of South Carolina is

Reversed.

* * *

Mr. Justice Rehnquist, dissenting.

* * *

Neither *Button* nor any other decision of this Court compels a State to permit an attorney to engage in uninvited solicitation on an individual basis. Further, I agree with the Court's statement in the companion case that the State has a strong interest in forestalling the evils that result "when a lawyer, a professional trained in the art of persuasion, personally solicits an unsophisticated, injured, or distressed lay person." The reversal of the judgment of the Supreme Court of South Carolina thus seems to me quite unsupported by previous decisions or by any principle which may be abstracted from them.

* * *

I cannot share the Court's confidence that the danger of such consequences is minimized simply because a lawyer proceeds from political conviction rather than for pecuniary gain. A State may reasonably fear that a lawyer's desire to resolve "substantial civil liberties questions," may occasionally take precedence over his duty to advance the interests of his client. It is even more reasonable to fear that a lawyer in such circumstances will be inclined to pursue both culpable and blameless defendants to the last ditch in order to achieve his ideological goals. Although individual litigants, including the ACLU, may be free to use the courts for such purposes, South Carolina is likewise free to restrict the activities of the members of its Bar who attempt to persuade them to do so.

I can only conclude that the discipline imposed upon Primus does not violate the Constitution, and I would affirm the judgment of the Supreme Court of South Carolina.

C. Advertising

If the term "solicitation" refers to "targeted communication initiated by the lawyer directed to a specific person," the term "advertising" applies to indirect contacts. Indirect contacts vary widely. They include broadcast and print media materials that are easily recognizable as advertising. However, they also include websites or blogs, which are probably more commonly viewed as information resources rather than advertising. In a similar vein, targeted mailings and e-communications seem to be more in the nature of solicitation, not advertising. Nevertheless, these types of marketing efforts likewise fall within the regulatory ambit of the rules of professional conduct that govern advertising.

The pertinent rules reflect a balance between the bar's general ambivalence toward advertising, the commercial speech rights of lawyers, and the public's need for information about the availability of legal services. For most of the Twentieth Century, the bar considered lawyer advertising unprofessional and therefore prohibited it. The Supreme Court struck down this blanket ban in *Bates v. State Bar of Arizona*, 433 U.S. 350 (1977). Although the ethics rules generally permit lawyer advertising, states continue to test the boundaries of permissible restrictions.

The basic rule governing "communication concerning a lawyer's services," including both advertising and solicitation, is Rule 7.1. *See* Delaware Rule 7.1 (based on pre-2018 Model Rule 7.1). It provides that "[a] lawyer shall not make a false or misleading communication about the lawyer or the lawyer's services." It then explains that "[a] communication is false or misleading if it contains a material misrepresentation of fact or law, or omits a fact necessary to make the statement considered as a whole not materially misleading." In addition, even a truthful advertisement that leads "a reasonable person to form an unjustified expectation" about the results that a lawyer can obtain may be misleading. Delaware Rule 7.1, cmt. 3.

Take Note

The ABA made no changes to the text of Model Rule 7.1 in 2018 but did substantially revise the Comment, including by incorporating much of former Rule 7.5, which it deleted. *See* Connecticut Rule 7.1 & cmt. (based on post-2018 Model Rule 7.1).

Delaware Rule 7.2 (based on the Pre-2018 Model Rule) explains that "a lawyer may advertise services through written, recorded or electronic communication, including public media" and requires that "[a]ny communication made pursuant to this rule shall include the name and office address of at least one lawyer or law firm responsible for its content." Delaware Rule 7.2(a), (c).

Revised Model Rule 7.2 incorporates a number of noteworthy changes, including the replacement of the word "advertise" with "communicate information regarding the lawyer's services" and simply stating that such information can be communicated through "any media," rather than specifying examples. *See* Connecticut Rule 7.2(a) (based on post-2018 Model Rule 7.2(a)). In addition, the amended rule only requires the inclusion of the name and "contact information" of at least one attorney, instead of the "name and office address." *Compare* Connecticut Rule 7.2(e) *with* Delaware Rule 7.2(c) (based on pre-2018 Model Rule 7.2(c)).

[Question 3-3]

An attorney who graduated two years ago is struggling to develop a personal injury practice. To assist in this effort, the attorney hired a marketing firm to prepare a website featuring flashy photos of the attorney addressing a jury, arguing before a judge, and shaking hands with satisfied-looking clients. The website includes a disclaimer stating that results will vary depending upon the particular legal and factual circumstances. The attorney has never actually appeared in court.

Is the attorney subject to discipline?

> (A) **Yes, because the information was prepared by a marketing firm, rather than the attorney.**
>
> (B) **Yes, because the website implied that the attorney had appeared in court when in fact the attorney had not.**
>
> (C) **No, because the attorney's marketing efforts constitute protected commercial speech under the First Amendment.**
>
> (D) **No, because the website contained an express disclaimer about the results a client could expect.**

Review Delaware Rule 7.1 and the accompanying Comment (based on pre-2018 Model Rule 7.1) and Connecticut Rule 7.1 and Comment (based on post-2018 Model Rule 7.1).

FYI

Before the Twentieth Century, lawyers were generally able to advertise. In 1835, David Hoffman, the first American legal ethics scholar, placed the following advertisement:

AMERICAN LAW AGENCY.

THE American and British Public are informed that the undersigned have established Law Agencies in each of the United States, and that claims of every description will be carefully attended to through the medium of eminent and responsible counsel in each State, and personally by the undersigned in the State of Maryland, and at Washington, in the District of Columbia.

Please address them under the firm of Hoffman & Dobbin, Counsellors at Law, Baltimore, Maryland.

DAVID HOFFMAN,
GEORGE W. DOBBIN.

Baltimore, Jan. 1, 1833.

REFERENCES:

We are of opinion that entire confidence may be placed in David Hoffman, Esq. LL. D. Counsellor-at-law in the Supreme Court of the United States, and in his associate George W. Dobbin, Esq. and that claims entrusted to them will be attended to with ability, integrity, and promptitude.

John Marshall, Chief Justice U. S. Richmond.
Edward Livingston, Secretary of State, S. Washington.
N. Biddle, President Bank U. S. Philadelphia.
Prime, Ward, King & Co. New York.
Thomas H. Perkins & Sons, Boston.
Robert Gilmor & Sons, }
Hoffman, Bend & Co. } Baltimore.
Baring, Brothers & Co. }
Thos. Wilson & Co. } London.
Bolton, Ogden & Co. }
W. & G. Brown & Co. } Liverpool.

Baltimore, Jan. 10—col m2am5m

Daily National Intelligencer, July 11, 1835, at 4, col. 2. Notice the first "reference" to vouch for Hoffman's "ability, integrity, and promptitude." Would Chief Justice Marshall's reference be considered ethical today?

Matter of Zang

741 P.2d 267 (Ariz. 1987), *cert. denied*, 484 U.S. 1067 (1988)

FELDMAN, VICE CHIEF JUSTICE.

* * *

II. False and Misleading Advertising

A. Background

Zang and Whitmer are charged with false and misleading advertising[.] * * * This charge is based on four print and nine video advertisements that appeared in Phoenix-area newspapers and on Phoenix-area television stations during 1982 and 1983.

All four print advertisements contained the bold-faced caption **"Law is Civilized Warfare!"** above a picture of Zang and Whitmer and to the left of the following language:

> **We're the [or "a"] personal injury law firm:**
>
> > *with the medical experience to understand complicated injuries
> >
> > *with investigators to find witnesses and hidden evidence
> >
> > *with computers for speed, accuracy and research
>
> **Free Consultation**
>
> > No recovery-no attorneys' fee

Each print advertisement also contained a photograph and a statement emphasizing some aspect of respondents' practice. The photographs featured either a judge in a courtroom, a computer circuit board leaning against several books about accident cases and medicine, a large reproduction of a fingerprint, or a woman sitting in a witness box. Beneath one of these photographs, each advertisement featured one of the following statements:

> If you're in an accident . . . You need a lawyer with facts and know-how, not just words.
>
> **Detailed Preparation**
>
> > is part of Zang & Whitmer, Chtd. because: the better your case is *prepared for trial*, the more likely your case will settle out of court without delay or hassles.
> >
> > (emphasis added).
> >
> > If you're in an accident . . . You need more than a lawyers' [sic] words!
>
> **Medicine and Law**
>
> > are combined at Zang & Whitmer, Chtd. because: to prove serious injury and future suffering, your lawyer must have the knowledge to *make complicated medical facts clear for the jury.*

(emphasis added).

If you're hurt in an accident . . . You need more than a lawyer's words!

Licensed Investigators

are part of Zang & Whitmer, Chtd. because: an investigator searches out witnesses, examines evidence at the accident scene, and discovers the facts *essential for victory in the courtroom.*

(emphasis added).

If you're hurt in an accident. . . . You need a lawyer with facts and know-how, not just words.

Evidence

is part of Zang & Whitmer, Chtd. because: *the defense* will use words and opinions to minimize their fault and your injuries. Only proof of facts will stop them.

(emphasis added).

Like the print advertisements, respondents' television advertisements emphasized the advantages of investigators and medical knowledge. The television advertisements also were very dramatic. They featured an authoritative-sounding narrator and either frenetic or peaceful music as a backdrop for pictures of an automobile accident, a worried couple in a hospital waiting room, or a father kissing his daughter goodbye, apparently for the last time. Each of the television advertisements ended with a climactic scene showing Mr. Zang arguing before a jury in a courtroom, with the viewer visually located behind the jury box.

The [State Bar] Committee and the [Disciplinary] Commission [of the Supreme Court of Arizona] concluded that respondents' advertisements portrayed respondents as willing and able to take, and as actually taking, personal injury cases to trial. The Committee and the Commission concluded that the advertisements were false and misleading because, in fact, respondents "scrupulously avoided" taking cases to trial.

B. Discussion

1. Constitutional Protection

We note at the outset that respondents' advertisements are "commercial speech" protected by the First Amendment. As respondents candidly acknowledge, however, the proscription of false and misleading advertising in DR 2-101 is constitutionally unobjectionable.

"[T]he extension of First Amendment protection to commercial speech is justified principally by the value to consumers of the information such speech provides. . . ." Consequently, false or misleading commercial speech has little or no constitutional value and may be "prohibited entirely." "Indeed, the elimination of false and deceptive claims serves to promote the one facet of commercial . . . advertising that warrants First Amendment protection-its contribution to the flow of accurate and reliable information relevant to public and private decision making."

In short, the constitution does not prevent discipline in this case if respondents' advertisements were false and misleading. We therefore must determine (1) what message respondents' advertisements conveyed, and (2) whether that message was false or inherently misleading.

2. The Message

The Committee and the Commission found that at least one of the messages conveyed by respondents' advertisements was that the law firm of Zang & Whitmer was willing and able to try, and actually did try, personal injury cases. The Commission concluded that respondents' print advertisements plainly suggest that attorneys at Zang & Whitmer "prepare cases for trial, combine medicine and law to present facts clearly to the jury, do presentations to juries, use investigators to aid in obtaining victory in the courtroom, and prove facts and defeat defenses in court." In like manner, it found that respondents' television advertisements suggest "that Zang and Whitmer take cases to court and argue before juries." After reviewing the record, we agree that respondents' advertisements would "be interpreted by a reasonable person as representations that Respondents have an unusually high level of expertise and experience in personal injury law, specifically including trial experience."

Both the bar and the respondents called advertising and advertising law experts. The experts gave their opinions regarding the message conveyed by respondents' advertisements. With all deference to the experts, and without deprecating or passing upon the admissibility of their opinions, we find no need to rely upon expert testimony to interpret the messages conveyed by the advertisements in evidence. As a matter of common sense, we find that depicting a lawyer trying a case conveys the idea that the lawyer tries cases. When Zang is shown arguing a case to a jury, the message is that Zang argues cases to juries. Accordingly, we hold that one message conveyed by respondents' advertisements was that Zang & Whitmer had tried personal injury cases in the past and were ready and able to prepare future cases for trial and to try them.

3. Were Respondents' Advertisements Misleading?

The Committee and the Commission found that respondents' advertisements were false and misleading because they did not accurately portray respondents' practice. Zang & Whitmer was formed in 1979. From that time until the advertisements at issue appeared in 1982 and 1983, no attorney at Zang & Whitmer had tried a personal injury case to a conclusion. Zang and Whitmer personally started only one trial, but a mistrial was declared after the first witness testified.

Zang, who holds a medical as well as a legal degree, has experience as a medical trial consultant, but has never tried a personal injury case. He conceded that although he felt fully capable of preparing personal injury cases for trial, he is not competent to try a personal injury case. Whitmer has criminal trial experience, having spent several years with the county attorney's office shortly after he graduated from law school. His only personal injury trial experience, however, consists of three or four trials that occurred more than ten years ago.

Most importantly, Zang & Whitmer consciously followed a firm policy of not taking cases to trial. Respondents believed that pretrial settlements invariably obtained better results for their clients. They settled cases before trial whenever possible. In the few cases where a trial was necessary, respondents' policy was to refer cases to trial lawyers in other firms. Thus, as the Commission concluded, "while [respondents] represented themselves as having the willingness to try cases, they in fact scrupulously avoided" litigation or trial work of any kind.

The evidence clearly demonstrates that respondents did not offer the trial services portrayed in their advertisements. Contrary to their print advertisements, respondents had not and did not prepare cases for trial, "make complicated medical facts clear for the jury," or strive for "victory in the courtroom." Nor did they argue cases in front of juries as their television advertisements suggested. Their intention was to settle all cases. Even if a settlement could not be reached, respondents had no intention of personally taking their clients' cases to trial.

We agree with the Committee and the Commission that respondents' advertisements were false and misleading. When consumers "choose[ ] a lawyer through the advertising process, [they] ha[ve] a right to expect that [their] lawyer will be able and willing to act in the manner represented. In this case, it is clear that respondents had no intention of taking a case personally to trial, and that express and implied representations of their courtroom abilities were false, misleading, and untruthful."

4. Respondents' Objections

Respondents argue that their advertisements were not false because they accurately suggest only that Zang & Whitmer has an unusually high level of expertise in personal injury law, which occasionally includes trial work. Respondents support this assertion with two pieces of evidence: the expert testimony of Professor Gerald Thain and statistics about the frequency of litigation in personal injury cases.

According to Professor Thain, a law professor specializing in advertising law, respondents' advertisements suggest that Zang & Whitmer will do what is necessary to get the best possible result for its clients, including going to court, if necessary. This suggestion is not misleading, according to Professor Thain, because the references to trial work add little to the public's preexisting perception that all lawyers appear in court. Because the public already incorrectly believes that all lawyers appear in court, consumers will not be misled further by respondents' references to trial work.

Professor Thain's testimony does not aid respondents' cause. As Professor Thain conceded, because respondents personally were unwilling and unable to take cases to court, their advertisements technically were false. Furthermore, that some consumers incorrectly believe that all lawyers routinely appear in court, does not give respondents license to present their practice in a false light. Disciplinary Rule 2-101(A) prohibits false and misleading claims, even if those claims serve only to reinforce consumers' prior misconceptions.

* * *

Respondents' final argument is that their advertisements never actually harmed anyone. This argument, inherently difficult to prove or disprove, also is unpersuasive. Although there may be little specific evidence of consumer injury or dissatisfaction, we think it self-evident that the message conveyed by respondents' advertisements was inherently misleading and potentially dangerous. * * *

Even if no client has yet been damaged, discipline is appropriate to protect consumers from misleading advertising. The rules governing attorneys are designed to prevent harm and protect consumers. * * * Advertisements falsely suggesting a willingness and ability to do trial work necessarily create a danger that consumers will turn to respondents for help with matters that may need to be litigated. This danger alone is sufficient justification for enforcing DR 2-101(A) without requiring proof of actual harm in the past.

Our conclusion that respondents' advertisements were false and misleading should not be read too broadly. Although it seems unlikely that personal injury lawyers can achieve the best results for their clients without earning and maintaining a proven willingness and competence to take cases to trial when necessary, we do not criticize respondents' practice of settling most cases or of referring trial work to outside counsel. Respondents were not charged with providing incomplete or incompetent legal services, nor was evidence adduced on this point. Thus, it may be, as the evidence at the disciplinary hearing suggested, that respondents' use of computers, investigators, and medical knowledge secured a fair settlement for many of their clients. The same, perhaps, could be said of a competent firm of public adjusters. The fact remains, however, that respondents' advertisements painted a false picture, portraying Zang and Whitmer as trial lawyers who prepared cases for trial, who were willing and able to try, and who actually tried, personal injury cases. That portrait was flattering past the point of deception.

C. Directions for the Future

As our prior discussion indicates, we intend strict enforcement of the rule against false and misleading advertising. As a guide for the future, we take this opportunity to outline some principles that may prove helpful in determining whether a particular advertisement is false or misleading. Although the comments that follow pertain to our present rules and are truly dicta in an adjudicatory sense (we cannot fairly evaluate respondents' conduct by standards announced today), they should provide some future direction for the bar.

The Rules of Professional Conduct regulate various aspects of commercial advertisements about a lawyer and his or her services. The only truly substantive regulation, however, is ER 7.1's prohibition of "false or misleading communication[s] about the lawyer or the lawyer's services." According to ER 7.1, an advertisement is false or misleading if it misrepresents or omits a material fact, creates an unjustified expectation about the results a lawyer can achieve, or makes unsubstantiated comparisons of legal services.

Lawyers who choose to advertise should remember that they are professionals charged with an important public trust: preserving and protecting the public's commercial, civil, and constitutional rights. Advertising that informs consumers about their rights and about the availability and cost of legal services is a valuable method of increasing access to legal representation and of furthering the rule of law. This type of advertising is fully deserving of constitutional protection, and is apparently what the Supreme Court had in mind when it extended first amendment protection to lawyer advertising.

We recognize, of course, that another primary purpose of advertising is to convince consumers to call a particular lawyer. While this focus is not objectionable standing alone, it often leads attorneys to stretch the truth or to focus on dramatic, "sophisticated" sales techniques that all too often provide little helpful information and consequently have a greater tendency to mislead consumers. While no doubt effective in attracting clients, dramatic, nonfactual advertisements are more likely to misrepresent or omit material facts, or to create unjustified expectations about the results a lawyer can achieve than are advertisements that primarily convey factual information that will help consumers make rational decisions about whether to seek legal services.

Thus, attorneys attempting to produce advertisements that are neither false nor misleading should keep in mind that the sale and use of legal services is fundamentally different than the sale and use of ordinary consumer products. It matters less which brand of beer or soap consumers choose than what kind of lawyer they choose. Legal representation may affect the consumer's basic rights and may have long-term consequences; consumers easily can discard a disappointing beer or bar of soap and try a different brand next time. Furthermore, consumers are less likely to be "taken in" by advertisements for consumer products than by advertisements for legal services. People usually have much more experience with consumer products than they have with legal services. Consequently, the Rules of Professional Conduct do not tolerate the same sort of sales pitch for legal services that the Federal Trade Commission tolerates for most consumer products.

The dramatic sales pitch is especially troublesome when it is broadcast on radio or television, which leave little time for reflection and rational deliberation. The Iowa and New Jersey Supreme Courts have responded to this potential danger by expanding their rules of professional conduct to require that television advertisements be "predominately informational." Reasoning that dramatic television advertisements are inherently misleading, both courts have severely limited the use of music, pictures, and dramatic presentations in television advertisements by attorneys. Although the Supreme Court has not reviewed either Iowa's or New Jersey's rules, its consistent refusal to explicitly extend its prior holdings to "the electronic broadcast media," and its dismissal of the appeal in Humphrey for want of a substantial federal question, suggest that even such stringent rules may be constitutional.

Our own rules do not yet place any special restrictions on television or radio broadcasts, nor do we think it necessary to take that step today. Some music or drama may help convey the attorney's message. We believe, however, that lawyer advertising, particularly on the electronic media, should be predominately informational in nature. This is consistent with the rationale for extending first amendment protection to lawyer advertising and with the public's interest in access to and knowledge about lawyers and legal services.

Advertisements are likely to minimize the danger of violating ER 7.1 if they are designed to inform consumers of their rights and of the methods available to meet legal problems and crises; to inform the public of the availability and costs of services; or to convey accurate information relevant to making informed, rational choices of counsel, including information about counsel's availability and areas of practice. In the future, the bar should examine lawyers' advertisements to determine whether, taken as a whole, they are predominately informational or are simply emotional, irrational sales pitches. While the latter may not be prohibited by ER 7.1, they should be examined carefully to assure that they are neither false nor misleading.

* * *

VIII. CONCLUSION

For the reasons discussed in this opinion, Stephen M. Zang is suspended from the practice of law for one year, commencing on the date of the mandate in this case. As a condition of reinstatement, he is required to make restitution to State Farm and to Rebecca Drummond as specified in section VII-A. Pursuant to former Rule 37(g), Mr. Zang is ordered to pay the State Bar of Arizona $15,441.06 for costs and expenses incurred in prosecuting this action.

* * *

Peter Whitmer is suspended for thirty days, commencing on the date of the mandate in this case, for engaging in false and misleading advertising. As a condition of reinstatement, he is ordered to make restitution to Rebecca Drummond as provided in section VII-A. Pursuant to former Rule 37(g), Mr. Whitmer is ordered to pay the State Bar $11,166.97 for costs and expenses.

———————————

[Question 3-4]

An attorney seeking to build a client base posted a flyer on a community bulletin board in a local library. The flyer listed the attorney's name, office address, telephone number, and law school. The flyer also stated: "I am an attorney specializing in wills and estate planning. You can find me sitting on the bench outside the library front door." All information on the flyer is factually accurate.

Is the attorney subject to discipline?

(A) **Yes, because the attorney's flyer indicated that he could be found sitting outside the library front door.**

(B) **Yes, because the flyer indicated that the attorney specializes in wills and estate planning.**

(C) **Yes, because the attorney's flyer constitutes solicitation.**

(D) **No, because the content of the advertisement is not false or misleading and contains the required contact information.**

Review Delaware Rules 7.1, 7.4, 7.5, and the accompanying Comments (based on the pre-2018 Model Rules).

Take Note

In its 2018 amendments to the Model Rules dealing with advertising and solicitation, the ABA deleted Model Rules 7.4 and 7.5, and incorporated much of their content into Model Rule 7.2 (and its Comment) and the Comment to Model Rule 7.1, respectively. *See* Connecticut Rules 7.1 & 7.2 (which are substantially similar to post-2018 Model Rules 7.1 & 7.2).

[Question 3-5]

Four lawyers formed a partnership and named it Alpha & Partners, using the last name of the most senior partner, Attorney Alpha. Over the next two decades, one partner died, another retired, and the third moved laterally to a new firm, leaving only one partner remaining, Attorney Alpha. Attorney Alpha did not change the firm's name even though no other partners remained. He believed the name was still accurate because the paralegals and assistants working at the law firm were essentially his "partners" when they assisted with cases.

Is Attorney Alpha subject to discipline?

    (A) Yes, because the departure of his three partners makes the firm name misleading.

    (B) Yes, because firms organized as partnerships must include the name of at least two partners.

    (C) No, because Attorney Alpha remained at the firm and only his name appeared in the firm's name.

    (D) No, because the paralegals were essentially Attorney Alpha's "partners" when they assisted with cases.

Delaware Rule 7.5 (based on pre-2018 Model Rule 7.5) governs firm names and letterheads. It prohibits firm names or letterheads that violate Rule 7.1, but it permits use of "a trade name" in private practice as long as that name does not imply a connection with a government agency or a public or charitable legal services organization. Delaware Rule 7.5(a). Similarly, Delaware Rule 7.5(c) provides that a firm may not use the name of a "lawyer holding public office . . . during any substantial period in which the lawyer is not actively and regularly practicing with the firm."

The rule also takes into account the multijurisdictional nature of some practices. Specifically, Delaware Rule 7.5(b) permits the use of the "same name or other professional designation in each jurisdiction, but identification of the lawyers in an office of the firm shall indicate the jurisdictional limitations on those not licensed to practice in the jurisdiction where the office is located."

Delaware Rule 7.5(d) allows lawyers to "state or imply that they practice in a partnership or other organization only when that is the fact."

Global Perspective

Some countries have more restrictive lawyer advertising rules than most U.S. state rules. For example, in 2003, an EU-commissioned report indicated that in 10 of the 18 jurisdictions surveyed, most lawyer advertising was prohibited. (See Table 3-8 on p. 49) Although there have been some significant regulatory changes since that study, a 2012 EU report noted that there is huge variation between EU countries that is "very likely connected to national regulation on advertising." The Report noted (at p. 184) that in Sweden, 57% of the surveyed lawyers reported the use of the media for advertisement, whereas in Italy, it was only 3%. A 2010 World Bank report on East Africa observed that advertising was prohibited in all of the surveyed countries and recommended that these countries work toward regulatory change.

Keep in mind that the ABA deleted Model Rule 7.5 in 2018 and moved much of its substance to Model Rule 7.1's Comment, and likewise deleted Model Rule 7.4 and incorporated its substance, with revisions, into Model Rule 7.2. Although the scope and content remain essentially the same, be sure to compare the pre-2018 version with the post-2018 revisions. *Compare* Delaware Rule 7.4 & 7.5 *with* Connecticut Rules 7.1 & 7.2.

In addition, it is important to note that another significant revision was added to Rule 7.2. Under the former version, there was a virtually blanket prohibition on compensating or giving anything of value to a person in return for recommending a lawyer's services, with several noted exceptions, including one for reciprocal referral arrangements. *See* Colorado Rule 7.2(b)(4) (based on pre-2018 Model Rule 7.2(b)(4)). Amended Rule 7.2 now contains an additional exception for a "nominal" gift given "as an expression of appreciation," provided that it is not "intended nor reasonably expected to be a form of compensation for recommending a lawyer's services." *See* Connecticut Rule 7.2(c)(5) (which is substantially similar to post-2018 Model Rule 7.2(b)(5)). The Comment to Model Rule 7.2(b)(5) indicates that a nominal gift cannot be more than a "token item," such as a holiday gift or "ordinary social hospitality." Interestingly, the Connecticut version is more specific, providing that no more than two gifts per year can be given to the same recipient, and individual gifts cannot exceed the value of $50. *See* Connecticut Rule 7.2(c)(5) & Comment.

For More Information

Considering that online conduct crosses state, national, and international boundaries, how do the advertising and solicitation rules govern attorney conduct in this realm? Many ethics experts have considered their application to blogs, web advertising, social networking, online referral services, chat rooms, and other online activities. *See, e.g.,* J.T. Westermeier, *Ethics and the Internet*, 17 Geo. J. Legal Ethics 267 (2004).

Food for Thought

In *Florida Bar v. Went for It, Inc.*, <u>515 U.S. 618 (1995)</u>, the Supreme Court approved of a state-imposed, thirty-day moratorium on lawyers contacting injured persons to offer representation, but the regulation at issue did not impose a similar restraint on insurance companies seeking to resolve injured persons' claims. Professors Monroe Freedman and Abbe Smith argue that:

> Discouraging victims and their survivors from retaining lawyers is a familiar practice of insurance companies . . . . * * * Clearly, this is a controversy of public importance— whether an accident victim should retain a lawyer to assert her First Amendment right of petition, and whether a particular settlement is in the interest of a particular victim. Just as clearly, one side of that controversy is being permitted to speak, while the other is being gagged.

Monroe H. Freedman & Abbe Smith, *Understanding Lawyers' Ethics* 343 (5th ed. 2016). What do you think of their argument? For another case upholding a moratorium on lawyers contacting individuals with potential personal injury or wrongful death claims, see *Alexander v. Cahill*, <u>598 F.3d 79 (2d Cir. 2010)</u>. In *Alexander*, the Second Circuit also held that regulations intended to control certain aspects of the content and tenor of lawyer advertisements violated the First Amendment.

III. Fees and Billing

Today, hourly billing and contingent fees remain the most prevalent attorney compensation approaches. Hourly billing is especially dominant in large firm practices. Contingent fees are most commonly employed for representation of plaintiffs,[1] although some lawyers have utilized such arrangements on the defense side as well.[2] Lawyers can always charge a flat fee for their services, and many do, especially for relatively routine services. Probably due to the extensive use of the venture capital model to finance high tech businesses, many lawyers for such entities have accepted an equity interest in their client as payment for services. Lawyers can use any of these approaches consistent with their ethical obligations. This Chapter explains how.

As a general matter, the rationale for the fee rules is consumer protection—ensuring that fees are reasonable and that lawyers do not take advantage of clients. In some respects, though, the rules retain a historical concern with maintaining lawyer independence and prohibiting lawyers from encouraging litigation. These concerns shape the modern restrictions on holding a proprietary interest in the subject matter of litigation, and on contingent fees in domestic relations and criminal matters, as well as the special rules preventing a third-party who is paying a client's fees from inappropriately influencing the representation.

---

1   Herbert M. Kritzer, *Holding Back the Floodtide: The Role of Contingent Fee Lawyers*, <u>70 Wis. Law., March 1997</u>, at 10 (describing author's research "reporting that relatively few individual litigants use fee structures other than contingent fees for nondivorce cases; even in practice areas such as contracts, contingent fees are the most common type of fees for individuals").

2   *See, e.g.*, D.C. Bar Ethics Op. 347 (2009) (recognizing the ethical propriety of reverse contingent fees based on the percentage of savings that a client realizes in a judgment or settlement, so long as the fee is reasonable and the terms are are agreed to in a writing consistent with Rule 1.5(c)).

As the Chapter reveals, lawyer's fees are a controversial topic. An American Bar Association study found that "[c]onsumers complain about the fees charged by all types of lawyers."[3] At the same time, lawyers have debated the propriety of each method of billing. They question whether particular approaches are more or less likely to align the lawyer's interests with those of the client.

Food for Thought

Historically, leading lawyers believed that professional excellence alone would result in lawyers earning a good living. George Sharswood, the nineteenth century scholar whose 1854 essay would become the basis of our modern legal ethics codes,[4] advised:

> [L]et business seek the young attorney; and though it may come in slowly, and at intervals, and promise in its character neither fame nor profit, still, if he bears in mind that it is an important part of his training that he should understand the business he does thoroughly, that he should especially cultivate, in transacting it, habits of neatness, accuracy, punctuality, and dispatch, candor toward his client, and strict honor toward his adversary, it may be safely prophesied that his business will grow as fast as it is good for him that it should grow[.]

George Sharswood, *An Essay on Professional Ethics*, 32 American Bar Association Reports 131–32 (5th ed. 1907).

[Question 3-6]

A lawyer contacted by telephone a nationally-recognized malpractice defense attorney after being sued by a client for negligently handling a case. The defense attorney, who had never worked for the lawyer before, accepted the representation and promptly began working on the matter. The two met in person the following week to discuss details about the representation. During the conversation, the defense attorney explained her customary hourly fee and expense reimbursement policy. The lawyer felt the fee was high but agreed to pay it. The defense attorney intended to follow up with a letter to document the conversation; however, she forgot to do so. The defense attorney continued to work on the matter for several months, and after it was successfully resolved, submitted a bill to the lawyer that accurately reflected the hours worked and expenses incurred. The fees and expenses charged were reasonable.

Is the defense attorney subject to discipline?

  Yes, because the hourly rate was not disclosed prior to commencement of the representation.

---

3   Am. Bar Ass'n Sec. of Lit., *Public Perceptions of Lawyers: Consumer Research Findings* 15 (Leo J. Shapiro & Assoc. 2002).

4   For biographical background on Sharswood and his influence on the legal ethics codes, see Russell G. Pearce, *Rediscovering the Republican Origins of the Legal Ethics Codes*, 6 Geo. J. Legal Ethics 241 (1992).

(B) **Yes, because the defense attorney did not document the conversation about fees and expenses in writing.**

(C) **No, because the defense attorney successfully handled the representation.**

(D) **No, because the defense attorney disclosed the basis of her fee within a reasonable time after commencing the representation.**

Rule 1.5 provides in part:

(a)   A lawyer shall not make an agreement for, charge, or collect an unreasonable fee or an unreasonable amount for expenses. The factors to be considered in determining the reasonableness of a fee include the following:

(1)   the time and labor required, the novelty and difficulty of the questions involved, and the skill requisite to perform the legal service properly;

(2)   the likelihood, if apparent to the client, that the acceptance of the particular employment will preclude other employment by the lawyer;

(3)   the fee customarily charged in the locality for similar legal services;

(4)   the amount involved and the results obtained;

(5)   the time limitations imposed by the client or by the circumstances;

(6)   the nature and length of the professional relationship with the client;

(7)   the experience, reputation, and ability of the lawyer or lawyers performing the services; and

(8)   whether the fee is fixed or contingent.

(b)   The scope of the representation and the basis or rate of the fee and expenses for which the client will be responsible shall be communicated to the client, preferably in writing, before or within a reasonable time after commencing the representation, except when the lawyer will charge a regularly represented client on the same basis or rate. Any changes in the basis or rate of the fee or expenses shall also be communicated to the client.

* * *

A.   The Hourly Billing Controversy

[Question 3-7]

In defending a major securities fraud action, a law firm used outside contract lawyers whom it paid $100 per hour. However, the firm billed the client $150 per hour for work performed by the lawyers on the case. The $150 per hour billable rate and the overall amount charged to the client for the contract lawyers' work were reasonable. The firm did not memorialize its fee arrangement with the client in writing. Was the firm's fee arrangement with the client proper?

(A) Yes, because the rate billed to the client and the overall amount charged were reasonable.

(B) Yes, because law firms have broad discretion in billing for work performed by outside contract lawyers.

(C) No, because the firm must bill the client $100 per hour, consistent with the contract lawyers' hourly rate of pay.

 (D) No, because the firm did not memorialize its fee arrangement with the client in writing.

Simulation

Assume the role of a lawyer who does ethics consulting, and be prepared to provide advice to the attorney based on the following facts: An attorney previously represented a client in drafting a master lease for a shopping mall. It was the first time that the attorney drafted such a master lease, and it took the attorney six hours, for which the attorney billed that client. Before sending the bill, the attorney asked around and learned that most lawyers in the area billed between four and eight hours for drafting master leases, so the attorney thought that the fee was reasonable. Now, a new client asks the attorney to draft a master lease for an outlet mall that the new client is planning. The attorney has the template for such a master lease because of his previous work for the first client. It takes the attorney only two hours to make the necessary revisions to complete the lease for the client. The attorney wants to know whether the new client may be billed four hours for the master lease, which would be at the low end of what other lawyers would have charged. The attorney does not plan to explain the basis for billing at this amount to the new client, out of concern that the new client may not appreciate the time involved for initially creating the master lease. Also, in order to further recoup expenses, the attorney plans to charge the new client for expenses like photocopying at rates 2% above his actual cost.

Advise the attorney as to the ethical propriety of charging the new client for the fees and expenses as proposed.

William G. Ross, *The Ethics of Hourly Billing by Attorneys*

44 Rutgers L. Rev. 1, 8–12, 88–90 (1991)

* * *

During early years of the Republic, many states followed the colonial practice of fee schedules by enacting fee regulations and providing penalties for lawyers who charged more than the prescribed amounts. * * * Similar to the fee schedules enacted prior to the Revolution, the fee regulations of the early Republic generally provided that the losing party would pay the fees of the prevailing party. * * * As the nineteenth century progressed, the courts gradually recognized the right of lawyers to collect fees that were larger than anything that was recoverable under the fee statutes. * * * The abolition of fee schedules also may have reflected the hostility of conservative middle class attorneys toward incipient trade unionism. For example, the fee schedules and other regulations that were established by the Massachusetts bar associations notably were similar to the restrictive rules of the early trade associations. * * *

As a result of the repeal of fee schedules, law firms began to use time, as well as the difficulty of the work and the results achieved, in assessing client bills. The repeal of the fee schedules also encouraged the use of contingent fees. * * * The American Bar Association reluctantly approved the use of contingent fees in 1908. Until the 1960s, few lawyers kept time records and most fees were based upon uniform schedules approved by bar associations or the courts, or upon the evaluation of various factors discussed in the canons of ethics.

During the 1960s, management experts concluded from various studies that lawyers who kept time records earned more than attorneys who did not. As one member of a legal consulting firm has explained, hourly billing appealed to clients because it was "based on something tangible that they could understand rather than on a 'value of services' concept." Similarly, hourly billing enabled business clients to "correlate the 'product' that they were buying to the products that they themselves produced and sold," and made it easier for corporate managers of outside counsel to justify to their superiors the payment of legal bills. * * * However, during the 1970s bills increasingly came to be based solely upon time. * * *

Time-based billing creates serious abuses and raises difficult ethical questions. Although the most obvious abuses are the temptation of attorneys to exaggerate the number of their billable hours or perform patently unnecessary work, "padding" and "churning" are so obviously wrong that these practices raise no ambiguous ethical questions. * * *

Far more troublesome than simple "padding" or "churning" are more complex practices that ultimately may amount to no more than sophisticated versions of those same two abuses. Through liberal methods of time recordation, attorneys may unduly inflate their hours without actually padding any entries. Similarly, over-zealous attorneys may perform tasks that yield a benefit to the client that is disproportionately small compared to the expense. These situations present the more profound ethical difficulties, because clear ethical standards often are difficult to formulate in these instances.

Perhaps the greatest danger is that some attorneys have become so accustomed to rationalizing their liberal time recordation techniques or their decisions to perform endless services for their clients regardless of cost that they may not even recognize that their actions are ethically questionable. How else, aside from preternatural stamina or lying, does one account for the views of one respondent to the author's survey who stated that he and most other attorneys who regularly bill more than 3,600 hours each year do not perform unnecessary work or exaggerate their hours?

* * *

Attorneys need to recognize that unethical time-based billing practices harm not only the client but also the legal profession, the courts, and the public. The fetish for accumulation of billable hours which increasingly pervades many law firms has eroded standards of professionalism by breeding a clock-punching mentality that until recently was the hallmark only of certain forms of industrial labor. Moreover, excessively clever strategies for accumulation of hours and the protraction of litigation for the conscious or unconscious purpose of generating more billable hours have aggravated a widespread cynicism about the legal profession that ultimately calls into question the integrity of the judicial system and weakens public faith in the quality of the nation's justice.

Since alternatives to time-based billing create their own ethical difficulties and lawyers seem loath to abandon hourly billing, both private practitioners and clients must try to purge the time-based billing system of unethical practices. Ethical billing requires constant sensitivity to the inherent conflict between the economic interests of the attorney and the real needs of the client. Ethical billing also requires a vigilant awareness of the potentials for abuse that are endemic to a system of time-based billing. It is encouraging that an increasing number of attorneys, clients, and commentators are admitting that hourly billing has encouraged a considerable measure of inefficiency and fraud and are beginning to call for more scrupulous billing practices.

Douglas R. Richmond, *In Defense of the Billable Hour*

14 Prof. Law. 1 (Winter 2003)

* * *

Of the many criticisms leveled at hourly billing, the most common is that it encourages and rewards inefficiency, and encourages billing fraud. This is nonsense for several reasons.

First, at least in the litigation context, billing by the hour forces clients and their counsel to think carefully about strategy and the need to perform particular tasks when budgeting a project, thereby controlling costs and preventing needless expenditures. * * * [A]re the alternatives any better? So-called "flat fees" have their own problems. Among other things, they are a potential disincentive to zealous advocacy. Flat fees encourage attorneys to do as little work as possible. * * *

Contingent fees are not necessarily the solution. Like all forms of compensation they can be abused by lawyers who are so inclined. * * *

Make the Connection

For further discussion of contingent fees, *see infra.*

Even were the billable hour the source of the problems that its critics contend, lawyers' duties * * * under various ethics rules and their common law fiduciary duties, protect clients against the abuses chiefly alleged. Indeed, to believe that hourly billing causes all of the problems attributed to it is to also believe that as a general rule lawyers who bill by the hour are either incompetent, inefficient or unethical. Because such a position defies logic, it must be that the problem is not the billable hour, but the few dishonest, misguided, and incompetent attorneys who misuse it. * * *

Billing pressure has been identified as the key culprit responsible for attorney dissatisfaction. Although billable hour pressure is reported to have negatively affected law firm partners, associates are thought to be "the most disenchanted casualties of the billable hour derby." In Professor Susan Saab Fortney's recent survey of 1,000 young lawyers working for Texas law firms, 74 percent of the respondents working in law firms of 100 or more lawyers indicated that billable hour pressures had taken a toll on their personal lives. * * * There is no doubt that professional success requires hard work, and that hard work sometimes takes a personal toll. * * * But, again, the problem is not the billable hour. The problem, if there is one, appears to be lawyers' income expectations or career aspirations. * * *

Jonathan D. Glater, *Billable Hours Giving Ground at Law Firms*

N.Y. Times, January 30, 2009, at A1

* * *

Clients have complained for years that the practice of billing for each hour worked can encourage law firms to prolong a client's problem rather than solve it. But the rough economic climate is making clients more demanding, leading many law firms to rethink their business model.

"This is the time to get rid of the billable hour," said Evan R. Chesler, presiding partner at Cravath, Swaine & Moore in New York, one of a number of large firms whose most senior lawyers bill more than $800 an hour.

"Clients are concerned about the budgets, more so than perhaps a year or two ago," he added, with a lawyer's gift for understatement.

* * *

With a sigh that is simultaneously proud and pained, lawyers will talk about charging clients for 3,000 or more hours in a year—a figure that means a lawyer spent about 12 hours a day of every weekday drafting motions or contracts and reviewing other lawyers' motions and contracts.

"Does this make any sense?" said David B. Wilkins, professor of legal ethics and director of the program on the legal profession at Harvard. "It makes as much sense as any other kind of effort to measure your value by some kind of objective, extrinsic measure. Which is not much." * * *

> **Food for Thought**
>
> What do you think of the controversy regarding hourly billing? Do you agree with Evan Chesler that "This is the time to get rid of the billable hour?"

B. The Controversy Regarding Contingent Fees and Other Issues Related to Fees and Fiduciary Duties

[Question 3-8]

A plaintiff, who was an experienced oil and gas developer, asked an attorney to represent her in a suit to establish ownership of certain oil and gas royalties. The plaintiff could not afford the attorney's reasonable hourly rate; and instead, proposed to pay the attorney 20% of the value of the proceeds received from the first-year royalties the plaintiff might recover in the suit. The attorney accepted the proposal and memorialized the terms in a written fee agreement, which the plaintiff signed. The attorney did not advise the plaintiff of the desirability of seeking the advice of independent legal counsel before signing the agreement.

Is the attorney subject to discipline?

(A) Yes, because the agreement gave the attorney a proprietary interest in the plaintiff's cause of action.

(B) Yes, because the attorney did not advise the plaintiff of the desirability of seeking the advice of independent legal counsel before signing the agreement.

(C) No, because the plaintiff, rather than the attorney, proposed the fee arrangement.

(D) No, because a lawyer may contract with a client for a reasonable contingent fee.

[Question 3-9]

An attorney entered into a written engagement agreement with a client in a divorce proceeding. The client agreed in writing to provide the attorney 10% of the final settlement if the divorce was finalized within three months. The attorney secured a one-million dollar settlement two weeks prior to the deadline and sent the client a bill for $100,000. The client happily paid the bill, thanking the attorney for handling the matter efficiently.

Is the attorney subject to discipline for entering into this agreement?

(A) Yes, because the attorney agreed to a fee contingent on the securing of a divorce.

(B) Yes, because $100,000 was not a reasonable fee for the legal services rendered.

(C) No, because the client was happy with the attorney's legal services.

(D) No, because the client agreed in writing to the contingent-fee arrangement.

Rule 1.5

* * *

(c) A fee may be contingent on the outcome of the matter for which the service is rendered, except in a matter in which a contingent fee is prohibited by paragraph (d) or other law. A contingent fee agreement shall be in a writing signed by the client and shall state the method by which the fee is to be determined, including the percentage or percentages that shall accrue to the lawyer in the event of settlement, trial or appeal; litigation and other expenses to be deducted from the recovery; and whether such expenses are to be deducted before or after the contingent fee is calculated. The agreement must clearly notify the client of any expenses for which the client will be liable whether or not the client is the prevailing party. Upon conclusion of a contingent fee matter, the lawyer shall provide the client with a written statement stating the outcome of the matter and, if there is a recovery, showing the remittance to the client and the method of its determination.

(d)   A lawyer shall not enter into an arrangement for, charge, or collect:

   (1)   any fee in a domestic relations matter, the payment or amount of which is contingent upon the securing of a divorce or upon the amount of alimony or support, or property settlement in lieu thereof; or

   (2)   a contingent fee for representing a defendant in a criminal case.

* * *

Comment

* * *

[6] This provision does not preclude a contract for a contingent fee for legal representation in connection with the recovery of post-judgment balances due under support, alimony or other financial orders because such contracts do not implicate the same policy concerns.

* * *

Food for Thought

The justifications for the prohibition of contingent fees in criminal cases include the absence of a res, conflicts of interest that might weigh against the lawyer seeking a plea bargain or asking for an instruction on a lesser included offense, and the availability of court appointed counsel for indigent defendants. Pamela S. Karlan, *Contingent Fees and Criminal Cases*, 93 Colum. L. Rev. 595, 602–06 (1993); Peter Lushing, *The Fall and Rise of the Criminal Contingent Fee*, 82 J. Crim. L. & Criminology 498 (1992). However, Professor Peter Lushing argues that:

> The prohibition on criminal contingent fees springs from irrelevant conceptual thinking, unverified concerns regarding conflict of interest, and prejudice against criminal attorneys and what they do. These concerns do not provide sufficient reason to bar lawyers and clients from entering into beneficial agreements. Repeal of the ban on criminal contingent fees would be of particular benefit to the middle class, who will be eager to pay for results instead of services.

Lushing, *supra*, at 546.

Do you agree or disagree with restriction on contingent fees in criminal cases?

With regard to the restriction on contingent fees in domestic relations matters, Restatement § 35, Comment g explains that "[t]he traditional grounds of the prohibition in divorce cases are that such a fee creates incentives inducing lawyers to discourage reconciliation and encourages bitter and wounding court battles." The Restatement acknowledges that this rationale has less force where "no-fault divorce legislation" indicates that "public policy does not clearly favor the continuation of a marriage that one spouse wishes to end." Another argument "is that such a fee arrangement is usually unnecessary in order to secure an attorney in a divorce proceeding or custody dispute [because if the opposing spouse] has assets, the courts will usually require that spouse to pay the first spouse reasonable attorney fees."

Do you agree or disagree with the restriction on contingent fees in domestic relations matters?

Rule 1.8(i)

A lawyer shall not acquire a proprietary interest in the cause of action or subject matter of litigation the lawyer is conducting for a client, except that the lawyer may:

(1) acquire a lien authorized by law to secure the lawyer's fee or expenses; and

(2) contract with a client for a reasonable contingent fee in a civil case.

Restatement § 35 Comment b:

First, [contingent fees] enable persons who could not otherwise afford counsel to assert their rights, paying their lawyers only if the assertion succeeds. Second, contingent fees give lawyers an additional incentive to seek their clients' success and to encourage only those clients with claims having a substantial likelihood of succeeding. Third, such fees enable a client to share the risk of losing with a lawyer, who is usually better able to assess the risk and to bear it by undertaking similar arrangements in other cases.

Global Perspective

In contrast to the American practice of generally permitting contingent fees, the Code of Conduct for European Lawyers (which is also known as the CCBE Code of Conduct) prohibits contingent fees unless a jurisdiction specifically permits them. It provides as follows:

3.3. Pactum de Quota Litis

3.3.1. A lawyer shall not be entitled to make a pactum de quota litis.

3.3.2. By "pactum de quota litis" is meant an agreement between a lawyer and the client entered into prior to final conclusion of a matter to which the client is a party, by virtue of which the client undertakes to pay the lawyer a share of the result regardless of whether this is represented by a sum of money or by any other benefit achieved by the client upon the conclusion of the matter.

3.3.3. "Pactum de quota litis" does not include an agreement that fees be charged in proportion to the value of a matter handled by the lawyer if this is in accordance with an officially approved fee scale or under the control of the Competent Authority having jurisdiction over the lawyer.

Commentary on Article 3.3—Pactum de Quota Litis

These provisions reflect the common position in all Member States that an unregulated agreement for contingency fees (pactum de quota litis) is contrary to the proper administration of justice because it encourages speculative litigation and is liable to be abused. The provisions are not, however, intended to prevent the maintenance or introduction of arrangements under which lawyers are paid according to results or only if the action or matter is successful, provided that these arrangements are under sufficient regulation and control for the protection of the client and the proper administration of justice.

Although CCBE Rule 3.3.3 refers to "an officially approved fee scale," these kinds of fee scales have come under scrutiny by EU antitrust authorities and by the European Court of Justice. *See* Laurel S. Terry, *The European Commission Project Regarding Competition in Professional Services,* 29 Northwestern J. Int'l L. & Bus. 1 (2009).

JEFFREY D. SWETT, *COMMENT, DETERMINING A REASONABLE PERCENTAGE IN ESTABLISHING A CONTINGENCY FEE: A NEW TOOL TO REMEDY AN OLD PROBLEM*

77 Tenn. L. Rev. 653, 654, 657–58, 661–65, 670–72 (2010)

* * *

Generally, the one-third contingency fee is the industry standard when determining a contingency fee percentage. However, in certain circumstances, the traditional one-third contingency fee may over-compensate the lawyer for his services, and in other situations the traditional fee may under-compensate the lawyer. * * *

Since the 1960s, the effective hourly rate of tort lawyers has increased dramatically, while the risk of non-recovery has remained relatively constant. Professor Brickman asserts that part of this problem is that when a client hires a lawyer on a contingent fee basis, the lawyer initially assigns the case a value of zero. This occurs even if the lawsuit already has significant value because a large settlement is virtually certain. Therefore, the standard contingency fee applied not only to the value that the lawyer added but also to the substantial value that the claim already possessed. Furthermore, "contingency fee lawyers not only charge fees against settlement offers previously obtained, but also routinely charge standard contingency fees in cases where they know at the outset that there is no meaningful litigation risk and that little work will need to be required to produce a settlement." Overall, " '[f]or every case in which a one-third fee is justified, there are dozens where that amount is excessive by any standard of reasonableness." '

On the other hand, numerous advocates argue that contingency fees are not unreasonable. Professor Charles Silver maintains that there is no empirical evidence to show that attorneys are overpaid in contingency fee representations. He further asserts that "there is some evidence that attorneys who handle class actions are often underpaid." He points out that there are many instances when the lawyer receives nothing after losing at trial, despite doing extensive legal work. According to Lawrence Fox, a contingency fee expert, an evaluation of the contingency fee system must include instances where the plaintiff is unsuccessful. Fox contends that you will never hear a client offer more money in the wake of an unexpectedly low recovery when the lawyer deserved more for the time spent on the lawsuit. He states, "[T]he question is whether the reasonableness of the fee should be measured by time or by result. I favor result." In regards to the risk contingent fee lawyers assume, Robert Peck, the senior director of legal affairs for the Association of Trial Lawyers of America, reasons that by opting for a contingency fee arrangement, the client is, in effect, subsidizing other cases where the recovery is not sufficient, "much like the concept of insurance." When taken as a whole, Peck states that contingency fee lawyers "do not earn excessive returns, particularly when this risk is taken into account." * * *

Many states have enacted tort reform legislation. Most of the legislation focuses on placing different limits on a lawyer's contingency fee recovery based on the amount a plaintiff recovers in medical liability cases. * * *

Four proposals for improving the current contingency fee system have received considerable discussion in the United States, including: the early offer proposal, the New American rule, the abolishment of contingency fees, and more effective enforcement of the current ethical mandates.

A. Early Offer Proposal

In conjunction with Professor Jeffrey O'Connell and Michael Horowitz, Professor Lester Brickman designed the early offer proposal to help protect "from fee-gouging lawyers." The proposal attempts "to confine [the lawyer's] fee percentage to the value that [the lawyer] added to the claim." The proposal provides five mandates. First, a contingency fee may not be levied against settlement offers made before counsel was obtained. Second, "all defendants are given an opportunity to make settlement offers covered by the proposal, but no later than 60 days from the receipt of a notice of claim from plaintiffs' counsel." Third, the "[n]otices of claim submitted by plaintiffs' counsel are required to include basic, routinely discoverable information designed to assist defendants in evaluating plaintiff claims," and similar information in possession of the defendant must be made available to the plaintiff. Fourth, if the "plaintiff[] reject[s the] defendants' early offers, contingency fees may only be charged against net recoveries in excess of such offers." Finally, if no settlement offer is made, the contingency fee is unaffected. Therefore, "the proposal would prohibit plaintiff lawyers in personal injury cases from charging standard contingency fees where alleged responsible parties made early settlement offers before the lawyer added any significant value to the claim." * * *

B. New American Rule

In cooperation with Jim Wooton, Professor [Richard] Painter drafted the New American rule. Generally, the New American rule "requires the lawyer charging a contingent fee to say to the client in advance that 'my fee will be X% of any judgment or settlement in this case but will be no higher than Y dollars per hour.' " The lawyer and the client would be able to freely agree on the numbers X and Y. This proposal is not tied to whether there is a settlement offer or any other action by the defendant. X and Y are determined by the price the plaintiff would pay for services in an unregulated market except for the fact that the lawyer, instead of the market, must specify both X and Y. At the conclusion of the lawsuit, the client can choose to pay either X or Y.

* * *

C. Abolishment

In response to unreasonable fees, John Barry and Bert Rein propose that "[t]he only appropriate solution is to prohibit lawyers from entering into any arrangement" in which they may obtain a financial interest in a client's claim. Barry and Rein believe that "a better approach would be to undertake a fundamental restructuring of the manner in which legal services are delivered to claim holders, preserving the societal benefits of the contingent fee system while getting attorneys out of the contingent fee business altogether." Under this plan, "parties could obtain legal representation by marketing their claims to 'claim brokers" ' who would act as intermediaries between plaintiffs and lawyers. This market would preserve the current efficiencies of scale, introduce healthy competition, and may "make compensation available to many holders of low-dollar claims" who would not otherwise receive representation because some lawyers refuse to pursue small claims. Finally, since the brokers would be "purchasers rather than providers," they would have the incentive to purchase the claims that reflect their value rather than just charging a standard fee.

* * *

V. Another Way to Approach Unreasonable Contingency Fees

The biggest problem with the current method of determining a contingency fee is that the lawyer does not evaluate each case on an individual basis. The standard fee is applied to most cases without regard to whether this fee under-or over-compensates the lawyer for his or her services. I believe the first step in reform is for the lawyer to evaluate each individual lawsuit on its merits and offer a reasonable contingency fee percentage based off of this evaluation. * * *

To begin evaluating an individual case, there are a number of factors that a lawyer should consider. Basically, when a lawyer takes a case on a contingency fee basis, he or she must be compensated for the time spent on the case and the risk of no payment. This compensation for time and risk will be a percentage of the recovery obtained in the lawsuit. Therefore, an estimate of a proper contingency fee percentage must take on a similar form.

A starting point in determining a proper contingency fee percentage would be to estimate the probable hours spent, the hourly wage, the costs fronted, and the probable recovery. Using this simple formula:

$$\frac{(\text{Estimated Hours x Estimated Hourly Wage}) + (\text{Estimated Costs Fronted x Risk Multiplier})}{\text{Estimated Recovery}}$$

A better estimate of a contingency fee can be determined. Rather than just blindly guessing at a proper percentage (or worse blindly assigning the standard percentage to every case), this formula will force the lawyer to evaluate each case individually.

However, I propose that the lawyer needs to expand on this simple formula. To determine a better contingency fee, the lawyer should perform a much more in-depth analysis of each phase of the lawsuit. Experienced litigators can project the tasks that will need to be performed and estimate how many hours will be required to complete each task. An in-depth analysis of each phase of the lawsuit will yield a more precise fee tied to the particular risks associated with the lawsuit. To help lawyers calculate a more accurate and individualized contingency fee, I have expanded on the formula outlined above and developed a mathematical program that helps perform an in-depth analysis of the client's case. * * *

> **FYI**
>
> The Tennessee Supreme Court recently found that an attorney violated Rules 1.5 and 1.8(i) by entering into a contingent fee agreement that entitled the attorney to 40% of a rejected settlement offer made to his client. Specifically, the attorney's agreement provided that if the client refused to accept a settlement offer that the attorney advised the client was reasonable and should be accepted, the attorney's fee would be based on the amount of that offer. The court held this to be unreasonable, as the contingency involved was not based on the outcome, but rather on the attorney's "recommendation of a settlement offer which he deemed reasonable." In addition, the agreement gave the attorney a proprietary interest in any settlement offer in violation of Rule 1.8(i). *Moore v. Bd. of Prof'l Responsibility*, 576 S.W.3d 341 (Tenn. 2019).

[Question 3-10]

Software Start-up, Inc. sought to retain a high-profile transactional attorney to represent it in connection with its initial public offering. However, because Software believed it could not afford the attorney's hourly billing rate, Software offered the attorney an equity interest in the company in exchange for legal assistance. The attorney agreed to represent Software for a 2% equity interest and provided Software with a written agreement, explained the fee arrangement, advised Software of the desirability of seeking

the advice of independent legal counsel regarding the agreement, and gave Software a reasonable opportunity to obtain such advice. The attorney also orally explained that potential conflicts might arise as a result of her acquiring an equity interest but that no significant risk of a conflict existed under the circumstances. The terms of the agreement were objectively fair and reasonable. Software decided not to consult independent legal counsel and signed the agreement.

The initial public offering was far more successful than expected and raised the total equity value of Software to $500 million. The $10 million in stock that the attorney obtained as a fee was much higher than the amount she would have received if she had billed Software on an hourly basis. Software believed that the attorney's fee was excessive and filed a disciplinary complaint against her. Is the attorney subject to discipline?

(A) Yes, because lawyers cannot take a proprietary interest in their clients.

(B) Yes, because the ultimate fee was much higher than it would have been if the attorney had billed Software on an hourly basis.

(C) Yes, because the attorney failed to ensure that Software consulted independent legal counsel before signing the fee agreement.

(D) No, because the attorney satisfied the ethical requirements for entering into a business transaction with a client.

Rule 1.5, Comment [4] provides in part that:

A lawyer may accept property in payment for services, such as an ownership interest in an enterprise, providing this does not involve acquisition of a proprietary interest in the cause of action or subject matter of the litigation contrary to Rule 1.8(i). However, a fee paid in property instead of money may be subject to the requirements of Rule 1.8(a) because such fees often have the essential qualities of a business transaction with the client.

Rule 1.8(a) provides that:

A lawyer shall not enter into a business transaction with a client or knowingly acquire an ownership, possessory, security or other pecuniary interest adverse to a client unless:

(1) the transaction and terms on which the lawyer acquires the interest are fair and reasonable to the client and are fully disclosed and transmitted in writing in a manner that can be reasonably understood by the client;

(2) the client is advised in writing of the desirability of seeking and is given a reasonable opportunity to seek the advice of independent legal counsel on the transaction; and

(3) the client gives informed consent, in a writing signed by the client, to the essential terms of the transaction and the lawyer's role in the transaction, including whether the lawyer is representing the client in the transaction.

Also review the Comment to Rule 1.8, part of which indicates that: "[Rule 1.8(a)] does not apply to ordinary fee arrangements between client and lawyer, which are governed by Rule 1.5, although its requirements must be met when the lawyer accepts an interest in the client's business or other nonmonetary property as a payment of all or part of a fee."

Hear from the Authors

To hear more from the authors on proprietary interests, click here.

THERESE MAYNARD, *ETHICS FOR BUSINESS LAWYERS REPRESENTING START-UP COMPANIES*

11 Wake Forest J. Bus. & Intell. Prop. L. 401 (2011)

The very essence of the attorney-client relationship rests on the long-standing, fundamental premise that the client depends on the lawyer to provide sound legal advice and independent judgment that is not tainted by concerns regarding the lawyer's personal financial wellbeing.

As a result, the long-standing practice of lawyers has been to avoid taking stock in their corporate clients in lieu of fees. In fact, until quite recently, even Silicon Valley law firms avoided making equity investments in their clients. One rather high profile example of such traditional reticence to take stock in law firm clients in lieu of fees was recounted by Bill Fenwick, one of the founders of the well-known Palo Alto, California, law firm of Fenwick & West, who turned down shares in Apple Computer's IPO:

> "[W]e incorporated Apple Computer and represented them exclusively for a number of years. At one point, at a very young point in their development, they wanted us to take $50,000 off of our fees in stock. And, quite frankly, I had come from the East and . . . there are a host of problems you've got to deal with if you're going to do that. Well, that $50,000 that they wanted us to take in stock was worth $12 million when they went public, so that is a pretty humbling experience."

This long-standing perspective on equity billing arrangements began to erode in the 1990s and quickly became the subject of numerous lawyer requests for guidance from their bar ethics committees as to the propriety of such fee arrangements. Ultimately, in 2000, the American Bar Association (ABA) issued its guidance under ABA Rule 1.8 (the ABA's general rule on conflicts of interest with respect to current clients) concerning equity billing arrangements. Without a doubt, those who object to the use of equity billing arrangements largely base their objections on the ethical implications of these fee arrangements. The ABA's 2000 Ethics Opinion emphasized that, at the very minimum, the lawyer considering taking stock in lieu of fees must ensure that the lawyer's investment in the client complies with the requirements of the relevant professional responsibility rules.

* * *

While the ABA and other commentators have analogized equity billing arrangements to the well-established lawyer billing practice of relying on contingency fee arrangements in the litigation context, at least one bar association ethics committee has questioned this proposition: "The ABA accepted without question the proposition that taking stock was like a contingent fee. The Committee is not so sure. A contingent fee in a civil case depends in large measure on the efforts of the lawyer, whereas the value of stock usually depends on the client's efforts and other factors little influenced by the lawyer's work, unless as part of her representation she is to find sources of financing or otherwise contribute directly to the client's financial success." At the same time, however, equity billing arrangements do resemble contingent fee arrangements in that the problems inherent in assessing the reasonableness of an equity-based fee are very similar to the problems in evaluating a contingency fee arrangement. In other words, in the case of both contingency fee and equity billing arrangements, the lawyer stands to collect nothing or to collect a windfall. Today, courts regularly uphold contingency fee arrangements (particularly in connection with personal injury litigation) even though the personal injury lawyer may collect a fee that, with the benefit of hindsight, seems unreasonable.

JOHN S. DZIENKOWSKI & ROBERT J. PERONI, *THE DECLINE IN LAWYER INDEPENDENCE: LAWYER EQUITY INVESTMENTS IN CLIENTS*

81 Tex. L. Rev. 405, 546-49 (2002)

* * *

We believe that the rush to accept equity investments as proper vehicles for law firm compensation is misplaced. First, we expressly take issue with the ABA and state and city bar ethics opinions as downplaying the risks arising from these equity investments. As we have argued, the opinions are not consistent with the extensive body of case law examining the obligations of lawyers engaging in client business transactions, including, in particular, making investments in clients. The legal profession should return to the time when equity investments in clients were viewed with great caution and undertaken in rare circumstances. Firms that do invest in client equity should implement an extensive client consent process and an understandable form for memorializing the consent, as well as strict procedures to limit the actual and potential conflicts of interests. Second, we challenge the view that most lawyers are only involved in direct investment in a client rather than receiving equity as part of the fee. In the vast majority of cases, lawyers receive client equity at an offering price not available to most public investors. In each of these circumstances, the lawyers must comply with both the business transaction rule and the reasonable fee rule. Third, we strongly disagree with the practice of demanding equity in exchange for performing legal work for a client. The requirement of client consent necessitates that a lawyer allow a client to decline to bring lawyers into the ownership circle. Fourth, firms that accept equity investments should monitor possible conflicts of interest from the continuing representation and should consider withdrawing from future representations because of the ongoing investment. This is particularly true in the down round venture capital financing context when the client's business venture experiences financial pressures. Fifth, we urge courts and disciplinary committees to strictly construe the ethics requirements and to place the burden on the lawyer to demonstrate compliance with all of the rules.

* * *

Clients hire lawyers to provide legal advice and independent judgment. It is unrealistic to believe that lawyers who have an interest in the venture do not consider their personal financial well-being while advising the client. The disparity between the lawyer's goals and the client's goals exists in virtually every circumstance. The lawyer's personal financial goals, which may be tied almost exclusively to the short-run performance of the client's stock, will inevitably color the lawyer's judgment in advising the client. Lawyers cannot simultaneously discharge their duty of loyalty to clients and be venture capitalists. The business and legal relationships between the founding entrepreneurs and the venture capitalists must be negotiated at arm's length in every representation. The terms of the agreement have potentially dire consequences to the entrepreneur if the venture is not successful. How can the lawyers for the entrepreneurs provide independent advice when the lawyers have aligned themselves economically with the venture capitalists? Lawyer investments in client equity have been driven by lawyer greed and receive client "consent" because of a perceived value of being associated with a major Silicon Valley law firm. As long as the clients were successful in the marketplace and stock prices were dramatically rising, the negative effect of the equity investment on the independence of the lawyers (including the many actual and potential conflicts of interest) stayed below the surface. But financial and market pressures resulting from equity investment in clients in Silicon Valley have fundamentally altered the dynamics of the lawyer-client relationship and threaten to undermine the attorney's role as an independent legal adviser.

ANTHONY SEBOK, *LITIGATION INVESTMENT AND LEGAL ETHICS: WHAT ARE THE REAL ISSUES?*

55 Canadian Business Law Journal 111 (2014)

Litigation investment has become increasingly more visible and controversial in the United States. One of the concerns raised in the United States is that litigation investment places lawyers at risk of acting unethically. In this short article I will address this concern. My argument, in brief, is that there are ethical pitfalls for American attorneys whose clients take litigation investment from third parties, but those pitfalls are not what some commentators and bar committees have identified. I will then frame the ethical pitfalls that I see as real and potentially serious, and make some tentative suggestions about how to solve them.

As an initial matter, it is important to define litigation investment. The practice can mean different things to different people, and sometimes controversy over lawyers' ethics in litigation investment is really disagreement over a practice that, regardless of its ethical status, is not really litigation investment (as I and many people understand it). In this article, I will define litigation investment narrowly. Litigation investment is an investment by a non-lawyer in the proceeds of litigation. Litigation investment is sometimes called "alternative litigation finance" (ALF) or "litigation funding."

* * *

IV. The Bar Confronts the Ethical Challenge of Litigation Investment: An Example

On April 16, 2013, the Ethics Committee of the Commercial and Federal Litigation Section of the New York State Bar Association (the "Committee") published a report "On the Ethical Implications of Third-Party Litigation Funding" (the "Report"). * * *

* * *

The Report is very comprehensive—in fact, its only flaw, I would suggest, is that it is too comprehensive. The Report lists some putative ethical concerns that are pure fiction, and thereby provides a pretext to those whose real objection to litigation investment is that they simply don't like it as a matter of public policy. Five issues are identified by the Report: (1) conflicts of interest, (2) privilege and confidentiality, (3) "control over the proceeding", (4) champerty and maintenance, and (5) fee-sharing with non-attorneys. In fact, only some of these reflect the "real" ethical issues that confront lawyers whose clients receive litigation investment. Some pruning is therefore in order.

The category of "conflicts of interest' is one that gets a lot of attention in the Model Rules and litigation. But actually, there is not much opportunity for conflicts of interest between a lawyer and her client in the context of litigation investment. The Report mentions referral fees paid to lawyers by funders, but these are a red herring. First, there is almost no evidence that they are paid in New York, and second, it isn't even obvious that there is any incentive for a lawyer to take a referral fee from a funder (rather than, in truth, the reverse). Dig a little deeper, and the real conflict of interest identified by the Report arises:

. . . in the commercial litigation context [where] . . . agreements are often entered into directly with the attorney or law firm rather than with the plaintiff and thus, the attorney or law firm has contractual duties to the corporate [litigation funder] that are independent of the attorney's professional duties to the plaintiff.

There are two problems with this sentence. First, it simply states, in more general language, the third ethical issue in the list above. The first victim of a side-agreement with a third party would be the lawyer's duty under Model Rule 5.4(c), the lawyer's duty of independent professional judgment owed to the client. But second, and more important, the concern is based on a myth. Litigation investment in New York does not involve side-agreements between lawyers and funders. It is extremely unlikely that such agreements are sought outside of New York, either. Whether or not they are permissible, and if they are, what ethical issues they raise, is simply beside the point—they are a myth.

Litigation investment involves a contract between just two parties: the claimholder and the funder. The claimholder's lawyer is not part of the transaction, has no duties to the funder, and remains at all times the claimholder's agent with undivided loyalties to the claimholder.

While conflicts of interest may arise between the lawyer and her client if the client seeks funding, they don't arise because the lawyer is ever under a (conflicting) contractual or ethical obligation to the funder. So, ethical issue (3) collapses into (1). This insight also tells us that ethical issue (5)—fee-splitting with non-lawyers—is a fiction. If the lawyer has no contract with the funder, then obviously the lawyer isn't transferring money to the funder, and so the risk of fee-splitting is eliminated.

V. Separating the Genuine from the Fake

The Report does identify ethical issues that need to be addressed. The first concerns the real conflicts of interest that may arise when the client seeks the lawyer's frank and honest advice about whether the client should seek funding. The second concerns the malpractice risks that arise on numerous fronts, including (but not limited to) the scope of the lawyer's obligation to competently advise a client who is attempting to get outside funding about whether to take funding, the terms of the investment agreement, the legality of the underlying investment agreement, and the risks to the client's case posed by allegations of waiver of privilege by the opposing party for any documents or communications provided by the client or the lawyer to the funder. Finally, although this is not technically a matter of concern for legal ethics, there is a larger concern about the social consequences of litigation investment, and consequently what role these concerns should play in the interpretation of the law and rules of professional responsibility. For example, if there were objective reasons to believe that consumers were ill-equipped to understand the costs and benefits of what they were selling when they sold contingent shares of their future personal injury recoveries, it might make sense to either interpret existing New York laws and regulations or demand new laws or regulations to protect consumers.

* * *

Recently the President of the U.K. Supreme Court argued in a major address that the same reasons that originally compelled the English legal system to suppress champerty and maintenance (*e.g.* litigation investment) now compel the opposite:

The public policy rationale regarding maintenance and champerty has turned full circle . . . [public policy] appears positively to support the development of litigation investment, as a means of securing effective access to justice.

Rather than viewing litigation investment with suspicion, Lord Neuberger called on attorneys and judges to embrace it, albeit with the appropriate protections and regulations that would accompany any new innovative financial product.

W. BRADLEY WENDEL, *ARE THERE ETHICAL PITFALLS IN THE USE OF THIRD-PARTY LITIGATION FINANCING?*

80 The Advocate (Texas) 51, 51–52 (2017)

A SMALL COMPANY INVENTS A NIFTY PIECE of technology and brings it to market. It is a success—so successful, in fact, that a huge multinational corporation with whom the small company had a longstanding commercial relationship steals confidential information and uses the technology in its own products. Now the small company wants to pursue an action for misappropriation of trade secrets, but is understandably worried about being able to finance the litigation. * * * A reasonable budget for the litigation, assuming a law firm compensated on an hourly basis, is about $5 million through trial. Could the plaintiff secure counsel on a contingency fee arrangement? Perhaps, although the law firms that tend to represent clients in complex commercial tort cases generally avoid contingency fees. Although it is apparently meritorious, the company's case is not a slam-dunk, so there is sufficient risk to deter firms that might otherwise take the case on a contingency. It appears that the company may be financially unable to pursue a claim against a much larger and wealthier defendant.

This is the backstory of *Miller, U.K. v. Caterpillar,* a case that resulted in a written opinion in federal district court in Chicago, and ultimately a $74 million jury verdict for the small company. The plaintiff in that case was able to obtain funding not from its own working capital or in the form of an advance from its lawyer, but from a third-party funding company. In a typical commercial litigation financing transaction, a funder agrees to invest some amount—let's say, $4 million—in a claimant's case. The agreement is between the funder and the claimant. It provides that upon recovery of any amount, by judgment or settlement, the funder will be entitled to the return of its investment plus some premium, generally calculated as a multiplier of the investment amount. The investment is non-recourse, so that if there is no recovery, the funder's investment is lost. Hypothetically speaking, after two years of litigation, the funder may receive a multiplier of three times the amount invested, which in this case would be $12 million. The client therefore winds up with $58 million (the judgment less the return of investment and the premium), less attorneys' fees and litigation expenses, but it did not have to come up with the capital to finance the litigation on an ongoing basis. Nor did it have to sign away one-third or more of the proceeds in exchange for a law firm agreeing to bear the risk of non-recovery, in addition to financing the value of its services and the expenses of litigation. The investor also realizes a nice return, commensurate with the risk of losing the full amount of its investment. Sounds like a win-win all around.

Even when presented with this type of good outcome all around, lawyers tend to be a bit skeptical about third-party litigation financing. * * * But American lawyers may also have a sense that it is happening elsewhere, including the U.K. and Australia, and that foreign lawyers may be using their access to investors' capital to gain an advantage over their competitors in the U.S. For this reason, the American Bar Association's Ethics 20/20 Commission ("Commission") decided to study third-party litigation financing, along with other recent developments related to information technology and globalization. The Commission wanted to know, in particular, whether any changes to the ABA's Model Rules of Professional Conduct were required to preserve the core values of the legal profession in the face of global and digital competition.

I was one of two co-Reporters to the Working Group ("Working Group") [the other was Anthony Sebok] formed by the Commission to study third-party litigation financing (which is also called "alternative" legal financing, or ALF). The Working Group and the Commission considered a number of proposed changes to the Model Rules and commentary, but eventually reached the following conclusion: The existing Model Rules are adequate to deal with whatever ethical problems may arise for lawyers as a result of third-party litigation financing. Ethics issues in connection with litigation financing are very fact-specific, and thus it is impossible to say anything of general significance about competence, confidentiality and privilege, conflicts of interest, or independent professional judgment. The better approach would instead be to provide detailed, comprehensive guidance for lawyers, organized around hypothetical cases that illustrate the ways in which these issues can arise in practice. The result was a so-called White Paper on Alternative Litigation Finance ("White Paper"), available on the Commission's website.

* * *

Take Note

In 2018 the New York City Bar issued an ethics opinion finding that it would violate Rule 5.4's prohibition on sharing fees with non-lawyers for a lawyer to make her repayment of funds provided by a third-party financier contingent on the lawyer's receipt of legal fees in the matter. N.Y.C. Bar, Formal Op. 2018-5 (July 30, 2018). To review the opinion, click here.

Global Perspectives

The White Paper on ALF, referenced in the Wendel article, notes that alternative litigation funding is available to clients in markets such as the United Kingdom, Australia, Germany, and Spain, and then seeks "to define general principles of professional responsibility that are applicable to lawyers representing clients who are involved in ALF funding." As the White Paper predicted, litigation funding has continued to grow. For example, the headline of a July 2016 ABA Journal story stated "Third-party financing is growing, and lawyers are big players." Providers include global companies who invest in litigation in the United States and elsewhere.

Hear from the Authors

To hear from the authors on types of fees, click here.

What special considerations are involved if a fee contract is entered into after a matter has commenced?

Restatement § 18, Comment e:

Client-lawyer fee contracts entered into after the matter in question is under way are subject to special scrutiny. * * *

The lawyer may enforce the contract by persuading the tribunal that the contract was fair and reasonable to the client under the circumstances in which it was entered. The showing of fairness and reasonableness must encompass two elements.

First, the lawyer must show that the client was adequately aware of the effects and any material disadvantages of the proposed contract, including, if applicable, circumstances concerning the need for modification. The more experienced the client is in such dealings with lawyers, the less the lawyer need inform the client. Likewise, less disclosure is required when an independent lawyer is advising the client about the proposed contract. It will also be relevant to sustaining the contract if the client initiated the request for the modification, such as when a client who is facing unexpected financial difficulty requests that the lawyer change an hourly fee contract to one involving a contingent fee. Second, the lawyer must show that the client was not pressured to accede in order to avoid the problems of changing counsel, alienating the lawyer, missing a deadline or losing a significant opportunity in the matter, or because a new lawyer would have to repeat significant work for which the client owed or had paid the first lawyer. * * * In general, the lawyer must show that a reasonable client might have chosen to accept the late contract, typically because it benefited the client in some substantial way (other than by relieving the client from having to find a new lawyer). Although fairness and reasonableness to the client is the issue, the strength and legitimacy of the lawyer's need for the terms of the late contract are relevant to that issue. If the client and lawyer made an initial contract and the postinception contract in question is a modification of that contract, the client may avoid the contract unless the lawyer makes the showings indicated in Subsection (1)(a). Postinception modification beneficial to a lawyer, although justifiable in some instances, raises questions why the original contract was not itself sufficiently fair and reasonable. Yet, the scope of the representation and the relationship between client and lawyer cannot always be foreseen at the time of an initial contract. Both client and lawyer might sometimes benefit from adjusting their terms of dealing. Sometimes, indeed, a new contract may be unavoidable, as when a client asks a lawyer to expand the scope of the representation.* * *

> **Food for Thought**
>
> You have now read arguments for and against lawyers' accepting an equity interest in their clients as payment for services and lawyers' use of alternative litigation funding. What is your view? What will you do when you are a lawyer? Should the ethics rules permit this practice?

Lawyers must follow special rules for certain financial transactions with clients. For example, Rule 1.8(e) provides:

A lawyer shall not provide financial assistance to a client in connection with pending or contemplated litigation, except that:

(1) a lawyer may advance court costs and expenses of litigation, the repayment of which may be contingent on the outcome of the matter; and

(2) a lawyer representing an indigent client may pay court costs and expenses of litigation on behalf of the client.

The limitation on financial assistance to clients results both from a concern for lawyer independence and for removing the incentive for stirring up litigation. Comment [10] to Rule 1.8 explains:

Lawyers may not subsidize lawsuits or administrative proceedings brought on behalf of their clients, including making or guaranteeing loans to their clients for living expenses, because to do so would encourage clients to pursue lawsuits that might not otherwise be brought and because such assistance gives lawyers too great a financial stake in the litigation. These dangers do not warrant a prohibition on a lawyer lending a client court costs and litigation expenses, including the expenses of medical examination and the costs of obtaining and presenting evidence, because these advances are virtually indistinguishable from contingent fees and help ensure access to the courts. Similarly, an exception allowing lawyers representing indigent clients to pay court costs and litigation expenses regardless of whether these funds will be repaid is warranted.

What about the assistance at issue in Question 3-11?

[Question 3-11]

A legal services attorney represents a client in an eviction proceeding. The client does not have enough money to buy his child shoes required for school. If the child does not have the required shoes, she cannot attend school, and evidence of her nonattendance would weigh against the client in the eviction proceeding. The attorney bought the shoes for the client's child. Was the attorney's conduct proper?

(A) Yes, because the attorney bought the shoes for the child personally, rather than giving the client the money to do so.

(B) Yes, because the attorney was a legal services lawyer.

(C) No, because the attorney provided financial assistance to the client in connection with the eviction proceeding.

(D) No, because lawyers may never provide financial assistance to clients.

Notwithstanding the general prohibition on providing financial assistance to clients in litigation matters, some jurisdictions include a "humanitarian exception" in their versions of Rule 1.8(e), which allows lawyers to make loans or gifts to clients when necessity dictates. D.C. Rule 1.8(d), for instance, permits a lawyer to provide "[o]ther financial assistance which is reasonably necessary to permit the client to institute or maintain the litigation or administrative proceedings."

Rule 1.8 also contains limits on the manner in which lawyers can be compensated for legal services:

(d) Prior to the conclusion of representation of a client, a lawyer shall not make or negotiate an agreement giving the lawyer literary or media rights to a portrayal or account based in substantial part on information relating to the representation.

* * *

(f) A lawyer shall not accept compensation for representing a client from one other than the client unless:

(1) the client gives informed consent;

(2) there is no interference with the lawyer's independence of professional judgment or with the client-lawyer relationship; and

(3) information relating to representation of a client is protected as required by Rule 1.6.

Safe-Keeping Client Funds

Rule 1.15 deals with safeguarding of client funds and property, as well as those of third persons in connection with a representation. This rule varies somewhat from jurisdiction to jurisdiction. As a result, you should be sure to consult the version in the state in which you will be practicing. Utah's Rule 1.15 captures the essence of the provision and is virtually identical to Model Rule 1.15:

(a) A lawyer shall hold property of clients or third persons that is in a lawyer's possession in connection with a representation separate from the lawyer's own property. Funds shall be kept in a separate account maintained in the state where the lawyer's office is situated or elsewhere with the consent of the client or third person. * * * Other property shall be identified as such and appropriately safeguarded. Complete records of such account funds and other property shall be kept by the lawyer and shall be preserved for a period of five years after termination of the representation.

(b) A lawyer may deposit the lawyer's own funds in a client trust account for the sole purpose of paying bank service charges on that account, but only in an amount necessary for that purpose.

Hear from the Authors

Insurance defense often raises ethical issues relating to an insurance company serving as a third-party payor of an insured's legal fees. *See, e.g.,* Stephen L. Pepper, *Applying the Fundamentals of Lawyers' Ethics to Insurance Defense Practice,* 4 Conn. Insurance L.J. 27 (1997). To hear more from the authors on ethical issues relating to the insurance company as a third-party payer, click here.

(c) A lawyer shall deposit into a client trust account legal fees and expenses that have been paid in advance, to be withdrawn by the lawyer only as fees are earned or expenses incurred.

(d) Upon receiving funds or other property in which a client or third person has an interest, a lawyer shall promptly notify the client or third person. Except as stated in this Rule or otherwise permitted by law or by agreement with the client, a lawyer shall promptly deliver to the client or third person any funds or other property that the client or third person is entitled to receive and, upon request by the client or third person, shall promptly render a full accounting regarding such property.

(e) When in the course of representation a lawyer is in possession of property in which two or more persons (one of whom may be the lawyer) claim interests, the property shall be kept separate by the lawyer until the dispute is resolved. The lawyer shall promptly distribute all portions of the property as to which the interests are not in dispute.

[Question 3-12]

An attorney received a $10,000 retainer from a client for a new matter, and promptly placed the money in her client trust account. The attorney anticipated doing at least 10 hours of work per week on the matter over the next four weeks. Her standard rate is $250/ hour. In order to cover some unusual office expenses that month, the attorney decided to transfer $2,000 of anticipated earnings from the client's matter into an account used for business expenses. The attorney explained to the client that the $2,000 had been moved from her client trust account. The client approved and, as the attorney expected, the matter did in fact require 10 hours of time each week for four weeks.

Is the attorney subject to discipline?

(A) **Yes, because the attorney withdrew money from her client trust account before the fees were earned or expenses incurred.**

(B) **Yes, because lawyers are not permitted to use client funds to pay business expenses.**

(C) **No, because the client approved of the attorney's conduct.**

(D) **No, because the attorney accurately predicted the number of hours that would be worked over the four weeks.**

[Question 3-13]

A client paid an attorney a $10,000 retainer to defend the client in a property dispute with a neighbor. The attorney promptly deposited the funds into his client trust account. The day after receiving the retainer, the attorney spent 10 hours on the matter, primarily conducting research. Late that evening, the client sent the attorney the following message:

> **"Please don't perform any work on my property dispute matter. My neighbor has agreed to settle."**

The attorney subsequently sent the client a bill for $2,000 for his 10 hours of work on the matter at his standard hourly rate of $200. The client refused to pay the bill and demanded a full refund the $10,000, because the attorney's work was not necessary.

What should the attorney do with the $10,000?

(A) Transfer $2,000 to the attorney's operating account and return $8,000 to the client.

(B) Leave $2,000 in the client trust account until the fee dispute is resolved and return $8,000 to the client.

(C) Keep the full $10,000 in the client trust account until the fee dispute is resolved.

(D) Return the entire $10,000 to the client.

C. Court-Awarded Attorneys' Fees

Another source of fees is court-awarded fees. As the Restatement notes, "[p]revailing litigants in some types of litigation are entitled to recover attorney fees from an opposing party." § 38, Comment f. These cases can range from matrimonial and contempt matters to federal and state statutes providing court-awarded attorneys' fees in an effort to provide an incentive to enforce particular laws. These latter provisions exist in a variety of areas of law, including securities, antitrust, civil rights, and *qui tam* actions.

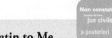

It's Latin to Me

Black's Law Dictionary defines *qui tam action* as "[a]n action brought under a statute that allows a private person to sue for a penalty, part of which the government or some specified public institution will receive."

ASHLEY E. COMPTON, *NOTE, SHIFTING THE BLAME: THE DILEMMA OF FEE-SHIFTING STATUTES AND FEE-WAIVER SETTLEMENTS*

22 Geo. J. Legal Ethics 761, 763–64 (2009)

* * *

Most federal civil rights are not self-executing; the law depends on government enforcement and private litigation in which plaintiff's counsel acts as a private attorney general. As a general rule of American common law, litigants pay their own legal fees. Congress, however, created fee-shifting statutes to support the private litigation of federal rights by giving the prevailing party the right to seek attorney's fees and costs.

Illustrating the importance of fee-shifting statutes for the enforcement of a federal civil right, Supreme Court Associate Justice Thomas Clark stated that not awarding attorney's fees in civil rights cases would be "tantamount to repealing the [Civil Rights] Act itself." Between 1870 and 1976, Congress passed over fifty fee-shifting statutes. Fee-shifting provisions are common "in laws under which 'private attorneys general' play a significant role in enforcing [Congressional civil rights] policies." In 1976, to close irregular gaps in civil rights laws caused by a Supreme Court holding, Congress passed the Civil Rights Attorney's Fees Award Act (the Fees Act), which provides that "the court, in its discretion, may allow the prevailing party . . . a reasonable attorney's fee as part of the costs." State civil rights statutes include similar fee-shifting provisions.

Fee-shifting statues generally have at least four common characteristics. First, the statutes attempt to promote private enforcement of individual rights in cases too discrete to ordinarily warrant Department of Justice enforcement. Recognizing the danger of relying on private enforcement, Congress feared that "if the cost of private enforcement becomes too great, there will be no private enforcement." Second, the statues often implicate civil rights cases in which "the citizen who must sue to enforce the law has little or no money with which to hire a lawyer." Therefore, Congress wanted these plaintiffs to "recover what it costs them to vindicate these rights in court." Third, the sought-after relief in civil rights suits is often injunctive and non-monetary. Thus, plaintiffs' attorneys cannot utilize traditional contingency fee agreements. Finally, Congress hoped the fee-shifting statutes would "deter[] frivolous suits" which would be "litigated in 'bad faith' under the guise of attempting to enforce" federal rights.

As out-of-court settlements became more popular than disposition by trial, the Supreme Court held that prevailing through settlement rather than litigation did not weaken a plaintiff's claim to fees. The Court also clarified that the statutory language "prevailing party" required that the attorney's fees are the right of the client, not the attorney.

MICHAEL WATERSTONE, *A NEW VISION OF PUBLIC ENFORCEMENT*

92 Minn. L. Rev. 434, 443–47 (2007)

* * *

To the extent that [the 1960s and 1970s] was a golden or even classic era, it did not last very long. The private attorney general as enforcer of civil rights soon faced a multilevel assault by the courts and Congress. In *Buckhannon Board & Care Home, Inc. v. West Virginia Department of Health and Human Resources*, the Court dramatically changed the ways that plaintiffs could recover attorneys' fees in civil rights cases. Rather than qualifying as "prevailing parties" by showing that their lawsuit was a catalyst for voluntary change by the defendant (the previously accepted "catalyst theory"), the Court held that plaintiffs must achieve a "material alteration of the legal relationship of the parties," such as a favorable judgment on the merits or a consent decree. This judicially imposed limitation has undermined the ability of the private attorney general to bring cases for injunctive relief. In other cases the Court has curtailed Congress's ability to authorize private damage suits against states and restricted private rights of action to enforce the disparate impact regulations promulgated under Title VI of the Civil Rights Act of 1964.

Perhaps unintentionally, statutory developments have also been unkind to the private attorney general. In 1991, Congress amended Title VII to allow plaintiffs claiming intentional discrimination to seek compensatory and punitive damages and to request jury trials. These changes were intended to bolster the private enforcement scheme. Ironically, however, by complicating the class certification inquiry, they have stymied the ability of the private parties and their lawyers to bring civil rights class actions.

The political capital and popularity of the civil rights plaintiffs' bar has also faded. The first step was the dismantling of the Legal Services Corporation (LSC). Organizations that had been effective private attorneys general in civil rights cases had their funds cut. Then, in 1996, Congress enacted a series of restrictions on the LSC, including prohibiting organizations that receive funding from the Corporation from bringing class actions. This was devastating to the LSC's ability to prosecute large cases on the public's behalf.

The civil rights private attorney general came to be viewed less as a social advocate and more akin to his mass tort or securities counterpart. The * * * passage of the Class Action Fairness Act (CAFA) demonstrates the decreased political power of the plaintiffs' civil rights bar. Amongst other things, CAFA moves certain class action cases from state to federal court on the stated rationale that the civil litigation system had been abused by plaintiffs' class action lawyers. Various civil rights groups argued that CAFA was unnecessary in civil rights cases because there was no history of civil rights class action abuses in state court. Despite vehement pursuit, the civil rights community was unable to get a carve-out for civil rights class actions.

Commentators also soured on the private attorney general. In a series of articles in the 1980s, Professor John Coffee started questioning the extent to which we could "sensibly rely on private litigation as a method of law enforcement." In criticizing the private attorney general as a legal institution that had not lived up to its early promise to promote the public interest, Coffee noted that private lawyers may have different incentives than their clients, which leads to either poor representation (where plaintiffs' lawyers sell out their clients) or excessive litigation (because the parties to the litigation do not bear its costs). Although Professor Coffee's work focused on securities litigation, his basic criticisms have * * * been extended to the civil rights private attorney general. Professor Michael Selmi conducted a * * * study of high-profile employment class action cases with large settlements, all of which were brought by the private bar. Professor Selmi found, quite discouragingly, that these cases have little or no effect on stock price, create little or no meaningful substantive change within corporations, and produce only modest financial benefits for class members, despite the fact that the remedial focus of these cases was monetary relief. He concludes that one of the few things these cases actually accomplished was enriching the lawyers that were involved.

* * *

[Question 3-14]

After the plaintiffs in a civil rights class action won a lengthy, difficult case against the State, the judge entered an award for attorneys' fees under the applicable federal fee-shifting statute based upon the lodestar, which is determined by multiplying the number of hours worked by the customary hourly rate. The judge felt the amount was far too low given the time and effort expended by the plaintiffs' attorneys over many years, during which they went uncompensated and were forced to cover substantial expenses. May the judge award the attorneys additional compensation?

(A) Yes, because the lodestar may be increased due to superior performance and results provided that the judge identifies extraordinary circumstances to justify the enhancement.

(B) Yes, because the lodestar may be increased at the judge's discretion.

(C) No, because a judge does not have authority to award a fee enhancement under federal fee-shifting statutes.

(D) No, because the judge did not have a sufficiently compelling reason to enhance the fees in this case.

Perdue v. Kenny A. ex rel. Winn

559 U.S. 542 (2010)

ALITO, J. delivered the opinion of the Court.

This case presents the question whether the calculation of an attorney's fee, under federal fee-shifting statutes, based on the "lodestar," *i.e.*, the number of hours worked multiplied by the prevailing hourly rates, may be increased due to superior performance and results. We have stated in previous cases that such an increase is permitted in extraordinary circumstances, and we reaffirm that rule. But as we have also said in prior cases, there is a strong presumption that the lodestar is sufficient; factors subsumed in the lodestar calculation cannot be used as a ground for increasing an award above the lodestar; and a party seeking fees has the burden of identifying a factor that the lodestar does not adequately take into account and proving with specificity that an enhanced fee is justified. Because the District Court did not apply these standards, we reverse the decision below and remand for further proceedings consistent with this opinion.

* * * Respondents (plaintiffs below) are children in the Georgia foster-care system and their next friends. They filed this class action on behalf of 3,000 children in foster care and named as defendants the Governor of Georgia and various state officials (petitioners in this case). Claiming that deficiencies in the foster-care system in two counties near Atlanta violated

their federal and state constitutional and statutory rights, respondents sought injunctive and declaratory relief, as well as attorney's fees and expenses.

The United States District Court for the Northern District of Georgia eventually referred the case to mediation, where the parties entered into a consent decree, which the District Court approved. The consent decree resolved all pending issues other than the fees that respondents' attorneys were entitled to receive under 42 U.S.C. § 1988. * * *

Respondents submitted a request for more than $14 million in attorney's fees. Half of that amount was based on their calculation of the lodestar-roughly 30,000 hours multiplied by hourly rates of $200 to $495 for attorneys and $75 to $150 for non-attorneys. In support of their fee request, respondents submitted affidavits asserting that these rates were within the range of prevailing market rates for legal services in the relevant market.

The other half of the amount that respondents sought represented a fee enhancement for superior work and results. Affidavits submitted in support of this request claimed that the lodestar amount "would be generally insufficient to induce lawyers of comparable skill, judgment, professional representation and experience" to litigate this case. * * * Petitioners objected to the fee request, contending that some of the proposed hourly rates were too high, that the hours claimed were excessive, and that the enhancement would duplicate factors that were reflected in the lodestar amount.

The District Court awarded fees of approximately $10.5 million. * * * The District Court found that the hourly rates proposed by respondents were "fair and reasonable," * * * but that some of the entries on counsel's billing records were vague and that the hours claimed for many of the billing categories were excessive. The court therefore cut the non-travel hours by 15% and halved the hourly rate for travel hours. This resulted in a lodestar calculation of approximately $6 million.

The court then enhanced this award by 75%, concluding that the lodestar calculation did not take into account "(1) the fact that class counsel were required to advance case expenses of $1.7 million over a three-year period with no on[-]going reimbursement, (2) the fact that class counsel were not paid on an on-going basis as the work was being performed, and (3) the fact that class counsel's ability to recover a fee and expense reimbursement were completely contingent on the outcome of the case." * * * The court stated that respondents' attorneys had exhibited "a higher degree of skill, commitment, dedication, and professionalism . . . than the Court has seen displayed by the attorneys in any other case during its 27 years on the bench." * * * The court also commented that the results obtained were " 'extraordinary' " and added that "[a]fter 58 years as a practicing attorney and federal judge, the Court is unaware of any other case in which a plaintiff class has achieved such a favorable result on such a comprehensive scale." * * * The enhancement resulted in an additional $4.5 million fee award.

Relying on prior Circuit precedent, a panel of the Eleventh Circuit affirmed. * * * The panel held that the District Court had not abused its discretion by failing to make a larger reduction in the number of hours for which respondents' attorneys sought reimbursement, but the panel commented that it "would have cut the billable hours more if we were deciding the matter in the first instance" and added that the hourly rates approved by the District Court also "appear[ed] to be on the generous side." * * * On the question of the enhancement, however, the panel splintered, with each judge writing a separate opinion.

Judge Carnes concluded that binding Eleventh Circuit precedent required that the decision of the District Court be affirmed, but he opined that the reasoning in our opinions suggested that no enhancement should be allowed in this case. He concluded that the quality of the attorneys' performance was "adequately accounted for 'either in determining the reasonable number of hours expended on the litigation or in setting the reasonable hourly rates.' " * * * He found that an enhancement could not be justified based on delay in the recovery of attorney's fees and reimbursable expenses because such delay is a routine feature of cases brought under 42 U.S.C. § 1983. * * * The Eleventh Circuit denied rehearing en banc over the dissent of three judges. * * *

We granted certiorari.

* * *

The general rule in our legal system is that each party must pay its own attorney's fees and expenses,* * * but Congress enacted 42 U.S.C. § 1988 in order to ensure that federal rights are adequately enforced. Section 1988 provides that a prevailing party in certain civil rights actions may recover "a reasonable attorney's fee as part of the costs."[3] Unfortunately, the statute does not explain what Congress meant by a "reasonable" fee, and therefore the task of identifying an appropriate methodology for determining a "reasonable" fee was left for the courts.

* * *

Our prior decisions concerning the federal fee-shifting statutes have established six important rules that lead to our decision in this case.

First, a "reasonable" fee is a fee that is sufficient to induce a capable attorney to undertake the representation of a meritorious civil rights case. * * * Section 1988's aim is to enforce the covered civil rights statutes, not to provide "a form of economic relief to improve the financial lot of attorneys." * * *

Second, the lodestar method yields a fee that is presumptively sufficient to achieve this objective. * * *

Third, although we have never sustained an enhancement of a lodestar amount for performance, * * * we have repeatedly said that enhancements may be awarded in " 'rare' " and " 'exceptional' " circumstances. * * *

Fourth, we have noted that "the lodestar figure includes most, if not all, of the relevant factors constituting a 'reasonable' attorney's fee," * * * and have held that an enhancement may not be awarded based on a factor that is subsumed in the lodestar calculation * * * . We have thus held that the novelty and complexity of a case generally may not be used as a ground for an

---

3   Virtually identical language appears in many of the federal fee-shifting statutes. * * *

enhancement because these factors "presumably [are] fully reflected in the number of billable hours recorded by counsel." We have also held that the quality of an attorney's performance generally should not be used to adjust the lodestar "[b]ecause considerations concerning the quality of a prevailing party's counsel's representation normally are reflected in the reasonable hourly rate." * * *

Fifth, the burden of proving that an enhancement is necessary must be borne by the fee applicant. * * *

Finally, a fee applicant seeking an enhancement must produce "specific evidence" that supports the award. * * * This requirement is essential if the lodestar method is to realize one of its chief virtues, i.e., providing a calculation that is objective and capable of being reviewed on appeal.

* * *

In light of what we have said in prior cases, we reject any contention that a fee determined by the lodestar method may not be enhanced in any situation. The lodestar method was never intended to be conclusive in all circumstances. Instead, there is a "strong presumption" that the lodestar figure is reasonable, but that presumption may be overcome in those rare circumstances in which the lodestar does not adequately take into account a factor that may properly be considered in determining a reasonable fee.

* * *

In this case, we are asked to decide whether either the quality of an attorney's performance or the results obtained are factors that may properly provide a basis for an enhancement. We treat these two factors as one. When a plaintiff's attorney achieves results that are more favorable than would have been predicted based on the governing law and the available evidence, the outcome may be attributable to superior performance and commitment of resources by plaintiff's counsel. Or the outcome may result from inferior performance by defense counsel, unanticipated defense concessions, unexpectedly favorable rulings by the court, an unexpectedly sympathetic jury, or simple luck. Since none of these latter causes can justify an enhanced award, superior results are relevant only to the extent it can be shown that they are the result of superior attorney performance. Thus, we need only consider whether superior attorney performance can justify an enhancement. And in light of the principles derived from our prior cases, we inquire whether there are circumstances in which superior attorney performance is not adequately taken into account in the lodestar calculation. We conclude that there are a few such circumstances but that these circumstances are indeed "rare" and "exceptional," and require specific evidence that the lodestar fee would not have been "adequate to attract competent counsel[.]"

First, an enhancement may be appropriate where the method used in determining the hourly rate employed in the lodestar calculation does not adequately measure the attorney's true market value, as demonstrated in part during the litigation. This may occur if the hourly rate is determined by a formula that takes into account only a single factor (such as years since admission to the bar) or perhaps only a few similar factors. In such a case, an enhancement may be appropriate so that an attorney is compensated at the rate that the attorney would receive in cases not governed by the federal fee-shifting statutes. But in order to provide a calculation that is objective and reviewable, the trial judge should adjust the attorney's hourly rate in accordance with specific proof linking the attorney's ability to a prevailing market rate.

Second, an enhancement may be appropriate if the attorney's performance includes an extraordinary outlay of expenses and the litigation is exceptionally protracted. As Judge Carnes noted below, when an attorney agrees to represent a civil rights plaintiff who cannot afford to pay the attorney, the attorney presumably understands that no reimbursement is likely to be received until the successful resolution of the case, * * * and therefore enhancements to compensate for delay in reimbursement for expenses must be reserved for unusual cases. In such exceptional cases, however, an enhancement may be allowed, but the amount of the enhancement must be calculated using a method that is reasonable, objective, and capable of being reviewed on appeal, such as by applying a standard rate of interest to the qualifying outlays of expenses.

Third, there may be extraordinary circumstances in which an attorney's performance involves exceptional delay in the payment of fees. An attorney who expects to be compensated under § 1988 presumably understands that payment of fees will generally not come until the end of the case, if at all. * * * Compensation for this delay is generally made "either by basing the award on current rates or by adjusting the fee based on historical rates to reflect its present value." * * * But we do not rule out the possibility that an enhancement may be appropriate where an attorney assumes these costs in the face of unanticipated delay, particularly where the delay is unjustifiably caused by the defense. In such a case, however, the enhancement should be calculated by applying a method similar to that described above in connection with exceptional delay in obtaining reimbursement for expenses.

We reject the suggestion that it is appropriate to grant performance enhancements on the ground that departures from hourly billing are becoming more common. As we have noted, the lodestar was adopted in part because it provides a rough approximation of general billing practices, and accordingly, if hourly billing becomes unusual, an alternative to the lodestar method may have to be found. However, neither respondents nor their *amici* contend that that day has arrived. Nor have they shown that permitting the award of enhancements on top of the lodestar figure corresponds to prevailing practice in the general run of cases.

We are told that, under an increasingly popular arrangement, attorneys are paid at a reduced hourly rate but receive a bonus if certain specified results are obtained, and this practice is analogized to the award of an enhancement such as the one in this case. The analogy, however, is flawed. An attorney who agrees, at the outset of the representation, to a *reduced hourly rate* in exchange for the opportunity to earn a performance bonus is in a position far different from an attorney in a § 1988 case who is compensated at the *full prevailing rate* and then seeks a performance enhancement in addition to the lodestar amount after the litigation has concluded. Reliance on these comparisons for the purposes of administering enhancements, therefore, is not appropriate.

* * *

In the present case, the District Court did not provide proper justification for the large enhancement that it awarded. The court increased the lodestar award by 75% but, as far as the court's opinion reveals, this figure appears to have been essentially arbitrary. Why, for example, did the court grant a 75% enhancement instead of the 100% increase that respondents sought? And why 75% rather than 50% or 25% or 10%?

The District Court commented that the enhancement was the "minimum enhancement of the lodestar necessary to reasonably compensate [respondents'] counsel." * * * But the effect of the enhancement was to increase the top rate for the attorneys to more than $866 per hour, and the District Court did not point to anything in the record that shows that this is an appropriate figure for the relevant market.

The District Court pointed to the fact that respondents' counsel had to make extraordinary outlays for expenses and had to wait for reimbursement, * * * but the court did not calculate the amount of the enhancement that is attributable to this factor. Similarly, the District Court noted that respondents' counsel did not receive fees on an ongoing basis while the case was pending, but the court did not sufficiently link this factor to proof in the record that the delay here was outside the normal range expected by attorneys who rely on § 1988 for the payment of their fees or quantify the disparity. Nor did the court provide a calculation of the cost to counsel of any extraordinary and unwarranted delay. * * *

Finally, insofar as the District Court relied on a comparison of the performance of counsel in this case with the performance of counsel in unnamed prior cases, the District Court did not employ a methodology that permitted meaningful appellate review. Needless to say, we do not question the sincerity of the District Court's observations, and we are in no position to assess their accuracy. But when a trial judge awards an enhancement on an impressionistic basis, a major purpose of the lodestar method-providing an objective and reviewable basis for fees * * * is undermined.

Determining a "reasonable attorney's fee" is a matter that is committed to the sound discretion of a trial judge, see 42 U.S.C. § 1988 (permitting court, "in its discretion," to award fees), but the judge's discretion is not unlimited. It is essential that the judge provide a reasonably specific explanation for all aspects of a fee determination, including any award of an enhancement. Unless such an explanation is given, adequate appellate review is not feasible, and without such review, widely disparate awards may be made, and awards may be influenced (or at least, may appear to be influenced) by a judge's subjective opinion regarding particular attorneys or the importance of the case. In addition, in future cases, defendants contemplating the possibility of settlement will have no way to estimate the likelihood of having to pay a potentially huge enhancement. * * *

Section 1988 serves an important public purpose by making it possible for persons without means to bring suit to vindicate their rights. But unjustified enhancements that serve only to enrich attorneys are not consistent with the statute's aim. In many cases, attorney's fees awarded under § 1988 are not paid by the individuals responsible for the constitutional or statutory violations on which the judgment is based. Instead, the fees are paid in effect by state and local taxpayers, and because state and local governments have limited budgets, money that is used to pay attorney's fees is money that cannot be used for programs that provide vital public services. * * *

* * *

For all these reasons, the judgment of the Court of Appeals is reversed, and the case is remanded for proceedings consistent with this opinion.

It is so ordered.

* * *

FYI

During the same term as *Perdue*, the Supreme Court considered two other fee-shifting cases. In *Hardt v. Reliance Standard Life Insurance Co.*, 560 U.S. 242 (2010), the Court held that a litigant need not be a "prevailing party" to receive attorney's fees so long as she achieves "some degree of success on the merits" under the federal Employment Retirement Income Security Act. In *Astrue v. Ratliff*, 560 U.S. 586 (2010), the Court held that a federal fee-shifting statute award belongs to the client, not the lawyer. Thus the government could use the fee award to offset the client's tax debt, leaving the lawyer unpaid despite a successful representation.

[Question 3-15]

An attorney represented a class of plaintiffs in a civil rights case against the State, which offered to provide substantially all of the relief the plaintiffs sought so long as the attorney agreed to waive court-awarded attorney's fees under 42 U.S.C. § 1988. The attorney agreed to waive her fee award, and the parties settled the case.

The plaintiffs later appealed the settlement on the ground that the demand for a waiver of court-awarded attorney's fees undermined the important public policy goal of encouraging lawyers to undertake such representations. How is the appeals court likely to rule?

(A) The court will uphold the settlement because Section 1988 does not prohibit settlement conditioned on waiver of attorney's fees.

(B) The court will uphold the settlement because the lawsuit was a class action.

(C) The court will set the settlement aside because the waiver of attorney's fees is inconsistent with the purpose of encouraging lawyers to undertake such representations.

(D) The court will set the settlement aside because the trial court was prohibited from approving a settlement conditioned on an attorney's waiver of court-awarded fees.

Evans v. Jeff D.

475 U.S. 717 (1986)

JUSTICE STEVENS delivered the opinion of the Court.

* * *

In March 1983, one week before trial, petitioners presented respondents with a new settlement proposal. As respondents themselves characterize it, the proposal "offered virtually all of the injunctive relief [they] had sought in their complaint." * * * [H[owever, petitioners' offer included a provision for a waiver by respondents of any claim to fees or costs. Originally, this waiver was unacceptable to the Idaho Legal Aid Society, which had instructed Johnson to reject any settlement offer conditioned upon a waiver of fees, but Johnson ultimately determined that his ethical obligation to his clients mandated acceptance of the proposal. The parties conditioned the waiver on approval by the District Court. * * * After the stipulation was signed, Johnson filed a written motion requesting the District Court to approve the settlement "except for the provision on costs and attorney's fees," and to allow respondents to present a bill of costs and fees for consideration by the court. At the oral argument on that motion, Johnson contended that petitioners' offer had exploited his ethical duty to his clients-that he was "forced," by an offer giving his clients "the best result [they] could have gotten in this court or any other court," to waive his attorney's fees. The District Court, however, evaluated the waiver in the context of the entire settlement and rejected the ethical underpinnings of Johnson's argument. Explaining that although petitioners were "not willing to concede that they were obligated to [make the changes in their practices required by the stipulation], . . . they were willing to do them as long as their costs were outlined and they didn't face additional costs," it concluded that "it doesn't violate any ethical considerations for an attorney to give up his attorney fees in the interest of getting a better bargain for his client[s]." Accordingly, the District Court approved the settlement and denied the motion to submit a costs bill.

When respondents appealed from the order denying attorney's fees and costs, petitioners filed a motion requesting the District Court to suspend or stay their obligation to comply with the substantive terms of the settlement. Because the District Court regarded the fee waiver as a material term of the complete settlement, it granted the motion. The Court of Appeals however, granted two emergency motions for stays requiring enforcement of the substantive terms of the consent decree pending the appeal. More dramatically, after ordering preliminary relief, it invalidated the fee waiver and left standing the remainder of the settlement; it then instructed the District Court to "make its own determination of the fees that are reasonable" and remanded for that limited purpose. * * *

The question this case presents, then, is whether the Fees Act requires a district court to disapprove a stipulation seeking to settle a civil rights class action under Rule 23 when the offered relief equals or exceeds the probable outcome at trial but is expressly conditioned on waiver of statutory eligibility for attorney's fees. For reasons set out below, we are not persuaded that Congress has commanded that all such settlements must be rejected by the District Court. Moreover, on the facts of record in this case, we are satisfied that the District Court did not abuse its discretion by approving the fee waiver.

* * *

The text of the Fees Act provides no support for the proposition that Congress intended to ban all fee waivers offered in connection with substantial relief on the merits. On the contrary, the language of the Act, as well as its legislative history, indicates that Congress bestowed on the "prevailing *party*" (generally plaintiffs) a statutory eligibility for a discretionary award of attorney's fees in specified civil rights actions. It did not prevent the party from waiving this eligibility anymore than it legislated against assignment of this right to an attorney, such as effectively occurred here. Instead, Congress enacted the fee-shifting provision as "an integral part of the remedies necessary to obtain" compliance with civil rights laws, * * * to further the same general purpose-promotion of respect for civil rights-that led it to provide damages and injunctive relief. The statute and its legislative history nowhere suggest that Congress intended to forbid *all* waivers of attorney's fees—even those insisted upon by a civil rights plaintiff in exchange for some other relief to which he is indisputably not entitled—anymore than it intended to bar a concession on damages to secure broader injunctive relief. Thus, while it is undoubtedly true that Congress expected fee shifting to attract competent counsel to represent citizens deprived of their civil rights, it neither bestowed fee awards upon attorneys nor rendered them nonwaivable or nonnegotiable; instead, it added them to the arsenal of remedies available to combat violations of civil rights, a goal not invariably inconsistent with conditioning settlement on the merits on a waiver of statutory attorney's fees.

In fact, we believe that a general proscription against negotiated waiver of attorney's fees in exchange for a settlement on the merits would itself impede vindication of civil rights, at least in some cases, by reducing the attractiveness of settlement. Of particular relevance in this regard is our recent decision in *Marek v. Chesny*, 473 U.S. 1, 105 S.Ct. 3012, 87 L.Ed.2d 1 (1985). In that case, which admittedly was not a class action and therefore did not implicate the court's approval power under Rule 23(e), we specifically considered and rejected the contention that civil rights actions should be treated differently from other civil actions for purposes of settlement. As THE CHIEF JUSTICE explained in his opinion for the Court, the settlement of litigation provides benefits for civil rights plaintiffs as well as defendants and is consistent with the purposes of the Fees Act:

> "There is no evidence, however, that Congress, in considering § 1988, had any thought that civil rights claims were to be on any different footing from other civil claims insofar as settlement is concerned. Indeed, Congress made clear its concern that civil rights plaintiffs not be penalized for 'helping to lessen docket congestion' by settling their cases out of court. * * *

> ". . . Some plaintiffs will receive compensation in settlement where, on trial, they might not have recovered, or would have recovered less than what was offered. And, even for those who would prevail at trial, settlement will provide them with

compensation at an earlier date without the burdens, stress, and time of litigation. In short, settlements rather than litigation will serve the interests of plaintiffs as well as defendants." * * *

To promote both settlement and civil rights, we implicitly acknowledged in *Marek v. Chesny* the possibility of a tradeoff between merits relief and attorney's fees when we upheld the defendant's lump-sum offer to settle the entire civil rights action, including any liability for fees and costs.

In approving the package offer in *Marek v. Chesny* we recognized that a rule prohibiting the comprehensive negotiation of all outstanding issues in a pending case might well preclude the settlement of a substantial number of cases:

> "If defendants are not allowed to make lump-sum offers that would, if accepted, represent their total liability, they would understandably be reluctant to make settlement offers. As the Court of Appeals observed, 'many a defendant would be unwilling to make a binding settlement offer on terms that left it exposed to liability for attorney's fees in whatever amount the court might fix on motion of the plaintiff.' * * *

Most defendants are unlikely to settle unless the cost of the predicted judgment, discounted by its probability, plus the transaction costs of further litigation, are greater than the cost of the settlement package. If fee waivers cannot be negotiated, the settlement package must either contain an attorney's fee component of potentially large and typically uncertain magnitude, or else the parties must agree to have the fee fixed by the court. Although either of these alternatives may well be acceptable in many cases, there surely is a significant number in which neither alternative will be as satisfactory as a decision to try the entire case.

The adverse impact of removing attorney's fees and costs from bargaining might be tolerable if the uncertainty introduced into settlement negotiations were small. But it is not. The defendants' potential liability for fees in this kind of litigation can be as significant as, and sometimes even more significant than, their potential liability on the merits. This proposition is most dramatically illustrated by the fee awards of district courts in actions seeking only monetary relief. Although it is more difficult to compare fee awards with the cost of injunctive relief, in part because the cost of such relief is seldom reported in written opinions, here too attorney's fees awarded by district courts have "frequently outrun the economic benefits ultimately obtained by successful litigants." * * * Undoubtedly there are many other civil rights actions in which potential liability for attorney's fees may overshadow the potential cost of relief on the merits and darken prospects for settlement if fees cannot be negotiated.

The unpredictability of attorney's fees may be just as important as their magnitude when a defendant is striving to fix its liability. Unlike a determination of costs, which ordinarily involve smaller outlays and are more susceptible of calculation, * * * "[t]here is no precise rule or formula" for determining attorney's fees * * * . Among other considerations, the district court must determine what hours were reasonably expended on what claims, whether that expenditure was reasonable in light of the success obtained, * * * and what is an appropriate hourly rate for the services rendered. Some District Courts have also considered whether a "multiplier" or other adjustment is appropriate. The consequence of this succession of necessarily judgmental decisions for the ultimate fee award is inescapable: a defendant's liability for his opponent's attorney's fees in a civil rights action cannot be fixed with a sufficient degree of confidence to make defendants indifferent to their exclusion from negotiation is therefore not implausible to anticipate that parties to a significant number of civil rights cases will refuse to settle if liability for attorney's fees remains open, thereby forcing more cases to trial, unnecessarily burdening the judicial system, and disserving civil rights litigants. Respondents' own waiver of attorney's fees and costs to obtain settlement of their educational claims is eloquent testimony to the utility of fee waivers in vindicating civil rights claims. We conclude, therefore, that it is not necessary to construe the Fees Act as embodying a general rule prohibiting settlements conditioned on the waiver of fees in order to be faithful to the purposes of that Act.

* * *

The question remains whether the District Court abused its discretion in this case by approving a settlement which included a complete fee waiver. As noted earlier, Rule 23(e) wisely requires court approval of the terms of any settlement of a class action. The potential conflict among members of the class-in this case, for example, the possible conflict between children primarily interested in better educational programs and those primarily interested in improved health care-fully justifies the requirement of court approval.

The Court of Appeals, respondents, and various *amici* supporting their position, however, suggest that the court's authority to pass on settlements, typically invoked to ensure fair treatment of class members, must be exercised in accordance with the Fees Act to promote the availability of attorneys in civil rights cases. Specifically, respondents assert that the State of Idaho could not pass a valid statute precluding the payment of attorney's fees in settlements of civil rights cases to which the Fees Act applies. * * * From this they reason that the Fees Act must equally preclude the adoption of a uniform state-wide policy that serves the same end, and accordingly contend that a consistent practice of insisting on a fee waiver as a condition of settlement in civil rights litigation is in conflict with the federal statute authorizing fees for prevailing parties, including those who prevail by way of settlement. Remarkably, there seems little disagreement on these points. Petitioners and the *amici* who support them never suggest that the district court is obligated to place its stamp of approval on every settlement in which the plaintiffs' attorneys have agreed to a fee waiver. The Solicitor General, for example, has suggested that a fee waiver need not be approved when the defendant had "no realistic defense on the merits," * * * or if the waiver was part of a "vindictive effort . . . to teach counsel that they had better not bring such cases[.]" * * *

We find it unnecessary to evaluate this argument, however, because the record in this case does not indicate that Idaho has adopted such a statute, policy, or practice. Nor does the record support the narrower proposition that petitioners' request to waive fees was a vindictive effort to deter attorneys from representing plaintiffs in civil rights suits against Idaho. It is true that a fee waiver was requested and obtained as a part of the early settlement of the education claims, but we do not understand respondents to be challenging that waiver, * * * and they have not offered to prove that petitioners' tactics in this case merely implemented a routine state policy designed to frustrate the objectives of the Fees Act. Our own examination of the record reveals no such policy.

In light of the record, respondents must-to sustain the judgment in their favor-confront the District Court's finding that the extensive structural relief they obtained constituted an adequate *quid pro quo* for their waiver of attorney's fees. The Court of Appeals did not overturn this finding. Indeed, even that court did not suggest that the option of rejecting the entire settlement and requiring the parties either to try the case or to attempt to negotiate a different settlement would have served the interests of justice. Only by making the unsupported assumption that the respondent class was entitled to retain the favorable portions of the settlement while rejecting the fee waiver could the Court of Appeals conclude that the District Court had acted unwisely.

What the outcome of this settlement illustrates is that the Fees Act has given the victims of civil rights violations a powerful weapon that improves their ability to employ counsel, to obtain access to the courts, and thereafter to vindicate their rights by means of settlement or trial. For aught that appears, it was the "coercive" effect of respondents' statutory right to seek a fee award that motivated petitioners' exceptionally generous offer. Whether this weapon might be even more powerful if fee waivers were prohibited in cases like this is another question, but it is in any event a question that Congress is best equipped to answer. Thus far, the Legislature has not commanded that fees be paid whenever a case is settled. Unless it issues such a command, we shall rely primarily on the sound discretion of the district courts to appraise the reasonableness of particular class-action settlements on a case-by-case basis, in the light of all the relevant circumstances. In this case, the District Court did not abuse its discretion in upholding a fee waiver which secured broad injunctive relief, relief greater than that which plaintiffs could reasonably have expected to achieve at trial.

The judgment of the Court of Appeals is reversed.

It is so ordered.

Test Your Knowledge

To assess your understanding of the material in this Chapter, click here to take a quiz.

CHAPTER 4

Attorney-Client Privilege and the Lawyer's Duty of Confidentiality

Learning Outcomes

At the end of Units I and II, you will be able to:

- Distinguish between attorney-client privilege and the duty of confidentiality

At the end of Unit III, you will be able to:

- Explain the duties of an attorney receiving privileged information

- Evaluate the impact of mistaken disclosures on attorney-client privilege

- Identify the rationale for and necessary elements of attorney-client privilege

- Identify who has the authority to waive attorney-client privilege

- Recognize the crime-fraud exception to attorney-client privilege

At the end of Unit IV, you will be able to:

- Assess whether the duty of confidentiality and exceptions to confidentiality serve clients' interests, lawyers' interests, or society's interests

- Develop your own view on whether the duty of confidentiality should be modified

- Evaluate the debate over whether there should be additional exceptions to the duty of confidentiality

- Identify the scope of information within the duty of confidentiality and exceptions to the duty of confidentiality

Topic Outline for Chapter 4

TOPIC	RELEVANT AUTHORITY	CHAPTER QUESTIONS
I. Introduction	1.6	

I. Introduction

The duty of confidentiality is one of the most fundamental obligations that a lawyer has towards a client. But it can also be one of the most controversial obligations because a lawyer's duty of confidentiality may conflict with other obligations the lawyer has, such as serving as an officer of the court. As a result, you should know that this is one of the topics for which you are most likely to find significant state variations. This Chapter addresses two separate doctrines: the legal rule of attorney-client privilege and the ethical duty of confidentiality. (This Chapter does not cover work-product.) While there is some overlap between them, both may apply in a particular situation and a lawyer needs to be familiar with both. The attorney-client privilege is a rule of evidence, defined in each jurisdiction by common law or statute, that applies in testimonial settings, such as when testifying, when deposed, or when documents are sought. Each court system has developed its own law on attorney-client privilege, although there obviously are commonalities.

The lawyer's duty of confidentiality is set forth in Rule 1.6, which provides that a lawyer "shall not reveal information relating to the representation of a client unless the client gives informed consent, the disclosure is impliedly authorized in order to carry out the representation or the disclosure is permitted by" some designated exceptions, as discussed later in this Chapter.

As seen later in this Chapter, there are a number of exceptional situations in which a lawyer may disclose information that is "confidential" within the Rule 1.6 definition. For introductory purposes, the point is that the lawyer must keep secret a broad range of information that she learns when representing a client.

As noted earlier, many states have adopted a version of Rule 1.6 which varies in significant ways from ABA Model Rule 1.6, which is the same as Delaware Rule 1.6. The ABA maintains charts that highlight some of these variations. To see the variations in Rule 1.6, click here; to see the variations in Rule 1.6(b)(2) and (b)(3), click here.

II. The Relationship Between the Duty of Confidentiality and the Attorney-Client Privilege

Hear from the Authors

To hear from the authors on the relationship between the duty of confidentiality and attorney-client privilege, click here.

There are similarities and differences between the attorney-client privilege and the lawyer's ethical duty of confidentiality. The duty of confidentiality is both broader and narrower than the attorney-client privilege. The duty of confidentiality is broader in the initial scope of its coverage because it covers information the lawyer receives from third parties, as well as information the lawyer receives directly from the client. As you will see elsewhere in this Chapter, as a threshold matter, Rule 1.6 prohibits a lawyer from *revealing* "information relating to the representation," regardless of the source of that information. In contrast to Rule 1.6 and the ethical duty of confidentiality, the attorney-client privilege is narrower and applies only to information between "privileged persons," which usually is defined as communications between the client and the lawyer (or between agents of either who facilitate communication between them).

Rule 1.6's duty of confidentiality is also broader than the attorney-client privilege because it applies to a lawyer 24/7. The privilege, in contrast, is a rule of evidence that is asserted in testimonial settings. On the other hand, Rule 1.6's duty of confidentiality is narrower than the attorney-client privilege because it has permissive exceptions that allow disclosure in situations in which the attorney-client privilege would not. The following graphic helps to illustrate the relationship between client confidentiality and attorney-client privilege.

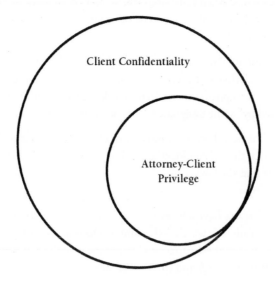

[Question 4-1]

An attorney represents a client who suffered injuries when the client was run down by a car in a crosswalk. The attorney investigates the matter and comes upon a surveillance tape indicating that the client, one minute before the accident, had exited from an XXX-rated adult theater with someone who was not the client's spouse. At a dinner party, the attorney tells everyone the "ironic" story of "a client," who got run down after being so "naughty."

Was the attorney's conduct proper?

(A)   Yes, because the information about the client's whereabouts was not protected by the attorney-client privilege.

(B)   Yes, because the attorney did not violate any duties to the client because the information was not secret—it was known by the person who was with the client at the time.

(C)   No, because the attorney violated the duty of confidentiality by disclosing information protected by attorney-client privilege.

(D)   No, because the attorney violated the duty of confidentiality by disclosing information related to the representation that was not covered by any of the exceptions.

So what difference does it make whether information is protected by the attorney-client privilege or the broader duty of confidentiality? *See* Rule 1.6(b)(6) (information that is confidential—not privileged—is subject to disclosure to comply with other law or a court order).

[Question 4-2]

An attorney represents a client who suffered injuries when the client was run down by a car in a crosswalk. The attorney investigates the matter and comes upon a surveillance tape indicating that the client, one minute before the accident, had exited from an XXX-rated adult theater with a person who was not the client's spouse. Before trial, the attorney receives a discovery request from defense counsel, demanding production of any surveillance tapes that are or may be relevant to the action. The attorney refuses to produce the surveillance tape.

Is the attorney's conduct proper?

(A)   Yes, because the surveillance tape is privileged.

(B)   Yes, because producing the surveillance tape would violate the duty of confidentiality.

(C)   No, because the information on the surveillance tape is not privileged, and the attorney must turn over non-privileged information if a lawful demand is made.

(D)   No, because even though the information on the surveillance tape is privileged, the attorney must comply with the discovery request.

III. Basics of the Attorney-Client Privilege

While the duty of confidentiality covers more information than that protected by the attorney-client privilege, it is important to determine the scope of the privilege. The privilege is a rule of evidence and the duty of confidentiality is a rule of professional responsibility, and the lawyer's duty to invoke and protect the privilege is a critical part of the lawyer's duty of confidentiality under Rule 1.6.

A.   Rationale for the Attorney-Client Privilege

> **Make the Connection**
>
> The attorney-client privilege is an important subject in most evidence courses—the privilege is after all a rule of evidence and not a rule of ethics. But covering the privilege is important in a professional responsibility course because a lawyer needs to know how to argue convincingly the client's claims of privilege. Privilege arguments are won and lost by proper lawyering in advance of any disclosure between a client and a lawyer.

The Supreme Court set forth the commonly-accepted rationale for the attorney-client privilege in *Upjohn Co. v. United States*, 449 U.S. 383 (1981):

The attorney-client privilege is the oldest of the privileges for confidential communications known to the common law. 8 J. Wigmore, *Evidence* § 2290 (McNaughton rev. 1961). Its purpose is to encourage full and frank communication between attorneys and their clients and thereby promote broader public interests in the observance of law and administration of justice. The privilege recognizes that sound legal advice or advocacy serves public ends and that such advice or advocacy depends upon the lawyer's being fully informed by the client. As we stated last Term in *Trammel v. United States*, 445 U.S. 40, 51 (1980): "The lawyer-client privilege rests on the need for the advocate and counselor to know all that relates to the client's reasons for seeking representation if the professional mission is to be carried out." And in *Fisher v. United States*, 425 U.S. 391, 403 (1976), we recognized the purpose of the privilege to be "to encourage clients to make full disclosure to their attorneys." This rationale for the privilege has long been recognized by the Court, see *Hunt v. Blackburn*, 128 U.S. 464, 470 (1888) (privilege "is founded upon the necessity, in the interest and administration of justice, of the aid of persons having knowledge of the law and skilled in its practice, which assistance can only be safely and readily availed of when free from the consequences or the apprehension of disclosure").

Upjohn concludes that without the privilege, clients would not be truthful, and the lawyer would be operating under an informational deficit and would thereby be less effective as an advocate for the client. Thus, attorney-client privilege rests on a claim about human behavior that no one has demonstrated empirically.

Can you see any other reason for the privilege, which, after all, deprives the court of relevant and

> **Make the Connection**
>
> So you can see that while the privilege is a rule of evidence, it bears directly on the lawyer's ethical duty to effectively represent the client—as well as the duty to preserve secret information to the extent allowed by law.

reliable evidence and thus is contrary to the search for truth? If there were no privilege, how would the now-unprotected communication between lawyer and client be proven in court?

The attorney-client privilege is not without its detractors. *See, e.g., Developments in the Law: Privileged Communications,* 98 Harv. L. Rev. 1450 (1985) (arguing that lawyers establish privileges, so it is not surprising that there is an aggressively enforced attorney-client privilege, but no accountant-client privilege in common law); Roger C. Cramton et al., *Legal and Ethical Duties of Lawyers After Sarbanes-Oxley,* 49 Vill. L. Rev 725 (2004) (noting that there is no evidence that longstanding exceptions to attorney-client privilege or duty of confidentiality have restrained the candor between co-agents and lawyers); Elizabeth G. Thornburg, *Sanctifying Secrecy: The Mythology of the Corporate Attorney-Client Privilege,* 69 Notre Dame L. Rev. 157 (1993) (arguing that the corporate attorney-client privilege gives unjustified protection to entrenched interests); Fred C. Zacharias, *Rethinking Confidentiality,* 74 Iowa L. Rev. 351 (1989) (criticizing the attorney-client privilege as a means of driving up lawyer fees, because clients pay a premium so that they can obtain a privilege for their communications, even though nonlawyers may be able to provide similar services more cheaply).

B.   Criteria for Attorney-Client Privilege

The attorney-client privilege applies only in testimonial or evidentiary settings, such as those involved when a witness is called to testify in court, is subject to a deposition, or is asked to produce records in connection with a court proceeding. The attorney-client privilege is based on state law when asserted in state court and is based on federal law when asserted in federal court. The American Law Institute's (ALI's) *Restatement of the Law Governing Lawyers* addresses the topic of attorney-client privilege in Sections 68–86. Section 68 defines the privilege as follows:

> Except as otherwise provided in this Restatement, the attorney-client privilege may be invoked as provided in § 86 with respect to:
>
> (1)   a communication
>
> (2)   made between privileged persons
>
> (3)   in confidence
>
> (4)   for the purpose of obtaining or providing legal assistance for the client.

The Restatement sections that follow § 68 define each of these elements and set forth exceptions to the privilege. While the Restatement constitutes secondary authority, rather than a binding source of law, it represents the ALI's best efforts to articulate the law of attorney-client privilege as found in state courts throughout the U.S.

The Federal Rules of Evidence (FRE) apply to lawsuits filed in federal court. FRE 501 provides that, absent certain exceptions, federal common law governs claims of privilege, except in civil cases, in which case state law will apply if state law supplies the rule for a claim or defense:

The Federal common law—as interpreted by United States courts in the light of reason and experience—governs a claim of privilege unless any of the following provides otherwise:

- the United States Constitution;

- a federal statute; or

- rules prescribed by the Supreme Court.

But in a civil case, state law governs privilege regarding a claim or defense for which state law supplies the rule of decision.

The Federal Rules of Evidence were amended in 2008 to add FRE 502, which addresses the topic of when disclosure of a communication or information covered by the attorney-client privilege or work-product protection will constitute a waiver. FRE 502 sets forth the waiver consequences, in both state and federal court, for disclosures made in the specified manner. FRE 502 does not, however, provide a general definition of the attorney-client privilege but instead defines it as "the protection that applicable law provides for confidential attorney-client communications."

Although there currently is no Federal Rule of Evidence that sets forth the scope of the attorney-client privilege in federal court, efforts to develop such a rule have been underway for several years. In 2010, the Judicial Conference Advisory Committee on Evidence Rules attempted to codify the federal law on attorney-client privilege, and the committee proposed the following draft. There has not been any further action since 2010 on this proposed rule, it is included because it is a useful and succinct overview of the privilege:

Lawyer-Client Privilege (Draft, March 1, 2010)

(a) Definitions. As used in this rule:

(1)   A "communication" is any expression through which a privileged person intends to convey information to another privileged person or any record containing such an expression;

(2)   A "client" is a person who or an organization that consults a lawyer to obtain professional legal services.

(3)   An "organization" is a corporation, unincorporated association, partnership, trust, estate, sole proprietorship, governmental entity, or other for-profit or not-for-profit association.

(4)   A "lawyer" is a person who is authorized to practice law in any domestic or foreign jurisdiction or whom a client reasonably believes to be a lawyer;

(5)   A "privileged person" is a client, that client's lawyer, or an agent of either who is reasonably necessary to facilitate communications between the client and the lawyer.

(6)   A communication is "in confidence" if, at the time and in the circumstances of the communication, the communicating person reasonably believes that no one except a privileged person will learn the contents of the communication.

(b) General Rule of Privilege.

A client has a privilege to refuse to disclose and to prevent any other person from disclosing a communication made in confidence between or among privileged persons for the purpose of obtaining or providing legal assistance for the client.

(c) Who May Claim the Privilege.

A client, a personal representative of an incompetent or deceased client, or a person succeeding to the interest of a client may invoke the privilege. A lawyer, agent of the lawyer, or an agent of a client from whom a privileged communication is sought may invoke the privilege on behalf of the client if implicitly or explicitly authorized by the client.

(d) Standards for Organizational Clients.

With respect to an organizational client, the lawyer-client privilege extends to a communication that

(1)   is otherwise privileged;

(2)   is between an organization's agent and a privileged person where the communication concerns a legal matter of interest to the organization within the scope of the agent's agency or employment; and

(3)   is disclosed only to privileged persons and other agents of the organization who reasonably need to know of the communication in order to act for the organization.

(e) Privilege of Co-Clients and Common-Interest Arrangements.

If two or more clients are jointly represented by the same lawyer in a matter or if two or more clients with a common interest in a matter are represented by separate lawyers and they agree to pursue a common interest and to exchange information concerning the matter, a communication of any such client that is otherwise privileged and relates to matters of common interest is privileged as against third persons. Any such client may invoke the privilege unless the client making the communication has waived the privilege. Unless the clients agree otherwise, such a communication is not privileged as between the clients. Communications between clients or agents of clients outside the presence of a lawyer or agent of a lawyer representing at least one of the clients are not privileged.

(f) Exceptions.

The lawyer-client privilege does not apply to a communication

(1)   from or to a deceased client if the communication is relevant to an issue between parties who claim an interest through the same deceased client, either by testate or intestate succession or by an inter vivos transaction;

(2)   that occurs when a client consults a lawyer to obtain assistance to engage in a crime or fraud or aiding a third person to do so. Regardless of the client's purpose at the time of consultation, the communication is not privileged if the client uses the lawyer's advice or other services to engage in or assist in committing a crime or fraud;

(3)   that is waived by the client;

(4)   between a trustee of an express trust or a similar fiduciary and a lawyer or other privileged person retained to advise the trustee concerning the administration of the trust that is relevant to a beneficiary's claim of breach of fiduciary duties; and

(5)   between an organizational client and a lawyer or other privileged person, if offered in a proceeding that involves a dispute between the client and shareholders, members, or other constituents of the organization toward whom the directors, officers, or similar persons managing the organization bear fiduciary responsibilities, provided the court finds

>   (A)   those managing the organization are charged with breach of their obligations toward the shareholders, members, or other constituents or toward the organization itself;
>
>   (B)   the communication occurred prior to the assertion of the charges and relates directly to those charges; and
>
>   (C)   the need of the requesting party to discover or introduce the communication is sufficiently compelling and the threat to confidentiality sufficiently confined to justify setting the privilege aside.

This proposed federal codification of the attorney-client privilege is similar to the ALI Restatement of the Law governing lawyers. The casebook sections that follow examine many of these elements and exceptions in greater depth.

1. Client Must Be Seeking Legal Advice

A client may not "buy" a privilege by retaining an attorney to do something that a nonlawyer could do just as well. *See, e.g., In re Feldberg*, 862 F.2d 622, 626 (7th Cir. 1988) ("A business that gets marketing advice from a lawyer does not acquire a privilege in the bargain; so too a business that obtains the services of a records custodian from a member of the bar."). The client must be seeking legal advice and assistance from the lawyer. *See, e.g., In re Grand Jury Subpoena, Peek*, 682 F. Supp. 1552, 1556 (M.D. Ga. 1987) (personal loan transaction between attorney and another person is not privileged: "Otherwise, everything that a lawyer does for himself or herself would be cloaked with a privilege just because he or she is a lawyer."); *SCM Corp. v. Xerox Corp.*, 70 F.R.D. 508, 515 (D. Conn. 1976) ("Legal departments are not citadels in which public, business or technical information may be placed to defeat discovery and thereby ensure confidentiality."). Restatement § 72 frames this element as follows:

> A communication is made for the purpose of obtaining or providing legal assistance within the meaning of § 68 if it is made to or to assist a person:
>
> (1) who is a lawyer or who the client or prospective client reasonably believes to be a lawyer; and
>
> (2) whom the client or prospective client consults for the purpose of obtaining legal assistance.

Food for Thought

If you hire a lawyer to prepare your tax return, are your private communications to the lawyer privileged? *See, e.g., United States v. Frederick*, 182 F.3d 496 (7th Cir. 1999) ("There is no common law accountant's or tax preparer's privilege, and a taxpayer must not be allowed, by hiring a lawyer to do the work that an accountant, or other tax preparer, or the taxpayer himself or herself, normally would do, to obtain greater protection from government investigators than a taxpayer who did not use a lawyer as his tax preparer would be entitled to do."). *In re Schroeder*, 842 F.2d 1223, 1224 (11th Cir. 1987) ("Courts generally have held that the preparation of tax returns does not constitute legal advice within the scope of the privilege.").

If you hire a lawyer to prepare your tax return, are your private communications to the lawyer protected by the lawyer's duty of confidentiality? See Rule 1.6, above. If it is so protected, what difference does it make that it is not privileged?

[Question 4-3]

A client retains an attorney for assistance in a real estate transaction. The client asks the attorney in confidence whether the attorney thinks it is "a good and workable deal."

Is this communication privileged?

    (A) Yes, because the client was speaking in confidence to the attorney.

    (B) Yes, because it is privileged if the dominant intent is to seek legal advice.

    (C) No, because the client asked for the attorney's opinion.

    (D) No, because the client was not seeking legal advice.

Sometimes a client seeks both legal and non-legal advice from the attorney. Should the privilege apply in these circumstances? The following case provides guidance on the subject.

In re County of Erie

473 F.3d 413 (2d Cir. 2007)

JACOBS, CHIEF JUDGE:

In the course of a lawsuit by a class of arrested persons against Erie County (and certain of its officials) alleging that they were subjected to unconstitutional strip searches, the United States District Court for the Western District of New York (Curtin, J.) ordered the discovery of emails (and other documents) between an Assistant Erie County Attorney and County officials that solicit, contain and discuss advice from attorney to client. The County defendants petition for a writ of mandamus directing the district court to vacate that order. The writ is available because: important issues of first impression are raised; the privilege will be irreversibly lost if review awaits final judgment; and immediate resolution of this dispute will promote sound discovery practices and doctrine. Upon consideration of the circumstances, we issue the writ ordering the district court: to vacate its order, to determine whether the privilege was otherwise waived, and to enter an interim order to protect the confidentiality of the disputed communications.

I

On July 21, 2004, plaintiffs-respondents Adam Pritchard, Edward Robinson and Julenne Tucker commenced suit under 42 U.S.C. § 1983, individually and on behalf of a class of others similarly situated, alleging that, pursuant to a written policy of the Erie County Sheriff's Office and promulgated by County officials, every detainee who entered the Erie County Holding Center or Erie County Correctional Facility (including plaintiffs) was subjected to an invasive strip search, without regard to individualized suspicion or the offense alleged, and that this policy violates the Fourth Amendment. They sued the County of Erie, New York, as well as [certain officials] * * * (collectively, the "County").

Practice Pointer

FRCP 26(b)(5) sets forth requirements for how a claim of attorney-client privilege is asserted in federal court. The document is often referred to as a "privilege log." For advice on preparing a privilege log, click here.

During the course of discovery, the County withheld production of certain documents as privileged attorney-client communications; a privilege log was produced instead * * *. In August 2005, plaintiffs moved to compel production of the logged documents, almost all of which were emails. The County submitted the documents to Magistrate Judge Hugh B. Scott for inspection in camera. In January 2006, Judge Scott ordered production of ten of the withheld emails, which (variously) reviewed the law concerning strip searches of detainees, assessed the County's current search policy, recommended alternative policies, and monitored the implementation of these policy changes.

Judge Scott reasoned that:

These communications "go beyond rendering 'legal analysis' [by] propos[ing] changes to existing policy to make it constitutional, including drafting of policy regulations";

The "drafting and subsequent oversight of implementation of the new strip search policy ventured beyond merely rendering legal advice and analysis into the realm of policy making and administration"; and

"[N]o legal advice is rendered apart from policy recommendations."

Judge Scott ordered the County to deliver these ten emails to the plaintiffs.

After considering the County's objections to this order, the district court independently reviewed the disputed emails in camera and, applying a "clearly erroneous" standard, overruled the objections, and directed production. This petition for a writ of mandamus followed.

II

[The Court held that mandamus was appropriate because "[t]o await resolution of this issue pending final judgment risks the development of discovery practices and doctrine that unsettle and undermine the governmental attorney-client privilege."]

III

The attorney-client privilege protects confidential communications between client and counsel made for the purpose of obtaining or providing legal assistance. Its purpose is to encourage attorneys and their clients to communicate fully and frankly and thereby to promote broader public interests in the observance of law and administration of justice. "The availability of sound legal advice inures to the benefit not only of the client who wishes to know his options and responsibilities in given circumstances, but also of the public which is entitled to compliance with the ever growing and increasingly complex body of public law." *In re Grand Jury Subpoena Duces Tecum Dated Sept. 15, 1983*, 731 F.2d 1032, 1036–37 (2d Cir. 1984).

At the same time, we construe the privilege narrowly because it renders relevant information undiscoverable; we apply it "only where necessary to achieve its purpose." *Fisher v. United States*, 425 U.S. 391, 403. The burden of establishing the applicability of the privilege rests with the party invoking it. *In re Grand Jury Proceedings*, 219 F.3d 175, 182 (2d Cir. 2000). * * *

In civil suits between private litigants and government agencies, the attorney-client privilege protects most confidential communications between government counsel and their clients that are made for the purpose of obtaining or providing legal assistance. See, e.g., *Ross v. City of*

Take Note

Does waiting until after a final judgment to appeal a disclosure order compromise the attorney-client privilege protection? Lawyers argued yes, because one cannot "unlearn" information after it has been revealed. The Supreme Court disagreed, holding that the post-judgment appeals process offers sufficient safeguards. What do you think? See *Mohawk Industries Inc. v. Carpenter*, 558 U.S. 100 (2009).

Memphis, 423 F.3d 596, 601 (6th Cir. 2005) ("[A] government entity can assert attorney-client privilege in the civil context.").

The attorney-client privilege accommodates competing values; the competition is sharpened when the privilege is asserted by a government. On the one hand, non-disclosure impinges on open and accessible government. On the other hand, public officials are duty-bound to understand and respect constitutional, judicial and statutory limitations on their authority; thus, their access to candid legal advice directly and significantly serves the public interest.

We believe that, if anything, the traditional rationale for the [attorney-client] privilege applies with special force in the government context. It is crucial that government officials, who are expected to uphold and execute the law and who may face criminal prosecution for failing to do so, be encouraged to seek out and receive fully informed legal advice. Upholding the privilege furthers a culture in which consultation with government lawyers is accepted as a normal, desirable, and even indispensable part of conducting public business. Abrogating the privilege undermines that culture and thereby impairs the public interest. * * * At least in civil litigation between a government agency and private litigants, the government's claim to the protections of the attorney-client privilege is on a par with the claim of an individual or a corporate entity.

IV

A party invoking the attorney-client privilege must show (1) a communication between client and counsel that (2) was intended to be and was in fact kept confidential, and (3) was made for the purpose of obtaining or providing legal advice. At issue here is the third consideration: whether the communications were made for the purpose of obtaining or providing legal advice, as opposed to advice on policy.

The rule that a confidential communication between client and counsel is privileged only if it is generated for the purpose of obtaining or providing legal assistance is often recited. The issue usually arises in the context of communications to and from corporate in-house lawyers who also serve as business executives. So the question usually is whether the communication was generated for the purpose of obtaining or providing legal advice as opposed to business advice.

Fundamentally, legal advice involves the interpretation and application of legal principles to guide future conduct or to assess past conduct. It requires a lawyer to rely on legal education and experience to inform judgment. But it is broader, and is not demarcated by a bright line. * * *

The complete lawyer may well promote and reinforce the legal advice given, weigh it, and lay out its ramifications by explaining: how the advice is feasible and can be implemented; the legal downsides, risks and costs of taking the advice or doing otherwise; what alternatives exist to present measures or the measures advised; what other persons are doing or thinking about the matter; or the collateral benefits, risks or costs in terms of expense, politics, insurance, commerce, morals, and appearances. So long as the predominant purpose of the communication is legal advice, these considerations and caveats are not other than legal advice or severable from it. The predominant purpose of a communication cannot be ascertained by quantification or classification of one passage or another; it should be assessed dynamically and in light of the advice being sought or rendered, as well as the relationship between advice that can be rendered only by consulting the legal authorities and advice that can be given by a nonlawyer. The more careful the lawyer, the more likely it is that the legal advice will entail follow-through by facilitation, encouragement and monitoring.

V

The County asserts that the Assistant County Attorney whose advice was solicited could not have been conveying non-legal policy advice because the Erie County Charter (§ 602) confines her authority to that of a "legal advisor," and because "only the County Sheriff and his direct appointees ha[ve] policy-making authority for the [Sheriff's] department." This argument does not assist the analysis much. A lawyer's lack of formal authority to formulate, approve or enact policy does not actually prevent the rendering of policy advice to officials who do possess that authority. A similar consideration may be useful in different circumstances. When an attorney is consulted in a capacity other than as a lawyer, as (for example) a policy advisor, media expert, business consultant, banker, referee or friend, that consultation is not privileged. * * *

In the government context, one court considered relevant the fact that the attorney seeking to invoke the privilege held two formal positions: Assistant to the President (ostensibly non-legal) and Deputy White House Counsel (ostensibly legal). *In re Lindsey*, 148 F.3d at 1103, 1106-07. The same is true in the private sector where "in-house attorneys are more likely to mix legal and business functions." *Bank Brussels Lambert*, 220 F. Supp. 2d at 286. In short, an attorney's dual legal and non-legal responsibilities may bear on whether a particular communication was generated for the purpose of soliciting or rendering legal advice; but here, the Assistant County Attorney's lack of formal policymaking authority is not a compelling circumstance.

The predominant purpose of a particular document—legal advice, or not—may also be informed by the overall needs and objectives that animate the client's request for advice. For example, Erie County's objective was to ascertain its obligations under the Fourth Amendment and how those requirements may be fulfilled, rather than to save money or please the electorate (even though these latter objectives would not be beyond the lawyer's consideration).

VI

After reviewing in camera the documents listed on the County's privilege log, Judge Scott determined that the ten emails at issue here are not privileged. These emails, dated between December 23, 2002 and December 11, 2003, passed between the Assistant County Attorney and various officials in the Sheriff's Office (primarily petitioners). The ten emails are an amalgam of the following six broad issues:

(i)   The compliance of the County's search policy with the Fourth Amendment;

(ii)   Any possible liability of the County and its officials stemming from the existing policy;

(iii)   Alternative search policies, including the availability of equipment to assist in conducting searches that comply with constitutional requirements;

(iv)   Guidance for implementing and funding these alternative policies;

(v)   Maintenance of records concerning the original search policy; and

(vi)   Evaluations of the County's progress implementing the alternative search policy.

* * * Because the emails "go beyond rendering legal analysis," the judge concluded that they were not privileged. We disagree.

It is to be hoped that legal considerations will play a role in governmental policymaking. When a lawyer has been asked to assess compliance with a legal obligation, the lawyer's recommendation of a policy that complies (or better complies) with the legal obligation—or that advocates and promotes compliance, or oversees implementation of compliance measures—is legal advice. Public officials who craft policies that may directly implicate the legal rights or responsibilities of the public should be encouraged to seek out and receive fully informed legal advice in the course of formulating such policies. * * *

We conclude that each of the ten disputed emails was sent for the predominant purpose of soliciting or rendering legal advice. They convey to the public officials responsible for formulating, implementing and monitoring Erie County's corrections policies, a lawyer's assessment of Fourth Amendment requirements, and provide guidance in crafting and implementing alternative policies for compliance. This advice—particularly when viewed in the context in which it was solicited and rendered—does not constitute general policy or political advice unprotected by the privilege.

Food for Thought

Even if information is not privileged because the lawyer is being retained predominately for non-legal services, the information may still be subject to Rule 1.6—meaning the lawyer cannot disclose it voluntarily.

Although the emails at issue were generated for the predominant purpose of legal advice, we remand for the district court to determine whether the distribution of some of the disputed email communications to others within the Erie County Sheriff's Department constituted a waiver of the attorney-client privilege.

* * *

2. The Communications Requirement

Restatement § 69 defines the communication element of the attorney-client privilege as follows:

A communication within the meaning of § 68 is any expression through which a privileged person, as defined in § 70, undertakes to convey information to another privileged person and any document or other record revealing such an expression.

How would you apply this definition to Question 4-4?

[Question 4-4]

An attorney represents a client in a personal injury action. The client is in a bodycast and claims extensive injuries after a car accident. About a month before the trial date, the attorney goes on a skiing vacation. As the attorney is swooshing down the slopes, the attorney sees the client—bodycast-free—swooshing down ahead of the attorney. The defendant now subpoenas the attorney to provide any information the attorney has about the client's medical condition. The attorney—who has since withdrawn from the representation—refuses to supply any information and invokes both the attorney-client privilege and the duty of confidentiality.

Is the attorney's conduct proper?

  (A) Yes, because turning over the information could subject the attorney to discipline for violating Rule 1.6.

  (B) Yes, because the privilege means that the attorney cannot be forced to testify against the client.

  (C) No, because the information is not a communication and therefore is not protected by the privilege.

  (D) No, because the attorney no longer represents the client.

Because the privilege protects only communications, it does not protect the underlying facts pertinent to the representation. Thus, in *In re Six Grand Jury Witnesses*, 979 F.2d 939 (2d Cir. 1992), corporate employees were instructed by counsel to analyze certain contracts in anticipation of litiga-

> **Food for Thought**
>
> Did the lawyer in the above question *have to withdraw? See* Rule 1.16.

tion. The Court held that the "underlying factual information" obtained by these employees was not protected by the privilege. They were not communications to an attorney. However, questions such as "With whom did you discuss this analysis?" were impermissible because the employee, in responding, "might be understood to be implying * * * that he had conveyed privileged information to the lawyer."

But if a lawyer discovers underlying facts, does she have any duty to *try* to keep them secret? At least until there is a lawful demand for the information? Where can that duty be found?

3. Communication Between Client and Lawyer

a. Who Is the Client?

Restatement § 70 defines the "privileged persons" element in the following manner:

> Privileged persons within the meaning of § 68 are the client (including a prospective client), the client's lawyer, agents of either who facilitate communications between them, and agents of the lawyer who facilitate the representation.

It is not always easy, however, to determine who is the client. Consider the following Supreme Court case, which addressed this issue.

Upjohn Co. v. United States

449 U.S. 383 (1981)

Justice Rehnquist delivered the opinion of the Court.

We granted certiorari in this case to address important questions concerning the scope of the attorney-client privilege in the corporate context and the applicability of the work-product doctrine in proceedings to enforce tax summonses. * * *

I

Petitioner Upjohn Co. manufactures and sells pharmaceuticals here and abroad. In January 1976 independent accountants conducting an audit of one of Upjohn's foreign subsidiaries discovered that the subsidiary made payments to or for the benefit of foreign government officials in order to secure government business. The accountants so informed petitioner, Mr. Gerard Thomas, Upjohn's Vice President, Secretary, and General Counsel. Thomas is a member of the Michigan and New York Bars, and has been Upjohn's General Counsel for 20 years. He consulted with outside counsel and R.T. Parfet, Jr., Upjohn's Chairman of the Board. It was decided that the company would conduct an internal investigation of what were termed "questionable payments." As part of this investigation the attorneys prepared a letter containing a questionnaire which was sent to "All Foreign General and Area Managers" over the Chairman's signature. The letter began by noting recent disclosures that several American companies made "possibly illegal" payments to foreign government officials and emphasized that the management needed full information concerning any such payments made by Upjohn. The letter indicated that the Chairman had asked Thomas, identified as "the company's General Counsel," "to conduct an investigation for the purpose of determining the nature and magnitude of any payments made by the Upjohn Company or any of its subsidiaries to any employee or official of a foreign government." The questionnaire sought detailed information concerning such payments. Managers were instructed to treat the investigation as "highly confidential" and not to discuss it with anyone other than Upjohn employees who might be helpful in providing the requested information. Responses were to be sent directly to Thomas. Thomas and outside counsel also interviewed the recipients of the questionnaire and some 33 other Upjohn officers or employees as part of the investigation.

On March 26, 1976, the company voluntarily submitted a preliminary report to the Securities and Exchange Commission on Form 8-K disclosing certain questionable payments. A copy of the report was simultaneously submitted to the Internal Revenue Service, which immediately began an investigation to determine the tax consequences of the payments. Special agents conducting the investigation were given lists by Upjohn of all those interviewed and all who had responded to the questionnaire. On November 23, 1976, the Service issued a summons pursuant to 26 U.S.C. § 7602 demanding production of:

> "All files relative to the investigation conducted under the supervision of Gerard Thomas to identify payments to employees of foreign governments and any political contributions made by the Upjohn Company or any of its affiliates since January 1, 1971 and to determine whether any funds of the Upjohn Company had been improperly accounted for on the corporate books during the same period.
>
> The records should include but not be limited to written questionnaires sent to managers of the Upjohn Company's foreign affiliates, and memorandums or notes of the interviews conducted in the United States and abroad with officers and employees of the Upjohn Company and its subsidiaries."

The company declined to produce the documents specified in the second paragraph on the grounds that they were protected from disclosure by the attorney-client privilege and constituted the work product of attorneys prepared in anticipation of litigation. On August 31, 1977, the United States filed a petition seeking enforcement of the summons * * *.

* * *

II

* * * The attorney-client privilege is the oldest of the privileges for confidential communications known to the common law. 8 J. Wigmore, *Evidence* § 2290 (McNaughton rev. 1961). Its purpose is to encourage full and frank communication between attorneys and their clients and thereby promote broader public interests in the observance of law and administration of justice. The privilege recognizes that sound legal advice or advocacy serves public ends and that such advice or advocacy depends upon the lawyer's being fully informed by the client. * * * Admittedly complications in the application of the privilege arise when the client is a corporation, which in theory is an artificial creature of the law, and not an individual; but this Court has assumed that the privilege applies when the client is a corporation, and the Government does not contest the general proposition.

The Court of Appeals, however, considered the application of the privilege in the corporate context to present a "different problem," since the client was an inanimate entity and "only the senior management, guiding and integrating the several operations, * * * can be said to possess an identity analogous to the corporation as a whole." The first case to articulate the so-called "control group test" adopted by the court below, *Philadelphia v. Westinghouse Electric Corp.*, 210 F. Supp. 483, 485 (E.D. Pa. 1962) reflected a similar conceptual approach:

Keeping in mind that the question is, Is it the corporation which is seeking the lawyer's advice when the asserted privileged communication is made?, the most satisfactory solution, I think, is that if the employee making the communication, of whatever rank he may be, is in a position to control or even to take a substantial part in a decision about any action which the corporation may take upon the advice of the attorney, * * * then, in effect, *he is (or personifies) the corporation* when he makes his disclosure to the lawyer and the privilege would apply." (Emphasis supplied.)

Such a view, we think, overlooks the fact that the privilege exists to protect not only the giving of professional advice to those who can act on it but also the giving of information to the lawyer to enable him to give sound and informed advice. The first step in the resolution of any legal problem is ascertaining the factual background and sifting through the facts with an eye to the legally relevant. *See* ABA Code of Professional Responsibility, Ethical Consideration 4-1:

> "A lawyer should be fully informed of all the facts of the matter he is handling in order for his client to obtain the full advantage of our legal system. It is for the lawyer in the exercise of his independent professional judgment to separate the relevant and important from the irrelevant and unimportant. The observance of the ethical obligation of a lawyer to hold inviolate the confidences and secrets of his client not only facilitates the full development of facts essential to proper representation of the client but also encourages laymen to seek early legal assistance."

* * *

In the case of the individual client the provider of information and the person who acts on the lawyer's advice are one and the same. In the corporate context, however, it will frequently be employees beyond the control group as defined by the court below—"officers and agents * * * responsible for directing [the company's] actions in response to legal advice"—who will possess the information needed by the corporation's lawyers. Middle-level—and indeed lower-level—employees can, by actions within the scope of their employment, embroil the corporation in serious legal difficulties, and it is only natural that these employees would have the relevant information needed by corporate counsel if he is adequately to advise the client with respect to such actual or potential difficulties.

* * *

The control group test adopted by the court below thus frustrates the very purpose of the privilege by discouraging the communication of relevant information by employees of the client to attorneys seeking to render legal advice to the client corporation. The attorney's advice will also frequently be more significant to noncontrol group members than to those who officially sanction the advice, and the control group test makes it more difficult to convey full and frank legal advice to the employees who will put into effect the client corporation's policy. * * *

The narrow scope given the attorney-client privilege by the court below not only makes it difficult for corporate attorneys to formulate sound advice when their client is faced with a specific legal problem but also threatens to limit the valuable efforts of corporate counsel to ensure their client's compliance with the law. In light of the vast and complicated array of regulatory legislation confronting the modern corporation, corporations, unlike most individuals, "constantly go to lawyers to find out how to obey the law," Burnham, *The Attorney-Client Privilege in the Corporate Arena*, 24 Bus. Law. 901, 913 (1969), particularly since compliance with the law in this area is hardly an instinctive matter. * * * The test adopted by the court below is difficult to apply in practice, though no abstractly formulated and unvarying "test" will necessarily enable courts to decide questions such as this with mathematical precision. But if the purpose of the attorney-client privilege is to be served, the attorney and client must be able to predict with some degree of certainty whether particular discussions will be protected. An uncertain privilege, or one which purports to be certain but results in widely varying applications by the courts, is little better than no privilege at all. The very terms of the test adopted by the court below suggest the unpredictability of its application. The test restricts the availability of the privilege to those officers who play a "substantial role" in deciding and directing a corporation's legal response. Disparate decisions in cases applying this test illustrate its unpredictability. * * *

The communications at issue were made by Upjohn employees to counsel for Upjohn acting as such, at the direction of corporate superiors in order to secure legal advice from counsel. As the Magistrate found, "Mr. Thomas consulted with the Chairman of the Board and outside counsel and thereafter conducted a factual investigation to determine the nature and extent of the questionable payments *and to be in a position to give legal advice to the company with respect to the payments.*" * * * Information, not available from upper-echelon management, was needed to supply a basis for legal advice concerning compliance with securities and tax laws, foreign laws, currency regulations, duties to shareholders, and potential litigation in each of these areas. The communications concerned matters within the scope of the employees' corporate duties, and the employees themselves were sufficiently aware that they were being questioned in order that the corporation could obtain legal advice. The questionnaire identified Thomas as "the company's General Counsel" and referred in its opening sentence to the possible illegality of payments such as the ones on which information was sought. A statement of policy accompanying the questionnaire clearly indicated the legal implications of the investigation. The policy statement was issued "in order that there be no uncertainty in the future as to the policy with respect to the practices which are the subject of this investigation." * * * This statement was issued to Upjohn employees worldwide, so that even those interviewees not receiving a questionnaire were aware of the legal implications of the interviews. Pursuant to explicit instructions from the Chairman of the Board, the communications were considered "highly confidential" when made, and have been kept confidential by the company. Consistent with the underlying purposes of the attorney-client privilege, these communications must be protected against compelled disclosure.

The Court of Appeals declined to extend the attorney-client privilege beyond the limits of the control group test for fear that doing so would entail severe burdens on discovery and create a broad "zone of silence" over corporate affairs. Application of the attorney-client privilege to communications such as those involved here, however, puts the adversary in no worse position than if the communications had never taken place. The privilege only protects disclosure of communications; it does not protect disclosure of the underlying facts by those who communicated with the attorney:

> "[T]he protection of the privilege extends only to *communications* and not to facts. A fact is one thing and a communication concerning that fact is an entirely different thing. The client cannot be compelled to answer the question,

Food for Thought

If the government had questioned the employees—who were suspected of violations of federal <u>criminal law</u>—wouldn't they have invoked their Fifth Amendment privilege? In which case is the Court's argument that the government didn't need the communications to the corporate attorney convincing?

'What did you say or write to the attorney?' but may not refuse to disclose any relevant fact within his knowledge merely because he incorporated a statement of such fact into his communication to his attorney." *Philadelphia v. Westinghouse Electric Corp.*, 205 F. Supp. 830, 831 (E.D. Pa. 1962).

Here the Government was free to question the employees who communicated with Thomas and outside counsel. Upjohn has provided the IRS with a list of such employees, and the IRS has already interviewed some 25 of them. While it would probably be more convenient for the Government to secure the results of petitioner's internal investigation by simply subpoenaing the questionnaires and notes taken by petitioner's attorneys, such considerations of convenience do not overcome the policies served by the attorney-client privilege. * * *

Needless to say, we decide only the case before us, and do not undertake to draft a set of rules which should govern challenges to investigatory subpoenas. Any such approach would violate the spirit of Federal Rule of Evidence 501. *See* S.Rep. No. 93–1277, p. 13 (1974) ("the recognition of a privilege based on a confidential relationship * * * should be determined on a case-by-case basis"). * * * While such a "case-by-case" basis may to some slight extent undermine desirable certainty in the boundaries of the attorney-client privilege, it obeys the spirit of the Rules. At the same time we conclude that the narrow "control group test" sanctioned by the Court of Appeals, in this case cannot, consistent with "the principles of the common law as * * * interpreted * * * in the light of reason and experience," Fed. Rule Evid. 501, govern the development of the law in this area.

III

Our decision that the communications by Upjohn employees to counsel are covered by the attorney-client privilege disposes of the case so far as the responses to the questionnaires and any notes reflecting responses to interview questions are concerned. The summons reaches further, however, and Thomas has testified that his notes and memoranda of interviews go beyond recording responses to his questions. * * * To the extent that the material subject to the summons is not protected by the attorney-client privilege as disclosing communications between an employee and counsel, we must reach the ruling by the Court of Appeals that the work-product doctrine does not apply to summonses issued under 26 U.S.C. § 7602.

The Government concedes, wisely, that the Court of Appeals erred and that the work-product doctrine does apply to IRS summonses. * * * This doctrine was announced by the Court over 30 years ago in *Hickman v. Taylor.* * * * In that case the Court rejected "an attempt, without purported necessity or justification, to secure written statements, private memoranda and personal recollections prepared or formed by an adverse party's counsel in the course of his legal duties." * * * The Court noted that "it is essential that a lawyer work with a certain degree of privacy" and reasoned that if discovery of the material sought were permitted "much of what is now put down in writing would remain unwritten. An attorney's thoughts, heretofore inviolate, would not be his own. Inefficiency, unfairness and sharp practices would inevitably develop in the giving of legal advice and in the preparation of cases for trial. The effect on the legal profession would be demoralizing. And the interests of the clients and the cause of justice would be poorly served." * * *

The "strong public policy" underlying the work-product doctrine was reaffirmed recently in *United States v. Nobles*, 422 U.S. 225, 236–240, 95 S.Ct. 2160, 2169-2171, 45 L.Ed.2d 141 (1975), and has been substantially incorporated in Federal Rule of Civil Procedure 26(b)(3).

* * * While conceding the applicability of the work-product doctrine, the Government asserts that it has made a sufficient showing of necessity to overcome its protections. The Magistrate apparently so found. * * *

Rule 26 accords special protection to work product revealing the attorney's mental processes. The Rule permits disclosure of documents and tangible things constituting attorney work product upon a showing of substantial need and inability to obtain the equivalent without undue hardship. This was the standard applied by the Magistrate * * *. Rule 26 goes on, however, to state that "[i]n ordering discovery of such materials when the required showing has been made, the court shall protect against disclosure of the mental impressions, conclusions, opinions or legal theories of an attorney or other representative of a party concerning the litigation." Although this language does not specifically refer to memoranda based on oral statements of witnesses, the *Hickman* court stressed the danger that compelled disclosure of such memoranda would reveal the attorney's mental processes. It is clear that this is the sort of material the draftsmen of the Rule had in mind as deserving special protection. * * *

Based on the foregoing, some courts have concluded that *no* showing of necessity can overcome protection of work product which is based on oral statements from witnesses. * * * Those courts declining to adopt an absolute rule have nonetheless recognized that such material is entitled to special protection. * * * *See, e. g., In re Grand Jury Investigation*, 599 F.2d 1224, 1231 (3rd Cir. 1979) ("special considerations * * * must shape any ruling on the discoverability of interview memoranda * * * ; such documents will be discoverable only in a 'rare situation' ") * * *.

We do not decide the issue at this time. It is clear that the Magistrate applied the wrong standard when he concluded that the Government had made a sufficient showing of necessity to overcome the protections of the work-product doctrine. The Magistrate applied the "substantial need" and "without undue hardship" standard articulated in the first part of Rule 26(b)(3). The notes and memoranda sought by the Government here, however, are work product based on oral statements. If they reveal communications, they are, in this case, protected by the attorney-client privilege. To the extent they do not reveal communications, they reveal the attorneys' mental processes in evaluating the communications. As Rule 26 and *Hickman* make clear, such work product

Take Note

If the Upjohn agent is the client's representative when communicating to the Upjohn lawyer, does that mean the agent can invoke the privilege and prevent the Upjohn lawyer from disclosing the information? The answer is no—because while the agent is speaking on behalf of the client, it is Upjohn's privilege, not the agent's. What does this mean for the agent? *See* the next case.

cannot be disclosed simply on a showing of substantial need and inability to obtain the equivalent without undue hardship.

While we are not prepared at this juncture to say that such material is always protected by the work-product rule, we think a far stronger showing of necessity and unavailability by other means than was made by the Government or applied by the Magistrate in this case would be necessary to compel disclosure.

* * *

Accordingly, the judgment of the Court of Appeals is reversed, and the case remanded for further proceedings.

[The concurring opinion of Chief Justice Burger is omitted.]

Hear from the Authors

To hear from the authors on *Upjohn* and Restatement Section 73, click here.

Because of the importance of the issues addressed in *Upjohn*, the ALI drafted a separate section that applies to organizational clients. Section 73 provides as follows:

> When a client is a corporation, unincorporated association, partnership, trust, estate, sole proprietorship, or other for-profit or not-for-profit organization, the attorney-client privilege extends to a communication that:
>
> (1)   otherwise qualifies as privileged under §§ 68–72;
>
> (2)   is between an agent of the organization and a privileged person as defined in § 70;
>
> (3)   concerns a legal matter of interest to the organization; and
>
> (4)   is disclosed only to:
>
>   (a)   privileged persons as defined in § 70; and
>
>   (b)   other agents of the organization who reasonably need to know of the communication in order to act for the organization.

Restatement § 75 addresses the Privilege of Co-Clients and § 76 addresses the Privilege in Common-Interest Arrangements. Despite the ALI's adoption of these provisions in 2000, disputes can still arise. Consider the following case.

In re Grand Jury Subpoena: Under Seal

415 F.3d 333 (4th Cir. 2005)

Wilson, District Judge.

This is an appeal by three former employees of AOL Time Warner ("AOL") from the decision of the district court denying their motions to quash a grand jury subpoena for documents related to an internal investigation by AOL. Appellants argued in the district court that the subpoenaed documents were protected by the attorney-client privilege. Because the district court concluded that the privilege was AOL's alone and because AOL had expressly waived its privilege, the court denied the appellants' motion. We affirm.

I.

In March of 2001, AOL began an internal investigation into its relationship with PurchasePro, Inc. AOL retained the law firm of Wilmer, Cutler & Pickering ("Wilmer Cutler") to assist in the investigation. Over the next several months, AOL's general counsel and counsel from Wilmer Cutler * * * interviewed appellants, AOL employees Kent Wakeford, John Doe 1, and John Doe 2.1

The investigating attorneys interviewed Wakeford, a manager in the company's Business Affairs division, on six occasions. At their third interview, and the first one in which Wilmer Cutler attorneys were present, Randall Boe, AOL's General Counsel, informed Wakeford, "We represent the company. These conversations are privileged, but the privilege belongs to the company and the company decides whether to waive it. If there is a conflict, the attorney-client privilege belongs to the company." Memoranda from that meeting also indicate that the attorneys explained to Wakeford that they represented AOL but that they "could" represent him as well, "as long as no conflict appear[ed]." The attorneys interviewed Wakeford again three days later and, at the beginning of the interview, reiterated that they represented AOL, that the privilege belonged to AOL, and that Wakeford could retain personal counsel at company expense.

The investigating attorneys interviewed John Doe 1 three times. Before the first interview, Boe told him, "We represent the company. These conversations are privileged, but the privilege belongs to the company and the company decides whether to waive it. You are free to consult with your own lawyer at any time." Memoranda from that interview indicate that the attorneys also told him, "We can represent [you] until such time as there appears to be a conflict of interest, [but] * * * the attorney-client privilege belongs to AOL and AOL can decide whether to keep it or waive it." At the end of the interview, John Doe 1 asked if he needed personal counsel. A Wilmer Cutler attorney responded that he did not recommend it, but that he would tell the company not to be concerned if Doe retained counsel.

AOL's attorneys interviewed John Doe 2 twice and followed essentially the same protocol they had followed with the other appellants. They noted, "We represent AOL, and can represent

[you] too if there is not a conflict." In addition, the attorneys told him that, "the attorney-client privilege is AOL's and AOL can choose to waive it."

In November, 2001, the Securities and Exchange Commission ("SEC") began to investigate AOL's relationship with PurchasePro. In December 2001, AOL and Wakeford, through counsel, entered into an oral "common interest agreement," which they memorialized in writing in January 2002. The attorneys acknowledged that, "representation of [their] respective clients raise[d] issues of common interest to [their] respective clients and that the sharing of certain documents, information, * * * and communications with clients" would be mutually beneficial. As a result, the attorneys agreed to share access to information relating to their representation of Wakeford and AOL, noting that "the oral or written disclosure of Common Interest Materials * * * [would] not diminish in any way the confidentiality of such Materials and [would] not constitute a waiver of any applicable privilege."

Wakeford testified before the SEC on February 14, 2002, represented by his personal counsel. Laura Jehl, AOL's general counsel, and F. Whitten Peters of Williams & Connolly, whom AOL had retained in November 2001 in connection with the PurchasePro investigation, were also present, and both stated that they represented Wakeford "for purposes of [the] deposition." During the deposition, the SEC investigators questioned Wakeford about his discussions with AOL's attorneys. When Wakeford's attorney asserted the attorney-client privilege, the SEC investigators followed up with several questions to determine whether the privilege was applicable to the investigating attorneys' March-June 2001 interviews with Wakeford. Wakeford told them he believed, at the time of the interviews, that the investigating attorneys represented him and the company.

John Doe 1 testified before the SEC on February 27, 2002, represented by personal counsel. No representatives of AOL were present. When SEC investigators questioned Doe about the March-June 2001 internal investigation, his counsel asserted that the information was protected and directed Doe not to answer any questions about the internal investigation "in respect to the company's privilege." He stated that Doe's response could be considered a waiver of the privilege and that, "if the AOL lawyers were [present], they could make a judgment, with respect to the company's privilege, about whether or not the answer would constitute a waiver."

On February 26, 2004, a grand jury in the Eastern District of Virginia issued a subpoena commanding AOL to provide "written memoranda and other written records reflecting interviews conducted by attorneys for [AOL]" of the appellants between March 15 and June 30, 2001. While AOL agreed to waive the attorney-client privilege and produce the subpoenaed documents, counsel for the appellants moved to quash the subpoena on the grounds that each appellant had an individual attorney-client relationship with the investigating attorneys, that his interviews were individually privileged, and that he had not waived the privilege. Wakeford also claimed that the information he disclosed to the investigating attorneys was privileged under the common interest doctrine.

The district court denied John Doe 1's and John Doe 2's motions because it found they failed to prove they were clients of the investigating attorneys who interviewed them. The court based its conclusion on its findings that: (1) the investigating attorneys told them that they represented the company; (2) the investigating attorneys told them, "we *can* represent you," which is distinct from "we *do* represent you"; (3) they could not show that the investigating attorneys agreed to represent them; and (4) the investigating attorneys told them that the attorney-client privilege belonged to the company and the company could choose to waive it.

The court initially granted Wakeford's motion to quash because it found that his communications with the investigating attorneys were privileged under the common interest agreement between counsel for Wakeford and counsel for AOL. Following a motion for reconsideration, the court reversed its earlier ruling and held that the subpoenaed documents relating to Wakeford's interviews were not privileged because it found that Wakeford's common interest agreement with AOL postdated the March–June 2001 interviews. In addition, the court held that Wakeford failed to prove that he was a client of the investigating attorneys at the time the interviews took place. The court based its conclusion on its findings that: (1) none of the investigating attorneys understood that Wakeford was seeking personal legal advice; (2) the investigating attorneys did not provide any personal legal advice to him; and (3) the investigating attorneys believed they represented AOL and not Wakeford. This appeal followed.

II.

Appellants argue that because they believed that the investigating attorneys who conducted the interviews were representing them personally, their communications are privileged. However, we agree with the district court that essential touchstones for the formation of an attorney-client relationship between the investigating attorneys and the appellants were missing at the time of the interviews. There is no evidence of an objectively reasonable, mutual understanding that the appellants were seeking legal advice from the investigating attorneys or that the investigating attorneys were rendering personal legal advice. Nor, in light of the investigating attorneys' disclosure that they represented AOL and that the privilege and the right to waive it were AOL's alone, do we find investigating counsel's hypothetical pronouncement that they *could* represent appellants sufficient to establish the reasonable understanding that they *were* representing appellants. Accordingly, we find no fault with the district court's opinion that no individual attorney-client privilege attached to the appellants' communications with AOL's attorneys.

* * *

The person seeking to invoke the attorney-client privilege must prove that he is a client or that he affirmatively sought to become a client. "The professional relationship * * * hinges upon the client's belief that he is consulting a lawyer in that capacity and his manifested intention to seek professional legal advice." *United States v. Evans*, 113 F.3d 1457, 1465 (7th Cir. 1997). An individual's subjective belief that he is represented is not alone sufficient to create an attorney-client relationship. See *United States v. Keplinger*, 776 F.2d 678, 701 (7th Cir. 1985) ("We think no individual attorney-client relationship can be inferred without some finding that the potential client's subjective belief is minimally reasonable."). Rather, the putative client must show that his subjective belief that an attorney-client relationship existed was reasonable under the circumstances.

With these precepts in mind, we conclude that appellants could not have reasonably believed that the investigating attorneys represented them personally during the time frame covered by the subpoena. First, there is no evidence that the investigating attorneys told the appellants that they represented them, nor is there evidence that the appellants asked the investigating attorneys to represent them. To the contrary, there is evidence that the investigating attorneys relayed to Wakeford the company's offer to retain personal counsel for him at the company's expense, and that they told John Doe 1 that he was free to retain personal counsel. Second, there is no evidence that the appellants ever sought personal legal advice from the investigating attorneys, nor is there any evidence that the investigating attorneys rendered personal legal advice. Third, when the appellants spoke with the investigating attorneys, they were fully apprised that the information they were giving could be disclosed at the company's discretion. Under these circumstances, appellants could not have reasonably believed that the investigating attorneys represented them personally. Therefore, the district court's finding that appellants had no attorney-client relationship with the investigating attorneys is not clearly erroneous.

The appellants argue that the phrase "we *can* represent you as long as no conflict appears," manifested an agreement by the investigating attorneys to represent them. They claim that, "it is hard to imagine a more straightforward assurance of an attorney-client relationship than 'we can represent you.' " We disagree. As the district court noted, "we *can* represent you" is distinct from "we *do* represent you." If there was any evidence that the investigating attorneys had said, "we *do* represent you," then the outcome of this appeal might be different. Furthermore, the statement actually made, "we *can* represent you," must be interpreted within the context of the entire warning. The investigating attorneys' statements to the appellants, read in their entirety, demonstrate that the attorneys' loyalty was to the company. That loyalty was never implicitly or explicitly divided. In addition to noting at the outset that they had been retained to represent AOL, the investigating attorneys warned the appellants that the content of their communications during the interview "belonged" to AOL. This protocol put the appellants on notice that, while their communications with the attorneys were considered confidential, the company could choose to reveal the content of those communications at any time, without the appellants' consent.

Food for Thought

The court is saying the lawyer would be operating under a conflict of interest by representing both the corporation and the corporate agents. Why? Wasn't the basic idea for everyone to try to defend against an investigation into suspected corporate misconduct? *See* Chapter 5, Section II.

We note, however, that our opinion should not be read as an implicit acceptance of the watered-down "*Upjohn* warnings" the investigating attorneys gave the appellants. It is a potential legal and ethical mine field. Had the investigating attorneys, in fact, entered into an attorney-client relationship with appellants, as their statements to the appellants professed they could, they would not have been free to waive the appellants' privilege when a conflict arose. It should have seemed obvious that they could not have jettisoned one client in favor of another. Rather, they would have had to withdraw from all representation and to maintain all confidences. Indeed, the court would be hard pressed to identify how investigating counsel could robustly investigate and report to management or the board of directors of a publicly-traded corporation with the necessary candor if counsel were constrained by ethical obligations to individual employees. However, because we agree with the district court that the appellants never entered into an attorney-client relationship with the investigating attorneys, they averted these troubling issues.

III.

Wakeford also claims that the documents in question are protected by the joint defense privilege because of his common interest agreement with AOL. However, the district court found that no common interest agreement existed at the time of the interviews in March-June 2001. This finding was not clearly erroneous.

The joint defense privilege, an extension of the attorney-client privilege, protects communications between parties who share a common interest in litigation. *United States v. Schwimmer*, 892 F.2d 237, 243-44 (2d Cir. 1989). The purpose of the privilege is to allow persons with a common interest to "communicate with their respective attorneys and with each other to more effectively prosecute or defend their claims." *In re Grand Jury Subpoenas 89-3 and 89-4, John Doe 89-129*, 902 F.2d 244, 249 (4th Cir. 1990). For the privilege to apply, the proponent must establish that the parties had "some common interest about a legal matter." *Sheet Metal Workers Int'l Assoc. v. Sweeney*, 29 F.3d 120, 124 (4th Cir. 1994). An employee's cooperation in an internal investigation alone is not sufficient to establish a common interest; rather "some form of joint strategy is necessary." *United States v. Weissman*, 195 F.3d 96, 100 (2d Cir. 1999).

The district court found that "an agreement to share information pursuant to a common interest did not exist prior to December 2001." * * *

IV.

After review of the district court's factual findings and legal conclusions, we find no clear error. We find no error in the district court's conclusion that the appellants were not clients of the investigating attorneys and therefore could not assert the attorney-client privilege to prevent disclosure of the subpoenaed documents. Further, we agree with the district court's finding that, because Wakeford failed to establish that he and AOL were cooperating in a common defense before December 2001, he has no joint defense privilege before that time. The district court therefore properly denied the appellants' motions.

b. Lawyer's Ethical Duty to Notify Corporate Agent That There Is No Attorney-Client Relationship

Colorado Rule 1.13, which follows the ABA Model Rule, provides as follows:

> (f)   In dealing with an organization's directors, officers, employees, members, shareholders or other constituents, a lawyer shall explain the identity of the client when the lawyer knows or reasonably should know that the organization's interests are adverse to those of the constituents with whom the lawyer is dealing.

Rule 1.13(f) provides the ethical grounding for what the AOL court, *supra*, refers to as the *Upjohn* warning. But as the court notes, the warning must be more than "I represent the corporation." It must also include "and I do not represent you."

Practice Pointer

A common interest agreement allows multiple clients to pool information without waiving the privilege, at least to anyone outside the common interest unit. But a common interest agreement will not be enforceable if the parties are pursuing fundamentally different interests. Note that if the parties to a common interest arrangement end up adverse to each other in a subsequent litigation, the communications they made during their common interest arrangement can be used by each against the other—the reason being that there was no expectation of confidentiality with respect to members of the common interest arrangement. Also, in that later lawsuit, lawyers for the former common interest parties are ordinarily disqualified and may be viewed as having acted in a manner inconsistent with Rule 1.9(c)(1), because cross-examining a member of the former common interest unit is the equivalent of using a former client's communications against them. *See United States v. Anderson*, 790 F. Supp. 231 (W.D. Wash. 1992) (an attorney who acquires information from a potential witness pursuant to a joint defense agreement is in no different position than would be an attorney who acquires such information from a prior or jointly represented client). For more on common interest arrangements, *see* 2 Saltzburg, Martin & Capra, *Federal Rules of Evidence Manual* at § 501.02[5][e].

Global Perspective

This section has considered the issue of "who is the client?" But when considering attorney-client privilege issues, one must also take into account the issue of "who is the lawyer?" For example, if an in-house counsel is the lawyer doing the communicating, is that communication necessarily privileged? What if a U.S. lawyer is communicating with its U.S. client about an EU antitrust investigation but those communications can be found (and seized) on a law firm network located in Europe? In the EU, the answer to both of these questions may be "no attorney-client privilege attaches." In 2010, the European Court of Justice, which is the EU's equivalent to the U.S. Supreme Court, decided the Akzo Nobel case in which it reaffirmed its prior AM&S decision and concluded that there was no EU-level attorney-client privilege for communications between a client and its in-house counsel who was a licensed Dutch lawyer. (There may be a national-level privilege, but not an EU-level privilege.) The Court reasoned that the in-house counsel's employment status meant that he or she could not be viewed as "independent," which is a necessary prerequisite for the privilege. The Court also used language that might suggest that the privilege is limited to *European* independent counsel, excluding U.S. lawyers from the European privilege. *See Akzo Nobel Chems. Ltd. v. Commission (E.C.J.), Introductory Note by Laurel S. Terry*, 50 I.L.M. 1 (2011).

c. Communications to Nonlawyer Agents of the Representation

In re New York Renu with Moistureloc Product Liability Litigation

2008 WL 2338552 (D.S.C.)

DANIEL J. CAPRA, SPECIAL MASTER:

In this litigation, Defendant Bausch & Lomb has refused to produce a number of otherwise responsive documents on the ground that they are protected by the attorney-client privilege * * *. The documents that are subject to this Order have been set forth in exhibits to an affidavit by Robert Bailey, Esq., Vice President and General Counsel for Bausch & Lomb. [Ed. note: This is a federal-state multi-district litigation involving thousands of claims against Bausch & Lomb for alleged contamination of its contact lens solution. The emails reviewed concerned steps considered and taken after the contamination came to light.]

* * *

In evaluating the privilege claims, I applied four fundamental legal principles:

1)   Defendant, as the party invoking the privilege, has the burden of showing that the requirements of the privilege are met. *See, e.g., United States v. Landof,* 591 F.2d 36 (9th Cir. 1978) (as the privilege is in derogation of the search for truth, the party who seeks to invoke it has the burden of establishing it).

2)   Intra-corporate communications to counsel may fall within the privilege if the predominant intent is to seek legal advice. *United States v. IBM,* 66 F.R.D. 206, 212-13 (S.D.N.Y. 1974) (applying the test of predominant intent).

3)   Intra-corporate communications to and from counsel can retain a privilege if disclosure is limited to those who have a "need to know" the advice of counsel; the company's burden "is to show that it limited its dissemination of the documents in keeping with their asserted confidentiality, not to justify each determination that a particular employee should have access to the information therein." *Federal Trade Comm'n v. GlaxoSmithKline,* 294 F.3d 141, 147-48 (D.C. Cir. 2002).

4)   As this case is in diversity, the applicable privilege law is state law. *See* Fed. R. Evid. 501. And of course state privilege law applies to the actions in New York state court. Choice of law principles appear to point to New York privilege law as determinative, as that is the location of defendant's principal place of business. Federal courts have recognized that the New York law of privilege is substantially similar to federal common law. *See, e.g., Bank of Am., N.A. v. Terra Nova Ins. Co. Ltd.,* 211 F. Supp. 2d 493 (S.D.N.Y. 2002) ("New York law governing attorney-client privilege is generally similar to accepted federal doctrine."). This statement is helpful

when the federal common law is itself clear and undisputed. But a difficulty arises where the federal courts are in dispute about the federal common law, and there appears to be no clear state law on the subject. Where such a situation arises, I have chosen the result that appears most consistent with the approach to privilege questions undertaken by the New York Court of Appeals; that approach is to use a utilitarian analysis to provide protection to communications to and from counsel that would not be made in absence of the privilege. *See generally* Martin & Capra, *New York Evidence Handbook* § 5.2 (2d ed. 2003).

* * *

Exhibit 3

This exhibit consists of two email strings regarding a contact with the FDA about a planned public statement about MoistureLoc [the contaminated contact lens solution]. The first email is from Barbara Kelley [corporate executive] to Ron Zarella [CEO of Bausch & Lomb], Bob Bailey [General Counsel], and others, including two public relations consultants from Hill & Knowlton, a public relations firm employed by Bausch & Lomb. Plaintiffs contend that any privilege is lost because of the disclosure to Hill & Knowlton. For the reasons discussed below, I agree with plaintiffs and accordingly find that this email is not privileged and must be produced in its entirety.

Communications to nonlawyers can be brought within the privilege under the so-called *Kovel* doctrine. The court in *United States v. Kovel*, 296 F.2d 918, 921 (2d Cir. 1961) held that confidential communications to nonlawyers could be protected by the privilege if the nonlawyer's services are *necessary to the legal representation*. But the *Kovel* protection is applicable only if the services performed by the nonlawyer are necessary to promote the lawyer's effectiveness; it is not enough that the services are beneficial to the client in some way unrelated to the legal services of the lawyer. *Id.* at 922 (the "communication must be made in confidence for the purpose of obtaining legal advice from the lawyer. * * * If what is sought is not legal advice but only accounting services * * * or if the advice sought is the accountant's rather than the lawyer's, no privilege exists."). See also *United States v. Ackert*, 169 F.3d 136, 139 (2d Cir. 1999) (ruling that the communication "between an attorney and a third party does not become shielded by the attorney-client privilege solely because the communication proves important to the attorney's ability to represent the client").

Courts are in some dispute on whether public relations firms are "necessary to the representation" so as to fall within the *Kovel* protection. Most courts agree, however, that basic public relations advice, from a consultant hired by the corporate client, is not within the privilege. * * *

Judge Cote in *Haugh v. Schroder Inv. Mgmt. North Am. Inc.*, 2003 WL 21998674, at *8 (S.D.N.Y. 2003) summed up the basic law, and held that disclosure to a public relations firm lost the privilege, in the following passage:

> Plaintiff has not shown that Murray [the p.r. consultant] performed anything other than standard public relations services for Haugh, and more importantly,

she has not shown that her communications with Murray or Murray's with Arkin [the lawyer] were necessary so that Arkin could provide Haugh with legal advice. The conclusory descriptions of Murray's role supplied by plaintiff fail to bring the sixteen documents within the ambit of the attorney-client privilege. The documents transmitted from plaintiff to Murray and the one document from Murray to Arkin are consistent with the design of a public relations campaign. Plaintiff has not shown that Murray was "performing functions materially different from those that any ordinary public relations" advisor would perform. *Calvin Klein Trademark Trust v. Wachner et al.*, 198 F.R.D. 53, 55 (S.D.N.Y. 2000). As such, Haugh's transmission of documents to Murray, even simultaneously with disclosure to former counsel, and Murray's transmission of a meeting agenda to Arkin, vitiates the application of the attorney-client privilege to these documents.

Judge Cote relied on the compelling point that "[a] media campaign is not a litigation strategy. Some attorneys may feel it is desirable at times to conduct a media campaign, but that decision does not transform their coordination of a campaign into legal advice."

It is true that a few cases have found communications to public relations consultants to be within the attorney-client privilege. But those cases arise from unusual and extreme facts and do not involve the basic provision of public relations advice by a company retained by the client, as in the instant case. For example, in *In re Copper Market Antitrust Litig.*, 200 F.R.D. 13 (S.D.N.Y. 2001), a foreign company found itself in the midst of a high profile scandal involving both regulatory and civil litigation aspects, and hired a public relations firm because it lacked experience both in English-speaking and in dealing with Western media. The public relations firm acted as the corporation's spokesperson when dealing with the Western press and conferred with the company's U.S. litigation counsel. Judge Swain upheld the attorney-client privilege claim, reasoning that the public relations firm, in the extreme circumstances of the case, was the functional equivalent of an in-house department of the corporation and thus part of the "client." Obviously the facts of *Copper Market* do not approach those of this case, in which a public relations consulting firm provides basic consulting advice.

Likewise, the facts of *In re Grand Jury Subpoenas*, 265 F. Supp. 2d 321 (S.D.N.Y. 2003) are vastly different from the instant case. Judge Kaplan held that the privilege applied to a public relations consulting firm hired to assist counsel to create a climate in which prosecutors might feel freer not to indict the client. He concluded that this was an area in which counsel were presumably unskilled and that the task constituted "legal advice." As Judge Cote stated in *Haugh*: "There is no need here to determine whether *In re Grand Jury Subpoenas* was correctly decided." Bausch & Lomb has not identified with particularity any legal advice that required the assistance of a public relations consultant; Bailey's affidavit simply states, in conclusory fashion, that Hill & Knowlton's presence was "necessary." Bausch & Lomb has not, for example, identified any nexus between the consultant's work and the attorney's role in defending against possible litigation or a regulatory action or proceeding.

I am most reluctant to rely on the broad applications in *Copper Market* and *In re Grand Jury Subpoenas* in light of the well-reasoned case law indicating that the privilege is lost when the corporate client communicates to an outside consultant, hired by the corporation, and providing nothing more than basic public relations advice. *See, e.g.,* Ann M. Murphy, *Spin Control and the High-Profile Client—Should the Attorney-Client Privilege Extend to Communications with Public Relations Consultants?,* 55 Syracuse L.Rev. 545 (2005) (concluding that "expanding the attorney-client privilege to communications with public relations consultants is inadvisable and against the interests of justice"). A conservative approach is, indeed, mandated by New York law, which appears to recognize the *Kovel* doctrine only in narrow circumstances in which the nonlawyer's services are absolutely necessary to effectuate the lawyer's legal services. *See, e.g., People v. Edney,* 39 N.Y.2d 620, 385 N.Y.S.2d 23, 350 N.E.2d 400 (1976).

Accordingly, the email from Barbara Kelley dated May 11, 2006 is not privileged because it was routed to employees of Hill & Knowlton. (If not for that routing, the email would be privileged because it was implicitly seeking Bob Bailey's legal advice on discussions with the FDA).

In contrast, the second email in the string, dated May 11, 2006 at 11:07 p.m., is privileged. It discusses the need to seek legal advice from Bob Bailey, and this email was *not* sent or routed to Hill & Knowlton.

Privilege claim sustained in part and denied in part.

* * *

FYI

> In a subsequent opinion involving other emails withheld by Bausch & Lomb, the Special Master found that emails sent to nonlawyer experts on regulatory matters were protected under the *Kovel* doctrine, because the experts were necessary to the legal representation. Outside counsel hired the experts to help prepare a response to the FDA on technical regulatory issues. *See In re New York Renu with Moistureloc Product Liability Litigation,* 2009 WL 2842745 (D.S.C. 2009).

Exhibit 11

Exhibit 11 contains four email chains discussing the arrangement for handling consumer returns of ReNu products. All of these emails were sent to employees of Hill & Knowlton and for reasons discussed above under Exhibit 3, these documents are not privileged.

Investigation of Hill & Knowlton's contributions on these emails only fortifies the determination that Hill & Knowlton was not involved in furthering (much less necessary to providing) legal advice. In one email, Christina Cheang, an employee of Hill & Knowlton, suggests that optical shops

Practice Pointer

The *Kovel* doctrine protects confidential communications to non-lawyers—but only if they are necessary to the legal representation. In close cases, what can the lawyer do in advance of a communication to help assure that a court will find that the non-lawyer was necessary to the legal representation?

should be used for redemptions, as a means of establishing good business relations with these shops. She has to be told, later on in the email string * * * that Bausch & Lomb cannot legally use optical shops for redemption. Clearly she is not necessary to providing legal advice—indeed she is providing business advice that is contrary to legal advice.

Privilege claim denied.

Global Perspective

Societies around the world have struggled with the issue of how to balance the attorney-client privilege against national security concerns. In 2016, the CCBE issued recommendations "on the protection of client confidentiality within the context of surveillance activities." As that document noted on p. 31, "Ever since the Snowden revelations of 2013, the CCBE has been releasing statements, studies, and letters to denounce the violations of professional secrecy by states and governmental bodies carrying out unlawful surveillance activities." In 2019, the CCBE issued an assessment of the U.S. CLOUD Act, which is the "Clarifying Lawful Overseas Use of Data Act." For additional information about the CCBE"s work in this area, you can consult the webpage of the CCBE's "Surveillance" Working Group.

4. Expectation of Confidentiality

Restatement § 71 provides additional information about what it means for a communication to be "in confidence." It states:

> A communication is in confidence within the meaning of § 68 if, at the time and in the circumstances of the communication, the communicating person reasonably believes that no one will learn the contents of the communication except a privileged person as defined in § 70 or another person with whom communications are protected under a similar privilege.

Consider this definition and the materials that follow as you answer Question 4-5.

[Question 4-5]

The board of directors of a client corporation votes to do a public offering of stock. The client hires an outside law firm to prepare the necessary documentation. An attorney from the outside law firm communicates with the client's corporate personnel and obtains factual information relevant to the public offering that would put the client in a negative light. Upon review of this information, the attorney recommends that the client terminate its plan to do a public offering. The client's board of directors agrees.

If the information was subpoenaed, would the negative information obtained by the attorney be protected by attorney-client privilege?

   (A) Yes, because corporate personnel were communicating with the attorney on behalf of the client.

(B) Yes, because corporate personnel were communicating with the attorney to assist the attorney with the attorney's legal representation of the client.

(C) No, because the attorney communicated with multiple corporate personnel.

(D) No, because the information was provided to the attorney for the purpose of making it public.

United States v. Hatcher

323 F.3d 666 (8th Cir. 2003)

RICHARD S. ARNOLD, CIRCUIT JUDGE.

This case involves the convictions of Michael Hatcher, Angelo Porrello, and Joseph Anthony Porrello on charges stemming from the armed robberies of jewelry stores in the Kansas City area. Appellants were convicted of charges including conspiracy, interference with interstate commerce by armed robbery, the use of a firearm during a crime of violence, attempted money laundering, and criminal forfeiture. On appeal, appellants raise numerous claims. We reject all but one of appellants' claims as without merit. As to that one claim—having to do with taped recordings of certain conversations in prison—further proceedings in the District Court will be necessary.

I

A career criminal by the name of Clarence Burnett organized a group of robbers who successfully robbed numerous jewelry stores. * * * In each robbery, a group of men entered the jewelry store with at least one gun drawn and proceeded to ransack the jewelry cases. * * * In each case, Mr. Burnett took the jewels to J's Pawnshop, operated by Angelo and Joseph Porrello, to fence the jewels to the Porrellos. According to the evidence at trial—which came primarily through the testimony of Clarence Burnett himself—the Porrellos were involved not only in the fencing of the jewelry but also in the planning of the robberies themselves, by, for instance, providing guns, bulletproof vests, and jewelry-store floor plans for the robberies.

* * *

At trial, the majority of the evidence came from cooperating co-conspirators in exchange for reduced sentences. * * * [The defendants were convicted.].

Angelo Porrello argues that the District Court erred in refusing to order the government to turn over tapes of conversations between the cooperating co-conspirators and their attorneys. These conversations took place while the co-conspirators were incarcerated, and the parties to these conversations were aware that they were being recorded by the prison. The District Court ruled that these tapes were protected by the attorney-client privilege and therefore would not order their disclosure to the defendants. The government defends the District Court's decision on the ground that the defendants failed to establish a factual record to support the argument that the attorney-client privilege had been waived.

We respectfully disagree. The presence of the prison recording device destroyed the attorney-client privilege. Because the inmates and their lawyers were aware that their conversations were being recorded, they could not reasonably expect that their conversations would remain private. The presence of the recording device was the functional equivalent of the presence of a third party. These conversations were not privileged. *See e.g., Fisher v. Mr. Harold's Hair Lab, Inc.,* 215 Kan. 515, 519, 527 P.2d 1026, 1030 (1974) (stating that conversations are privileged only when made outside the presence of third parties); *Lipton Realty, Inc. v. St. Louis Housing Authority,* 705 S.W.2d 565, 570 (Mo. App.1986) (stating that the attorney-client privilege is waived when the client voluntarily shares the communications with third parties). The very existence of the tapes, which were made by and are now in the custody of the United States, was factually sufficient to demonstrate that the co-conspirators waived the attorney-client privilege.

We conclude that the District Court erred in refusing to order the disclosure of the taped conversations on the ground that they were privileged. Because the tapes were never disclosed to the Court or to the defendants, we do not know what was said. We therefore cannot assess whether defendants were prejudiced by the non-disclosure. Thus, we remand the case to the District Court to consider what effect, if any, the disclosure would have had on this prosecution. This will provide the government with the opportunity to argue that the non-disclosure of the tapes was harmless error.

* * *

In general, the attorney-client privilege is personal and cannot be asserted by anyone other than the client. In this case, the United States is asserting the co-defendants' attorney-client privilege as a defense to the request for disclosure of the tapes. On remand, if the District Court deems it appropriate, it may allow the parties to pursue the issue of the government's standing by supplemental briefs, evidence, or otherwise.

BYE, CIRCUIT JUDGE, concurring.

* * *

We have previously held that inmates impliedly consent to having their telephone conversations taped when they know a policy of recording all inmate telephone calls exists. *See United States v. Eggleston,* 165 F.3d 624, 626 (8th Cir. 1999); *United States v. Horr,* 963 F.2d 1124, 1126 (8th Cir. 1992). These same cases, however, recognize that such policies specifically exempt telephone calls made to attorneys. *Eggleston,* 165 F.3d at 626 (referencing a county jail policy excepting calls made to inmates' attorneys from the jail's monitoring policy); *Horr,* 963 F.2d at 1125 (referencing the Bureau of Prison's policy of recording all inmate telephone calls, except those between inmates and their attorneys). Because the record in this case does not show whether a similar policy existed or whether the co-conspirators knew of its existence, we have insufficient information to conclude the privilege was waived.

I recognize the attorney/client telephone calls at issue may have been placed without following the procedures necessary to protect their confidentiality. If so, the co-conspirators may well have waived any protections afforded by the privilege. There is, however, insufficient information in this record to satisfy me such was the case. Therefore, I cannot agree with the majority's conclusion that the privilege was waived simply because the conversations were taped.

Despite these concerns with the majority holding, I agree the district court should have allowed the defendants access to the tapes because the government lacks standing to lay claim to the co-conspirators' attorney/client privilege. The attorney/client privilege is personal in nature and cannot be asserted vicariously. Because the government failed to establish any basis for asserting the co-conspirators' attorney/client privilege, the district court should have ordered disclosure of the taped conversations.

* * *

Practice Pointer

If a client tells his/her attorney confidentially about the location of evidence that would hurt the client's case, may the attorney remove the evidence?

In *People v. Meredith*, 631 P.2d 46 (Cal. 1981), the court held that statements between the defendant and his attorney concerning the location of a piece of evidence, a partially burned wallet, were confidential communications protected by the attorney-client privilege. However, when the defense team removed the wallet from the trash bin where the defendant had left it, the privilege disappeared with regard to the location and condition of the wallet. "When defense counsel alters or removes physical evidence, he necessarily deprives the prosecution of the opportunity to observe that evidence in its original condition or location. * * * To extend the attorney-client privilege to a case in which the defense removed evidence might encourage defense counsel to race the police to seize critical evidence. * * * We therefore conclude that whenever defense counsel removes or alters evidence, the statutory privilege does not bar revelation of the original location or condition of the evidence in question. We thus view the defense decision to remove evidence as a tactical choice. If defense counsel leaves the evidence where he discovers it, his observations derived from privileged communications are insulated from revelation. If, however, counsel chooses to remove evidence to examine or test it, the original location and condition of that evidence loses the protection of the privilege." Rule 3.4(a) states: "A lawyer shall not: (a) unlawfully obstruct another party's access to evidence or unlawfully alter, destroy or conceal a document or other material having potential evidentiary value. A lawyer shall not counsel or assist another person to do any such act." For more on Rule 3.4, see Chapter 6, Section III.

See also New York Rule 3.4(a)(1): A lawyer may not "suppress any evidence that the lawyer or the client has a legal obligation to reveal or produce." How do these rules differ, if at all?

Simulation: Privilege Review, "You Be the Judge"

Assume you are a judge presiding over a dispute concerning which emails are covered by attorney-client privilege. The parties involved are Corporation A, which provides bookstore services, and University X, which has a dispute with Corporation A. Your jurisdiction follows the Restatement's approach to attorney-client privilege. Also, the law in your jurisdiction is clear that communications between in-house counsel and a corporate client are protected by attorney-client privilege to the same extent as communications between the corporation and outside counsel.

You are reviewing the following emails, and you must make rulings on each. What are your rulings and why?

1. President of Corporation A sends an email to Corporation A's General Counsel, "What are the requirements of a binding contract for a bookstore service contract with University X?"

2. General Counsel emails the President with a list of the requirements for such a contract.

3. President of Corporation A sends an email to Corporation A's Vice President, who, as part of her job, is engaged in negotiations with University X, and the email states: "Our General Counsel has advised me that in order to form a binding contract with University X, we need to agree on requirements 1, 2, and 3."

4. Email from Vice President to Corporation A's Sales Manager: "President has instructed us to proceed to negotiate a contract for bookstore services with University X. Get to this ASAP."

5. Email from Sales Manager to Vice President: "I've just met with Manager of Univesity X and we have a handshake deal. How much detail do we need in the written contract?"

6. Email from Vice President to President: "Sales Manager reached a great deal for us. Let's keep the written contract simple and direct to close the deal ASAP."

7. Email from President to General Counsel: "Draft this contract as quickly as possible. Draft a contract including 1, 2, 3 and also 4, 5 and 6."

8. Email from General Counsel to in-house Paralegal: "The President wants a contract with 1 through 6. Please take language from our prior contract with University Z to get the process started."

9. Email from General Counsel to Vice President: "Here is my proposed contract attached to this email. Show this to University X, but tell them it is non-negotiable."

> 10. Email from Vice President to University X: "Here is our proposed contract. Our General Counsel says since we are giving you such a good deal, we must insist on these terms as written. Please send it back with your signature."
>
> 11. Emails by non-lawyers within each party, and between Corporation A and University X, following execution of the contract, disputing its interpretation, and at times indicating they rely on their counsel's advice.
>
> 12. As a result of a dispute on contract interpretation between the parties, Vice President discusses this with President and then contacts General Counsel about her interpretation of the contract and General Counsel responds with an email. Vice President forwards this email to University X.

C. Waiver of Attorney-Client Privilege

1. Introduction

Even where all the elements of the privilege are otherwise present, the privilege will not be recognized if it has been waived. The term "waiver" as used by the courts actually encompasses more than the traditional definition of a knowing and voluntary waiver of a right. Courts often find a "waiver" in circumstances that might more appropriately be considered a "forfeiture." Judge Richard Posner has stated that many of the waiver doctrines—such as the doctrine finding a waiver of the privilege in some circumstances when the party has mistakenly disclosed the privileged information—are not "waiver in the standard sense in which the word is used in the law: the deliberate relinquishment of a right." Rather, a "waiver" of the privilege is sometimes found "in order to punish the person claiming the privilege for a mistake." *International Oil, Chem. & Atomic Workers Local 7-517 v. Uno-Ven Co.*, 170 F.3d 779 (7th Cir. 1999).

"Waiver" in this broad sense includes the concept of forfeiture and follows from any conduct by the client that would make it unfair for the client thereafter to assert the privilege. *See United States v. Yerardi*, 192 F.3d 14 (1st Cir. 1999) ("The concept of waiver by conduct exists, but often amounts simply to a determination that the privilege holder's conduct makes it unfair to allow subsequent assertion of the privilege.").

2. Authority to Waive the Privilege

Under U.S. law, the client holds the privilege and the power to waive it. The lawyer generally has implicit authority to waive the privilege as well in the course of the representation.

The identity of the client for purposes of waiver is a problematic issue in the corporate context. The Supreme Court held in *CFTC v. Weintraub*, 471 U.S. 343, 349 (1985), that "the power to waive the corporate attorney-client privilege rests with the corporation's management and is normally exercised by its officers and directors." Therefore, in *Weintraub*, a person who had resigned as an officer no longer had authority to exercise or waive the privilege. The *Weintraub*

Court further stated that "when control of a corporation passes to new management, the authority to assert and waive the corporation's attorney-client privilege passes as well." Applying this rule, the *Weintraub* Court held that a trustee in bankruptcy succeeded to management's authority to waive the corporate privilege, over the objection of former and present corporate officers. *See also United States v. Campbell,* 73 F.3d 44 (5th Cir. 1996) (a partnership, like a corporation, is an artificial person that can act only through its agents: "Accordingly, the same rule that applies to corporations in bankruptcy should apply to a bankrupt limited partnership."); *Odmark v. Westside Bancorp., Inc.,* 636 F. Supp. 552 (W.D. Wash. 1986) (after a bank's failure, the FSLIC was held to control the privilege).

Global Perspective

U.S. clients hold the attorney-client privilege and the power to waive it, but this is not a universal approach to this topic. *See, e.g.,* the CCBE Edward Report and the CCBE Updated Edward Report. Additional information about attorney-client privilege in European Union countries is available in an online PDF prepared by a leading law firm.

3. "Selective" Waiver

Please review the materials in this section and then consider the following question:

[Question 4-6]

A client corporation is being investigated by the Environmental Division of the Department of Justice (DOJ) on suspicion that it had illegally dumped toxic chemicals for a number of years. Before the DOJ investigation began, the client had hired an attorney with an outside law firm to investigate how the client was disposing of the chemicals. The attorney interviewed corporate agents of the client and filed a report with the client. The DOJ requests this report from the client. The client agrees to turn over the report "in the spirit of cooperation" but only if the DOJ signs a confidentiality agreement under which the DOJ will not turn over the report to any private parties.

After receiving the report, the DOJ concludes its investigation of the client. But private parties allegedly injured by the client's activities bring a lawsuit against the client. They serve a discovery demand for the report. The client refuses to turn over the report, citing the attorney-client privilege.

Is the report privileged?

(A) **Yes, because the client was forced to turn over the report to the DOJ in order to avoid a criminal prosecution.**

(B) **Yes, because the disclosure of the report was not a general waiver and the private parties cannot take advantage of the selective waiver, and the DOJ agreed to keep the disclosure confidential.**

(C) **No, because the attorney was acting as a factual investigator, and the "legal advice" requirement of the privilege is not met.**

(D) **No, because the client waived any privilege by disclosing the report to the DOJ.**

An example of the selective waiver problem arose in *Westinghouse Elec. Corp. v. Republic of the Philippines*, 951 F.2d 1414 (3d Cir. 1991), where Westinghouse received a report from outside counsel who had conducted an internal corporate investigation. The internal investigation was in response to an inquiry by the SEC into allegations that Westinghouse had obtained certain contracts by bribing officials of the Philippine Government. Westinghouse cooperated with the SEC inquiry by turning over outside counsel's report. Later, the Department of Justice began to investigate whether Westinghouse obtained contracts from the Philippines through bribery. Again, Westinghouse cooperated by turning over the investigative report prepared by counsel. Thereafter, the Republic brought suit against Westinghouse for damages stemming from the alleged bribery of Philippine officials by agents of Westinghouse. The Republic sought access to counsel's investigative report.

The Court rejected the Westinghouse argument that the attorney-client privilege could be *selectively* waived—that is, it rejected the concept that a party who voluntarily discloses privileged material to the government nonetheless retains the privilege as to private parties. In rejecting selective waiver the *Westinghouse* Court sided with the clear majority of circuits. *See, e.g., In re Quest Communications Int'l, Inc.,* 450 F.3d 1179 (10th Cir. 2006) (concluding that the case has not been made that selective waiver protection is required to assure cooperation with law enforcement); *United States v. Billmyer,* 57 F.3d 31 (1st Cir. 1995) (corporation's disclosure of report to the government constituted a waiver of the privilege: "A risk of unfairness is evident where information is provided to one side in a case (here, the United States) and then an inquiry into its origin is shielded by a claim of privilege."); *In re Columbia/HCA Healthcare Corp. Billing Practices Litigation,* 293 F.3d 289 (6th Cir. 2002) (rejecting the concept of selective waiver, even in the face of an express confidentiality agreement). *But see Diversified Industries v. Meredith,* 572 F.2d 596 (8th Cir. 1977) *(en banc)* (adopting selective waiver).

The argument in favor of selective waiver is that it is necessary to assure cooperation with government investigations—corporations are less likely to cooperate if the consequence of disclosure is that privileged reports can be used by plaintiffs in private litigation. And if corporations don't cooperate, this will increase the costs of government investigations—the regulator will have to investigate from the ground up, rather than being able to work off the report that was prepared by corporate counsel. But the courts have countered that selective waiver is not required to encourage cooperation with government investigations, as the corporation is already fully incentivized to cooperate, given the risks of fines, indictments, and general regulatory obligations. As the Court in *Westinghouse* noted, Westinghouse disclosed the investigative report to the government even though the selective waiver rule was far from clearly established at the time.

It could be argued that *Westinghouse* places the client in a dilemma: If the client wants to cooperate with the government, it can do so but only at the expense of completely waiving the privilege. However, this supposed "tough choice" is one that attorneys and clients routinely make in a variety of contexts. Waiver of the privilege often has advantages and disadvantages. For example, in *In re John Doe Corp.*, 675 F.2d 482 (2d Cir. 1982), a corporation conducted through counsel an internal investigation of its business practices. The resulting investigative report was shown to a lawyer representing an underwriter in connection with a public offering of the corporation's securities, so that underwriter's counsel could complete a due diligence review. The corporation argued that disclosure to underwriter counsel should not be considered a waiver because disclosure was "required" by the legal duty of due diligence and the millions of dollars riding on the public offering of registered securities. Hence the waiver, according to the corporation, was not voluntary. The Second Circuit responded:

> We view this argument with no sympathy whatsoever. A claim that a need for confidentiality must be respected in order to facilitate the seeking and rendering of informed legal advice is not consistent with selective disclosure when the claimant decides that the confidential materials can be put to other beneficial purposes. Once a corporate decision is made to disclose them for commercial purposes, no matter what the economic imperatives, the privilege is lost. * * * We hold that the calculated use of otherwise privileged materials for commercial purposes will waive the privilege.

4. Mistaken Disclosures

One of the most difficult problems of waiver occurs when the disclosure of confidential information is a mistake. For example, the lawyer mistakenly includes an opposing lawyer on an email, and privileged information is thereby sent to the adversary. A more common example arises where the lawyer painstakingly complies with a voluminous discovery request for thousands of emails, and a privileged email is mistakenly included in the CD sent to the adversary. Again, the loss of privilege that might occur here is really grounded in a theory of forfeiture rather than traditional waiver, which speaks in terms of intentional relinquishment of a known right. The question is, what sort of conduct should be subject to the sanction of the loss of a privilege.

The risks of mistaken disclosure are obviously profound, and these risks increase in complex cases with voluminous discovery of electronic information. The costs of privilege review, in order to avoid the consequences of waiver, can rise to the millions of dollars. Lawyers, especially in complex litigation, often enter into arrangements to control the risks of waiver when privileged electronic data is disclosed during discovery. These arrangements can cover inadvertent disclosure, or can more broadly cover even intentional disclosures. Generally speaking there are two kinds of agreements: "claw back" and "quick peek." The 2006 Advisory Committee Note to Rule 26 discusses the costs of preproduction privilege review of electronic data, as well as the use of "claw back and "quick peek" agreements:

Parties may attempt to minimize these costs and delays by agreeing to protocols that minimize the risk of waiver. They may agree that the responding party will provide certain requested materials for initial examination without waiving any privilege or protection—sometimes known as a "quick peek." The requesting party then designates the documents it wishes to have actually produced. This designation is the Rule 34 request. The responding party then responds in the usual course, screening only those documents actually requested for formal production and asserting privilege claims as provided in Rule 26(b)(5)(A). On other occasions, parties enter agreements—sometimes called "clawback agreements"—that production without intent to waive privilege or protection should not be a waiver so long as the responding party identifies the documents mistakenly produced, and that the documents should be returned under those circumstances. Other voluntary arrangements may be appropriate depending on the circumstances of each litigation. In most circumstances, a party who receives information under such an arrangement cannot assert that production of the information waived a claim of privilege or of protection as trial-preparation material.

Although these agreements may not be appropriate for all cases, in certain cases they can facilitate prompt and economical discovery by reducing delay for the discovering party in obtaining access to documents, and by reducing the cost and burden of review by the producing party.

Practice Pointer

The way these agreements often work in practice is that the disclosing party takes a "first cut" of the material and removes all the data that is clearly privileged upon a cursory review—for example, emails from or to counsel. The rest of the material is then produced and if it turns out on further review that it is privileged, it is returned. Such agreements limit the multiple levels of intensive review of all the electronic data that would otherwise be required for pre-production privilege review. If a party has signed such an agreement, it waives any argument that a mistaken disclosure of privileged information by the other side is a waiver. *See, e.g., Prescient Partners, L.P. v. Fieldcrest Cannon, Inc.,* No. 96 Civ. 7590, 1997 WL 736726 (S.D.N.Y. Nov. 26, 1997) (enforcing a confidentiality agreement and refusing to find a waiver from an inadvertent disclosure of privileged information).

There are a number of factors that limit the utility of "claw back" and "quick peek" agreements. Most important, *they provide protection only in the proceeding in which they are entered.* An agreement between two parties in another litigation does not estop a third party, in a subsequent litigation, from arguing that a waiver occurred by disclosing the privileged information in the previous matter. Because enforceability of such agreements is uncertain, they may do little to limit the costs of pre-production privilege review. Lawyers have to be certain that mistaken disclosures of privileged information will not result in a waiver—otherwise they have no choice but to engage in the multiple levels of privilege review of all the electronic data.

Another limitation on such agreements is obvious—the parties must agree. Where the discoverable electronic data on both sides is relatively equal, then all parties have an incentive to enter such an agreement. But where one side has most of the data—*e.g.*, an employment discrimination case brought by a fired employee, where all the emails are on the employer's server—then the party with few (if any) documents to produce may not be inclined to limit the costs of the adversary's pre-production privilege review. (One factor that may still provide an incentive is if the party has an interest in *expedited* discovery; if there is no non-waiver agreement in effect, then the court is very likely to allow the party with custody of the data greater time to conduct a full pre-production privilege review.)

Concerned about the rising costs of electronic discovery and privilege review, the House Judiciary Committee asked the Advisory Committee on Evidence Rules to prepare a rule that would provide some protection against these costs, by providing a more liberal, and a uniform, rule on waiver. The rule as prepared by the Advisory Committee was enacted by Congress in September, 2010 as Rule 502 of the Federal Rules of Evidence. Among other things, the Rule provides for the possibility of a court order that will protect against the consequences of waiver.

FEDERAL RULE OF EVIDENCE 502

Rule 502. Attorney-Client Privilege and Work Product; Limitations on Waiver

The following provisions apply, in the circumstances set out, to disclosure of a communication or information covered by the attorney-client privilege or work-product protection.

(a)   Disclosure made in a federal proceeding or to a federal office or agency; scope of a waiver. When the disclosure is made in a federal proceeding or to a federal office or agency and waives the attorney-client privilege or work-product protection, the waiver extends to an undisclosed communication or information in a federal or state proceeding only if:

(1)   the waiver is intentional;

(2)   the disclosed and undisclosed communications or information concern the same subject matter; and

(3)   they ought in fairness to be considered together.

(b)   Inadvertent disclosure. When made in a federal proceeding or to a federal office or agency, the disclosure does not operate as a waiver in a federal or state proceeding if:

(1)   the disclosure is inadvertent;

(2)   the holder of the privilege or protection took reasonable steps to prevent disclosure; and

(3)   the holder promptly took reasonable steps to rectify the error, including (if applicable) following Fed. R. Civ. P. 26(b)(5)(B).

(c)   **Disclosure made in a state proceeding.** When the disclosure is made in a state proceeding and is not the subject of a state-court order concerning waiver, the disclosure does not operate as a waiver in a federal proceeding if the disclosure:

> (1)   would not be a waiver under this rule if it had been made in a federal proceeding; or

> (2)   is not a waiver under the law of the state where the disclosure occurred.

(d)   **Controlling effect of a court order.** A federal court may order that the privilege or protection is not waived by disclosure connected with the litigation pending before the court—in which event the disclosure is also not a waiver in any other federal or state proceeding.

(e)   **Controlling effect of a party agreement.** An agreement on the effect of disclosure in a federal proceeding is binding only on the parties to the agreement, unless it is incorporated into a court order.

(f)   **Controlling effect of this rule.** Notwithstanding Rules 101 and 1101, this rule applies to state proceedings and to federal court-annexed and federal court-mandated arbitration proceedings, in the circumstances set out in the rule. And notwithstanding Rule 501, this rule applies even if state law provides the rule of decision.

(g)   **Definitions.** In this rule:

> 1)   "attorney-client privilege" means the protection that applicable law provides for confidential attorney-client communications; and

> 2)   "work-product protection" means the protection that applicable law provides for tangible material (or its intangible equivalent) prepared in anticipation of litigation or for trial.

Explanatory Note on Rule 502

Prepared by the Judicial Conference Advisory Committee on Evidence Rules

This new rule has two major purposes:

1) It resolves some longstanding disputes in the courts about the effect of certain disclosures of communications or information protected by the attorney-client privilege or as work product—specifically those disputes involving inadvertent disclosure and subject matter waiver.

2) It responds to the widespread complaint that litigation costs necessary to protect against waiver of attorney-client privilege or work product have become prohibitive due to the concern that any disclosure (however innocent or minimal) will operate as a subject matter waiver of all protected communications or information. This concern is especially troubling in cases involving electronic discovery. *See, e.g., Hopson v. City of Baltimore*, 232 F.R.D. 228, 244 (D. Md. 2005) (electronic discovery may encompass "millions of documents" and to insist upon "record-by-record pre-production privilege review, on pain of subject matter waiver, would

impose upon parties costs of production that bear no proportionality to what is at stake in the litigation") .

The rule seeks to provide a predictable, uniform set of standards under which parties can determine the consequences of a disclosure of a communication or information covered by the attorney-client privilege or work product protection. Parties to litigation need to know, for example, that if they exchange privileged information pursuant to a confidentiality order, the court's order will be enforceable. Moreover, if a federal court's confidentiality order is not enforceable in a state court then the burdensome costs of privilege review and retention are unlikely to be reduced.

The rule makes no attempt to alter federal or state law on whether a communication or information is protected under the attorney-client privilege or work product immunity as an initial matter. Moreover, while establishing some exceptions to waiver, the rule does not purport to supplant applicable waiver doctrine generally.

The rule governs only certain waivers by disclosure. Other common-law waiver doctrines may result in a finding of waiver even where there is no disclosure of privileged information or work product. *See, e.g., Nguyen v. Excel Corp.*, 197 F.3d 200 (5th Cir. 1999) (reliance on an advice of counsel defense waives the privilege with respect to attorney-client communications pertinent to that defense); *Byers v. Burleson*, 100 F.R.D. 436 (D.D.C. 1983) (allegation of lawyer malpractice constituted a waiver of confidential communications under the circumstances). The rule is not intended to displace or modify federal common law concerning waiver of privilege or work product where no disclosure has been made.

* * *

Subdivision (b). Courts are in conflict over whether an inadvertent disclosure of a communication or information protected as privileged or work product constitutes a waiver. A few courts find that a disclosure must be intentional to be a waiver. Most courts find a waiver only if the disclosing party acted carelessly in disclosing the communication or information and failed to request its return in a timely manner. And a few courts hold that any inadvertent disclosure of a communication or information protected under the attorney-client privilege or as work product constitutes a waiver without regard to the protections taken to avoid such a disclosure. *See generally Hopson v. City of Baltimore*, 232 F.R.D. 228 (D. Md. 2005), for a discussion of this case law.

The rule opts for the middle ground: inadvertent disclosure of protected communications or information in connection with a federal proceeding or to a federal office or agency does not constitute a waiver if the holder took reasonable steps to prevent disclosure and also promptly took reasonable steps to rectify the error. This position is in accord with the majority view on whether inadvertent disclosure is a waiver.

Cases such as *Lois Sportswear, U.S.A., Inc. v. Levi Strauss & Co.*, 104 F.R.D. 103, 105 (S.D.N.Y. 1985) and *Hartford Fire Ins. Co. v. Garvey*, 109 F.R.D. 323, 332 (N.D. Cal. 1985), set out a multi-factor test for determining whether inadvertent disclosure is a waiver. The stated factors (none of which are dispositive) are the reasonableness of precautions taken, the time taken to rectify the error, the scope of discovery, the extent of disclosure and the overriding issue of fairness. The rule does not explicitly codify that test, because it is really a set of non-determinative guidelines that vary from case to case. The rule is flexible enough to accommodate any of those listed factors. Other considerations bearing on the reasonableness of a producing party's efforts include the number of documents to be reviewed and the time constraints for production. Depending on the circumstances, a party that uses advanced analytical software applications and linguistic tools in screening for privilege and work product may be found to have taken "reasonable steps" to prevent inadvertent disclosure. The implementation of an efficient system of records management before litigation may also be relevant.

The rule does not require the producing party to engage in a post-production review to determine whether any protected communication or information has been produced by mistake. But the rule does require the producing party to follow up on any obvious indications that a protected communication or information has been produced inadvertently.

The rule applies to inadvertent disclosures made to a federal office or agency, including but not limited to an office or agency that is acting in the course of its regulatory, investigative or enforcement authority. The consequences of waiver, and the concomitant costs of pre-production privilege review, can be as great with respect to disclosures to offices and agencies as they are in litigation.

* * *

Subdivision (d). Confidentiality orders are becoming increasingly important in limiting the costs of privilege review and retention, especially in cases involving electronic discovery. But the utility of a confidentiality order in reducing discovery costs is substantially diminished if it provides no protection outside the particular litigation in which the order is entered. Parties are unlikely to be able to reduce the costs of pre-production review for privilege and work product if the consequence of disclosure is that the communications or information could be used by non-parties to the litigation.

———————

There is some dispute on whether a confidentiality order entered in one case is enforceable in other proceedings. *See generally Hopson v. City of Baltimore*, 232 F.R.D. 228 (D. Md. 2005), for a discussion of this case law. The rule provides that when a confidentiality order governing the consequences of disclosure in that case is entered in a federal proceeding, its terms are enforceable against non-parties in any federal or state proceeding. For example, the court order may provide for return of documents without waiver irrespective of the care taken by the disclosing party; the rule contemplates enforcement of "claw-back" and "quick peek" arrangements as a way to avoid the excessive costs of pre-production review for privilege and work product. See *Zubulake v. UBS Warburg LLC*, 216 F.R.D. 280, 290 (S.D.N.Y. 2003) (noting that parties may enter into "so-called 'claw-back' agreements that allow the parties to forego privilege review altogether in favor of an agreement to return inadvertently produced privilege documents"). The rule provides a party with a predictable protection from a court order—predictability that is needed to allow the party to plan in advance to limit the prohibitive costs of privilege and work product review and retention.

Under the rule, a confidentiality order is enforceable whether or not it memorializes an agreement among the parties to the litigation. Party agreement should not be a condition of enforceability of a federal court's order.

* * *

If Federal Rule of Evidence 502 is applicable, it will override state privilege law on the consequences of disclosure in a federal proceeding. If it is applicable, then Restatement §§ 77–80 may be useful resources. Restatement § 79 provides: "The attorney-client privilege is waived if the client, the client's lawyer, or another authorized agent of the client voluntarily discloses the communication in a nonprivileged communication." Although FRE 502 is a relatively new rule, there already has been a significant amount of discussion about it and whether it is living up to its potential. *See, e.g.,* John M. Barkett, Evidence Rule 502: The Solution to the Privilege-Protection Puzzle in the Digital Era, 81 Fordham L. Rev. 1589 (2013); Paul W. Grimm, Lisa Yurwit Bergstrom, and Matthew Kraeuter, Fed. R. Evid. 502: Has It Lived Up to Its Potential?, 17 Rich. J.L. & Tech. 8 (2011). Here is a model draft of a Rule 502(d) court order that the privilege is not waived by disclosure connected with the litigation pending before the court.

[Question 4-7]

A corporation sued the client, another corporation, for fraud after a deal went sour. Each sought discovery of thousands of emails that were relevant to the case. At the client's request, and over the corporation's objection, the court entered an order providing that any disclosure of information protected by the attorney-client privilege during discovery would not constitute a waiver of the privilege. After the order was entered, the client produced 650,000 emails; 1000 emails involved confidential attorney-client communications. Subsequently the client was sued for fraud by a third party, another corporation, which was involved in the deal that went bad. The third party, the plaintiff in this second case, sought to use as evidence the 1000 privileged emails that the client produced in the previous litigation—arguing that the client waived the privilege by producing them in that litigation.

Are the client's emails privileged in the second case?

    (A)   **Yes, because there has been no showing that any waiver was intentional.**

    (B)   **Yes, because the court order protects against a waiver in any subsequent litigation.**

    (C)   **No, because the order in the previous case cannot bind a person who was not a party in that case.**

    (D)   **No, because the order was entered in the absence of agreement between the parties in the case.**

5. Duties of an Attorney Receiving Privileged Information

The prior section addressed the legal consequences of disclosure on the attorney-client privilege. This section explores how an attorney that receives privileged information should respond. (This topic is also addressed in Chapter 6.)

Ethics authorities have become increasingly aware of and concerned with the disclosure of information protected by an attorney's duty of confidentiality, including attorney-client privileged materials. Since the early 2000s, many jurisdictions have amended their rules of professional conduct to address inadvertent disclosure by specifically addressing the issue in Rule 4.4, which provides: "(b) A lawyer who receives a document or electronically stored information relating to the representation of the lawyer's client and knows or reasonably should know that the document or electronically stored information was inadvertently sent shall promptly notify the sender." Comment [2] to Rule 4.4 specifically addresses ethical duties with respect to electronically stored information, commonly known as Metadata, and this topic is explored in greater depth in Chapter 6.

Make the Connection

Rule 4.4(b) governs inadvertent receipt of a document. *See* Chapter 6.

There is some variation among jurisdictions in the obligations they impose on the recipient of a misdirected email, and a chart comparing state versions of Rule 4.4 is found here. Many take the approach outlined above, but some take an approach that seeks to protect the sender from such a mistake, mandating that the recipient not read such an email and notify the sender of her mistake. For example, New Jersey Rule of Professional Conduct 4.4 states: "(b) A lawyer who receives a document and has reasonable cause to believe that the document was inadvertently sent shall not read the document or, if he or she has begun to do so, shall stop reading the document, promptly notify the sender, and return the document to the sender." Other jurisdictions adopt a less protective approach allowing the recipient to read and use the content of such a misdirected email. (*See, e.g., Mt. Hawley Ins. Co. v. Felman Production, Inc.,* 271 F.R.D. 125, 130–131 (S.D. W. Va. 2010)).

In re Nitla S.A. de C.V.

92 S.W.3d 419 (Tex. 2002)

PER CURIAM

The issue here is whether the trial court abused its discretion when it refused to disqualify Nitla's counsel, who had reviewed privileged documents that the trial court ordered the opposing party to produce. * * *

Nitla, a Mexican pharmaceutical company, sued Bank of America (BOA) in 1996. Nitla claimed that BOA misappropriated over $24 million of Nitla's funds on deposit. During discovery, Nitla asked BOA to produce certain documents. BOA resisted and asserted the attorney-client and work-product privileges. After an in camera inspection and a hearing, the trial court identified numerous documents that it determined BOA should produce. BOA asked the trial court to stay production until BOA decided whether to seek emergency relief in the court of appeals. Rather than issue an order, the trial court requested additional briefing and scheduled another hearing. The trial court also indicated it would order BOA to produce any nonprivileged documents at that time.

At the second hearing, after considering the additional briefing and oral arguments, the trial court ordered BOA to produce the previously identified documents. BOA again asked the trial court to stay production, arguing that if Nitla's counsel reviewed the documents, BOA would be irreparably harmed. Moreover, BOA argued that if Nitla's counsel reviewed the documents and the court of appeals determined them privileged, Nitla's counsel could be disqualified. Nevertheless, the trial court granted, in part, Nitla's motion to compel production. The trial court next handed the documents, which were under the trial court's control, directly to Nitla's counsel. This enabled Nitla's counsel to review the documents before BOA could seek mandamus relief.

Later that same day, BOA notified Nitla by fax that it still believed all the tendered documents were privileged. BOA also asked Nitla not to review or distribute the documents, because BOA would seek mandamus relief. However, Nitla's counsel relied on the trial court's order and reviewed the documents.

After BOA filed for mandamus relief, the court of appeals abated the proceeding to allow the trial court's new judge to reconsider his predecessor's decision. After another hearing, the trial court again overruled BOA's objection that the documents were privileged. However, the trial court ordered Nitla to return the documents to BOA pending appellate review. Nitla complied with this order. BOA then reurged its mandamus petition in the court of appeals, and the court of appeals held that most of the documents were privileged.

BOA then moved to disqualify Nitla's counsel, alleging that Nitla's counsel "disregarded their ethical and professional obligations to gain an unfair advantage" when they reviewed the privileged documents. BOA also argued that the *Meador* factors support disqualification. *See In re Meador*, 968 S.W.2d 346, 351-52 (Tex.1998) (discussing six factors a trial court should consider when deciding whether to disqualify an attorney who receives privileged information outside the normal course of discovery).

After a hearing, the trial court denied BOA's motion to disqualify. Even though the trial court found that Nitla had extensively reviewed the documents and that BOA had "clean hands," the trial court denied the disqualification motion because it found: (1) Nitla's counsel did not act unprofessionally or violate any disciplinary rules; (2) Nitla's counsel did not obtain the documents wrongfully, but rather, after a judicial proceeding; and (3) no competent evidence showed that Nitla's counsel had developed its trial strategy based on the documents. Moreover, the trial court determined that it had less severe measures available to prevent Nitla from using the privileged information to gain unfair advantage.

* * * Nitla contends that the trial court correctly refused to disqualify Nitla's counsel, because BOA did not prove the disqualification grounds with specificity and did not prove it would suffer actual harm. * * * In response, BOA claims that * * * Nitla improperly reviewed the documents when it knew BOA intended to seek appellate relief; Nitla's actions irreparably harmed BOA; and there is no evidence that disqualification would harm Nitla.

* * *

"Disqualification is a severe remedy." It can result in immediate and palpable harm, disrupt trial court proceedings, and deprive a party of the right to have counsel of choice. In considering a motion to disqualify, the trial court must strictly adhere to an exacting standard to discourage a party from using the motion as a dilatory trial tactic. This Court often looks to the disciplinary rules to decide disqualification issues. However, the disciplinary rules are merely guidelines—not controlling standards—for disqualification motions. Even if a lawyer violates a disciplinary rule, the party requesting disqualification must demonstrate that the opposing lawyer's conduct caused actual prejudice that requires disqualification. And, under appropriate circumstances, a trial court has the power to disqualify a lawyer even if he has not violated a specific disciplinary rule.

In *Meador*, we acknowledged that there are undoubtedly some situations when a party's lawyer who reviews another party's privileged information must be disqualified, even though the lawyer did not participate in obtaining the information. However, we did not articulate a bright-line standard for disqualification in such situations. Instead, we determined that a trial court must consider the importance of our discovery privileges along with all the facts and circumstances to decide "whether the interests of justice require disqualification." We then identified six factors a trial court should consider when a lawyer receives an opponent's privileged materials. However, we emphasized that "these factors apply only when a lawyer receives an opponent's privileged materials outside the normal course of discovery."

Here, the trial court determined that Nitla's counsel did not violate a disciplinary rule. Consequently, the disciplinary rules provide no guidance. Moreover, Nitla's counsel received the documents directly from the trial court in a discovery hearing. Thus, the six *Meador* factors do not apply. We have not defined a precise standard for disqualification in such circumstances. Nevertheless, the trial court referred to the appropriate guiding principles when it denied BOA's motion to disqualify.

Food for Thought

If you receive privileged information that you weren't supposed to get, are you content to rely on the authorities above and exploit the information as much as a court will allow? Or would you be concerned about getting a reputation as a "Rambo" lawyer?

In disqualification cases, our analysis begins with the premise that disqualification is a severe measure that can result in immediate harm, because it deprives a party of its chosen counsel and can disrupt court proceedings. Consequently, when a party receives documents from a trial court, and a reviewing court later deems the documents privileged, the party moving to disqualify opposing counsel must show that: (1) opposing counsel's reviewing the privileged documents caused actual harm to the moving party; and (2) disqualification is necessary, because the trial court lacks any lesser means to remedy the moving party's harm.

We conclude that the trial court correctly applied these principles. Thus, we hold that the trial court did not abuse its discretion when it denied BOA's motion to disqualify Nitla's counsel. At the disqualification hearing, the trial court focused on whether BOA proved it suffered actual prejudice. BOA argued that the mere fact that Nitla had extensively reviewed the privileged documents demonstrated prejudice to BOA. However, BOA could not show that Nitla's trial strategy had significantly changed after reviewing the documents. Indeed, BOA could only demonstrate that reviewing the documents might have enabled Nitla's counsel to identify four new witnesses to depose, and that this additional testimony could potentially harm BOA. Recognizing that disqualification is a severe measure, the trial court determined that less severe measures, such as quashing depositions, could cure BOA's alleged harm. Accordingly, the trial court [properly] concluded that disqualification was neither a necessary nor an appropriate remedy.

* * *

D.   The Crime-Fraud Exception to the Attorney-Client Privilege

Hear from the Authors

To hear from the authors on the crime-fraud exception, click here.

Restatement § 82 sets forth the crime-fraud exception to its attorney-client privilege. This section states:

> The attorney-client privilege does not apply to a communication occurring when a client:
>
> (a)   consults a lawyer for the purpose, later accomplished, of obtaining assistance to engage in a crime or fraud or aiding a third person to do so, or
>
> (b)   regardless of the client's purpose at the time of consultation, uses the lawyer's advice or other services to engage in or assist a crime or fraud.

Consider this definition and the materials that follow as you answer Question 4-8.

[Question 4-8]

An attorney's client is a used car salesman. The client has been sued by a buyer who claims the buyer bought a car with a turned-back odometer. The client retains the attorney to defend the case. When the attorney asks the client to describe the background of the dispute, the client makes the following statements to the attorney in confidence:

1) "I've destroyed a number of documents that could be used to prove the buyer's case."

2) "I still think there might be some documents in the files that could be relevant to the buyer's case. Could you look through the files and let me know what you think the buyer might ask for in discovery?"

Are both of these statements privileged?

    (A)   **Yes, because the client sought advice on a legal matter and both statements were made in confidence.**

    (B)   **Yes, provided the client abandons any plan to destroy more records.**

    (C)   **No, because each statement can be used to prove that the client engaged in crime or fraud.**

    (D)   **No, only the first statement is privileged and the second is not privileged because the second statement was made to further a crime or fraud.**

Statements made by the client to the attorney, even though in confidence, are not privileged if the purpose of the communication is to further crime or fraud. The crime-fraud exception is triggered when the party seeking the information provides *prima facie* evidence that the client was seeking the attorney's advice and services in furtherance of a plan of wrongdoing. The Court in *In re Grand Jury*, 845 F.2d 896 (11th Cir. 1988) set forth the standards many jurisdictions follow for applying the crime-fraud exception:

> First, there must be a prima facie showing that the client was engaged in criminal or fraudulent conduct when he sought the advice of counsel, that he was planning such conduct when he sought the advice of counsel, or that he committed a crime or fraud subsequent to receiving the benefit of counsel's advice. Second, there must be a showing that the attorney's assistance was obtained in furtherance of the criminal or fraudulent activity or was closely related to it.

Note that the Court in *In re Grand Jury* held that the exception can apply even if the client never actually committed a fraudulent or criminal act, provided the client communicates with the attorney with the *intent* to further a plan of crime or fraud. *See In re Grand Jury Proceedings*, 87 F.3d 377 (9th Cir. 1996) ("the crime-fraud exception does not require a *completed* crime or fraud but only that the client have consulted the attorney in an *effort* to complete one"). As discussed in greater detail below, the Court's position in *In re Grand Jury* that *the client must consult the attorney with the intent* to further a crime or fraud differs from Restatement § 82(b) that the exception applies when a client, "*regardless of the client's purpose* at the time of consultation, uses the lawyer's advice or other services to engage in or assist a crime or fraud."

The crime-fraud exception can apply even if the attorney is an unwitting instrument in the crime or fraud. The basis of the exception is that the client may not in bad faith exploit the privilege by using the attorney as an instrument of crime or fraud. Therefore it does not matter whether the attorney was knowingly involved in the client's scheme. The Court in *In re Grand Jury Proceedings*, 87 F.3d 377 (9th Cir. 1996) explained this result as follows:

> Inasmuch as today's privilege exists for the benefit of the client, not the attorney, it is the client's knowledge and intentions that are of paramount concern to the application of the crime-fraud exception; the attorney need know nothing about the client's ongoing or planned illicit activity for the exception to apply.

The crime-fraud exception applies only when the attorney is being used to further a *future or ongoing* scheme of misconduct. It does not apply to communications seeking legal representation with respect to a past act of crime or fraud; such statements are at the heart of the protection provided by the privilege. *See, e.g., Coleman v. American Broadcasting Co.,* 106 F.R.D. 201 (D.D.C. 1985) ("Only communications in regard to ongoing or future misconduct fall outside the scope of the privilege. This distinction goes to the very core of the policies underlying the privilege."). Moreover, the exception will not apply if the client consulted with an attorney *in order to determine whether a prospective course of conduct was lawful.* As one Court put it:

> The crime-fraud exception has a precise focus: It applies only when the communications between the client and his lawyer further a crime, fraud or other misconduct. * * * [The exception should not be applied to deny a client] the privilege where even its stern critics acknowledge that the justification for the shield is strongest—where a client seeks counsel's advice to determine the legality of conduct *before* the client takes any action.

United States v. White, 887 F.2d 267 (D.C. Cir. 1989); *see In re Grand Jury Proceedings,* 87 F.3d 377 (9th Cir. 1996) (crime-fraud exception should not be applied in such a way as to "discourage many would-be clients from consulting an attorney about entirely legitimate legal dilemmas").

On the other hand, the crime-fraud exception will apply if the client already knows that a prospective course of conduct is impermissible and is simply using counsel in an attempt to effectuate the plan. *See, e.g., United States v. Reeder,* 170 F.3d 93 (1st Cir. 1999) (client conferred with counsel in order to obtain "some ideas" on how to cover up a series of questionable loans, and proposed that the loans could be backdated; these communications were within the crime-fraud exception and not privileged); *United States v. Jacobs,* 117 F.3d 82 (2d Cir. 1997) (crime-fraud exception was found where "the wrong-doer had set upon a criminal course *before* consulting counsel").

Likewise, any communications made with a view to covering up past acts of misconduct are in fact made with the purpose of perpetrating a crime or fraud, and hence are not privileged. *See United States v. Edwards,* 303 F.3d 606 (5th Cir. 2002) (crime-fraud exception applied where the legal services sought by the defendant were "to conceal and cover up the crimes committed"; "[r]ather than merely defending himself from wrongdoing, [the client] was actively continuing the cover-up of extortion and perpetuating his tax fraud").

The fact that a communication with counsel can be used to *prove* a crime or fraud is not sufficient to trigger the exception. The Reporter's Note to Restatement § 82 states that some courts differ on whether there must be proof that the client intended to commit a crime or fraud at the time the client consulted with the client's lawyer. For some courts, unless the scheme of crime or fraud was afoot at the time of the communication, the statements remain privileged.

For example, assume that a corporation seeks legal advice to determine whether a large account receivable is, in fact, legally collectible. Counsel investigates and informs the corporation that the receivable is not legally collectible. A few months later, the corporation sells the receivable without informing the buyer about the advice received from counsel. Of course, counsel's report would be relevant to prove that the seller-client acted fraudulently. But in order for the crime-fraud exception to apply, some courts require that the buyer establish a *prima facie* case that the seller had a fraudulent intent *at the time that counsel's advice was sought*. If not, the privilege will apply even though the client acted fraudulently subsequent to receiving the legal advice. *See, e.g., Pritchard-Keang Nam Corp. v. Jaworski,* 751 F.2d 277 (8th Cir. 1984):

> That the report may help *prove* that a fraud occurred does not mean that it was *used* in perpetrating the fraud.* * * Timing is critical, for the prima facie showing requires that the client was engaged in or planning a criminal or fraudulent scheme when he sought the advice of counsel to further the scheme.

See also In re Sealed Case, 107 F.3d 46 (D.C. Cir. 1997) (the mere fact that a person commits a fraud after consulting with counsel does not establish a *prima facie* case that the consultation was in furtherance of the fraud). These federal courts take a position that is at odds with Restatement § 82(b) that "attorney-client privilege does not apply to a communication occurring when a client * * * regardless of the client's purpose at the time of the consultation, uses the lawyer's advice or other services to engage in or assist a crime or fraud." There is also variation among state courts on whether there must be proof that the client intended to commit a crime or fraud at the time the client consulted with the client's lawyer. *See, e.g., Whetstone v. Olson,* 732 P.2d 159 (Wash.Ct.App. 1986) (holding that the exception applies only when the client seeks advice for a wrongful purpose). The fact that some courts differ from the Restatement on this aspect reinforces the need to know the law on attorney-client privilege in the jurisdiction in which a lawyer practices rather than assuming that the Restatement reflects a uniform position on the matter.

IV. The Basics of the Duty of Confidentiality Under Rule 1.6

As discussed above, the lawyer's duty of confidentiality covers more information than is protected by the evidentiary attorney-client privilege. As a threshold matter, Rule 1.6(a) prohibits a lawyer from *revealing* "information related to the representation of a client" unless an exception applies. Rule 1.6's exceptions are permissive, rather than mandatory. Two exceptions are found within Rule 1.6(a): a lawyer may reveal information if the client gives informed consent, which is a term defined in Rule 1.0, or if the disclosure is impliedly authorized to carry out the representation. An additional seven exceptions are found in Rule 1.6(b).

A.   Individuals to Whom a Duty of Confidentiality Is Owed

Rule 1.6(a) applies to information related to representation of a client. Chapter 2 discussed the formation of a lawyer-client relationship. As that Chapter noted, none of the ABA Model

Rules addresses this point. <u>Restatement § 14</u>, however, can be useful in analyzing whether an attorney-client relationship exists. In light of Rule 1.6, it is clear that the duty of confidentiality certainly applies once an attorney-client relationship has been formed. But it can also apply when a lawyer and prospective client have preliminary discussions about *whether* to form an attorney-client relationship, even if they decide *not* to go forward.

[Question 4-9]

A homeowner meets with an attorney to discuss a possible property claim against an apartment building owner. After the homeowner explains the claim, the attorney determines that the homeowner cannot afford the attorney's services and refuses the case. The apartment building owner then meets with the attorney and offers to meet all of the attorney's financial terms. In representing the apartment building owner, the attorney uses the information the homeowner provided, reasoning that because they never had an attorney-client relationship, the attorney did not owe the homeowner a duty of confidentiality.

Is the attorney subject to discipline?

> **(A)   Yes, because the homeowner was a client.**
>
> **(B)   Yes, because the homeowner was a prospective client.**
>
> **(C)   No, because the homeowner was not a client.**
>
> **(D)   No, because the information was not dispositive of the property claim.**

Rule 1.18: Duties to Prospective Clients

(a)   A person who consults with a lawyer about the possibility of forming a client-lawyer relationship with respect to a matter is a prospective client.

(b)   Even when no client-lawyer relationship ensues, a lawyer who has learned information from a prospective client shall not use or reveal that information, except as Rule 1.9 would permit with respect to information of a former client.

(c)   A lawyer subject to paragraph (b) shall not represent a client with interests materially adverse to those of a prospective client in the same or a substantially related matter if the lawyer received information from the prospective client that could be significantly harmful to that person in the matter, except as provided in paragraph (d). If a lawyer is disqualified from representation under this paragraph, no lawyer in a firm with which that lawyer is associated may knowingly undertake or continue representation in such a matter, except as provided in paragraph (d).

(d)   When the lawyer has received disqualifying information as defined in paragraph (c), representation is permissible if:

> (1)   both the affected client and the prospective client have given informed consent, confirmed in writing, or:

(2)   the lawyer who received the information took reasonable measures to avoid exposure to more disqualifying information than was reasonably necessary to determine whether to represent the prospective client; and

(i)   the disqualified lawyer is timely screened from any participation in the matter and is apportioned no part of the fee therefrom; and

(ii)   written notice is promptly given to the prospective client.

Under Rule 1.18, two key elements must be fulfilled to become a prospective client. First, Rule 1.18(a) requires that a person *consults* with a lawyer about the possibility of forming a client-lawyer relationship. The phrase "consults with a lawyer" suggests that there must be some reciprocity on the part of the lawyer— that there is some mutual communication between the person and the lawyer whether the communication is written, oral, or electronic. Second, Comment [2] explains that a person who sends an email to a lawyer and otherwise communicates unilaterally with the lawyer without a *reasonable expectation* that the lawyer is willing to discuss forming a client-lawyer relationship will not be a prospective client. This comment reinforces the need for reciprocity on the lawyer's part. Lawyers using websites and social media to communicate with nonclients, prospective clients, and clients need to understand Rule 1.18 and should take extra care to avoid forming unintended prospective client and client relationships. *See, e.g,* Peter A. Joy & Kevin C. McMunigal, *Client or Prospective Client: What's the Difference?*, 27 Crim. Just. 51 (Fall 2012) (analyzing Rule 1.18 and unintended client and prospective client relationships).

A lawyer does not owe a prospective client the full set of obligations a lawyer owes a client. But Rule 1.18 does impose both confidentiality and conflict-of-interest obligations to a prospective client. A lawyer also owes a duty of confidentiality to former clients. This obligation is specified in Rule 1.9, which incorporates by reference the provisions of Rule 1.6 (and other Rule provisions):

Rule 1.9: Duties to Former Clients

[Rule 1.9(a and b) address the issue of representation adverse to a former client]

(c)   A lawyer who has formerly represented a client in a matter or whose present or former firm has formerly represented a client in a matter shall not thereafter:

(1)   use information relating to the representation to the disadvantage of the former client except as these Rules would permit or require with respect to a client, or when the information has become generally known; or

(2)   reveal information relating to the representation except as these Rules would permit or require with respect to a client.

Thus, if one learns the confidentiality rules and exceptions applicable to current clients, one has also learned the confidentiality rules and exceptions applicable to former clients, except that a lawyer may also use information about a former client when it has become generally known.

B.   Scope of Information Within the Duty of Confidentiality

1. General Obligations with Respect to Rule 1.6 Information

Rule 1.6 prohibits a lawyer from "revealing" information related to the representation of a client. But there are other things that a lawyer might do with respect to confidential client information that also are problematic. Rule 1.8(b) is found in the conflicts of interest section of the Rules and prohibits a lawyer from "using" information related to the representation of a client to the disadvantage of the client (unless the client gives informed consent or it is permitted or required by the Rules.) Rule 1.9(c) sets forth a lawyer's obligation not to reveal or use confidential information from a former client. Rule 1.18(b), as noted earlier, sets forth the lawyer's obligations with respect to prospective (but rejected) clients.

Given heightened concern about the need to be cautious with confidential client information, Rule 1.6 was amended to provide:

> (c)   A lawyer shall make reasonable efforts to prevent the inadvertent or unauthorized disclosure of, or unauthorized access to, information relating to the representation of a client.

Comment [8] to Rule 1.1 on competence makes clear that the duty of competence is dynamic rather than static. It states: "To maintain the requisite knowledge and skill, a lawyer should *keep abreast of changes* in the law and its practice, including the benefits and risks associated with relevant technology * * *" Competence requires that a lawyer stay aware of the technology currently used in law practice, the risks it poses, and the security measures available to reduce those risks. Competence mandates that a lawyer keep pace with professional peers in addressing the risks of technology. Comment [5] to Rule 1.1 states that competence includes "use of methods and procedures meeting the standards of competent practitioners." As more lawyers adopt heightened measures to protect client information, such as encryption software for email and scrubbing software for metadata in electronic files, a lawyer who lags behind other lawyers in using such security measures runs the risk of being found incompetent in safeguarding client information.

Many jurisdictions, such as Ohio, have adopted Comment [18] to Rule 1.6, which "requires a lawyer to act competently to safeguard information relating to the representation of a client against inadvertent or unauthorized disclosure" by either the lawyer or others working with the lawyer. Comment [18] provides additional guidance about how a lawyer can competently safeguard confidential client information, including a list of factors to be considered in determining the reasonableness of the lawyer's efforts such as the sensitivity of the information, the likelihood of disclosure if additional safeguards are not employed, the cost of employing additional safeguards, the difficulty of implementing the safeguards, and the extent to which the safeguards adversely affect the lawyer's ability to represent clients (*e.g.*, by making a device or important piece of software excessively difficult to use). Comment [19] states, inter alia, that when transmitting a communication that includes information relating to the representation of a client, the lawyer must take reasonable precautions to prevent the information from coming into the hands of unintended recipients. Both Comments [18] and [19] state that a client may require the lawyer to implement special security measures not required by Rule 1.6(c) or may give informed consent to forgo security measures that would otherwise be required by the Rule.

Thus, when dealing with confidential client information, the lawyer needs to be concerned with all three of these verbs: *revealing* client information, *using* information, and *preventing* improper disclosures. This is especially true with the many inadvertent disclosures a lawyer may make without thinking, for example: discussing a client's matter with the client's family or roommate without the client's consent; identifying clients in a firm brochure or a website without the first obtaining the clients' permission; discussing a client matter in an elevator or other public place where others may overhear the conversation; reviewing a client's file or documents in a coffee shop or elsewhere where others may be able to see client information; or discussing a client matter with a family member or friend.

Practice Pointer

Under Rule 1.6, it does not appear to matter that information held by the lawyer is in fact widely known. It is still subject to the lawyer's duty of confidentiality. Compare New York Rule 1.6, which provides that confidential information "does not ordinarily include * * * information that is generally known in the local community or in the trade, field or profession to which the witness relates." As a practical matter, it is unlikely that a lawyer would be disciplined for disclosing client information that is widely known. But it will always be prudent to obtain client consent in advance of any disclosure.

2. The Duty of Confidentiality Applies to Information Related to the Representation

[Question 4-10]

An attorney represents a client who is under indictment for murder and attempted murder. In the course of the representation, the client told the attorney that the client had previously killed three other people. These other murders are completely unrelated to pending charges against the client. The client tells the attorney that the bodies of the other victims are buried in a ravine near the corner of a local cemetery. The attorney goes to the location described by the client, and the attorney finds the bodies at the bottom of the ravine. The attorney does not touch or disturb the dead bodies in any way. The attorney does some investigation, and learns that three persons have been reported missing and that the authorities have an ongoing investigation into their whereabouts. The attorney does not disclose the location of these bodies to the authorities or any other information provided to the attorney by the client.

Is the attorney subject to discipline?

(A) Yes, because as an officer of the court, the attorney is required to disclose information the attorney has concerning the commission of the prior crimes by the attorney's client.

(B)   **Yes, because the attorney is impeding the authorities access to significant evidence.**

(C)   **No, because the attorney obtained the information about the dead bodies in the course of representing the client.**

(D)   **No, because the attorney did not represent or advise the client with respect to the prior crimes.**

Rule 1.6 covers information "relating to the representation of the client." But of course "relating to" can be broad and, depending on the matter, it could cover all types of background and personal information about the client. Some states have defined confidential information even more broadly than the Model Rule. *See, e.g.,* New York Rule 1.6 (confidential information defined as that gained "during or relating to" the representation of a client). Other states have defined confidential information more narrowly and limit it to information from third parties that is embarrassing or detrimental to the client or that the client has asked to be held inviolate. *See, e.g.,* District of Columbia Rule 1.6(b); Michigan Rule 1.6(a).

To consider the breadth of the duty of confidentiality, consider the following landmark case.

People v. Belge

372 N.Y.S.2d 798 (Sup. Ct. Onondaga Cty 1975)

ORMAND N. GALE, JUDGE.

In the summer of 1973 Robert F. Garrow, Jr. stood charged in Hamilton County with the crime of MURDER. The Defendant was assigned two attorneys, Frank H. Armani and Francis R. Belge. A defense of insanity had been interposed by counsel for Mr. Garrow. During the course of the discussions between Garrow and his two counsel, three other murders were admitted by Garrow, one being in Onondaga County. On or about September of 1973 Mr. Belge conducted his own investigation based upon what his client had told him and with the assistance of a friend the location of the body of Alicia Hauck was found in Oakwood Cemetery in Syracuse. Mr. Belge personally inspected the body and was satisfied, presumably, that this was the Alicia Hauck that his client had told him that he murdered.

This discovery was not disclosed to the authorities, but became public during the trial of Mr. Garrow in June of 1974, when to affirmatively establish the defense of insanity, these three other murders were brought before the jury by the defense in the Hamilton County trial. Public indignation reached the fever pitch; statements were made by the District Attorney of Onondaga County relative to the situation and he caused the Grand Jury of Onondaga County, then sitting, to conduct a thorough investigation. As a result of this investigation Frank Armani was No Billed by the Grand Jury but Indictment No. 75-55 was returned as against Francis R. Belge, Esq., accusing him of having violated section 4200(1) of the Public Health Law, which, in essence, requires that a decent burial be accorded the dead, and section

4143 of the Public Health Law, which, in essence, requires anyone knowing of the death of a person without medical attendance, to report the same to the proper authorities. Defense counsel moves for a dismissal of the Indictment on the grounds that a confidential, privileged communication existed between him and Mr. Garrow, which should excuse the attorney from making full disclosure to the authorities.

* * *

In the most recent issue of the New York State Bar Journal (June 1975) there is an article by Jack B. Weinstein, entitled "Educating Ethical Lawyers." In a sub-caption to this article is the following language which is pertinent:

> "The most difficult ethical dilemmas result from the frequent conflicts between the obligation to one's client and those to the legal system and to society. It is in this area that legal education has its greatest responsibility, and can have its greatest effects."

In the course of his article Mr. Weinstein states that there are three major types of pressure facing a practicing lawyer. He uses the following language to describe these:

> "First, there are those that originate in the attorney's search for his own well-being. Second, pressures arise from the attorney's obligation to his client. Third, the lawyer has certain obligations to the courts, the legal system, and society in general."

Our system of criminal justice is an adversary system and the interests of the state are not absolute, or even paramount.

* * *

The effectiveness of counsel is only as great as the confidentiality of its client-attorney relationship. If the lawyer cannot get all the facts about the case, he can only give his client half of a defense. This, of necessity, involves the client telling his attorney everything remotely connected with the crime.

Apparently, in the instant case, after analyzing all the evidence, and after hearing of the bizarre episodes in the life of their client, they decided that the only possibility of salvation was in a defense of insanity. For the client to disclose not only everything about this particular crime but also everything about other crimes which might have a bearing upon his defense, requires the strictest confidence in, and on the part of, the attorney.

When the facts of the other homicides became public, as a result of the defendant's testimony to substantiate his claim of insanity, members of the public were shocked at the apparent callousness of these lawyers, whose conduct was seen as typifying the unhealthy lack of concern of most lawyers with the public interest and with simple decency. A hue and cry went up from the press and other news media suggesting that the attorneys should be found guilty of such crimes as obstruction of justice or becoming an accomplice after the fact. From a layman's standpoint, this certainly was a logical conclusion. However, the constitution of the United States of America attempts to preserve the dignity of the individual and to do that guarantees him the services of an attorney who will bring to the bar and to the bench every conceivable protection from the inroads of the state against such rights as are vested in the constitution for one accused of crime. Among those substantial constitutional rights is that a defendant does not have to incriminate himself. His attorneys were bound to uphold that concept and maintain what has been called a sacred trust of confidentiality.

* * *

'Garrow was constitutionally exempt from any statutory requirement to disclose the location of the body. And Attorney Belge, as Garrow's attorney, was not only equally exempt, but under a positive stricture precluding such disclosure. Garrow, although constitutionally privileged against a requirement of compulsory disclosure, was free to make such a revelation if he chose to do so. Attorney Belge was affirmatively required to withhold disclosure. The criminal defendant's self-incrimination rights become completely nugatory if compulsory disclosure can be exacted through his attorney.'

* * *

In the case at bar we must weigh the importance of the general privilege of confidentiality in the performance of the defendant's duties as an attorney, against the inroads of such a privilege, on the fair administration of criminal justice as well as the heart tearing that went on in the victim's family by reason of their uncertainty as to the whereabouts of Alicia Hauck. In this type situation the Court must balance the rights of the individual against the rights of society as a whole. There is no question

Food for Thought

To read an interview with one of the lawyers, thirty years after the case, see Lisa G. Lerman, Frank H. Armani, Thomas D. Morgan, and Monroe H. Freedman, *The Buried Bodies Case: Alive and Well after Thirty Years*, 2007 Prof. Law. 19, which is available here.

but Attorney Belge's failure to bring to the attention of the authorities the whereabouts of Alicia Hauck when he first verified it, prevented bringing Garrow to the immediate bar of justice for this particular murder. This was in a sense, obstruction of justice. This duty, I am sure, loomed large in the mind of Attorney Belge. However, against this was the Fifth Amendment right of his client, Garrow, not to incriminate himself. * * *

It is the decision of this Court that Francis R. Belge conducted himself as an officer of the Court with all the zeal at his command to protect the constitutional rights of his client. Both on the grounds of a privileged communication and in the interests of justice the Indictment is dismissed.

Practice Pointer

After Garrow was convicted and incarcerated, he escaped. When officers searched his cell, they found a list of names. Belge was on that list, as was his daughter, and a number of other people against whom Garrow held a grudge. (During Garrow's trial, Garrow had made several inappropriate comments about Belge's daughter, who was in the courtroom.) When police informed Belge that Garrow had escaped and about the list in his cell, Belge volunteered information concerning where he thought Garrow might be hiding. He learned this information—Garrow's favorite haunts—during the representation. Should Belge have been disciplined for disclosing these locations? *See* Chapter 8 for further discussion.

C. Exceptions to the Duty of Confidentiality

Rule 1.6(b) provides a number of exceptions under which a lawyer is permitted to disclose the client's confidential information:

> (b)   A lawyer may reveal information relating to the representation of a client to the extent the lawyer reasonably believes necessary:
>
>> (1)   to prevent reasonably certain death or substantial bodily harm;
>>
>> (2)   to prevent the client from committing a crime or fraud that is reasonably certain to result in substantial injury to the financial interests or property of another and in furtherance of which the client has used or is using the lawyer's services;
>>
>> (3)   to prevent, mitigate or rectify substantial injury to the financial interests or property of another that is reasonably certain to result or has resulted from the client's commission of a crime or fraud in furtherance of which the client has used the lawyer's services;
>>
>> (4)   to secure legal advice about the lawyer's compliance with these Rules;
>>
>> (5)   to establish a claim or defense on behalf of the lawyer in a controversy between the lawyer and the client, to establish a defense to a criminal charge or civil claim against the lawyer based upon conduct in which the client was involved, or to respond to allegations in any proceeding concerning the lawyer's representation of the client;
>>
>> (6)   to comply with other law or a court order; or
>>
>> (7)   to detect and resolve conflicts of interest arising from the lawyer's change of employment or from changes in the composition or ownership of a firm, but only if the revealed information would not compromise the attorney-client privilege or otherwise prejudice the client.

The remainder of this Chapter discusses some of the problems of applying these exceptions. Note that the exceptions in the Rule 1.6 do not *require* disclosure of confidential information. They *permit* it—so the lawyer cannot be disciplined for disclosing or not disclosing. Some states, however, such as New Jersey, *require* disclosure of some of the Rule 1.6(b) exceptions.

1. To Prevent Death or Serious Bodily Harm

FYI

For more on the ethical dilemma of disclosing a confidence to protect against reasonably certain death or bodily harm, see the Symposium in Volume 29 of the Loyola L.A. Law Review (1996): Executing the Wrong Person: The Professionals' Ethical Dilemmas.

[Question 4-11]

An attorney represents a client charged with murder. When interviewing the client about what happened, the client says, "I hope they don't find out about that other murder I did in Virginia. If they do, they'll put me on death

row if they find me guilty now." At the attorney's request, the client then gives the details about the other murder. The attorney does some surfing on the internet and finds out that another person has been convicted of that murder in Virginia, and is awaiting execution for the crime. The attorney discloses the information to the authorities. Eventually the person convicted of that murder is released, and the client is convicted and sentenced to death.

Is the attorney subject to discipline?

- (A) Yes, because the attorney caused the death of the client.

- (B) Yes, because the death of the other person convicted was not reasonably certain.

- No, because the attorney was required to disclose to prevent the death of another.

- (D) No, because the attorney was permitted to disclose to prevent a death of another.

[Question 4-12]

An attorney lawyer is representing a client who has been charged with murder. The murder weapon, a gun, has never been found. In a conference with the attorney, the client says: "I'm worried about them finding that gun. I can't see any way out other than to get rid of it. I'm going to throw it in the swamp tonight; they'll never find it there." After the client leaves, the attorney calls the police and tells them about the client's plan. The police then follow the client and arrest the client just before the client is going to throw the gun away.

Is the attorney subject to discipline?

- (A) Yes, because there is no exception to the duty of confidentiality under these circumstances.

- No, because the attorney should not have to sit silently while the client commits a future crime.

- No, because the information was not privileged because the client was not seeking legal advice.

- (D) No, because disposing of a weapon could lead to death or serious bodily harm.

[Question 4-13]

An attorney has been hired by a client to represent the client in a civil commitment proceeding initiated by the state. The client is now undergoing psychiatric evaluation to determine whether civil commitment should be ordered. The client told the attorney that the client intends to commit suicide as soon as the tests are completed, and the attorney believes that the client will carry out this threat. Suicide and attempted suicide are crimes in the state. The attorney discloses the client's intentions to the authorities.

Is the attorney subject to discipline?

(A) Yes, because there is no evidence that the attorney knows that the client has attempted suicide in the past.

(B) Yes, because disclosure would aid the state in its civil commitment case against the client.

(C) No, because the information concerns a future crime and is not protected by the attorney-client privilege.

(D) No, because disclosure of the information might prevent the client's death.

It can sometimes be difficult to determine whether the exception found in Rule 1.6(b)(1) applies. Rule 1.6, Comment [6] provides additional guidance:

Food for Thought

The exception in Rule 1.6(b) permitting disclosure to prevent reasonably certain death or bodily harm did not exist at the time of People v. Belge, *supra*. If it had, could Belge have used it to disclose the location of the body? Could Belge have used it to disclose Garrow's whereabouts after Garrow escaped from prison?

[6] Although the public interest is usually best served by a strict rule requiring lawyers to preserve the confidentiality of information relating to the representation of their clients, the confidentiality rule is subject to limited exceptions. Paragraph (b)(1) recognizes the overriding value of life and physical integrity and permits disclosure reasonably necessary to prevent reasonably certain death or substantial bodily harm. Such harm is reasonably certain to occur if it will be suffered imminently or if there is a present and substantial threat that a person will suffer such harm at a later date if the lawyer fails to take action necessary to eliminate the threat. Thus, a lawyer who knows that a client has accidentally discharged toxic waste into a town's water supply may reveal this information to the authorities if there is a present and substantial risk that a person who drinks the water will contract a life- threatening or debilitating disease and the lawyer's disclosure is necessary to eliminate the threat or reduce the number of victims.

People v. Belge is one of the landmark lawyer confidentiality cases. Despite the heart-rending facts, many commentators agree that under the circumstances recited in the case, the lawyers owed their client Garrow a duty of confidentiality. The facts of *Belge* did not lead to any changes in the exceptions currently found in ABA Model Rule 1.6.

Two other landmark lawyer confidentiality cases, however, illustrate how difficult cases can lead to discussions about lawyer confidentiality and sometimes can lead to rule changes. The landmark case of *Spaulding v. Zimmerman,* 116 N.W.2d 704 (Minn. 1962) gave rise to discussions that led to changes to the exception found in Rule 1.6(b)(1). The more recent case of Alton Logan has given rise to some calls for changes in the Rule 1.6(b)(1) exception. The facts of *Spaulding*

Make the Connection

Chapter 8(II) includes an additional discussion of *Belge* and role morality.

v. Zimmerman and Alton Logan will help you better understand these debates about the proper boundaries of Rule 1.6(b)(1).

Spaulding v. Zimmermann affirmed a trial court order that vacated and set aside a settlement agreement made on behalf of a 20-year old minor. The original lawsuit was brought by Theodore Spaulding, as father and natural guardian of David Spaulding, for injuries sustained by David in an automobile collision that occurred August 24, 1956, between an automobile driven by John Zimmerman, in which David was a passenger, and one owned by John Ledermann and driven by Florian Ledermann. The defendants were Florian Lederman, John Zimmerman, and their parents who owned the vehicles. Under the terms of the Zimmerman and Lederman insurance policies, the insurance companies were required to pay for lawyers to defend the case; the insurance companies also had the right to select those lawyers.

After the automobile accident, David Spaulding was examined by two of his own doctors, neither of whom discovered the fact that he had an aortic aneurysm, which is a weakened area in the aorta [the main artery leading into and out of the heart]. To the contrary, one of his doctor's reports stated: "The lung fields are clear. The heart and aorta are normal."

Although David's own doctors did not find the aneurysm, a neurologist hired by the defendants to examine David discovered the aneurysm. This doctor included the following language in the report he wrote to defendants' lawyers:

> "The one feature of the case which bothers me more than any other part of the case is the fact that this boy of 20 years of age has an aneurysm, which means a dilatation of the aorta and the arch of the aorta. Whether this came out of this accident I cannot say with any degree of certainty and I have discussed it with the Roentgenologist and a couple of Internists. * * * Of course an aneurysm or dilatation of the aorta in a boy of this age is a serious matter as far as his life. This aneurysm may dilate further and it might rupture with further dilatation and this would cause his death.

> "It would be interesting also to know whether the X-ray of his lungs, taken imme-diately following the accident, shows this dilatation or not. If it was not present immediately following the accident and is now present, then we could be sure that it came out of the accident."

Although the neurologist who examined David on behalf of the defendants found that this aneurysm could be life-threatening, defendants' counsel did not disclose this report or the existence of this aneurysm to David Spaulding, his parents, his physicians, or his lawyer. In 1957, after this lawsuit was set for trial, it was settled for $6500.

Because David Spaulding was a minor, court approval of the settlement was necessary. David's lawyer presented to the court a petition for approval of the settlement which described David's injuries. The petition included as attachments affidavits of David's physicians. Defendants' counsel urged the court to approve the settlement. The Supreme Court later found that at "no time was there information disclosed to the [trial] court that David was then suffering from an aorta aneurysm which may have been the result of the accident." Based upon the petition for settlement and the affidavits of David's doctors, the trial court entered an order on May 8, 1957 approving the settlement.

In 1959, David was required by the army reserve, of which he was a member, to have a physical checkup. This checkup was performed by his personal physician, who had examined him after the accident. In this checkup, however, his doctor discovered the aorta aneurysm. This doctor reexamined the X-Rays that had been taken shortly after the automobile accident and found that they disclosed the beginning of the process which produced the aneurysm. He promptly sent David to a specialist for further examination and opinion. The latter confirmed the finding of the aorta aneurysm and recommended immediate surgery, which was performed in Minneapolis on March 10, 1959.

Shortly thereafter, David, having attained his majority, filed suit for additional damages due to the more serious injuries including the aorta aneurysm which he alleged proximately resulted from the accident. Defendants objected on the grounds of the prior settlement. The trial court vacated the prior settlement on the grounds of the nondisclosure of the aortic aneurysm and the Minnesota Supreme Court affirmed this decision. The Court reasoned as follows:

> [T]he Court finds that although the aneurysm now existing is causally related to the accident, such finding is for the purpose of the motions only and is based solely upon the opinion expressed by Dr. Cain * * * which, so far as the Court can find from the numerous affidavits and statements of fact by counsel, stands without dispute. * * *

> From the foregoing it is clear that in the instant case the court did not abuse its discretion in setting aside the settlement which it had approved on plaintiff's behalf while he was still a minor. It is undisputed that neither he nor his counsel nor his medical attendants were aware that at the time settlement was made he was suffering from an aorta aneurysm which may have resulted from the accident. The seriousness of this disability is indicated by Dr. Hannah's report indicating the imminent danger of death therefrom. This was known by counsel for both defendants but was not disclosed to the court at the time it was petitioned to approve the settlement. While no canon of ethics or legal obligation may have required them to inform plaintiff or his counsel with respect thereto, or to advise the court therein, it did become obvious to them at the time, that the settlement then made did not contemplate or take into consideration the disability described. This fact opened the way for the court to later exercise its discretion in vacating the settlement and under the circumstances described we cannot say that there was any abuse of discretion on the part of the court in so doing under Rule 60.02(6) of Rules of Civil Procedure.

Make the Connection

Chapter 8(II) includes additional commentary and links regarding *Spaulding v. Zimmerman.*

> * * *

> Affirmed.

Rule 1.6(b)(1) currently states "A lawyer may reveal information relating to the representation of a client to the extent the lawyer reasonably believes necessary: (1) to prevent reasonably certain death or substantial bodily harm." *If this exception had governed the conduct of the lawyers in* **Spaulding v. Zimmerman,** *would the defendants' counsel have been permitted to reveal the aneurysm to plaintiff or his counsel?*

The current version of Rule 1.6(b)(1) was adopted after the ABA changed its Model Rule in 2002 as part of the ABA Ethics 2000 Commission's review of the ABA Model Rule. Previously, the exception in Rule 1.6(b)(1) stated that a lawyer may reveal information "1) to prevent the client from committing a criminal act that the lawyer believes is likely to result in imminent death or substantial bodily harm." *If the pre-2002 version of the exception had governed the conduct of the lawyers in* **Spaulding v. Zimmerman,** *would the defendants' counsel have been permitted to reveal the aneurysm to plaintiff or his counsel?*

Do you agree with the modifications that expanded the information that may be disclosed pursuant to Rule 1.6(b)(1)? *Should the exception require disclosure of the information about the aneurysm?*

Alton Logan is another landmark case that has led some to call for changes to the exception found in Rule 1.6(b)(1). *See, e.g.,* Peter A. Joy & Kevin C. McMunigal, *Confidentiality and Wrongful Conviction,* 23 Crim. Just. 46 (Sum. 2008); James E. Moliterno, *Rectifying Wrongful Convictions: May a Lawyer Reveal Her Client's Confidences to Rectify the Wrongful Conviction of Another?,* 38 Hastings Const. L. Q. 811 (2011). The facts of Alton Logan are as follows.

In 1982, defendant Alton Logan was convicted of killing a security guard at a McDonald's restaurant in Chicago. Alton Logan was innocent, however, and two lawyers knew that.

The lawyers in question represented Andrew Wilson, who had been arrested a few days after Alton Logan in connection with the unrelated murder of two policemen. Wilson confessed to his public defenders that he not only had killed the policemen, but that he was one of the two men who committed the crime with which Alton Logan was charged. In the absence of client consent, Wilson's lawyers saw no exception that would permit them to reveal this information, which would have exposed their client to a third capital case charge. The lawyers, however, prepared a notarized affidavit stating that they had gotten information through privileged sources that Alton Logan was not in fact guilty of killing the security officer and that somebody else committed this crime.

At trial, Alton Logan, his mother, and his brother all testified that he was at home asleep when the crime was committed, but three witnesses, including a second security guard, identified Alton Logan as one of the two perpetrators. Alton Logan was convicted. One of Wilson's lawyers was in the courtroom the day Alton Logan was sentenced. Wilson's lawyers were prepared to speak up if Alton Logan had received the death penalty, but Logan was sentenced to life in prison (after a jury vote of 10–2 in favor of the death penalty). For twenty-six years, Alton Logan remained in prison, wrongfully convicted. For decades, the affidavit prepared by Wilson's lawyers sat in a locked metal box under the bed of one of the lawyers.

Before Wilson's death, his lawyers had received permission from Wilson to reveal Alton Logan's innocence after Wilson died. In November 2007, Wilson died. Wilson's lawyers contacted Alton Logan's current lawyer. Thereafter, in March 2008, Wilson's former lawyers appeared on the TV news magazine show *60 Minutes,* which aired a story on Alton Logan's situation. This TV show led to substantial publicity. On April 4, 2008, a retrial was ordered, but the attorney general ultimately refused to proceed and on September 4, 2008, a judge vacated Logan's conviction, and all charges were formally dropped. Logan later filed a wrongful conviction lawsuit. In December 2012, the parties agreed to settle this case for $10.25 million. The settlement avoided a trial in which a convicted Chicago police detective would have been asked to testify by video from prison; the detective had been fired in 1993 (and later convicted) after the Police Department Review Board ruled that he had used torture to obtain confessions. Alton Logan planned to introduce evidence that one of the witnesses against him was tortured until he provided evidence against Logan.

1. Consider the Alton Logan case in light of Rule 1.6. Do you think that Wilson's confession to his lawyers was "information related to the representation?"

2. Now examine the exception found in Rule 1.6(b)(1). If the same events occurred today in a jurisdiction that had adopted the Rule 1.6(b)(1), would Wilson's lawyers be able to reveal the information he told them and explain that Alton Logan was wrongfully convicted?

3. Should the Rules of Professional Conduct be revised to either permit or require Wilson's lawyers to reveal the information he told them indicating that Alton Logan was wrongfully convicted? Massachusetts, for example, has adopted a version of Rule 1.6(b) that includes an exception to prevent wrongful execution or incarceration:

   "A lawyer may reveal, and to the extent required by Rule 3.3, Rule 4.1(b), or Rule 8.3 must reveal, such information * * * (1) to prevent reasonably certain death or substantial bodily harm or to prevent the wrongful execution or incarceration of another."

2. To Protect Victims When the Client Has Misused the Lawyer's Services

One of the most controversial set of exceptions in Rule 1.6 are those related to a lawyer's obligation when the client has injured or will injure the financial interests or property of another and the lawyer's services have been used. The exceptions found in Rule 1.6(b)(2) and (b)(3) were not part of the original ABA Model Rules of Professional Conduct nor were they part of the Ethics 2000 amendments approved by the ABA House of Delegates. (The ABA Ethics 2000 Commission had recommended these exceptions, but they were rejected by the ABA House of Delegates.) The exceptions currently found in Rule 1.6(b)(2) and (3) were adopted in 2003 in the wake of the Enron scandal and Congress' adoption of the Sarbanes-Oxley Act of 2002 (see Chapter 6). It is noteworthy that there are so many state variations of the exceptions found in ABA Model Rule 1.6(b)(2) and (3) that the ABA maintains a separate comparison chart for these exceptions. It is also noteworthy that many states had these types of exceptions long before the ABA incorporated them into its Model Rules, but not all jurisdictions have adopted them.

The O.P.M. Leasing case, which is described in the article by Stuart Taylor, Jr., *Ethics and the Law: A Case History*, N.Y. Times Mag., Jan. 9, 1983 at 33, has been cited as an example of the reason why these types of exceptions are necessary. As Taylor describes in his article, two business partners, Myron S. Goodman and his brother-in-law, Mordecai Weissman, were convicted and sentenced to several years in prison for defrauding banks and other lenders of more than $210 million (in 1981 dollars) before their computer leasing company, O.P.M. (short for "other peoples' money") Leasing, went bankrupt in 1981. O.P.M.'s law firm, Singer Hunter, continued to close new loans for O.P.M. even after being warned by an O.P.M. employee that the leasing company was engaged in massive fraud by falsifying documents to overstate the value of leases and computers. Singer Hunter had issued legal opinion letters based upon the false documents, and lenders had relied on Singer Hunter's opinion letters in making the loans.

Taylor explains the dilemma for O.P.M.'s law firm, Singer Hunter, as follows: "Warned that it might be in the midst of a massive fraud orchestrated by its most important client, the law firm sought the advice of respected legal experts, and with their approval proceeded to close new loans for O.P.M. Even after learning that more than $60 million of these new loans was fraudulent, Singer Hutner kept its silence while bowing out of the picture. Thus Goodman was able to use new lawyers [the law firm of Kaye Scholer] to swindle lenders out of another $15 million before his house of cards collapsed early in 1981." It is important to note that Taylor's article covers an event that occurred before the ethics rules were amended to allow a lawyer to disclose confidences to protect victims if the lawyer's services have been misused. Singer Hunter later paid approximately $10 million to settle suits against the firm arising from its representation of O.P.M.

As you consider the scope of Rule 1.6(b)(2) and 1.6(b)(3), do comments [7] and [8] to Rule 1.6 provide you with any additional guidance?

Comments [7] and [8] to Rule 1.6

[7] Paragraph (b)(2) is a limited exception to the rule of confidentiality that permits the lawyer to reveal information to the extent necessary to enable affected persons or appropriate authorities to prevent the client from committing a crime or fraud, as defined in Rule 1.0(d), that is reasonably certain to result in substantial injury to the financial or property interests of another and in furtherance of which the client has used or is using the lawyer's services. Such a serious abuse of the client-lawyer relationship by the client forfeits the protection of this Rule. The client can, of course, prevent such disclosure by refraining from the wrongful conduct. Although paragraph (b)(2) does not require the lawyer to reveal the client's misconduct, the lawyer may not counsel or assist the client in conduct the lawyer knows is criminal or fraudulent. *See* Rule 1.2(d). *See also* Rule 1.16 with respect to the lawyer's obligation or right to withdraw from the representation of the client in such circumstances.

* * *

[Ed note: Comment [7] to both the Delaware Rule and the ABA Model Rule references Rule 1.13 (b) or (c) respectively to discuss the limited circumstances where the lawyer may be permitted to reveal information relating to the representation.]

Food for Thought

If the exception to confidentiality for situations in which the lawyer's services have been misused had been applicable at the time of O.P.M., would Singer Hutner have been subject to discipline for refusing to inform victims of the fraud?

Note that there are two things going on in O.P.M.—not informing the victims of fraud with regard to past and existing leases, and helping O.P.M. with new leases that appear to be fraudulent. Rule 1.6 governs the former situation. Rule 1.2(d) governs the latter situation:

(d) A lawyer shall not counsel a client to engage, or assist a client, in conduct that the lawyer knows is criminal or fraudulent, but a lawyer may discuss the legal consequences of any proposed course of conduct with a client and may counsel or assist a client to make a good faith effort to determine the validity, scope, meaning or application of the law.

Did Singer Hutner violate Rule 1.2(d) by continuing to assist O.P.M. in its transactions? Did it "know" at the time that O.P.M. was up to no good?

Comment [8] to Rule 1.6 provides:

[8] Paragraph (b)(3) addresses the situation in which the lawyer does not learn of the client's crime or fraud until after it has been consummated. Although the client no longer has the option of preventing disclosure by refraining from the wrongful conduct, there will be situations in which the loss suffered by the affected person can be prevented, rectified or mitigated. In such situations, the lawyer may disclose information relating to the representation to the extent necessary to enable the affected persons to prevent or mitigate reasonably certain losses or to attempt to recoup their losses.

* * *

[Ed note: Comment [8] to both the Delaware Rule and the ABA Model Rule proceed to explain that disclosure is not permitted under paragraph (b)(3) when a person who has committed a crime or fraud thereafter employs a lawyer for representation concerning that offense if that lawyer's services were not used in the initial crime or fraud.]

———

To understand how ethics authorities consider the scope of the exception "to prevent, mitigate, or rectify financial injury or property damage from a client's crime or fraud," consider this ethics opinion from the Maryland State Bar Committee on Ethics.

Maryland State Bar Association, Inc. Committee on Ethics

Ethics Docket No. 2001-18 (2001)

Duty to Report Improper Conduct by a Personal Representative and Duty to Report Client's Failure to Comply With Withholding Tax Requirements

Your letter of inquiry requests an opinion as to an attorney's duty to report suspected criminal activity of a client in two different factual scenarios.

In the first scenario you indicate that you were engaged by the personal representative of an estate to prepare various probate documents, including accountings. During your work on the accountings, you discovered a serious discrepancy between the amount of cash in the decedent's various bank accounts and the amount of cash used to open the estate account. You also state that there is other evidence of misuse of estate assets, however, you have not indicated the nature of that evidence.

You state that the sole beneficiary of the estate is an elderly woman in a nursing home. You have received information that her bills are not being paid. You also indicate that you have been completely unable to reach your client through both telephone and mail. A final accounting in due shortly on the estate and you are continuing your efforts to reach your client. You indicate that you plan to advise your client that you are withdrawing as counsel of record. You request an opinion as to whether you may report your suspicions of the misuse of estate assets to Adult Protective Services

Rule 1.6 of the Maryland Rules of Professional Conduct states:

>   (a)   A lawyer shall not reveal information relating to representation of a client unless the client consents after consultation, except for disclosures that are impliedly authorized in order to carry out the representation, and except as stated in paragraph (b).
>
>   (b)   A lawyer may reveal such information to the extent the lawyer reasonably believes necessary:
>
>   (1)   to prevent the client from committing a criminal or fraudulent act that the lawyer believes is likely to result in death or substantial bodily harm or in substantial injury to the financial interests or property of another;
>
>   (2)   to rectify the consequences of a client's criminal or fraudulent act in the furtherance of which the lawyer's services were used;
>
>   (3)   to establish a claim or defense on behalf of the lawyer in a controversy between the lawyer and the client, or to establish a defense to a criminal charge, civil claim, or disciplinary complaint against the lawyer based upon conduct in which the client was involved or to respond to allegations in any proceedings concerning the lawyer's representation of the client;

(4)   To comply with these Rules, court order or other law.

Your inquiry does not specifically identify whether your client is the personal representative in an individual capacity, the personal representative in her capacity as a fiduciary for the estate, or the estate itself. However, you indicate that you were engaged by the personal representative of the estate to prepare various documents involving the estate. This suggests that you were retained by the personal representative in her fiduciary capacity, but your agreement, whether written or oral, with the client as to whom you represent, governs. If you do represent the personal representative in her fiduciary capacity, that representation does not give rise to duties to the sole beneficiary. *See Ferguson v. Cramer*, 349 Md. 760 (1998). You would owe the beneficiary a duty only if you separately agreed to represent her. However, because we find no duty to disclose in any event, the question of whom you represent is immaterial for the purposes of this opinion.

The rationale for maintaining the confidentiality of client information is clearly set forth in the comments to Rule 1.6. With this Rule in place, the client is encouraged to communicate fully and frankly with the lawyer even as to embarrassing or legally damaging subject matter. The rule applies not only to matters communicated in confidence by the client but also to all information relating to the representation, whatever its source. As such, the Rule mandates that an attorney shall not reveal confidential information absent client consent unless the information falls within one of the exceptions found in subsection (b).

You indicate that you uncovered discrepancies in the amount of cash that was in the decedent's bank accounts and the amount used to open the estate. It is assumed that you believe that the personal representative of the estate may have converted these funds to a use for which she had no authority. Rule 1.6 (b) (1) allows an attorney to divulge confidential information to prevent the client from committing a criminal or fraudulent act that the lawyer believes is likely to result in substantial injury to the financial interests or property of another. This exception deals with prospective conduct of the client. If you believe that it is likely that your client's future conduct will result in substantial injury as indicated above you may reveal that information to the extent that you believe is necessary to rectify the situation. If the only fraudulent conduct of which you are aware is conduct that has already occurred, Rule 1.6(b)(1) does not permit disclosure of that conduct.

An attorney may also disclose information to rectify the consequences of a client's criminal of fraudulent act in the furtherance of which the lawyer's services were used. You have not indicated any facts that would indicate that your client's used your services to further a criminal or fraudulent act. Absent facts that would support disclosure under the above exceptions, you may not disclose information obtained during the course of representing your client to the authorities.

You state that you intend to withdraw from the representation of your client. Please keep in mind that the confidentiality of information survives that the attorney client relationship. As such, your termination of representation would not change your obligations under Rule 1.6.

If you choose to continue with your representation, it is assumed that it will become necessary to file certain information with the Court. If you do continue with the representation, you should review Rule 3.3, "Candor toward the tribunal" and Rule 4.1, "Truthfulness in statements to others." Both of these Rules of Professional Conduct state that an attorney shall not knowingly make a false statement or fail to disclose facts when disclosure is necessary to avoid assisting a criminal or fraudulent act by a client. Unlike Rule 1.6, which permits but does not mandate disclosures under certain circumstances, Rules 3.3 and 4.1 are mandatory and must be complied with even if compliance requires the disclosure of information otherwise protected by Rule 1.6.

In your second scenario you state you were recently consulted by a client who had been caring for her elderly husband at home. During your conversation, which was not related to the scope of your representation, she revealed that she had been engaging caregivers and paying then in cash at their request. She indicated that she had not withheld FICA, paid household employment taxes, worker's compensation or unemployment insurance. She indicated that her Certified Public Account had advised her that she did not need to pay any of the above. Although your inquiry does not state that you advised her that her CPA was in error and that she was required to pay for those items, we infer that you did. Further, she asked if she had to pay for those items with respect to her household cleaning person and you told her that she did. She refused further counseling on the subject matter.

You now inquire whether you have a duty to report her failure to meet these obligations. Even though the conversation was not relevant to the matter that the client had initially consulted you about it seems clear that you were engaging the client in a conversation in your capacity as her attorney. As such the attorney-client privilege would exist. As stated above, Rule 1.6 of the Maryland Rules of Professional Conduct would prohibit the disclosure of confidential information. If she advised you that she intended to continue her practice of not deducting FICA, paying household taxes, or paying for required insurance coverages, then under Rule 1 .6(b)(1), you would be permitted, but not required, to disclose this only if it would result in "substantial injury to the financial interests or property of another." Whether such omissions fall within the reach of 1.6(b)(1) is a factual question upon which the Committee cannot opine. However, nothing in your description of the conversation suggested that your client indicated that she intended to continue her unlawful practices. Accordingly, it does not appear that the information you received would trigger one of the exceptions to the Rule.

We hope the foregoing is responsive to your inquiry and we thank you for consulting the Committee on this matter.

In the first scenario of suspected criminal or fraudulent activity, it is important to note that the ethics committee would have permitted disclosure of the discrepancies in the amount of cash in the decedent's bank accounts and the amount used to open the estate under two circumstances – if the client had used the attorney's services to further a criminal or fraudulent act, or if the attorney believed it was likely that his client's future conduct would result in substantial injury to the financial interests or property of the beneficiary. The committee also discusses the attorney's candor to the tribunal obligation under Rule 3.3. Based on the facts presented, neither circumstance existed. In the second scenario, the ethics committee would have permitted disclosure of the client's failure to pay taxes if the client had advised her attorney that she intended to continue not to pay taxes and the attorney determined that it would result in "substantial injury to the financial interests or property of another."

3. Lawyer Self-Protection

[Question 4-14]

An attorney represented a client in the sale of a printing business owned by the client. The purchaser of the printing business has filed suit against the client and the attorney, alleging that they committed fraud by misstating the financial condition of the client's printing business. The attorney had advised the client to disclose all of the financial information concerning the printing business to the purchaser. The client and the attorney each have separate lawyers to defend against the purchaser. The purchaser's lawyer has subpoenaed the attorney to attend a deposition. Under questioning by the purchaser's lawyer, the attorney reveals, to the extent the attorney reasonably believes necessary to defend herself, confidential information about the client that will be favorable to the attorney but damaging to client.

Is the attorney's conduct proper?

    (A) Yes, unless the client objects to the disclosure.

    (B) Yes, because the attorney may reveal such information to defend herself against a civil claim.

    (C) No, because such disclosure of confidential information may only be made by attorney to defend against criminal charges, not a civil claim.

    (D) No, because attorney made the disclosure knowing it would be detrimental to the client.

In answering this question, consider Rule 1.6(b)(5) and Comments [10] and [11]. Rule 1.6(b)(5) provides:

> (b) A lawyer may reveal information relating to the representation of a client to the extent the lawyer reasonably believes necessary:
>
> > (5) to establish a claim or defense on behalf of the lawyer in a controversy between the lawyer and the client, to establish a defense to a criminal charge

or civil claim against the lawyer based upon conduct in which the client was involved, or to respond to allegations in any proceeding concerning the lawyer's representation of the client.

Comments [10] and [11] to Rule 1.6 provide:

[10] Where a legal claim or disciplinary charge alleges complicity of the lawyer in a client's conduct or other misconduct of the lawyer involving representation of the client, the lawyer may respond to the extent the lawyer reasonably believes necessary to establish a defense. The same is true with respect to a claim involving the conduct or representation of a former client. Such a charge can arise in a civil, criminal, disciplinary or other proceeding and can be based on a wrong allegedly committed by the lawyer against the client or on a wrong alleged by a third person, for example, a person claiming to have been defrauded by the lawyer and client acting together. The lawyer's right to respond arises when an assertion of such complicity has been made. Paragraph (b)(5) does not require the lawyer to await the commencement of an action or proceeding that charges such complicity, so that the defense may be established by responding directly to a third party who has made such an assertion. The right to defend also applies, of course, where a proceeding has been commenced.

[11] A lawyer entitled to a fee is permitted by paragraph (b)(5) to prove the services rendered in an action to collect it. This aspect of the rule expresses the principle that the beneficiary of a fiduciary relationship may not exploit it to the detriment of the fiduciary.

Global Perspective

Although Rule 1.6 imposes confidentiality obligations on lawyers, it is not the only rule or law to do so. In recent years, U.S. lawyers and law firms have been trying to understand and comply with the European Union's General Data Protection Regulation or GDPR, which took effect in May 2018. One of the first ethics opinions to address the impact of the GDPR on U.S. lawyers is Opinion 2018-06 of the Maryland State Bar Committee on Ethics.

Simulation: Lawyer Self-Protection

Law Firm believes that an "unhappy" Former Client has unfairly characterized Law Firm's representation of Former Client on a website that provides reviews of lawyers. Former Client gave Law Firm a rating of "1" on a scale of 1 to 4, and posted a note that stated: "I regret the day that I hired Law Firm. Law Firm did not provide me with the type of representation I wanted, poorly communicated with me, and did not achieve my goals."

Assume you are admitted to practice and one of your areas of practice is providing legal ethics advice to lawyers and law firms. Law Firm comes to see you for advice about how to respond to Former Client's depiction of its representation. Law Firm tells you that it achieved a good result for Former Client given the underlying facts, and it wants to respond to Former Client's criticism by telling Law Firm's side of the story. Law Firm asks you if it may post a response on the website to rebut the accusations by including information relating to Former Client and its representation of Former Client?

(A) Before giving your advice, are there any other facts you need?

(B) What is your advice and why?

4. Other Exceptions to Rule 1.6

There are three exceptions in <u>Rule 1.6(b)</u> beyond the four exceptions already covered in this Chapter. These relatively new exceptions codified practices that were common among lawyers, but for which there previously was no explicit exception. Rule 1.6(b)(4) permits a lawyer to reveal information the lawyer reasonably believes is necessary in order "to secure legal advice about the lawyer's compliance with these Rules." (It is not uncommon for lawyers to seek ethics advice from lawyers outside their own firm.) Rule 1.6(b)(6) permits a lawyer to reveal information the lawyer reasonably believes is necessary "to comply with other law or a court order." (This permissive exception gives a lawyer discretion under the duty of confidentiality when responding to a court order denying attorney-client privilege. The lawyer can reveal the information allegedly protected by the attorney-client privilege if ordered to do so by the court or the lawyer may choose not to reveal the allegedly privileged information and risk a contempt of court citation.) The third additional exception is Rule 1.6(b)(7), which was added by many states after 2012 at the recommendation of the ABA Commission on Ethics 20/20. This exception states:

Make the Connection

Sarbanes-Oxley, commonly referred to as "Sox," is an example of the "other law" a lawyer might rely on to justify the disclosure of confidential client information. For a discussion of Sox and <u>Rule 1.13</u>, see Chapter 6.

(b) A lawyer may reveal information relating to the representation of a client to the extent the lawyer reasonably believes necessary: * * * (7) to detect and resolve conflicts of interest arising from the lawyer's change of employment or from changes in the composition or ownership of a firm, but only if the revealed information would not compromise the attorney-client privilege or otherwise prejudice the client.

Food for Thought

There is great variation among states both in the language of Rule 1.6 and the comments to the rule. For example, some states require an attorney to reveal confidential information if there is an exception under Rule 1.6(b), but most states give the attorney discretion by stating that the attorney "may" reveal confidential information when the circumstances fit an exception under Rule 1.6(b). Which approach do you think is better? What is your reasoning for your position? Do you think that Delaware's version of Rule 1.6, which comes close to tracking the ABA Model Rule, accomplishes a good balance of the client's interest, the attorney's interest, and society's interest? If so, why? If not, how do you think Rule 1.6 can be improved to achieve a better balance? Finally, do you think that there should be additional exceptions to Rule 1.6? If so, what would you include? Would you make those new exceptions mandatory (shall reveal) or discretionary (may reveal)?

Test Your Knowledge

To assess your understanding of the material in this Chapter, click here to take a quiz.

CHAPTER 5

Conflicts of Interest

Learning Outcomes

At the end of Units I, II, III, and IV, you will be able to:

- Analyze whether a concurrent conflict of interest exists

- Evaluate whether representation is permitted when a concurrent conflict of interest exists

- Evaluate what constitutes proper informed consent to representation

At the end of Units V, VI, VII, and VIII, you will be able to:

- Analyze whether a former client conflict of interest exists

- Evaluate whether representation is permitted when a former client conflict of interest exists

- Analyze when conflicts of interest are imputed to lawyers associated in a firm

- Determine when representation is permitted even though there are conflicts of interest imputed to a tainted lawyer's firm

- Evaluate when criminal defense attorney conflicts of interest result in ineffective assistance of counsel

Topic Outline for Chapter 5

TOPIC			RELEVANT AUTHORITY	CHAPTER QUESTIONS
I.	Introduction			
II.	Simultaneous Representations of Multiple Clients			
	A.	Is There a Current Attorney-Client Relationship? [Dow Chemical; Murray]		
	B.	Simultaneous Representation Standards	1.7	
		1. "Directly Adverse" Under Rule 1.7(a)(1)	1.7	5-1 to 5-4

I. Introduction

From a client's perspective, the lawyer's duty of loyalty signifies more than a mere ethical obligation. For clients whose civil or criminal liability hangs in the balance, or for those whose business interests depend upon the successful completion of a transaction, the retention of counsel carries with it an implied expectation that the attorney will advocate devotedly and diligently, and will avoid conduct harmful to the clients' interests. Clients often come to the lawyer-client relationship in a position of vulnerability, and as a practical imperative, are entitled to demand of their counsel undivided loyalty during and after the culmination of the representation. The lawyer's duty of loyalty is independent of the relative strength or weakness of the client's position. As the U.S. Supreme Court noted long ago:

> There are few business relations of life involving a higher trust and confidence than those of attorney and client, or generally speaking one more honorably and faithfully discharged, few more anxiously guarded by the law or governed by sterner principles of morality and justice; and it is the duty of the court to administer them in a corresponding spirit, and to be watchful and industrious, to see that confidence thus reposed shall not be used to the detriment of prejudice of the rights of the party bestowing it.

Stockton v. Ford, 52 U.S. (11 How.) 232, 247 (1850).

In the following materials, notice the many scenarios in which attorneys use confidences entrusted to them "to the detriment of . . . the party bestowing it," and the ways in which contemporary ethical guidelines "anxiously guard" the attorney-client relationship.

II. Simultaneous Representations of Multiple Clients

A. Is There a Current Attorney-Client Relationship?

Rohm and Haas Co. v. Dow Chemical Co.

2009 WL 445609 (Del. Ch. 2009)

William B. Chandler, III, Chancellor.

Dear Counsel:

Before me is defendants' motion to disqualify Wachtell, Lipton, Rosen & Katz ("Wachtell") from conducting discovery against The Dow Chemical Company and examining Dow witnesses. I have considered the parties' briefs, and oral argument was presented to the Court on February 11, 2009. For the reasons set forth briefly below, the motion to disqualify is denied.

Practice Pointer

Prior to analyzing an alleged conflict of interest, courts may need to resolve the threshold question of whether an attorney-client relationship in fact came into existence. What factors are dispositive to the courts' determinations in the following decisions?

Dow argues that Wachtell should be disqualified because the firm's representation of Rohm and Haas Company in this matter presents a conflict of interest as a result of Wachtell's representation of Dow. Dow alleges that Wachtell is in violation of the Delaware Rules of Professional Conduct because Dow is both a current client of Wachtell and a client whom Wachtell has previously represented in matters substantially related to the instant proceedings. Dow alleges that it is prejudiced in this action because Wachtell was privy to sensitive information in its capacity as Dow's counsel.

Dow argues that it is a current client of Wachtell because the firm never took steps to inform Dow that it was no longer a client following Wachtell's representation of Dow in 2007 and 2008 in connection with the termination of two Dow executives and potential defensive measures in response to rumors of a takeover bid. * * *

Plaintiff Rohm and Haas counters that there is not a concurrent conflict of interest because Dow is no longer a Wachtell client. According to Rohm and Haas, it should have been clear to Dow that Dow was no longer a Wachtell client when the firm appeared opposite Dow in its representation of Rohm and Haas in the negotiations of the initial confidentiality agreement and the merger agreement in mid-2008. * * *

After careful consideration of the parties' arguments, * * * I am not convinced by the argument that Dow reasonably believes it is a current client of Wachtell or that Dow relied on such a belief. Dow knew that Wachtell was representing Rohm and Hass during the negotiations of the merger agreement and did not object. Rather, Dow obtained its own separate counsel to represent Dow in the merger negotiations. Wachtell sent its final bill to Dow in June 2008, and there is no convincing evidence that Wachtell continued to perform services for Dow that would justify a reasonable belief by Dow that it is a current Wachtell client. I am also not convinced by Dow's argument that there was an implicit promise by Wachtell that they would represent Rohm and Haas in the negotiations but would discontinue the representation if litigation arose. In short, if Dow truly felt that they were a current client of Wachtell and that they should not be "across the table" from their own lawyers, then Dow should have objected at the outset of the negotiations of the merger agreement that eventually led to this litigation rather than waiting until this expedited litigation was commenced to attempt to make Rohm and Haas obtain new counsel.

* * *

For the foregoing reasons, the motion to disqualify is denied.

Very truly yours,

William B. Chandler III

Murray v. Metropolitan Life Ins. Co.

583 F.3d 173 (2d Cir. 2009)

DENNIS JACOBS, CHIEF JUDGE:

Plaintiffs in this class action were policyholders of Metropolitan Life Insurance Company when it was a mutual insurance company. They complain that they were misled and shortchanged in the transaction by which the company demutualized in 2000. Nine years after the action was commenced and five weeks before trial was scheduled to begin, plaintiffs moved to disqualify the lead counsel for Metropolitan Life Insurance Company and MetLife, Inc. ("MetLife"), Debevoise & Plimpton LLP ("Debevoise"). The grounds alleged related to that firm's representation of MetLife in the underlying demutualization. * * *

The district court disqualified Debevoise on the ground that its representation of MetLife in the 2000 demutualization made it counsel to the policyholders as well. On appeal, plaintiffs urge affirmance on that ground * * * .

We conclude that * * * Debevoise did not have an attorney-client relationship with the policyholders by virtue of its representation of MetLife * * * . Accordingly, we reverse.

I

In 1915, MetLife converted from a stock life insurance company to a mutual insurance company. On April 7, 2000, MetLife completed a months-long process of demutualization back to a stock insurance company. Debevoise served as MetLife's corporate counsel in that transaction.

On April 18, 2000, plaintiffs filed this class action lawsuit in the Eastern District of New York, alleging that MetLife violated federal securities laws by misrepresenting or altogether omitting certain information from the materials provided to its policyholders during the demutualization process. In June 2007, MetLife invoked the attorney-client privilege to prevent plaintiffs' discovery of particular communications between MetLife and its in-house and outside counsel. The district court denied a protective order on the ground that the plaintiff policyholders were the owners of the mutual company and were therefore clients of Debevoise during the demutualization.

Following discovery and the usual preliminaries, the trial was set to begin on September 8, 2009. When last-minute settlement negotiations failed, plaintiffs moved to disqualify Debevoise on July 31, 2009—more than nine years after the action was commenced, more than two years after the court ruled that plaintiffs were clients of Debevoise, and five weeks before trial. Plaintiffs argued that disqualification was appropriate for the same reason articulated by the district court to support its 2007 discovery ruling: Debevoise had been counsel to plaintiffs in the demutualization and cannot now jump sides to become adverse to plaintiffs at trial. * * *

Food for Thought

Why does the Court make so much about the timing of the disqualification motion?

MetLife's response invoked the doctrine of laches; argued that as a matter of law the policyholders of a mutual insurance company are not *a priori* the clients of that company's corporate counsel; * * * and charged that the motion was made for improper tactical purposes.

* * *

III

We conclude that plaintiffs were not clients of Debevoise. It is well-settled that outside counsel to a corporation represents the corporation, not its shareholders or other constituents. This rule is entirely consonant with Rule 1.13 of the New York Rules of Professional Conduct, N.Y. R. Prof'l Conduct § 1.13(a) ("[A] lawyer employed or retained by an organization . . . is the lawyer for the organization and not for any of the constituents."), and with the Restatement (Third) of the Rule [sic] Governing Lawyers, § 96 cmt. b (explaining that a lawyer retained by a corporation has an attorney-client relationship with the corporation, but the lawyer "does not thereby also form a client-lawyer relationship with all or any individuals employed by it or who direct its operations or who have an ownership or other beneficial interest in it, such as shareholders").

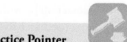

Practice Pointer

It's clear that if a lawyer does not want to be saddled with the obligation of an attorney-client relationship, she must clarify any ambiguity on the subject. What would you do to clarify that you have not entered into an attorney-client relationship with a prospective client?

These principles apply as well to a mutual insurance company. Under New York law, "[a] mutual insurance company is a cooperative enterprise in which the policyholders constitute the members for whose benefit the company is organized, maintained and operated." But a policyholder, "even in a mutual company, [is] in no sense a partner of the corporation which issued the policy, and . . . the relation between the policy-holder and the company [is] one of contract, measured by the terms of the policy."

The district court's 2007 decision reasoned that plaintiffs were clients of Debevoise during the demutualization "because they were MetLife's beneficiaries and the beneficiaries of MetLife counsel's advice." But this does not distinguish a mutual insurance company from any other corporation.

Not every beneficiary of a lawyer's advice is deemed a client. *See* N.Y. R. Prof'l Conduct 2.3(a) ("A lawyer may provide an evaluation of a matter affecting a client for the use of *someone other than the client* if the lawyer reasonably believes that making the evaluation is compatible with other aspects of the lawyer's relationship with the client.") (emphasis added) * * * .

In light of these principles, and without any extraordinary circumstances raised by the parties, we conclude that the policyholders in this case were not clients of Debevoise.

* * *

For More Information

Recall from Chapter 2, the *Restatement* is an excellent starting point for further reading on the formation of an attorney-client relationship. Section 14 of the Restatement may provide some clarity with respect to when an attorney-client relationship has been created:

> A relationship of client and lawyer arises when:
>
> > (1) a person manifests to a lawyer the person's intent that the lawyer provide legal services for the person; and either
> >
> > > (a) the lawyer manifests to the person consent to do so; or
> > >
> > > (b) the lawyer fails to manifest lack of consent to do so, and the lawyer knows or reasonably should know that the person reasonably relies on the lawyer to provide the services; or
> >
> > (2) a tribunal with power to do so appoints the lawyer to provide the services.

See the Comment and Reporter's Note accompanying § 14 for further applications of the general rule.

B. Simultaneous Representation Standards

See It

Here is a helpful model for analyzing Rule 1.7 problems.

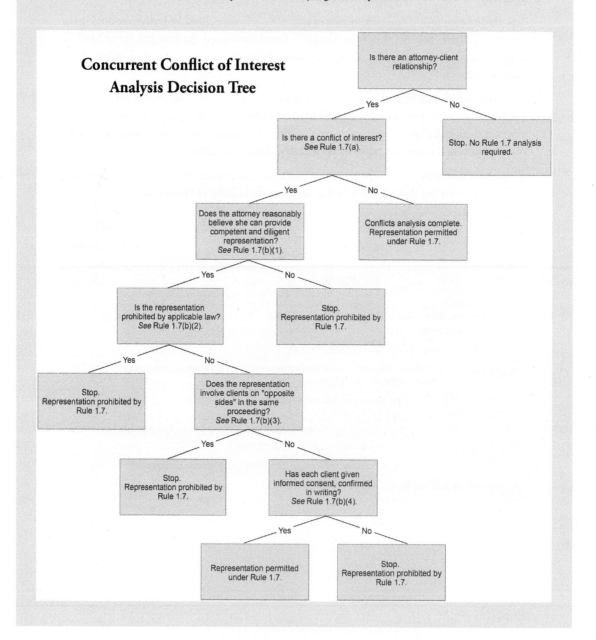

Rule 1.7—Conflict of Interest: Current Clients

(a)   Except as provided in paragraph (b), a lawyer shall not represent a client if the representation involves a concurrent conflict of interest. A concurrent conflict of interest exists if:

(1)   the representation of one client will be directly adverse to another client; or

(2)   there is a significant risk that the representation of one or more clients will be materially limited by the lawyer's responsibilities to another client, a former client or a third person or by a personal interest of the lawyer.

(b)   Notwithstanding the existence of a concurrent conflict of interest under paragraph (a), a lawyer may represent a client if:

(1)   the lawyer reasonably believes that the lawyer will be able to provide competent and diligent representation to each affected client;

(2)   the representation is not prohibited by law;

(3)   the representation does not involve the assertion of a claim by one client against another client represented by the lawyer in the same litigation or other proceeding before a tribunal; and

Hear from the Authors

To hear from the authors on Rule 1.7 analysis, click here.

(4)   each affected client gives informed consent, confirmed in writing.

1. "Directly Adverse" Under Rule 1.7(a)(1)

Litigation Conflicts

[Question 5-1]

A construction company's equipment and crew were involved in an accident in which a bystander was injured. The construction company notified its insurer, which retained and paid an attorney to defend the company when the bystander sued it. Unknown to the construction company, based on information disclosed by the company to the attorney, the attorney correctly advised the insurer that it had no obligation to provide coverage because the construction company had made a misrepresentation in its insurance application. The insurer subsequently sought a declaratory judgment relieving it of responsibility to the construction company.

Is the attorney subject to discipline?

(A)   **No, because the attorney was permitted to disclose the construction company's misrepresentation to the insurer to protect it from prejudice.**

(B)   **No, because the insurer retained and paid the attorney, and therefore the attorney was permitted to share the company's confidential information with the insurer.**

(C)   Yes, because an attorney may not represent two clients at the same time.

(D)   Yes, because the attorney disclosed the construction company's confidential information to the insurer.

[Question 5-2]

For the past three months, an attorney has represented a local manufacturing company in a contract dispute with the company's landlord. Last week, an employee of the manufacturing company asked the attorney to represent the employee in an action against the manufacturing company for failing to comply with wage and hour laws. The contract dispute and the wage and hour matter have no common issues of law or fact, and the attorney reasonably believed that he could competently represent the clients in the respective matters. Without discussing it with the manufacturing company, the attorney accepted and began representation of the employee in the wage and hour matter.

Is the attorney subject to discipline?

   (A)   No, because the attorney reasonably believed that he could represent both the company and the employee competently in the respective matters.

   (B)   No, because there were no common issues of law or fact in the respective lawsuits.

   (C)   Yes, because the attorney did not terminate the representation of the company before agreeing to represent the employee.

   (D)   Yes, because the attorney's representation of the employee was directly adverse to the manufacturing company.

[Question 5-3]

For the past three months, an attorney has represented a local manufacturing company in a contract dispute with the company's landlord. Last week, an employee of the manufacturing company asked the attorney to represent the employee in an action against the manufacturing company for failing to comply with wage and hour laws. The contract dispute and the wage and hour matter have no common issues of law or fact, and the attorney reasonably believes that he can competently represent the clients in the respective matters. The attorney accepted and began representation of the employee in the wage and hour matter after both the employee and the manufacturing company provided informed consent in writing.

Is the attorney subject to discipline?

   (A)   No, because the attorney is confident that the lease negotiations and the wage and hour matter have no common issues.

   (B)   No, because both the employee and the manufacturing company gave informed consent to the representation.

(C) Yes, because the employee and the manufacturing company are directly adverse.

(D) Yes, because the new client is an employee of the manufacturing company.

Non-Litigation Conflicts

[Question 5-4]

An attorney represented an employee in an employment negotiation with a company for whom the employee works. The company asked the attorney to represent it in real estate negotiations with a property owner in another state. With informed consent from both the employee and the company, the attorney agreed to represent the company in the real *[handwritten: So far So good.]* estate negotiations. Neither the employee nor the company consulted with independent counsel before giving consent, and the attorney did not recommend that they do so. In the course of the real estate negotiation, the attorney learned in confidence that the company plans to relocate the employee to the state. The attorney knew that this would be important information for the employee to know in connection with her employment negotiations, but the attorney concluded the employment negotiations without disclosing this information to her. Six months later, the company relocated the employee, who was upset that the employment contract negotiated by the attorney did not protect her from the adverse impact of the relocation.

> ### Take Note
>
> Directly adverse conflicts from simultaneous representation of multiple clients are not limited to litigation; such conflicts arise also in transactional matters. For example, many courts have held that a lawyer cannot represent both sides of a commercial real estate transaction. *See, e.g. N.C. State Bar v. Merrell,* 777 S.E.2d 103 (N.C. Ct. App. 2015). Courts also have held that representing borrower and lender in a residential real estate transaction is a concurrent conflict of interest. *See, e.g., Iowa Supreme Court Board of Prof'l Ethics & Conduct v. Wagner,* 599 N.W.2d 721 (Iowa 1999). Why?

[handwritten: Lombard to this]

Is the attorney subject to discipline?

(A) No, because the clients gave informed consent to the representation.

(B) No, because the attorney did not represent both clients adversely to one another in the same matter.

(C) Yes, because the attorney did not withdraw from representing the employee after he learned confidential information from the company that was important to the employee.

(D) Yes, because the attorney did not advise the clients to consult independent counsel before giving informed consent.

Comment 6 to Rule 1.7

Loyalty to a current client prohibits undertaking representation directly adverse to that client without that client's informed consent. Thus, absent consent, a lawyer may not act as an advocate in one matter against a person the lawyer represents in some other matter, even when the matters are wholly unrelated. The client as to whom the representation is directly adverse is likely to feel betrayed, and the resulting damage to the client-lawyer relationship is likely to impair the lawyer's ability to represent the client effectively. In addition, the client on whose behalf the adverse representation is undertaken reasonably may fear that the lawyer will pursue that client's case less effectively out of deference to the other client, i.e., that the representation may be materially limited by the lawyer's interest in retaining the current client. Similarly, a directly adverse conflict may arise when a lawyer is required to cross-examine a client who appears as a witness in a lawsuit involving another client, as when the testimony will be damaging to the client who is represented in the lawsuit. On the other hand, simultaneous representation in unrelated matters of clients whose interests are only economically adverse, such as representation of competing economic enterprises in unrelated litigation, does not ordinarily constitute a conflict of interest and thus may not require consent of the respective clients.

Global Perspective

Some countries define conflicts of interest differently than ABA Model Rule 1.7. For example, solicitors in England and Wales may—in essence—oppose a current client if the matters are not related. Whereas the premise of the ABA Model Rules is loyalty in the *relationship*, the premise of the English rules is loyalty in the *matter*. Because of the ABA Model Rules' imputation rules, many U.S. law firms with offices in England feel they are at a competitive disadvantage because they must comply with the stricter U.S. conflicts rules. In 2010, the Association of the Bar of the City of New York issued a Report recommending a change to Rule 1.10, which is the firm imputation rule. The proposed amendment stated "(d) Notwithstanding the foregoing, no conflict will be imputed hereunder where (i) a conflict arises under these rules from the conduct of lawyers practicing in another jurisdiction in accordance with such jurisdiction's rules of professional conduct, and (ii) such conduct is permitted by the rules of professional conduct of that other jurisdiction." The recommended amendment would allow U.S. lawyers (and law firms) practicing in London to apply the English conflicts of interest rules rather than the U.S. conflicts rules to matters handled in their London office. The ABA did not adopt this recommendation, but in February 2013, it voted to add the following sentence about choice of law matters affecting conflicts of interest to Comment [5] in Rule 8.5 (Delaware has added this sentence as a separate Comment [8]): "With respect to conflicts of interest, in determining a lawyer's reasonable belief under paragraph (b)(2), a written agreement between the lawyer and client that reasonably specifies a particular jurisdiction as within the scope of that paragraph may be considered if the agreement was obtained with the client's informed consent confirmed in the agreement."

2. "Materially Limited" Under Rule 1.7(a)(2)

[Question 5-5]

A father and his two adult children, a son and a daughter, retained an attorney for business purposes. Later, the father had the attorney draft the father's will, which the

father signed in the presence of his children. A month later, at the father's request, the attorney drafted a new will that was less favorable to the daughter, and the father directed the attorney not to tell his daughter about it. The father subsequently executed the new will, and neither the son nor the daughter was present. Several weeks later, the daughter consulted the attorney regarding her estate plan. The daughter assumed that her father's earlier will was in effect, and she made estate plan decisions based on that assumption. The attorney provided the daughter legally correct advice in light of the information provided by the daughter. The attorney did not disclose that the father had executed a will that was less favorable to her.

Is the attorney subject to discipline?

> (A) No, because the attorney followed the father's instructions not to tell the daughter about the second will.
>
> (B) No, because the attorney provided legally correct advice to the daughter.
>
> (C) Yes, because the attorney did not tell the daughter about the father's new will.
>
> (D) Yes, because the attorney did not withdraw from representing the daughter regarding her estate planning.

FYI

As Comment 8 to Rule 1.7 below notes, a conflict of interest may exist if there is a significant risk that a lawyer's ability "to consider, recommend or carry out an appropriate course of action" will be materially limited due to the lawyer's other interests, even where there is no direct adverseness.

> [A] lawyer asked to represent several individuals seeking to form a joint venture is likely to be materially limited in the lawyer's ability to recommend or advocate all possible positions that each might take because of the lawyer's duty of loyalty to the others. The conflict in effect forecloses alternatives that would otherwise be available to the client. The mere possibility of subsequent harm does not itself require disclosure and consent. The critical questions are the likelihood that a difference in interests will eventuate and, if it does, whether it will materially interfere with the lawyer's independent professional judgment in considering alternatives or foreclose courses of action that reasonably should be pursued on behalf of the client.

---

3. "Reasonably Believes" and "Competent and Diligent Representation" Under Rule 1.7(b)(1)

[Question 5-6]

A mother and daughter are partners in a business venture to develop a software program. Their business is not incorporated, but is a general partnership, with a partnership agreement. The daughter is the primary creative contributor and the mother is the primary business contributor. The mother wants to retire, but their partnership agreement is unclear about certain issues related to the financial settlement upon dissolution. State law is also ambiguous on these issues.

The mother and daughter both want an amicable dissolution, and they agree on what constitutes a fair distribution of the partnership assets. They obtained a dissolution agreement from a legal website, tailored it to their situation, and executed it. To ensure that the agreement was legally enforceable, they wanted a lawyer's opinion.

A good friend has been the attorney for the partnership since its inception and had provided individual representation to the mother in her estate planning and the daughter in a personal injury lawsuit.

Make the Connection

For more on the sale of legal forms, see Chapter 2, Part II, *supra*; for more on limited scope representation, see Chapter 2, Part V, *supra*.

The mother and daughter met with the attorney together and asked if he would review the dissolution agreement for enforceability. During this meeting, the attorney advised the mother and daughter that he would be representing each of them equally in reviewing the agreement and that their communications with him would not be confidential from one another. The attorney also told the two women that if they began to disagree on how to distribute the partnership assets, or if any other conflict arose, the attorney would withdraw from the representation. Reasonably believing that he could competently and diligently carry out the representation, the attorney prepared an engagement agreement detailing these terms, which the mother and daughter signed. The attorney did not inform the mother and daughter of the desirability of seeking the advice of independent legal counsel before signing the agreement.

Is the attorney subject to discipline?

(A) No, because lawyers should, when possible, review legal documents that originate from websites.

(B) No, because the attorney reasonably believed he could provide competent and diligent representation.

(C) Yes, because the attorney previously represented the mother and daughter in other matters.

(D) Yes, because the attorney did not inform the mother and daughter of the desirability of seeking the advice of independent legal counsel before signing the agreement.

Make the Connection

Paragraph (b)(1) of Rule 1.7 provides that, despite the existence of a current conflict, representation may be permissible only if the lawyer "reasonably believes" that the lawyer will be able to provide "competent" and "diligent" representation to each client.

"Competent" representation requires that a lawyer employ the legal knowledge, skill, thoroughness and preparation that are reasonably necessary for the representation. Rule 1.1. "Diligent" representation requires that the lawyer act with "reasonable diligence and promptness in representing a client." Rule 1.3.

Sanford v. Commonwealth of Virginia

687 F.Supp.2d 591 (E.D. Va. 2009)

ROBERT E. PAYNE, SENIOR DISTRICT JUDGE.

[Plaintiff's decedent, John Sanford, had been admitted to a Virginia-run hospital for the removal of his kidney. Sanford was mentally and physically disabled due to a neurological condition. His head and body shook almost continuously; he was able to walk only with the assistance of a walker, and he wore leg braces from knee to foot. Two days after his surgery, Sanford's brother found Sanford naked, delirious, and hallucinating in the hallway of the hospital, struggling to hold himself upright without the assistance of his walker. The medical staff were aware of Sanford's condition and summoned police officers (the "VCUPD") to restrain him. The next day, other family members found Sanford partially disrobed on the floor in his hospital room cleaning imaginary blood. Sanford became delirious again the following day, allegedly as a result of medications he had been prescribed by the hospital's staff. The nurses summoned the VCUPD, who allegedly seized Sanford, wrestled him to the ground, handcuffed him and held him "prone." Sanford remained in this position for approximately thirty minutes, during which time he was injected with Haldol, a sedative. When the VCUPD finally turned Sanford over, they discovered that he was dead.

> **Food for Thought**
>
> Assuming there is a conflict of interest on the part of defense counsel, why should the plaintiffs be able to complain about it? Wouldn't the conflict of interest actually help them? If the plaintiffs are just trying to make the defendants' lives miserable by making them find their own counsel, should that motivation be considered by the court in determining whether to disqualify the defense lawyers?

Sanford's family sued the VCUPD and the hospital staff (the "MCV defendants") on claims including gross negligence, battery, false imprisonment, intentional infliction of emotional distress and a violation of Sanford's rights under the Fourth and Fourteenth Amendments. The same lawyer represented all of the VCUPD defendants. Another lawyer represented the MCV defendants. The plaintiffs have moved to disqualify the lawyers for operating under a conflict of interest.]

DISCUSSION

[*Ed.'s Note*—The court recites Virginia State Bar Rule of Professional Conduct 1.7, which tracks the Delaware Rule.]

* * *

A. VCUPD Officer Defendants

First, there is, according to the Plaintiffs, the conflict between Colonel Fuller and all of the subordinate VCU police officers respecting the adequacy of training for dealing with hospital patients. * * * In sum, it is the position of Colonel Fuller that his officers are adequately trained to deal with hospital patients because their general training about how to deal with handcuffed persons includes instruction to check for signs of physical distress and for difficulty in breathing.

The testimony of Officer LaVigne is that subordinate officers received no training for handling patients in a health care setting and Officer Carter testifies that she is not trained to look for signs of distress or difficulty in breathing. * * *

Thus, on this topic, the adequacy of training, there appears to be a substantial discrepancy in the testimony of the VCUPD officer defendants and an incompatibility in positions that the VCUPD officer defendants occupy vis-à-vis Colonel Fuller. The possibilities for settlement also appear to be substantially different on the claims and liabilities in question as to Colonel Fuller, on one hand, and the VCUPD officer defendants, on the other.

It is also asserted by the Plaintiffs that there is conflict between the VCUPD officer defendants who initially responded to the summons to Sanford's room and effectuated the seizure by handcuffing Sanford and keeping him facedown on the floor, and those officers who arrived on the scene later. This conflict arises out of the undisputed evidence that the accepted protocol for the VCUPD in situations such as the one here at issue is that the first responding officer provides the lead and that subsequently responding officers follow the instructions of the lead officer. * * *

[The subsequently responding officers] would be able to assert that their conduct was governed by protocol, which had been set in place when they arrived upon the scene and by the instructions of [first responder] Officer Bailey. Thus, they could argue that the reasonableness of their conduct, which lies at the heart of their ability to defend a number of the claims against them, must be assessed differently than the conduct of Officer Bailey who was the one who first laid hands on Sanford and who also dictated that Sanford be kept in handcuffs and be kept facedown in the prone position. The positional incompatibility in presenting a defense is obvious. * * *

* * *

B. VCU Medical Defendants

The motion asserts several conflicts among the VCU medical defendants. First, Dr. Meguid diagnosed Sanford's condition as opium withdrawal rather than delirium, a condition which Dr. Meguid stated might be present in Sanford only in its waning stages. Several defense experts (a pharmacist, a toxicologist, and a psychiatrist) have expressed the opinion that Sanford's symptoms were consistent with delirium, not with opium withdrawal. The Plaintiffs intend to offer evidence that Dr. Meguid's diagnosis was erroneous and that, as a consequence of the misdiagnosis, certain of Sanford's medications were resumed without the necessary, precedent tests. As a consequence, it will be said by other expert witnesses that certain drug levels reached toxic levels and created episodes of delirium which led to the decision to restrain Sanford and hence to his death.

In other words, the expert opinions of the defense experts will support the conclusion that Dr. Meguid misdiagnosed Sanford. There is a medical malpractice claim against Dr. Meguid and an attorney representing Dr. Meguid would certainly want to present expert testimony that Dr. Meguid's diagnosis was correct. However, there appears to be no such evidence offered on his behalf and, indeed, the defense experts render opinions which make it quite difficult for Dr. Meguid to assert that his diagnosis was a correct one. On this record, there is a significant incompatibility in position between Dr. Meguid and the other medical professionals on this issue. * * *

Second, it is undisputed that Dr. Meguid made a medical note that Haldol should be avoided for Sanford, if possible. Further, Dr. Meguid recognized that Haldol might not be appropriate for a patient with Biemond's Syndrome and that the drug could have adverse cardiac side effects. Dr. Maiberger, however, prescribed Haldol and Nurse Brown or Nurse Ferguson administered Haldol. Neither of the three were aware of Dr. Meguid's cautions respecting the use of Haldol for Sanford. At oral argument on the disqualification motion, counsel for the medical defendants asserted that it was the position of Dr. Maiberger and Nurse Brown that they had no reason to be aware of Dr. Meguid's caution because Dr. Meguid had not entered his note in the computerized system which, in turn, would have alerted the nurses to Dr. Meguid's cautionary advice. That failure is a further indictment of Dr. Meguid.

Quite clearly there are conflicting positions presented by the testimony. Dr. Meguid certainly is entitled to present, as part of his defense, that he cautioned against the use of Haldol. At the same time, Dr. Maiberger and the nurses intend to say that they had no reason to know of this caution because Dr. Meguid did not act in accord with established procedure at the Hospital to take the necessary actions to alert them to his caution. Counsel for Dr. Maiberger and the nurses, therefore, would certainly want to point the finger of fault toward Dr. Meguid as part of the means of defending Dr. Maiberger and the nurses.

* * *

C. The Legal Principles

* * * Rule 1.7 of the Virginia Rules of Professional Conduct governs conflicts of interest. * * * Rule 1.7 prohibits a lawyer from representing a client if the representation involves a concurrent conflict of interest, which exists if "there is a significant risk that the representation of one or more clients will be materially limited by the lawyer's responsibilities to another client." The notes to Rule 1.7 make clear that "[l]oyalty and independent judgment are essential elements in the lawyer's relationship to a client." This assessment ought to be undertaken at the beginning of the representation of multiple clients in the same action, but the rules make clear that if the conflict arises after the representation has been undertaken, it is the obligation of the lawyer to withdraw from the representation.

* * * It is also important to note that "[s]imultaneous representation of parties whose interests in litigation may conflict, such as co-plaintiffs or co-defendants, is governed by paragraph (a)(2)" of Rule 1.7. "An impermissible conflict may exist by reason of substantial discrepancy in the parties' testimony, incompatibility in positions in relation to an opposing party or the fact that there are substantially different possibilities of settlement of the claims or liabilities in question."

* * *

It is, of course, important in our system of justice that parties be free to retain counsel of their choice. However, this Court has held that the right of one to retain counsel of his choosing is secondary in importance to the Court's duty to maintain the highest ethical standards of professional conduct to insure and preserve trust in the integrity of the bar. Accordingly, there must be a balance between the client's free choice of counsel and the maintenance of the highest and ethical and professional standards in the legal community. Moreover, the party seeking disqualification has a high standard of proof to show that disqualification is warranted. These principles are well settled.

The rules of professional responsibility make clear that the resolution of conflict of interest questions is principally the responsibility of the lawyer undertaking the litigation. However, those rules also make equally clear that, during litigation, it is appropriate for a court to raise the question in certain circumstances, or the conflict can be raised properly by opposing counsel. Such an objection should be viewed with caution, however, for it can be misused as a technique of harassment. * * *

[T]he asserted conflict must be a real one and not a hypothetical one or a fanciful one. Put another way, disqualification simply cannot be based on mere speculation that a chain of events whose occurrence theoretically could lead counsel to act counter to his client's interests might in fact occur. The applicable rule requires disqualification when the independent professional judgment of the lawyer is likely to be affected. Accordingly, some stronger indicator than judicial intuition or surmise on the part of opposing counsel is necessary to warrant the drastic step of disqualification of counsel.

* * *

It is obvious from reviewing the motions for summary judgment and the expert opinions that counsel, both for the VCUPD officers and the VCU medical defendants, have staked out defensive positions that they think are the best positions for the defense side of the case considered as a whole. It does not appear, however, that counsel have considered, or that they appreciate, how the assertion of those positions could affect the ability of each individual defendant to defend herself or himself by presenting arguments that other defendants are really responsible for Sanford's tragic death even though another defendant may have had some involvement in the circumstances leading up to that death. * * *

* * * [T]he Court must conclude that the conflicts alleged here are real ones that are currently in existence. The conflicts also present very real risks of serious, adverse consequences for the rights of the litigants, mostly the defendants, but also those of the plaintiffs.

Moreover, the nature of the conflicts is such that disqualification is necessary to ensure and preserve trust in the integrity of the bar. The present record contains testimony that tends to inculpate the VCUPD officers in different degrees. That same testimony would permit some VCUPD officer defendants to urge their exoneration by arguing that other VCUPD officer defendants are the cause of Sanford's death. The same is true respecting the VCU medical defendants.

Each defendant is entitled to use the record to exonerate himself or herself even if to do so inculpates another defendant in the same category of defendants (*i.e.*, the same group of clients).

The pleadings, motions and briefs filed thus far afford no indication that such a course in being pursued on behalf of any defendant who, from the record evidence, could take it. * * * The option can be exercised by the asking of questions, or by refraining from asking questions and by asking for instructions. And, most importantly, it can be pursued in closing argument. Of course, a lawyer who represents all defendants is not free to pursue such a course on behalf of any defendant because to do so would be to act adversely to one or more of his other clients. On the other hand, the failure to pursue such a course compromises the interest of any defendant on whose behalf that approach could be taken at trial.

* * *

Counsel for each group of defendants asserts that disqualification is not required because all of the defendants have consented to multiple representations. It is true that Rule 1.7(b) provides that the written consent of the client may allow counsel to represent clients who otherwise would not be representable under Rule 1.7(a)(2). However, there are four conditions to a representation under the consent process: (1) the lawyer must reasonably believe that he will be able to provide competent representation to each affected client; (2) the representation must not be prohibited by law; (3) the representation does not involve the assertion of a claim by one client against another; and (4) the waiver of conflict must be in writing. Rule 1.7(b). The second and third conditions above do not present any problems for the counsel in this case. As will be explained below, the fourth condition, for purposes of the Plaintiff's motion, is not dispositive, and the Court will assume compliance therewith. However, the Court cannot conclude that any lawyer reasonably could believe, as the first condition requires, that he would be able to provide competent and diligent representation to each of the affected clients identified in the foregoing discussion of conflicts.

* * *

For consent to be effective under Rule 1.7(b), it must be meaningful and that, in turn, necessitates that the clients be advised clearly about the conflicts that might very well arise.

The record shows that each of the VCUPD defendants, including the legal guardian for the now incompetent Colonel Fuller, signed documents stating the following:

> I, [Defendant's name], hereby declare that, notwithstanding the existence of any possible conflicts of interest, I knowingly and voluntarily consent to the continued representation by [counsel for the VCUPD Defendants] in this matter. This informed consent is made after consultation with my attorney.

Although counsel for these defendants asserts that the consent was provided knowingly and voluntarily, there is no basis in the record to conclude that the affected defendants had the very real conflicts described to them thoroughly and accurately. And, such a showing is essential especially where, as here, the conflicts are so patent and so numerous and have such potentially adverse consequences for many of the defendant clients. The absence of that showing alone renders the record on consent here insufficient to animate the exception permitted by Rule 1.7(b).

* * *

Setting aside the importance of obtaining properly executed written consent, to focus on the particularities of the conflict waivers is to miss the key point. As provided in Note [19] to Rule 1.7, "when a disinterested lawyer would conclude that the client should not agree to the representation under the circumstances, the lawyer involved cannot properly ask for such agreement or provide representation on the basis of the client's consent." In this case, neither of these counsel were in position to request a waiver because, for the reasons set forth fully above, neither reasonably could have believed that, under the circumstances of this case, they could represent all of the defendants whom they undertook to represent.

CONCLUSION

For the foregoing reasons, the [plaintiff's motion to disqualify] is granted. The question arises whether the grant of this motion to disqualify permits existing counsel to remain in the case for any of the defendants. The approach taken in the Virginia Rules of Professional Responsibility is that "[o]rdinarily, the lawyer would be forced to withdraw from representing all of the clients if the common representation fails." This commentary leaves open the possibility that a lawyer might remain as counsel to one or more defendants even if he is disqualified from representing all defendants. Considering the complex issues presented in this record and the rather significant nature of the conflict, it appears that this case ought to be one in which counsel, having been disqualified, should not further remain in the case. However, it is appropriate to leave that prospect open and to allow for discussion and further assessment of that issue after each defendant is separately advised by counsel not laboring under conflicts.

Take Note

Although paragraph (b)(3) does not preclude a lawyer's representation of opposing parties to a mediation—which does not constitute a "tribunal" within the meaning of Rule 1.0(m)—such representation is nonetheless likely to violate Paragraph (b)(1) of Rule 1.7. However, you should distinguish lawyers representing opposing parties to a mediation from lawyers *acting as mediators*. Lawyer/mediators do not operate under a conflict of interest because there is no attorney-client relationship between the mediator and the mediatee—and the mediator must so inform the parties. *See* Rule 2.4. *See also* N.Y. Ethics Opinion 1178 (2019).

4. "Not Prohibited by Law" Under Rule 1.7(b)(2)

Rule 1.7(b)(2) precludes clients from consenting to conflicted representations that are prohibited under the applicable substantive law. For example, as the Comment to Rule 1.7 notes, some states prohibit a lawyer from representing more than one defendant in a capital case, regardless of whether the defendants would consent to the representation. Because such a representation is barred under state law, it is also non-consentable under Rule 1.7.

5. "Assertion of a Claim by One Client Against Another" Under Rule 1.7(b)(3)

Rule 1.7(b)(3) prevents lawyers from representing opposing parties in the same litigation, regardless of the parties' consent. The Comment to Rule 1.7 explains that the "institutional interest in vigorous development of each client's position" renders consent ineffective when the clients are "aligned directly against each other in the same litigation or other proceeding before a tribunal."

6. "Informed Consent, Confirmed in Writing" Under Rule 1.7(b)(4)

Clients must consent in writing to allow the lawyer to represent multiple clients with adverse interests. But it is important to remember that while informed consent is *necessary*, it is not *sufficient* to permit representation.

[Question 5-7]

A homeowner wanted to buy a piece of property adjacent to his home to avoid future development on the property. The homeowner wanted to use a home equity line of credit for the financing, but he lacked sufficient equity. The seller offered to loan the homeowner the money if the homeowner could get a surety, or cosigner. The homeowner's grandmother agreed to serve as surety, and the seller agreed to the loan with the grandmother as the surety.

The grandmother wanted her attorney, who had worked for the family for many years, to serve as her counsel and the homeowner's counsel in the transaction. The seller uses the same attorney for real estate work and wanted the attorney to also serve as counsel to the seller. This type of representation is permitted in the jurisdiction. Given the circumstances and the familiarity among the parties, the attorney reasonably believed he could adequately represent the interests of each of the three parties. All three parties gave informed consent, in writing, and the attorney began the representation.

Is the attorney subject to discipline?

    (A) No, because the attorney was familiar with and had worked previously with each of the parties.

    (B) No, because this was a consentable conflict of interest, and the parties properly consented.

    (C) Yes, because the attorney, having done real estate work for the seller before, would inherently favor the seller's interest.

    (D) Yes, because an attorney is prohibited from representing three parties with differing interests.

[Question 5-8]

A mother and daughter are partners in a business venture to develop a software program. Their business is not incorporated, but is a general partnership, with a partnership agreement. The daughter is the primary creative contributor and the mother is the primary business contributor. The mother wants to retire, but their partnership agreement is unclear about certain issues related to the financial settlement upon dissolution. State law is also ambiguous on these issues.

The mother and daughter both agreed that they only wanted a fair distribution of the partnership assets, but they needed help determining what was fair under the applicable law. A good friend has been the attorney for the partnership since its inception and had provided individual representation to the mother in her estate planning and the daughter in a personal injury lawsuit.

The mother and daughter asked the attorney whether he could represent them jointly in determining a fair distribution of the partnership assets. The attorney reasonably believed he could provide competent and diligent representation to them jointly. Without discussing the risks of joint representation and the alternative of obtaining separate counsel, the attorney accepted the representation.

Doesn't matter

The attorney's engagement agreement detailed the scope and cost of the representation and confirmed that the parties agreed to be represented jointly. Both the mother and daughter signed the agreement, and the attorney proceeded with the representation.

Is the attorney subject to discipline?

   (A) No, because the attorney has represented the partnership since its inception.

   (B) No, because both the mother and daughter agreed that they wanted a fair distribution, and the attorney reasonably believed he could provide competent and diligent representation to them jointly.

   (C) Yes, because the attorney previously had represented the mother and daughter individually.

   (D) Yes, because the mother and daughter did not provide informed consent to the joint representation.

Comments 18-21 to Rule 1.7(b)(4)

Informed Consent

Informed consent requires that each affected client be aware of the relevant circumstances and of the material and reasonably foreseeable ways that the conflict could have adverse effects on the interests of that client. * * * The information required depends on the nature of the conflict and the nature of the risks involved. When representation of multiple clients in a single matter is undertaken, the information must include the implications of the common representation, including possible effects on loyalty, confidentiality and the attorney-client privilege and the advantages and risks involved. * * *

Under some circumstances it may be impossible to make the disclosure necessary to obtain consent. For example, when the lawyer represents different clients in related matters and one of the clients refuses to consent to the disclosure necessary to permit the other client to make an informed decision, the lawyer cannot properly ask the latter to consent. In some cases the alternative to common representation can be that each party may have to obtain separate representation with the possibility of incurring additional costs. These costs, along with the benefits of securing separate representation, are factors that may be considered by the affected client in determining whether common representation is in the client's interests.

Consent Confirmed in Writing

Paragraph (b) requires the lawyer to obtain the informed consent of the client, confirmed in writing. * * * The requirement of a writing does not supplant the need in most cases for the lawyer to talk with the client, to explain the risks and advantages, if any, of representation burdened with a conflict of interest, as well as reasonably available alternatives, and to afford the client a reasonable opportunity to consider the risks and alternatives and to raise questions and concerns. Rather, the writing is required in order to impress upon clients the seriousness of the decision the client is being asked to make and to avoid disputes or ambiguities that might later occur in the absence of a writing.

Revoking Consent

A client who has given consent to a conflict may revoke the consent and, like any other client, may terminate the lawyer's representation at any time. Whether revoking consent to the client's own representation precludes the lawyer from continuing to represent other clients depends on the circumstances, including the nature of the conflict, whether the client revoked consent because of a material change in circumstances, the reasonable expectations of the other client and whether material detriment to the other clients or the lawyer would result.

> ### Global Perspective
>
> U.S. observers may find it puzzling that some of the conflicts of interest provisions in foreign jurisdictions do not contain a consent or waiver provision. Some of these differences may be attributable to the very different contexts in which conflicts of interest provisions appear. In Germany, for example, conflict of interest provisions are found in the criminal code (StGB Sec. 356); a lawyer's violation of these provisions constitutes a criminal violation. Accordingly, in a situation in which a U.S. lawyer might find a Rule 1.7(a) conflict that requires "consent plus" in order to proceed, a German lawyer might conclude there was no "legal" conflict under the German criminal code. The German lawyer, however, might conclude that it would be prudent, from a client-relations or business perspective, to treat the situation as one that involved a "business conflict" and obtain client consent. *See also* Hans-Jürgen Hellwig, *At the Intersection of Legal Ethics and Globalization: International Conflicts of Law in Lawyer Regulation*, 27 Penn St. Int'l L. Rev. 395 (2008).

Hear from the Authors

To hear more from the authors on informed consent, click here.

7. Waiving Future Conflicts Under Rule 1.7(b)

[Question 5-9]

An attorney represented a first-time entrepreneur in lease negotiations with a local university for lab space. The attorney and the entrepreneur executed an engagement

agreement in which the entrepreneur agreed to "waive in advance any conflict of interest that might arise in the future."

Last week, the president of the university sought to retain the attorney to defend the university in an action brought by an employee for wrongful termination. The attorney disclosed to the president that he represented the entrepreneur in the lease negotiations and described the general nature of the legal work involved. The president indicated that he saw no problem with the attorney's concurrent representation of the entrepreneur. The attorney then accepted the representation of the university and commenced working on the wrongful termination matter.

Is the attorney subject to discipline?

(A)   No, because clients can waive their right to object to future conflicts of interest.

(B)   No, because the lease negotiations and the wrongful termination action were not substantially related.

(C)   Yes, because clients cannot waive their right to object to future conflicts of interest.

(D)   Yes, because the entrepreneur has not provided informed consent to the representation.

Consent to Future Conflict

Practice Pointer

Lawyers today often limit the scope of the representation specifically for the purpose of avoiding a future conflict of interest. How does limiting the scope decrease the risk of future conflicts of interest? How might a lawyer ensure that an engagement agreement appropriately limits the scope for this purpose? For more on limiting the scope of representation, see Chapter 2, Part V, *supra.*

Whether a lawyer may properly request a client to waive conflicts that might arise in the future is subject to the test of paragraph (b). The effectiveness of such waivers is generally determined by the extent to which the client reasonably understands the material risks that the waiver entails. The more comprehensive the explanation of the types of future representations that might arise and the actual and reasonably foreseeable adverse consequences of those representations, the greater the likelihood that the client will have the requisite understanding. Thus, if the client agrees to consent to a particular type of conflict with which the client is already familiar, then the consent ordinarily will be effective with regard to that type of conflict. If the consent is general and open-ended, then the consent ordinarily will be ineffective, because it is not reasonably likely that the client will have understood the material risks involved. On the other hand, if the client is an experienced user of the legal services involved and is reasonably informed regarding the risk that a conflict may arise, such consent is more likely to be effective, particularly if, *e.g.*, the client is independently represented by other counsel in giving consent and the consent is limited to future conflicts unrelated to the subject of the representation. In any case, advance consent cannot be effective if the circumstances that materialize in the future are such as would make the conflict nonconsentable under paragraph (b).

Sheppard, Mullin, Richter & Hampton, LLP v. J-M Manufacturing Co.

6 Cal. 5th 59 (Cal. 2018)

KRUGER, J.

[The law firm of Sheppard Mullin represented J-M Manufacturing Company (J-M) in a federal qui tam action brought on behalf of a number of public entities, including South Tahoe Public Utility District (South Tahoe). During the same time period, Sheppard Mullin, through a single partner, also represented South Tahoe in certain employment matters. Both J-M and South Tahoe had executed engagement agreements that purported to waive all current and future conflicts of interest, but the agreements did not refer to any particular conflict. In addition, Sheppard Mullin did not tell either client about its representation of the other. South Tahoe discovered the conflict and successfully moved to have the firm disqualified in the qui tam action. A dispute over J-M's $3.8 million in outstanding law firm bills followed, and the dispute was sent to arbitration (in accordance with an arbitration clause in the engagement agreement).

The arbitrators ruled in Sheppard Mullin's favor, noting that "the better practice" would have been for the firm to disclose to and seek consent from J-M to its representation of South Tahoe, but concluding that the violation was not egregious or serious enough to warrant the disgorgement of fees. The superior court confirmed the arbitrator's award. However, the Court of Appeal reversed, concluding that Sheppard Mullin's undisclosed conflict of interest violated the rules of professional conduct, and that this ethical violation rendered the parties' agreement, including the arbitration clause, unenforceable in its entirety. The Court of Appeal further held that the conflict of interest "pervaded the entire relationship" and precluded Sheppard Mullin from receiving any fees.

J-M's conflict waiver, which was very similar to South Tahoe's, read as follows:

"Conflicts with Other Clients. *Sheppard, Mullin, Richter & Hampton LLP has many attorneys and multiple offices. We may currently or in the future represent one or more other clients (including current, former, and future clients) in matters involving [J-M]. We undertake this engagement on the condition that we may represent another client in a matter in which we do not represent [J-M], even if the interests of the other client are adverse to [J-M] (including appearance on behalf of another client adverse to [J-M] in litigation or arbitration) and can also, if necessary, examine or cross-examine [J-M] personnel on behalf of that other client in such proceedings or in other proceedings to which [J-M] is not a party* provided *the other matter is not substantially related to our representation of [J-M] and in the course of representing [J-M] we have not obtained confidential information of [J-M] material to representation of the other client.* By consenting to this arrangement, [J-M] is waiving our obligation of loyalty to it so long as we maintain confidentiality and adhere to the foregoing limitations. *We seek this consent to allow our Firm to meet the needs of existing and future clients, to remain available to those other clients and to render legal services with vigor and competence. Also, if an attorney does not continue an engagement or must withdraw therefrom, the client may incur delay, prejudice or additional cost such as acquainting new counsel with the matter."]*

* * *

I

We granted Sheppard Mullin's petition for review. * * *

III

J-M argues, and the Court of Appeal agreed, that the engagement agreement at issue is unenforceable because it violated rule 3-310(C)(3) of the [California] Rules of Professional Conduct (rule 3-310(C)(3)). That rule provides that an attorney "shall not, without the informed written consent of each client . . . [¶] . . . [¶] . . . [r]epresent a client in a matter and at the same time in a separate matter accept as a client a person or entity whose interest in the first matter is adverse to the client in the first matter. "Simply put," without informed written consent, "an attorney (and his or her firm) cannot simultaneously represent a client in one matter while representing another party suing that same client in another matter." * * * This general prohibition applies even if "the simultaneous representations may have *nothing* in common." * * * " 'Informed written consent' " is defined to mean "written agreement to the representation following written disclosure," and "[d]isclosure" is defined as "informing the client . . . of the relevant circumstances and of the actual and reasonably foreseeable adverse consequences to the client. . . ." (Rules Prof. Conduct, rule 3-310(A)(2), (1).)

Sheppard Mullin does not dispute that its concurrent representation of J-M and South Tahoe came within the scope of rule 3-310(C)(3), but maintains that it obtained J-M's informed consent to that representation by means of the conflict waiver provision of the parties' engagement agreement. We conclude that Sheppard Mullin's concurrent representation of J-M and South Tahoe violated rule 3-310(C)(3) and rendered the engagement agreement between Sheppard Mullin and J-M unenforceable. Our conclusion rests on three subsidiary points: First, at the time Sheppard Mullin agreed to represent J-M in the qui tam action, the law firm also represented a client with conflicting interests, South Tahoe; second, because Sheppard Mullin knew of that conflicting interest and failed to inform J-M of it, J-M's consent was not "informed" within the meaning of the Rules of Professional Conduct; and third, Sheppard Mullin's unconsented-to conflict of interest affected the whole of its engagement agreement with J-M, rendering it unenforceable in its entirety.

* * *

B.

As noted, J-M consented to waive current conflicts, as well as future ones. The waiver thus, by its terms, covers the conflict with South Tahoe. We must therefore consider whether the waiver constituted effective consent to Sheppard Mullin's concurrent representation of adverse interests.

The limitations in rule 3-310(C)(3) serve to enforce "the attorney's duty—and the client's legitimate expectation—of *loyalty*, rather than confidentiality." It is for this reason that the rules encompass simultaneous representation even in unrelated matters where there is no risk that confidential information will be transmitted. The purpose of these rules, we have explained, "is evident, even (or perhaps especially) to the nonattorney. A client who learns that his or her lawyer is also representing a litigation adversary, even with respect to a matter *wholly unrelated* to the one for which counsel was retained, cannot long be expected to sustain the level of confidence and trust in counsel that is one of the foundations of the professional relationship."

Because rule 3-310(C)(3) embodies a core aspect of the duty of loyalty, the disclosure required for informed consent to dual representation must also be measured by a standard of loyalty. To be informed, the client's consent to dual representation must be based on disclosure of all material facts the attorney knows and can reveal. An attorney or law firm that knowingly withholds material information about a conflict has not earned the confidence and trust the rule is designed to protect.

Assessed by this standard, the conflicts waiver here was inadequate. By asking J-M to waive current conflicts as well as future ones, Sheppard Mullin did put J-M on notice that a current conflict *might* exist. But by failing to disclose to J-M the fact that a current conflict *actually* existed, the law firm failed to disclose to its client all the "relevant circumstances" within its knowledge relating to its representation of J-M. (Rules Prof. Conduct, rule 3-310(A)(1).)

Sheppard Mullin contends the blanket disclosure and waiver was sufficient in light of J-M's size and sophistication and the participation of J-M's own general counsel in the engagement negotiations. * * *

Whether the client is an individual or a multinational corporation with a large law department, the duty of loyalty demands an attorney or law firm provide the client all material information in the attorney or firm's possession. No matter how large and sophisticated, a prospective client does not have access to a law firm's list of other clients, and cannot check for itself whether the firm represents adverse parties. Nor can it evaluate for itself the risk that it may be deprived, via motion for disqualification, of its counsel of choice, as happened here. In any event, clients should not have to investigate their attorneys. Simply put, withholding available information about a known, existing conflict is not consistent with informed consent.

Because this case concerns the failure to disclose a current conflict, we have no occasion here to decide whether, or under what circumstances, a blanket advance waiver * * * would be permissible. We conclude, rather, that without full disclosure of existing conflicts known to the attorney, the client's consent is not informed for purposes of our ethics rules. Sheppard Mullin failed to make such full disclosure here.

C.

Sheppard Mullin argues that even if it failed to secure adequate consent to the dual representation of J-M in the qui tam action, the ethical violation does not invalidate the entire engagement agreement because the agreement encompassed other matters as well. But as noted, the object of the agreement was representation in the qui tam action. The agreement states that Sheppard Mullin is engaged to represent J-M "in connection with the lawsuit filed by Qui Tam plaintiff John Hendrix." The agreement further states that the representation will terminate upon completion of that action and any related proceedings. The only reference to work outside that scope is a general statement that, except as the parties otherwise agree, the agreement's terms will also apply to "other engagements for [J-M] that [Sheppard Mullin] *may undertake.*" (Italics added.) And while the agreement states that certain provisions on responding to possible third party document requests survive termination of the representation, those provisions were not independent of the qui tam representation but dependent on it. They do not change the fact that the agreement was one for representation in the qui tam action, a representation that violated rule 3-310(C)(3).

As explained* * * [a] violation of a Rule of Professional Conduct in the formation of a contract can render the contract unenforceable as against public policy. That is what happened here when Sheppard Mullin agreed to represent J-M in the qui tam action, while also representing South Tahoe on other matters, without obtaining J-M's informed consent. It is true that Sheppard Mullin rendered J-M substantial legal services pursuant to the agreement, and J-M has not endeavored to show that it suffered damages as a result of the law firm's conflict of interest. But the fact remains that the agreement itself is contrary to the public policy of the state. The transaction was entered under terms that undermined an ethical rule designed for the protection of the client as well as for the preservation of public confidence in the legal profession. The contract is for that reason unenforceable.

IV

Because Sheppard Mullin's ethical breach renders the engagement agreement unenforceable in its entirety * * * Sheppard Mullin is not entitled to the benefit of the arbitrators' decision awarding it unpaid contractual fees. * * *

Trust and confidence are central to the attorney-client relationship, and maintaining them requires an ethical attorney to display all possible candor in his or her disclosure of circumstances that may affect the client's interests. Sheppard Mullin's failure to exhibit the necessary candor in this case has rendered its contract with J-M unenforceable and has thus disentitled it to the benefit of the unpaid contract fees awarded by the arbitrators in this case. Whether Sheppard Mullin is nevertheless entitled to a measure of compensation for its work is, along with the other unresolved noncontract issues raised by the pleadings, a matter for the trial court to consider in the first instance.

V

We affirm the judgment of the Court of Appeal insofar as it reversed the superior court's judgment entered on the arbitration award. We reverse the judgment of the Court of Appeal insofar as it ordered disgorgement of all fees collected, and remand for further proceedings consistent with our opinion.

CHIN, J.

I agree with the majority that the conflict rendered the engagement agreement, including its arbitration clause, unenforceable as against public policy. However, I disagree with the majority that, notwithstanding the conflict and the agreement's invalidity, Sheppard Mullin may be entitled to recover from J-M in quantum meruit for the value of the legal services it provided in the qui tam action. I would instead hold that Sheppard Mullin's failure to disclose its known conflict of interest precludes it from any recovery. I dissent insofar as the majority holds otherwise.

C. Additional Applications of Rule 1.7

1. Positional Conflicts

Positional conflicts may arise where a lawyer advocates contrary positions with respect to the same substantive legal issue on behalf of separate clients. For example, a lawyer who represents clients seeking to enforce an environmental rule against a manufacturer may have a positional conflict if the lawyer represents a different manufacturer who will be subject to the legal ruling the lawyer seeks.

Practice Pointer

If the rule is that positional conflicts are disabling, consider the difficulty of running conflicts checks, especially in a big firm. Typically, if a new client comes to the firm with a matter, a conflicts check is run to determine if anyone in the firm has represented the new client's adversary. But this would not work with a positional conflict, because it is not the adversary that is the problem. Rather, it is the fact that the firm represents current clients in a similar position as the adversary. What might be required is some kind of checklist of interests in the existing client database—*e.g.*, pro-or-anti NAFTA? pro-or-anti environmental protection? Is this a practical solution, given the nature of law practice today?

For More Information

Comment (f) to § 128 of the Restatement provides further tools and illustrations helpful to the positional conflicts analysis:

* * * Factors relevant in determining the risk of such an effect include whether the issue is before a trial court or an appellate court; whether the issue is substantive or procedural; the temporal relationship between the matters; the practical significance of the issue to the immediate and long-run interests of the clients involved; and the clients' reasonable expectations in retaining the lawyer. If a conflict of interest exists, absent informed consent of the affected clients under § 122, the lawyer must withdraw from one or both of the matters. Informed client consent is provided for in § 122. On circumstances in which informed client consent would not allow the lawyer to proceed with representation of both clients, *see* § 122(2)(c) and Comment g(iv) thereto.

Illustrations:

5. Lawyer represents two clients in damage actions pending in different United States District Courts. In one case, representing the plaintiff, Lawyer will attempt to introduce certain evidence at trial and argue there for its admissibility. In the other case, representing a defendant, Lawyer will object to an anticipated attempt by the plaintiff to introduce similar evidence. Even if there is some possibility that one court's ruling might be published and cited as authority in the other proceeding, Lawyer may proceed with both representations without obtaining the consent of the clients involved.

6. The same facts as in Illustration 5, except that the cases have proceeded to the point where certiorari has been granted in each by the United States Supreme Court to consider the common evidentiary question. Any position that Lawyer would assert on behalf of either client on the legal issue common to each case would have a material and adverse impact on the interests of the other client. Thus, a conflict of interest is presented. Even the informed consent of both Client A and Client B would be insufficient to permit Lawyer to represent each before the Supreme Court.

2. Aggregate Settlements

[Question 5-10]

An attorney represented six homeowners, who live in the same housing development, against their developer. The suit arose after the developer built a road adjacent to the homeowners' property line. As a result of the new road, each of the six homeowners lost a strip of their property. The developer compensated them for the land but has refused to pay the cost of replacing the grass or landscaping on these strips of property, leaving the property unimproved.

After the suit was filed, the developer called the attorney and offered $12,000 to settle with all six homeowners. Because the homeowners each owned different amounts of land, the attorney determined that it was fair to divide the total settlement based on the percentage of the total impacted land owned by the homeowners, respectively.

The attorney prepared agreements for each of the six homeowners, detailing how much money they would receive of the total settlement amount. The attorney then met individually with each of them and explained the settlement, including how much each homeowner would receive. All of the homeowners agreed to the settlement and signed the agreements.

Was the attorney's conduct proper?

 No, because lawyers may not represent all parties on one side of an action.

 No, because the attorney shared with the homeowners the settlement amounts of the other homeowners.

 Yes, because each homeowner was informed of the amounts received by all of the other homeowners and agreed to the settlement allocation in writing.

 Yes, because an attorney must seek to effectuate settlements and avoid litigation.

Rule 1.8(g)

A lawyer who represents two or more clients shall not participate in making an aggregate settlement of the claims of or against the clients * * * unless each client gives informed consent, in a writing signed by the client. The lawyer's disclosure shall include the existence and nature of all the claims or pleas involved and of the participation of each person in the settlement.

Comment 13 to Rule 1.8(g)

Differences in willingness to make or accept an offer of settlement are among the risks of common representation of multiple clients by a single lawyer. Under Rule 1.7, this is one of the risks that should be discussed before undertaking the representation, as part of the process of obtaining the clients' informed consent. In addition, Rule 1.2(a) protects each client's right to have the final say in deciding whether to accept or reject an offer of settlement. The rule stated in this paragraph is a corollary of both of these Rules and provides that, before any settlement offer or plea bargain is made or accepted on behalf of multiple clients, the lawyer must inform each of them about all the material terms of the settlement, including what the other clients will receive or pay if the settlement or plea offer is accepted. * * * Lawyers representing a class of plaintiffs or defendants, or those proceeding derivatively, may not have a full client-lawyer relationship with each member of the class; nevertheless, such lawyers must comply with applicable rules regulating notification of class members and other procedural requirements designed to ensure adequate protection of the entire class.

III. Conflicts Between Client's Interests and Personal or Financial Interests of the Lawyer

A. Transactions Between Lawyer and Client

[Question 5-11]

An attorney's oldest daughter is to begin college this fall at a prestigious university. The attorney did not have enough money to pay the tuition but did not want the daughter to take out student loans. After sharing this information with a long-time client who owns a successful petroleum engineering firm, the client offered to loan the attorney the money for the tuition with no interest, if the attorney would agree to recommend that the daughter come to work for the client after graduation. The attorney was hesitant but ultimately agreed, without discussing the arrangement with his daughter.

The next day, the attorney prepared a promissory note reflecting what the client and the attorney agreed to and mailed a copy to the client to sign. The client signed the note and returned it to the attorney, who also signed the note and sent the client a fully executed copy.

Was the attorney's conduct proper?

(A) No, because this is an improper business transaction with a client.

(B) No, because the attorney should never have made such an agreement without the daughter's input.

(C) Yes, because the loan was the client's idea, not the attorney's.

(D) Yes, because the terms of the loan were fair and reasonable to the client.

Rule 1.8—Conflict of Interest: Business Transactions Between Client and Lawyer

(a) A lawyer shall not enter into a business transaction with a client or knowingly acquire an ownership, possessory, security or other pecuniary interest adverse to a client unless:

> **Make the Connection**
>
> To review conflicts that arise when clients pay fees with equity, *see* Chapter 3, Part III, *supra*. Conflicts that may arise with regard to contingent fees are also discussed in Chapter 3, Part III. *supra*. To review conflicts regarding prospective limits on malpractice liability, *see* Chapter 2, Part V, *supra*.

(1) the transaction and terms on which the lawyer acquires the interest are fair and reasonable to the client and are fully disclosed and transmitted in writing to the client in a manner that can be reasonably understood by the client;

(2) the client is advised in writing of the desirability of seeking and is given a reasonable opportunity to seek the advice of independent legal counsel on the transaction; and

(3)   the client gives informed consent, in a writing signed by the client, to the essential terms of the transaction and the lawyer's role in the transaction, including whether the lawyer is representing the client in the transaction.

* * *

Comment 1 to Rule 1.8

A lawyer's legal skill and training, together with the relationship of trust and confidence between lawyer and client, create the possibility of overreaching when the lawyer participates in a business, property or financial transaction with a client, for example, a loan or sales transaction or a lawyer investment on behalf of a client. The requirements of paragraph (a) must be met even when the transaction is not closely related to the subject matter of the representation, as when a lawyer drafting a will for a client learns that the client needs money for unrelated expenses and offers to make a loan to the client. The Rule applies to lawyers engaged in the sale of goods or services related to the practice of law, for example, the sale of title insurance or investment services to existing clients of the lawyer's legal practice. * * * [T]he Rule does not apply to standard commercial transactions between the lawyer and the client for products or services that the client generally markets to others, for example, banking or brokerage services, medical services, products manufactured or distributed by the client, and utilities' services. In such transactions, the lawyer has no advantage in dealing with the client, and the restrictions in paragraph (a) are unnecessary and impracticable.

* * *

B.   Literary and Media Rights Issues

[Question 5-12]

A woman was charged with the first-degree murder of her spouse. The court appointed a public defender to represent the woman, but she and her family wanted a lawyer in private practice. The family found an attorney who was willing to accept the representation, primarily because of the potential media exposure for his practice, as the murder had received extensive local and national attention.

Neither the woman nor her family, however, had the resources to pay the attorney. As a result, the woman offered to give the attorney ten percent of the proceeds from any motion picture made about the case. The attorney prepared an engagement agreement, detailing the arrangement, including how any expenses would be paid. The attorney presented the engagement agreement to the woman and advised her of the desirability of seeking the advice of inde-

Food for Thought

Assume a lawyer is paid through an assignment of media rights. What decisions might that lawyer make to benefit himself that would not be in the client's best interest? Wouldn't the ability of a client to assign media rights actually benefit the client—by allowing him to hire an attorney that he could not otherwise afford?

pendent legal counsel before signing. After consulting with another lawyer, the woman signed the agreement, and the attorney proceeded with the representation.

Is the attorney subject to discipline?

(A) No, because the attorney advised the woman of the desirability of seeking the advice of independent legal counsel before signing the engagement agreement.

(B) No, because the attorney was permitted to enter a business transaction with the woman.

(C) Yes, because the attorney primarily accepted the representation of the woman for the potential media exposure for his practice.

(D) Yes, because this fee agreement gave the attorney media rights to the woman's story while the case was still pending.

Rule 1.8—Conflict of Interest: Business Transactions Between Client and Lawyer

(d) Prior to the conclusion of representation of a client, a lawyer shall not make or negotiate an agreement giving the lawyer literary or media rights to a portrayal or account based in substantial part on information relating to the representation.

Beets v. Collins

986 F.2d 1478 (5th Cir. 1993)

EDITH H. JONES, CIRCUIT JUDGE:

* * *

I

BACKGROUND

* * * Beets's fifth husband, Jimmy Don, disappeared on August 6, 1983. His fishing boat was found drifting on Lake Athens, Texas, suggesting that he had drowned. More than a year later, a trailer home that was Jimmy Don's separate property before his death was destroyed by fire. When the insurer refused Beets's claim for the loss, Beets sought the counsel of E. Ray Andrews, an attorney who had represented Beets since 1981 or '82. During their discussions, they also decided that Andrews would pursue any insurance or pension benefits to which Beets might be entitled.

Beets and Andrews entered into a contingent fee arrangement whereby Andrews would pursue collection on both Beets's fire insurance claim and any death benefits to which she might have been entitled in connection with Jimmy Don's disappearance. Andrews determined that certain benefits existed and so informed Beets. * * * Jimmy Don's former employer, the City of Dallas Fire Department, agreed to provide benefits to Beets.

Before Beets received the first check from the Fire Department, she was arrested on June 8, 1985, and was charged with the capital murder of Jimmy Don. Beets was charged with shooting and killing her husband and, with the assistance of her son, Robbie Branson, burying him under a planter in her front yard. Beets allegedly disposed of her fourth husband, Doyle Wayne Barker, in a similar fashion. Barker's body was found buried in the back yard underneath a patio upon which a storage shed had been erected. Beets had also shot another former husband, Bill Lane, although he survived.

Andrews agreed to extend his representation of Beets to the capital murder charge. The case generated significant media interest on both a local and national level. On October 8, just after Beets's trial commenced, she signed a contract transferring all literary and media rights in her case to Andrews's son, E. Ray Andrews, Jr. The trial judge never became aware of the media rights contract during trial, although he did learn of it three months later during a hearing on Beets's motion to appoint counsel for appeal when the prosecutor asked Beets if she had signed over the book rights to her case to Andrews's son. The judge did not inquire whether Beets was willing to waive her Sixth Amendment right to conflict-free counsel.

Beets was convicted of murder for remuneration and the promise of remuneration on the theory that she killed her husband in order to obtain his insurance and pension benefits.

* * *

II

DISCUSSION

* * *

C. Media Rights Conflict

The contract granting E. Ray Andrews, Jr., full literary and motion picture rights to Beets's story represented full satisfaction of the fee arrangement between Beets and Andrews. * * *

Courts, scholars, and the bar have not hesitated to denounce these types of fee arrangements. Virtually every court to consider a conflict of interest arising from a media rights contract executed in favor of trial counsel has unequivocally condemned the practice. * * * Particularly in a capital murder case, it is odious to think that counsel hopes to gain his fee by marketing the tragedy and misery of his client, her family and, worst, the victim and his loved ones.

Notwithstanding Andrews's apparent breach of his ethical obligations, this court sits not to discipline counsel, but to determine whether Andrews's ethical breach violated Beets's Sixth Amendment rights. The state has the duty to punish an attorney for unethical behavior. (Why the State Bar of Texas did not discipline Andrews is not revealed in the record.) This court will not succumb to Beets's invitation to punish her attorney by granting relief to his client.

The media rights contract posed a serious potential conflict of interest, but Beets failed to show how it ripened into an actual conflict of interest. The media rights contract was almost surely unethical, but on the facts before us, it did not by itself create an actual conflict or adversely affect Andrews's performance.

* * *

C.   Client-Lawyer Sexual Relationships

[Question 5-13]

An associate at a large law firm is working on a transaction for a corporation. The associate works regularly with another lawyer, the corporation's in-house general counsel who is supervising the matter. Their working relationship grew into a close personal and eventually a sexual relationship. Before the sexual aspect of their relationship began, however, the associate stopped working on the matter and transferred it to another lawyer in the firm.

Is the associate subject to discipline?

   (A)   No, because the corporation's general counsel was also a lawyer.

   (B)   No, because the associate stopped representing the corporation before the sexual aspect of his relationship with the corporation's general counsel began.

   (C)   Yes, because the associate transferred the matter to another lawyer in the firm.

   (D)   Yes, because the associate had a close personal relationship with the corporation's general counsel while representing the corporation.

Rule 1.8(j)

A lawyer shall not have sexual relations with a client unless a consensual sexual relationship existed between them when the client-lawyer relationship commenced.

Comment 17 to Rule 1.8(j)

The relationship between lawyer and client is a fiduciary one in which the lawyer occupies the highest position of trust and confidence. The relationship is almost always unequal; thus, a sexual relationship between lawyer and client can involve unfair exploitation of the lawyer's fiduciary role, in violation of the lawyer's basic ethical obligation not to use the trust of the client to the client's disadvantage. In addition, such a relationship presents a significant danger that, because of the lawyer's emotional involvement, the lawyer will be unable to represent the client without impairment of the exercise of independent professional judgment. Moreover, a blurred line between the professional and personal relationships may make it difficult to predict to what extent client confidences will be protected by the attorney-client evidentiary privilege, since client confidences are protected by privilege only when they are imparted in the context of the client-lawyer relationship. Because of the significant danger of harm to client interests and because the client's own emotional involvement renders it unlikely that the client could give adequate informed consent, this Rule prohibits the lawyer from having sexual relations with a client regardless of whether the relationship is consensual and regardless of the absence of prejudice to the client.

* * *

When the client is an organization, paragraph (j) of this Rule prohibits a lawyer for the organization (whether inside counsel or outside counsel) from having a sexual relationship with a constituent of the organization who supervises, directs or regularly consults with that lawyer concerning the organization's legal matters.

IV. Lawyer Advocate as Witness

[Question 5-14]

An attorney spent more than a year representing a company that was being sold. The attorney and the company's accountant reviewed and analyzed the company's value to establish a proper valuation for the sale.

There are several accepted valuation standards. Throughout the negotiations, the attorney and the accountant agreed on the proper valuation standard, and the deal closed based on a valuation standard that was favorable to the company.

Several months after the closing, the buyer brought an action against the company for fraud, alleging that the company used an improper valuation standard which artificially inflated the value of its assets. The company wanted the attorney to defend it in the action at trial. While the attorney knew he might be called as a witness in the action, he nevertheless accepted the representation, after obtaining the company's written informed consent.

Is the attorney subject to discipline?

(A) **No, because the attorney obtained the company's written informed consent to the representation.**

(B) **No, because the accountant can testify about the same information as the attorney.**

(C) **Yes, because the attorney violated duties owed to the company in closing on a possibly fraudulent deal.**

(D) **Yes, because the attorney might be called as a witness in the action.**

Rule 3.7—Lawyer As Witness

(a)   A lawyer shall not act as advocate at a trial in which the lawyer is likely to be a necessary witness unless:

(1) the testimony relates to an uncontested issue;

(2) the testimony relates to the nature and value of legal services rendered in the case; or

(3) disqualification of the lawyer would work substantial hardship on the client.

(b) A lawyer may act as advocate in a trial in which another lawyer in the lawyer's firm is likely to be called as a witness unless precluded from doing so by Rule 1.7 or Rule 1.9.

Comments 1-7 to Rule 3.7

Combining the roles of advocate and witness can prejudice the tribunal and the opposing party and can also involve a conflict of interest between the lawyer and client.

Advocate-Witness Rule

The tribunal has proper objection when the trier of fact may be confused or misled by a lawyer serving as both advocate and witness. The opposing party has proper objection where the combination of roles may prejudice that party's rights in the litigation. A witness is required to testify on the basis of personal knowledge, while an advocate is expected to explain and comment on evidence given by others. It may not be clear whether a statement by an advocate-witness should be taken as proof or as an analysis of the proof.

To protect the tribunal, paragraph (a) prohibits a lawyer from simultaneously serving as advocate and necessary witness except in those circumstances specified in paragraphs (a)(1) through (a)(3).

* * *

Because the tribunal is not likely to be misled when a lawyer acts as advocate in a trial in which another lawyer in the lawyer's firm will testify as a necessary witness, paragraph (b) permits the lawyer to do so except in situations involving a conflict of interest.

Conflict of Interest

In determining if it is permissible to act as advocate in a trial in which the lawyer will be a necessary witness, the lawyer must also consider that the dual role may give rise to a conflict of interest that will require compliance with Rules 1.7 or 1.9. For example, if there is likely to be substantial conflict between the testimony of the client and that of the lawyer, the representation involves a conflict of interest that requires compliance with Rule 1.7. * * * Determining whether or not such a conflict exists is primarily the responsibility of the lawyer involved. If there is a conflict of interest, the lawyer must secure the client's informed consent, confirmed in writing. In some cases, the lawyer will be precluded from seeking the client's consent. * * *

Paragraph (b) provides that a lawyer is not disqualified from serving as an advocate because a lawyer with whom the lawyer is associated in a firm is precluded from doing so by paragraph (a). If, however, the testifying lawyer would also be disqualified by Rule 1.7 or Rule 1.9 from representing the client in the matter, other lawyers in the firm will be precluded from representing the client by Rule 1.10 unless the client gives informed consent under the conditions stated in Rule 1.7.

V. Representation Adverse to a Former Client

A. The General Rules

[Question 5-15]

An attorney spent nearly a decade working in house for a large amusement park. The attorney did all of the human resources legal work for the amusement park. This included oversight and review of all hiring policies, including references and background checks, employment contracts, and benefits.

Over a year ago, the attorney left the amusement park and joined a multi-national law firm as a senior associate in the employment law practice group. Because of a decline in the firm's employment law workload, the attorney began working with other practice groups.

Recently, the attorney has been working with the litigation practice group on a nuisance action brought by an adjacent property owner against the amusement park for alleged excessive noise and lighting. The law firm represented the adjacent property owner in the action. Without obtaining the amusement park's informed consent, the attorney assisted with the representation of the adjacent proper owner.

Is the attorney subject to discipline?

(A) No, because the attorney's previous work for the amusement park was not substantially related to the nuisance action.

(B) No, because the attorney had not done any work for the amusement park in over a year.

(C) Yes, because the attorney failed to obtain informed consent from the amusement park to the representation of the adjacent property owner.

(D) Yes, because the attorney breached his duty of loyalty to the amusement park.

[Question 5-16]

An attorney spent nearly a decade working in house for a large amusement park. The attorney did all of the human resources legal work for the amusement park. This included oversight and review of all hiring policies, including references and background checks, employment contracts, and benefits.

Last year, the attorney left the amusement park and joined a multi-national law firm as a senior associate in the employment law practice group. Because of a decline in the firm's employment law workload, the attorney began working with other practice groups.

The attorney has been working mostly with the litigation practice group in various capacities. In one matter, the law firm represented a young child and his parents in an action against the amusement park for injuries the child suffered on a water slide. The claim against the amusement park was for the alleged negligent hiring of the water slide operator. Before working on the representation, the attorney fully disclosed the extent of his prior work for the amusement park to the child and his parents, and they each gave their informed consent to his participation in the representation.

Is the attorney subject to discipline?

(A) No, because there was no substantial risk that the attorney has confidential information relevant to the action.

(B) No, because the attorney obtained informed consent from the child and his parents to his participation in the representation.

(C) Yes, because the negligent hiring action was substantially related to work the attorney did for the amusement park.

(D) Yes, because the attorney was prohibited from jointly representing the child and his parents.

Rule 1.9—Duties to Former Clients

(a)   A lawyer who has formerly represented a client in a matter shall not thereafter represent another person in the same or a substantially related matter in which that person's interests are materially adverse to the interests of the former client unless the former client gives informed consent, confirmed in writing.

(b)   A lawyer shall not knowingly represent a person in the same or a substantially related matter in which a firm with which the lawyer formerly was associated had previously represented a client

(1)   whose interests are materially adverse to that person; and

(2)   about whom the lawyer had acquired information protected by Rules 1.6 and 1.9(c) that is material to the matter;

unless the former client gives informed consent, confirmed in writing.

(c)   A lawyer who has formerly represented a client in a matter or whose present or former firm has formerly represented a client in a matter shall not thereafter:

(1)   use information relating to the representation to the disadvantage of the former client except as these Rules would permit or require with respect to a client, or when the information has become generally known; or

(2)   reveal information relating to the representation except as these Rules would permit or require with respect to a client.

Comment 3 to Rule 1.9

* * *

Matters are "substantially related" for purposes of this Rule if they involve the same transaction or legal dispute or if there otherwise is a substantial risk that confidential factual information as would normally have been obtained in the prior representation would materially advance the client's position in the subsequent matter. For example, * * * a lawyer who has previously represented a client in securing environmental permits to build a shopping center would be precluded from representing neighbors seeking to oppose rezoning of the property on the basis of environmental considerations; however, the lawyer would not be precluded, on the grounds of substantial relationship, from defending a tenant of the completed shopping center in resisting eviction for nonpayment of rent. Information that has been disclosed to the public or to other parties adverse to the former client ordinarily will not be disqualifying. Information acquired in a prior representation may have been rendered obsolete by the passage of time, a circumstance that may be relevant in determining whether two representations are substantially related. In the case of an organizational client, general knowledge of the client's policies and practices ordinarily will not preclude a subsequent representation; on the other hand, knowledge of specific facts gained in a prior representation that are relevant to the matter in question ordinarily will preclude such a representation. A former client is not required to reveal the confidential information learned by the lawyer in order to establish a substantial risk that the lawyer has confidential information to use in the subsequent matter. A conclusion about the possession of such information may be based on the nature of the services the lawyer provided the former client and information that would in ordinary practice be learned by a lawyer providing such services.

Westinghouse Elec. Corp. v. Gulf Oil Corp.

588 F.2d 221 (7th Cir. 1978)

SPRECHER, CIRCUIT JUDGE.

In this case we review the propriety of a district court's refusal to grant a motion to disqualify opposing counsel. The issues presented are whether there is a sufficient relationship between matters presented by the pending litigation and matters which the lawyers in question worked on in behalf of the party now seeking disqualification and whether the party seeking disqualification has given legally sufficient consent to the dual representation.

I

This case arises as one aspect of the complex litigation filed by Westinghouse against a number of parties engaged in, or having interests in, the mining of uranium. That suit alleged that increases in the price of uranium, which had encouraged Westinghouse to default on long-term uranium supply contracts, resulted from an international cartel which was alleged to have "fixed and increased the price of uranium to purchasers within the United States; * * *

[and] otherwise eliminated competition among defendants. . . ." The movant here, Gulf Oil Corporation (Gulf), and the respondent, United Nuclear Corporation (UNC) are two of the named defendants in this action. UNC is being represented by the Santa Fe, New Mexico firm of Bigbee, Stephenson, Carpenter & Crout (Bigbee), which had previously performed legal work on behalf of Gulf. Gulf, accordingly, moved to disqualify the Bigbee firm.

The history of the relationship between Gulf and Bigbee had its origin in 1968, when substantial reserves of uranium ore were discovered on tracts of land located near Grants, New Mexico. By 1971 Gulf owned a substantial majority interest in a joint venture which had acquired a portion, designated as the Mt. Taylor properties, of these uranium reserves. After having acquired its interests, Gulf retained the Bigbee firm to represent it on legal matters relating to Gulf's uranium operations in New Mexico. During a five year period of representation from 1971 through 1976, the Bigbee firm through nine of its twelve attorneys performed numerous services for Gulf including the patenting of fifty-nine mining claims, drafting leases required for uranium exploration, representing Gulf in litigation involving title disputes, counseling Gulf in relation to the resolution of certain problems relating to mine waters, and lobbying on behalf of Gulf in front of the New Mexico state legislature on tax and environmental matters. One of Bigbee's name partners, G. Stanley Crout, alone spent over 2,000 hours working on behalf of Gulf.

Gulf argued before the district court that these matters on which Bigbee represented Gulf were substantially related to the matters raised in the Westinghouse litigation. Gulf delineated this relationship by arguing that since the Mt. Taylor properties constituted Gulf's largest supply of uranium and was not currently in production, the reasons for Gulf's failure to produce from this property would be material to the allegation of the Westinghouse suit that Gulf, as well as the other defendants, withheld uranium supplies from the market. Further, Gulf argued, in relation to Bigbee's prior representation of Gulf, Gulf had entrusted Bigbee with confidential information relating to the quantity and quality of uranium reserves in the Mt. Taylor properties. Finally, even though Bigbee represented UNC, a co-defendant in Westinghouse, the position between the two parties was adverse because UNC was attempting to exculpate itself by inculpating Gulf.

The district court accepted Gulf's argument of actual adverseness but nonetheless declined to disqualify the Bigbee firm. The court concluded that Bigbee "certainly did gain knowledge of Gulf's uranium properties during its work" but reasoned that nevertheless there was not a substantial relationship between the matters encompassed by the prior representation and those of the Westinghouse litigation, because the prior representation "focused on real estate transactions connected with Gulf's untapped and undeveloped uranium reserves," whereas the "heart of the complaint" details a price-fixing conspiracy, the evidence of which "will focus on meetings and communications among the alleged co-conspirators, as well as evidence on uranium prices, terms and conditions of sale, and market availability." Thus, the court concluded that there was no substantial relationship between the matters.

II

The district court set out and attempted to apply what is clearly settled as the relevant test in disqualification matters: where an attorney represents a party in a matter in which the adverse party is that attorney's former client, the attorney will be disqualified if the subject matter of the two representations are "substantially related."

* * *

[I]t is clear that the determination of whether there is a substantial relationship turns on the possibility, or appearance thereof, that confidential information might have been given to the attorney in relation to the subsequent matter in which disqualification is sought. The rule thus does not necessarily involve any inquiry into the imponderables involved in the degree of relationship between the two matters but instead involves a realistic appraisal of the possibility that confidences had been disclosed in the one matter which will be harmful to the client in the other. * * * [I]t is not appropriate for the court to inquire into whether actual confidences were disclosed.

The substantial relationship test is not a rule of substantive law but a measure of the quantum of evidence required for proof of the existence of the professional obligation. The evidence need only establish the scope of the legal representation and not the actual receipt of the allegedly relevant confidential information. * * * Doubts as to the existence of an asserted conflict of interest should be resolved in favor of disqualification.

The substantial relationship is determined by asking whether it could reasonably be said that during the former representation that attorney might have acquired information related to the subject matter of the subsequent representation. * * * Essentially then, disqualification questions require three levels of inquiry. Initially, the trial judge must make a factual reconstruction of the scope of the prior legal representation. Second, it must be determined whether it is reasonable to infer that the confidential information allegedly given would have been given to a lawyer representing a client in those matters. Finally, it must be determined whether that information is relevant to the issues raised in the litigation pending against the former client.

Although the district court properly identified this rule of law, it erred in its application. * * * It was established that Bigbee prepared numerous mining patents and handled real estate transactions relating to Gulf uranium properties. Given this reconstruction, the second step in the analysis is to inquire whether it is reasonable to presume that Gulf would have transmitted to the Bigbee firm the class of confidential information allegedly given.

Gulf alleges that three types of confidential information were imparted: 1) that relating to the quantity and quality of uranium reserves at Mt. Taylor, 2) the reasons for delaying the production of those reserves, and 3) information detailing Gulf's relationship with one of the joint owners of the properties. Regardless of the reasonableness of inferring knowledge of the reasons for production delay from the scope of the former representation, we think it is clearly reasonable to presume that the information regarding quantity and quality of uranium was given. Indeed, it seems difficult to believe that Bigbee would not have acquired rather detailed information relating to the quantity and quality of the uranium reserves in the course of its filing of mining patents and resolution of conflicting claims. * * *

Having established the presumption that this information was given, disqualification must result if that information is relevant to the issues in the suit pending against Gulf. Relevance must be gauged by the violations alleged in the complaint and assessment of the evidence useful in establishing those allegations. Judge Marshall did not consider the information allegedly given to Bigbee to be relevant to the cartel litigation. He reasoned that the violation charged was essentially price fixing, not conspiratorial control of uranium production. * * *

The lower court erred, both in identifying the issues raised by an allegation of price fixing, and in assessing the relevance of circumstantial economic evidence to proof of a price fixing conspiracy. The lower court found that the "heart of the (Westinghouse) complaint is directed at alleged price-fixing arrangements." However, an agreement to restrict the production of uranium unquestionably is a price fixing arrangement. * * * Thus, the lower court's view that conspiracy to fix prices and conspiracy to restrict output are distinct offenses is in error. * * *

The lower court also erred in its determination of what evidence was relevant to proof of the alleged price fixing conspiracy. * * * Proof that Gulf was restricting its output of uranium would be highly relevant circumstantial evidence if its competitors were behaving in a parallel fashion. Although evidence of parallel behavior alone may not be sufficient to establish conspiracy, it is given great weight. Furthermore, it has been suggested that proof that an individual competitor has un-utilized productive capacity in excess of demand may in itself suggest collusive behavior within an industry. Information possibly demonstrating that Gulf had uranium reserves available for production which were not brought on to the market would be central to this mode of proof. Thus, even though Westinghouse could prove its claim of price fixing solely through direct evidence of collusive agreements, evidence of Gulf's quantity and quality of uranium reserves could serve as a central element in an alternative method of proof of the Section One Sherman Act violation alleged. * * * Therefore the incentives to disclose and abuse the confidential information are present, and disqualification is required.

Food for Thought

To detect conflicts of interest among new associates or partners, law firms generally conduct thorough conflict screening, soliciting information from new hires regarding past representation. At the same time, these attorneys owe their former clients a duty of confidentiality. How might attorneys resolve this apparent conflict? For an in depth examination, see Paul R. Tremblay, *Migrating Lawyers and the Ethics of Conflict Checking*, 19 Geo. J. Legal Ethics 498 (2006).

Rule 1.6(b)(7) permits lawyers to disclose certain confidential client information to "detect and resolve conflicts of interest arising from the lawyer's change of employment* * *."

In one of the most recent Second Circuit cases, a lawyer upon graduation from law school became associated with a firm representing Cook Industries, which was being sued in connection with a shipment of soybeans from Louisiana to Taiwan which was 254 tons short of the amount stated on the bills of lading and weight certificates. After putting in more than 100 hours over three years on behalf of Cook, the young lawyer left his firm and became associated with another firm where he was assigned to represent the government of India which was suing Cook Industries for delivery of grain of inferior quality and grade and of short weight. Although the two representations involved different shipments at different times to different parties, they shared similar loading and weighing procedures of Cook to which the lawyer had become privy in his first representation. The Second Circuit concluded that "[i]t would be difficult to think of a closer nexus between issues."

Here it could reasonably be said that during the former representation the attorneys might have acquired information related to the subject matter of the subsequent representation, that the former representation was lengthy and pervasive, that the former representation was more than peripheral, and that the relationship between the two matters is sufficiently close to bring the later representation within the prohibition of the canons. Therefore there was clearly a substantial relationship between the two representations.

* * *

REVERSED AND REMANDED.

B. Former and Current Government Lawyers

[Question 5-17]

Several years ago, while working at the state Environmental Protection Agency (EPA), an attorney worked on a lawsuit against several hog farming companies for contaminating groundwater with hog waste. The action resulted in a permanent injunction against the companies. Currently, the attorney is in private practice in a rural area of the same state.

One of the companies hired the attorney to seek an exception to the injunction based on a variation in its waste disposal process. The attorney was certain that he could maintain the confidentiality of all information learned during his work with the EPA.

Is the attorney subject to discipline?

   (A) No, because the attorney was certain that he could maintain the confidentiality of all information learned during his work with the EPA.

   (B) No, because the Rules attempt to encourage private lawyers to enter public practice.

   (C) Yes, because these two actions at issue involve the same matter.

   (D) Yes, because the representation would be adverse to the attorney's former employer, the EPA.

[Question 5-18]

Several years ago, while working at the state Environmental Protection Agency (EPA), an attorney worked on a lawsuit against several hog farming companies for contaminating groundwater with hog waste. The action resulted in a permanent injunction against the companies. Currently, the attorney is in private practice in a rural area of the same state.

One of the companies filed an action seeking an exception to the injunction based on a variation in its waste disposal process. The attorney represented a local environmental group in its opposition to the company's request for an exception. Prior to beginning the representation, the attorney disclosed to the environmental group her previous work on the injunctions at the EPA, but she did not notify the EPA of her representation of the local environmental group.

Is the attorney subject to discipline?

(A) No, because the representation of the local environmental group is not adverse to the attorney's former employer, the EPA.

(B) No, because the attorney disclosed to the environmental group her previous work on the injunctions at the EPA.

(C) Yes, because while at the EPA, the attorney personally and substantially participated in the lawsuit against the hog farmers, which constituted the same matter as the action by the company.

(D) Yes, because once the attorney left the EPA, he was prohibited from working on environmental matters.

Rule 1.11—Special Conflicts of Interest for Former and Current Government Officers and Employees

Former Government Officers and Employees

(a)　Except as law may otherwise expressly permit, a lawyer who has formerly served as a public officer or employee of the government:

(1)　is subject to Rule 1.9(c); and

(2)　shall not otherwise represent a client in connection with a matter in which the lawyer participated personally and substantially as a public officer or employee, unless the appropriate government agency gives its informed consent, confirmed in writing, to the representation.

(b)　When a lawyer is disqualified from representation under paragraph (a), no lawyer in a firm with which that lawyer is associated may knowingly undertake or continue representation in such a matter unless:

(1)　the disqualified lawyer is timely screened from any participation in the matter and is apportioned no part of the fee therefrom; and

(2)   written notice is promptly given to the appropriate government agency to enable it to ascertain compliance with the provisions of this rule.

(c)   Except as law may otherwise expressly permit, a lawyer having information that the lawyer knows is confidential government information about a person acquired when the lawyer was a public officer or employee, may not represent a private client whose interests are adverse to that person in a matter in which the information could be used to the material disadvantage of that person. As used in this Rule, the term "confidential government information" means information that has been obtained under governmental authority and which, at the time this Rule is applied, the government is prohibited by law from disclosing to the public or has a legal privilege not to disclose and which is not otherwise available to the public. A firm with which that lawyer is associated may undertake or continue representation in the matter only if the disqualified lawyer is timely screened from any participation in the matter and is apportioned no part of the fee therefrom.

Current Government Officers and Employees

(d)   Except as law may otherwise expressly permit, a lawyer currently serving as a public officer or employee:

(1)   is subject to Rules 1.7 and 1.9; and

(2)   shall not:

(i)   participate in a matter in which the lawyer participated personally and substantially while in private practice or nongovernmental employment, unless the appropriate government agency gives its informed consent, confirmed in writing; or

(ii)   negotiate for private employment with any person who is involved as a party or as lawyer for a party in a matter in which the lawyer is participating personally and substantially, except that a lawyer serving as a law clerk to a judge, other adjudicative officer or arbitrator may negotiate for private employment as permitted by Rule 1.12(b) and subject to the conditions stated in Rule 1.12(b).

(e)   As used in this Rule, the term "matter" includes:

(1)   any judicial or other proceeding, application, request for a ruling or other determination, contract, claim, controversy, investigation, charge, accusation, arrest or other particular matter involving a specific party or parties, and

(2)   any other matter covered by the conflict of interest rules of the appropriate government agency.

Take Note

The term "matter" for purposes of Rule 1.11 has a different definition and scope from Rule 1.9. Section 133A of the Restatement provides:

> The term "matter," as applied to former government employees, is often defined as a judicial or other proceeding, application, request for a ruling or other determination, contract, claim, controversy, investigation, charge, accusation, arrest, or other particular matter involving a specific party or parties. Drafting of a statute or regulation of general applicability is not included under that definition, nor is work on a case of the same type (but not the same parties) as the one in which the lawyer seeks to be involved. The definition is narrower than that governing former-client conflicts of interest under § 132.

Hear from the Authors

To hear from the authors on matter in Rule 1.9, click here.

Babineaux v. Foster

2005 WL 711604 (E.D. La. 2005)

Africk, J.

Before the Court is a motion to disqualify plaintiff's counsel filed on behalf of defendants, the City of Hammond and Mayor Mayson Foster. Defendants argue that plaintiff's counsel, Douglas D. Brown, should be disqualified because his previous employment as an Assistant City Attorney for the City of Hammond creates a conflict of interest. After considering the law, the arguments of the parties, and the record, defendants' motion to disqualify is DENIED.

BACKGROUND

Plaintiff, Tysonia Babineaux ("Babineaux"), was the City of Hammond's Recreation Director until she was dismissed in July 2003. In connection with her dismissal, she has sued the City of Hammond and Mayor Foster (collectively "the City") for violations of Title VII of the 1964 Civil Rights Act and Louisiana's anti-employment discrimination statute.

Babineaux retained attorney Douglas D. Brown to represent her in her employment discrimination lawsuit. Brown was an Assistant City Attorney for the City of Hammond during the administration of former Mayor Louis J. Tallo which ended on December 31, 2002, when the City's current mayor, defendant Mayson Foster, took office. Since leaving the Hammond City Attorney's office, Brown has entered private practice, representing a number of individuals in lawsuits against the City of Hammond.

The thrust of the City's motion to disqualify centers around an employment grievance filed by Babineaux in 2001, while Brown was an Assistant City Attorney for the City of Hammond. Specifically, the City alleges that (1) the subject matter of Babineaux's 2001 grievance is "similar in all material respects" to plaintiff's current allegations and (2) Brown presumably has knowledge of confidential information relating to the prior complaint. Therefore, the City argues that Louisiana law and the Louisiana Rules of Professional Conduct require Brown to withdraw from the case.

Brown argues, on behalf of the plaintiff, that no conflict of interest exists because all of the events giving rise to the current allegations occurred after he left the Hammond City Attorney's office. Further, Brown claims that the City and the Mayor hold a grudge against him for "making a living suing his former client," and, that the defendants are only bringing this motion to disqualify him because of "secondary motives." Brown also points out that he has offered to amend Paragraph 35 of plaintiff's complaint to limit the temporal reach of the action to events occurring after he left the City Attorney's office. Finally, Brown argues that Babineaux's right to counsel of her choice should outweigh any relationship between this case and Babineaux's 2001 complaint.

LAW AND ANALYSIS

* * *

II. Inapplicability of Louisiana Rule of Professional Conduct 1.9

The City bases much of this motion to disqualify on Louisiana Rule of Professional Conduct 1.9(a). [Identical to Rule 1.9(a), *supra*] * * * Brown responds that Rule 1.9 is inapplicable to this case because he never "represented" the City of Hammond in relation to Babineaux's 2001 grievance.

Brown is correct that subsection (a) of Rule 1.9 is inapplicable to this case, but not because he did not represent the City of Hammond in 2001. Rather, because Brown is a former government attorney, any conflict with his former employer is governed by Rule 1.11. [Identical to Rule 1.11, *supra*].

* * *

Because Rule 1.9 would require disqualification of former non-government attorneys who have formerly represented a client in any "substantially related" matter, regardless of the attorney's involvement, it imposes a higher ethical duty on attorneys exclusively engaged in private practice. On the other hand, Rule 1.11 requires a former government attorney to have "personally and substantially" participated in a previous "matter" which, therefore, requires a higher threshold for disqualification. If parties seeking to disqualify any opposing attorney (even former government counsel) could rely on Rule 1.9(a), it would render 1.11(a) surplusage in adverse representations. In other words, if the City is correct that 1.9(a) applies in cases like this one, no party seeking disqualification of a former government attorney would ever rely on Rule 1.11(a), considering that it provides a former government attorney substantially less chance of disqualification.

* * *

ABA Model Rule 1.11 was intended to "deal with the problems peculiar to government service." ABA Formal Op. 409. Although the Louisiana version of Rule 1.11 does not include official comments, this Court finds the ABA comments to Model Rule 1.11 persuasive. In particular, comment 4 to Rule 1.11 states the reasons behind the more lenient standard for former government lawyers:

> [T]he rules governing lawyers presently or formerly employed by a government agency should not be so restrictive as to inhibit transfer of employment to and from the government. The government has a legitimate need to attract qualified lawyers as well as to maintain high ethical standards. Thus a former government lawyer is disqualified only from particular matters in which the lawyer participated personally and substantially.

Governments need and want good young lawyers to devote some time to public service without depriving themselves of the ability to obtain employment thereafter.

For the above reasons, this Court finds that Rule 1.11, and not Rule 1.9(a) or (c), applies to this case. The City, however, does not solely rely on Rule 1.9 in its motion to disqualify Brown. It also argues that Rule 1.11 requires disqualification because Brown was "personally and arguably substantially involved as counsel for Mayor Tallo" in connection with the 2001 grievance.

III. Applying Rule 1.11

The current version of Louisiana Rule of Professional Conduct 1.11(a) and (c) requires the party moving for disqualification to show either that the former government attorney participated "personally and substantially" in a previous "matter" or that the attorney actually possesses confidential government information.

A. Personal and Substantial Involvement

Neither the Fifth Circuit nor the Louisiana Supreme Court has clearly defined what constitutes "personal and substantial" participation in a previous matter. However, the Fifth Circuit has suggested that if a lawyer is only "tenuously and nominally" connected to the prior case, the personal and substantial requirement is not met. *See Hernandez v. Johnson*, 108 F.3d 554, 560 (5th Cir. 1997). * * * In a Formal Ethics Opinion addressing Rule 1.11's predecessor, DR 9-101(B), the ABA stated that:

> "substantial responsibility" envisages a much closer and more direct relationship than that of a mere perfunctory approval or disapproval of the matter in question. It contemplates a responsibility requiring the official to become personally involved to an important, material degree, in the investigative or deliberative processes regarding the transactions or facts in question.

With these guidelines in mind, the Court turns to the City's arguments.

The City contends that Brown should be disqualified pursuant to Rule 1.11 for two reasons. First, the City argues that Brown was "personally and substantially" involved in Babineaux's 2001 grievance. Second, the City argues that Brown was privy to confidential information in connection with the 2001 grievance. Specifically, the City claims that Mayor Tallo copied Brown on a "confidential" response to Babineaux's complaint. The City also argues that, based on Brown's receipt of this response letter, "it can be presumed that other confidential information transpired during Brown's representation of the City of Hammond."

In *United States v. Clark*, 333 F. Supp. 2d 789, 794 (E.D. Wis. 2004) the district court disqualified a former Assistant United States Attorney from representing a criminal defendant where the attorney (1) was currently defending a client on the same charge that he was previously assigned to prosecute; (2) had received and reviewed investigative reports in connection with the prosecution; and (3) had previously discussed the matter with the head law enforcement agent in charge of the investigation and arrest. In *United States v. Phillip Morris, Inc.*, 312 F. Supp. 2d 27 (D.D.C. 2004) the district court disqualified a former Food and Drug Administration attorney from representing a tobacco company after the government produced timesheets indicating that the attorney had logged 382 hours on substantially-related litigation.

Neither *Clark* nor *Phillip Morris* is analogous to this case. There is no evidence that Brown conducted any investigation in connection with the 2001 complaint. There is also no evidence that Brown spent any substantial amount of time on the matter. While Brown does not dispute receiving the two letters in connection with the 2001 matter, he has submitted a declaration that he does not recall receiving the letters. Further, Brown has stated, under penalty of perjury, that any involvement he did have in the 2001 matter was limited to being copied on those two letters. * * * The City has not submitted any evidence that questions the validity of these statements.

"Professional ethics are self-enforcing, and lawyers are entitled to the presumption of being ethical, until the contrary is shown in specific instances." Therefore, this Court finds that Brown's cursory involvement in the 2001 matter does not rise to the level of "personal and substantial" participation in a matter which would require his disqualification pursuant to Rule 1.11.

B. Possession of Confidential Information

Even if Brown did not "personally and substantially participate" in the 2001 matter, Rule 1.11(c) requires disqualification if he possesses information he knows to be confidential and that information could be used to the material disadvantage of his former client. "Confidential government information" is defined * * * as "information that has been obtained under governmental authority and which, at the time [the] Rule is applied, the government is prohibited by law from disclosing to the public or has a legal privilege not to disclose and which is not otherwise available to the public." La. R. Prof. Cond. 1.11(c). * * *

The City does not contend that Brown possesses any specific confidential information beyond the information contained in the two letters on which Brown was copied. Rather, the City contends that "it can be presumed that other confidential communications transpired" during Brown's 2001 representation of the City of Hammond. Considering all of the evidence submitted, this Court finds that Brown does not possess confidential government information that could be used to the material disadvantage of the City. Consequently, the Court finds that the City has not carried its burden in showing that Brown personally and substantially participated in the 2001 grievance or possesses confidential information, and, therefore, Brown should not be disqualified pursuant to Rule 1.11.

* * *

VI. Lawyers as Third-Party Neutrals

Rule 2.4—Lawyer Serving As Third-Party Neutral

(a)   A lawyer serves as a third-party neutral when the lawyer assists two or more persons who are not clients of the lawyer to reach a resolution of a dispute or other matter that has arisen between them. Service as a third-party neutral may include service as an arbitrator, a mediator or in such other capacity as will enable the lawyer to assist the parties to resolve the matter.

(b)   A lawyer serving as a third-party neutral shall inform unrepresented parties that the lawyer is not representing them. When the lawyer knows or reasonably should know that a party does not understand the lawyer's role in the matter, the lawyer shall explain the difference between the lawyer's role as a third-party neutral and a lawyer's role as one who represents a client.

Comments 3–4 to Rule 2.4

* * *

Make the Connection

How does the concept of "matter" for purposes of Rule 1.11 compare to "matter" as defined in Rule 1.12? *See* below for further discussion on this point.

Unlike nonlawyers who serve as third-party neutrals, lawyers serving in this role may experience unique problems as a result of differences between the role of a third-party neutral and a lawyer's service as a client representative. The potential for confusion is significant when the parties are unrepresented in the process. Thus, paragraph (b) requires a lawyer-neutral to inform unrepresented parties that the lawyer is not representing them. For some parties, particularly parties who frequently use dispute-resolution processes, this information will be sufficient. For others, particularly those who are using the process for the first time, more information will be required. Where appropriate, the lawyer should inform unrepresented parties of the important differences between the lawyer's role as third-party neutral and a lawyer's role as a client representative, including the inapplicability of the attorney-client evidentiary privilege. * * *

A lawyer who serves as a third-party neutral subsequently may be asked to serve as a lawyer representing a client in the same matter. The conflicts of interest that arise for both the individual lawyer and the lawyer's law firm are addressed in Rule 1.12.

Global Perspective

Countries differ from each other with respect to the way they treat, in international trade agreements, lawyers who serve as third-party neutrals. For example, when the United States and the European Union were engaged in the T-TIP trade talks, the Council of Bars and Law Societies of Europe [CCBE] treated the issue of lawyer third party neutrals as an issue that involved legal services regulation. The American Bar Association, on the other hand, responded that it did not have a policy on that issue; implicit in Rule 2.4 is the assumption that a lawyer who serves as a third-party neutral does not represent a client and is not engaged in activities for which a law license is required. For information on legal services international trade discussions, click here.

* * *

Rule 1.12—Former Judge, Arbitrator, Mediator Or Other Third-Party Neutral

(a)   Except as stated in paragraph (d), a lawyer shall not represent anyone in connection with a matter in which the lawyer participated personally and substantially as a judge or other adjudicative officer or law clerk to such a person or as an arbitrator, mediator or other third-party neutral, unless all parties to the proceeding give informed consent, confirmed in writing.

* * *

(c)   If a lawyer is disqualified by paragraph (a), no lawyer in a firm with which that lawyer is associated may knowingly undertake or continue representation in the matter unless:

    (1)   the disqualified lawyer is timely screened from any participation in the matter and is apportioned no part of the fee therefrom; and

    (2)   written notice is promptly given to the parties and any appropriate tribunal to enable them to ascertain compliance with the provisions of this rule.

(d)   An arbitrator selected as a partisan of a party in a multimember arbitration panel is not prohibited from subsequently representing that party.

Comments 2–3 to Rule 1.12

* * *

Like former judges, lawyers who have served as arbitrators, mediators or other third-party neutrals may be asked to represent a client in a matter in which the lawyer participated personally and substantially. This Rule forbids such representation unless all of the parties to the proceedings give their informed consent, confirmed in writing. * * * Other law or codes of ethics governing third-party neutrals may impose more stringent standards of personal or imputed disqualification. See Rule 2.4.

Although lawyers who serve as third-party neutrals do not have information concerning the parties that is protected under Rule 1.6, they typically owe the parties an obligation of confidentiality under law or codes of ethics governing third-party neutrals. Thus, paragraph (c) provides that conflicts of the personally disqualified lawyer will be imputed to other lawyers in a law firm unless the conditions of this paragraph are met.

Take Note

A law firm may be disqualified from representation when an attorney in the firm previously has served as a third-party neutral in the same matter and there is a risk that confidential information has been shared within the firm. *Fields-D'Arpino v. Restaurant Associates, Inc.*, 39 F. Supp. 2d 412 (S.D.N.Y. 1999).

The plaintiff in *Restaurant Associates* filed suit against her employer alleging gender and pregnancy discrimination, and sought an order disqualifying the Dornbush firm as counsel for Defendants. Plaintiff argued that the Dornbush firm's earlier involvement as a "neutral, third-party" in attempting to resolve her discrimination claim prior to litigation precluded the firm's later representation of Defendant in the same dispute. According to Plaintiff, the firm lured her into disclosing certain confidences because it held itself out as a "neutral" mediator.

Judge Pauley found that, although the Dornbush firm did not conceal or misrepresent its relationship with Defendant, the firm—through its attorney-mediator—purported to be an impartial mediator for Plaintiff's grievance. The firm failed to implement screening procedures that would have prevented the attorney-mediator from sharing with other attorneys in the firm the confidential information disclosed by Plaintiff during the mediation. Rather, the firm attempted to exploit what the attorney-mediator learned during the mediation, and even intended to call the attorney-mediator as a witness at trial.

In disqualifying the Dornbush firm, the court emphasized the "strong public policy favoring mediation."

* * *

VII. Vicarious Disqualification Under Rule 1.10: Disqualification of an Entire Firm Because of a Tainted Lawyer

[Question 5-19]

A law firm specializes in products liability litigation. Eight years ago, an attorney in the firm defended a motorcycle manufacturer that was sued by a purchaser who alleged that he was seriously injured because of the defective design of his motorcycle. The case was settled twelve months later after extensive discovery. Recently, a plaintiff who was injured while riding the same model of motorcycle retained the attorney to bring a products liability lawsuit against the same manufacturer. The attorney did not seek informed consent to the representation from the manufacturer, nor did he disclose to the client that he previously represented the manufacturer.

Is the attorney subject to discipline?

   (A) No, because a significant period of years has passed since the attorney represented the manufacturer.

(B) No, because the lawsuit involves a different plaintiff, a different motorcycle, and an accident at a different time and place from the lawsuit in which the attorney defended the manufacturer.

 (C) Yes, because the matters are substantially related, and the plaintiff's interests are materially adverse to those of the manufacturer.

 (D) Yes, because a lawyer may not represent a plaintiff adversely to a former client.

[Question 5-20]

A law firm specializes in products liability litigation. Eight years ago, an attorney in the firm defended a motorcycle manufacturer that was sued by a purchaser who alleged that he was seriously injured because of the defective design of his motorcycle. The case was settled twelve months later after extensive discovery. Recently, a plaintiff who was injured while riding the same model of motorcycle retained one of the attorney's law firm partners to bring a products liability action against the manufacturer. The partner had not participated in the previous litigation in which the attorney had represented the manufacturer. The attorney had no involvement in the partner's representation of the plaintiff against the manufacturer, but the attorney was not formally screened from the matter.

Is it proper for the partner to represent the plaintiff without the manufacturer's informed consent?

 (A) No, because the attorney was not formally screened from the plaintiff's action.

 (B) No, because the attorney's disqualifying conflict of interest was imputed to the partner.

 (C) Yes, because the plaintiff's action against the manufacturer is not substantially related to the matter in which the attorney previously represented the manufacturer.

(D) Yes, because the partner had not participated in the previous representation of the manufacturer.

[Question 5-21]

A law firm specializes in products liability litigation. Eight years ago, a partner and an associate in the firm defended a motorcycle manufacturer that was sued by a rider who alleged that he was seriously injured because of the defective design of his motorcycle. The case was settled twelve months later after extensive discovery in which both the partner and the associate were integrally involved. Shortly thereafter, the partner retired from practice.

Recently, a plaintiff hired an attorney at the firm to represent him in an action against the motorcycle manufacturer for injuries sustained while riding the same model of motorcycle at issue in the previous case. The associate is still employed by the firm.

Is the attorney subject to discipline?

  (A) No, because a significant period of time has passed since the partner represented the manufacturer.

 (B) No, because a significant period of time has passed since the partner retired from the firm.

 (C) Yes, because the associate has confidential information material to the plaintiff's action against the manufacturer.

(D) Yes, because a firm may not accept a representation adverse to a former client when a lawyer that previously represented the former client remains employed by the firm.

[Question 5-22]

An attorney in a small law firm represents a pro-gun control organization seeking to overturn a statute that limits restrictions on gun ownership. One of the attorney's partners is a strong advocate for gun owners' rights. The attorney knows that if the partner were to participate in the representation, the partner could not provide competent representation because of the partner's strongly held beliefs. Therefore, the attorney screened the partner from the matter. The attorney supports restrictions on gun ownership and reasonably believes that the attorney will not be influenced by the partner's views. The attorney did not advise the organization of the partner's views nor obtain the organization's informed consent, confirmed in writing.

Is the attorney's conduct proper?

 (A) No, because the partner's conflict is automatically imputed to all the lawyers in the firm, including the attorney.

(B) No, because the attorney did not advise the organization of the partner's views and obtain the organization's informed consent, confirmed in writing.

(C) Yes, because the partner's views will not influence the attorney.

  (D) Yes, because the partner was screened from the matter.

Rule 1.10—Imputation of Conflicts of Interest

(a) While lawyers are associated in a firm, none of them shall knowingly represent a client when any one of them practicing alone would be prohibited from doing so by Rules 1.7 or 1.9, unless:

(1) the prohibition is based on a personal interest of the disqualified lawyer and does not present a significant risk of materially limiting the representation of the client by the remaining lawyers in the firm; or

(2) the prohibition is based upon Rule 1.9(a) or (b) and arises out of the disqualified lawyer's association with a prior firm, and

(i)   the disqualified lawyer is timely screened from any participation in the matter and is apportioned no part of the fee therefrom;

(ii)   written notice is promptly given to any affected former client to enable the former client to ascertain compliance with the provisions of this Rule, which shall include a description of the screening procedures employed; a statement of the firm's and of the screened lawyer's compliance with these Rules; a statement that review may be available before a tribunal; and an agreement by the firm to respond promptly to any written inquiries or objections by the former client about the screening procedures; and

> **Take Note**
>
> The rationale for allowing screening, a relatively recent addition to the Rules, was that most courts were already allowing it anyway, and so the Rules should keep up with what the courts are doing. Another rationale was that screening was important for allowing lawyer mobility—especially in a difficult market for lawyers.

(iii)   certifications of compliance with these Rules and with the screening procedures are provided to the former client by the screened lawyer and by a partner of the firm, at reasonable intervals upon the former client's written request and upon termination of the screening procedures.

(b)   When a lawyer has terminated an association with a firm, the firm is not prohibited from thereafter representing a person with interests materially adverse to those of a client represented by the formerly associated lawyer and not currently represented by the firm, unless:

(1)   the matter is the same or substantially related to that in which the formerly associated lawyer represented the client; and

(2)   any lawyer remaining in the firm has information protected by Rules 1.6 and 1.9(c) that is material to the matter.

(c)   A disqualification prescribed by this rule may be waived by the affected client under the conditions stated in Rule 1.7.

(d)   The disqualification of lawyers associated in a firm with former or current government lawyers is governed by Rule 1.11.

[*Ed. Note*—The above is Connecticut's Rule 1.10; Delaware Rule 1.10, like many states, differs substantially.]

LaSalle Nat'l Bank v. County of Lake

703 F.2d 252 (7th Cir. 1983)

CUDAHY, CIRCUIT JUDGE.

*** Lake County, Illinois, one of the parties to this appeal, is the former employer of an attorney now practicing law with the firm representing the plaintiffs-appellants. Lake County moved to disqualify the plaintiffs' law firm because of the County's former relationship with one of the firm's associates. The district court granted the motion, finding that the past association gave rise to an appearance of impropriety and holding that both the attorney and the entire law firm must be disqualified. * * * We affirm the order of the district court.

I

Marc Seidler, the attorney upon whose career our attention must focus in this case, served as an Assistant State's Attorney in Lake County from 1976 until January 31, 1981. On December 1, 1976, Mr. Seidler was appointed Chief of the Civil Division of the Lake County State's Attorney's office, and in September 1979, he was appointed First Assistant State's Attorney. As such, he had general supervisory responsibility with respect to all civil cases handled by the State's Attorney's office. On February 2, 1981, Mr. Seidler joined the Chicago law firm of Rudnick & Wolfe as an associate, working in the firm's Northbrook, Illinois office. * * *

On June 5, 1981, Rudnick & Wolfe filed suit against the County of Lake and the Village of Grayslake, on behalf of its clients, the LaSalle National Bank as Trustee ("LaSalle National") and Lake Properties Venture ("Lake Properties"). * * *

[The Court found that Seidler represented the defendant County on a substantially related matter, and therefore that Seidler would be personally disqualified from this action.]

IV

Having found that Mr. Seidler was properly disqualified from representation of the plaintiffs in this case, we must now address whether this disqualification should be extended to the entire law firm of Rudnick & Wolfe. Although the knowledge possessed by one attorney in a law firm is presumed to be shared with the other attorneys in the firm, this court has held that this presumption may be rebutted. The question arises here whether this presumption may be effectively rebutted by establishing that the "infected" attorney was "screened," or insulated, from all participation in and information about a case, thus avoiding disqualification of an entire law firm based on the prior employment of one member.

* * * If past employment in government results in the disqualification of future employers from representing some of their long-term clients, it seems clearly possible that government attorneys will be regarded as "Typhoid Marys." Many talented lawyers, in turn, may be unwilling to spend a period in government service, if that service makes them unattractive or risky for large law firms to hire. In recognition of this problem, several other circuits have begun either explicitly or implicitly to approve the use of screening as a means to avoid disqualification of an entire law firm by "infection." * * *

* * *

Scholarly commentary has also generally approved screening as a device to avoid the wholesale disqualification of law firms with which former government attorneys are associated.

The screening arrangements which courts and commentators have approved, however, contain certain common characteristics. [In one case permitting screening, the screened attorney was] denied access to relevant files and did not share in the profits or fees derived from the representation in question; discussion of the suit was prohibited in his presence and no members of the firm were permitted to show him any documents relating to the case; and both the disqualified attorney and others in his firm affirmed these facts under oath. [Another] case was similarly specific: all other attorneys in the firm were forbidden to discuss the case with the disqualified attorney and instructed to prevent any documents from reaching him; the files were kept in a locked file cabinet, with the keys controlled by two partners and issued to others only on a "need to know" basis. In both cases, moreover, * * *, the screening arrangement was set up at the time when the potentially disqualifying event occurred, either when the attorney first joined the firm or when the firm accepted a case presenting an ethical problem.

Practice Pointer

There is no uniform rule on whether screening will protect a law firm from disqualification, when one of the lawyers in the firm is personally disqualified. Lawyers need to be aware of the case law in the particular court. And the uncertainty of the efficacy of screening means that law firms will be cautious about hiring lawyers who carry with them the taint of conflict with respect to matters the firm is currently pursuing.

In the case at hand, by contrast, Mr. Seidler joined the firm of Rudnick & Wolfe on February 2, 1981; yet screening arrangements were not established until the disqualification motion was filed in August 1981. * * * Although Mr. Seidler states in his affidavit that he did not disclose to any person associated with the firm any [confidential] information * * * on any matter relevant to this litigation, no specific institutional mechanisms were in place to insure that that information was not shared, even if inadvertently, between the months of February and August.[3] Recognizing that this is an area in which the relevant information is singularly within the ken of the party defending against the motion to disqualify and in which the reputation of the bar as a whole is implicated, we hold that the district court did not abuse its discretion in extending the disqualification of Marc Seidler to the entire firm of Rudnick & Wolfe. The district court order is therefore

Affirmed.

Hear from the Authors

To hear more from the authors on screening, click here.

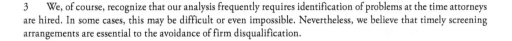

3   We, of course, recognize that our analysis frequently requires identification of problems at the time attorneys are hired. In some cases, this may be difficult or even impossible. Nevertheless, we believe that timely screening arrangements are essential to the avoidance of firm disqualification.

Kassis v. Teacher's Ins. and Annuity Ass'n

93 N.Y.2d 611, 695 N.Y.S.2d 515 (1999)

SMITH, J.

Plaintiffs Henry Kassis and North River Insurance Company retained the law firm of Weg & Myers to represent them in an action premised upon property damage to a building owned by Kassis in New York City. Thurm & Heller, a firm of approximately 26 attorneys, is counsel for defendants and third-party plaintiffs, Teacher's Insurance and Annuity Association and Cauldwell-Wingate Company, Inc. The decisive issue on this appeal is whether Thurm & Heller should be disqualified from continued representation of defendants on the basis that it hired Charles Arnold, a former associate of Weg & Myers who participated in the Kassis litigation while employed there. For the reasons that follow, we hold that Thurm & Heller should be disqualified, and we reverse the order of the Appellate Division that permitted the continued representation.

In 1994, two years after commencement of the underlying action, Weg & Myers was substituted as counsel for plaintiffs. Joshua Mallin, a partner at Weg & Myers, was in charge of the case, conducting most of the discovery and planning the litigation strategy. Charles Arnold, a first-year associate, assisted Mallin. Specifically, Arnold conducted five depositions of nonparties and co-plaintiff North River, attended two court-ordered mediation sessions as sole counsel for the client, appeared as Kassis' attorney at a physical examination of the subject building, and conversed with Kassis on a regular basis. Moreover, the record indicates that Weg & Myers conducted weekly staff meetings where all associates were privy to discussions of law and strategy regarding litigation the firm handled. In addition, Arnold reviewed certain portions of the litigation file in order to conduct the depositions, but allegedly "never read the overwhelming majority of the documents contained within the file."

In February 1997, following a deposition in the Kassis matter, Arnold informed Roula Theofanis, the partner at Thurm & Heller who was primarily in charge of the Kassis litigation, that he was leaving Weg & Myers. At the suggestion of Theofanis, Arnold was interviewed by Thurm & Heller, and began working there in March 1997. During the interview and upon commencement of his employment, Thurm & Heller cautioned Arnold that he would not be permitted to participate in the Kassis litigation and that he was not to discuss that matter with anyone at the firm.

Upon learning of Arnold's employment, Mallin requested that Theofanis detail the precautionary measures that the firm planned to take in order to prevent Arnold's inadvertent disclosure of confidential information he had obtained while at Weg & Myers. By written response, Theofanis detailed the following safeguards:

> "1. The entire file which presently consists of 15 redwells will be kept in my office in lieu of our general filing area.

> "2. Mr. Arnold's office will be at a substantial distance from my office.

"3. Mr. Arnold upon commencement of his employment with the firm on March 3, 1997 will be instructed not to touch the Kassis file nor to discuss the Kassis matter with any partner, associate or staff member of the firm.

"4. There will be no meetings, conferences or discussions in the presence of Mr. Arnold concerning the Kassis' litigation.

"5. All future associates who may work on the Kassis matter with me in preparation for trial will be instructed not to discuss this file with Mr. Arnold."

On March 6, 1997, three days after Arnold began working at Thurm & Heller, Mallin moved on behalf of plaintiffs to disqualify the firm from further participation in the Kassis litigation. Supreme Court denied plaintiffs' motion, finding Arnold's involvement in the Kassis litigation while employed at Weg & Myers limited. The Appellate Division affirmed, holding that the safeguards employed by Thurm & Heller eliminated the danger of Arnold inadvertently transmitting information he might have gained from his previous employment at Weg & Myers. * * *

What's That?

Many professional responsibility scholars argue that the "appearance of impropriety" is a meaningless, indeed dangerous term that allows courts to disqualify lawyers on completely subjective grounds.

Attorneys owe a continuing duty to former clients not to reveal confidences learned in the course of their professional relationship. It is this duty that provides the foundation for the well-established rule that a lawyer may not represent a client in a matter and thereafter represent another client with interests materially adverse to interests of the former client in the same or a substantially related matter. Indeed, such "side switching" clearly implicates the policies both of maintaining loyalty to the first client and of protecting that client's confidences. These same principles give rise to the general rule that, where an attorney working in a law firm is disqualified from undertaking a subsequent representation opposing a former client, all the attorneys in that firm are likewise precluded from such representation.

In addition to ensuring that attorneys remain faithful to the fiduciary duties of loyalty and confidentiality owed by attorneys to their clients, the rule of imputed disqualification reinforces an attorney's ethical obligation to avoid the appearance of impropriety.

* * *

[I]mputed disqualification is not an irrebuttable presumption. A per se rule of disqualification * * * is unnecessarily preclusive because it disqualifies all members of a law firm indiscriminately, whether or not they share knowledge of former client's confidences and secrets. Such a rule also imposes significant hardships on the current client and is subject to abusive invocation purely to seek tactical advantages in a lawsuit. Additionally, a per se disqualification rule conflicts with public policies favoring client choice and restricts an attorney's ability to practice.

* * *

Thus, where one attorney is disqualified as a result of having acquired confidential client information at a former law firm, the presumption that the entirety of the attorney's current firm must be disqualified may be rebutted. Of course, no presumption of disqualification will arise if either the moving party fails to make any showing of a risk that the attorney changing firms acquired any client confidences in the prior employment or the nonmoving party disproves that the attorney had any opportunity to acquire confidential information in the former employment. In either case, it would not have been established that the side-switching attorney actually "represented the former client in a matter," and neither the attorney nor the firm would need to be disqualified.

Food for Thought

Note the difference between *Kassis* and Rule 1.10, which provides that if proper screening is in place before the tainted attorney comes into the firm, it doesn't matter *how tainted* that attorney may be. In contrast, *Kassis* says screening works only if the tainted lawyer had access to insignificant confidential information. In other words, it only works if the lawyer is a little bit tainted. But how do you determine when the tainted lawyer has crossed the line from significant to insignificant taint? Because of that uncertainty, in New York, screening cannot be relied on as a means of avoiding disqualification. Doesn't this put a damper on the mobility of lawyers?

Where the presumption does arise, however, the party seeking to avoid disqualification must prove that any information acquired by the disqualified lawyer is unlikely to be significant or material in the litigation. In that factual scenario, with the presumption rebutted, a "Chinese Wall" around the disqualified lawyer would be sufficient to avoid firm disqualification.

To determine whether the presumption of shared confidences and disqualification has been rebutted, consideration must be given to the particular facts of each case. Where, for example, a disqualified attorney formerly worked in a small law firm characterized by a certain informality and conducive to "constant cross-pollination" and a "cross current of discussion and ideas' among all attorneys on all matters which the firm handled," there will be a greater likelihood of acquiring material client confidences. Similarly, where offices are not physically isolated and files are made open and available to all lawyers, the probability that an attorney gained significant confidential information increases.

Other factors also weigh in the balance. In *Solow v. Grace & Co.*, 83 N.Y.2d 303, 610 N.Y.S.2d 128 (1994), for example, this Court declined to disqualify the law firm of Stroock & Stroock & Lavan, a 372-lawyer firm which represented plaintiff in a suit against defendant W.R. Grace & Co. Members of Stroock had previously defended Grace in another action, and Grace moved to disqualify the firm from participating in the action. While recognizing the importance of the presumption of shared confidences, the Court nevertheless permitted Stroock to continue as counsel against Grace, its former client. Aside from being a very large firm, the Stroock partner, associate and paralegals who actively participated in the litigation involving the former client had all left the firm long before the current litigation. Sworn affidavits by the remaining partner and associate at Stroock established that their involvement in the prior Grace litigation had been negligible.

Demonstrating that no significant client confidences were acquired by the disqualified attorney, however, does not wholly remove the imputation of disqualification from a law firm. Because even the appearance of impropriety must be eliminated, it follows that even where it is demonstrated that the disqualified attorney possesses no material confidential information, a firm must nonetheless erect adequate screening measures to separate the disqualified lawyer and eliminate any involvement by that lawyer in the representation.

Here, the undisputed facts in the record evidence that Arnold played an appreciable role as counsel for plaintiff in the Kassis litigation while at Weg & Myers. He was sufficiently knowledgeable and steeped in the files of this case to conduct several depositions that resulted in extensive transcripts; he appeared as sole counsel for the client in two court-ordered mediation sessions; and he conversed regularly with the client. Given Arnold's extensive participation in the Kassis litigation and Thurm & Heller's representation of the adversary in the same matter, defendants' burden in rebutting the presumption that Arnold acquired material confidences is especially heavy. Defendants' conclusory averments that Arnold did not acquire such confidences during the prior representation failed to rebut that presumption as a matter of law. The erection of a "Chinese Wall" in this case, therefore, was inconsequential. Thus, we hold, as a matter of law, that disqualification is required.

VIII. Conflicts of Interest in Criminal Cases

[Question 5-23]

Three defendants were charged with the murder of a local woman. The defendants retained the same attorney and consented to their joint representation by her. Each defendant was tried separately. The first defendant was convicted, while the other two were acquitted. On appeal, the convicted defendant claimed, for the first time, that his attorney provided ineffective assistance because she had an impermissible conflict of interest. As evidence of this, the first defendant pointed to the fact that the attorney did not call the second and third defendants as witnesses in his trial. In response, the attorney conceded that the testimony of the second and third defendants could have helped the first defendant's case. However, she explained that she refrained from calling them as witnesses because of her concern regarding the harm that such testimony might cause to the subsequent trials.

Is the attorney subject to discipline?

(A) No, because the first defendant consented to the representation.

(B) No, because the first defendant did not object to the conflict of interest until his appeal.

(C) Yes, because the attorney breached her duty of loyalty to first defendant.

(D) Yes, because the first defendant was convicted of the murder.

[Question 5-24]

Two defendants, a brother and a sister, were indicted in connection with the robbery and fatal shooting of a store owner. There were no eyewitnesses to the robbery, but the defendants were seen leaving the store shortly after the store owner was shot, and merchandise from the store was found in their possession. The defendants agreed to be represented jointly by an attorney. The attorney did not secure their informed consent, confirmed in writing, to the joint representation.

The defendants told the attorney truthfully that the brother committed the robbery and shooting without the sister's advanced knowledge or participation. But the brother was unwilling to plead guilty, because he believed the prosecution's case was weak. The attorney knew that it was in the sister's best interest to present her version of the events to the prosecutor and to offer to testify against her brother in exchange for dismissal of the charges against her, or for her to testify in her own defense. However, the attorney did not advise her of these options, because he did not want to prejudice the brother. Even if the attorney had given this advice, it is uncertain whether the sister would have followed it and testified in her own defense or against her brother.

Both defendants were convicted following a trial at which neither testified. Afterward, the sister retained a new lawyer who argued on appeal that her conviction should be overturned because her trial attorney had a conflict of interest.

Is the court likely to set aside the sister's conviction?

 (A) No, because the defendants' interests were aligned, since neither wanted to be convicted.

 (B) No, because it is uncertain whether the sister would have taken the attorney's advice to testify in her own defense or against her brother.

 (C) Yes, because the attorney's conflict of interest adversely affected the attorney's performance.

 (D) Yes, because the defendants did not give informed consent, confirmed in writing.

[Question 5-25]

Three defendants have been indicted for the armed robbery of a cashier at a grocery store. Two of the defendants retained an attorney to represent them jointly. Before agreeing to the representation, however, the attorney required that the two defendants allow him to interview them separately.

During the interviews, each defendant told the attorney that the robbery had been committed by the third defendant while they sat in the third defendant's car outside the store. The defendants both stated that the third defendant said he needed some cigarettes and maintained that they knew nothing about the third defendant's plan to rob the cashier. Following the interviews, the attorney agreed to represent both defendants jointly.

One week before the trial, one of the two defendants told the attorney that he wanted to plea bargain and that he was prepared to testify that his co-defendant had loaned the third defendant the gun used in the robbery. This same defendant also said that he and his co-defendant had shared in the proceeds of the robbery. The attorney recognized that a conflict of interest had arisen and therefore obtained consent, in writing, from each of the two co-defendants to his continued representation of them.

Is the attorney subject to discipline?

 (A) No, because the attorney obtained the co-defendants' consent, in writing, to his continued representation of them.

  (B) No, because the attorney interviewed the defendants separately before accepting the joint representation.

 (C) Yes, because the defendant's desire to plea bargain created a non-consentable conflict of interest.

 (D) Yes, because there is a per-se prohibition on the joint representation of multiple defendants.

A. The Right to Conflict-Free Representation

The Sixth Amendment provides as follows:

> In all criminal prosecutions, the accused shall enjoy the right to a speedy and public trial, by an impartial jury of the State and district where in the crime shall have been committed, which district shall have been previously ascertained by law, and to be informed of the nature and cause of the accusation; to be confronted with the witnesses against him; to have compulsory process for obtaining witnesses in his favor, and to have the Assistance of Counsel for his defence.

U.S. Const. amend. VI.

The right to effective assistance of counsel may be denied because defense counsel has a conflict of interest, and cannot or does not properly protect a client's interests. One situation that presents the potential for a conflict of interest is when counsel represents multiple defendants. Co-defendants may have divergent interests at all stages of a prosecution. A plea bargain advantageous to one defendant may produce testimony adverse to another defendant. Defendants may have inconsistent defense or wish to testify in ways that incriminate co-defendants. *See, e.g., United States v. Hall*, 200 F.3d 962 (6th Cir. 2000) (conflict of interest where defense counsel represents two brothers, and one has a public authority defense while the other does not). Evidence inculpating one defendant might exculpate another, forcing counsel to make unsatisfactory choices in response to offered testimony. Separate counsel also might choose differing approaches to closing argument that a counsel to multiple defendants might not be able to choose.

Conflicts also might arise when defense counsel has a personal interest that could be negatively affected by aggressive representation of the defendant. For example, in one notorious case, a lawyer represented the defendant in a felony prosecution while simultaneously having a sexual relationship with the defendant's wife. Counsel's ardor for the wife may well have dampened his ardor to have the defendant set free. *Hernandez v. State*, 750 So.2d 50 (Fla. App. 1999).

Another possibility is that the interests of the defendant may be in conflict with the interests of defense counsel's client in another matter, or with the interests of a former client. For example, if counsel represents two defendants charged with the same crime in separate matters, the decision whether to call one defendant to testify in the other's trial may be impacted by counsel's conflicting loyalties. *See, e.g., United States v. Elliot*, 463 F.3d 858 (9th Cir. 2006) (conflict where two clients are separately tried for the same crime and their best defense is to shift blame to each other: "To represent Elliot adequately, Gordon needed to interview, aggressively examine, and possibly place blame on Hevia, all of which clashed with his attorney-client relationship with Hevia."). And the lawyer's duty to preserve the confidences and secrets of a former client may impair a current client's representation if the former client is called as a witness for the prosecution.

For More Information

While the 6th Amendment provides a right to counsel of one's choosing, this right is not absolute and is qualified by the trial court's authority to disqualify a defense lawyer operating under a conflict of interest. *See Wheat v. United States*, 486 U.S. 153 (1988). Wheat is criticized in Bruce A. Green, *"Through a Glass, Darkly": How the Court Sees Motions to Disqualify Criminal Defense Lawyers*, 89 Colum. L. Rev. 1201 (1989). Among other criticisms, Professor Green notes that "the Court relied on an unwarranted assumption that if the defendant is willing to waive potential conflict of interest claims his attorney probably has not complied with the ethical standards governing the investigation and disclosure of potential conflicts." *Wheat* is defended in William J. Stuntz, *Waiving Rights in Criminal Procedure*, 75 Va. L. Rev. 761 (1989). Professor Stuntz argues that clients jointly represented by a single counsel may or may not have improper motives.

1. The Duty of Court Inquiry

Per Se Reversal: Holloway v. Arkansas

In *Holloway v. Arkansas*, 435 U.S. 475 (1978), the Court made it clear that joint representation of co-defendants by a single attorney is not a per se violation of the right to effective assistance of counsel. The Court noted that a common defense often gives strength against a common attack. Under some circumstances, however, joint representation may create a conflict that can deny a defendant effective assistance of counsel. In *Holloway*, the defense counsel made pretrial motions for appointment of separate counsel for each defendant because of possible conflicts of interest. The trial court denied the motions, and refused defense counsel's renewed request, during the trial, for separate counsel when the three co-defendants each wished to testify. Counsel felt that he would be unable to examine or cross-examine any defendant to protect the interests of the others.

Without ever reaching the issue of whether there was an actual conflict of interest, the Supreme Court reversed the defendants' convictions. Reversal was required because the judge, after timely motions, erred in failing to "either appoint separate counsel, or to take adequate steps to ascertain whether the risk was too remote to warrant separate counsel." The Court held that in these circumstances, prejudice to the defendants must be presumed:

> Joint representation of conflicting interests is suspect because of what it tends to prevent the attorney from doing. For example, in this case it may well have precluded defense counsel for [one of the codefendants] from exploring possible plea negotiations and the possibility of an agreement to testify for the prosecution, provided a lesser charge or a favorable sentencing recommendation would be acceptable. Generally speaking a conflict may also prevent an attorney from challenging the admission of evidence prejudicial to one client but perhaps favorable to another, or from arguing at the sentencing hearing the relative involvement and culpability of his clients in order to minimize the culpability of one by emphasizing that of another. Examples can be readily multiplied. * * *

> [A] rule requiring a defendant to show that a conflict of interests—which he and his counsel tried to avoid by timely objections to the joint representation—prejudiced him in some specific fashion would not be susceptible to intelligent, evenhanded application. In the normal case where a harmless error rule is applied, the error occurs at trial and its scope is readily identifiable. Accordingly, the reviewing court can undertake with some confidence its relatively narrow task of assessing the likelihood that the error materially affected the deliberations of the jury. But in a case of joint representation of conflicting interests the evil—it bears repeating—is in what the advocate finds himself compelled to *refrain* from doing, not only at trial but also as to possible pretrial plea negotiations and in the sentencing process. * * * Thus, an inquiry into a claim of harmless error here would require, unlike most cases, unguided speculation.

Federal Rule 44

Fed. R. Crim. P. 44 attempts to address the problem of joint representation, and the need for a hearing, that the Court was concerned with in Holloway:

Rule 44. Right to and assignment of counsel

* * *

(c)(2) **Court's Responsibilities in Cases of Joint representation.**—The court must promptly inquire about the propriety of joint representation and must personally advise each defendant of the right to the effective assistance of counsel, including separate representation. Unless there is good cause to believe that no conflict of interest is likely to arise, the court must take appropriate measure to protect each defendant's right to counsel.

It should be apparent that Rule 44 does not address all the conflict situations that can arise in a criminal case. Rule 44 addresses only questions of multiple representation in the same criminal proceeding. It does not apply if defense counsel has previously represented a person who is now a government witness in the case against the defendant. It also does not apply if the lawyer has a personal interest conflict, such as his possible involvement in the defendant's alleged crime.

Such conflicts, however, are often reviewed by the court at a hearing when they are raised, usually by the prosecutor. Why would the prosecution raise these conflicts?

2. Active Conflict Impairing the Representation

A Different Kind of Prejudice Test: Cuyler v. Sullivan

In *Cuyler v. Sullivan,* 446 U.S. 335 (1980), the Court considered the propriety of relief where defense counsel operated under a conflict of interest that was not brought to the attention of the trial judge. Justice Powell's opinion for the Court rejected the petitioner's claim that *Holloway* requires a trial judge to inquire in every case into the propriety of joint representation, even in the absence of the defendant's timely motion. He reasoned as follows:

> Defense counsel have an ethical obligation to avoid conflicting representations and to advise the court promptly when a conflict of interest arises during the course of a trial. Absent special circumstances, therefore, trial courts may assume that multiple representation entails no conflict or that the lawyer and his clients knowingly accept such risk of conflict as may exist.

The opinion reiterated the suggestion in *Holloway* that multiple representation does give rise to a possibility of an improper conflict of interest and that a defendant "must have the opportunity to show that potential conflicts impermissibly imperil his right to a fair trial." But, said the Court, "a defendant who raised no objection at trial must demonstrate that an actual conflict of interest adversely affected his lawyer's performance." Thus, the Court created a limited presumption of prejudice in cases where a defendant fails to make a timely objection to conflicted simultaneous representation: prejudice is presumed, but only if the defendant demonstrates that counsel "actively represented conflicting interests" and that "an actual conflict of interest adversely affected his lawyer's performance."

The *Cuyler* prejudice standard applies when a defendant fails to bring a potential conflict to the trial court's attention. But it also applies when the defendant notifies the trial court of a potential conflict and the trial court, after a full hearing, finds that there is no actual or potential conflict and orders the multiple representation to continue. *See Freund v. Butterworth,* 165 F.3d 839 (11th Cir. 1999) (en banc). *Holloway* applies when the court refuses to hold a hearing after the defense counsel brings a potential conflict to its attention.

Application of the Cuyler Standard: Burger v. Kemp

The Supreme Court found no ineffective assistance of counsel under the *Cuyler* standards in *Burger v. Kemp*, 483 U.S. 776 (1987), a capital case in which Burger and a co-defendant were represented by law partners. The defendants were soldiers charged with the murder of a fellow soldier who worked part-time driving a taxi. Each defendant confessed, and Burger took military police to the place where the victim had been drowned. Leaphart, an experienced lawyer, was appointed to represent Burger, and he insisted that his law partner represent the co-defendant. The two defendants were tried separately, and at their trials each defendant sought to avoid the death penalty by emphasizing the other's culpability. Burger was sentenced to death and attacked his representation in a habeas corpus proceeding on the ground that Leaphart's partnership relationship with counsel for the other defendant created a conflict of interest for him. A federal district court denied relief, and the court of appeals affirmed.

Justice Stevens wrote for the Court in affirming the denial of relief. He conceded that "[t]here is certainly much substance to petitioner's argument that the appointment of two partners to represent coindictees in their respective trials creates a possible conflict of interest that could prejudice either or both clients," and that "the risk of prejudice is increased when the two lawyers cooperate with one another in planning and conduct of trial strategy." He observed, however, that the Court's decisions do not presume prejudice in all cases, and he concluded that "the overlap of counsel, if any, did not so infect Leaphart's representation as to constitute an active representation of competing interests." Justice Stevens added that "[p]articularly in smaller communities where the supply of qualified lawyers willing to accept the demanding and unrewarding work of representing capital prisoners is extremely limited, the two defendants may actually benefit from the joint efforts of two partners who supplement one another in their preparation." He noted that "we generally presume that the lawyer is fully conscious of the overarching duty of complete loyalty to his or her client," and that trial courts "appropriately and necessarily rely in large measure upon the good faith and good judgment of defense counsel." Justice Stevens also emphasized that each defendant was tried separately, and that separate trials significantly reduce the risk of a conflict of interest. The Court declined to disturb the lower courts' findings that there was no actual conflict of interest.

Go Online

A comprehensive discussion of the problems that can result when one lawyer, firm, or public agency represents successive criminal defendants is found in Gary T. Lowenthal, *Successive Representation By Criminal Lawyers*, 93 Yale L.J. 1 (1983).

B. Waiver of the Right to Conflict-Free Counsel

The premise of Federal Rule 44 is that if the defendant is properly warned of the possible conflicts that could arise, then he can knowingly and voluntarily waive the right to conflict-free representation. Generally speaking, a knowing and voluntary waiver of conflict-free representation can be found if the trial court informs the defendant about the ways in which conflicted counsel can impair the representation—particularly that one client could shift blame to another, or testify against another, and defense counsel would be impaired in representing the multiple interests. The trial court must assure itself that the defendant understands the consequences and has made a rational decision to proceed with counsel despite the conflict.

As a matter of practice, some judges require the defendant to articulate, in his own words, what counsel's conflict is, and how it could impair the representation. Such a practice may help to assure that the defendant is making a knowing and intelligent waiver, or, to the contrary, could indicate that the defendant doesn't really know what he is giving up. *But see United States v. Flores,* 5 F.3d 1070 (7th Cir. 1993).

Test Your Knowledge

To assess your understanding of the material in this Chapter, click here to take a quiz.

CHAPTER 6

The Lawyer's Duties to the Legal System and Nonclients

Learning Outcomes

At the end of Unit I, you will be able to:

- Recognize the tension between the lawyer's role as a "zealous advocate" and the lawyer's role as an "officer of the court"

- Analyze the duties lawyers owe to the court and other tribunals

- Explain the interplay between the duties related to perjury and the duty of confidentiality

At the end of Unit II, you will be able to:

- Analyze the duties requiring truthfulness in statements to others

- Analyze the duties that apply to inadvertent disclosures of confidential information

- Analyze the prohibition against communications with a represented party

- Analyze the duties relating to unrepresented persons

At the end of Unit III, you will be able to:

- Analyze the duties to comply with the law

- Analyze the subordinate lawyer's duty to comply with the ethical rules

- Analyze the organizational lawyer's duty to report certain matters up-the-ladder under the ethical rules and the Sarbanes-Oxley regulations

- Analyze when a prohibition that restricts the practice of law is proper

- Determine when a lawyer must report misconduct by another lawyer or a judge

Topic Outline for Chapter 6

	TOPIC	RELEVANT AUTHORITY	CHAPTER QUESTIONS
I.	Duties to the Court and Other Tribunals		
	A. Meritorious Claims and Contentions	3.1; F.R. Civil P. 11	6-1
	B. Law, Evidence, and False Testimony	1.6; 3.3	6-2 to 6-6
	C. Argument	3.4(e)	6-7
	D. Witnesses	3.4(b),(f); Restatement § 117	6-8 to 6-9
	E. Improper Communication with Judges and Jurors	3.3(d); 3.5; Restatement § 113	6-10 to 6-11
	F. Nonadjudicative Proceeding	3.9	6-12
	G. Stating or Implying Improper Influence	8.4(e)	6-13
	H. Trial Publicity [Cutler, Silver]	3.6; 3.8(f)	6-14 to 6-15
	I. Criticism of Judges [Yagman]	8.2(a)	6-16
	J. Decorum, Civility, and Obedience to Court Rulings [Jones, GMAC]	3.5(b); F.R. Civil P. 30(d)(2)	
II.	Duties to Opposing Parties and Third Parties		
	A. Truthfulness	4.1; 1.6	6-17
	B. Inadvertent Disclosures	4.4(b)	6-18
	C. Communications with a Represented Party	4.2; 8.4(a)	6-19 to 6-20
	D. Unrepresented Persons	4.3	6-21
III.	Duties Regarding the Law and the Legal Profession		
	A. Obedience to Law [Heinen]	Restatement § 56; 1.2(d); 1.13; 4.1; 4.4(a); 5.1; 5.2; Hazard test	6-22 to 6-25
	B. The Sarbanes-Oxley Act of 2002	17 CFR Part 205	6-26
	C. Restrictions on Practice	5.6(b)	6-27
	D. Reporting Lawyer and Judge Misconduct [Himmel]	8.3; 1.6	6-28 to 6-29

In this Chapter, we turn from the lawyer's duties to clients to the lawyer's responsibilities as an officer of the court, a member of an organized profession, and a citizen. Professor Eugene

Gaetke contrasts the lawyer's obligation to clients with the lawyer's obligations as an officer of a court. He explains:

> Two antagonistic models describe the role of lawyers in our legal system. More familiar to the public, and more comfortable to lawyers, is the model of the lawyer as a 'zealous advocate,' the devoted champion of the client's cause. Indeed, the image of the lawyer as loyal advocate for the beleaguered client is perpetuated by the bar itself and reinforced by the media, in literature, and in common lore.
>
> In its public assertions, the legal profession promotes a different model: lawyers are officers of the court in the conduct of their professional, and even their personal, affairs. The organized bar has expressly emphasized this obligation in each of its major codifications of the ethical obligations of the profession[.]* * * The very words 'officer of the court' connote a mandatory public interest role for lawyers and suggest that lawyers sometimes must act in a quasi-judicial or quasi-official capacity despite duties owed to their clients. The primary distinguishing characteristic of the duties making up the officer of the court obligation, therefore, must be their subordination of the interests of the client and the lawyer to those of the judicial system and the public.*

The ethical rules deal with the tension between these two models. The Preamble to the Rules states that "[v]irtually all difficult ethical problems arise from conflict between a lawyer's responsibilities to clients, to the legal system and to the lawyer's own interest in remaining an ethical person while earning a satisfactory living." How does a lawyer resolve these "difficult ethical problems"? The Rules suggest that these "issues must be resolved through the exercise of sensitive professional and moral judgment guided by the basic principles underlying the Rules. These principles include the lawyer's obligation zealously to protect and pursue a client's legitimate interests, within the bounds of the law, while maintaining a professional, courteous and civil attitude toward all persons." The ABA Commission on Professionalism proposed a somewhat different emphasis:

> The profession's view has long been that the lawyer best serves the system of justice when he or she represents a client honestly and effectively, whether in court or in the office. Nothing that we say should be understood

Food for Thought

Professors Russell Pearce and Eli Wald argue that the notion of two antagonistic models of lawyering presumes that people live as autonomous individuals, rather than as participants in a web of inter-connected relationships. They suggest that, under the latter view, a difference between the perspective of the lawyer and the perspective of the client do not inevitably lead to conflict. Rather, the lawyer may be able to resolve differences through dialogue with the client regarding how to find a mutually acceptable resolution of the lawyer's and client's obligations, given that they both live their lives in a web of relationships. Russell G. Pearce & Eli Wald, *Rethinking Lawyer Regulation: How a Relational Approach Would Improve Professional Rules and Roles*, 2012 Mich. St. L. Rev. 513 (2012).

---

*   Eugene R. Gaetke, Lawyers as Officers of the Court, 42 Vand. L. Rev. 39, 40–41, 48 (1989).

as inconsistent with that general observation. However, there are limitations on such representation.

First, lawyers must avoid identifying too closely with their clients. Unless the advice provided by a lawyer is truly objective and independent, the client's own interests will not be well served.

Second, lawyers must communicate openly and fully with their clients about limitations on their ability to serve. Where necessary, they should explain to their clients what their duties are to the court or to the system of justice in a given case, beginning with the obvious prohibition against participating in any way in the giving of perjured testimony.

Unit I of this Chapter explores the lawyer's role as officer of the court. Unit II examines the lawyer's duties to opposing parties and third parties. Unit III discusses the lawyer's responsibilities regarding the law and the legal profession.

I. Duties to the Court and Other Tribunals

This section examines the "duties of lawyers as officers of the court to avoid conduct that undermines the integrity of the adjudicative process." See Comment [1] to Rule 3.3. The particular obligations range from avoiding frivolous claims and contentions to remedying client perjury and limiting trial publicity.

A. Meritorious Claims and Contentions

Lawyers must be able to distinguish between a frivolous claim or argument on the one hand and a good faith claim or argument on the other. Doing so ordinarily requires some investigation to determine whether there is sufficient legal and factual basis to make the claim or argument.

[Question 6-1]

An attorney is employed in the legal department of a large retail clothing company and represents that company in litigation. A group of current and former employees of the company filed a class action alleging that the company has and continues to engage in racial and gender discrimination. After discussing the lawsuit with the attorney, the board of directors of the company instructed the attorney to defend the case. Accordingly, the attorney filed (on behalf of the company) an answer in which the attorney asserted a defense to plaintiffs' claims. Although the attorney was aware that in the prior year the U.S. Supreme Court had rejected the use of that defense for racial and gender discrimination claims, the attorney genuinely and reasonably believed and argued in the answer that the Supreme Court's rejection of that defense should not apply to the factual circumstances of this case. The plaintiffs' lawyer moved for summary judgment and for sanctions against the attorney for asserting a frivolous defense. Four weeks later, the court

granted plaintiffs' summary judgment motion, rejecting the attorney's defense based on the Supreme Court precedent. The court has not yet ruled on the motion for sanctions.

Is the attorney subject to litigation sanction and discipline?

 No, because in asserting the company's defense, the attorney had a good faith argument for a modification or reversal of existing law.

 No, because the attorney was following the instructions of the board, which is authorized to direct the attorney in legal matters.

 Yes, because the attorney should have withdrawn the defense within the time limits prescribed by Rule 11, which is 21 days after service of a motion for sanctions.

 (D) Yes, because the attorney never should have asserted the defense in light of the Supreme Court's recent rejection of that defense.

Rule 11 of the Federal Rules of Civil Procedure requires all papers filed with the court to be signed by the represented party's attorney and provides for sanctions against the attorney or client for harassment, frivolous arguments, or a lack of factual investigation. Under Rule 11(b), legal contentions must be "warranted by existing law or by a nonfrivolous argument for extending, modifying, or reversing existing law or for establishing new law." Factual assertions must "have evidentiary support or, if specifically so identified, [must be] likely [to] have evidentiary support after a reasonable opportunity for further investigation or discovery." Courts have fairly broad discretion regarding the nature of the sanction, and sanctions may be imposed on the court's own initiative or by motion, but "[the motion] must not be filed or be presented to the court if the challenged paper, claim, defense, contention, or denial is withdrawn or appropriately corrected within 21 days after service or within another time the court sets."

Rule 3.1 governs "Meritorious Claims and Contentions." It provides that:

A lawyer shall not bring or defend a proceeding, or assert or controvert an issue therein, unless there is a basis in law and fact for doing so that is not frivolous, which includes a good faith argument for an extension, modification or reversal of existing law. A lawyer for the defendant in a criminal proceeding, or the respondent in a proceeding that could result in incarceration, may nevertheless so defend the proceeding as to require that every element of the case be established.

The Comment to Rule 3.1 further explains:

[2] The filing of an action or defense or similar action taken for a client is not frivolous merely because the facts have not first been fully substantiated or because the lawyer expects to develop vital evidence only by discovery. What is required of lawyers, however, is that they inform themselves about the facts of their clients' cases and the applicable law and determine that they can make good faith arguments in support of their clients' positions. Such action is not frivolous even though the lawyer believes that the client's position ultimately will not prevail. The action is frivolous, however, if the lawyer is unable either to make a good faith argument

on the merits of the action taken or to support the action taken by a good faith argument for an extension, modification or reversal of existing law.

B. Law, Evidence, and False Testimony

Once a case has been filed in court, lawyers are subject to a plethora of ethical and court rules that set forth a lawyer's obligations to the tribunal. As Comment [2] to Rule 3.3 explains, lawyers have special duties as officers of the court "to avoid conduct that undermines the integrity of the adjudicative process." Because the focus of Rule 3.3 is on the integrity of the adjudicative process, rather than the outcome for a particular client, lawyers are subject to more stringent obligations to volunteer adverse law than they are to volunteer adverse facts. At the same time, Rule 3.3 prohibits lawyers from knowingly presenting false testimony and requires lawyers to correct known false testimony. Although the "duty of candor" applies to both criminal and civil contexts, states have varied in their approaches to criminal contexts considering the high stakes of criminal proceedings.

[Question 6-2]

A toy manufacturer was sued in a products liability case in State A. The defendant toy manufacturer's lawyer filed a motion to dismiss plaintiff's complaint but, in the brief that accompanied defendant's motion, failed to cite a 25-year-old State A supreme court decision that supported the defendant's position. Although the plaintiff's attorney was aware of that prior state supreme court decision and knew that it was directly adverse to the plaintiff's position, plaintiff's attorney did not cite the State A supreme court decision in plaintiff's opposition brief because the attorney had a good faith basis for arguing that the state supreme court decision should be reversed in light of subsequent legal developments and because the client wished not to cite it.

Is plaintiff's attorney subject to discipline?

- (A) **No, because it was the responsibility of the defendant's lawyer to cite the state supreme court decision that supported the defendant's position.**

- (B) **No, because the plaintiff's attorney had a good faith argument that the state supreme court decision should be reversed.**

- (C) **Yes, because the client does not have the right to decide whether to cite the state supreme court decision.**

- (D) **Yes, because the plaintiff's attorney knowingly failed to disclose the directly adverse state supreme court decision after the opposing counsel failed to disclose it.**

Rule 3.3(a)(2) provides that:

(a)   A lawyer shall not knowingly:

　　　　* * *

(2)   fail to disclose to the tribunal legal authority in the controlling jurisdiction known to the lawyer to be directly adverse to the position of the client and not disclosed by opposing counsel[.]

* * *

The Comment to Rule 3.3 further explains:

Legal Argument

[4] Legal argument based on a knowingly false representation of law constitutes dishonesty toward the tribunal. A lawyer is not required to make a disinterested exposition of the law, but must recognize the existence of pertinent legal authorities. Furthermore, as stated in paragraph (a)(2), an advocate has a duty to disclose directly adverse authority in the controlling jurisdiction that has not been disclosed by the opposing party. The underlying concept is that legal argument is a discussion seeking to determine the legal premises properly applicable to the case.

* * *

Although lawyers have an obligation to disclose directly adverse controlling law, they do not have a corollary obligation to disclose to the opposing party facts that are adverse to the lawyer's client. On the other hand, if the opposing party asks about adverse facts during discovery, the lawyer must either object to the discovery request or comply. Rule 3.4(a) says that a lawyer shall not "unlawfully obstruct another party's access to evidence or unlawfully alter, destroy, or conceal a document or other material having potential evidentiary value." Question 6-3 and the material that follows will help you better understand the ethical rules that prohibit the lawyer from knowingly presenting false testimony and require lawyers to correct known false testimony.

[Question 6-3]

An attorney represents a criminal defendant charged with racketeering. The attorney called a witness, who testified that the defendant was not a member of an organized crime family of which the witness was a member. During the break, the witness openly admitted to the attorney that he lied under oath and that, in fact, the defendant was a member of the organized crime family, but the witness insisted that the attorney not disclose this information to anyone. The attorney tried to persuade the witness to disclose his lie to the court, but the witness refused.

Must the attorney disclose the perjury to the tribunal?

   (A)   No, because the perjury related to a statement of a witness and not a statement of the client.

   (B)   No, because the witness did not consent to the attorney's disclosure of the perjury.

(C) **Yes, because the information is not protected by the attorney's duty of confidentiality.**

(D) **Yes, because the attorney has learned that the witness has perpetrated a fraud on a tribunal.**

Global Perspective

Although some non-U.S. lawyers will have to grapple with the "client perjury" problem, this is not true of all non-U.S. lawyers. In some countries, for example, criminal suspects are not permitted to testify under oath. As Professor Geoffrey C. Hazard Jr. and Angelo Dondi explain in their book entitled *Legal Ethics: A Comparative Study* 36 (Stanford Press 2004):

> A further nuance in the ethical obligations of [U.S.] criminal defense lawyers concerns the problem of perjury by a criminal accused or a witness on behalf of the accused. This problem is much discussed in American professional discourse. . . . This absurdity [of the U.S. system] is avoided in civil law systems. In those systems, an accused is permitted to present statements that are not on oath and are not regarded as evidence in the full sense. The court is required to hear and to consider the statements, but they are not "testimony" governed by the same legal obligation of truth-telling that applies to other witnesses. (In many civil law systems the same distinction between parties and independent witnesses is also made in civil litigation.)

Rule 3.3 governs "candor to the tribunal." Rule 3.3(a) provides the general rule with regard to false statements and false evidence. It provides that:

(a)   A lawyer shall not knowingly:

    (1)   make a false statement of fact or law to a tribunal or fail to correct a false statement of material fact or law previously made to the tribunal by the lawyer;

    * * *

    (3)   offer evidence that the lawyer knows to be false. If a lawyer, the lawyer's client, or a witness called by the lawyer, has offered material evidence and the lawyer comes to know of its falsity, the lawyer shall take reasonable remedial measures, including, if necessary, disclosure to the tribunal. A lawyer may refuse to offer evidence, other than the testimony of a defendant in a criminal matter, that the lawyer reasonably believes is false.

Take Note

Note two points: First, the duty to rectify false evidence and other frauds on the court continues until the relevant proceedings are over; and second, the duty "trumps" the confidentiality duty of Rule 1.6. This means that in some cases, lawyers will have to disclose their clients' confidential information. This was not true under Disciplinary Rule 7-102(B)(1) of the ABA Model Code of Professional Responsibility when a client perpetrated a fraud on the tribunal. Under the earlier provision, the lawyer was instructed to call upon the client to rectify the fraud, but if the client refused, the lawyer was required to reveal the fraud to the tribunal only when the information was not protected as a privileged communication. Which alternative do you think is better?

Rule 3.3(b) establishes a duty to rectify frauds on the court in addition to the presentation of false evidence, which is covered by Rule 3.3(a)(3). Rule 3.3(b) provides that:

(b) A lawyer who represents a client in an adjudicative proceeding and who knows that a person intends to engage, is engaging or has engaged in criminal or fraudulent conduct related to the proceeding shall take reasonable remedial measures, including, if necessary, disclosure to the tribunal.

Rule 3.3(c) identifies the proceedings to which these duties apply. It provides: "The duties stated in paragraphs (a) and (b) continue to the conclusion of the proceeding, and apply even if compliance requires disclosure of information otherwise protected by Rule 1.6."

* * *

The Comment to Rule 3.3 further explains:

Preserving Integrity of Adjudicative Process

[12] Lawyers have a special obligation to protect a tribunal against criminal or fraudulent conduct that undermines the integrity of the adjudicative process, such as bribing, intimidating or otherwise unlawfully communicating with a witness, juror, court official or other participant in the proceeding, unlawfully destroying or concealing documents or other evidence or failing to disclose information to the tribunal when required by law to do so. Thus, paragraph (b) requires a lawyer to take reasonable remedial measures, including disclosure if necessary, whenever the lawyer knows that a person, including the lawyer's client, intends to engage, is engaging or has engaged in criminal or fraudulent conduct related to the proceeding.

[Question 6-4]

An attorney represents a client in a personal injury lawsuit against the driver of a truck that collided with the client's car. In preparation for a deposition, the attorney interviewed the client, who claimed to be in perfect health before the accident. However, as the interview progressed, the attorney noticed a number of inconsistencies in the client's story. The attorney now reasonably believes, but is uncertain, that the client is lying about her health prior to the accident. The deposition is scheduled for tomorrow, and the client intends to testify about the previous "perfect health."

May the attorney allow the client to testify about her health at the deposition?

    (A) Yes, because the duty not to offer false evidence does not apply to depositions.

    (B) Yes, because the attorney is not certain that the client intends to provide false testimony.

    (C) No, because the attorney is an officer of the court and has the obligation to prevent the trier of fact from being misled by false evidence.

    (D) No, because the attorney is prohibited from offering false evidence in a proceeding.

Review the provisions of <u>Rule 3.3</u> above. In addition, the Comment to Rule 3.3 elaborates:

Offering Evidence

[5] Paragraph (a)(3) requires that the lawyer refuse to offer evidence that the lawyer knows to be false, regardless of the client's wishes. This duty is premised on the lawyer's obligation as an officer of the court to prevent the trier of fact from being misled by false evidence. * * *

[6] If a lawyer knows that the client intends to testify falsely or wants the lawyer to introduce false evidence, the lawyer should seek to persuade the client that the evidence should not be offered. If the persuasion is ineffective and the lawyer continues to represent the client, the lawyer must refuse to offer the false evidence. If only a portion of a witness's testimony will be false, the lawyer may call the witness to testify but may not elicit or otherwise permit the witness to present the testimony that the lawyer knows is false.

[7] The duties stated in paragraphs (a) and (b) apply to all lawyers, including defense counsel in criminal cases. In some jurisdictions, however, courts have required counsel to present the accused as a witness or to give a narrative statement if the accused so desires, even if counsel knows that the testimony or statement will be false. The obligation of the advocate under the Rules of Professional Conduct is subordinate to such requirements. *See also* Comment [9].

[8] The prohibition against offering false evidence only applies if the lawyer knows that the evidence is false. A lawyer's reasonable belief that evidence is false does not preclude its presentation to the trier of fact. A lawyer's knowledge that evidence is false, however, can be inferred from the circumstances. *See* Rule 1.0(f). Thus, although a lawyer should resolve doubts about the veracity of testimony or other evidence in favor of the client, the lawyer cannot ignore an obvious falsehood.

[9] Although paragraph (a)(3) only prohibits a lawyer from offering evidence the lawyer knows to be false, it permits the lawyer to refuse to offer testimony or other proof that the lawyer reasonably believes is false. Offering such proof may reflect adversely on the lawyer's ability to discriminate in the quality of evidence and thus impair the lawyer's effectiveness as an advocate. Because of the special protections historically provided criminal defendants, however, this Rule does not permit a lawyer to refuse to offer the testimony of such a client where the lawyer reasonably believes but does not know that the testimony will be false. Unless the lawyer knows the testimony will be false, the lawyer must honor the client's decision to testify. *See also* Comment [7].

Remedial Measures

[10] Having offered material evidence in the belief that it was true, a lawyer may subsequently come to know that the evidence is false. Or, a lawyer may be surprised when the lawyer's client, or another witness called by the lawyer, offers testimony the lawyer knows to be false, either during the lawyer's direct examination or in response to cross-examination by the opposing lawyer. In such situations or if the lawyer knows of the falsity of testimony elicited from the client during a deposition, the lawyer must take reasonable remedial measures. In such situations, the advocate's proper course is to remonstrate with the client confidentially,

advise the client of the lawyer's duty of candor to the tribunal and seek the client's cooperation with respect to the withdrawal or correction of the false statements or evidence. If that fails, the advocate must take further remedial action. If withdrawal from the representation is not permitted or will not undo the effect of the false evidence, the advocate must make such disclosure to the tribunal as is reasonably necessary to remedy the situation, even if doing so requires the lawyer to reveal information that otherwise would be protected by Rule 1.6. It is for the tribunal then to determine what should be done—making a statement about the matter to the trier of fact, ordering a mistrial or perhaps nothing.

[11] The disclosure of a client's false testimony can result in grave consequences to the client, including not only a sense of betrayal but also loss of the case and perhaps a prosecution for perjury. But the alternative is that the lawyer cooperate in deceiving the court, thereby subverting the truth-finding process which the adversary system is designed to implement. *See* Rule 1.2(d). Furthermore, unless it is clearly understood that the lawyer will act upon the duty to disclose the existence of false evidence, the client can simply reject the lawyer's advice to reveal the false evidence and insist that the lawyer keep silent. Thus the client could in effect coerce the lawyer into being a party to fraud on the court.

[Question 6-5]

An attorney represents a client who is charged with murder. The client insists that he wants to take the stand, claiming to have an alibi. The client claims he was with his sister at the movies when the crime took place. The attorney interviewed the client's sister. At first, the sister did not recall where she was that evening, but later developed a vivid recollection confirming the details of the client's story. The attorney reasonably believes, but is uncertain, that the client and the sister are both lying. The attorney attempts to persuade the client not to take the stand, but the client ignores the attorney's pleas.

Must the attorney allow the client to testify about his alibi?

(A) No, because the attorney is prohibited from offering false evidence in a proceeding.

(B) No, because the attorney retains the discretion to disallow his client from testifying if the attorney reasonably believes the client intends to provide false testimony.

(C) Yes, because, in a criminal trial, if the attorney is not certain that the client intends to provide false testimony, then the question of whether to testify in one's own defense is one reserved to the client.

(D) Yes, because the duty not to offer false evidence does not apply to the testimony of criminal defendants.

Review Rule 3.3, including the excerpts provided earlier in this section.

[Question 6-6]

An attorney represented a client who was charged with murder. The client insisted on taking the stand. Certain that the client intended to provide false testimony, the attorney told the client that if the client lied on the stand, the attorney would have no choice but to inform the judge of the client's perjury. The client took the stand but testified truthfully because of the attorney's threat. After the trial, the jury convicted the client.

Does the client have a claim of ineffective assistance of counsel?

(A) Yes, because clients have an unfettered right to testify in their own defense in capital cases.

(B) Yes, because it is never proper for an attorney to threaten a client.

(C) No, because the attorney's conduct fell within accepted standards of professional conduct and did not undermine confidence in the outcome of the trial.

(D) No, because the client's refusal to commit perjury showed that the attorney's threat was effective.

Review Rule 3.3 and the following materials before answering this question.

When a criminal defense attorney believes that her client is about to commit perjury, she faces a particularly difficult dilemma that bears on the right to effective assistance of counsel.

Hear from the Authors

To hear more from the authors on this perjury dilemma, click here.

Applying Strickland v. Washington to Client Perjury: Nix v. Whiteside

In a highly publicized case, *Nix v. Whiteside*, 475 U.S. 157 (1986), the defendant pleaded self-defense, but in his initial statement to defense counsel, he did not mention that the victim had a gun. In a later interview, the defendant stated that he now remembered that he saw the victim with "something metallic" in his hand. When challenged about the discrepancy by defense counsel, the defendant referred to a case in which an acquaintance was acquitted after testifying that his victim wielded a gun. In apparent comparison with that case, the defendant concluded: "If I don't say I saw a gun, I'm dead." The defense counsel told the client that any statement about a gun would be perjury; that if the defendant testified about a gun at trial, the lawyer would advise the court of the perjury, would probably be permitted to impeach the testimony, and would seek to withdraw. The client succumbed to the threats. He testified at trial that he believed the victim was reaching for a gun, but he had not seen one. The client challenged his second degree murder conviction on the ground of ineffective assistance of counsel. Although the state courts commended the lawyer's integrity, a federal court of appeals granted habeas corpus relief.

The Supreme Court unanimously reversed the Court of Appeals in an opinion by Chief Justice Burger. He reasoned that no defendant has a right to commit perjury, so that no defendant has a right to rely upon counsel to assist in the development of false testimony. The Court noted that under *Strickland v. Washington*, 466 U.S. 668 (1984) the defendant alleging ineffective assistance must prove prejudice, and Whiteside "has no valid claim that confidence in the result of his trial has been diminished by his desisting from the contemplated perjury."

Even if the jury would have been persuaded by the perjury, the Court concluded that under *Strickland*, "a defendant has no entitlement to the luck of a lawless decisionmaker." The Chief Justice reasoned that "if a 'conflict' between a client's proposal and counsel's ethical obligation gives rise to a presumption that counsel's assistance was prejudicially ineffective, every guilty criminal's conviction would be suspect if the defendant had sought to obtain an acquittal by illegal means."

Although lack of cognizable prejudice was enough to decide the case, the Chief Justice went further and held that Whiteside's counsel had not been ineffective in discouraging his client from committing perjury. He concluded that for the purposes of this case, effectiveness could be determined by reference to the prevailing rules of professional

> **Make the Connection**
>
> For further discussion of *Strickland*'s 2-pronged test for ineffective assistance of counsel, *see* Chapter 2.

responsibility governing the conduct of lawyers. He noted that Disciplinary Rule 7-102(A)(4) of the ABA Code of Professional Responsibility (then in effect in Iowa and in a small minority of states) provided that a lawyer shall not "knowingly use perjured testimony or false evidence;" and that Rule 3.3 of the Model Rules requires disclosure of client perjury to the tribunal as a last resort. The Chief Justice found that the prevailing ethical standards "confirm that the legal profession has accepted that an attorney's ethical duty to advance the interests of his client is limited by an equally solemn duty to comply with the law and standards of professional conduct." He concluded as follows:

> [U]nder no circumstances may a lawyer either advocate or passively tolerate a client's giving false testimony. * * * The rule adopted by the Court of Appeals, which seemingly would require an attorney to remain silent while his client committed perjury, is wholly incompatible with the established standards of ethical conduct and the laws of Iowa and contrary to professional standards promulgated by that State. * * * Since there has been no breach of any recognized professional duty, it follows that there can be no deprivation of the right to assistance of counsel under the *Strickland* standard.

Justice Brennan wrote an opinion concurring in the judgment. He agreed with the majority's analysis on the "prejudice" prong of *Strickland*. As to the "performance" prong, however, he argued that the Court "has no constitutional authority to establish rules of ethical conduct for lawyers practicing in the state courts," and that "the Court's essay regarding what constitutes the correct response to a criminal client's suggestion that he will perjure himself is pure discourse without force of law." Justice Blackmun wrote an opinion concurring in the judgment, joined by Justices Brennan, Marshall, and Stevens. He agreed that Whiteside had not shown prejudice from his lawyer's conduct but saw no need to "grade counsel's performance." Justice Stevens also wrote an opinion concurring in the judgment, emphasizing that it is often difficult to determine whether the client's proposed testimony is perjurious.

Whiteside Was Too Easy

Even if the propriety of counsel's performance is considered, *Whiteside* is an easy case. Most lawyers would think it entirely appropriate to try to discourage the client from a planned course of perjury. Indeed, discouragement of perjury is effective advocacy, because the jury may disbelieve the lie, the prosecutor may easily tear it apart on cross-examination, and obviously the client may subject himself to a perjury charge. Moreover, if the trial judge believes that a defendant lied on the stand, this will be taken into account at sentencing. So it certainly makes sense to do everything reasonable to discourage a client from committing perjury on the witness stand.

Harder Questions

The difficult questions, not presented by *Whiteside*, are three. First, what if the client refuses to be dissuaded from a course of perjury and demands to testify? Second, what if the client appears to have been dissuaded from testifying falsely, but then commits perjury after taking the stand? Third, what if the lawyer discovers after the testimony that the client has perjured himself? *See* Monroe H. Freedman, *Client Confidences and Client Perjury: Some Unanswered Questions*, 136 U. Pa. L. Rev. 1939 (1988) (arguing that all of these problems should be left to the adversary system and to cross-examination by the prosecutor). After *Whiteside*, the ABA Standing Committee on Ethics issued ABA Formal Op. 87-353 (1987), which provides that if the lawyer is convinced that a witness is going to commit perjury, and all discussions with the client fail, then the lawyer should inform the court. And if the lawyer discovers perjury after the fact but before the proceedings are terminated, the lawyer must inform the court as well. The opinion justifies its position by noting that the lawyer's obligations to the client have long been constrained by the bounds of law. Those bounds have recognized and continue to recognize that the lawyer should not be complicit in the corruption of the judicial process by assisting the client in the introduction of false testimony. Because of the lawyer's role as an officer of the court, the lawyer is required to prevent perjury and, if unsuccessful, to prevent perjury's ability to pervert the judgment of the court. The opinion further notes that the guarantee of client confidentiality is not applicable where the client seeks to corrupt the judicial process with false evidence.

Food for Thought

What about the lawyers who "follow a practice of not questioning the client about the facts in the case"? ABA Formal Op. 87-353 (1987). According to Professor Stephen Ellmann, "this sort of denial of knowledge has two tremendous, and in our view fatal, disadvantages. The first is that it requires lawyers, who like everyone else no doubt believe that they 'know' many things about many subjects, to profess utter lack of knowledge about matters they should be studying especially carefully, namely the facts of their cases. In other words, it requires lawyers to disclaim common sense. The second disadvantage to disclaiming knowledge in this fashion is that it requires lawyers to assert that the many provisions in the professional codes of ethics which forbid lawyers from using or uttering knowing falsehoods are actually mere pretense, because they will never, ever have any bearing on lawyers' actual duties. * * *

We worry, also, that a relationship marked at its inception by avoidance of truth may grow worse rather than better over time. Clients who have avoided one truth with the lawyer's aid may avoid other truths as well, even against the lawyer's wishes. Lawyers who might seek, for example, to counsel their clients about ethical matters may find that their standing to do so has been impaired." Stephen Ellman, *Truth and Consequences*, 69 Fordham L. Rev. 895, 902–06 (2000).

One difficulty with the ABA solution is that criminal defendants have a constitutional right to testify. They do not, of course, have a constitutional right to commit perjury; but perjury occurs only when the defendant actually testifies. A common scenario proceeds like this: defense counsel believes that the client is adamant about committing perjury, even after counsel gives the defendant *Whiteside* warnings. According to the ABA, counsel must now inform the trial judge that her client intends to commit perjury. The trial judge cannot at this point, on defense counsel's word alone, prevent the defendant from testifying. To do so would risk almost certain reversal for violating the defendant's constitutional right to testify (because perjury will not have been shown to a reviewing court's satisfaction). So the trial judge would have to hold some kind of hearing. At that hearing, the defendant will likely insist that he will tell the truth if permitted to testify. The trial judge will be extremely reluctant to get into a quagmire of confidential communications between client and counsel in determining who is right about whether perjury is planned. By the end of the hearing, the trial judge will likely be uncertain as to whether the defendant is going to commit perjury. Hence, the judge will not want to risk violating the constitutional right to testify by keeping the defendant off the stand. So in the vast majority of cases, defense counsel will have accomplished little by informing the tribunal of the client's planned perjury—the defendant will be permitted to testify anyway. The destruction of the attorney-client relationship, however, will be guaranteed.

> **Food for Thought**
>
> Because reporting on one's client will invariably lead to the destruction of the attorney-client relationship, would it be better to handle the perjury problem through cross-examination by the prosecutor? When a district attorney was asked what the defense lawyer should do when a client intends to commit perjury, he responded, "Do me a favor. Let him try it" (quoting Monroe H. Freedman, *Client Confidences and Client Perjury: Some Unanswered Questions,* 136 U. Pa. L. Rev. 1939 (1988)). Would most prosecutors respond similarly? Is the existence of a lawyer-client relationship a sufficient reason to permit defense lawyers, but not prosecutors, to offer perjured testimony? *See* Stephen A. Saltzburg, *Lawyers, Clients, and the Adversary System,* 37 Mercer L. Rev. 647 (1986).

Compare the ABA solution with the solution proposed by Professor Monroe Freedman, who addressed the perjury problem in *Lawyer's Ethics in an Adversary System* 31–37 (1985):

> In my opinion, the attorney's obligation in such a situation would be to advise the client that the proposed testimony is unlawful, but to proceed in the normal fashion in presenting the testimony and arguing the case to the jury if the client makes the decision to go forward. Any other course would be a betrayal of the assurances of confidentiality given by the attorney in order to induce the client to reveal everything, however damaging it might appear.

Professor Freedman argues that none of the other alternatives, including withdrawal, is workable:

> The most obvious way to avoid the ethical difficulty is for the lawyer to withdraw from the case, at least if there is sufficient time before trial for the client to retain

another attorney. The client will then go to the nearest law office, realizing that the obligation of confidentiality is not what it has been represented to be, and withhold incriminating information or the fact of guilt from the new attorney. In terms of professional ethics, the practice of withdrawing from a case under such circumstances is difficult to defend, since the identical perjured testimony will ultimately be presented. Moreover, the new attorney will be ignorant of the perjury and therefore will be in no position to attempt to discourage the client from presenting it. Only the original attorney, who knows the truth, has that opportunity, but loses it in the very act of evading the ethical problem.

Professor Freedman describes the "Free Narrative" proposal, in which defense counsel lets the defendant tell his story on the stand, without asking questions and without referring to the statement in closing argument. He finds the free narrative solution also unworkable for two principal reasons—one practical and the other strategic. First, the prosecutor may object to the defendant testifying in a narrative form, rather than in the conventional manner, because narrating effectively deprives the prosecutor of the opportunity to object to inadmissible evidence prior to the jury hearing it. Second, seasoned trial attorneys have often concluded, based on their experience, that jurors will likely draw a negative inference about the credibility of the defendant if "the defendant's own attorney turns his or her back on the defendant at the most critical point in the trial, and then, in closing argument, sums up the case with no reference to the fact that the defendant has given exculpatory testimony."

Despite the rejection of the "Free Narrative" solution by the ABA, the Court in *Whiteside*, and Professor Freedman, the free narrative "continues to be a commonly accepted method of dealing with client perjury." *See Shockley v. State*, 565 A.2d 1373 (Del. 1989) (holding that use of free narrative was ethically permissible and did not constitute ineffective assistance of counsel); *People v. Guzman*, 755 P.2d 917 (Cal. 1988) (holding that use of free narrative did not constitute ineffective assistance of counsel); *see also The Florida Bar v. Rubin*, 549 So. 2d 1000 (Fla. 1989) (lawyer jailed for thirty days for refusing to defend client who intended to commit perjury; proper solution would have been to use a free narrative).

Some states have expressly endorsed the "Free Narrative" solution for criminal trials. For example, Rule 3.3(b) of the D.C. Rules of Professional Conduct requires the lawyer to try to dissuade the client from lying and, if unsuccessful, to make a motion to withdraw. If the motion is denied, the lawyer may allow the client to testify "in a narrative fashion" but may not argue the probative value of the client's testimony in closing argument. Also, Comments [11D] and [11E] of the Massachusetts Rules of Professional Conduct provide that "[i]f the lawyer learns of the client's intention to commit perjury during trial, and is unable to dissuade the client from testifying falsely, the lawyer may not stand in the way of the client's absolute right to take the stand and testify." But "the lawyer must not assist the client in presenting the perjured testimony and must not argue the false testimony to a judge, or jury or appellate court as true or worthy of belief." Both D.C. and Massachusetts also prohibit lawyers from disclosing their client's perjury to a tribunal. These jurisdictions obviously place a higher value in preserving client confidentiality than on promoting candor to the tribunal.

The National Association of Criminal Defense Lawyers issued an ethics opinion in support of Professor Freedman's view that client perjury should be treated by defense counsel as a non-event. *See The Champion*, March, 1993, p. 28:

> In the relatively small number of cases in which the client who has contemplated perjury rejects the lawyer's advice and decides to proceed to trial, to take the stand, and to give false testimony, the lawyer should go forward at trial in the ordinary way. That is, the lawyer should examine the client in the normal professional manner and should argue the client's testimony to the jury in summation to the extent that sound tactics justify doing so.

The NACDL also emphasized that the "perjury dilemma" does not arise unless the lawyer *knows* that the client committed perjury and opined that counsel in *Whiteside* lacked actual knowledge. Do you agree with the NACDL that counsel in *Whiteside* did not actually know that his client intended to commit perjury? Do you think it is ethical for the lawyer to refer to the client's testimony during closing argument even though she believes that testimony to be perjurious?

Regardless of your position on these issues, you should know that a lawyer who follows the Freedman/NACDL approach risks discipline in jurisdictions that follow Rule 3.3, which *requires* the lawyer to notify the court as a last resort. Most states have similar language to Rule 3.3. State variations on Rule 3.3 can be found here.

C. Argument

To avoid prejudicing the judgment of jurors and to protect the truth-finding purpose of adjudicatory proceedings, lawyers are restricted in what they may say in court, particularly in their closing statements, even if their statements represent genuine views. These restrictions have also been justified as respecting the obligation of fairness owed to opposing party and counsel, which is covered in Unit II of this Chapter.

[Question 6-7]

A member of a national gun rights organization was being criminally prosecuted for assaulting a member of a national gun control organization during a protest march. During closing arguments to the jury, the defense attorney, who was a member of the gun rights organization, said to the jury, "As a juror, you have a unique opportunity to defend your Second Amendment rights. Do you want a world where only thieves have guns? I certainly don't. As a proud gun owner for 20 years, I personally cherish our Second Amendment rights to own guns as the last bastion of liberty. Therefore, I support my client who was merely asserting his Second Amendment right. You should, too."

Was the defense attorney's statement proper?

(A) **No, because the attorney attempted to influence the jurors with emotion.**

(B) **No, because the attorney asserted a personal opinion as to the justness of the cause of the Second Amendment.**

(C) Yes, because the attorney properly reminded the jury of their solemn responsibility in the case.

(D) Yes, because the attorney genuinely believes in the justness of the Second Amendment cause.

Rule 3.4(e) states that "a lawyer shall not . . . in trial, allude to any matter that the lawyer does not reasonably believe is relevant or that will not be supported by admissible evidence, assert personal knowledge of facts in issue except when testifying as a witness, or state a personal opinion as to the justness of a cause, the credibility of a witness, the culpability of a civil litigant or the guilt or innocence of an accused."

Rules 3.1 and 3.3 may also be relevant to a lawyer's arguments.

Rule 3.4(e) is especially directed at closing arguments in a jury trial. Improper statements during summation may result in having a conviction overturned, a mistrial, or reversal of a verdict. Additionally, the offending lawyer may be sanctioned by the trial judge or by a disciplinary body.

In *United States v. Young*, 470 U.S. 1 (1985), the Supreme Court emphasized the prosecutor's special responsibility for closing arguments: "The prosecutor's vouching for the credibility of witnesses and expressing his personal opinion concerning the guilt of the accused pose two dangers: such comments can convey the impression that evidence not presented to the jury, but known to the prosecutor, supports the charges against the defendant and can thus jeopardize the defendant's right to be tried solely on the basis of the evidence presented to the jury; and the prosecutor's opinion carries with it the imprimatur of the Government and may induce the jury to trust the Government's judgment rather than its own view of the evidence." The Court also made clear this doctrine applies equally to defense attorneys. "Defense counsel, like the prosecutor, must refrain from interjecting personal beliefs into the presentation of his case.* * * Defense counsel, like his adversary, must not be permitted to make unfounded and inflammatory attacks on the opposing advocate."

Although state and federal law vary regarding the specifics of what is permissible and impermissible to say during summation or closing arguments, some broad categories are observable. Generally, a lawyer must avoid misstating evidence, referring to facts not introduced in trial, offering a personal opinion about the credibility of witnesses, offering a personal opinion about guilt or liability, presenting their own testimony about evidence, or appealing to irrelevant factors for decision-making such as sympathy, passion or prejudice.

Simulation: Good and Bad Arguments

Suppose that you are the trial judge listening to closing arguments. Which of the following statements made to juries during closing arguments violates Rule 3.4(e)? Why? Which violations warrant a new trial?

- Defense attorney in a civil case commenting on the damages request: "I added all this up at $461,775 and the only thing that I see is [plaintiffs' counsel] getting rich. That's all that I see with $461,000." *Aetna Cas. & Sur. Co. v. Kaufman*, 463 So. 2d 520 (Fla. Dist. Ct. App. 1985).

- In a medical malpractice action, plaintiff's counsel describes defendants' actions as "the most ridiculous decision that anybody has ever made in history. * * * Here's a patient laying there * * * and these idiots are coming in with Life Flight and picking him up and actually taking off 30 minutes later, when time is of the essence, minutes and seconds count. * * * It's a tragedy of errors. Everything these people did while he's sitting there is ridiculous." *Baptist Hosp., Inc. v. Rawson*, 674 So. 2d 777 (Fla. Dist. Ct. App. 1996).

- In a child abuse case, the prosecutor comments on the defendant's testimony: "The number one reason why you should not believe what [the defendant] says is nobody, nobody in this country has more reason to lie than a defendant in a criminal trial. [Defense attorney] told you about motives to lie. The Judge told you you can consider that. [Defense attorney] gave a ridiculous motive for [prosecution witness] to lie. But this defendant has every reason to lie. She is a defendant. Other reasons why you should not believe the defendant, her testimony is inconsistent with her statement." *Degren v. State*, 722 A.2d 887 (Maryland 1999).

- Prosecutor commenting on trial witnesses and evidence: "You have the statement of [a witness]. He's very believable. You can rely on him. You have the statement of [another witness], believable. * * * I don't know how many of you have worked on vehicles. I've never seen a carburetor float scale that looked like that. But I've seen a lot of crackheads arrested with that same thing in their pocket, a little tin scale." *State v. Hayden*, 190 P.3d 1091 (Mont. 2008).

- During closing rebuttal, a prosecutor said: "The only question you've got is you've got to get back here and determine beyond a reasonable doubt is did he do it? Did he do it? Because we've proven all the elements of the offense. I submit to you, we proved he did it. But that's the question for you. I don't get to go back there with you. My vote was cast a long time ago when I charged him with what he did." *Brown v. State*, 74 So. 3d 984 (Ala. Crim. App. 2010).

D. Witnesses

Because a central purpose of an adjudicative proceeding is to discover facts and to determine the best legal basis on which to grant or deny relief, the Rules limit a lawyer's ability to prevent a party's access to witnesses or evidence. These rules are designed to ensure that lawyers play fairly and that their zeal does not unduly obstruct the court's pursuit of truth.

[Question 6-8]

An attorney represents a client in a slip-and-fall accident claim against the owner of a local burger restaurant. The client alleged that he fell on a banana peel while walking toward the drink machine at the restaurant. Three weeks prior to the date designated for trial, the attorney discovered a customer who witnessed the accident. The attorney interviewed the customer-witness, who contradicted the testimony of the client. The witness claimed that there was no banana peel on the floor and that the client's kids were running around the restaurant and tripped the client, who then fell on the floor. The witness asked the attorney, "Do I have to appear in court? I really can't take time off of work to appear in court." The attorney replied, "If you can't take time off of work, then you shouldn't answer your phone." The attorney never mentioned this conversation with the witness to the opposing counsel, who knew nothing about this witness.

Is the attorney subject to discipline?

 Yes, because the attorney failed to notify opposing counsel of a witness who had relevant adverse evidence.

 (B) Yes, because the attorney improperly suggested that the witness refrain from speaking about what the witness saw, and the witness is not a relative, employee, or agent of the client.

 No, because the opposing counsel had not yet subpoenaed the witness to testify.

 No, because the attorney has an ethical obligation to represent her client zealously.

Rule 3.4, relating to "fairness to opposing party and counsel," includes a number of provisions relating to evidence and witnesses. It states that:

[a] lawyer shall not:

(a)   unlawfully obstruct another party's access to evidence or unlawfully alter, destroy or conceal a document or other material having potential evidentiary value. A lawyer shall not counsel or assist another person to do any such act;

(b)   falsify evidence, counsel or assist a witness to testify falsely, or offer an inducement to a witness that is prohibited by law;

* * *

(f)   request a person other than a client to refrain from voluntarily giving relevant information to another party unless:

> (1)   the person is a relative or an employee or other agent of a client; and

> (2)   the lawyer reasonably believes that the person's interests will not be adversely affected by refraining from giving such information.

The Comment explains that "[t]he procedure of the adversary system contemplates that the evidence in a case is to be marshalled competitively by the contending parties. Fair competition in the adversary system is secured by prohibitions against destruction or concealment of evidence, improperly influencing witnesses, obstructive tactics in discovery procedure, and the like."

Global Perspective

Standards about acceptable lawyer behavior toward witnesses can vary from country to country. In the U.S., for example, we consider it improper to pay "fact" witnesses, but we do not consider it improper to interview fact witnesses ahead of time or to "prep" them for their testimony, so long as the lawyer does not cross the line of encouraging false testimony. Indeed, U.S. lawyers might say that the duty of competence found in Rule 1.1 requires that lawyers meet with and prepare their witnesses for trial. In some jurisdictions, however, it is considered unethical and improper for a lawyer to discuss a case with a witness prior to the witness' testimony in court. These differing views about acceptable lawyer actions have led to misunderstandings in international criminal cases and international arbitration matters, both of which may involve lawyers from different jurisdictions. Because of these differing norms, witness preparation is one of the topics addressed in the International Bar Association's Rules on the Taking of Evidence in International Arbitration (2010). Article 4(3) states: "It shall not be improper for a Party, its officers, employees, legal advisors or other representatives to interview its witnesses or potential witnesses and to discuss their prospective testimony with them." (The IBA Rules are not binding, but may be incorporated by an international tribunal or the parties.) The introduction to this IBA document explains that its suggested rules "may be particularly useful when the parties come from different legal cultures."

[Question 6-9]

An attorney represents a client in a sexual harassment claim against her former boss, a west coast software company executive. The attorney learned from the client that another former employee of the software company was an eyewitness to the alleged incidents of sexual harassment. That witness, however, had moved back east to live with his ailing parents. The attorney contacted and interviewed the witness and ultimately concluded that the witness's testimony would be helpful to the client's case. The attorney asked the witness to travel back to the west coast to testify at trial. The witness complained that as a salaried employee, he would lose income from traveling to the west coast for trial. As a result, the attorney offered to pay for the witness's actual travel expenses, the witness's lost income from his employment, and $200 in the event that the client recovers from the defendant. The witness accepted the offer.

Is the attorney subject to discipline?

> (A)   Yes, because the attorney may not pay the witness the $200 contingent fee.

Yes, because the attorney may not enter into a contract with a witness to appear in court.

No, because the attorney may offer an inducement to a witness in exchange for favorable testimony.

(D) No, because the amount promised to the witness for appearing and testifying was reasonable.

Rule 3.4(b) leaves it to other law, including especially court opinions, to establish what payments may be made to witnesses. Restatement § 117 summarizes the law on compensating witnesses. It provides that:

[a] lawyer may not offer or pay to a witness any consideration:

(1) in excess of the reasonable expenses of the witness incurred and the reasonable value of the witness's time spent in providing evidence, except that an expert witness may be offered and paid a noncontingent fee;

(2) contingent on the content of the witness's testimony or the outcome of the litigation; or

(3) otherwise prohibited by law.

Early court decisions recognized that it is unlawful to compensate a witness for his or her testimony because of the danger that the payment might influence the witness's testimony (or appear to the trier of fact to have done so) and because witnesses have a duty to testify even without compensation. Thus, long before the adoption of the Codes, lawyers were subject to professional discipline for agreeing to pay witnesses in connection with their testimony, and such agreements were deemed unenforceable as against public policy. Disciplinary Rule ("DR") 7-109(c) of the ABA Model Code of Professional Responsibility ("ABA Model Code") sought to codify the understanding reflected in the case law. It generally prohibited compensating a fact witness "contingent on the content of his testimony or the outcome of the case." An exception was recognized, however, for providing fact witnesses reimbursement of expenses and compensation for lost time in testifying. This was explicitly codified in DR 7-109(C)(1)&(2), which provided that "a lawyer may . . . acquiesce in the payment of. . . [e]xpenses reasonably incurred by a witness in attending or testifying" and "[r]easonable compensation to a witness for the loss of time in attending or testifying."

ABA Formal Op. 96–402 (1996) addresses some of the challenges of calculating a witness's "reasonable compensation . . . for the loss of time" in testifying and preparing to testify. When the witness is a salaried employee who loses income in order to testify or prepare, the measure of reasonable compensation is lost income. It may be somewhat less straightforward to calculate the value of lost time when dealing with a witness who is self-employed, but the opinion provides that when the self-employed individual loses time from that employment, the fee may be based upon the witness' hourly rate. The calculation is far less simple when the witness is unemployed or retired. The opinion concludes that unemployed and retired individuals may be compensated for their lost time in testifying and preparing to testify, and that "the lawyer must determine the reasonable value of the witness's time based on all relevant circumstances."

E. Improper Communications with Judges and Jurors

While lawyers are expected to deploy their skills and resources to persuade judges and jurors, there are limits to what they can do. For example, Rule 3.5(a) provides that a lawyer shall not "seek to influence a judge, juror, prospective juror or other official by means prohibited by law[.]" Accordingly, lawyers are prohibited from bribing jurors and judges, which would be a violation of federal and state criminal statutes. In addition, other provisions of Rule 3.5 have highlighted ex parte communications with judges and jurors as being vulnerable to unfair manipulation by lawyers.

[Question 6-10]

A company's board of directors discovered evidence that someone had embezzled $30,000 from the company's treasury. The board members believed that the likely embezzler was an officer and that the officer was about to transfer the money and flee the country. However, the board recognized that there was also evidence that the embezzler was the officer's secretary who might have stolen the funds without the officer's knowledge. The company asked its attorney to obtain an emergency court order to freeze the officer's bank account until responsibility for the embezzlement could be conclusively determined. In accordance with the state's procedural rules on emergency orders, the attorney sought the court order and appeared in court without giving notice to the officer. The attorney then presented the evidence supporting the theory that the officer embezzled the money. The attorney did not present the evidence that the secretary may have been responsible. The court granted the emergency motion.

Is the attorney subject to discipline?

    (A) **No, because there is no duty to present evidence that is adverse to the client's motion.**

    (B) **No, because the attorney's duty to present contrary evidence was superseded by the company's right to confidentiality.**

    (C) **Yes, because the attorney failed to disclose evidence indicating that the secretary, acting alone, may have embezzled the money on her own.**

    (D) **Yes, because the attorney communicated with the court without including the opposing party.**

Rule 3.5 of the Pennsylvania Rules of Professional Conduct, which is identical to the ABA Model Rule, governs "impartiality and decorum of the tribunal." Rule 3.5(b) provides that "[a] lawyer shall not * * * communicate ex parte with [a judge, juror, prospective juror or other official] during the proceeding unless authorized to do so by law or court order[.]"

Restatement § 113 Comment (c) explains that the prohibition on ex parte communications "does not apply to routine and customary communications for the purpose of scheduling a hearing or similar communications[.]" As Comment (d) notes, the law generally permits ex parte communications for purposes of obtaining a temporary restraining order, but that in such circumstances a "special duty of candor" arises. Rule 3.3(d) codifies this duty by requiring a lawyer "[i]n an ex parte proceeding [to] inform the tribunal of all material facts known to the lawyer that will enable the tribunal to make an informed decision, whether or not the facts are adverse."

[Question 6-11]

After a long trial, a jury awarded the plaintiff a large sum of money in an employment discrimination suit. The attorney for the defendant former employer interviewed the jurors to get a sense of why they awarded such a large sum to the plaintiff. The attorney's communication was cordial and truthful. This communication was not prohibited by law or a court order.

Is the attorney subject to discipline?

Take Note

Disciplinary Rule 7-108 of the ABA Model Code of Professional Responsibility had a slightly different approach to communications with jurors. It contained provisions addressing what was impermissible *before, during* and *after* the trial of a case. DR 7-108(D) addresses the "after" phase and provides, "After discharge of the jury from further consideration of a case with which the lawyer was connected, the lawyer shall not ask questions of or make comments to a member of that jury that are calculated merely to harass or embarrass the juror or to influence his actions in future jury service."

(A) Yes, because ex parte communications with jurors are not permitted.

(B) Yes, because the judge did not expressly permit the communication.

(C) No, because the rules do not regulate communications with jurors after a proceeding is over.

(D) No, because the communication was cordial and truthful and not prohibited by law or a court order.

Rule 3.5(c) of the Pennsylvania Rules of Professional Conduct provides that

a lawyer shall not * * * communicate with a juror or prospective juror after discharge of the jury if:

(1)   the communication is prohibited by law or court order;

(2)   the juror has made known to the lawyer a desire not to communicate; or

(3)   the communication involves misrepresentation, coercion, duress or harassment[.]

F.   Nonadjudicative Proceeding

Although courts and other adjudicative proceedings, such as arbitral tribunals, easily come to mind when thinking about the lawyer's "officer of the court" role, special duties are by no means confined to adjudicative settings. Lawyers owe a duty to deal honestly with nonadjudicative bodies. Comment [1] of Rule 3.9 justifies this prescription by noting, "In representation before bodies such as legislatures, municipal councils, and executive and administrative agencies acting in a rule-making or policy-making capacity, lawyers present facts, formulate issues and advance argument in the matters under consideration. The decision-making body, like a court, should be able to rely on the integrity of the submissions made to it."

[Question 6-12]

An attorney is a notable expert on financial regulation. The attorney was asked to appear before Congress to present the attorney's views about the problems afflicting the banking sector during the recent financial crisis. Before Congress, the attorney testified that the best reform was no reform because regulation is bad for banks and bad for America. These were, in fact, the attorney's genuine views. However, the attorney declined to mention that a large bank, a client of the attorney, was compensating the attorney for the appearance and time before Congress.

Is the attorney subject to discipline?

   (A) **Yes, because an attorney may not accept a fee for providing congressional testimony.**

   (B) **Yes, because an attorney representing a client before a legislative body must disclose that the appearance is in a representative capacity.**

   (C) **No, because the attorney presented only genuine views.**

   (D) **No, because the attorney's comments to Congress are protected by the First Amendment's guarantee of the freedom of speech.**

Rule 3.9 provides that "[a] lawyer representing a client before a legislative body or administrative agency in a nonadjudicative proceeding shall disclose that the appearance is in a representative capacity[.]" The Rule also requires lawyers in non-adjudicative proceedings "to conform to the provisions of Rules 3.3(a) through (c), 3.4(a) through (c), and 3.5."

G. Stating or Implying Improper Influence

As the competition for clients continues to increase and the practice of law comes to resemble more and more a business, the temptation to push the envelope in promotional marketing intensifies. What restrictions are imposed on lawyers' abilities to brag to their existing or prospective clients? Can the lawyer, for example, boast about her connections to the judiciary?

[Question 6-13]

An attorney is a well-known patent litigator who often defends cases in a bench trial and who strives to maintain good relationships with judges. Once, the attorney received an unsolicited letter from a judge, whom the attorney happened to know well. In that letter, the judge praised the quality of the attorney's briefing and argument. At a meeting with

a prospective client, the attorney boasted about this letter and said, "I can tell you that if you retain me, you will be guaranteed to be represented by an attorney who not only has fans on the bench but also has some of the tightest relationships with many of the judges deciding patent cases. Many of them are my good friends and go out of their way to rule in my favor."

Is the attorney subject to discipline?

    (A)   No, because the attorney's statements were true.

    (B)   No, because the attorney's statements would fail to persuade and impress the reasonable prospective client.

    (C)   Yes, because it is inappropriate to refer to private letters from judges to prospective clients.

    (D)   Yes, because the attorney stated or implied an ability to influence improperly an official.

Rule 8.4(e) defines it as "professional misconduct [to] state or imply an ability to influence improperly a government agency or official or to achieve results by means that violate the Rules of Professional Conduct or other law."

H. Trial Publicity

Lawyers may be tempted to try their case in the court of public opinion, especially if the case involves gruesome criminal acts, celebrities, well-known corporations, or alleged civil rights violations. Out-of-court statements, however, are regulated by ethical rules designed to preserve the parties' right to a fair trial, to avoid prejudicing the pending proceeding by tainting the jury, and to preserve the integrity of the legal profession in the eyes of the public.

[Question 6-14]

An attorney represents a famous actress who is being prosecuted for the brutal murder of her husband. The case is being tried before a jury. After police officers took the stand and testified as to what they saw at the scene of the crime, the court recessed. During the court recess, the attorney held a press conference on the courthouse steps. Before television cameras, the attorney said, "We expect to prove that my client had nothing to do with this man's death. In fact, we have definitive forensic evidence that proves beyond any doubt that my client is not the killer. We do not know who the real killer is but we have reason to believe, based on the nature of the heinous crime, that this person is very dangerous. If anyone has any information relating to the killing, please contact us immediately so that we can bring the real killers to justice."

Is the attorney subject to discipline?

(A) Yes, because the attorney should not have made the statement regarding proof based on forensic evidence, as that statement has a substantial likelihood of being materially prejudicial.

(B) Yes, because the attorney inappropriately made melodramatic statements about the dangerousness of the real killer.

(C) No, because the attorney was acting appropriately as a zealous advocate for the client.

(D) No, because criminal defense attorneys are granted a wide range of discretion with respect to extra-judicial statements.

[Question 6-15]

The police apprehended a defendant who confessed to murder. At a press conference convened the day after the defendant's confession, the prosecutor said, "We have a murder confession from the individual we apprehended, and this individual provided incredible details that only the murderer would have known. We're very confident that we have apprehended the right person." The day after the press conference, the police filed charges against the defendant for the murder. The filed statement of charges stated: "The defendant provided a full and detailed account of the assault and murder . . . . The defendant provided details about the murder that would only be known by the perpetrator of the crime."

Is the prosecutor subject to discipline?

(A) Yes, because the prosecutor should not have made the statement regarding the confession as that statement has a substantial likelihood of materially prejudicing an adjudicative proceeding.

(B) Yes, because a prosecutor should never announce that a defendant has confessed.

(C) No, because the error was harmless because the prosecutor's statement appeared in the charges against the defendant.

(D) No, because the prosecutor's statement regarding the confession is protected under the safe harbor provisions of the rule governing trial publicity.

Rule 3.6 governs "trial publicity." It forbids "[a] lawyer who is participating or has participated in the investigation or litigation of matter" from "mak[ing] an extrajudicial statement that the lawyer knows or reasonably should know will be disseminated by means of public communication and will have a substantial likelihood of materially prejudicing an adjudicative proceeding in the matter." Rule 3.6(b) sets forth a series of statements that a lawyer is expressly permitted to make. These "safe harbors" are:

(1) the claim, offense or defense involved and, except when prohibited by law, the identity of the persons involved;

(2)   information contained in a public record;

(3)   that an investigation of a matter is in progress;

(4)   the scheduling or result of any step in litigation;

(5)   a request for assistance in obtaining evidence and information necessary thereto;

(6)   a warning of danger concerning the behavior of a person involved, when there is reason to believe that there exists the likelihood of substantial harm to an individual or to the public interest; and

(7)   in a criminal case, in addition to subparagraphs (1) through (6):

> (i)   the identity, residence, occupation and family status of the accused;
>
> (ii)   if the accused has not been apprehended, information necessary to aid in apprehension of that person;
>
> (iii)   the fact, time and place of arrest; and
>
> (iv)   the identity of investigating and arresting officers or agencies and the length of the investigation.

Rule 3.6(c) provides for counsel's right to counter adverse publicity. It is known as the "fair reply" provision and provides that "a lawyer may make a statement that a reasonable lawyer would believe is required to protect a client from the substantial undue prejudicial effect of recent publicity not initiated by the lawyer or the lawyer's client." It further limits such a statement to "such information as is necessary to mitigate the recent adverse publicity." Rule 3.6(d) applies the provisions of Rule 3.6 to the colleagues in a firm or the government of a lawyer covered by Rule 3.6(a).

The Comment to Rule 3.6 explains:

* * *

[4] Paragraph (b) identifies specific matters about which a lawyer's statements would not ordinarily be considered to present a substantial likelihood of material prejudice, and should not in any event be considered prohibited by the general prohibition of paragraph (a). Paragraph (b) is not intended to be an exhaustive listing of the subjects upon which a lawyer may make a statement, but statements on other matters may be subject to paragraph (a).

[5] There are, on the other hand, certain subjects that are more likely than not to have a material prejudicial effect on a proceeding, particularly when they refer to a civil matter triable to a jury, a criminal matter, or any other proceeding that could result in incarceration. These subjects relate to:

> (1)   the character, credibility, reputation or criminal record of a party, suspect in a criminal investigation or witness, or the identity of a witness, or the expected testimony of a party or witness;

(2) in a criminal case or proceeding that could result in incarceration, the possibility of a plea of guilty to the offense or the existence or contents of any confession, admission, or statement given by a defendant or suspect or that person's refusal or failure to make a statement;

(3) the performance or results of any examination or test or the refusal or failure of a person to submit to an examination or test, or the identity or nature of physical evidence expected to be presented;

(4) any opinion as to the guilt or innocence of a defendant or suspect in a criminal case or proceeding that could result in incarceration;

(5) information that the lawyer knows or reasonably should know is likely to be inadmissible as evidence in a trial and that would, if disclosed, create a substantial risk of prejudicing an impartial trial; or

(6) the fact that a defendant has been charged with a crime, unless there is included therein a statement explaining that the charge is merely an accusation and that the defendant is presumed innocent until and unless proven guilty.

* * *

Rule 3.6 is not the only provision that deals with trial publicity. Recognizing that prosecutors' extrajudicial statements may deprive defendants of their right to an impartial jury, Rule 3.8(f) imposes additional ethical obligations on prosecutors in criminal cases.

Rule 3.8 provides that:

The prosecutor in a criminal case shall:

* * *

(f) except for statements that are necessary to inform the public of the nature and extent of the prosecutor's action and that serve a legitimate law enforcement purpose, refrain from making extrajudicial comments that have a substantial likelihood of heightening public condemnation of the accused and exercise reasonable care to prevent investigators, law enforcement personnel, employees or other persons assisting or associated with the prosecutor in a criminal case from making an extrajudicial statement that the prosecutor would be prohibited from making under Rule 3.6 or this Rule.

Of course, whenever speech is restricted, First Amendment concerns are raised. Consider the following case, which upheld a district judge's contempt order against lawyer Bruce Cutler for violating the Southern and Eastern Districts of New York Local Criminal Rule 7 governing trial publicity, which provides in part: "It is the duty of the lawyer or law firm not to release or authorize the release of information or opinion which a reasonable person would expect to be disseminated by means of public communication, in connection with pending or imminent criminal litigation with which a lawyer or law firm is associated, if there is a reasonable likelihood that such dissemination will interfere with a fair trial or otherwise prejudice the due administration of justice . . . ." What interpretation of the local rule did the *Cutler* Court adopt in order to avoid running afoul of the First Amendment?

United States v. Cutler

58 F.3d 825 (2d Cir. 1995)

MCLAUGHLIN, CIRCUIT JUDGE:

* * *

BACKGROUND

[Ed note: Notorious mob boss John Gotti was arrested on December 11, 1990 on racketeering charges. In announcing the indictment at a press conference, the U.S. Attorney Andrew Maloney called Gotti a "murderer, not a folk hero" and boasted that the government's evidence, which included extensive wiretap recordings, was much stronger than in prior failed prosecution attempts. Gotti's lawyer, Bruce Cutler, a member of the New York bar, waged a publicity campaign, emphatically denying that Gotti was a mob boss. The federal district court found both prosecution's and defense counsel's extra-judicial statements to be in tension with Local Criminal Rule 7 of the Southern and Eastern Districts of New York ("Local Rule 7"), which provides, "It is the duty of the lawyer . . . not to release or authorize the release of information or opinion which a reasonable person would expect to be disseminated by means of public communication, in connection with pending or imminent criminal litigation with which a lawyer . . . is associated, if there is a reasonable likelihood that such dissemination will interfere with a fair trial or otherwise prejudice the due administration of justice. . . ." Local Rule 7 also enumerates six categories of extrajudicial statements which lawyers are prohibited from making. Despite the district court's pre-trial admonition and formal orders to comply with Local Rule 7, Cutler continued to hold numerous press conferences and continued to give numerous interviews to print and broadcast media, including *60 Minutes* and a live television show called *9 Broadcast Plaza*. In these interviews, Cutler accused the prosecutors of, among other things, lying and "dealing in vendettas," "framing people" and conducting "a witch hunt." District court Judge Glasser issued an order to show cause why Cutler should not be held in criminal contempt. Judge Glasser then recused himself, and the matter was reassigned to Chief Judge Platt. After a

> **FYI**
>
> Cutler won acquittals for Gotti on three previous occasions (which is how Gotti earned the nickname "the Teflon Don") and has represented other high-profile criminal defendants such as Phil Spector. Thanks to his over-the-top courtroom style and engagement of the press, Cutler became a media favorite, appearing in movies and even playing a judge for a televised courtroom series, "Jury Duty." For an example of Cutler's courtroom demeanor, watch this video of Cutler being reproached by the judge in the Spector trial.

five-day bench trial, the district court found Cutler guilty of criminal contempt. The court sentenced Cutler to ninety days' house arrest and three years' probation, and also suspended him from practicing law in the Eastern District of New York for 180 days.]

Cutler now appeals.

Take Note

In *Commonwealth v. Lambert,* 723 A.2d 684 (Pa. Super. Ct. 1998), a first-degree murder prosecution resulted in a conviction and a life sentence, but the defendant sought relief in state court under Pennsylvania's Post-Conviction Relief Act. The Court issued an order saying that both sides were precluded from public comment except as allowed by Pennsylvania Rule of Professional Conduct 3.6. The Court held that Rule 3.6 provides clear guidance as to what may be discussed regarding a pending case and that some generality is permissible so that the rule will apply to a multitude of cases. In *Lambert* and *Cutler* the court issued an order essentially instructing attorneys to abide by the local ethical rules. Why would such an order be necessary when lawyers already have an obligation to follow the rules? Issuing an order compelling lawyers to adhere to a rule to which they were already bound allows the court to use its contempt power to enforce the rule.

DISCUSSION

Cutler challenges the validity of the orders, contending that Local Rule 7 is unconstitutional. In addition, he argues that, under the heightened scrutiny employed in First Amendment cases, the evidence does not support his conviction. Finally, he challenges various aspects of his sentence.

* * *

II. Sufficiency of the Evidence

* * *

To hold Cutler in criminal contempt, the government had to prove beyond a reasonable doubt that: (1) the court entered a reasonably specific order; (2) defendant knew of that order; (3) defendant violated that order; and (4) his violation was willful.

A. Reasonably Specific Orders

[The Court finds that Cutler was on notice to follow definite and specific orders by the judge.]

B. Violations of the Orders

Next, Cutler mounts a two-pronged challenge to the finding that he violated the orders. He argues that: (1) even when comments fall within the six categories specifically mentioned in Local Rule 7, the rule proscribes them only if they are reasonably likely to prejudice the proceedings; and (2) none of the comments cited in the order to show cause were reasonably likely to prejudice the proceedings. The first argument has merit; the second does not.

Local Rule 7 proscribes generally any statements by counsel that "a reasonable person would expect to be disseminated by means of public communication, in connection with pending or imminent criminal litigation . . ., if there is a reasonable likelihood that such dissemination will interfere with a fair trial or otherwise prejudice the due administration of justice." The rule then enumerates several specific categories of forbidden speech, but without repeating the "reasonable likelihood" standard. For example, an attorney cannot offer his opinion as to his client's guilt or innocence, or as to the merits of the case. Reasoning that the reasonable likelihood standard did not apply to comments within the six categories, the district court held that if a comment fell within a category and if a reasonable person would expect that the comment would be disseminated by the press, the comment was prohibited. This goes too far. Were we writing on a completely clean slate, we might adopt the district court's approach.

But, the Fourth Circuit has already rejected it. Reviewing a local rule virtually identical to Local Rule 7, the *Hirschkop* court held that a per se proscription of certain types of speech was overbroad and violated the First Amendment. To pass muster, speech that fell within a proscribed category had to be reasonably likely to interfere with a fair trial or otherwise prejudice the due administration of justice.

FYI

Many cases concerning Rule 3.6 reference *Gentile v. State Bar of Nevada*, 501 U.S. 1030 (1991), in which a criminal defense attorney was sanctioned for holding a press conference the day after his client was indicted on charges of theft of money and cocaine used in undercover police operations. Gentile said his client was innocent and blamed the theft on corrupt police officers. In a case pitting regulation of lawyer speech against the First Amendment, the Court found that Nevada's specific application of the state's version of Rule 3.6 was unconstitutional for vagueness, but that such regulations would be permissible under other circumstances.

The Court determined that regulation of lawyer speech must pass a "substantial likelihood of material prejudice" standard: imposing "only narrow and necessary limitations" aimed at curtailing "comments that are likely to influence the actual outcome of the trial, and . . . comments that are likely to prejudice the jury venire, even if an untainted panel can ultimately be found." Chief Justice Rehnquist explained "The restraint on speech is narrowly tailored to achieve those objectives. The regulation of attorneys' speech is limited—it applies only to speech that is substantially likely to have a materially prejudicial effect; it is neutral as to points of view, applying equally to all attorneys participating in a pending case; and it merely postpones the attorneys' comments until after the trial. While supported by the substantial state interest in preventing prejudice to an adjudicative proceeding by those who have a duty to protect its integrity, the Rule is limited on its face to preventing only speech having a substantial likelihood of materially prejudicing that proceeding."

In a separate opinion, Justice Kennedy placed greater weight on protecting speech. He argued that Gentile's speech should have been analyzed as political speech under a stricter standard of preventing a "clear and present danger" of "actual prejudice or an imminent threat." Justice Kennedy maintained "[Gentile's] words were directed at public officials and their conduct in office. There is no question that speech critical of the exercise of the State's power lies at the very center of the First Amendment." Justice Kennedy argued that the public has a legitimate interest in knowing how the judicial system operates and emphasized the important role of publicity in informing public opinion, which acts as an effective restraint on possible abuse of judicial power. Which standard do you think is better?

We see no need to adopt an interpretation of Local Rule 7 that might offend the Constitution. Accordingly, we conclude that speech falling within the six categories violates Local Rule 7 only if it is also reasonably likely to interfere with a fair trial or the administration of justice.

That said, we believe there is a strong, albeit rebuttable, presumption that speech falling within the six categories violates Local Rule 7, as these categories "furnish the context in which the 'reasonable likelihood' standard is intended to operate."

Despite our different approach to Local Rule 7, we need not disturb the result reached by the district court. The district court, at the government's request, made findings of fact under the assumption that the reasonable likelihood standard did apply to speech that fell within proscribed categories, and concluded that, under that standard, Cutler had still violated the orders. Cutler challenges this finding on several grounds. They all lack merit.

First, he contends that the district court ignored his expert witnesses' testimony. We disagree. The experts, criminal trial lawyers, stated their opinion that Cutler's extensive comments could have had no prejudicial effect. The court characterized this testimony as self-serving and worthy of little weight, given that as defense lawyers, the experts shared an inherent bias. Thus, the court did not ignore the testimony; it simply discounted its probative value, which was well within its discretion.

Next, Cutler argues that the voir dire of the Gotti jury venire demonstrates that his comments were not reasonably likely to prejudice the proceedings. Again, we disagree. True, evidence that the Cutler-generated publicity did not in fact taint the jury pool may be relevant to the issue whether those statements were likely to interfere with a fair trial. But *Gentile* never said that such evidence was dispositive, nor did *Gentile* require that actual prejudice be shown. Instead, Local Rule 7's "standard for controlling pretrial publicity must be judged at the time a statement is made."

Finally, Cutler chastises the district court for taking his comments out of context. He notes that Gotti's trial received more press coverage and publicity than any other trial in New York history. He contends that in the midst of a veritable firestorm of anti-Gotti publicity, the few cinders he added could not possibly have tainted the proceedings. He adds that the timing of his comments—made five months before the trial began—underscores their relative harmlessness. We are not persuaded, however, by Cutler's Uriah Heep pose.

Cutler vastly understates the effect defense lawyers can have on prospective jurors. As *Gentile* cautions, "lawyers' statements are likely to be received as especially authoritative" because "lawyers have special access to information through discovery and client communications." Indeed, *Gentile* affirmed the very portion of Nevada's pre-trial publicity rule that considered statements of the sort Cutler made as "ordinarily" likely to have a "substantial likelihood of materially prejudicing" a pending criminal proceeding.

Moreover, although the timing of Cutler's comments may be significant, this factor does not necessarily weigh in Cutler's favor. Our review of the record makes clear that his "statements were timed to have a maximum impact, when public interest in the case was at its height immediately after" the disqualification briefs and record were unsealed.

Finally, we note that in *Gentile*, four Justices were prepared to hold that relatively innocuous statements made at a single press conference some six months before trial in the midst of extensive and sensationalized publicity were substantially likely to materially prejudice the proceedings. In contrast, Cutler spoke repeatedly and heatedly to the press in the months preceding Gotti's trial. Given the more lenient "reasonable likelihood" standard here, coupled with Cutler's performance on 9 Broadcast Plaza alone, we do not doubt that a majority of the *Gentile* Court would find that Cutler violated the orders.

We thus find that Cutler's comments were reasonably likely to prejudice the Gotti proceedings.

C. Willfulness

Criminal contempt generally "requires a specific intent to consciously disregard an order of the court." Cutler contends that he did not willfully disobey the orders because he did not know the comments listed in the order to show cause were reasonably likely to prejudice the proceedings. This argument taxes the most generous credulity.

We hold attorneys to a higher standard of conduct than we do lay persons. Cutler's persistent attempts to try Gotti's case in the media, despite Judge Glasser's repeated warnings, belie any notion that he did not intend these particular comments to prejudice the proceedings, or that he did not recklessly disregard the orders.

Any doubt about this is dispelled by Cutler's participation in a Brooklyn Law School symposium on April, 25, 1991, before the Gotti trial began. There, he expounded upon the virtues of a friendly press:

> I've really grown to appreciate and respect Anthony DeStefano from *New York Newsday*[,] Pete Bowles for *New York Newsday*, Lenny Buder for *The New York Times*, and Arnie Lubasch from *The New York Times* and some of the other reporters who I think do a conscientious job. Do I have selfish reasons? I have honest reasons that I don't want to alienate them, that I want the prospective veniremen out there to feel that I mean what I say and say what I mean, and if that can spill over and help my client, then I feel it's important for me to do that.

With a smoking gun like this, we cannot fault the district court for finding that the government proved Cutler's willfulness "not only beyond any reasonable doubt, but beyond any possible doubt."

In short, the record amply supports findings that the orders were specific, and that Cutler's comments were reasonably likely to prejudice prospective jurors and were willfully made with the intent of prejudicing prospective jurors. Accordingly, we affirm Cutler's criminal contempt conviction.

* * *

CONCLUSION

We have considered all of Cutler's arguments, and find them without merit. We recognize that Cutler did not singlehandedly generate the media circus that threatened the fairness of the final Gotti trial; federal prosecutors and law enforcement officials deserve their share of the blame. Moreover, we sympathize with the plight of a defense lawyer torn between his duties to act as an officer of the court and to zealously defend his client. Nonetheless, a lawyer, of all people, should know that in the face of a perceived injustice, one may not take the law into his own hands. Defendant did, and now he must pay the price.

For More Information

Despite courts' displeasure when lawyers "try a case in the press," a high-profile case may require some level of engagement with the media. During the investigations of Martha Stewart on insider trading charges, a federal judge held attorney-client privilege was not waived when lawyers retained and communicated with public relations consultants in order to obtain advice about how to counteract negative publicity in the media that might influence prosecutors to bring charges against Stewart. The court considered these communications legitimate because the attorneys "were not skilled at public relations" and "needed outside help" to provide legal advice and assistance to their client. *See* Michele DeStefano Beardslee, *Advocacy in the Court of Public Opinion, Installment One: Broadening the Role of Corporate Attorneys*, 22 Geo. J. Legal Ethics 1259 (2009); Michael P. Richman, *Ethical Considerations for Media Advocacy or, Why Martha Stewart Should Matter to You*, Am. Bankr. Inst. J., April 2004, at 24.

For high-profile clients, media coverage of a criminal case may permanently impair the client's reputation regardless of the outcome. Is there a tension between the lawyer's ethical duties under Rule 3.6 and her fiduciary duties to the client where a client relies on the lawyer to also protect him in the court of public opinion? *See* Lonnie T. Brown, Jr., *"May It Please the Camera, . . . I Mean the Court"-an Intrajudicial Solution to an Extrajudicial Problem*, 39 Ga. L. Rev. 83 (2004); Nicholas A. Battaglia, *The Casey Anthony Trial and Wrongful Exonerations: How "Trial by Media" Cases Diminish Public Confidence in the Criminal Justice System*, 75 Alb. L. Rev. 1579, 1584 (2012); Leigh A. Krahenbuhl, Note: *Advocacy in the Media: The Blagojevich Defense and A Reformulation of Rule 3.6*, 61 Duke L.J. 167 (2011).

In some quarters, doubtless, this affirmance will elicit thunderbolts that we are chilling effective advocacy. Obviously, that is neither our intention nor our result. The advocate is still entitled—indeed encouraged—to strike hard blows, but not unfair blows. Trial practice, whether criminal or civil, is not a contact sport. And, its tactics do not include eye-gouging or shin-kicking.

In this case, a conscientious trial judge tried mightily to limit the lawyers to press statements that were accurate and fair. The defendant's statements were dipped in venom and were deliberately couched to poison the well from which the jury would be selected. Such conduct goes beyond the pale, by any reasonable standard, and cannot be condoned under the rubric of "effective advocacy."

We are not unaware that it has become de rigueur for successful criminal defense lawyers to cultivate cozy relationships with the media. Indeed, in this very case, defendant urged law students to do just that. As Seneca once observed, "quae fuerant vitia mores sunt" ("what once were vices are now the manners of the day"). The Bruce Cutler case must now stand as a caution that enough of the "old ethics" survive to bar flouting the Canons of Professional Conduct.

Lord Henry Brougham, who defended Queen Caroline on a criminal charge of adultery, was an early apostle of what today would be known as Rambo litigation tactics. In his argument before the House of Lords, he summed up his view of the advocate's role: "the first great duty of an advocate [is] to reckon everything subordinate to the interests of his client." Twenty-three years later, at a dinner for barristers, with the eighty-six-year-old Lord Brougham in the audience, Chief Justice Alexander Cockburn responded—to loud cheers from the distinguished assembly—"[t]he arms which an advocate wields he ought to use as a warrior, not as an assassin. He ought to uphold the interests of his clients *per fas*, not *per nefas*. He ought to know how to reconcile the interests of his clients with the eternal interests of truth and justice."

The judgment of conviction and sentence are AFFIRMED.

For More Information

The intersection between professional rules and First Amendment speech continues to challenge attorneys and academics. For much more commentary on attorney speech, *see* John Q. Barrett, *The Leak and the Craft: A Hard Line Proposal to Stop Unaccountable Disclosures of Law Enforcement Information*, 68 Fordham L. Rev. 613 (1999); Esther Berkowitz-Caballero, Notes: *In the Aftermath of* Gentile: *Reconsidering the Efficacy of Trial Publicity Rules*, 68 N.Y.U.L. Rev. 494 (1993); Erwin Chemerinsky, *The Sound of Silence: Reflections on the Use of the Gag Order: Lawyers Have Free Speech Rights, Too: Why Gag Orders on Trial Participants are Almost Always Unconstitutional*, 17 Loy. L.A. Ent. L.J. 311 (1997); Kevin Cole & Fred C. Zacharias, *The Agony of Victory and the Ethics of Lawyer Speech*, 69 S. Cal. L. Rev. 1627 (1996); Suzanne F. Day, *The Supreme Court's Attack on Attorneys' Freedom of Expression: The* Gentile v. State Bar of Nevada *Decision*, 43 Case W. Res. 1347 (1993); Rita M. Glavin, Note, *Prosecutors Who Disclose Prosecutorial Information for Literary or Media Purposes: What About the Duty of Confidentiality?*, 63 Fordham L. Rev. 1809 (1995); Gabriel G. Gregg, *ABA Rule 3.6 and California Rule 5-120: A Flawed Approach to the Problem of Trial Publicity*, 43 UCLA L. Rev. 1321 (1996); Peter R. Jarvis, *Legal Ethics Limitations on Pretrial Publicity and the Case of Ron Hoevet*, 31 Willamette L. Rev. 1 (1995); Jonathan M. Moses, Note, *Legal Spin Control: Ethics and Advocacy in the Court of Public Opinion*, 95 Colum. L. Rev. 1811 (1995); Robert S. Stephen, *Prejudicial Publicity Surrounding a Criminal Trial: What a Trial Court Can Do to Ensure a Fair Trial in the Face of a "Media Circus,"* 26 Suffolk U.L. Rev. 1063 (1992); Lynn Weisberg, *On a Constitutional Collision Course: Attorney No-Comment Rules and the Right of Access to Information*, 83 J. Crim. L. & Criminology 644 (1992).

———————

Consider the following case involving the extrajudicial statements of former U.S. Attorney for the Southern District of New York Preet Bharara relating to a grand jury indictment of Sheldon Silver, a former New York State Assembly speaker who was charged with corruption. Although the Court ultimately denied Silver's motion to dismiss the indictment (or, alternatively, to poll the grand jurors or review the grand jury minutes), the Court found that Bharara's statements pushed the envelope "so close to the edge of the rules" that Bharara risked prejudicing the grand jury proceedings. What concerns did the Court express about the content or timing of Bharara's extrajudicial statements, including statements made on Twitter? What guidelines did the Court articulate for staying safely within the rules? Do you agree with the Court's conclusion?

United States v. Silver

103 F.Supp.3d 370 (S.D.N.Y. 2015)

* * *

CAPRONI, DISTRICT JUDGE:

The Court starts with several inarguable principles. First, criminal defendants are entitled to a fair trial. Second, the public has a right to know about criminal prosecutions, perhaps particularly those involving charges of public corruption. Third, criminal cases should be tried in the courtroom and not in the press. Finally, people who venture close to the edge of a rule risk falling over the edge. The rules that govern public statements by federal prosecutors regarding accused defendants are designed to balance the first three principles, with a heavy thumb on the side of defendants' fair trial rights. In this case, the U.S. Attorney, while castigating politicians in Albany for playing fast and loose with the ethical rules that govern their conduct, strayed so close to the edge of the rules governing his own conduct that Defendant Sheldon Silver has a non-frivolous argument that he fell over the edge to the Defendant's prejudice.

Although the Court does not condone the Government's brinksmanship relative to the Defendant's fair trial rights or the media blitz orchestrated by the U.S. Attorney's Office in the days following Mr. Silver's arrest, for the reasons stated below, the Defendant's Motion to Dismiss the Indictment based on allegedly improper and prejudicial extrajudicial statements by the U.S. Attorney (the "Motion") is DENIED.

BACKGROUND

On January 21, 2015, the Government filed a 35-page, single-spaced, sealed Complaint before Chief Magistrate Judge Maas, charging Defendant Silver, the then-Speaker of the New York Assembly, with honest services fraud, conspiracy and extortion. * * * Finding probable cause, Magistrate Judge Maas issued an arrest warrant. * * * In the weeks prior to the issuance of the arrest warrant, there had been numerous newspaper articles reporting on the U.S. Attorney's investigation, including lengthy investigative journalism pieces on Silver's relationship with Weitz & Luxenberg and with Goldberg & Iryami. Shortly after midnight on January 22, 2015, although the Government's Complaint had not yet been unsealed, the press began reporting that that Silver would be arrested imminently along with the substance of the charges against him. * * *

Pursuant to an arrangement between Silver's attorneys and the U.S. Attorney's Office, on the morning of January 22, 2015, Silver surrendered to federal authorities at the Jacob J. Javits Federal Building, where he was processed and then driven in an unmarked car to the basement of the federal courthouse. * * * Silver was presented to Magistrate Judge Maas and granted bail. * * * Upon leaving the courthouse, Silver issued a short statement to the press. * * *

Later that day, the U.S. Attorney for the Southern District of New York and the FBI Special Agent–in–Charge held a press conference, during which the U.S. Attorney described the substance of the Government's charges against Silver, while also criticizing the "the show-me-the-money culture of Albany." Unofficial Transcript of U.S. Attorney's Press Conference, Jan. 22, 2015 * * *. During the press conference, the U.S. Attorney dutifully noted that the charges at that point were only allegations. * * * ("The central allegation in this case is that Speaker Silver successfully sought ways to monetize his public office and that he did so in violation of Federal law."). Certain portions of the U.S. Attorney's comments, however, could reasonably have been interpreted to reflect the U.S. Attorney's personal views as to Silver's character or guilt with respect to the charges filed against him. * * * ("For many years New Yorkers have asked the question 'How could Speaker Silver, one of the most powerful men in all of New York, earn millions of dollars in outside income without deeply compromising his ability to honestly serve his constituents?' Today we provide the answer. He didn't."); * * * ("And as the charges also show, the greedy art of secret self-reward was practiced with particular cleverness and cynicism by the Speaker himself."). Given Silver's status as one of the three most powerful politicians in New York State government, it is not surprising that the U.S. Attorney's comments were covered widely in the press. * * *

For members of the media who missed the press conference, the U.S. Attorney's Office also issued a press release. *See* U.S. Attorney's Office, *New York State Assembly Speaker Sheldon Silver Arrested on Corruption Charges*, Jan. 22, 2015 * * *. The press release highlighted some of the U.S. Attorney's most salient comments, in particular regarding the relationship between the charges against Silver and a broader "culture of corruption" in Albany. * * * ("Politicians are supposed to be on the people's payroll, not on secret retainer to wealthy special interests they do favors for. These charges go to the very core of what ails Albany—a lack of transparency, lack of accountability, and lack of principle joined with an overabundance of greed, cronyism, and self-dealing."). At the same time, the press release referred to the charges as "allegations," and closed by stating that "the charges contained in the Complaint are merely accusations, and the defendant * * * is presumed innocent unless and until proven guilty." * * *

In addition to the press release, following the press conference, the U.S. Attorney's Office transmitted several of the U.S. Attorney's comments via Twitter. One of the "tweets" announced that Silver had been charged with public corruption offenses and referred readers to a link to the press release. * * * Other tweets issued at the same time stated: "Bharara: Silver monetized his position as Speaker of the Assembly in two principal ways & misled the public about his outside income," * * *, and "Bharara: Politicians are supposed to be on the ppl's payroll, not on secret retainer to wealthy special interests they do favors for." * * *

The following day, the U.S. Attorney gave a previously-scheduled speech at New York Law School that was broadcast live on local television and covered by the press. * * * In his opening remarks, the U.S. Attorney said he had decided to address public corruption "given the timing" and the likelihood of interest in the topic. Unofficial Transcript of U.S. Attorney's Speech at New York Law School, Jan. 23, 2015 * * *. Addressing the recent charges brought against Silver, the U.S. Attorney noted that, apart from "the standing and stature of the person who was charged," the Government's charges against Silver were essentially "business as usual in our public corruption unit. Case after case after case we have brought has had at its base money and specifically a person who is in the public trust who is supposed to hold the public trust and sought ways to monetize his or her position." * * * At other points, the U.S. Attorney noted that he was "not talking about anything outside of the four corners of the complaint and nothing beyond what [he] said [the day before]" and emphasized that he was speaking about the "allegations" made in Silver's case. * * *

A couple of weeks later, but still before Silver was indicted, the U.S. Attorney was interviewed on MSNBC. When asked about the recent arrest of "one of the most powerful Democrats in New York," the U.S. Attorney discussed the importance of public corruption prosecutions generally, and then added:

> [W]hen you see somebody who's been charged with (and we've convicted many, many people before this case)—and you see somebody who has basically sold his office to line his pockets and compromised his integrity and ethics with respect to how to make decisions on all those issues I mentioned that affect people's lives, that's a big problem. And it's a big problem for democracy.

MSNBC, *In Conversation, Preet Bharara and Ari Melber*, Feb. 12, 2015 * * *.

On February 19, 2015, the grand jury returned the Indictment charging Silver with honest services mail fraud, honest services wire fraud and extortion. * * * On February 24, 2015, Silver filed the instant Motion claiming that, through his conduct, the U.S. Attorney has "caused [him] irreparable harm." * * * In order to remedy any prejudice that he may have suffered and to deter future misconduct, Silver urges the Court to dismiss the Indictment, or, at a minimum, to poll the grand jury and order disclosure of the grand jury minutes to determine whether the grand jurors were influenced in any improper way. * * *

DISCUSSION

An individual charged with a felony is "constitutionally entitled to have his case considered by an impartial and unbiased grand jury." * * * The proceedings of a grand jury are "accorded a presumption of regularity, which generally may be dispelled only upon particularized proof of irregularities in the grand jury process." * * *

The Defendant argues that this standard has been satisfied because the U.S. Attorney's extrajudicial statements are "*presumed* prejudicial" pursuant to this Court's Local Criminal Rules, Department of Justice ("DOJ") regulations, and the New York Rules of Professional Conduct. * * * Local Criminal Rule 23.1(d) states that "opinion[s] as to the accused's guilt or innocence or as to the merits of the case or the evidence in the case" are matters that "presumptively involve a substantial likelihood" of interference with a fair trial or prejudice to the administration of justice. L.Crim. R. 23.1(d)(7). DOJ regulations similarly state that "[o]bservations about a defendant's character" and "[a]ny opinion as to the accused's guilt" will "generally tend[ ] to create dangers of prejudice without serving a significant law enforcement function." 28 C.F.R. § 50.2(b)(6)(i), (vi). The New York Rules of Professional Conduct are in accord, stating that "any opinion as to the guilt or innocence of a defendant or suspect in a criminal matter" is "ordinarily . . . likely to prejudice materially an adjudicative proceeding." N.Y. R. Prof'l Conduct 3.6(b)(4). The Defendant argues that, because the U.S. Attorney's comments amount to "opinions" as to the Defendant's guilt, they are presumptively prejudicial.

As an initial matter, the Court notes that this is not a disciplinary proceeding and therefore the question of whether the U.S. Attorney's extrajudicial remarks violated any ethical rules is not, per se, before the Court. * * * Rather, the issue before the Court is whether the U.S. Attorney's comments were sufficiently prejudicial to overcome the presumption of regularity accorded to grand jury proceedings and to warrant the extreme sanction of dismissing the Indictment, or in the alternative, polling of the grand jurors or reviewing the grand jury minutes.

I. There Is No Basis to Dismiss the Indictment

FYI

Do you agree with the *Silver* Court that there is no basis to dismiss the grand jury indictment? Professor Bennett L. Gershman believes that some of U.S. Attorney Bharara's statements may have "contaminated the ability of people who might be selected to serve on juries to evaluate the evidence dispassionately and render fair judgements." *See* Bennett L. Gershman, *Mouthing Off: Preet Bharara is an entertaining speaker, but he goes too far*, SLATE. com (March 2, 2015). For a video that includes excerpts of Bharara's press conference and MSNBC interview, click here.

Dismissal of an indictment because of a defect in the grand jury proceedings is a "drastic remedy" that is "rarely used." * * * The district court's authority to dismiss an indictment, whether to eliminate prejudice or to deter official misconduct, is narrowly circumscribed to instances where the misconduct at issue "amounts to a violation of one of those 'few, clear rules which were carefully drafted and approved by [the Supreme] Court and by Congress to ensure the integrity of the grand jury's functions.'" *United States v. Williams*, 504 U.S. 36, 46, 112 S.Ct. 1735, 118 L.Ed.2d 352 (1992) * * * Notably, the Defendant does not argue that this Court's Local Rules, the DOJ Regulations or the New York Rules of Professional Conduct were drafted by the Supreme Court or Congress to ensure the integrity of the grand jury's functions; nor does he cite a single post-*Williams* case in which an indictment has been dismissed due to a violation of such rules. Thus, even if the U.S. Attorney's extrajudicial comments violated applicable disciplinary or ethical rules (and the Court is not saying that they did), that alone would be insufficient grounds to dismiss the Indictment.

Turning to controlling authority, the Defendant argues that the U.S. Attorney's extrajudicial statements and conduct violated the standards set forth in *Bank of Nova Scotia v. United States*, 487 U.S. 250, 255–256, 108 S.Ct. 2369, 101 L.Ed.2d 228 (1988). In that case, the Supreme Court held that dismissal of an indictment for non-constitutional error may be appropriate " 'if it is established that the violation substantially influenced the grand jury's decision to indict,' or if there is 'grave doubt' that the decision to indict was free from the substantial influence of such violations." * * *

The Defendant argues that the U.S. Attorney improperly and "substantially" influenced the grand jury in several ways. First, the Defendant complains that the Government improperly initiated this case by means of its 35-page Complaint, rather than by indictment, and claims the Government did so solely for the purpose of "maximiz[ing] exposure" and prejudicing the Defendant before the grand jury. * * * Second, the Defendant asserts that the Government improperly leaked news of the Defendant's arrest to the press hours before the Complaint was unsealed or the arrest was made. * * * Third, the Defendant claims that the Government "orchestrated the arrest and arraignment to maximize the opportunity for a 'photo op' " to enhance the "perp walk" effect. * * * Finally, the Defendant argues that the U.S. Attorney created a "media circus" around Silver's arrest through his improper and prejudicial comments during the press conference, New York Law School speech and MSNBC interview. * * *

The Court finds little merit in the Defendant's first three arguments. The Government has discretion to proceed via complaint pursuant to the Federal Rules of Criminal Procedure; although the Complaint filed against Silver may have included more information than was absolutely necessary to establish probable cause, the Defendant does not argue that the Complaint itself was improper or the source of any prejudice. As to the Defendant's claim that the Government improperly leaked news of Silver's arrest to the press, which the Government denies, the Court finds that even if the leaks occurred as the Defendant alleges, the speculative news stories published between 1:55 a.m. and 8:00 a.m. on the day of Silver's arrest could hardly have had any prejudicial impact inasmuch as Silver was arrested, the Complaint was unsealed and he appeared in court later that day. * * * Finally, the Court agrees with the Government that its decision to permit Silver to surrender (rather than be arrested) and then to drive him in an unmarked car to the basement of the federal courthouse showed considerable sensitivity, rather than an improper effort to set Silver up for a prejudicial "perp walk."

On the other hand, the Defendant's argument focused on the substance and timing of the U.S. Attorney's public remarks merits further discussion. While the Court does not endorse the Defendant's view that the U.S. Attorney's comments reflected his "uncensored views" as to Silver's guilt and character, * * *, neither does it accept the Government's suggestion that any prejudicial effect of otherwise improper comments is magically dispelled by sprinkling the words "allege(d)" or "allegation(s)" liberally throughout the press conference or speech, or by inserting a disclaimer that the accused is "innocent unless and until proven guilty" at the end of an otherwise improper press release. In particular, the Court is troubled by remarks by the U.S. Attorney that appeared to bundle together unproven allegations regarding the Defendant with broader commentary on corruption and a lack of transparency in certain aspects of New York State politics. In this regard, the Court finds that it would not be unreasonable for members of the media or the public to interpret some of the U.S. Attorney's statements—for example, "[p]oliticians are supposed to be on the people's payroll, not on secret retainer to wealthy special interests they do favors for"—as a commentary on the character or guilt of the Defendant. * * * The rules afford prosecutors considerable latitude to speak about the facts of a case, the offenses charged, and even "the public policy significance of a case," to the extent that such discussion is in furtherance of "law enforcement goals." * * * Remarks that associate the accused with a long line of convicted criminals or a broader pattern of recognized wrongdoing, however, are of concern specifically because they tend to blur the distinction between legitimate public commentary and improper opinion.[8]

Finally, the Court finds the Government's argument that the timing of the U.S. Attorney's speech at the New York Law School event was merely coincidental to be pure sophistry. While the New York Law School speaking engagement was apparently scheduled long before Silver's arrest, it was the Government that decided when to arrest Silver. Given the fact that the U.S. Attorney apparently wanted to address the topic of public corruption in his speech, a far more prudent course—and one that would have been far more respectful of the Defendant's presumption of innocence and fair trial rights—would have been to delay the arrest until after the U.S. Attorney's speech and for the U.S. Attorney to stay focused on politicians who have actually been convicted.

Nevertheless, dismissal of the Indictment is not appropriate. Even if the Court were to accept the Defendant's view that the U.S. Attorney's comments were improper, there is no evidence that the U.S. Attorney's comments "substantial[ly] influenced" the grand jury's decision to indict. * * * The Court reaches this conclusion not in a vacuum but in the wake of established precedent holding that the existence of negative pretrial publicity is generally not sufficient to show substantial influence or actual prejudice.

* * * [Ed note: After citing precedent, the Court rejected the Defendant's attempt to establish the inapplicability of such precedent. The Court noted that, unlike a petit jury, the grand jury "is not confined to a passive role" and "therefore presumptively has access to the media without being prejudiced in the absence of evidence to the contrary." The Court concluded, "While dismissal might be appropriate in instances where the defendant can show 'a history of prosecutorial misconduct, spanning several cases, that is so systematic and pervasive as to raise a substantial and serious question about the fundamental fairness of the process which resulted in the indictment,' the Court finds that standard has not been met here."] * * *

II. There is No Basis to Poll the Grand Jury or Review the Grand Jury Minutes

* * * [Ed note: The Court rejected the Defendant's argument that the grand jurors may have been prejudiced by the U.S. Attorney's extrajudicial statements. Citing precedent, the Court concluded that the Defendant failed to establish a "particularized need" that outweighs the presumption of secrecy accorded grand jury proceedings. In its reasoning, the Court emphasized

---

8   This is especially true in the context of Twitter communications. The Government argues that the Court should read a tweet stating "Silver monetized his position as Speaker of the Assembly in two principal ways & misled the public about his outside income" not in "isolation" but "in the context of the statements in the press release (and the Complaint linked to the press release)." This argument ignores the fact that the most problematic tweets, including the one quoted above and "Politicians are supposed to be on the ppl's payroll, not on secret retainer to wealthy special interests they do favors for," contained no links to the press release or Complaint. Moreover, this argument disregards the substantial known risk that, in communicating via a platform that limits messages to 140 characters and permits readers to "retweet" a single communication, one's statements will in fact be read in isolation.

that, unlike petit juries, the grand jury "need not deliberate in a sterile chamber, completely immunized from reports of those events transpiring about it."] * * *

CONCLUSION

For the foregoing reasons, the Defendant's Motion is DENIED. Nevertheless, the parties are cautioned that this case is to be tried in the courtroom and not in the press. * * *

SO ORDERED.

I. Criticism of Judges

Given the crucial role that the judiciary and law enforcement play in our legal system and the need for public trust, lawyers may be disciplined for false statements that they make about judges and other legal officials.

[Question 6-16]

An attorney representing tenants in landlord-tenant disputes has often litigated before a particular state court judge in a state in which judges are elected to the bench. That judge is now running for reelection. Based on the attorney's previous observations and interactions with this judge, the attorney genuinely believes that this judge is well-mannered, polite and judicious. However, the attorney also genuinely believes that a judge with a more activist judicial philosophy would better serve the attorney's many clients, who are in desperate need of overhauling the law governing landlord-tenant relationships. Once, on the way to the courtroom, a local news reporter approached the attorney and asked the attorney to rate the judicial candidate running for reelection. The attorney responded, "Well, I don't normally discuss judicial candidates but—since you asked me—I believe this candidate is unsuited for the bench and does not possess what I would call 'proper judicial temperament.' "

Were the attorney's remarks proper?

    (A) No, because the attorney should not make disparaging public remarks about a candidate because such remarks threaten the independence of the judiciary.

    (B) No, because the attorney was not truthful in expressing views about the candidate.

    (C) Yes, because the attorney was exercising the First Amendment right to freedom of speech.

    (D) Yes, because the attorney was acting as a zealous advocate for the attorney's clients.

Rule 8.2(a) provides the general rule governing lawyers' statements regarding "judicial and legal officials." It states that:

A lawyer shall not make a statement that the lawyer knows to be false or with reckless disregard as to its truth or falsity concerning the qualifications or integrity of a judge, adjudicatory officer or public legal officer, or of a candidate for election or appointment to judicial or legal office.

The Comment to Rule 8.2 explains:

[1] Assessments by lawyers are relied on in evaluating the professional or personal fitness of persons being considered for election or appointment to judicial office and to public legal offices, such as attorney general, prosecuting attorney and public defender. Expressing honest and candid opinions on such matters contributes to improving the administration of justice. Conversely, false statements by a lawyer can unfairly undermine public confidence in the administration of justice. * * *

————————

Can a lawyer be sanctioned and suspended from practice for stating that a particular judge is "anti-Semitic," "dishonest," or "drunk on the bench" if that is what the lawyer truly believes? Consider the following case, which reversed a district judge's sanction against lawyer Stephen Yagman for violating the Central District of California Local Civil Rule 2.5.2, which enjoins lawyers from engaging in any conduct that "degrades or impugns the integrity of the Court" or "interferes with the administration of justice." What standards did the *Yagman* Court articulate for the two prongs of Local Civil Rule 2.5.2 so as to address First Amendment concerns?

Standing Committee on Discipline v. Yagman

55 F.3d 1430 (9th Cir. 1995)

Kozinski, Circuit Judge:

Never far from the center of controversy, outspoken civil rights lawyer Stephen Yagman was suspended from practice before the United States District Court for the Central District of California for impugning the integrity of the court and interfering with the random selection of judges by making disparaging remarks about a judge of that court. We confront several new issues in reviewing this suspension order.

I

The convoluted history of this case begins in 1991 when Yagman filed a lawsuit pro se against several insurance companies. The case was assigned to Judge Manuel Real, then Chief Judge of the Central District. Yagman promptly sought to disqualify Judge Real on grounds of bias.[1]

————————

1   [Ed note: The Court recounted background history in which Judge Real granted in a prior case a directed verdict against Yagman's clients and sanctioned Yagman personally in the amount of $250,000. The Ninth Circuit reversed Judge Real's sanctions and remanded the case for reassignment to another judge "to preserve the appearance of justice." Judge Real's petition for certiorari to the Supreme Court was subsequently denied.]

The disqualification motion was randomly assigned to Judge William Keller, who denied it * * * and sanctioned Yagman for pursuing the matter in an "improper and frivolous manner[.]" * * *

A few days after Judge Keller's sanctions order, Yagman was quoted as saying that Judge Keller "has a penchant for sanctioning Jewish lawyers: me, David Kenner and Hugh Manes. I find this to be evidence of anti-semitism." The district court found that Yagman also told the Daily Journal reporter that Judge Keller was "drunk on the bench," although this accusation wasn't published in the article. * * *

Around this time, Yagman received a request from Prentice Hall, publisher of the much-fretted-about Almanac of the Federal Judiciary, for comments in connection with a profile of Judge Keller. Yagman's response was less than complimentary.[4] * * * The district court found that Yagman mailed copies both to Prentice Hall and to Judge Keller, * * * and we have no basis for rejecting this finding.

A few weeks later, Yagman placed an advertisement (on the stationary of his law firm) in the *L.A. Daily Journal*, asking lawyers who had been sanctioned by Judge Keller to contact Yagman's office.

Soon after these events, Yagman ran into Robert Steinberg, another attorney who practices in the Central District. According to Steinberg, Yagman told him that, by levelling [sic] public criticism at Judge Keller, Yagman hoped to get the judge to recuse himself in future cases. Believing that Yagman was committing misconduct, Steinberg described his conversation with Yagman in a letter to the Standing Committee on Discipline of the U.S. District Court for the Central District of California * * *.

A few weeks later, the Standing Committee received a letter from Judge Keller describing Yagman's anti-Semitism charge, his inflammatory statements to Prentice Hall and the newspaper advertisement placed by Yagman's law firm. * * *

[The Standing Committee on Discipline pursued the matter and, after a hearing, the district court found Yagman had committed sanctionable misconduct and suspended him from practice for two years.]

III

* * *

---

4   The portion of the letter relevant here reads as follows:

It is outrageous that the Judge wants his profile redone because he thinks it to be inaccurately harsh in portraying him in a poor light. It is an understatement to characterize the Judge as "the worst judge in the central district." It would be fairer to say that he is ignorant, dishonest, ill-tempered, and a bully, and probably is one of the worst judges in the United States. If television cameras ever were permitted in his courtroom, the other federal judges in the Country would be so embarrassed by this buffoon that they would run for cover. One might believe that some of the reason for this sub-standard human is the recent acrimonious divorce through which he recently went: but talking to attorneys who knew him years ago indicates that, if anything, he has mellowed. One other comment: his girlfriend . . . , like the Judge, is a right-wing fanatic.

Local Rule 2.5.2 contains two separate prohibitions. First, it enjoins attorneys from engaging in any conduct that "degrades or impugns the integrity of the Court." Second, it provides that "[n]o attorney shall engage in any conduct which . . . interferes with the administration of justice." The district court concluded that Yagman violated both prongs of the rule. Because different First Amendment standards apply to these two provisions, we discuss the propriety of the sanction under each of them separately.

A

1. We begin with the portion of Local Rule 2.5.2 prohibiting any conduct that "impugns the integrity of the Court." As the district court recognized, this provision is overbroad because it purports to punish a great deal of constitutionally protected speech, including all true statements reflecting adversely on the reputation or character of federal judges. A substantially overbroad restriction on protected speech will be declared facially invalid unless it is "fairly subject to a limiting construction." * * *

To save the "impugn the integrity" portion of Rule 2.5.2, the district court read into it an "objective" version of the malice standard enunciated in *New York Times Co. v. Sullivan*, 376 U.S. 254 (1964). Relying on *United States Dist. Ct. v. Sandlin*, 12 F.3d 861 (9th Cir. 1993), the court limited Rule 2.5.2 to prohibit only false statements made with either knowledge of their falsity or with reckless disregard as to their truth or falsity, judged from the standpoint of a "reasonable attorney." * * *

Sandlin involved a First Amendment challenge to Washington Rule of Professional Conduct 8.2(a), which provided in part: "A lawyer shall not make a statement that the lawyer knows to be false or with reckless disregard as to its truth or falsity concerning the qualifications, integrity, or record of a judge." * * * Though the language of the rule closely tracked the *New York Times* malice standard, we held that the purely subjective standard applicable in defamation cases is not suited to attorney disciplinary proceedings. * * * Instead, we held that such proceedings are governed by an objective standard, pursuant to which the court must determine "what the reasonable attorney, considered in light of all his professional functions, would do in the same or similar circumstances." The inquiry focuses on whether the attorney had a reasonable factual basis for making the statements, considering their nature and the context in which they were made.

Yagman nonetheless urges application of the *New York Times* subjective malice standard in attorney disciplinary proceedings. *Sandlin* stands firmly in the way. In *Sandlin*, we held that there are significant differences between the interests served by defamation law and those served by rules of professional ethics. Defamation actions seek to remedy an essentially private wrong by compensating individuals for harm caused to their reputation and standing in the community. Ethical rules that prohibit false statements impugning the integrity of judges, by contrast, are not designed to shield judges from unpleasant or offensive criticism, but to preserve public confidence in the fairness and impartiality of our system of justice. * * *

Though attorneys can play an important role in exposing problems with the judicial system, * * * *false* statements impugning the integrity of a judge erode public confidence without serving to publicize problems that justifiably deserve attention. *Sandlin* held that an objective malice standard strikes a constitutionally permissible balance between an attorney's right to criticize the judiciary and the public's interest in preserving confidence in the judicial system: Lawyers may freely voice criticisms supported by a reasonable factual basis even if they turn out to be mistaken.

Food for Thought

The *Yagman* Court follows Ninth Circuit precedent in imposing an *objective* standard for evaluating lawyers' criticisms of courts under the Washington Rule of Professional Conduct 8.2(a), which provides: "A lawyer shall not make a statement that the lawyer knows to be false or with reckless disregard as to its truth or falsity concerning the qualifications, integrity, or record of a judge." The objective standard, which requires lawyers' criticisms to be supported by a "reasonable factual basis even if they turn out to be mistaken" has also been embraced by most states. Are you persuaded that an objective standard, rather than a subjective standard, better strikes the balance between an attorney's right to criticize the judiciary and the public's interest in preserving confidence in the judicial system? Consider that in *In re Holtzman*, 577 N.E.2d 30 (N.Y. 1991), District Attorney Holtzman was formally disciplined for publicly disseminating an allegation, which was later determined to be unsupported by evidence, about the specific conduct of a judge. In making the allegation, however, Holtzman had reportedly relied on the report of an Assistant District Attorney, although she failed to conduct an independent investigation of the allegation. In rejecting the subjective standard, the New York court argued that an objective standard was needed to "adequately protect the public interest and maintain the integrity of the judicial system . . . It is the reasonableness of the belief, not the state of mind of the attorney, that is determinative."

Attorneys who make statements impugning the integrity of a judge are, however, entitled to other First Amendment protections applicable in the defamation context. To begin with, attorneys may be sanctioned for impugning the integrity of a judge or the court only if their statements are false; truth is an absolute defense. * * * Moreover, the disciplinary body bears the burden of proving falsity. * * *

It follows that statements impugning the integrity of a judge may not be punished unless they are capable of being proved true or false; statements of opinion are protected by the First Amendment unless they "imply a false assertion of fact." * * * Even statements that at first blush appear to be factual are protected by the First Amendment if they cannot reasonably be interpreted as stating actual facts about their target. * * * Thus, statements of "rhetorical hyperbole" aren't sanctionable, nor are statements that use language in a "loose, figurative sense." * * *

With these principles in mind, we examine the statements for which Yagman was disciplined.

2. We first consider Yagman's statement in the Daily Journal that Judge Keller "has a penchant for sanctioning Jewish lawyers: me, David Kenner and Hugh Manes. I find this to be evidence of anti-semitism." Though the district court viewed this entirely as an assertion of fact, * * * we conclude that the statement contains both an assertion of fact and an expression of opinion.

Yagman's claim that he, Kenner and Manes are all Jewish and were sanctioned by Judge Keller is clearly a factual assertion: The words have specific, well-defined meanings and describe objectively verifiable matters. Nothing about the context in which the words appear suggests the use of loose, figurative language or "rhetorical hyperbole." Thus, had the Standing Committee proved that Yagman, Kenner or Manes were not sanctioned by Judge Keller, or were not Jewish, this assertion might have formed the basis for discipline. The committee, however, didn't claim that Yagman's factual assertion was false, and the district court made no finding to that effect. We proceed, therefore, on the assumption that this portion of Yagman's statement is true.

The remaining portion of Yagman's Daily Journal statement is best characterized as opinion; it conveys Yagman's personal belief that Judge Keller is anti-Semitic. As such, it may be the basis for sanctions only if it could reasonably be understood as declaring or implying actual facts capable of being proved true or false. * * *

In applying this principle, we are guided by section 566 of the Restatement (Second) of Torts, which distinguishes between two kinds of opinion statements: those based on assumed or expressly stated facts, and those based on implied, undisclosed facts. * * * The statement, "I think Jones is an alcoholic," for example, is an expression of opinion based on implied facts, because the statement "gives rise to the inference that there are undisclosed facts that justify the forming of the opinion". Readers of this statement will reasonably understand the author to be implying he knows facts supporting his view—*e.g.*, that Jones stops at a bar every night after work and has three martinis. If the speaker has no such factual basis for his assertion, the statement is actionable, even though phrased in terms of the author's personal belief.

A statement of opinion based on expressly stated facts, on the other hand, might take the following form: "[Jones] moved in six months ago. He works downtown, and I have seen him during that time only twice, in his backyard around 5:30 seated in a deck chair . . . with a drink in his hand. I think he must be an alcoholic." This expression of opinion appears to disclose all the facts on which it is based, and does not imply that there are other, unstated facts supporting the belief that Jones is an alcoholic.

A statement of opinion based on fully disclosed facts can be punished only if the stated facts are themselves false and demeaning. * * * The rationale behind this rule is straightforward: When the facts underlying a statement of opinion are disclosed, readers will understand they are getting the author's interpretation of the facts presented; they are therefore unlikely to construe the statement as insinuating the existence of additional, undisclosed facts. * * *, "an opinion which is unfounded reveals its lack of merit when the opinion-holder discloses the factual basis for the idea"; readers are free to accept or reject the author's opinion based on their own independent evaluation of the facts. * * * . A statement of opinion of this sort doesn't "imply a false assertion of fact," * * * and is thus entitled to full constitutional protection.

Yagman's Daily Journal remark is protected by the First Amendment as an expression of opinion based on stated facts. * * * Yagman disclosed the basis for his view that Judge Keller is anti-Semitic and has a penchant for sanctioning Jewish lawyers: that he, Kenner and Manes are all Jewish and had been sanctioned by Judge Keller. The statement did not imply the existence of additional, undisclosed facts; it was carefully phrased in terms of an inference drawn from the facts specified rather than a bald accusation of bias against Jews.[17] Readers were "free to form another, perhaps contradictory opinion from the same facts," as no doubt they did.

3. The district court also disciplined Yagman for alleging that Judge Keller was "dishonest." This remark appears in the letter Yagman sent to Prentice Hall in connection with the profile of Judge Keller in the Almanac of the Federal Judiciary. The court concluded that this allegation was sanctionable because it "plainly impl[ies] past improprieties." Had Yagman accused Judge Keller of taking bribes, we would agree with the district court. Statements that "could reasonably be understood as imputing specific criminal or other wrongful acts" are not entitled to constitutional protection merely because they are phrased in the form of an opinion. * * *

When considered in context, however, Yagman's statement cannot reasonably be interpreted as accusing Judge Keller of criminal misconduct. The term "dishonest" was one in a string of colorful adjectives Yagman used to convey the low esteem in which he held Judge Keller. The other terms he used—"ignorant," "ill-tempered," "buffoon," "sub-standard human," "right-wing fanatic," "a bully," "one of the worst judges in the United States"—all speak to competence and temperament rather than corruption; together they convey nothing more substantive than Yagman's contempt for Judge Keller. Viewed in context of these "lusty and imaginative expression[s]," * * * the word "dishonest" cannot reasonably be construed as suggesting that Judge Keller had committed specific illegal acts.[18] * * * Yagman's remarks are thus statements of rhetorical hyperbole, incapable of being proved true or false.

Were we to find any substantive content in Yagman's use of the term "dishonest," we would, at most, construe it to mean "intellectually dishonest"-an accusation that Judge Keller's rulings were overly result-oriented. Intellectual dishonesty is a label lawyers frequently attach to decisions with which they disagree. An allegation that a judge is intellectually dishonest, however, cannot be proved true or false by reference to a "core of objective evidence." * * * Because Yagman's allegation of

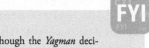

Even though the *Yagman* decision has not been overruled, it has proven controversial. For example, the Seventh Circuit noted that "[t]o the extent [the *Yagman* decision] may hold that attorneys are entitled to excoriate judges in the same way, and with the same lack of investigation, as persons may attack political officeholders, it is inconsistent with *Gentile* and our own precedents." *Matter of Palmisano*, 70 F.3d 483, 487 (7th Cir. 1995). Other courts have rejected the *Yagman* court's assertion that "prejudice to the administration of justice must be highly likely before speech may be published." *In re Comfort*, 159 P.3d 1011 (Kan. 2007).

---

17   Even if Yagman's statement were viewed as a bare allegation of anti-Semitism, it might well qualify for protection under the First Amendment as mere "name-calling." *Cf. Stevens v. Tillman*, 855 F.2d 394, 402 (7th Cir. 1988) (allegation that plaintiff was a "racist" held not actionable); *Buckley v. Littell*, 539 F.2d 882, 894 (2d Cir. 1976) (allegation that plaintiff was a "fascist" held not actionable); *Ward v. Zelikovsky*, 136 N.J. 516 (1994) (allegation that plaintiffs "hate Jews" held not actionable).

18   A lawyer accusing a judge of criminal misconduct would use a more pointed term such as "crooked" or "corrupt." *See Rinaldi*, 397 N.Y.S.2d at 951, 366 N.E.2d at 1307 (accusation that judge was "corrupt" not protected because it implied the judge had committed illegal acts).

"dishonesty" does not imply facts capable of objective verification, it is constitutionally immune from sanctions.

4. Finally, the district court found sanctionable Yagman's allegation that Judge Keller was "drunk on the bench." Yagman contends that, like many of the terms he used in his letter to Prentice Hall, this phrase should be viewed as mere "rhetorical hyperbole." The statement wasn't a part of the string of invective in the Prentice Hall letter, however; it was a remark Yagman allegedly made to a newspaper reporter. Yagman identifies nothing relating to the context in which this statement was made that tends to negate the literal meaning of the words he used. We therefore conclude that Yagman's "drunk on the bench" statement could reasonably be interpreted as suggesting that Judge Keller had actually, on at least one occasion, taken the bench while intoxicated. Unlike Yagman's remarks in his letter to Prentice Hall, this statement implies actual facts that are capable of objective verification. For this reason, the statement isn't protected * * *.

For Yagman's "drunk on the bench" allegation to serve as the basis for sanctions, however, the Standing Committee had to prove that the statement was false. * * * This it failed to do; indeed, the committee introduced no evidence at all on the point. While we share the district court's inclination to presume, "[i]n the absence of supporting evidence," that the allegation is untrue * * * the fact remains that the Standing Committee bore the burden of proving Yagman had made a statement that falsely impugned the integrity of the court. By presuming falsity, the district court unconstitutionally relieved the Standing Committee of its duty to produce evidence on an element of its case. Without proof of falsity Yagman's "drunk on the bench" allegation, like the statements discussed above, cannot support the imposition of sanctions for impugning the integrity of the court.

B

As an alternative basis for sanctioning Yagman, the district court concluded that Yagman's statements violated Local Rule 2.5.2's prohibition against engaging in conduct that "interferes with the administration of justice." The court found that Yagman made the statements discussed above in an attempt to "judge-shop"—*i.e.*, to cause Judge Keller to recuse himself in cases where Yagman appeared as counsel.

The Supreme Court has held that speech otherwise entitled to full constitutional protection may nonetheless be sanctioned if it obstructs or prejudices the administration of justice. * * * Given the significant burden this rule places on otherwise protected speech, however, the Court has held that prejudice to the administration of justice must be highly likely before speech may be punished.

In a trio of cases involving contempt sanctions imposed against newspapers, the Court articulated the constitutional standard to be applied in this context. Press statements relating to judicial matters may not be restricted, the Court held, unless they pose a "clear and present danger" to the administration of justice. * * * The standard announced in these cases is a demanding one: Statements may be punished only if they "constitute an imminent, not merely a likely, threat to the administration of justice. The danger must not be remote or even probable; it must immediately imperil." * * * There was no clear and present danger in these cases, the Court concluded, because any prospect that press criticism might influence a judge's decision was far too remote. In an oft-quoted passage, the Court noted that "the law of contempt is not made for the protection of judges who may be sensitive to the winds of public opinion. Judges are supposed to be men of fortitude, able to thrive in a hardy climate." * * *

[The Court considered the lower standard of review adopted in *Gentile*, that speech may be restricted where there is a "substantial likelihood" of material prejudice to the administration of justice, but found its rationale only applied to matters that are or may soon be taken up in pending cases.] We conclude, therefore, that lawyers' statements unrelated to a matter pending before the court may be sanctioned only if they pose a clear and present danger to the administration of justice. * * *

[The Court reviewed the rules for recusal of judges and determined that even if there is a possibility (or even a probability) of harm to the system of random assignment of judges and the administration of justice, it does not rise to the level of a clear and present danger.]

We conclude that "the danger under this record to fair judicial administration has not the clearness and immediacy necessary to close the door of permissible public comment." * * * As noted above, firm and long-standing precedent establishes that unflattering remarks like Yagman's cannot force the disqualification of the judge at whom they are aimed. The question remains whether the possibility of voluntary recusal is so great as to amount to a clear and present danger. We believe it is not. Public criticism of judges and the decisions they make is not unusual, * * * yet this seldom leads to judicial recusal. * * * Federal judges are well aware that "[s]ervice as a public official means that one may not be viewed favorably by every member of the public," and that they've been granted "the extraordinary protections of life tenure to shield them from such pressures." * * * Because Yagman's statements do not pose a clear and present danger to the proper functioning of the courts, we conclude that the district court erred in sanctioning Yagman for interfering with the administration of justice.

CONCLUSION

We can't improve on the words of Justice Black * * * :

The assumption that respect for the judiciary can be won by shielding judges from published criticism wrongly appraises the character of American public opinion. For it is a prized American privilege to speak one's mind, although not always with perfect good taste, on all public institutions. And an enforced silence, however limited, solely in the name of preserving the dignity of the bench, would probably engender resentment, suspicion, and contempt much more than it would enhance respect.

REVERSED.

J.   Decorum, Civility, and Obedience to Court Orders

Integral to the "officer of the court" role is the obligation to observe proper decorum and be civil during legal proceedings and to obey court orders. These obligations are generally reflected in Rule 3.5(d) of the Pennsylvania Rules of Conduct, which is identical to the ABA Model Rule and prohibits lawyers from engaging in "conduct intended to disrupt a tribunal."

The Comment explains that:

[4] The advocate's function is to present evidence and argument so that the cause may be decided according to law. Refraining from abusive or obstreperous conduct is a corollary of the advocate's right to speak on behalf of litigants. A lawyer may stand firm against abuse by a judge but should avoid reciprocation; the judge's default is no justification for similar dereliction by an advocate. An advocate can present the cause, protect the record for subsequent review and preserve professional integrity by patient firmness no less effectively than by belligerence or theatrics.

A violation of Rule 3.5(d) is punishable by way of a disciplinary action and a finding of contempt by the court. Typically, however, before issuing a contempt order, a judge must give the attorney "a reasonable opportunity to make a statement in his defense or in extenuation of his conduct." *See Kunstler v. Galligan*, 168 A.D.2d 146 (App. Div. 1991), *aff'd*, 587 N.E.2d 286 (upholding contempt order against lawyer for "disorderly, contemptuous, and insolent behavior").

In addition, Comment [1] of Rule 1.3 reminds us that the lawyer's duty of diligence and the obligation to be civil need not be mutually exclusive. It notes: "A lawyer is not bound . . . to press for every advantage that might be realized for a client . . . . The lawyer's duty to act with reasonable diligence does not require the use of offensive tactics or preclude the treating of all persons involved in the legal process with courtesy and respect."

Food for Thought

"When is 'civility' a duty, and when is it a trap?" asks ZZ Packer in a provocative New York Times article in 2018. Packer argues that there are at least two meanings of civility and that our society tends to emphasize one at the neglect of the other. The prevailing understanding of civility today is basically equated with "niceness" and ranges from "courtesy" and "consideration" to "the absence of rudeness." There is, however, an older and deeper understanding of civility that is connected to the notion of citizenship and social compact; it refers to a set of conventions that allows us to "communicate basic moral attitudes of respect, tolerance and considerateness." The danger, Packer contends, is that "an ethic of generalized niceness" can lead us to be suckered into accommodating "unjust social arrangements." For example, Dr. Martin Luther King Jr. was once heavily criticized by clergy for disturbing the peace with his organized demonstrations. In response, Dr. King wrote, "I am sorry that your statement did not express a similar concern for the conditions that brought the demonstrations into being."

Observing proper decorum and obeying court orders sound easy. But what if the judge orders you to engage in conduct that you genuinely believe would violate your ethical obligations toward your client? Can you stand your ground and defy the order? What if the judge finds you in contempt for disobeying the order? The following case explores this dilemma.

State v. Jones

2008-Ohio-6994 (Ohio Ct. App. 2008)

* * *

Appellant, an attorney with the Portage County Public Defender's Office, was appointed on August 15, 2007, to represent Jordan Scott ("defendant Scott") on a charge of misdemeanor assault * * *. The case was set for trial the following day.

According to appellant's affidavit, on the morning of the trial, he met with six other clients before receiving the Scott file. Appellant then met with defendant Scott for twenty minutes. * * * After Judge Plough stated that the matter was set for trial, appellant indicated that he had been appointed to the case the day before. Appellant voiced concerns that he would not be effective as defendant Scott's counsel and would not feel comfortable representing him. Appellant said that he would need more time to talk to the witnesses. Judge Plough replied that three witnesses were present and the trial would proceed after lunch. Appellant indicated that he needed to speak with other witnesses whom the state had not subpoenaed.

Following the break, the trial court reconvened and proceeded with the Scott case. As appellant attempted to raise a pretrial matter, Judge Plough asked him whether he was ready to start the trial. Appellant replied that he was not and that he did not have an opportunity to interview the witnesses. Judge Plough warned appellant that he would be held in contempt of court if he did not proceed with the trial. Over objection by defense counsel, Judge Plough ordered the trial to commence. Appellee, the state of Ohio, waived its opening statement and appellant informed the trial court that he was not able to participate in the case. Judge Plough threatened appellant that if he did not proceed, he would be taken to jail immediately. * * * Judge Plough wanted appellant to proceed with the trial, and if a conviction resulted, the defendant could file an appeal on the basis of ineffective assistance of counsel. Appellant did not comply. The trial court found appellant in direct criminal contempt and ordered him to be taken into custody.

[At a subsequent hearing before Judge Plough,] the trial court found appellant guilty of direct criminal contempt * * *[.]

[A]ppellant contends that the trial court improperly found him in direct criminal contempt of court for refusing to proceed with trial.

R.C. 2705.01 provides that a court "may summarily punish a person guilty of misbehavior in the presence of or so near the court or judge as to obstruct the administration of justice."

This court stated in *Cawley*:

"Contempt is an act or omission that substantially disrupts the judicial process in a particular case * * *. It is described as the disobedience of a court order, conduct that brings the administration of justice into disrespect, or conduct that tends to embarrass, impede or obstruct a court in the performance of its functions. * * * When reviewing a finding of contempt, an appellate court applies an abuse of discretion standard. * * * Abuse of discretion is more than an error of law; rather, it implies that the trial court's attitude is unreasonable, arbitrary or unconscionable."

* * *

[In *In re Sherlock*, 37 Ohio App.3d 204 (1987) the Court wrote:]

"Where a trial court denies a continuance in a criminal trial and, as a consequence, defense counsel refuses to participate in the trial for fear that the defendant would receive ineffective assistance of counsel and that counsel would be in violation of [Ohio's Code of Professional Conduct requirements of competency and zealous advocacy], the court may commit error under the circumstances of the particular case in finding defense counsel in contempt and in imposing a fine. * * * Defense counsel should not be required to violate his duty to his client as the price of avoiding punishment for contempt."

In the instant matter, the record reveals that appellant was appointed to represent defendant Scott the day before the case was set for trial. Appellant orally requested a continuance, which was denied by Judge Plough.

"In evaluating a motion for a continuance, a court should note, inter alia: the length of the delay requested; whether other continuances have been requested and received; the inconvenience to litigants, witnesses, opposing counsel and the court; whether the requested delay is for legitimate reasons or whether it is dilatory, purposeful, or contrived; whether the defendant contributed to the circumstance which gives rise to the request for a continuance; and other relevant factors, depending on the unique facts of each case."

Here, the facts demonstrate that a continuance was warranted. Although appellant did not request a specific length of time, the complete denial of any continuance by Judge Plough under the present circumstances was an abuse of discretion. Appellant had never requested and/or received any other meaningful continuances in this matter. Any inconvenience to the judicial system would have been minimal in comparison to Judge Plough's proposal to have this court reverse him.

In addition, the continuance requested by appellant was for legitimate reasons and his conduct did not give rise to the need for one. Again, appellant was permitted merely two hours to familiarize himself with the facts, the witnesses, and his client, before preparing and constructing a defense based upon his findings. The mere fact that defendant Scott was charged with misdemeanor assault does not render the matter simple or inconsequential. Based on the information available to appellant, there may have been any number of potential witnesses and defenses pertinent to the assault charge and it was his obligation to conduct a complete investigation.

Under these circumstances, effective assistance and ethical compliance were impossible as appellant was not permitted sufficient time to conduct a satisfactory investigation as required by * * * the Code of Professional Responsibility,* * * the Ohio Rules of Professional Conduct, and the Sixth Amendment of the United States Constitution. It would have been unethical for appellant to proceed with trial as any attempt at rendering effective assistance would have been futile. Appellant properly refused to put his client's constitutional rights at risk by proceeding to trial unprepared.

* * *

By denying appellant's motion for a continuance, Judge Plough improperly placed an administrative objective of controlling the court's docket above its supervisory imperative of facilitating effective, prepared representation and a fair trial.

[The Court also held that it was improper for Judge Plough to rely on the appellate process to correct any ineffective assistance of counsel resulting from the trial.]

* * * The judgment of the Portage County Municipal Court, Kent Division, is reversed with respect to holding appellant in contempt. It is ordered that appellee is assessed costs herein taxed. The court finds there were reasonable grounds for this appeal.

Global Perspective

Does Rule 3.5(d) require a lawyer to comply with a particular dress code? Controversies periodically erupt in the U.S. regarding the appropriate dress code for a lawyer appearing in court. For example, should a lawyer be sanctioned for refusing to remove a "Black Lives Matter" button in court? Should a woman be able to wear pants, rather than a skirt, to court? What, if anything, do the norms of professional attire for lawyers tell us about the role of the legal profession in a particular country? Does it matter whether a lawyer wears a suit, a robe, or a wig? Should all lawyers be able to wear the same clothes or is it appropriate to single out certain lawyers—such as Queen's Counsel—who wear different clothes (or robes) than other lawyers? One of the sessions at the 2016 International Conference of Legal Ethics was entitled "*Keeping Up Appearances: Legal Dress.*" The session description explained that "Professional dress codes (and court dress in particular), are regulated within social norms, ethical rules or court rules, but their meanings, rationales and consequences are neglected. In these sessions, we intend to initiate a new platform, a research group, to discuss the various aspects of professional dress codes and professional appearance. Historical, empirical, semiotic, literature and practical aspects will enable us to know more, and to understand better the rationales and consequences of professional (legal) dress codes and appearance."

Should the lawyer be responsible not just for her own conduct but also the conduct of her client? What about conduct that takes place at a deposition? Comment [5] of Rule 3.5(d) clarifies that the "duty to refrain from disruptive conduct applies to any proceeding of a tribunal, including a deposition." If you are in federal court, Federal Rule of Civil Procedure 30 governing depositions also applies. Specifically, Rule 30(d)(2) provides that if a person's conduct is so egregious such that it "impedes, delays, or frustrates the fair examination of the deponent," then the court may impose an "appropriate sanction" on that person, including "reasonable expenses and attorney's fees incurred by any party." If you encounter an obstreperous deponent, you may rely on Federal Rule of Civil Procedure 37(a)(3)(B)(i), which empowers a party seeking discovery to "move for an order compelling an answer . . . if a deponent fails to answer a question" during a deposition. Rule 37(a)(4) treats an "evasive or incomplete . . . response" as a "failure to . . . answer," and Rule 37(a)(5)(A) requires the party whose conduct is in question, the "attorney advising that conduct," or both to pay the successful movant's reasonable expenses, including attorney's fees. Can the lawyer's failure to restrain her client's obstreperous behavior at a deposition result in her being sanctioned? The following case explores this question.

GMAC Bank v. HTFC Corp.

248 F.R.D. 182, *aff'd* 252 F.R.D. 253 (E.D. Pennsylvania 2008)

ROBRENO, DISTRICT JUDGE:

I. INTRODUCTION

The issue of how to rein in incivility by counsel in depositions has been the subject of considerable interest in the legal profession for some time. Less discussed, perhaps because it is less frequent, but nevertheless just as pernicious, is what to do about uncivil conduct by a witness at a deposition. An important corollary to the issue is what is the duty of counsel who is confronted by uncivil conduct by his own witness.

The spectacular failure of the deposition process in this case occurred during two deposition sessions in the course of a commercial dispute. The deponent, Aaron Wider, is the owner and chief executive officer of Defendant HTFC Corp.

Before the Court are a motion to compel and for sanctions filed by Plaintiff GMAC Bank and a rule to show cause issued by the Court upon counsel for HTFC and Wider, Joseph Ziccardi, Esq., why sanctions should not be imposed upon counsel. A hearing was held on December 20, 2007, and the parties submitted supplemental briefing thereafter. For the reasons that follow, the motion to compel will be granted, and Wider and Ziccardi will be sanctioned.

II. BACKGROUND

Plaintiff GMAC Bank administers residential mortgage loans, and Defendant HTFC Corp. takes loan applications and sells residential mortgage loans to lenders, such as GMAC. GMAC and HTFC entered into a contract for the sale of certain loans. GMAC claims that HTFC breached the contract by selling it certain loans that were improperly underwritten and not investment quality, and refusing to repurchase them, as required by the contract. HTFC, in turn, asserts a counterclaim for tortious interference with contract based on GMAC's allegedly improper administration of certain loans to HTFC's clients.

On September 26 and November 8, 2007, GMAC sought to take the deposition of Aaron Wider, owner and chief executive officer of HTFC. According to GMAC, due to Wider's abusive conduct toward counsel, obstruction and delay of the deposition proceedings, and failure to answer and evasive responses to questions propounded at the deposition, GMAC was unable to complete the deposition. GMAC brings the instant motion to compel Wider's deposition and for sanctions.

III. MOTION TO COMPEL AND FOR SANCTIONS AGAINST WIDER

* * * [Ed note: The Court granted GMAC's motion to compel the deposition based on its finding that Wider's conduct at his deposition violated Federal Rules of Civil Procedure 37(a)(3)(B)(i). It also imposed sanctions on Wider based on the finding that Wider violated Fed.R.Civ.P. 30(d)(2). This section of the opinion also includes several excerpts from the deposition transcript, showing egregious conduct on the part of Wider] * * *

IV. RULE TO SHOW CAUSE AS TO SANCTIONS AGAINST ZICCARDI

The Court turns now to the question of whether defense counsel Joseph Ziccardi's conduct at Wider's deposition warrants sanctions under the Federal Rules of Civil Procedure.

A. Legal Standard

The Federal Rules specifically provide for sanctions if "a deponent['s] fail[ure] to answer a question" or "evasive or incomplete" answers at a deposition necessitate a motion to compel. Fed.R.Civ.P. 37(a)(3)(B)(i), (a)(4), (a)(5)(A). These sanctions can apply to attorneys: "If the motion is granted . . . the court must, after giving an opportunity to be heard, require the party or deponent whose conduct necessitated the motion, the party or *attorney advising that conduct*, or both to pay the movant's reasonable expenses incurred in making the motion, including attorney's fees." Fed.R.Civ.P. 37(a)(5)(A) (emphasis added). Therefore, an attorney who improperly "advis[es]" a deponent to provide evasive or incomplete answers or to refuse to answer questions propounded at a deposition is subject to sanctions. Sanctions must be imposed unless "circumstances make an award of expenses unjust." Fed.R.Civ.P. 37(a)(5)(A)(i)–(iii).

In addition, an attorney may be sanctioned for engaging in conduct that "impedes, delays, or frustrates the fair examination of the deponent." Fed.R.Civ.P. 30(d)(2) (empowering a court to impose an "appropriate sanction," including "reasonable expenses and attorney's fees incurred by any party") * * *.

B. Discussion

1. Summary of Ziccardi's conduct

As evidenced by the portions of the record quoted at length above, throughout the deposition, notwithstanding the severe and repeated nature of Wider's misconduct, Ziccardi persistently failed to intercede and correct Wider's violations of the Federal Rules. * * * Instead, Ziccardi sat idly by as a mere spectator to Wider's abusive, obstructive, and evasive behavior; and when he did speak, he either incorrectly directed the witness not to answer, dared opposing counsel to file a motion to compel, or even joined in Wider's offensive conduct.

2. *Ziccardi's defenses of his conduct*

a. *Adequacy of intervention*

Ziccardi argues that he made sufficient efforts to intervene and curb his client's misconduct. To that effect, the few attempts that Ziccardi did make to control his client were limited to mildly worded requests to Wider to answer a question or not interrupt counsel for GMAC. * * *

Ziccardi avers that many of his efforts to correct his client's misconduct occurred off the record. Even if this assertion is to be believed, Wider's continuing misconduct indicates that whatever efforts Ziccardi made were woefully ineffectual. In fact, Ziccardi's meek attempts to intercede and his otherwise silent toleration of Wider's conduct only emboldened Wider to further flout the procedural rules:

> MR. BODZIN: I'm going to ask the question again and I'll ask it a different way so as to make sure that I'm not characterizing this witness's testimony.
>
> THE WITNESS: Get his [Ziccardi's] permission.
>
> MR. BODZIN: I don't need his permission.
>
> THE WITNESS: Yes you do.
>
> Q. My question is in submitting loans originated by HTFC for purchase by GMAC, was it HTFC's policy that so long as there was an appraisal that supported the value of the property, it was not up to HTFC to report to GMAC flip activity?
>
> MR. ZICCARDI: Same objection. Go ahead.
>
> A. My attorney just told you to get fucked and so did I.
>
> MR. ZICCARDI: No.
>
> THE WITNESS: Okay. That's for the record.
>
> Q. First of all, your attorney didn't tell me that. You told me that and now you can answer the question.
>
> A. Go get fucked.
>
> Q. You're not answering the question?
>
> A. I did answer your question.
>
> Q. No, that's not an answer to the question.
>
> A. That's my answer to your question.
>
> Q. Okay.
>
> A. My attorney very nicely told you that he objects. Fuck you. And I'm telling you on behalf of my attorney, fuck you.

* * *

It is true that any attorney can be blindsided by a recalcitrant client who engages in unexpected sanctionable conduct at a deposition. An attorney faced with such a client cannot, however, simply sit back, allow the deposition to proceed, and then blame the client when the deposition process breaks down. * * *

Moreover, Ziccardi was not blindsided by Wider. Rather, he had ample notice of Wider's intent to frustrate the deposition. Wider's first outburst and unilateral interruption of the deposition occurred a mere *six* minutes after the deposition had begun. * * * Wider's first use of profanity and hostile behavior toward opposing counsel occurred only a few minutes later. * * * Therefore, Ziccardi was on notice at an early point during the deposition of his client's hostility toward opposing counsel and efforts to frustrate the deposition. Nonetheless, Ziccardi allowed the deposition to drag on for over two days and nearly twelve hours of testimony, much of which was an unmitigated waste of time and resources.

Ziccardi never once suggested that the ill-fated deposition be adjourned. In fact, even though the deposition was being taken over 100 miles away from counsel for GMAC's home office, it was counsel for GMAC who suggested adjournment several times, * * *, and who eventually adjourned the deposition after enduring the last of many onslaughts from Wider:

> Q. Yes or no, did he ask you if you had any documents?
>
> A. Shut the fuck up. Don't raise your voice to me.
>
> MR. BODZIN: We're adjourning this deposition.
>
> THE WITNESS: Good.
>
> MR. BODZIN: We're adjourning this deposition. We're going back to the Judge. We're going to let the Judge decide if this was an appropriate way for anybody to behave at a deposition. I'm not going to continue-
>
> THE WITNESS: You don't point your fucking fingers at me. You don't raise your fucking voice at me. And I'm going to spit right back at you.
>
> MR. BODZIN: I'm not going to continue to be subject to this harassment, this rudeness is absolutely inappropriate conduct and I'm going to adjourn this deposition right now.
>
> THE WITNESS: Good.

* * *

Based on the record, the Court rejects the argument that Ziccardi made adequate efforts to curb Wider's misconduct.

b. *Good faith*

* * * [Ed note: The Court rejected the argument that Ziccardi acted in good faith, noting that a finding of bad faith is not required for imposing sanctions and, even if it were, "the record, viewed as a whole, inexorably leads to the conclusion that Ziccardi's conduct was undertaken in bad faith." The Court noted that "Ziccardi's failure to intervene was not merely negligent,

but rather willful" and cited evidence of Ziccardi's indifference (e.g., telling opposing counsel to "file whatever motion you want to file" and "snickering at Wider's abusive conduct").] * * *

c. *Confidentiality*

* * * [Ed note: The Court rejected the argument that "the questions propounded at the deposition by counsel for GMAC sought confidential information and thus were properly not answered by Wider," noting that "Ziccardi did not generally object to the questions on that basis at the deposition, and he did not seek an adjournment to obtain a protective order."] * * *

3. *Rule to show cause as to sanctions*

Because he has failed to show cause why sanctions should not be imposed, the Court will impose sanctions upon Ziccardi.

a. *Violation of Rule 37(a)(3)(B)(i)*

As explained above, if a motion to compel is necessitated by a deponent's "evasive or incomplete" answers or "failure to answer" questions, the movant may seek sanctions against the "attorney advising that conduct." Fed.R.Civ.P. 37(a)(3)(B)(i), (a)(4), (a)(5)(A). It is beyond dispute that Wider provided evasive and incomplete answers and failed to answer questions propounded at his deposition. * * * The remaining question is whether Ziccardi "advis[ed]" Wider's misconduct.

It is true that, in most instances, Ziccardi did not actively counsel Wider on the record to provide evasive or incomplete answers or to refuse to answer questions. What is remarkable about Ziccardi's conduct is not his actions, but rather his failure to act. Despite the pervasiveness of Wider's evasive and incomplete answers and his repeated failure to answer questions, Ziccardi failed to take remedial steps to curb his client's misconduct.

The nature of Wider's misconduct was so severe and pervasive, and his violations of the Federal Rules of Civil Procedure so frequent and blatant, that any reasonable attorney representing Wider would have intervened in an effort to curb Wider's misconduct. Ziccardi's failure to address, then and there, Wider's misconduct could have no other effect but to empower Wider to persist in his behavior. Under these circumstances, the Court equates Ziccardi's silence with endorsement and ratification of Wider's misconduct. This endorsement and ratification by Ziccardi is the functional equivalent of "advising [Wider's] conduct" under Rule 37(a)(5)(A).

Rule 37(a)(5)(A) provides for sanctions against the "party or deponent whose conduct necessitated the motion, the party or attorney advising that conduct, or both." Fed.R.Civ.P. 37(a)(5)(A). Because Ziccardi's actions and inaction at Wider's deposition constitute the functional equivalent of "advising" Wider's misconduct, Ziccardi must compensate GMAC for the expense it incurred in having to file the instant motion to compel. * * *

Accordingly, because the circumstances here do not make the imposition of sanctions unjust, Ziccardi will be ordered to pay to GMAC, jointly and severally with Wider, the $13,026.00 in fees and expenses that GMAC incurred in connection with the motion to compel. * * *

b. *Violation of Rule 30(d)(2)*

As discussed above, "[t]he court may impose an appropriate sanction-including the reasonable expenses and attorney's fees incurred by any party-on a person who impedes, delays, or frustrates the fair examination of the deponent." Fed.R.Civ.P. 30(d)(2).

The Court has no difficulty finding that Ziccardi's inaction impeded, delayed, and frustrated Wider's fair examination. For example, had Ziccardi prevented Wider from improperly interposing his own objections, the deposition would have proceeded in a much more expeditious manner. Had Ziccardi curbed Wider's abusive bullying of counsel for GMAC, counsel for GMAC would not have been forced to adjourn the deposition before its completion. Had Ziccardi warned Wider that providing evasive and incomplete answers would result in sanctions, the deposition could have been completed without requiring the Court's intervention. Instead, Ziccardi's persistent inaction in the face of Wider's gross misconduct impeded, delayed, and contributed to the total frustration Wider's deposition.

Therefore, Ziccardi will be sanctioned for violating Rule 30(d)(2). The Court will order Ziccardi to pay to GMAC, jointly and severally with Wider, the $16,296.61 in costs and fees incurred by GMAC in connection with the deposition. * * *

V. CONCLUSION

Wider's conduct was outrageous. Ziccardi's complicity is inexcusable. Therefore, sanctions will be imposed.

It is the Court's hope that these sanctions will motivate Wider and HTFC to proceed in a civil and expeditious manner with this deposition and the remainder of discovery, and Ziccardi to adhere faithfully to the Federal Rules of Civil Procedure. Otherwise, more severe sanctions will follow.

The motion to compel and for sanctions * * * will be granted. Sanctions will be imposed on Aaron Wider and Joseph Ziccardi, jointly and severally, in the amount of $29,322.61. An appropriate order follows.

ORDER

AND NOW, this **29th** day of February, 2008, for the reasons stated in the accompanying Memorandum, it is hereby **ORDERED** that Plaintiff's motion to compel and for sanctions * * * is **GRANTED**.

IT IS FURTHER ORDERED that the deposition of Aaron Wider shall take place at the U.S. Courthouse, 601 Market Street, Philadelphia, PA, before a magistrate judge, within 30 days of the date of this order, at a date and time to be designated by the magistrate judge.

IT IS FURTHER ORDERED that Aaron Wider and Joseph Ziccardi shall pay, jointly and severally, to GMAC Bank the amount of $13,026.00, representing the fees and expenses incurred by GMAC Bank in connection with the instant motion to compel by **March 25, 2008.**

IT IS FURTHER ORDERED that Aaron Wider and Joseph Ziccardi shall pay, jointly and severally, the amount of $16,296.61, representing the expenses and 75% of the fees incurred by GMAC Bank in connection with Wider's deposition in New York, N.Y. on September 26 and November 8, 2007, by **March 25, 2008**.

IT IS FURTHER ORDERED that the motion for protective order * * * is **DENIED without prejudice**. * * *

AND IT IS SO ORDERED.

Food for Thought

Should civility be enforced against lawyers through discipline or court sanction? Should law schools teach civility? Consider that, according to one report, the 2007 Illinois Supreme Court Commission on Professionalism concluded that the vast majority of practicing lawyers experienced unprofessional behavior by fellow members of the bar. Seventy-one percent of respondents reported rudeness, including sarcasm, condescension, profanity, or inappropriate interruption at some point during the prior year. An even higher percentage of respondents reported being the victim of "strategic incivility," or the strategic deployment of uncivil behaviors for the purpose of gaining leverage, typically in litigation. Behaviors included, for example, the deliberate distortion of facts, refusal to consent to reasonable requests for accommodation, indiscriminate or frivolous use of pleadings, and inflammatory language in briefs or motions. The survey also reported that 95 percent of the respondents reported that incivility made the practice of law less satisfying. As of March 2017, there were more than 140 state and local bar associations with civility codes.

II. Duties to Opposing Parties and Third Parties

As a general rule, the law and the rules do not make a lawyer responsible for the impact on others resulting from the lawyer's representation of a client. Indeed, Rule 1.2(b) expressly states that "[a] lawyer's representation of a client * * * does not constitute an endorsement of the client's political, economic, social or moral views or activities." This

Make the Connection

This section deals with legal responsibility. Chapter 8 examines whether lawyers have a moral responsibility for their clients' conduct.

section describes significant exceptions to the general approach. This section also addresses lawyers' obligations of truthfulness and fairness to represented and unrepresented parties.

A. Truthfulness

When lawyers communicate with third parties on behalf of clients, they have a duty to avoid making material false statements and, under narrow circumstances, a duty to make affirmative disclosures.

[Question 6-17]

An attorney represented a terminated employee in a discrimination lawsuit against the former employer. The attorney for the employee retained and directed an expert to

prepare a report on the terminated employee's damages. In preparing the report, the expert erroneously assumed that the employee remained unemployed; thus, the expert's report vastly overstated the employee's damages as amounting to $50,000. In fact, as the terminated employee had testified during the employee's deposition, the employee had obtained new employment within one week after the termination and at a salary higher than the prior job with the former employer. As a result, the employee had actually incurred only $4,000 in damages. The attorney knew about the report's mistakes. During settlement negotiations, the attorney handed the expert's report to opposing counsel, declaring, "My client suffered $50,000 in damages and here's the report that supports it."

[handwritten margin note: Material fact]

Is the attorney subject to discipline?

(A) No, because the attorney's duty of confidentiality prevented the attorney from revealing the error in the expert's report.

(B) No, because the attorney made no false statement of material fact or law to a third person.

(C) Yes, because the attorney made a false statement of material fact.

(D) Yes, because the attorney should not have allowed the expert to prepare the report.

Simulation: At the Closing

Suppose that you are an attorney representing a borrower, a small business owner, in connection with a significant loan transaction, the proceeds of which will be used (as contemplated and required by the loan agreement) to purchase expensive equipment and machinery that will enable the borrower to increase output and significantly expand the business. You and your client, the borrower, are present at the closing of the loan transaction taking place in a conference room at the offices of the lender's lawyer. The borrower takes you aside and informs you that the borrower has just defaulted on a commercial real estate loan and that the business is on the verge of bankruptcy. The borrower wants to proceed with the closing but does not want to disclose these facts to the lender. What would you say to your client, the borrower? Suppose you respond by saying that if your client doesn't disclose the mortgage loan default to the lender, the client risks being charged with fraud and risks having the loan transaction set aside. After this conversation, you and your client return to the conference room and rejoin the lender and the lender's lawyer. The lender asks the borrower to orally affirm the representations contained in the loan agreement as of the closing date, as required by the terms of the loan agreement. Specifically, the lender asks the borrower to confirm that the borrower has not defaulted on any prior loans. To your surprise, the borrower responds, "Confirmed. There has been no default whatsoever." Then the lender proceeds to ask the borrower to confirm that there has been no material change in the borrower's financial condition. Would you say or do anything? Would you allow the borrower to proceed with the closing? What do Rules 1.2(d), 1.16(a), 1.6, and 4.1 require you to do?

Rule 4.1 is the general rule governing "truthfulness in statements" to non-clients. It provides that "[i]n the course of representing a client a lawyer shall not knowingly:

(a)   make a false statement of material fact or law to a third person; or

(b)   fail to disclose a material fact to a third person when disclosure is necessary to avoid assisting a criminal or fraudulent act by a client, unless disclosure is prohibited by Rule 1.6."

The Comment to the Rule explains:

Misrepresentation

[1] A lawyer is required to be truthful when dealing with others on a client's behalf, but generally has no affirmative duty to inform an opposing party of relevant facts. A misrepresentation can occur if the lawyer incorporates or affirms a statement of another person that the lawyer knows is false. Misrepresentations can also occur by partially true but misleading statements or omissions that are the equivalent of affirmative false statements. For dishonest conduct that does not amount to a false statement or for misrepresentations by a lawyer other than in the course of representing a client, *see* Rule 8.4.

Statements of Fact

[2] This Rule refers to statements of fact. Whether a particular statement should be regarded as one of fact can depend on the circumstances. Under generally accepted conventions in negotiation, certain types of statements ordinarily are not taken as statements of material fact. Estimates of price or value placed on the subject of a transaction and a party's intentions as to an acceptable settlement of a claim are ordinarily in this category, and so is the existence of an undisclosed principal except where nondisclosure of the principal would constitute fraud. Lawyers should be mindful of their obligations under applicable law to avoid criminal and tortious misrepresentation.

* * *

Make the Connection

Does the duty of confidentiality under Rule 1.6 trump the duty to disclose under Rule 4.1(b)? The wording of Rule 4.1(b) ("unless prohibited by Rule 1.6") would suggest that to be the case. *But* remember that Rule 1.6(b) provides for several instances in which the lawyer *may*, but is not required to, disclose information relating to the representation. Does mandatory disclosure under Rule 4.1(b) trump discretionary disclosure under Rule 1.6(b)? Stated another way, does Rule 4.1(b) convert the permissive disclosure under Rule 1.6(b) into a mandatory obligation? For analysis of the interaction between the two rules, see Peter R. Jarvis & Trisha M. Rich, *The Law of Unintended Consequences: Whether and When Mandatory Disclosure under Model Rule 4.1(b) Trumps Discretionary Disclosure under Model Rule 1.6(b)*, 44 Hofstra L. Rev. 421 (2015). *See also* Chapter 4(IV) for exceptions to the duty of confidentiality.

Notice that Rule 4.1(b) requires the lawyer to make a determination as to whether the lawyer's silence in the situation would amount to assistance in a crime or fraud. Of course, that determination requires analysis of the criminal or tort law in question. Ordinarily, if the lawyer's silence could reasonably be interpreted as affirming a false statement of fact by the lawyer's client, then such nondisclosure may be deemed a fraud under other law. The complex topic of the lawyer's obligations under *other law* is more fully addressed below in Unit III in the section discussing obedience to the law.

The Comment to Rule 4.1 identifies the various options available to the lawyer seeking to avoid assisting a crime or fraud. One of those alternatives is known as "noisy withdrawal"— withdrawing from representation and giving notice of the fact of withdrawal to a third party or disaffirming a legal opinion previously furnished by the lawyer. The Comment explains:

[3] * * * Ordinarily, a lawyer can avoid assisting a client's crime or fraud by withdrawing from the representation. Sometimes it may be necessary for the lawyer to give notice of the fact of withdrawal and to disaffirm an opinion, document, affirmation or the like. In extreme cases, substantive law may require a lawyer to disclose information relating to the representation to avoid being deemed to have assisted the client's crime or fraud. If the lawyer can avoid assisting a client's crime or fraud only by disclosing this information, then under paragraph (b) the lawyer is required to do so, unless the disclosure is prohibited by Rule 1.6.

* * *

Today, most states, including Texas and New York, permit lawyers to make a noisy withdrawal under specified circumstances. A few states, such as Tennessee, *require* the lawyer to make a noisy withdrawal under specified circumstances. By contrast, California prohibits the disclosure of confidential client information for purposes of preventing or rectifying financial harm.

B. Inadvertent Disclosures

What if counsel for the other side accidentally sends you a document that contains confidential information that you could use to your client's advantage in negotiations in connection with the settlement of a lawsuit or an ordinary business transaction? Can you use that confidential information to benefit your client? Should you alert opposing counsel that you are privy to such information?

[Question 6-18]

An attorney, who represents a client in connection with a settlement of a dispute over the sale of property, received an email from the lawyer representing the other side. The email attached a document representing the final version of a settlement offer to the attorney's client. The attorney began reading and quickly realized that the opposing party's lawyer had mistakenly sent a version of the document with the "tracked changes" feature enabled, which revealed the following comment inserted by the lawyer's client: "Settling for $100,000 would be a real home run, but I'm prepared to go to $150,000 if that's what it takes to get this over with."

Under the ethical rules, the attorney must:

    (A) **Notify the lawyer on the other side.**

    (B) **Notify the lawyer on the other side after reading the document.**

    (C) **Notify the lawyer on the other side and refuse to continue reading the document.**

    (D) **Keep silent about the receipt of the document.**

Rule 4.4(b) provides that "[a] lawyer who receives a document or electronically stored information relating to the representation of the lawyer's client and knows or reasonably should know that the document or electronically stored information was inadvertently sent shall promptly notify the sender."

Hear from the Authors

To hear more from the authors on Rule 4.4(b), click here.

The Comment to the Rule states:

[2] Paragraph (b) recognizes that lawyers sometimes receive a document or electronically stored information that was mistakenly sent or produced by opposing parties or their lawyers. * * * If a lawyer knows or reasonably should know that such a document or electronically stored information was sent inadvertently, then this Rule requires the lawyer to promptly notify the sender in order

Make the Connection

For discussion of the impact of the mistaken disclosure of confidential information on the attorney-client privilege, *see* Chapter 4(III).

to permit that person to take protective measures. Whether the lawyer is required to take additional steps, such as returning the document or electronically stored information, is a matter of law beyond the scope of these Rules, as is the question of whether the privileged status of a document or electronically stored information has been waived. Similarly, this Rule does not address the legal duties of a lawyer who receives a document or electronically stored information that the lawyer knows or reasonably should know may have been inappropriately obtained by the sending person. For purposes of this Rule, "document or electronically stored information" includes, in addition to paper documents, email and other forms of electronically stored information, including embedded data (commonly referred to as "metadata"), that is subject to being read or put into readable form. Metadata in electronic documents creates an obligation under this Rule only if the receiving lawyer knows or reasonably should know that the metadata was inadvertently sent to the receiving lawyer.

[3] Some lawyers may choose to return a document or delete electronically stored information unread, for example, when the lawyer learns before receiving it that it was inadvertently sent.

Where a lawyer is not required by applicable law to do so, the decision to voluntarily return such a document or delete electronically stored information is a matter of professional judgment ordinarily reserved to the lawyer. *See* Rules 1.2 and 1.4.

> **Food for Thought**
>
> What are the lawyer's ethical duties with regard to metadata? "Metadata" is often described as "data about data" or "hidden data." It consists mostly of information relating to a document's origins, including who created it, when it was opened, and what software was used. It can also contain more sensitive information, such as hidden comments, versions, revisions, a record of the author of any revisions, and work product or other privileged information. Jurisdictions that have examined metadata agree that the sender of metadata has a duty to exercise reasonable care to avoid inadvertently disclosing confidential information. Unfortunately, jurisdictions differ significantly about whether the recipient has a duty to avoid searching for or "mining" metadata. That said, there is fairly wide agreement that the recipient who discovers sensitive information is required to notify the sender in accordance with local variations of Rule 4.4, which explicitly notes that metadata triggers the notification duties of the Rule, but only when the receiving lawyer knows or has reason to know the inclusion of metadata was unintentional. Most jurisdictions also do not object to the lawyer's use of metadata if such metadata was readily accessible. A chart comparing state versions of Rule 4.4 is found here.

C. Communications with a Represented Party

When a lawyer communicates about a matter with an individual whom the lawyer knows to be represented by another lawyer in the matter, there is a risk that the lawyer will try to do an "end run" around the other lawyer. For example, the lawyer may try to extract sensitive information from that individual outside of the lawyer's presence. As a result, the ethical rules impose restrictions on communications with represented persons, regardless of whether there is pending litigation, whether the person is an adverse party, or whether the lawyer communicates through an agent. The restriction is commonly referred to as the "no contact" rule.

[Question 6-19]

An attorney represents a lender in all of its lending transactions. In the course of preparing for the closing of one loan transaction, the attorney received a phone call from the borrower's comptroller, who proceeded to ask the attorney what interest rate would apply to the borrowed funds. The attorney responded to the comptroller by asking, "Shouldn't your in-house lawyer be contacting me?" to which the comptroller replied, "Normally yes, but our lawyer is very busy, and this time I'm authorized to handle this matter." The attorney then communicated the rate to the comptroller.

Was the attorney's conduct proper?

    (A) Yes, because the communications between the attorney and the comptroller were not substantive in nature.

    (B) Yes, because the comptroller initiated contact with the attorney.

(C) No, because the attorney did not receive the express consent of the borrower's lawyer to speak with the comptroller.

(D) No, because the attorney had no basis for relying on the claim that the comptroller was authorized to handle the matter.

[Question 6-20]

A law firm employee hired a lawyer to file an employment lawsuit against the law firm. When the general counsel of the law firm approached the law firm's reception area, a process server handed the partner the summons and the complaint for the lawsuit. The general counsel immediately called the law firm's director of human resources and asked the director to talk to the employee about the employment claim. As requested, the director went to the employee's office and asked factual questions about the employee's claim.

Is the general counsel of the law firm subject to discipline?

(A) No, because the director of human resources only asked factual questions.

(B) No, because the director of human resources is entitled to discuss employment claims with employees.

(C) Yes, because the employee was represented by counsel.

(D) Yes, because the general counsel requested that the director of human resources engage in the unauthorized practice of law.

Rule 4.2 governs "communication with person[s] represented by counsel." It states that: "In representing a client, a lawyer shall not communicate about the subject of the representation with a person the lawyer knows to be represented by another lawyer in the matter, unless the lawyer has the consent of the other lawyer or is authorized to do so by law or a court order."

Rule 8.4(a) makes it "professional misconduct" for a lawyer to * * * violate or attempt to violate the Rules of Professional Conduct, knowingly assist or induce another to do so, or do so through the acts of another[.]"

D. Unrepresented Persons

In recognition of the risk that lawyers, with their greater legal knowledge and training, might take advantage of unrepresented third parties, the rules place limits on what lawyers can claim or advise.

[Question 6-21]

The court appointed a criminal defense attorney to represent a man who has been charged with contempt of court for violating a domestic violence restraining order. The order prohibited the man from visiting or communicating with his ex-girlfriend in any way. The ex-girlfriend claimed that the man had violated the order by calling her several times to beg her to resume their relationship. The attorney questioned the man, who vehemently denied violating the restraining order. Uncertain about whether to believe him, the attorney phoned the ex-girlfriend, identifying himself as "the court-appointed attorney," and asked her if she was represented by counsel. The ex-girlfriend responded that she was not represented by counsel but asked, "What do you mean by 'court-appointed attorney?'" to which the attorney responded, "The court ordered me to represent your ex-boyfriend." After discussing the facts surrounding the contempt order, the ex-girlfriend asked, "What do you think I should do?" The attorney paused for a moment and honestly responded, "I'm not your attorney but I don't think you want to be responsible for putting your ex-boyfriend behind bars."

Is the attorney subject to discipline?

(A) No, because the attorney's statements reflected his honest views.

(B) No, because the attorney clarified his role vis-à-vis his client.

(C) Yes, because the attorney implied that he was disinterested.

(D) Yes, because the attorney should not have given legal advice to the ex-girlfriend.

Rule 4.3 governs communications "with unrepresented persons * * * on behalf of a client with a person who is not represented by counsel[.]" It provides that "a lawyer shall not state or imply that the lawyer is disinterested." The lawyer's duty is even greater "[w]hen the lawyer knows or reasonably should know that the unrepresented person misunderstands the lawyer's role in the matter[.]" In that situation, "the lawyer shall make reasonable efforts to correct the misunderstanding." The lawyer has a further obligation "if the lawyer knows or reasonably should know that the interests of such a person are or have a reasonable possibility of being in conflict with the interests of the client." Where that occurs, "[t]he lawyer shall not give legal advice to an unrepresented person, other than the advice to secure counsel." In some jurisdictions, such as Pennsylvania and the District of Columbia, the rules go further: lawyers are prohibited from giving *any* advice, and not just legal advice, to unrepresented persons where there is a reasonable possibility of conflict.

Food for Thought

How do the Rules apply to social networking contact? The Philadelphia Professional Guidance Committee has found that Rules 4.1, 5.3, and 8.4 prohibit a lawyer or a person working on lawyer's behalf from "friending" an unrepresented witness on a social media site. Philadelphia Bar Op. 2009-02 (March 2009). But where "the Facebook and MySpace profiles of a party other than the lawyer's client in litigation [are] available to all members in the network and the lawyer neither 'friends' the other party nor directs someone else to do so[,]" another ethics committee has found it permissible for the lawyer to access and view the information under Rules 4.1, 5.3, and 8.4, as well as Rule 4.3 (contact with unrepresented party) or Rule 4.2 (contact with representing party), depending upon whether the party is represented. N.Y. Ethics Op. 843 (2010).

The Comment explains that:

[1] An unrepresented person, particularly one not experienced in dealing with legal matters,

Organizational clients are one context in which a lawyer may need to explain that the client has interests opposed to those of the unrepresented person. This is especially true where the lawyer is retained to conduct an internal investigation of possible wrongdoing by constituents, such as officers or employees. Familiarity with Rule 1.13(f) is essential to representing organizations. For more information regarding Rule 1.13(f), *see generally* D.C. Ethics Op. 269 (1997).

might assume that a lawyer is disinterested in loyalties or is a disinterested authority on the law even when the lawyer represents a client. In order to avoid a misunderstanding, a lawyer will typically need to identify the lawyer's client and, where necessary, explain that the client has interests opposed to those of the unrepresented person. For misunderstandings that sometimes arise when a lawyer for an organization deals with an unrepresented constituent, *see* Rule 1.13(f).

III. Duties Regarding the Law and the Legal Profession

A lawyer has duties relating to the law and the legal profession that can trump those owed to the client. These range from limits on the ability of lawyers to issue threats on behalf of their clients to the obligation to report the misconduct of judges and lawyers. Some of these duties are absolute trumps, such as the prohibition of agreements restricting the lawyer's practice even when the agreement would benefit the client. Other duties are limited by duties to the client, such as the duty to report professional misconduct, which is subject to the lawyer's confidentiality obligations.

A.   Obedience to Law

When studying the ethical rules governing lawyers, it is easy to lose sight of the fact that lawyers also have *legal* obligations, just as nonlawyers do, to comply with the law. The Restatement explains that as a general matter "a lawyer is subject to liability to a client or nonclient when a nonlawyer would be in similar circumstances." Restatement § 56. But this does *not* mean that clients' law violations are automatically imputed to their lawyers. The Restatement clarifies that "[a] lawyer, like other agents, is not as such liable for acts of a client that make the client liable." That said, lawyers remain responsible for their *own* actions that violate the law, such as when they knowingly assist law violations. Under principles of tort, agency and criminal law, assistance in the form of "legal services" is not categorically exempt from being classified as assistance in furtherance of illegality. The Restatement notes, "a lawyer is not always free of liability to a nonclient for assisting a client's act solely because the lawyer acting in the course of representation." *Id.* at (c). This section covers some common situations in which there is a heightened risk that the lawyer will run afoul of the law: when lawyers issue threats on behalf of their clients to gain leverage in civil lawsuits; when lawyers give advice about the legality of proposed courses of action; when lawyers encounter wrongdoing by clients or client representatives; and when subordinate lawyers are directed to undertake legally questionable actions by supervisory lawyers.

Practice Pointer

Remember that you can comply with the Rules and still face potential liability under law. In the Savings and Loan scandals of the 1980s, for example, the disciplinary authorities expressly cleared the lawyers at Kaye Scholer of any disciplinary violations. William H. Simon, *The Kaye Scholer Affair: The Lawyer's Duty of Candor and the Bar's Temptations of Evasion and Apology*, 23 Law & Soc. Inquiry 243, 265 (1998). Nonetheless, the firm paid $41 million to the government and $20 million to plaintiffs to settle legal claims arising from the same conduct. Alison Leigh Cowan, *Big Law and Auditing Firms to Pay Millions in S.&L. Suit*, N.Y. Times, Mar. 31, 1992, at A1.

[Question 6-22]

An attorney represents a client in a negligence action against a driver who accidently collided with her car. In the course of the representation, the attorney discovered evidence that could lead one to reasonably conclude that the driver had improperly entered the United States, which is a criminal misdemeanor. After discussing this issue with the client, the client consented to the attorney's using this information as leverage to negotiate a favorable settlement. The attorney phoned the opposing lawyer and said, "We have reason to believe that your client has entered the country unlawfully. If you give us $400,000, we can make your client's deportation go away. The local prosecutor happens to be one of my best friends." It was later determined that the driver had properly and lawfully entered the country.

Is the attorney subject to discipline?

- (A) No, because the attorney reasonably believed that the man was guilty of a crime.

- (B) No, because the attorney was required to report knowledge of criminal conduct.

- (C) Yes, because the criminal issue was unrelated to the client's civil claim and the attorney suggested that the attorney had improper influence over the criminal process.

- (D) Yes, because the attorney was mistaken about the legal status of the driver's entry into the United States and thus violated the driver's rights.

Rule 4.4(a) provides that "[i]n representing a client, a lawyer shall not use means that have no substantial purpose other than to embarrass, delay, or burden a third person, or use methods of obtaining evidence that violate the legal rights of such a person." Also consider the relevance of Rules 8.4(b), (d) and (e).

ABA Formal Op. 92–363 (1992) explains the ABA's current position on the use of threats of criminal prosecution to gain leverage in a civil lawsuit. The opinion clarifies that the Model Rules of Professional Conduct do not prohibit the lawyer from using the possibility of presenting criminal charges against an opposing party in a private civil litigation as a means of gaining leverage for his client in the civil litigation, provided that:

(i) the criminal matter is related to the client's civil claim;

(ii) the lawyer has a well-founded belief that both civil and criminal claims are supported by the facts and the law; and

(iii) the lawyer neither suggests that he has nor seeks to have improper influence over the criminal process.

So long as those conditions are met, the lawyer may agree in exchange for the satisfaction of his client's civil claim for relief, to refrain from pursuing criminal charges against the opposing party as part of a settlement agreement, so long as such an agreement does not violate *other law*.

Of course, this raises the question: *when* does a threat of criminal prosecution violate other law? Although the opinion provides no definitive answer to that question, it notes that threats of criminal prosecution are generally constrained by the criminal laws against *extortion* and *compounding a crime*. With respect to extortion, under the Model Penal Code, threats of prosecution are not considered a crime where the "property obtained by threat of accusation, exposure, lawsuit or other invocation of official action was honestly claimed as restitution for harm done in the circumstances to which such accusation, exposure, lawsuit or other official action relates, or as compensation for property or lawful services." Model Penal Code, § 223.4. In defining the crime of compounding, the Model Penal Code provides, "A person commits a misdemeanor if he accepts any pecuniary benefit in consideration of refraining from reporting to law enforcement authorities the commission of any offense or information relating to an offense. It is an affirmative defense to prosecution under this Section that the pecuniary benefit did not exceed an amount which the actor believed to be due as restitution or indemnification for harm caused by the offense." Model Penal Code, § 242.5. In sum, it seems that threats of criminal prosecution are unlikely to run afoul of the criminal laws in those jurisdictions that have adopted similar provisions to the Model Penal Code, where the recovery obtained from the settlement of the civil lawsuit (i) "was honestly claimed as restitution for harm done" and (ii) was not excessive compared to the amount of harm believed to be caused by the offense that is the basis of the civil claim. Also, it is helpful to note that compliance with the other conditions—that the criminal and civil claims are related to each other and are non-frivolous—helps avoid exposure to the charge of extortion or compounding a crime.

FYI

Douglas Richmond finds that some states have retained the express prohibition on using criminal charges solely to obtain an advantage in civil litigation. *See* Douglas R. Richmond, *Saber-Rattling and the Sound of Professional Responsibility*, 34 Am. J. Trial Advoc. 27 (2010), which also asks whether it is ethical to threaten disciplinary action to gain an advantage in litigation.

The opinion also clarifies why Rule 4.4 did not continue the express prohibition that was contained in Disciplinary Rule 7-105(A) of the Model Code of Professional Responsibility (1969, amended 1980). The Model Code provision prohibited the lawyer from threatening to present criminal charges *solely* to obtain an advantage in a civil matter. That provision was grounded in the rationale that threatening to use the criminal process to coerce an outcome in a private civil matter was a subversion of the criminal process and impaired the proper resolution of private civil disputes by deterring private litigants from asserting their legal rights in the civil process. Disciplinary Rule 7-105(A) was deliberately omitted from the subsequent Model Rules because it was seen as "redundant or overbroad or both," in light of the fact that "extortionate, fraudulent, or otherwise abusive threats were covered by other, more general prohibitions in the Model Rules."

The following provisions also constrain the lawyer's use of threats of criminal prosecution to gain an advantage in a civil matter:

> Rule 8.4(b), which provides that it is professional misconduct to engage in "criminal act[s] that reflect adversely on the lawyer's honesty, trustworthiness or fitness as a lawyer in other respects."

> Rule 8.4(d) and (e), which provide that it is professional misconduct to engage in conduct that is prejudicial to the administration of justice and to state or imply an ability to influence a government official or agency;

> Rule 4.1, which requires lawyers to be truthful when dealing with others on a client's behalf; and

> Rule 3.1, which prohibits an advocate from asserting frivolous claims.

[Question 6-23]

An attorney is retained by a client to lobby the state in favor of legalizing recreational marijuana. In that state, the cultivation, harvesting, and marketing of marijuana for non-medicinal purposes and without a doctor's medical prescription is a state crime. The attorney's client is an active cultivator and marketer of recreational marijuana. While the attorney personally believes that recreational marijuana should be legalized, the attorney has been careful not to counsel the client with respect to its cultivation and marketing activities. The attorney has only represented the client in correspondence with and appearances before the state legislature regarding the issue of legalization. In such correspondences and appearances, the attorney has been forthright about acting in a representative capacity but has not volunteered information about the client's illegal cultivation and marketing activities.

Is the attorney subject to discipline?

> **(A) No, because the attorney is not counseling or assisting the client to commit a crime.**

> **(B) No, because the attorney genuinely believes that recreational marijuana should be legalized.**

> **(C) Yes, because the client is engaging in continuing illegal conduct.**

(D) Yes, because the attorney has not volunteered information about the client's illegal cultivation and marketing activities during the attorney's appearances before the state legislature.

Rule 1.2(d) provides that "[a] lawyer shall not counsel a client to engage, or assist a client, in conduct that the lawyer knows is criminal or fraudulent, but a lawyer may discuss the legal consequences of any proposed course of conduct with a client and may counsel or assist a client to make a good faith effort to determine the validity, scope, meaning or application of the law."

The Comment to the Rule explains:

[9] Paragraph (d) prohibits a lawyer from knowingly counseling or assisting a client to commit a crime or fraud. This prohibition, however, does not preclude the lawyer from giving an honest opinion about the actual consequences that appear likely to result from a client's conduct. Nor does the fact that a client uses advice in a course of action that is criminal or fraudulent of itself make a lawyer a party to the course of action. There is a critical distinction between presenting an analysis of legal aspects of questionable conduct and recommending the means by which a crime or fraud might be committed with impunity.

Make the Connection

Comment [10] to Rule 1.2(d) is strikingly similar to Comment [3] to Rule 4.1(b), which was discussed in Unit II in the section on Truthfulness. Both comments discuss options available to the lawyer to avoid assisting a crime or fraud, including the option of "noisy withdrawal."

[10] When the client's course of action has already begun and is continuing, the lawyer's responsibility is especially delicate. The lawyer is required to avoid assisting the client, for example, by drafting or delivering documents that the lawyer knows are fraudulent or by suggesting how the wrongdoing might be concealed. A lawyer may not continue assisting a client in conduct that the lawyer originally supposed was legally proper but then discovers is criminal or fraudulent. The lawyer must, therefore, withdraw from the representation of the client in the matter. *See* Rule 1.16(a). In some cases, withdrawal alone might be insufficient. It may be necessary for the lawyer to give notice of the fact of withdrawal and to disaffirm any opinion, document, affirmation or the like. *See* Rule 4.1.

* * *

[12] Paragraph (d) applies whether or not the defrauded party is a party to the transaction. Hence, a lawyer must not participate in a transaction to effectuate criminal or fraudulent avoidance of tax liability. Paragraph (d) does not preclude undertaking a criminal defense incident to a general retainer for legal services to a lawful enterprise. The last clause of paragraph (d) recognizes that determining the validity or interpretation of a statute or regulation may require a course of action involving disobedience of the statute or regulation or of the interpretation placed upon it by governmental authorities.

Food for Thought

What if the lawyer's obligation to obey the law conflicts with the client's right of access to counsel? In 2010, lawyers from the Center for Constitutional Rights and the A.C.L.U. sought to challenge the legality of a reported government order authorizing the assassination of Anwar Al-Awlaki, a Yemeni cleric and United States citizen, whom the United States government has designated as a terrorist. When Al-Awalaki's father asked the civil liberties groups to represent him in contesting the reported assassination order, the groups were "in a Catch-22-like bind: because the government has designated Mr. Awlaki a terrorist, it would be a crime for the lawyers to file a lawsuit challenging the government's attempts to kill him." Charlie Savage, Lawyers Seeking Terror Suspect's Case Sue U.S., N.Y. Times, Aug. 3, 2010. The lawyers applied for permission to represent Mr. Al-Awlaki. When they did not receive a response, they "filed a lawsuit challenging a Treasury Department regulation that requires them to obtain permission to provide uncompensated legal service benefiting Mr. Awlaki[.]" *Id.* The Treasury Department then stated that "it would 'work with the A.C.L.U. to ensure that the legal services can be delivered.'" *Id.* One of the lead lawyers in this case was Professor Bill Quigley. He explains his position in Why We Sued to Represent Muslim Cleric Aulaqi, *Dissident Voice*, August 3, 2010. A September 20, 2011, drone strike killed Mr. Awlaki in Yemen. Mark Mazzetti, Charlie Savage, and Scott Shane, *How a U.S. Citizen Came to Be in America's Cross Hairs*, N.Y. Times, March 9, 2013. In *Humanitarian Law Project v. Holder*, 561 U.S. 1 (2010), the Court held that Congress can ban legal assistance to designated foreign terrorist organizations. David Cole, the attorney representing the Humanitarian Law Project, argued that the federal antiterrorism law violated the First Amendment. You can learn more by reading Cole's argument in *What Accounts as Abetting Terrorists?*, N.Y. Times, June 21, 2010.

While ethical rules prohibit lawyers from assisting a crime or fraud, lawyers also have tort and criminal law obligations to avoid aiding and abetting a crime or fraud. Although each jurisdiction has its own body of law, Professor Geoffrey C. Hazard, Jr. has offered a helpful test that should alert a lawyer to investigate further her potential liability:

> This analysis indicates the dimensions of the lawyer's duty under criminal and civil law to refrain from "assisting" a client in conduct that is "illegal." A lawyer violates that duty if:
>
> (1)   The client is engaged in a course of conduct that violates the criminal law or is an intentional violation of a civil obligation, other than failure to perform a contract or failure to sustain a good faith claim to property;
>
> (2)   The lawyer has knowledge of the facts sufficient to reasonably discern that the client's course of conduct is such a violation; and
>
> (3)   The lawyer facilitates the client's course of conduct either by giving advice that encourages the client to pursue the conduct or indicates how to reduce the risks of detection, or by performing an act that substantially furthers the course of conduct.

Geoffrey C. Hazard, Jr., *How Far May a Lawyer Go in Assisting a Client in Legally Wrongful Conduct?*, 35 U. Miami L. Rev. 669, 682–83 (1981). This test will be referred to as the "Hazard Test."

Food for Thought

What if complying with the law encumbers the lawyer's ability to communicate freely with her client and interferes with the lawyer-client relationship? That was the predicament faced by the most famous lawyer to have been punished for violating the criminal law. In *United States v. Stewart*, 590 F.3d 93 (2009), the Second Circuit affirmed the convictions of criminal defense lawyer Lynne Stewart and her associates for various crimes arising from their contacts with and behavior relating to government restrictions on communications and other contacts with their client, Sheikh Omar Ahmad Ali Abdel Rahman ("Rahman"), a Muslim cleric and spiritual leader of the group al-Gama'a. In 1997, the U.S. State Department designated al-Gama'a as a terrorist organization. In 1995, Rahman was convicted of conspiring to bomb several New York City landmarks, including the World Trade Center, and soliciting crimes of violence against the U.S. military and Egyptian President Hosni Mubarak, for which Rahman was sentenced to life (plus 65 years) in prison. After the appeals were exhausted, Stewart concentrated on improving the conditions of Rahman's confinement and obtaining his transfer from prison in the U.S. to Egypt. In 1997, the Bureau of Prisons imposed severely restrictive Special Administrative Measures ("SAMs") on Rahman, limiting his access to the mail, the media, the telephone and visitors, for the purpose of protecting "persons against the risk of death or serious bodily injury." During the seven-month trial of Stewart, evidence was presented that Stewart and her associates violated the SAMs by distracting prison guards to enable Rahman and his interpreter to covertly discuss issues relating to al-Gama'a governance, strategy and policy and to enable Stewart and her associates to transmit messages between Rahman and third parties, including leaders of al-Gama'a. Following the Court's decision, Stewart gave interviews justifying her actions. To listen to one of those interviews, click here. On remand, U.S. District Judge Koetl sentenced Stewart to 10 years in prison. He said that "postsentencing comments by Ms. Stewart in 2006, including a statement in a television interview that she would do 'it' again and would not 'do anything differently' influenced his decision to give a higher sentence than the one rejected as too light last year by the U.S. Court of Appeals for the Second Circuit." Mark Hamblett, *Stewart Gets a New 10-Year Prison Sentence*, N.Y. L.J. 1, July 16, 2010, at 1.

[Question 6-24]

An attorney is retained by a client corporation to register its initial public offering of stock to the public with the Securities & Exchange Commission (the "SEC"). After performing extensive research about the corporation's transactional history, the attorney concluded that the failure to disclose certain past transactions between the company and its chief executive officer (the "CEO") in its SEC filing would not only violate the disclosure requirements under the SEC regulations but would also amount to a material omission, rendering the corporation's disclosures in the SEC filing materially misleading. The attorney conferred with the CEO and properly advised that the intentional failure to disclose such transactions in the filing will likely give rise to a claim of securities fraud, opening the corporation up to shareholder lawsuits and possible delisting from the stock exchange. Moreover, the attorney correctly warned that the failure to disclose may completely derail the public offering, if the authorities detect the omission early enough. The CEO replied, "Just make the SEC filing without the disclosures. Why would we want to scare off investors? We're trying to sell our stock." The attorney vehemently argued with the CEO but, having failed to persuade, proceeded to make the filing without disclosing the transactions. The attorney was afraid of being fired by the CEO and believed that the CEO had the final say on disclosure matters. The SEC learned about the missing information and proceeded to initiate proceedings against the corporation.

Is the attorney subject to discipline and civil or criminal liability?

    (A) **No, because the attorney's role as an advisor means that the attorney must abide by the CEO's final decisions on key matters.**

    (B) **No, because the attorney fully discharged all professional and legal obligations by attempting to dissuade the CEO from engaging in misconduct.**

    (C) **Yes, because the attorney should have referred the matter to the corporation's board of directors and should not have complied with the CEO's instruction.**

    (D) **Yes, because the attorney should have avoided discussing this issue with the CEO and should have gone straight to the corporation's board of directors.**

Review Rule 1.2(d) and the Hazard test above preceding Question 6-24. Rule 1.13 of the Colorado Rules of Professional Conduct, which is identical to the ABA Model Rule, provides specific guidance for lawyers encountering organizational wrongdoing. As a threshold matter, Rule 1.13(a) clarifies who the client is when the lawyer represents an organization. It explains that "a lawyer employed or retained by an organization represents the organization acting through its duly authorized constituents." Thus, the client is the *organization*, a term that encompasses corporations and other associations. Accordingly, the lawyer for an organization ordinarily does not legally represent the organization's *constituents*, who may include officers, directors, employees, shareholders, and members. Some of these constituents are vested with the organizational authority to direct the lawyer's services and thus are often referred to colloquially as "clients." However, legally speaking, they are more accurately regarded as "client representatives."

Rule 1.13(b) explains the basic protocol:

If a lawyer for an organization knows that an officer, employee or other person associated with the organization is engaged in action, intends to act or refuses to act in a matter related to the representation that is a violation of a legal obligation to the organization, or a violation of law that reasonably might be imputed to the organization, and that is likely to result in substantial injury to the organization, then the lawyer shall proceed as is reasonably necessary in the best interest of the organization. Unless the lawyer reasonably believes that it is not necessary in the best interest of the organization to do so, the lawyer shall refer the matter to higher authority in the organization, including, if warranted by the circumstances to the highest authority that can act on behalf of the organization as determined by applicable law.

Rule 1.13(c) permits disclosure when the lawyer does not succeed in efforts under Rule 1.13(b). It states that:

[e]xcept as provided in paragraph (d), if

(1)   despite the lawyer's efforts in accordance with paragraph (b) the highest authority that can act on behalf of the organization insists upon or fails to address in a timely and appropriate manner an action, or a refusal to act, that is clearly a violation of law, and

(2)   the lawyer reasonably believes that the violation is reasonably certain to result in substantial injury to the organization,

then the lawyer may reveal information relating to the representation whether or not Rule 1.6 permits such disclosure, but only if and to the extent the lawyer reasonably believes necessary to prevent substantial injury to the organization.

Take Note

One area in which the lawyer must take care to avoid assisting a crime or fraud is money laundering, because successful money laundering often requires the services of a lawyer. If you are a fan of the popular television show, Breaking Bad, you will recall the episode in which rogue lawyer Saul Goodman carefully explains the mechanics of laundering money to Jesse Pinkman. As Chapter 2 explained, there is international and domestic interest in making sure that lawyers do not facilitate money laundering. The Financial Action Task Force is an inter-governmental body that establishes global standards against money laundering and terrorist financing. The International Bar Association sponsors an Anti-Money Laundering Forum, which helps lawyers comply with new anti-money laundering legislation. The ABA has a Task Force on Gatekeeper Regulation and the Profession, which helps educate lawyers about their responsibilities under anti-money laundering laws.

Rule 1.13(d) explains that the disclosure allowed under Rule 1.13(c) "shall not apply with respect to information relating to a lawyer's representation of an organization to investigate an alleged violation of law, or to defend the organization or an officer, employee or other constituent associated with the organization against a claim arising out of an alleged violation of law."

Rule 1.13(e) provides that "[a] lawyer who reasonably believes that he or she has been discharged because of the lawyer's actions taken pursuant to paragraphs (b) or (c), or who withdraws under circumstances that require or permit the lawyer to take action under either of those paragraphs, shall proceed as the lawyer reasonably believes necessary to assure that the organization's highest authority is informed of the lawyer's discharge or withdrawal."

Hear from the Authors

To hear more from the authors on Rule 1.13, click here.

Rule 1.13(f) provides that "[i]n dealing with an organization's directors, officers, employees, members, shareholders or other constituents, a lawyer shall explain the identity of the client when the lawyer knows or reasonably should know that the organization's interests are adverse to those of the constituents with whom the lawyer is dealing."

The Comment to the Rule explains:

[5] Paragraph (b) also makes clear that when it is reasonably necessary to enable the organization to address the matter in a timely and appropriate manner, the lawyer must refer the matter to higher authority, including, if warranted by the circumstances, the highest authority that can act on behalf of the organization under applicable law. The organization's highest authority to whom a matter may be referred ordinarily will be the board of directors or similar governing body. However, applicable law may prescribe that under certain conditions the highest authority reposes elsewhere, for example, in the independent directors of a corporation.

* * *

[10] There are times when the organization's interest may be or become adverse to those of one or more of its constituents. In such circumstances the lawyer should advise any constituent, whose interest the lawyer finds adverse to that of the organization of the conflict or potential conflict of interest,

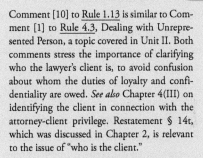

Make the Connection

Comment [10] to Rule 1.13 is similar to Comment [1] to Rule 4.3, Dealing with Unrepresented Person, a topic covered in Unit II. Both comments stress the importance of clarifying who the lawyer's client is, to avoid confusion about whom the duties of loyalty and confidentiality are owed. *See also* Chapter 4(III) on identifying the client in connection with the attorney-client privilege. Restatement § 14t, which was discussed in Chapter 2, is relevant to the issue of "who is the client."

that the lawyer cannot represent such constituent, and that such person may wish to obtain independent representation. Care must be taken to assure that the individual understands that, when there is such adversity of interest, the lawyer for the organization cannot provide legal representation for that constituent individual, and that discussions between the lawyer for the organization and the individual may not be privileged.

As noted above, under Rule 1.2(d), lawyers must not knowingly assist a client's crime or fraud. Lawyers who represent publicly traded companies frequently have to make judgment calls about whether they are complying with Rule 1.2(d). Public companies are required under the federal securities laws to file annual, quarterly and special reports (on Form 10-K, Form 10-Q, and Form 8-K respectively) with the Securities & Exchange Commission (the "SEC") for the benefit of the securities markets. These periodic filing reports must contain accurate and updated financial information. Lawyers not only draft the bulk of the narrative portions of these reports, but they also routinely facilitate and document the background transactions that underlie the numbers in the financial statements. Therefore, lawyers must take care to ensure as much as possible that there are no inaccurate or misleading statements about the company's financial condition in these reports.

A number of lawyers became ensnared in their client's securities fraud in the course of preparing the documentation of employee stock option grants. A "stock option" gives the recipient of the grant the right, but not the obligation, to purchase a stated number of shares of the company's stock on or after a specific date in the future at a stated price (the "exercise" or "strike" price) in accordance with the stated eligibility or "vesting" requirements. An option is said to be an "at-the-money" option if the assigned exercise price *equals* the fair market value of the stock on the date that the option is granted to the recipient. Once vested, the recipient of the option can purchase the company's shares by tendering to the company the exercise price assigned to the option. Once purchased, the recipient can then immediately resell those same shares on the open market at the prevailing market price, pocketing the difference between the prevailing market price and the exercise price as personal profit. Of course, this is only profitable if the prevailing market price of those shares on resale is *higher* than the stated exercise price of the option.

In late 2005 and throughout 2006, the *Wall Street Journal* published a series of reports suggesting that numerous public companies were *backdating* their executive stock option grants to reflect an earlier fictitious date of issuance, a date on which the market price of the company's shares was significantly *lower* than the market price on the actual grant date. Although backdating can take many forms, most backdating is intended to underreport the company's compensation expenses (and thus artificially inflate the company's net income figures on the financial statements). Prior to 2004, the accounting rules did not require at-the-money options to be recorded as a compensation expense of the company. But "in-the-money" options, which specify an exercise price *below*, rather than equal to, the fair market value at the time of the grant, were treated differently. In-the-money options were viewed as already having a positive value at the time of the grant. Accordingly, this positive value had to be accurately recorded and properly reflected as a compensation expense in the company's financial statements. The SEC investigated over a hundred companies and, according to one report, more than twenty former in-house counsel had been fired, demoted, or forced to resign following allegations of or investigations into the improper backdating of stock options. Perhaps the most famous of these scandals involved Nancy R. Heinen, the former general counsel of Apple Inc. In 2008, the SEC settled its case with Heinen. Note that, as part of the settlement, Heinen was suspended from "appearing or practicing before the" SEC as an attorney for three years. The SEC has the authority to discipline attorneys under its longstanding Rule 102(e) of its Rules of Practice. *See* 17 C.F.R. § 201.102(e) (2006).

Securities and Exchange Commission v. Nancy R. Heinen

SEC Litigation Release No. 20683 (2008)

SEC Settles Options Backdating Charges with Former Apple General Counsel for $2.2 Million

The Securities and Exchange Commission today announced that it has settled options backdating charges against Nancy R. Heinen, the former General Counsel of Apple, Inc. As part of the settlement Heinen, of Portola Valley, California, agreed (without admitting or denying the Commission's allegations) to pay $2.2 million in disgorgement, interest and penalties, be barred from serving as an officer or director of any public company for five years, and be suspended from appearing or practicing as an attorney before the Commission for three years.

The settlement stems from a complaint filed by the Commission in April 2007 in federal court in the Northern District of California. According to the complaint, Heinen caused Apple to fraudulently backdate two large options grants to senior executives of Apple—a February 2001 grant of 4.8 million options to Apple's Executive Team and a December 2001 grant of 7.5 million options to Apple Chief Executive Officer Steve Jobs—and altered company records to conceal the fraud. The complaint alleges that as a result of the backdating Apple underreported its expenses by nearly $40 million.

In the first instance, Apple granted 4.8 million options to six members of its Executive Team (including Heinen) in February 2001. Because the options were in-the-money when granted (*i.e.* could be exercised to purchase Apple shares at a below market price), Apple was required to report a compensation charge in its publicly-filed financial statements. The Commission alleges that, in order to avoid reporting this expense, Heinen caused Apple to backdate options to January 17, 2001, when Apple's share price was substantially lower. Heinen is also alleged to have directed her staff to prepare documents falsely indicating that Apple's Board had approved the Executive Team grant on January 17. As a result, Apple failed to record approximately $18.9 million in compensation expenses associated with the option grant.

The Commission's complaint also alleges improprieties in connection with a December 2001 grant of 7.5 million options to CEO Steve Jobs. Although the options were in-the-money at that time, Heinen—as with the Executive Team grant—caused Apple to backdate the grant to October 19, 2001, when Apple's share price was lower. As a result, the Commission alleges that Heinen caused Apple to improperly fail to record $20.3 million in compensation expense associated with the in-the-money options grant. The Commission further alleges that Heinen then signed fictitious Board minutes stating that Apple's Board had approved the grant to Jobs on October 19 at a "Special Meeting of the Board of Directors"—a meeting that, in fact, never occurred.

As part of the settlement, Heinen consented (without admitting or denying the allegations) to a court order that:

> (A)   enjoins her from violations of [various provisions of] the Securities Act of 1933 and [various provisions of] the Securities Exchange Act of 1934 . . . , and from aiding and abetting violations of [various provisions of] the Securities Exchange Act of 1934 . . . ;
>
> (B)   orders her to pay disgorgement of $1,575,000 (representing the in-the-money portion of the proceeds she received from exercising backdated options) plus $400,219.78 in interest;
>
> (C)   imposes a civil penalty of $200,000; and
>
> (D)   bars her from serving as an officer or director of any public company for five years.

In addition, Heinen agreed to resolve a separate administrative proceeding against her by consenting to a Commission order that suspends her from appearing or practicing before the Commission as an attorney for three years.

Simulation: Backdating Stock Options, Part I

The former chief financial officer for Apple has blamed Steve Jobs for the backdating of some of the options and alleged that Jobs knew about the accounting implications of the backdating. It is thus possible that Heinen faced pressure from Jobs and others to go along with the backdating scheme. In-house counsel can face pressures from senior executives, including the chief executive officer ("CEO"), to engage in questionable conduct such as the backdating of stock options. Suppose that you are the general counsel of a small public company and the CEO asks you to backdate *in-the-money* stock options previously granted to him, you, and other key members of management. (Remember that in-the-money options already have a positive value when granted because the exercise price assigned to those options is a price below the fair market value of the stock on the date of the grant.) The CEO wants you to make them appear *at-the-money* by assigning an earlier, fictitious grant date on which the fair market value of the stock matches the assigned exercise price of the options (and is also lower than the fair market value of the stock on the actual grant date). He wants you to do this because, among other reasons, he doesn't want to record the in-the-money options as a compensation expense in the company's books because he wants to report higher net income in the company's quarterly earnings report. He also wants you to make the "requisite editorial changes" to the board minutes authorizing the grants. What would you say to him? What do Rule 1.2(d) and Rule 1.13 require you to do? Assume, for purposes of this hypothetical, that the relevant accounting rules have retained the pre-2004 disparate treatment of in-the-money and at-the-money options indicated *supra*.

Take Note

Historically, private plaintiffs sued lawyers for facilitating frauds on an "aiding and abetting" cause of action under the federal securities laws. However, that avenue was largely foreclosed in 1993, when the Supreme Court in *Central Bank of Denver v. First Interstate Bank of Denver*, 511 U.S. 164 (1994), rejected aiding and abetting liability under Rule 10b-5 of the Securities Exchange Act of 1934. But *Central Bank* only impacted *secondary*, aiding-and-abetting liability for private securities lawsuits arising under Rule 10b-5. It remains theoretically possible to sue a lawyer for "making" a fraudulent statement as a *primary* violator of Rule 10b-5, at least to the extent that the plaintiff can demonstrate that a lawyer exercised "ultimate [corporate] authority" over a particular false or misleading statement. *See Janus Capital Group, Inc., et al. v. First Derivative Traders*, 564 U.S. 135 (2011). Lawyers are also still potentially liable to the extent they have provided expert certifications in connection with public offerings under Section 11 of the Securities Act of 1933. And the Securities & Exchange Commission still retains the power to pursue aiders and abettors of securities fraud, including lawyers, under their disciplinary authority. It is important to keep in mind that securities fraud (which is potentially criminal) is only one species of fraud in which lawyers must avoid becoming entangled. Recall that Rule 1.2(d) generally prohibits the lawyer from engaging or assisting a client in conduct that the lawyer knows is criminal or fraudulent.

[Question 6-25]

A law firm represented a savings and loan association in connection with an investigation conducted by a federal regulatory agency. The law firm was engaged in settlement discussions with the agency. An associate of the law firm brought to a partner's attention the fact that a board resolution that the law firm had previously prepared and filed with the agency had been backdated to give the appearance of contemporaneous board approval. The associate correctly believed that backdating materially violated a civil obligation of the corporation and that the knowing failure to correct the backdating in documents used and referred to in settlement discussions with the agency would amount to a fraud against the agency in any settlement concluded with the agency. After reviewing the relevant law and rules, the partner honestly but unreasonably concluded that it was proper not to correct the backdating and instructed the associate to proceed with the discussions as if no backdating had occurred. The associate believed that the partner had mistakenly applied the law and that the partner's interpretation was unreasonable. In discussions with the agency, the associate abided by the partner's instruction to continue referring to the incorrect date and withholding from the agency the date on which the resolution was actually signed.

Is the associate subject to discipline?

(A) Yes, because the associate made a false statement of material fact to the agency.

(B) Yes, because the associate was not entitled to rely on the partner's determination because the associate did not have a follow-up conversation with the partner.

(C) No, because the associate acted at the direction of the partner when the associate referred to the incorrect date in settlement discussions with the agency.

(D) No, because the associate acted reasonably in light of the associate's relative lack of experience.

Review the materials following Questions 6-17 and 6-23 *supra*.

Under Rule 5.2, all lawyers are "bound by the Rules of Professional Conduct notwithstanding that the lawyer acted at the direction of another person." Nonetheless, Rule 5.2(b) provides that "[a] subordinate lawyer does not violate the Rules of Professional Conduct if that lawyer acts in accordance with a supervisory lawyer's reasonable resolution of an arguable question of professional duty."

Under Rule 5.1(b), a supervising lawyer "shall make reasonable efforts to ensure that the [supervised] lawyer conforms to the Rules[.]"

Rule 5.1(c) makes a lawyer:

responsible for another lawyer's violation of the Rules * * * if:

(1)   the lawyer orders or, with knowledge of the specific conduct, ratifies the conduct involved; or

(2)   the lawyer is a partner or has comparable managerial authority in the law firm in which the other lawyer practices, or has direct supervisory authority over the other lawyer, and knows of the conduct at a time when its consequences can be avoided or mitigated but fails to take reasonable remedial action.

B.   The Sarbanes-Oxley Act of 2002

Although the ABA and others often refer to our system as one of "state judicial regulation of the practice of law," it is important to understand that certain federal government agencies, such as the Securities & Exchange Commission ("SEC"), the U.S. Patent and Trademark Office and the Internal Revenue Service, also regulate the professional conduct of those lawyers subject to their jurisdiction. In response to the scandals at Enron, WorldCom, Global Crossing and others, the U.S. Congress enacted the Sarbanes-Oxley Act of 2002 (the "Act"), which became effective on July 30, 2002. Under Section 307 of the Act, Congress delegated authority to the SEC to establish "minimum standards of professional conduct" for attorneys, representing the first time in its history that the SEC would have sweeping authority to establish disciplinary rules for attorneys "appearing or practicing before the [SEC]." The genesis of Section 307 was an amendment introduced during the Senate floor debate of the Sarbanes-Oxley bill. In proposing the amendment, Senator John Edwards noted:

> The truth is that executives and accountants do not work alone. Anybody who works in corporate America knows that wherever you see corporate executives and accountants working, lawyers are virtually always there looking over their shoulder. If executives and/or accountants are breaking the law, you can be sure that part of the problem is that the lawyers who are there and involved are not doing their jobs.
>
> . . . With Enron and WorldCom, and all the other corporate misconduct we have seen, it is again clear that corporate lawyers should not be left to regulate themselves no more than accountants should be left to regulate themselves.

148 Cong. Rec. S6551, 6551-52 (daily ed. July 10, 2002).

As a result, the SEC promulgated its detailed regulations on January 23, 2003 pursuant to the authority granted to it under the Act. Review the summary of the Sarbanes-Oxley regulations presented below before answering the following question.

[Question 6-26]

A senior in-house attorney was employed by a publicly traded energy corporation and oversaw all of the corporation's filings with the Securities & Exchange Commission ("SEC"). In the course of preparing an SEC filing, the attorney discovered that the chief financial officer had concealed various self-dealing transactions in which the chief financial officer made an enormous profit. Those transactions were never revealed to the board of directors. The attorney proceeded to report evidence relating to those

transactions to the corporation's top legal officer, the general counsel of the corporation. Upon receiving the report, the general counsel left a voicemail for the attorney, stating, "I saw your report. I'll look into it. Thanks." The attorney waited for a more detailed response from the general counsel but received none. The attorney suspected that the general counsel did not investigate the transactions and heard rumors that the general counsel and the chief financial officer were involved in a romantic relationship. However, the attorney honestly believed that the attorney had discharged the obligations required under the Sarbanes-Oxley regulations.

Is the attorney subject to discipline by the SEC for failure to comply with the Sarbanes-Oxley regulations?

> (A) No, because the attorney is not appearing and practicing before the SEC.
>
> (B) No, because the attorney properly reported the matter to the chief legal officer of the corporation.
>
> (C) Yes, because the attorney did not report the matter to the chief executive officer.
>
> (D) Yes, because the attorney lacked a reasonable belief that the attorney had received an appropriate response from the chief legal officer.

SARBANES-OXLEY REGULATIONS: A SUMMARY

17 C.F.R. Part 205—Standards of Professional Conduct for Attorneys Appearing and Practicing Before the Commission in the Representation of an Issuer

The SEC regulations promulgated under the Sarbanes-Oxley Act of 2002 apply to all attorneys "appearing and practicing before the [SEC] in the representation of an issuer [of securities]."[1] Those regulations specify two core rules: (1) a mandatory rule requiring attorneys to report "evidence of a material violation" up-the-ladder—*potentially* to the board of directors of the issuer and (2) a permissive rule allowing attorneys to report such evidence to the SEC, without the consent of the client issuer. "Evidence of a material violation" is defined as "credible evidence, based upon which it would be unreasonable, under the circumstances, for a prudent and competent attorney not to conclude that it is reasonably likely that a material violation has occurred, is ongoing, or is about to occur." 17 C.F.R. § 205.2(e). "Material violation" means a material violation of U.S. federal or state securities law, a material breach of fiduciary duty arising under any federal or state law, or a similar material violation of any federal or state law. *Id.* § 205.2(i).

Mandatory up-the-ladder reporting. An attorney must report any "evidence of a material violation" to the issuer's Chief Legal Officer ("CLO"), or to both the CLO and CEO, subject to what is colloquially referred to as the "futility exception." 17 C.F.R. § 205.3(b)(1). The futility

---

1   *See* 17 C.F.R. § 205.2(a)(1) for a definition of "appearing and practicing before the [SEC]." The definition comfortably covers attorneys who advise issuers with respect to any document to be filed with the SEC.

exception provides that if the attorney reasonably believes it would be futile to report to the CLO and the CEO, she may bypass the CLO and CEO and directly report to the board or a committee thereof. 17 C.F.R. § 205.3(b)(4). Unless the attorney reasonably believes that the CLO or CEO has provided an "appropriate response"[2] within a reasonable time, he must go over their heads and report further to the board or an appropriate board committee. *Id.* § 205.3(b)(3). If the attorney has taken the report "up the ladder" and does not reasonably believe that the issuer has made an appropriate response, the attorney must explain the reasons for this belief to the CLO, CEO, and the directors to whom the report was made. *Id.* § 205.3(b)(9).

Alternative QLCC reporting rule. In lieu of the mandatory up-the-ladder reporting rule, an attorney may report under an alternative reporting protocol if the issuer has previously and properly constituted a Qualified Legal Compliance Committee ("QLCC"), a committee of independent board members charged with adopting written procedures for confidentially receiving, retaining, and considering any report of evidence of a material violation, and with recommending remedial measures. Under this alternative rule, the attorney or the supervisory attorney may bypass the CEO and the CLO and submit a report directly to the QLCC and need not determine further whether the company has made an appropriate response. The QLCC will determine whether an investigation is necessary and may incur any expense (including retaining experts) in order to perform an investigation. The QLCC may notify the SEC if recommended remedial measures are not implemented. *Id.* § 205.3(c).

CLO's obligations. When the CLO receives a report of evidence of a material violation, she is responsible for piloting its investigation, taking any necessary remedial measures, and providing an "appropriate response" to the reporting attorney. If the company has previously formed a QLCC, the CLO can refer the matter directly to the QLCC (without making any further inquiry) and advise the reporting attorney of such referral. *Id.* § 205.3(b)(2).

Permissive "reporting out." An attorney may, but is not required to, reveal to the SEC, without the company's consent, confidential information relating to his representation. *Id.* § 205.3(d)(2). Not surprisingly, the triggering standard for "reporting out" is considerably more stringent than the triggering standard for the initial "reporting up."[3]

---

2   "Appropriate response" means a response as a result of which the reporting attorney reasonably believes that (1) no material violation has occurred, is ongoing, or is about to occur; or (2) the issuer has adopted appropriate remedial measures, including appropriate steps or sanctions to stop an ongoing material violation, to prevent a future violation, or to remedy (or otherwise appropriately address) a past violation and minimize the possibility of its recurrence; or (3) the issuer, with the consent of the board of directors or an appropriate committee thereof, has retained or directed an attorney to review the evidence of material violation and has either substantially implemented such attorney's remedial recommendations (after a reasonable investigation and evaluation of the reported evidence) or has been advised that such attorney may assert a colorable defense on behalf of the issuer (or its officers or agents) in any investigation or judicial or administrative proceeding. *Id.* § 205.2(b).

3   *See id.* § 205.3(d)(2). In contrast to the triggering standard for "reporting up," where an attorney is obligated to report credible evidence when it would be unreasonable for her not to conclude that a material violation is reasonably likely to occur (or have occurred, or is ongoing), the standard for "reporting out" is triggered when there is a clear sense of urgency. An attorney may "report out" if she reasonably believes reporting out is necessary to (a) prevent the company from committing a material violation that is likely to cause substantial injury to the financial interest or property of the issuer or investors; or (b) rectify the consequences of a material violation that caused (or may cause) such injury, if the attorney's services were used in furtherance of the violation; or (c) prevent the company from committing or suborning perjury, or perpetrating a fraud upon the SEC. *Id.*

Simulation: Backdating Stock Options, Part II

Revisit the simulation hypothetical, *supra*, immediately following *Securities and Exchange Commission v. Nancy R. Heinen*, SEC Litigation Release No. 20683 (2008). Now suppose further that you, the general counsel, have unsuccessfully attempted to dissuade the CEO from proceeding with the backdating scheme and that you have called a meeting of the board of directors to discuss the matter. How might you go about describing the problem to the board? Suppose that the board simply doesn't understand why you aren't acquiescing in the CEO's demands. What would you say to the board? What if the board insisted that you facilitate the backdating scheme on the ground that the company owes its success to the CEO, the scheme is in the best interest of the company, and the risk of getting caught is really low? How would you respond to the board? What are your options and obligations under Rule 1.2(d), Rule 1.13, Rule 1.16(a), Rule 4.1 and the Sarbanes-Oxley regulations?

C. Restrictions on Practice

The ethical rules prohibit agreements among lawyers that restrict the practice of law. Because lawyers are critical for laypersons to gain access to justice, many consider such agreements to be inherently problematic.

[Question 6-27]

A criminal defense attorney represents a spiritual leader of a terrorist organization, who is charged in federal court with directing and committing acts of terrorism. The government offers a plea deal, whereby the defendant will receive a reduced sentence if the defendant pleads guilty, but only if the attorney also agrees not to voluntarily represent members of any terrorist organizations in the future. The attorney believes that this plea agreement is favorable to the defendant.

Is this plea agreement proper?

   (A) **No, because the proposed plea agreement would restrict the attorney's right to practice.**

   (B) **No, because the attorney must not discriminate among clients based on their political views.**

   (C) **Yes, because the restriction on the attorney's right to practice is limited only to representing members of terrorist organizations, and this restriction is justified by national security concerns.**

   (D) **Yes, because the attorney believes that this plea agreement is in the best interest of the client.**

Rule 5.6(a) provides that a lawyer cannot participate in the making of an agreement that "restricts the right of a lawyer to practice after termination of the relationship, except an agreement concerning benefits upon retirement." Rule 5.6(b) prohibits a lawyer from making "an agreement in which a restriction on the lawyer's right to practice is part of the settlement of a client controversy." The Comment describes the rationale for Rule 5.6(a) as protecting both lawyers' "professional autonomy" and "the freedom of clients to choose a lawyer." This rationale would seem to be the basis for Rule 5.6(b) as well.

D. Reporting Lawyer and Judge Misconduct

The duty to report the serious misconduct of lawyers and judges to disciplinary authorities lays the foundation for the claim that state judicial regulation of the practice of law is adequate and need not be augmented. The Comment to Rule 8.3 of the Wyoming Rules of Professional Conduct, which is identical to the ABA Model Rule, explains that "[s]elf-regulation of the legal profession requires that members of the profession initiate disciplinary investigation when they know of a violation of the Rules[.]"

Food for Thought

Nikki A. Ott and Heather F. Newton have argued that the duty to report misconduct "embodies one of the most underenforced, and possibly unenforceable, mandates in legal ethics." Nikki A. Ott & Heather F. Newton, *A Current Look at Model Rule 8.3: How Is It Used and What Are Courts Doing About It?*, 16 Geo. J. Legal Ethics 747, 747 (2003).

[Question 6-28]

An attorney has been friends with a lawyer since their days as law school classmates. Recently, when she met with him during the workday, she smelled alcohol on his breath. She noticed him being nasty and abusive to colleagues, adversary lawyers, and even, on occasion, to clients. She recently litigated a case against him where his performance failed to meet even minimum standards as a matter of competence. The attorney then recommended to the lawyer that he seek help from the bar's lawyer assistance program for his alcohol problem. The lawyer angrily refused. Worried that any further action might jeopardize her longstanding friendship with the lawyer, the attorney does nothing.

Is the attorney subject to discipline?

(A) **Yes, because the attorney failed to inform the appropriate authorities about the lawyer's conduct.**

(B) **Yes, because the attorney did not ask the client in her recent case whether the client wanted her to inform the appropriate authorities.**

(C) **No, because the attorney suggested that the lawyer seek help from a lawyer assistance program.**

(D) **No, because the attorney reasonably feared that the lawyer would end their friendship if she reported him.**

Rule 8.3(a) requires a lawyer to "inform the appropriate professional authority" when the lawyer "knows that another lawyer has committed a violation of the Rules of Professional Conduct that raises a substantial question as to that lawyer's honesty, trustworthiness or fitness as a lawyer in other respects[.]" Rule 8.3(c) makes clear that "[t]his Rule does not require disclosure of information otherwise protected by Rule 1.6 or information gained by a lawyer or judge while participating in an approved lawyers assistance program." Also, Comment [4] clarifies that "[t]he duty to report professional misconduct does not apply to a lawyer retained to represent a lawyer whose professional conduct is in question."

Hear from the Authors

To hear more from the authors on this reporting duty, click here.

IN RE HIMMEL, 533 N.E.2D 790 (ILL. 1988): A SUMMARY

Himmel may be the first case in which an attorney was suspended for failure to report another lawyer's wrongdoing. In 1980, an accident victim hired attorney James Himmel to collect her share of the funds procured from a $35,000 settlement of her accident claim. Upon investigation, Himmel discovered that the victim's former lawyer, who had negotiated the settlement, illegally converted the settlement money from his client trust account for his personal use. Instead of reporting the former lawyer's misconduct, however, Himmel negotiated a settlement in which Himmel agreed not to report the lawyer's misconduct if that lawyer would pay $75,000 to the victim.

Make the Connection

Refer to Chapter 4 for further discussion of confidential information vs. privileged communications. How might the Illinois interpretation of the Rule 8.3 impact communications between lawyer and client?

The Illinois Supreme Court, reviewing the decisions of the disciplinary agency, concluded that Himmel violated the Illinois reporting rule and suspended him from practicing law for one year. The Illinois rule was substantially modeled after the ABA Model Rules with one important difference: the reporting duty under Model Rule 8.3 is "trumped" by the confidentiality duty of Rule 1.6, which protects "information relating to the representation of a client," a limitation that, many believe, virtually swallows up the reporting rule. By contrast, under the Illinois version, only attorney-client privileged information is protected from disclosure. The Court rejected Himmel's contention that the information relating to the lawyer's misconduct was privileged. It found that Himmel's communications with the victim had taken place in the presence of third parties (the victim's fiancé and mother). The *Himmel* decision has been widely criticized for its harshness, but Illinois lawyers seem to have gotten the message: more than 20 years after *Himmel*, Illinois reportedly has the nation's highest rate of attorney reports of misconduct.

For More Information

Another well-known case of an attorney being sanctioned under Rule 8.3 is *In re Michael G. Riehlmann*, 891 So. 2d 1239 (La. 2005). In *Riehlmann*, a former prosecutor confessed to his long-time friend, a New Orleans attorney named Michael Riehlmann, that he had failed to provide the defense with an exculpatory blood test that would have exonerated the accused in a death penalty case. The confessing friend soon died without taking remedial action. Five years later, when it was reported in the local newspaper that defendant's counsel in that case had discovered the exculpatory blood test, Riehlmann finally contacted the defense team and provided an affidavit detailing his friend's confession. The Louisiana Office of Disciplinary Counsel filed charges against Riehlmann, and the Louisiana Supreme Court found that Riehlmann's failure to report the confession to a tribunal with the power to act on attorney misconduct and Riehlmann's inordinate delay amounted to a "serious offense," and ordered that Riehlmann be publicly reprimanded.

Notwithstanding *Himmel* and *Riehlmann*, sanctions under Rule 8.3 are relatively rare, but the Rule has remained essentially unchanged since it was created. Many theories have been offered about why it is difficult to enforce the reporting requirement. Some vagueness about how and when to report the misconduct: "The few allegations that have been investigated, prosecuted, and sanctioned confirm that the rule's language, specifically its failure to prescribe a time period during which reporting misconduct must occur, contributes to the rule's infirmity." Laurel Fedder, Note: *Obstacles to Maintaining the Integrity of the Profession: Rule 8.3's Ambiguity and Disciplinary Board Complacency*, 23 Geo. J. Legal Ethics 571 (2010). The reporting lawyer has to make a judgment call as to whether the possible violation is sufficiently serious or "substantial" enough to require reporting. Douglas R. Richmond, *For A Few Dollars More: The Perplexing Problems of Unethical Billing Practices by Lawyers*, 60 S.C. L. Rev. 63 (2008). Violations of the rule are hard to detect and prove: "Knowledge is particularly difficult to impute from the outside. Furthermore, by failing to report, an attorney merely goes about his business as usual. There is nothing that would lead an outside party to investigate an attorney who has violated such a rule." Ryan Williams, Comment: *Reputation and the Rules: An Argument for A Balancing Approach Under Rule 8.3 of the Model Rules of Professional Conduct*, 68 La. L. Rev. 931, 939 (2008). And inadequate incentive and protection for the reporting attorneys: "One reason many attorneys may not report the misconduct of co-workers is the fear of retaliation. * * * Retaliation may take many forms, both professionally and socially. Some scholars seem to hold the belief that a fear of negative social repercussions from reporting another attorney should have no impact on the willingness to comply with reporting mandates. However, it probably does in practice, particularly when the misconduct which must be reported is that of a co-worker rather than an adversary." Cynthia L. Gendry, *Ethics-an Attorney's Duty to Report the Professional Misconduct of Co-Workers*, 18 S. Ill. U. L.J. 603 (1994).

[Question 6-29]

An attorney regularly appeared before a female divorce court judge in a state in which judges are elected to the bench. Once at a divorce law conference sponsored by the local bar association, numerous divorce lawyers, including the attorney, gathered together to complain about this judge's mistreatment of their female clients. These lawyers believed they had witnessed the judge repeatedly making disparaging remarks about women who are financially incapable of supporting themselves after the divorce, being rude and abrupt to female litigants seeking maintenance and child support payments from their spouses, and making rulings that were patently unfair to female litigants. These lawyers also openly wondered why a female judge would show such strong bias against women. After the conference, the attorney contacted many other divorce lawyers, who confirmed that they had similar experiences with this judge. The attorney then drafted a public petition and began mobilizing an effort to recall this judge, in accordance with the proper state recall procedures applicable to judges. When someone suggested that the attorney also contact the bar disciplinary authorities, the attorney dismissed that idea, noting, "Bar counsel will never prosecute anyone."

Is the attorney subject to discipline?

- (A) No, because the attorney's statement about bar counsel is the attorney's opinion.

- (B) No, because there is no rule prohibiting attorneys from mobilizing a recall effort.

- (C) Yes, because the attorney failed to inform the appropriate disciplinary authorities about the judge's misbehavior.

- (D) Yes, because the attorney has improperly mobilized a recall effort, which threatens the independence of the judiciary and the rule of law.

Rule 8.3(b) of the Wyoming Rules of Professional Conduct states that: "[a] lawyer who knows that a judge has committed a violation of applicable rules of judicial conduct that raises a substantial question as to the judge's fitness for office shall inform the appropriate authority."

Test Your Knowledge

To assess your understanding of the material in this Chapter, click here to take a quiz.

CHAPTER 7

Special Ethical Rules: Prosecutors and Judges

Learning Outcomes

At the end of Unit I, you will be able to:

*   Articulate the unique role of the prosecutor as minister of justice

*   Recognize the boundaries of the prosecutor's discretion to charge

*   Recognize prosecutors' duties to ensure a defendant's right to counsel and to refrain from seeking a waiver of pretrial rights from an unrepresented accused

*   Differentiate the constitutional obligation to disclose evidence (the Brady Rule) from the requirements under Rule 3.8

*   Analyze, and articulate the policy behind, the rules requiring prosecutors to rectify, as well as avoid, wrongful convictions

At the end of Unit II, you will be able to:

*   Recognize the sources of law governing the ethical standards for judges

*   Analyze prohibitions on external influences for sitting judges

*   Analyze grounds for judicial disqualification

*   Recognize limitations on extrajudicial activity

*   Recognize campaign limitations on candidates for judicial elections

Topic Outline for Chapter 7

	TOPIC	RELEVANT AUTHORITY	CHAPTER QUESTIONS
I.	Prosecutors	3.8	
	A. The Decision to Charge [McKittrick, Pugach]	3.8	7-1

In the previous Chapter, we explored the lawyer's duties to the legal system and the public. Most, but not all, of that analysis related to representation of private clients. In this Chapter, we explore two special roles for lawyers that diverge altogether from the paradigm of representing private clients—work as a prosecutor or a judge. But although prosecutors and judges share a primary obligation to the legal system and the public, their particular ethical duties differ in significant ways. Moreover, prosecutors are subject to the Rules like other lawyers, while judges are governed by the Code of Judicial Conduct.

I. Prosecutors

The prosecutor's basic job is to enforce the criminal law. Prosecutors decide whether to initiate criminal charges against individuals and, on occasion, entities believed to have violated the criminal law and prosecute the cases against them in court. In doing so, prosecutors wield the state's or federal government's vast criminal law enforcement power. In the process, prosecutors are governed by ethical rules and law and have broad discretion within the bounds of the law.

In most cases, a prosecutor's office is comprised of a chief prosecutor, such as a United States Attorney, a state Attorney General, or a District or County Attorney. On the federal level, the U.S. Attorney General and the United States Attorneys for each of the 94 federal districts are appointed by the President and confirmed by the Senate (although acting or interim

U.S. Attorneys may be appointed by the Attorney General or by the federal district court). State attorneys general are usually elected or appointed by the Governor. Many local chief prosecutors—*e.g.*, District or County Attorneys—are elected. Some, as in Alaska and New Jersey, are appointed. In some localities, a lawyer is hired on a part-time or full-time basis by the locality to prosecute low-level crimes.

Most prosecutors serve under the authority of the elected or appointed chief prosecutor. In a small rural community, an elected County Attorney may have no lawyers on staff, or only one or two full-time or part-time lawyers. In a large city or county, such as Manhattan or Los Angeles, the prosecutors' office may be staffed by several hundred prosecutors. While a newly elected or appointed chief prosecutor may bring in new lawyers to serve on the senior staff, lower level prosecutors in most jurisdictions are free to stay from one administration to the next. In some jurisdictions, prosecutors can be replaced "at will" by the chief prosecutor, but in others, prosecutors have civil service protection and can be fired only for good cause.

Global Perspective

There are a number of differences between prosecutors in the United States and prosecutors in other countries. For example, the U.S. has a unified legal profession which means that once someone is licensed as a lawyer by a particular state, that lawyer has an unrestricted license to practice law in all types of law settings in that state, including private law firms, as in-house (corporate) counsel, or as a prosecutor. In other countries, however, prosecutors may have a different title, may be regulated differently, and may not be able to easily transition into private practice, as a U.S. prosecutor can. For example, in Germany, the title of "lawyer" [Rechtsanwalt] is reserved to those in private practice. A prosecutor is a "Staatsanwalt" and is not regulated by the bar association. *See, e.g.*, the Germany Legal Professions: Prosecutor (Staatsanwalt) page in the European Union's E-Justice Portal. As the E-Justice Portal illustrates, prosecutors' roles and ethics depend on the country's adjudicative system. Some of the differences you are likely to encounter include whether a country has local prosecutors or only a centralized national prosecutor and differences such as whether prosecutors' charging and advocacy functions are separated. Although there is no international database with information about prosecutors, the EU's E-Justice Portal is a very useful website that provides information about prosecutors in EU Member States, as well as information on a wide variety of topics, including legal systems, legal professions, judicial training, rights of criminal defendants, mediation, and wills.

The nature of an office's legal personnel may vary in other respects as well. The junior or "line" prosecutors in a large urban office may mostly be made up of recent law school graduates and lawyers with less than five years of experience. A smaller number of senior lawyers may staff senior trial units such as homicide units and serve in supervisory positions. Few of the prosecutors may regard themselves as "career prosecutors." Most may view the job of prosecutor as a stepping stone to private employment, including as private criminal defense lawyer, that draws on trial experience. Or they may move to the private sector after several years to make more money. Elsewhere, many lawyers make a career in the prosecutor's office, because they are committed to the work, the pay and hours are relatively good compared to the other opportunities available in professional community, and the office's ethos and tradition do not encourage lawyers to leave after a short time.

Collectively, prosecutors in an office make a host of decisions and engage in a variety of conduct that substantially affects the lives of individuals—including importantly the lives of victims, witnesses and those suspected of committing crimes—as well as the lives of members of the community in general. Much of their work takes place outside the courtroom and is administrative in nature. State prosecutors work closely with the police department, sheriff's office, or other state office with investigative authority; federal prosecutors work with the F.B.I. and other federal investigative agencies. Prosecutors sometimes do not become involved in a case until the police arrest a suspect. But prosecutors often work with the police, who may need prosecutors' help to obtain search warrants, and prosecutors in some jurisdictions use the grand jury not only to approve of indictments but as an investigative tool. Prosecutors may interview or question witnesses, suspects and arrested individuals informally or question them in the grand jury.

See It

The 1990 shooting of a bouncer outside New York's Palladium nightclub led to one of the more controversial stories about the prosecutor's role. Assistant District Attorney Daniel Bibb claimed that he was ordered by District Attorney Robert M. Morgenthau to defend the original conviction of two men on the murder charge, despite new evidence suggesting their innocence which convinced Bibb the wrong men were convicted. The case highlights prosecutorial discretion, the political considerations of a prosecutor's office, and whether it is ethical to "throw the case" as Bibb said he did. Watch an MSNBC Dateline news report; *see also* David Luban, *The Conscience of a Prosecutor*, 45 Val. U. L. Rev. 1 (2010).

Besides deciding in many cases whom to investigate and by what means to conduct the investigation, prosecutors decide whether to initiate criminal charges in cases where they believe a suspect committed a crime, decide what charges to bring, offer plea bargains and conduct plea negotiations, and take positions at sentencing hearings. Often, though believing an individual to be guilty, prosecutors decline to bring charges for any of a host of reasons, such as that: the crime was a low-level and first offense so that a criminal conviction would be disproportionately harsh; the policies of the office encourage alternatives to a criminal conviction; a prosecution would require excessive resources; or the case is too weak for prosecutors to be confident of securing a conviction.

Approximately 95% of the cases that prosecutors bring are resolved by a plea of guilty rather than a trial. But the most visible and media-worthy work of prosecutors involves presenting cases against defendants charged with a crime who choose to exercise their right to trial. In the trial setting, the prosecutor is much like a civil litigator representing a private party. Although the procedural rules differ—for example, the prosecutor has the burden of proving guilt beyond a reasonable doubt—the prosecutor's basic task is to present the prosecution's proof and to argue the prosecution's positions as convincingly as possible.

As to any individual prosecutor, the daily work can vary. In some large, urban offices, prosecutors' work is compartmentalized based on particular tasks or phases of work. Prosecutors may be divided into units that arraign defendants, investigate cases and present them to the grand jury, prepare for and conduct trials, and handle appeals. Some offices have different units in which prosecutors focus on particular kinds of cases—*e.g.*, homicide, narcotics, white collar—or are divided between misdemeanor and felony units. Typically, more senior prosecutors handle the more important tasks (*e.g.*, trials) or types of cases (*e.g.*, homicides). Different units of a large office may develop different practices and cultures.

The fact that a chief prosecutor has broad discretion does not mean that each individual prosecutor has the same level of discretion. Where offices are divided into units along one or more lines, the units are generally supervised by an experienced prosecutor. Besides having a teaching role and serving as a source of guidance, supervisory lawyers typically have responsibility to make or approve certain decisions, such as whether to initiate an indictment, offer a particular plea bargain, grant immunity to a defendant in exchange for testifying against others, or take a particular position at a defendant's sentencing. Further, particularly in large offices, frequently recurring decisions may be governed by written or oral policies developed and approved by senior

FYI

On the allocation of decision making within a prosecutor's office, *see* Bruce A. Green & Fred C. Zacharias, *"The U.S. Attorneys Scandal" and the Allocation of Prosecutorial Power*, 69 Ohio St. L.J. 187 (2008). On the question of whether the President may give direction to federal prosecutors, see Bruce A Green & Rebecca Roiphe, *Can the President Control the Department of Justice?*, 70 Ala. L. Rev. 1 (2018).

supervisory prosecutors or by the chief prosecutor. The policies may or may not be publicized. For example, an office may decide to bring misdemeanor rather than felony charges for first-offenders in narcotics possession cases or to seek at least a year's imprisonment when a defendant possesses a firearm in the course of criminal conduct. The policies may or may not be subject to exception.

FYI

Professors Green and Zacharias discuss the importance of identifying internal principles and policies to guide the work of prosecutors in Bruce A. Green & Fred C. Zacharias, *Prosecutorial Neutrality*, 2004 Wis. L. Rev. 837. The best example of such guidelines is the U.S. Attorney's Manual, available here. The U.S. Attorney's Manual provides guidance to federal prosecutors, who may be subject to internal discipline for violating its provisions. The U.S. Department of Justice has an office, the Office of Professional Responsibility, which investigates alleged violations of ethics rules and internal guidelines by federal prosecutors and recommends sanctions when it finds wrongdoing. Another office, the Professional Responsibility Advisory Office, gives advice to federal prosecutors about their compliance with ethics rules.

In conducting their work, prosecutors have no need to pursue business or please clients. But their personal motivations may include advancing within the office or, in the case of those who are not career prosecutors, obtaining future outside employment. In any case, prosecutors are ordinarily interested in developing and preserving a favorable reputation within and/or outside the office. But this can be a double-edged sword, because the values of the relevant community may differ from prosecutors' perception of their role. The prosecutor's job prospects in or outside the office may be enhanced, on one hand, by a reputation for evenhandedness, balance, fairness and candor or, on the other hand, by a reputation for zealousness, fearlessness, and a willingness to go up to the limits of the law, and even to test the law where it is ambiguous, in order to win a case.

One of the distinctive aspects of prosecutors' work is that prosecutors do not answer to a client. Chief prosecutors may have to be accountable to the public in an abstract sense, but they do not take direction from the public. Prosecutors bring cases in the name of "the United States" or "the Commonwealth of Virginia" or the "People of the State of the New York," but they make decisions on behalf of the entity that they represent. Unlike lawyers for private clients, there is no other individual or entity who hires the prosecutor to bring a particular matter, who defines the objectives of the representation, who decides whether to bring or resolve a case, or with whom the prosecutor must confer. Although a prosecutor may work closely with the police department or other investigative agency, the investigators are not clients. Further, because prosecutors do not seek or represent private clients, professional conduct rules such as those governing the protection of client funds and the solicitation of business have no relevance to their work.

To be sure, a prosecutor has some of the professional obligations that historically grow out of the lawyer's obligation as agent of a client, but these do not pose the same kinds of difficulties that they often pose for privately retained lawyers. For example, prosecutors must maintain the confidentiality of information learned in a representation. But they also generally have authority to use or disclose the information for legitimate law-enforcement purposes. Prosecutors must avoid conflicts of interest. But because they represent only one client, conflicts of interest are rare.

More significant are the ethical rules governing trial lawyers generally, such as the rules against offering false testimony and false evidence; communicating ex parte with judges and jurors; trying the case in the press; and making jury arguments that refer to facts not in evidence, that play on the jury's sympathies or prejudices, or that are otherwise out of bounds.

Prosecutors are also subject to Rule 3.8, which identifies "Special Responsibilities of a Prosecutor." The rule is predicated on the understanding that prosecutors have an ethically exceptional status that carries with it special responsibilities. This understanding is captured by Comment 1 to Rule 3.8, which begins: "A prosecutor has the responsibility of a minister of justice and not simply that of an advocate. This responsibility carries with it specific obligations to see that the defendant is accorded procedural justice and that guilt is decided upon the basis of sufficient evidence." The counterpart Comment in the ABA Model Rules adds that prosecutors must take "special precautions . . . to rectify the convictions of innocent persons." The prosecutor's special responsibilities have sometimes been summed up by the "duty to seek justice."

Rule 3.8 does not set forth all of a prosecutor's special responsibilities. Other responsibilities are reflected in judicial decisions.

Prosecutorial discretion is central to the operation of all state and federal criminal justice systems. It pervades every aspect of a prosecutor's work and daily life including investigating, charging, bail and plea bargaining decisions as well as decisions in trial, sentencing and post conviction motions. Prosecutorial decision making may be guided by case law, statutes, procedural rules, and ethics provisions. Law and rules typically provide boundaries but insufficient guidance for the exercise of discretion. There are few enforceable laws that provide legal limitations on the exercise of discretion. Standards applicable to criminal cases may include informal constraints that courts can impose upon prosecutors to establish some norms of conduct for the exercise of discretion. But mostly, discretionary choices are guided by a potential range of other factors including norms within prosecutors' offices, and individual commitment to fairness. These choices may be guided by the internal and external supervisory and accountability systems. They may be guided by political realities. These norms are rarely explicit.

FYI

Commentators have disagreed to some extent about the reason why prosecutors are said to have a special "duty to seek justice." Fred Zacharias argued that this duty is explained by prosecutors' special power, and that prosecutors should therefore have special duties only when they exercise power that is different from that of ordinary trial advocates. Fred C. Zacharias, *Structuring the Ethics of Prosecutorial Trial Practice: Can Prosecutors Do Justice*, 44 Vand. L. Rev. 45 (1991). In response, Bruce Green suggested that the special duty comes primarily from the prosecutor's role in representing the government, whose objectives, which are implicit in the constitution and statutes, include avoiding punishment of those who are innocent, affording the accused, and others, a lawful, fair process, treating individuals with proportionality, and treating lawbreakers with rough equality. Bruce A. Green, Why Should Prosecutors "Seek Justice," 26 Fordham Urb. L.J. 607 (1999).

FYI

For a discussion of the reasons for the ABA's failure to make its Rule 3.8 more complete, and the types of additional issues that the rule might address, *see* Bruce A. Green, Prosecutorial Ethics as Usual, 2003 U. Ill. L. Rev. 1573. One of the suggestions in the article was adopted around five years later when the ABA amended its rule to add Rules 3.8(g) and (h) to address prosecutors' post-conviction obligations.

Commentators have long questioned whether there are sufficient standards, principles or policies to guide discretionary decision making and have sought to delineate the boundaries of legitimate discretionary decision making. Some of the literature on this subject is normative, identifying principles or standards that should exist to exercise discretion in certain areas. Other writings describe how prosecutors have made discretionary decisions, such as those regarding charging and plea bargaining.

A. The Decision to Charge

Discretion

[Question 7-1]

An assistant county prosecutor worked with the sheriff to investigate a drug-related murder. Several informants passed along rumors that the murder was committed by

a local shopkeeper. Although the prosecutor knew that the rumors did not amount to probable cause to believe that the shopkeeper committed the murder, the investigation did uncover sufficient evidence to convict the shopkeeper of rarely-enforced misdemeanor provisions governing the disposal of trash. In the prosecutor's jurisdiction, a prosecutor may file criminal charges without obtaining an indictment by a grand jury. The prosecutor filed charges alleging that the shopkeeper committed the murder in violation of a felony provision and that he violated misdemeanor provisions. After the sheriff arrested the shopkeeper, the prosecutor undertook the prosecution in the hope that witnesses would come forward with admissible evidence of the shopkeeper's role in the murder.

Is the prosecutor subject to discipline?

(A) Yes, because he prosecuted a murder charge that he knew was not supported by probable cause.

(B) Yes, because he prosecuted misdemeanor charges as a pretext for punishing the shopkeeper for a more serious crime for which there was insufficient evidence.

(C) No, because the rumors of the shopkeeper's commission of the murder justified initiating a prosecution with the hope that witnesses would come forward with admissible evidence.

(D) No, because there was sufficient evidence to convict the shopkeeper of the misdemeanor provisions.

Rule 3.8

The prosecutor in a criminal case shall:

(a) refrain from prosecuting a charge that the prosecutor knows is not supported by probable cause[.]

The "probable cause" standard in Rule 3.8(a) derives from criminal procedure law, including the Fourth Amendment. An individual may not be arrested or charged with a crime unless there is "probable cause" to believe the individual committed a crime. "Probable cause" is a burden of proof. It requires less than "a preponderance of the evidence" or "more likely than not," but more than a "reasonable suspicion."

Prosecutors are rarely disciplined for knowingly prosecuting charges without probable cause. In *Livingston v. Va. State Bar*, 744 S.E.2d 220 (Va. 2013), the prosecutor had charged a defendant on erroneous legal theories, but the court found that, because the prosecutor did so negligently, he could be sanctioned for incompetence under Rule 1.1, but not under Rule 3.8(a).

In ABA Formal Op. 486 (2019), the ABA's ethics committee addressed how Rule 3.8(a) and other rules apply to prosecutors in misdemeanor cases. Although prosecutors often carry heavy caseloads of misdemeanor cases, the opinion said, they must assess each case individually to ensure that the facts and law support a charge rather than relying uncritically on police reports.

Rule 3.8(a) is the only provision that specifically addresses prosecutors' decisions about whether to initiate criminal charges. However, prosecutors who grossly abuse their charging discretion may be subject to discipline under general provisions, such as Rule 8.4(d), which forbids "conduct that is prejudicial to the administration of justice." For a discussion of the role that discipline has served, and might serve, in this area, see Bruce A. Green & Samuel J. Levine, *Disciplinary Regulation of Prosecutors as a Remedy for Abuses of Prosecutorial Discretion: A Descriptive and Normative Analysis*, 14 Ohio St. J. Crim. L. 143 (2016).

State ex rel. McKittrick v. Wallach

182 S.W.2d 313 (Mo. 1944)

HYDE, JUDGE.

This case, recently coming to the writer by reassignment, is an original proceeding in *quo warranto* to declare forfeiture of the office of prosecuting attorney of St. Louis County, and to oust respondent therefrom. * * *

> **It's Latin to Me**
>
> *Quo warranto* is translated to mean "by what authority." Quo warranto is a common-law writ used to challenge the authority by which a public office is held. Here, Petitioner brings this action questioning the Respondent's authority as County prosecutor.
>
> Non constat
> jus civile
> á posteriori

Respondent was elected to the office of prosecuting attorney in 1938, 1940 and 1942. The Commissioner's report summarizes relator's charges (which were limited to the years 1941 and 1942, respondent's second term) placing them in four general classifications, as follows:

> '(1) That respondent willfully, knowingly, continuously, corruptly and unlawfully neglected, failed and refused to investigate, commence prosecutions of and prosecute various persons (95 persons named in the Information) for violations of the Liquor Control Act and Non-Intoxicating Beer Laws of Missouri;

> '(2) That without any reason, cause or justification therefor the respondent dismissed and caused to be dismissed various criminal cases (none designated by name or number in the Information) pending against persons charged in said county with felonies and misdemeanors;

> '(3) That although respondent was advised of the evidence thereof, he has failed and refused to commence and prosecute criminal actions against persons (none designated by name in the Information) who set up, kept and operated certain named gambling machines and devices;

> '(4) That respondent has failed and refused to commence and prosecute criminal actions against persons (none designated by name in the Information) who established, openly advertised and conducted lotteries:'

* * *

The duty of a prosecuting officer necessarily requires that he investigate, *i.e.*, inquire into the matter with care and accuracy, that in each case he examine the available evidence, the law and the facts, and the applicability of each to the other; that his duties further require that he intelligently weigh the chances of successful termination of the prosecution, having always in mind the relative importance to the county he serves of the different prosecutions which he might initiate. Such duties of necessity involve a good faith exercise of the sound discretion of the prosecuting attorney. 'Discretion' in that sense means power or right conferred by law upon the prosecuting officer of acting officially in such circumstances, and upon each separate case, according to the dictates of his own judgment and conscience uncontrolled by the judgment and conscience of any other person. Such discretion must be exercised in accordance with established principles of law, fairly, wisely, and with skill and reason. It includes the right to choose a course of action or non-action, chosen not willfully or in bad faith, but chosen with regard to what is right under the circumstances. Discretion denotes the absence of a hard and fast rule or a mandatory procedure regardless of varying circumstances. That discretion may, in good faith (but not arbitrarily), be exercised with respect to when, how and against whom to initiate criminal proceedings. * * * Such discretion exercised in good faith authorizes the prosecuting officer to personally determine, in conference and in collaboration with peace officers and liquor enforcement officers, that a certain plan of action or a certain policy of enforcement will be best productive of law enforcement, and will best result in general law observance. * * *

It appearing in the record that respondent did at all times and in each instance in good faith exercise his discretion, and it further not appearing anywhere in this record that respondent's discretion was at any time arbitrarily exercised, or that his discretion was corruptly exercised, or exercised in bad faith, the Special Commissioner concludes that in those cases wherein he exercised his discretion and did not prosecute * * * the respondent had the legal right to reach the conclusion he did reach with respect to prosecution or no prosecution. * * * And that respondent has not been guilty of any act, or conduct, or of any omission, meriting the forfeiture of his right to occupy the office of prosecuting attorney. * * *

Pugach v. Klein

193 F. Supp. 630 (S.D.N.Y 1961)

MACMAHON, DISTRICT JUDGE.

These applications by Pugach for habeas corpus, mandamus, and warrants for arrest and search raise once again the vexing question of whether a federal court ought to interfere at the preliminary stage of a state criminal prosecution allegedly resulting from wire tap evidence obtained in violation of the Federal Communications Act, but in compliance with the clashing law of the State of New York.

* * *

Mandamus

Petitioner seeks, by original petition for a writ of mandamus, to compel the United States Attorney to prosecute an officer of the New York City Police Department, an Assistant District Attorney, and a County Judge.

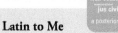

It's Latin to Me

Mandamus n. [Latin "we command"] A writ issued by a superior court to compel a lower court or a government officer to perform mandatory or purely ministerial duties correctly.

The petition, largely by resort to conclusions, purports to allege violations of, and conspiracy to violate, Sections 501 and 605 of the Communications Act of 1934, in that agents of the Bronx County District Attorney and the New York police obtained an order from the State Supreme Court authorizing them to intercept petitioner's telephone conversations, used information resulting from such interceptions, caused tapes to be made and divulged their contents and meaning both to newspapers and to the Bronx County Grand Jury, thereby causing his arrest, indictment and detention. The Judge is accused of aiding and abetting, resisting arrest, withholding evidence and remaining a fugitive.

Asserting the imminence of the trial, open defiance by New York of the wire tap prohibitions of the Communications Act, and failure of the District Attorney and the United States Attorney to enforce violations, notwithstanding admonitions by Judge Waterman of the Court of Appeals for this circuit, Pugach contends that there is no existing state process to protect his rights. He specifically alleges refusal of the United States Attorney to act on his complaints * * *.

* * *

With all deference to the concern of some over the lack of prosecutions against state officers for wire tapping in accordance with state law, it is, nevertheless, clear beyond question that it is not the business of the Courts to tell the United States Attorney to perform what they conceive to be his duties.

Article II, Section 3 of the Constitution, provides that "(the President) shall take Care that the Laws (shall) be faithfully executed." The prerogative of enforcing the criminal law was vested by the Constitution, therefore, not in the Courts, nor in private citizens, but squarely in the executive arm of the government. Congress has implemented the powers of the President by conferring the power and the duty to institute prosecution for federal offenses upon the United States Attorney for each district. In exercising his power, the United States Attorney acts in an administrative capacity as the representative of the public. * * *

It by no means follows, however, that the duty to prosecute follows automatically from the presentation of a complaint. The United States Attorney is not a rubber stamp. His problems are not solved by the strict application of an inflexible formula. Rather, their solution calls for the exercise of judgment. Judgment reached primarily by balancing the public interest in effective law enforcement against the growing rights of the accused.

There are a number of elements in the equation, and all of them must be carefully considered. Paramount among them is a determination that a prosecution will promote the ends of justice, instill respect for the law, and advance the cause of ordered liberty. Here, respect for, and cooperative relations with, state law enforcement agencies weigh heavily in the scale.

Surely it is for the United States Attorney to decide whether the public interest is better served by prosecuting or declining to prosecute state law enforcement agencies and besmirch a Judge on the eve of a trial on the feeble complaint of an accuser infected with self-interest in escaping trial on a grave charge. The reason for leaving the choice with the United States Attorney is all the more compelling in an area such as this, riven with controversy, fraught with friction, and confused by clashing law.

Other considerations are the likelihood of conviction, turning on choice of a strong case to test uncertain law, the degree of criminality, the weight of the evidence, the credibility of witnesses, precedent, policy, the climate of public opinion, timing, and the relative gravity of the offense. In weighing these factors, the prosecutor must apply responsible standards, based, not on loose assumptions, but, on solid evidence balanced in a scale demanding proof beyond a reasonable doubt to overcome the presumption of innocence. Just how thoroughly cases are screened to meet these basic criteria is reflected in the fact that 97% of all prosecutions commenced in this district end either in a plea of guilty or conviction after trial.

Still other factors are the relative importance of the offense compared with the competing demands of other cases on the time and resources of investigation, prosecution and trial. All of these and numerous other intangible and imponderable factors must be carefully weighed and considered by the conscientious United States Attorney in deciding whether or not to prosecute.

All of these considerations point up the wisdom of vesting broad discretion in the United States Attorney. The federal courts are powerless to interfere with his discretionary power. The Court cannot compel him to prosecute a complaint, or even an indictment, whatever his reasons for not acting. The remedy for any dereliction of his duty lies, not with the courts, but, with the executive branch of our government and ultimately with the people.

* * *

Accordingly, all of the applications are denied. It is so ordered.

Food for Thought

In 1989, the Wisconsin Supreme Court upheld a statute that allowed judges to hold a hearing and issue a criminal complaint if the judge had probable cause to believe a crime had been committed and the district attorney refused or was unavailable to issue a complaint. Citing the existence of a similar procedure that predated the state's constitution, the court determined "the statute does not impermissibly delegate exclusive powers of the executive branch to the judiciary." *State v. Unnamed Defendant*, 441 N.W.2d 696 (Wis. 1989). Would such a law violate the constitutional separation of powers doctrine in a state that didn't have a historical precedent for such judicial procedures? *See also Young v. U.S. ex rel. Vuitton et Fils S.A.*, 481 U.S. 787 (1987), where the Court held that a judge's inherent authority to initiate contempt proceedings for disobedience of court orders necessarily includes the ability to appoint private attorney to prosecute contempt.

1. Refusing to Prosecute a Certain Type of Crime

In some situations, a prosecutor might decide that a certain kind of crime will not be prosecuted. A prosecutor's decision not to prosecute a certain type of crime is often based on a judgment that prosecuting the conduct in question is simply not worth the resources that would have to be expended in a prosecution. Prosecutors might also be concerned about a public backlash in prosecuting certain crimes. Local and cultural conditions might be involved as well.

In 2018, the new Boston prosecutor was elected to office as a reformer. She promised to implement a <u>policy</u> under which, except in exceptional cases, the prosecutor's office would no longer prosecute more than a dozen crimes, including trespassing, shoplifting, disorderly conduct and drug possession. Rather, these charges would be dismissed outright or the conduct would be treated as a civil infraction.

Another example of the non-prosecution of a class of crime arose in Utah, as reported in an article in the *National Law Journal*, Aug. 10, 1998, A10:

> Facing criticism for suggesting that polygamy may fall under religious freedoms, Gov. Mike Leavitt turned to Utah's attorney general for advice on why the state fails to prosecute polygamists when the practice is widespread. * * * The Tapestry of Polygamy, a self-help group for former polygamist wives and children, held a news conference outside the governor's office July 27 and presented his chief of staff, Vicky Varela, a letter urging that the state constitutional ban on polygamy be enforced.
>
> * * *
>
> Ms. Varela drew a distinction between prosecuting the act of polygamy itself and prosecuting crimes that may occur within plural marriages. "Polygamy is against the law in Utah," she said. "We do not know why prosecutors do not choose to prosecute it."
>
> There has not been a prosecution of anyone solely for practicing polygamy in Utah since 1952, when federal and state agents raided the border community of Short Creek * * *. The raid turned into a public-relations debacle as children were pulled from their parents' arms and husbands were jailed.
>
> Ms. Varela said the governor will ask Utah Attorney General Jan Graham for a "policy statement" on polygamy prosecutions. But Ms. Graham's chief deputy, Reed Richards, said the policy is simple: "Crimes are prosecuted when we know about them, and the vast majority of these relationships are consenting adults."

Does the explanation given by Chief Deputy Graham make any sense? If crimes are prosecuted when the prosecutor knows about them, and consent is no defense to polygamy, then why is the fact of consent an answer to non-prosecution?

2. Suspected of Serious Crime, Charged with a Less Serious Crime

Daniel Richman and William Stuntz, in *Al Capone's Revenge: An Essay on the Political Economy of Pretextual Prosecution*, 105 Colum. L. Rev. 583 (2005), recall the government's prosecution of Chicago mobster Al Capone for income tax evasion after it was unable to prove far more serious crimes, such as "running illegal breweries" and "even slaughtering rival mobsters." They argue that pretextual decisions to charge create social costs:

> There is a strong social interest in non-pretextual prosecution, and that interest is much more important than the "fairness to defendants" argument that has preoccupied the literature on this subject. Criminal charges are not only a means of identifying and punishing criminal conduct. They are also a means by which prosecutors send signals to their superiors, including the voters to whom they are ultimately responsible. When a murderer is brought to justice for murder rather than for tax evasion, voters learn some important things about their community and about the justice system: that a given homicide has been committed in a particular way (if a criminal organization is involved, they may learn things about how the organization works and what kind of people comprise it); that the crime has been solved; that the police and prosecution have done a good job of assembling evidence against the killer, and so forth. If there is a legislative body that oversees the relevant law enforcement agencies, those same signals are sent to the legislative overseers. When a prosecutor gets a conviction—usually by inducing a guilty plea—for an unrelated lesser crime than the one that motivated the investigation, the signals are muddied. They may disappear altogether. * * *
>
> Another audience also gets a muddied signal: would-be criminals. Instead of sending the message that running illegal breweries and bribing local cops would lead to a term in a federal penitentiary, the Capone prosecution sent a much more complicated and much less helpful message: If you run a criminal enterprise, you should keep your name out of the newspapers and at least pretend to pay your taxes. * * * [T]he political economy of criminal law enforcement depends on a reasonably good match between the charges that motivate prosecution and the charges that appear on defendants' rap sheets. When crimes and charges do not coincide, no one can tell whether law enforcers are doing their jobs. The justice system loses the credibility it needs, and voters lose the trust they need to have in the justice system. Individual agents and prosecutors pay only a tiny fraction of that price, which is why they continue to follow the Capone strategy. The larger price is paid only over time—by crime victims, by law enforcement agencies, and (not least) by the voting public.

B.   Factors Bearing on Prosecutor's Discretion to Charge

Excerpt from motion: People v. Strauss-Kahn

August 22, 2011

Recommendation for Dismissal

SUMMARY

The People of the State of New York move to dismiss the above-captioned indictment, which charges the defendant with sexually assaulting the complainant at a hotel in midtown Manhattan on May 14, 2011. The crimes charged in the indictment require the People to prove beyond a reasonable doubt that the defendant engaged in a sexual act with the complainant using forcible compulsion and without her consent. After an extensive investigation, it is clear that proof of two critical elements—force and lack of consent—would rest solely on the testimony of the complaining witness at trial. The physical, scientific, and other evidence establishes that the defendant engaged in a hurried sexual encounter with the complainant, but it does not independently establish her claim of a forcible, nonconsensual encounter. Aside from the complainant and the defendant, there are no other eyewitnesses to the incident. Undeniably, then, for a trial jury to find the defendant guilty, it must be persuaded beyond a reasonable doubt that the complainant is credible. Indeed, the case rises and falls on her testimony.

At the time of the indictment, all available evidence satisfied us that the complainant was reliable. But evidence gathered in our post-indictment investigation severely undermined her reliability as a witness in this case. That an individual has lied in the past or committed criminal acts does not necessarily render them unbelievable to us as prosecutors, or keep us from putting them on the witness stand at trial. But the nature and number of the complainant's falsehoods leave us unable to credit her version of events beyond a reasonable doubt, whatever the truth may be about the encounter between the complainant and the defendant. If we do not believe her beyond a reasonable doubt, we cannot ask a jury to do so.

> **Go Online**
>
> Dominique Strauss-Kahn was the head of the International Monetary Fund until he was arrested on charges of sexual assault in 2011, prompting him to resign from the IMF. He was accused of assaulting a maid when she entered his hotel suite in New York. You can read the entire recommendation for dismissal of the charges against him, and you can read a news report about the dismissal in John Eligon, William K. Rashbaum and Colin Moynihan, "Prosecutor Asks Court to Drop Charges Against Strauss-Kahn" N.Y. Times (Aug. 22, 2011).

We have summarized below the circumstances that have led us to this conclusion. This is not a case where undue scrutiny or a heightened standard is being imposed on a complainant. Instead, we are confronted with a situation in which it has become increasingly clear that the complainant's credibility cannot withstand the most basic evaluation. In short, the complainant has provided shifting and inconsistent versions of the events surrounding the alleged assault, and as a result, we cannot be sufficiently certain of what actually happened on May 14, 2011, or what account of these events the complainant would give at trial. In virtually every substantive interview with prosecutors, despite entreaties to simply be truthful, she has not been truthful, on matters great and small, many pertaining to her background and some relating to the circumstances of the incident itself. Over the course of two interviews, for example, the complainant gave a vivid, highly-detailed, and convincing account of having been raped in her native country, which she now admits is entirely false. She also gave prosecutors and the grand jury accounts of her actions immediately after the encounter with the defendant that she now admits are false. This longstanding pattern of untruthfulness predates the complainant's contact with this Office. Our investigation revealed that the complainant has made numerous prior false statements, including ones contained in government filings, some of which were made under oath or penalty of perjury. All of these falsehoods would, of course, need to be disclosed to a jury at trial, and their cumulative effect would be devastating.

Finally, we have conducted a thorough investigation in an effort to uncover any evidence that might speak to the nature of the sexual encounter between the complainant and the defendant. All of the evidence that might be relevant to the contested issues of force and lack of consent is simply inconclusive.

We do not make this recommendation lightly. Our grave concerns about the complainant's reliability make it impossible to resolve the question of what exactly happened in the defendant's hotel suite on May 14, 2011, and therefore preclude further prosecution of this case. Accordingly, we respectfully recommend that the indictment be dismissed.

PROSECUTION STANDARDS

Along with the substantial power conferred upon prosecutors come unique responsibilities. Rather than serving only as a zealous advocate on behalf of a client, prosecutors have a broader set of obligations to the community, the victim, and the defendant:

> The [prosecutor] is the representative not of an ordinary party to a controversy, but of a sovereignty whose obligation to govern impartially is as compelling as its obligation to govern at all; and whose interest, therefore, in a criminal prosecution is not that it shall win a case, but that justice shall be done. As such, he is in a peculiar and very definite sense the servant of the law, the twofold aim of which is that guilt shall not escape or innocence suffer.[1]

New York's rules of professional conduct, which parallel the ethics rules in virtually all jurisdictions, and the American Bar Association's Criminal Justice Standards both rest on the same belief that the prosecutor's duty is to seek justice, not simply to win cases.[2]

---

1   *Berger v. United States*, 295 U.S. 78, 88 (1935).

2   *See* New York Rules of Prof'l Conduct R. 3.8 cmt 1, 6B (2011); ABA Standards for Criminal Justice: Prosecution Function 3-1.2(b), (c).

Prosecutors also must abide by unique rules that reflect our special role in the legal system. Most significantly, prosecutors must satisfy an exacting standard for conviction: proof of guilt beyond a reasonable doubt. This requirement is "bottomed on a fundamental value determination of our society that it is far worse to convict an innocent [person] than to let a guilty [person] go free."[3]

That standard of proof guides the decisions of prosecutors who must decide whether to proceed with a case, not just the jurors who must decide whether to convict. At the beginning of a case, prosecutors are frequently called upon to make charging decisions before all the relevant facts are capable of being known, or all investigative steps required for trial are complete. Under New York's legal ethics rules, charges may be brought against a defendant if they are supported by probable cause.[4] But for generations, before determining whether a case should proceed to trial, felony prosecutors in New York County have insisted that they be personally convinced beyond a reasonable doubt of the defendant's guilt, and believe themselves able to prove that guilt to a jury. The standards governing the conduct of federal prosecutors, as well as the American Bar Association's criminal justice standards, likewise recognize the need for prosecutors to act as a gatekeeper by making an independent assessment of the evidence before proceeding to trial.[5]

These core principles, by which this Office operates, are therefore clear. If, after a careful assessment of the facts, the prosecutor is not convinced that a defendant is guilty beyond a reasonable doubt, he or she must decline to proceed. While an abiding concern for victims of crime is an essential attribute for every prosecutor working in this Office, that concern cannot eclipse our obligation to act only on the evidence and the facts, mindful of the high burden of proof in a criminal prosecution.

* * *

REASONS FOR RECOMMENDATION OF DISMISSAL

The prosecution has the burden at trial to prove the guilt of an accused beyond a reasonable doubt. For a host of reasons, including those set forth below, the complainant's untruthfulness makes it impossible to credit her. Because we cannot credit the complainant's testimony beyond a reasonable doubt, we cannot ask a jury to do so. The remaining evidence is insufficient to satisfy the elements of the charged crimes. We are therefore required, as both a legal and ethical matter, to move for dismissal of the indictment.

* * *

---

3   *In re Winship*, 397 U.S. 358, 372 (1970) (Harlan, J., concurring).

4   New York Rules of Prof'l Conduct R. 3.8(a) (2011).

5   *See* US Dep't of Justice, United States Attorney's Manual § 9–27.220 (1997); ABA Standards for Criminal Justice: Prosecution Function 3-3.9(b)(i).

Food for Thought

Even before the prosecution made this recommendation, attorneys for Strauss-Kahn were engaged in challenging the character and reliability of his accuser in the press. The recommendation of dismissal by the prosecutors, therefore, was not without controversy as some legal scholars and advocates worry that it essentially put the alleged victim on trial.

> "There's the French former IMF chief, Dominique Strauss-Kahn, * * * a really powerful and really wealthy white man who was accused last summer of attempted rape by * * * a poor, black, female immigrant from Africa who was sent into his room to pick up his trash and wipe down his toilet * * *. [The case] was dismissed on the grounds that Strauss-Kahn's accuser had claimed rape before, and maybe had worked as a prostitute, maybe she had a shady boyfriend, and maybe was either a bad mother or a welfare cheat . . . the list goes on of classic ways to discredit a woman crying rape that were immediately applied to his accuser."

Tracey Jean Boisseau, *Response to "The Duke Rape Case Five Years Later: Lessons for the Academy, the Media, and the Criminal Justice System" by Dan Subotnik*, 45 Akron L. Rev. 927, 933 (2012); *see also* Cara Buckley, "After Strauss-Kahn, Fear of Rape Victim Silence," N.Y. Times (Aug. 24, 2011).

Does the prosecutor's decision in the Strauss-Khan case create a disincentive to women who suffer sexual violence to report their attackers? Or should the situation be considered sui generis because of the unusual facts of the case?

C. Respecting the Right to Counsel

[Question 7-2]

After arresting a young man for vandalism, a police officer notified the prosecutor, who directed that the man be brought to court rather than held in jail overnight. The prosecutor knew that, although the man had a statutory right to counsel, it was too late in the day to secure a court-appointed lawyer, but that a judge working in the courthouse that evening would be willing to arraign the man without a lawyer. When the police officer arrived with the man, the prosecutor met with the man and said, "I have a good deal for you. If you are willing to appear before a judge this evening and plead guilty without a lawyer, I will recommend that the judge release you, so that you can return for sentencing another day. Otherwise, you will have to spend the night in prison." The man agreed, and they proceeded to the judge's chambers, where the man pleaded guilty to vandalism. The judge then ordered the man to be released with instructions to return a week later to be sentenced. Neither the judge nor anyone else advised the man of his right to counsel.

Is the prosecutor subject to discipline?

(A)   Yes, because he sought to obtain a guilty plea from an unrepresented accused.

(B)   Yes, because he made no effort to assure that the man was advised of the right to counsel.

(C)   No, because it was the judge's responsibility to advise the man of his rights, and the prosecutor was not required to do so.

☞ **No, because, as a lawyer for the opposing party, a prosecutor is not permitted to advise the accused of his rights.**

Rule 3.8 The prosecutor in a criminal case shall:

* * *

(b) make reasonable efforts to assure that the accused has been advised of the right to, and the procedure for obtaining, counsel and has been given reasonable opportunity to obtain counsel;

(c) not seek to obtain from an unrepresented accused a waiver of important pretrial rights, such as the right to a preliminary hearing;

* * *

Only a handful of published opinions refer to Rules 3.8(b) and (c), and they do so mostly in passing. Importantly, these provisions do not prevent prosecutors from negotiating guilty pleas with defendants who are unrepresented either because they elect to represent themselves or because, in low-level cases, they simply cannot afford a lawyer and they have no legal right to court-appointed counsel. Although a guilty plea constitutes a waiver of *trial* rights, such as the right to a jury trial and the right to call and cross-examine witnesses, and arguably also constitutes a waiver of some "pretrial rights" such as the right to pretrial discovery, the inability to retain a lawyer is not regarded as a "waiver" of an "important pretrial right" under Rule 3.8(c). In any event, as a practical matter, prosecutors must be able to plea bargain directly with unrepresented defendants who have no ability to obtain a lawyer.

Before prosecutors enter into such negotiations, Rule 3.8(b) requires prosecutors to advise unrepresented defendants about their right to counsel. ABA Formal Op. 486 (2019) seems to imply that in misdemeanor cases, the rule does not apply unless the accused has a constitutional or statutory right to appointed counsel, but that is a debatable interpretation of the rule. Even when they have no right to court-appointed counsel, defendants have a constitutional right to retain a lawyer on a paid or pro bono basis, to receive that lawyer's advice, and to be represented by that lawyer in court. Rule 3.8(b) can be read to require the prosecutor to advise the defendant of that right and to give the defendant an opportunity to retain a lawyer.

Moreover, individuals who are in custody have *"Miranda* rights." Before questioning them, police must advise arrested persons that they have a right to counsel and a right to remain silent, and that if they give up these rights, their statements can be used against them. In *United States v. Acosta*, 111 F. Supp.2d 1082 (E.D. Wis. 2000), the court found that once *Miranda* rights attach, there is a "criminal case" under Rule 3.8, and therefore Rule 3.8(b) applies. Further, the court found, the rule requires more than *Miranda*—that is, more than just advising the individual of the right to counsel: the prosecutor must also describe the procedure for obtaining counsel and provide a reasonable opportunity to obtain counsel. *But see Paris v. Ky. Bar Ass'n*, 547 S.W.3d 766 (Ky. 2019) (noting that while serving as a prosecutor in Colorado, the lawyer had been charged with violating Rules 3.8(b) and (c) in his interactions with a murder suspect, but the Colorado Supreme Court dismissed the disciplinary charges on the ground that there was no "criminal case" at the time of the interaction).

In serious cases, such as felony cases, where indigent defendants have a constitutional right to appointed counsel, Rules 3.8(b) and (c) may restrict prosecutors from taking unfair advantage of defendants before a lawyer has been appointed. In *State v. Farfan-Galvan*, 389 P.3d 155 (2016), the Idaho Supreme Court observed: "[W]e are aware of the practice by certain prosecuting entities of initiating contact with defendants while they are in custody in advance of their initial appearance or arraignment in order to extend plea offers which, if not accepted, expire at the time of the initial appearance or arraignment. [¶] We take this opportunity to express our disapproval of this practice. In our view, the practice of establishing the initial appearance or arraignment as the time a plea bargain offer expires has the practical effect of dissuading indigent defendants from seeking the assistance of court-appointed counsel to evaluate the offer. At a minimum, we view such conduct as violating Idaho Rules of Professional Conduct 3.8(b), 3.8(c) and 8.4(d)."

These provisions of Rule 3.8 go beyond Rules 4.2 and 4.3, which govern lawyers' communications with represented and unrepresented persons. (Rules 4.2 and 4.3 are discussed in Chapter 6.) In the 1980's and 1990's, the question of how Rule 4.2 applies to prosecutors was highly contentious, especially in federal cases. The controversy was fueled by the Second Circuit's decision in *United States v. Hammad*, 858 F.2d 834 (2d Cir. 1988), in which federal prosecutors overseeing an arson investigation sent an informant, armed with a sham subpoena, to initiate and secretly record a conversation with Hammad, a co-conspirator, about how to respond to the investigation. Although the communication did not violate Hammad's constitutional rights, the Second Circuit found that the communication violated Rule 4.2, which forbids a lawyer (or the lawyer's agent) from communicating directly with a represented party on the subject of the representation. The opinion proved to be an outlier, with most courts finding that prosecutors were "authorized by law" to send agents and informants to speak with represented individuals as long as constitutional requirements were met. Nonetheless, the Department of Justice responded to *Hammad* by adopting regulations exempting federal prosecutors from Rule 4.2 and substituting less restrictive requirements. In 1998, Congress effectively superseded the federal regulations by adopting a law, known as the McDade Amendment, requiring federal prosecutors to abide by the ethics rules of the states in which they practice. For a review of three decades of prosecutorial ethics, in which the story of Rule 4.2 figures prominently, see Bruce A. Green, *Prosecutorial Ethics in Retrospect*, 30 Geo. J. Legal Ethics 461 (2017).

D. Plea Bargaining

[Question 7-3]

A state prosecutor oversaw the prosecution of a store manager for first-degree arson, which was punishable by up to a life sentence. The principal witness was a former employee who claimed that the store manager paid him $500 in cash to set the fire in order to enable the property owner to collect insurance proceeds. The defense lawyer asked the prosecutor to dismiss the charges, asserting that the store manager had fired the employee for coming late to work, and that the employee had set the fire out of malice. But the prosecutor declined.

In the course of preparing the employee to testify, the prosecutor began to question the employee's credibility. Instead of leaving it to the jury to decide for itself whether there was a reasonable doubt, the prosecutor contacted the defense lawyer and offered to dismiss the charges if the store manager pled guilty to criminal mischief. The former employee's testimony, if believed, would establish that the store manager was guilty of this misdemeanor, which involved intentionally damaging the property of another. The prosecutor knew that even if the store manager was innocent, he would accept this plea offer to avoid the risk of being convicted of first-degree arson.

Is the prosecutor subject to discipline?

(A) Yes, because he prosecuted the store manager even though he had a reasonable doubt about the principal witness's credibility.

(B) Yes, because he pressured the store manager to plead guilty to criminal mischief, a misdemeanor, by continuing the first-degree arson prosecution unless the store manager accepted the plea offer.

(C) No, because the prosecutor did not know that the former employee's testimony was false, and the testimony provided probable cause to believe that the store manager committed arson and criminal mischief.

(D) No, because a prosecutor may bring charges as long as they are not frivolous.

FYI

Suppose that in Question 7-3, the prosecutor wanted to make a plea offer, allowing the accused to plead guilty to a less serious offense than the one charged, but the prosecutor could not identify a less serious offense that the accused actually committed. May the prosecutor permit the accused to plead guilty to a crime that everyone—the accused, defense counsel, the prosecutor and the judge—know that the accused did not commit? For example, could the prosecutor offer to drop the arson charge if the accused pled guilty to illegally downloading music?

State courts in many parts of the country routinely enter judgments based on similar agreements. In 2018, while successfully campaigning for election as an Ohio Supreme Court Justice, Michael Donnelly condemned this practice, observing that baseless pleas "are inconsistent with the courts' main objective to seek the truth" and "undermine the public's confidence in the justice system." For more on the practice, and on legal ethics arguments made in support of and against the practice, *see* Mari Byrne, Note, *Baseless Pleas: A Mockery of Justice,* 78 Fordham L. Rev. 2961 (2010).

Justice Donnelly also raised this concern about what he called "dark pleas": "Attorneys file written motions for new trials for their incarcerated clients for a variety of reasons including: the discovery of new evidence undermining the theory used to convict them; that their convictions were based on junk science; or that material witnesses have recanted their testimony. Such motions are usually accompanied by a request for a formal hearing where the merits of the prisoner's allegations can be tested in open court. . . . If the prisoner . . . is fortunate to be granted a hearing, a dark plea will occur on some occasions prior to the hearing being held. The prosecutor essentially dangles the opportunity of freedom in exchange for a plea of guilty to the charges in which THEY HAVE ALREADY ACHIEVED A CONVICTION! It is the legal equivalent of putting a gun to someone's head to extract a confession—offering a plea when the prisoner is in a state of complete uncertainty with no leverage to negotiate."

Bordenkircher v. Hayes

434 U.S. 357 (1978)

Mr. Justice Stewart delivered the opinion of the Court.

The question in this case is whether the Due Process Clause of the Fourteenth Amendment is violated when a state prosecutor carries out a threat made during plea negotiations to reindict the accused on more serious charges if he does not plead guilty to the offense with which he was originally charged.

I

The respondent, Paul Lewis Hayes, was indicted by a Fayette County, Ky., grand jury on a charge of uttering a forged instrument in the amount of $88.30, an offense then punishable by a term of 2 to 10 years in prison. After arraignment, Hayes, his retained counsel, and the Commonwealth's Attorney met in the presence of the Clerk of the Court to discuss a possible plea agreement. During these conferences the prosecutor offered to recommend a sentence of five years in prison if Hayes would plead guilty to the indictment. He also said that if Hayes did not plead guilty and "save[d] the court the inconvenience and necessity of a trial," he would return to the grand jury to seek an indictment under the Kentucky Habitual Criminal Act, which would subject Hayes to a mandatory sentence of life imprisonment by reason of his two prior felony convictions. Hayes chose not to plead guilty, and the prosecutor did obtain an indictment charging him under the Habitual Criminal Act. It is not disputed that the recidivist charge was fully justified by the evidence, that the prosecutor was in possession of this evidence at the time of the original indictment, and that Hayes' refusal to plead guilty to the original charge was what led to his indictment under the habitual criminal statute.

A jury found Hayes guilty on the principal charge of uttering a forged instrument and, in a separate proceeding, further found that he had twice before been convicted of felonies. As required by the habitual offender statute, he was sentenced to a life term in the penitentiary. The Kentucky Court of Appeals [held] that the prosecutor's decision to indict him as a habitual offender was a legitimate use of available leverage in the plea-bargaining process.

* * *

II

It may be helpful to clarify at the outset the nature of the issue in this case. While the prosecutor did not actually obtain the recidivist indictment until after the plea conferences had ended, his intention to do so was clearly expressed at the outset of the plea negotiations. Hayes was thus fully informed of the true terms of the offer when he made his decision to plead not guilty. This is not a situation, therefore, where the prosecutor without notice brought an additional and more serious charge after plea negotiations relating only to the original indictment had ended with the defendant's insistence on pleading not guilty. As a practical matter, in short, this case would be no different if the grand jury had indicted Hayes as a recidivist from the outset, and the prosecutor had offered to drop that charge as part of the plea bargain.

* * *

III

We have recently had occasion to observe: "[W]hatever might be the situation in an ideal world, the fact is that the guilty plea and the often concomitant plea bargain are important components of this country's criminal justice system. Properly administered, they can benefit all concerned." The open acknowledgment of this previously clandestine practice has led this Court to recognize the importance of counsel during plea negotiations, * * * the need for a public record indicating that a plea was knowingly and voluntarily made, * * * and the requirement that a prosecutor's plea-bargaining promise must be kept* * * . * * *

IV

This Court held in *North Carolina v. Pearce*, 395 U.S. 711, 725, that the Due Process Clause of the Fourteenth Amendment "requires that vindictiveness against a defendant for having successfully attacked his first conviction must play no part in the sentence he receives after a new trial." The same principle was later applied to prohibit a prosecutor from reindicting a convicted misdemeanant on a felony charge after the defendant had invoked an appellate remedy, since in this situation there was also a "realistic likelihood of 'vindictiveness.' "

In those cases the Court was dealing with the State's unilateral imposition of a penalty upon a defendant who had chosen to exercise a legal right to attack his original conviction-a situation "very different from the give-and-take negotiation common in plea bargaining between the prosecution and defense, which arguably possess relatively equal bargaining power." The Court has emphasized that the due process violation in cases such as *Pearce* and *Perry* lay not in the possibility that a defendant might be deterred from the exercise of a legal right, but rather in the danger that the State might be retaliating against the accused for lawfully attacking his conviction.

To punish a person because he has done what the law plainly allows him to do is a due process violation of the most basic sort * * * . But in the "give-and-take" of plea bargaining, there is no such element of punishment or retaliation so long as the accused is free to accept or reject the prosecution's offer.

Plea bargaining flows from "the mutuality of advantage" to defendants and prosecutors, each with his own reasons for wanting to avoid trial. Defendants advised by competent counsel and protected by other procedural safeguards are presumptively capable of intelligent choice in response to prosecutorial persuasion, and unlikely to be driven to false self-condemnation. Indeed, acceptance of the basic legitimacy of plea bargaining necessarily implies rejection of any notion that a guilty plea is involuntary in a constitutional sense simply because it is the end result of the bargaining process. By hypothesis, the plea may have been induced by promises of a recommendation of a lenient sentence or a reduction of charges, and thus by fear of the possibility of a greater penalty upon conviction after a trial. * * *

While confronting a defendant with the risk of more severe punishment clearly may have a discouraging effect on the defendant's assertion of his trial rights, the imposition of these difficult choices is an inevitable—and permissible—attribute of any legitimate system which tolerates and encourages the negotiation of pleas. It follows that, by encouraging the negotiation of pleas, this Court has necessarily accepted as constitutionally legitimate the simple reality that the prosecutor's interest at the bargaining table is to persuade the defendant to forgo his right to plead not guilty.

It is not disputed here that Hayes was properly chargeable under the recidivist statute, since he had in fact been convicted of two previous felonies. In our system, so long as the prosecutor has probable cause to believe that the accused committed an offense defined by statute, the decision whether or not to prosecute, and what charge to file or bring before a grand jury, generally rests entirely in his discretion. Within the limits set by the legislature's constitutionally valid definition of chargeable offenses, the conscious exercise of some selectivity in enforcement is not in itself a federal constitutional violation so long as the selection was not deliberately based upon an unjustifiable standard such as race, religion, or other arbitrary classification. To hold that the prosecutor's desire to induce a guilty plea is an "unjustifiable standard," which, like race or religion, may play no part in his charging decision, would contradict the very premises that underlie the concept of plea bargaining itself. Moreover, a rigid constitutional rule that would prohibit a prosecutor from acting forthrightly in his dealings with the defense could only invite unhealthy subterfuge that would drive the practice of plea bargaining back into the shadows from which it has so recently emerged.

There is no doubt that the breadth of discretion that our country's legal system vests in prosecuting attorneys carries with it the potential for both individual and institutional abuse. And broad though that discretion may be, there are undoubtedly constitutional limits upon its exercise. We hold only that the course of conduct engaged in by the prosecutor in this case, which no more than openly presented the defendant with the unpleasant alternatives of forgoing trial or facing charges on which he was plainly subject to prosecution, did not violate the Due Process Clause of the Fourteenth Amendment.

Accordingly, the judgment of the Court of Appeals is

Reversed.

Mr. Justice Blackmun, with whom Mr. Justice Brennan and Mr. Justice Marshall join, dissenting.

* * *

It might be argued that it really makes little difference how this case * * * is decided. The Court's holding gives plea bargaining full sway despite vindictiveness. A contrary result, however, merely would prompt the aggressive prosecutor to bring the greater charge initially in every case, and only thereafter to bargain. The consequences to the accused would still be adverse, for then he would bargain against a greater charge, face the likelihood of increased bail, and run the risk that the court would be less inclined to accept a bargained plea. Nonetheless, it is far preferable to hold the prosecution to the charge it was originally content to bring and to justify in the eyes of its public.[6]

MR. JUSTICE POWELL, dissenting.

Although I agree with much of the Court's opinion, I am not satisfied that the result in this case is just or that the conduct of the plea bargaining met the requirements of due process.

* * *

The plea-bargaining process, as recognized by this Court, is essential to the functioning of the criminal-justice system. It normally affords genuine benefits to defendants as well as to society. And if the system is to work effectively, prosecutors must be accorded the widest discretion, within constitutional limits, in conducting bargaining. This is especially true when a defendant is represented by counsel and presumably is fully advised of his rights. Only in the most exceptional case should a court conclude that the scales of the bargaining are so unevenly balanced as to arouse suspicion. In this case, the prosecutor's actions denied respondent due process because their admitted purpose was to discourage and then to penalize with unique severity his exercise of constitutional rights. Implementation of a strategy calculated solely to deter the exercise of constitutional rights is not a constitutionally permissible exercise of discretion. I would affirm the opinion of the Court of Appeals on the facts of this case.

1. Inverted Sentencing

As a practical matter in multi-defendant cases, those who are more culpable sometimes have a chance to receive a lighter sentence than those who are less culpable. That is because prosecutors often need cooperation from some criminals in order to convict others, and plea bargaining is about the only tool that the prosecutor can legitimately employ to encourage cooperation. The incentives result in what Professor Richman terms "inverted sentencing": "The more serious the defendant's crimes, the lower the sentence—because the greater his wrongs, the more information and assistance he has to offer a prosecutor." Daniel C. Richman, *Cooperating Clients*, 56 Ohio St. L.J. 69 (1995). Judge Bright, dissenting in *United States v. Griffin*, 17 F.3d 269 (8th Cir. 1994), had this to ask about the phenomenon of inverted sentencing:

---

6   That prosecutors, without saying so, may sometimes bring charges more serious than they think appropriate for the ultimate disposition of a case, in order to gain bargaining leverage with a defendant, does not add support to today's decision, for this Court, in its approval of the advantages to be gained from plea negotiations, has never openly sanctioned such deliberate overcharging or taken such a cynical view of the bargaining process. Normally, of course, it is impossible to show that this is what the prosecutor is doing, and the courts necessarily have deferred to the prosecutor's exercise of discretion in initial charging decisions. * * *

What kind of a criminal justice system rewards the drug kingpin or near-kingpin who informs on all the criminal colleagues he or she has recruited, but sends to prison for years and years the least knowledgeable or culpable conspirator, one who knows very little about the conspiracy and is without information for the prosecution?

Is inverted sentencing an indictment of the plea bargaining system? Or is it an inevitable consequence of the prosecutor's need for cooperation from criminals? If plea bargaining were abolished, what incentive would a criminal have to cooperate with the government by giving away information about his confederates?

2. Package Deals

Suppose a prosecutor in a multi-defendant case proposes a global settlement: all the defendants can plead to specified crimes, but they must plead guilty as a group; if all the defendants do not agree, the deal is off. Does a "wired" plea or "package deal" present a greater risk of coercion than an individual plea? In *United States v. Pollard*, 959 F.2d 1011 (D.C. Cir. 1992), the defendant pled guilty to one count of conspiracy to deliver national defense information to the Government of Israel. He later claimed that the government coerced his guilty plea by linking his wife's plea to his own, especially as his wife was seriously ill at the time. But the court rejected his argument:

> To say that a practice is "coercive" or renders a plea "involuntary" means only that it creates improper pressure that would be likely to overbear the will of some innocent persons and cause them to plead guilty. Only physical harm, threats of harassment, misrepresentation, or promises that are by their nature improper as having no proper relationship to the prosecutor's business (*e.g.*, bribes) render a guilty plea legally involuntary. * * *
>
> * * * We must be mindful * * * that if the judiciary were to declare wired pleas unconstitutional, the consequences would not be altogether foreseeable and perhaps would not be beneficial to defendants. Would Pollard, for instance, have been better off had he not been able to bargain to aid his wife? Would his wife have been better off? Would the bargaining take place in any event, but with winks and nods rather than in writing?

FYI

The practice is discussed in Jonathan Liebman & Orin S. Snyder, *Joint Guilty Pleas: "Group Justice" In Federal Plea Bargaining*, N.Y. L.J., Sept. 8, 1994, at p.1, col.1 (noting that for the government, "group pleas dispose of cases in one fell swoop and thereby conserve scarce prosecutorial resources and, in some cases, avoid lengthy, costly or potentially embarrassing trials").

Nor do we believe that Mrs. Pollard's medical condition makes an otherwise acceptable linkage of their pleas unconstitutional. The appropriate dividing line between acceptable and unconstitutional plea wiring does not depend upon the physical condition or personal circumstances of the defendant; rather, it depends upon the conduct of the government. Where, as here, the government had probable cause to arrest and prosecute both defendants in a related crime, and there is no suggestion that the government conducted itself in bad faith in an effort to generate additional leverage over the defendant, we think a wired plea is constitutional.

Pollard considered the problem of a defendant "pressured" because of feelings toward the person to whom his plea is linked. The court in *United States v. Caro*, 997 F.2d 657 (9th Cir. 1993), considered a different problem that might be created by wired pleas—the possibility of coercion by other defendants. Caro moved to set aside his guilty plea on the ground that he was pressured by his codefendants into going along with the package deal. At the hearing in which his plea was entered, the judge was never informed that Caro's plea was part of a group settlement. Judge Kozinski analyzed the problem as follows:

> Though package deal plea agreements are not per se impermissible, they pose an additional risk of coercion not present when the defendant is dealing with the government alone. Quite possibly, one defendant will be happier with the package deal than his codefendants; looking out for his own interests, the lucky one may try to force his codefendants into going along with the deal. * * * We * * * have recognized that the trial court should make a more careful examination of the voluntariness of a plea when it might have been induced by threats or promises from a third party. We make it clear today that, in describing a plea agreement * * * the prosecutor must alert the district court to the fact that codefendants are entering into a package deal.

> **FYI**
>
> Professor Green, in *"Package" Plea Bargaining and the Prosecutor's Duty of Good Faith*, 25 Crim. L. Bull. 507 (1989), argues that prosecutors who offer multi-defendant deals have an ethical responsibility to avoid over-reaching.

The court held that the trial court's error—really the prosecutor's error in failing to tell the judge that the pleas were "wired"—was not harmless. It vacated Caro's guilty plea and remanded. *Compare United States v. Carr*, 80 F.3d 413 (10th Cir. 1996) (pressures of cohorts to accept a package deal "might have been palpable" to the defendant, but they did not vitiate the voluntariness of his plea because "it was still his choice to make").

E.   Discovery

[Question 7-4]

In a murder prosecution, the case against the defendant rests primarily on the testimony of a single eyewitness. The shooting occurred at dusk on a quiet suburban street. The eyewitness, whose house looked out on the scene of the crime, telephoned the police right after the shooting and, when they arrived, said that he heard a gunshot, looked out the window, and saw a man with a gun in his hand standing over the victim. The eyewitness said he recognized the man as the defendant, who lived in the neighborhood. Shortly before the scheduled trial date, the eyewitness told the prosecutor that he was recanting

his earlier statement, and that <u>he had not really</u> gotten a good look at the shooter. The prosecutor did not tell anyone about the eyewitness's recantation because she believed that the eyewitness's original identification was truthful and that he was now changing his story because he was afraid of the defendant. At trial, the eyewitness identified the defendant as the shooter and there was no mention of the eyewitness's earlier recantation. The jury found the defendant guilty. However, before sentencing, the defense lawyer learned about the eyewitness's recantation and moved for a new trial. The defense lawyer correctly alleged that, although the jury would not necessarily have acquitted if it had heard about the eyewitness's recantation, there was a reasonable probability that the verdict would have been different.

Is the court likely to grant a new trial?

 (A) Yes, because the prosecutor violated her constitutional duty to disclose exculpatory evidence.

 (B) Yes, because the prosecutor violated her ethical duty to disclose evidence helpful to the accused.

 (C) No, because it is defense counsel's responsibility in a criminal case to locate exculpatory evidence.

 (D) No, because the jury would not necessarily have acquitted if it had heard about the eyewitness's recantation.

1. Constitutional Obligation

Prosecutors have an ethical obligation to make timely disclosure to the defense of all evidence or information known to the prosecutor that negates the guilt of the accused or mitigates the seriousness of the offense. This is known as the *Brady* Rule, based on the holding of the Supreme Court in *Brady v. Maryland*, <u>373 U.S. 83 (1963)</u>. Brady and a companion, Boblit, were charged with first degree murder, a capital offense. Brady was tried first; he admitted participation in the crime, but claimed that Boblit did the actual killing. Prior to trial Brady's lawyer asked the prosecutor to allow him to see Boblit's statements. Several statements were shown to counsel, but one in which Boblit admitted the homicide was not revealed. The defense did not learn about that statement until after Brady's conviction and death sentence were affirmed. The Supreme Court found that the prosecutor has an obligation to disclose all materially exculpatory evidence, and that Boblit's admission would have had a material effect on Brady's death sentence. The Court declared that "[a] prosecution that withholds evidence on demand of an accused which, if made available, would tend to exculpate him or reduce the penalty helps shape a trial that bears heavily on the defendant. That casts the prosecutor in the role of an architect of a proceeding that does not comport with standards of justice * * *." The Court concluded as follows:

We now hold that the suppression by the prosecution of evidence favorable to an accused upon request violates due process where the evidence is material either to guilt or to punishment, irrespective of the good faith or bad faith of the prosecution.

In *Brady*, the Court extended their holding in *Mooney v. Holohan*, 294 U.S. 103, 112 (1935), in which the Court held that the prosecutor's deliberate use of perjured testimony violates the defendant's due process rights and is a denial of a fair trial.

It is a requirement that cannot be deemed to be satisfied by mere notice and hearing if a state has contrived a conviction through the pretense of a trial which in truth is but used as a means of depriving a defendant of liberty through a deliberate deception of court and jury by the presentation of testimony known to be perjured. Such a contrivance by a state to procure the conviction and imprisonment of a defendant is as inconsistent with the rudimentary demands of justice as is the obtaining of a like result by intimidation.

United States v. Agurs

427 U.S. 97 (1976)

MR. JUSTICE STEVENS delivered the opinion of the Court.

After a brief interlude in an inexpensive motel room, respondent repeatedly stabbed James Sewell, causing his death. She was convicted of second-degree murder. The question before us is whether the prosecutor's failure to provide defense counsel with certain background information about Sewell, which would have tended to support the argument that respondent acted in self-defense, deprived her of a fair trial under the rule of *Brady v. Maryland*.

* * *

I

At about 4:30 p.m. on September 24, 1971, respondent, who had been there before, and Sewell, registered in a motel as man and wife. They were assigned a room without a bath. Sewell was wearing a bowie knife in a sheath, and carried another knife in his pocket. Less than two hours earlier, according to the testimony of his estranged wife, he had had $360 in cash on his person.

About 15 minutes later three motel employees heard respondent screaming for help. A forced entry into their room disclosed Sewell on top of respondent struggling for possession of the bowie knife. She was holding the knife; his bleeding hand grasped the blade; according to one witness he was trying to jam the blade into her chest. The employees separated the two and summoned the authorities. Respondent departed without comment before they arrived. Sewell was dead on arrival at the hospital.

Circumstantial evidence indicated that the parties had completed an act of intercourse, that Sewell had then gone to the bathroom down the hall, and that the struggle occurred upon his return. The contents of his pockets were in disarray on the dresser and no money was found; the jury may have inferred that respondent took Sewell's money and that the fight started when Sewell re-entered the room and saw what she was doing.

On the following morning respondent surrendered to the police. She was given a physical examination which revealed no cuts or bruises of any kind, except needle marks on her upper arm. An autopsy of Sewell disclosed that he had several deep stab wounds in his chest and abdomen, and a number of slashes on his arms and hands, characterized by the pathologist as "defensive wounds."

Respondent offered no evidence. Her sole defense was the argument made by her attorney that Sewell had initially attacked her with the knife, and that her actions had all been directed toward saving her own life. The support for this self-defense theory was based on the fact that she had screamed for help. Sewell was on top of her when help arrived, and his possession of two knives indicated that he was a violence-prone person. It took the jury about 25 minutes to elect a foreman and return a verdict.

Three months later defense counsel filed a motion for a new trial asserting that he had discovered (1) that Sewell had a prior criminal record that would have further evidenced his violent character; (2) that the prosecutor had failed to disclose this information to the defense; and (3) that a recent opinion of the United States Court of Appeals for the District of Columbia Circuit made it clear that such evidence was admissible even if not known to the defendant. Sewell's prior record included a plea of guilty to a charge of assault and carrying a deadly weapon in 1963, and another guilty plea to a charge of carrying a deadly weapon in 1971. Apparently both weapons were knives.

The Government opposed the motion, arguing that there was no duty to tender Sewell's prior record to the defense in the absence of an appropriate request; that the evidence was readily discoverable in advance of trial and hence was not the kind of "newly discovered" evidence justifying a new trial; and that, in all events, it was not material.

The District Court denied the motion. * * *

The Court of Appeals reversed. The court found no lack of diligence on the part of the defense and no misconduct by the prosecutor in this case. It held, however, that the evidence was material, and that its nondisclosure required a new trial because the jury might have returned a different verdict if the evidence had been received.

The decision of the Court of Appeals represents a significant departure from this Court's prior holding; because we believe that that court has incorrectly interpreted the constitutional requirement of due process, we reverse.

II

The rule of *Brady v. Maryland* arguably applies in three quite different situations. Each involves the discovery, after trial, of information which had been known to the prosecution but unknown to the defense.

In the first situation, typified by *Mooney v. Holohan*, the undisclosed evidence demonstrates that the prosecution's case includes perjured testimony and that the prosecution knew, or should have known, of the perjury. In a series of subsequent cases, the Court has consistently held that a conviction obtained by the knowing use of perjured testimony is fundamentally unfair, and must be set aside if there is any reasonable likelihood that the false testimony could have affected the judgment of the jury. It is this line of cases on which the Court of Appeals placed primary reliance. In those cases the Court has applied a strict standard of materiality, not just because they involve prosecutorial misconduct, but more importantly because they involve a corruption of the truth-seeking function of the trial process. Since this case involves no misconduct, and since there is no reason to question the veracity of any of the prosecution witnesses, the test of materiality followed in the *Mooney* line of cases is not necessarily applicable to this case.

The second situation, illustrated by the *Brady* case itself, is characterized by a pretrial request for specific evidence. In that case defense counsel had requested the extrajudicial statements made by Brady's accomplice, one Boblit. This Court held that the suppression of one of Boblit's statements deprived Brady of due process, noting specifically that the statement had been requested and that it was "material." A fair analysis of the holding in *Brady* indicates that implicit in the requirement of materiality is a concern that the suppressed evidence might have affected the outcome of the trial.

* * *

In *Brady* the request was specific. It gave the prosecutor notice of exactly what the defense desired. Although there is, of course, no duty to provide defense counsel with unlimited discovery of everything known by the prosecutor, if the subject matter of such a request is material, or indeed if a substantial basis for claiming materiality exists, it is reasonable to require the prosecutor to respond either by furnishing the information or by submitting the problem to the trial judge. When the prosecutor receives a specific and relevant request, the failure to make any response is seldom, if ever, excusable.

In many cases, however, exculpatory information in the possession of the prosecutor may be unknown to defense counsel. In such a situation he may make no request at all, or possibly ask for "all *Brady* material" or for "anything exculpatory." Such a request really gives the prosecutor no better notice than if no request is made. If there is a duty to respond to a general request of that kind, it must derive from the obviously exculpatory character of certain evidence in the hands of the prosecutor. But if the evidence is so clearly supportive of a claim of innocence that it gives the prosecution notice of a duty to produce, that duty should equally arise even if no request is made. Whether we focus on the desirability of a precise definition of the prosecutor's duty or on the potential harm to the defendant, we conclude that there is no significant difference between cases in which there has been merely a general request for exculpatory matter and cases, like the one we must now decide, in which there has been no request at all. The third situation in which the *Brady* rule arguably applies, typified by this case, therefore embraces the case in which only a general request for "*Brady* material" has been made.

We now consider whether the prosecutor has any constitutional duty to volunteer exculpatory matter to the defense, and if so, what standard of materiality gives rise to that duty.

III

* * *

The Court of Appeals appears to have assumed that the prosecutor has a constitutional obligation to disclose any information that might affect the jury's verdict. That statement of a constitutional standard of materiality approaches the "sporting theory of justice" which the Court expressly rejected in *Brady*. For a jury's appraisal of a case "might" be affected by an improper or trivial consideration as well as by evidence giving rise to a legitimate doubt on the issue of guilt. If everything that might influence a jury must be disclosed, the only way a prosecutor could discharge his constitutional duty would be to allow complete discovery of his files as a matter of routine practice.

Whether or not procedural rules authorizing such broad discovery might be desirable, the Constitution surely does not demand that much. * * * The mere possibility that an item of undisclosed information might have helped the defense, or might have affected the outcome of the trial, does not establish "materiality" in the constitutional sense.

Nor do we believe the constitutional obligation is measured by the moral culpability, or the willfulness, of the prosecutor. If evidence highly probative of innocence is in his file, he should be presumed to recognize its significance even if he has actually overlooked it. Conversely, if evidence actually has no probative significance at all, no purpose would be served by requiring a new trial simply because an inept prosecutor incorrectly believed he was suppressing a fact that would be vital to the defense. If the suppression of evidence results in constitutional error, it is because of the character of the evidence, not the character of the prosecutor.

* * * [T]here are situations in which evidence is obviously of such substantial value to the defense that elementary fairness requires it to be disclosed even without a specific request. For though the attorney for the sovereign must prosecute the accused with earnestness and vigor, he must always be faithful to his client's overriding interest that "justice shall be done." He is the "servant of the law, the twofold aim of which is that guilt shall not escape or innocence suffer." *Berger v. United States*, 295 U.S. 78, 88 (1935). This description of the prosecutor's duty illuminates the standard of materiality that governs his obligation to disclose exculpatory evidence.

* * *

The proper standard of materiality must reflect our overriding concern with the justice of the finding of guilt. Such a finding is permissible only if supported by evidence establishing guilt beyond a reasonable doubt. It necessarily follows that if the omitted evidence creates a reasonable doubt that did not otherwise exist, constitutional error has been committed. This means that the omission must be evaluated in the context of the entire record. If there is no reasonable doubt about guilt whether or not the additional evidence is considered, there is no justification for a new trial. On the other hand, if the verdict is already of questionable validity, additional evidence of relatively minor importance might be sufficient to create a reasonable doubt.

This statement of the standard of materiality describes the test which courts appear to have applied in actual cases although the standard has been phrased in different language. It is also the standard which the trial judge applied in this case. He evaluated the significance of Sewell's prior criminal record in the context of the full trial which he recalled in detail. Stressing in particular the incongruity of a claim that Sewell was the aggressor with the evidence of his multiple wounds and respondent's unscathed condition, the trial judge indicated his unqualified opinion that respondent was guilty. He noted that Sewell's prior record did not contradict any evidence offered by the prosecutor, and was largely cumulative of the evidence that Sewell was wearing a bowie knife in a sheath and carrying a second knife in his pocket when he registered at the motel.

Since the arrest record was not requested and did not even arguably give rise to any inference of perjury, since after considering it in the context of the entire record the trial judge remained convinced of respondent's guilt beyond a reasonable doubt, and since we are satisfied that his firsthand appraisal of the record was thorough and entirely reasonable, we hold that the prosecutor's failure to tender Sewell's record to the defense did not deprive respondent of a fair trial as guaranteed by the Due Process Clause of the Fifth Amendment. * * *

MR. JUSTICE MARSHALL with whom MR. JUSTICE BRENNAN joins, dissenting.

* * *

* * * [The majority's] rule creates little, if any, incentive for the prosecutor conscientiously to determine whether his files contain evidence helpful to the defense. Indeed, the rule reinforces the natural tendency of the prosecutor to overlook evidence favorable to the defense, and creates an incentive for the prosecutor to resolve close questions of disclosure in favor of concealment.

* * * I would hold that the defendant in this case had the burden of demonstrating that there is a significant chance that the withheld evidence, developed by skilled counsel, would have induced a reasonable doubt in the minds of enough jurors to avoid a conviction. * * *

Take Note

The standard of materiality for *Brady* rulings has preoccupied the Supreme Court. In *United States v. Bagley*, 473 U.S. 667 (1985), the Court declined to overturn a conviction because of nondisclosure of exculpatory evidence. Bagley was charged with narcotics and firearms offenses and convicted in a bench trial only on the narcotics charges. Thereafter he learned that, despite his motion to discover any deals or promises between the government and its witnesses, the government had not disclosed that its two principal witnesses had signed contracts with the Bureau of Alcohol, Tobacco and Firearms to be paid for their undercover work. The Supreme Court found that nondisclosure of impeachment evidence requires reversal only if the evidence was material in the sense that it might have affected the outcome of the trial. No such showing was made on the facts of this case.

Justice Blackmun's opinion set forth a single "standard of materiality" applicable to nondisclosed exculpatory evidence:

> [Suppressed evidence] is material only if there is a reasonable probability that, had the evidence been disclosed to the defense, the result of the proceeding would have been different. A reasonable probability is a probability sufficient to undermine confidence in the outcome.

Justice Blackmun noted that this test was "sufficiently flexible" to cover no request, general request, and specific request cases.

In *Smith v. Cain*, 565 U.S. 73 (2012), the Court reversed, in an 8-to-1 opinion, the conviction of a man convicted of first degree murder. Prosecutors in New Orleans failed to disclose police notes regarding statements of Larry Boatner, an eyewitness to the murder.

> The notes from the night of the murder state that Boatner "could not . . . supply a description of the perpetrators other then [sic] they were black males." [Police investigator] Ronquillo also made a handwritten account of a conversation he had with Boatner five days after the crime, in which Boatner said he "could not ID anyone because [he] couldn't see faces" and "would not know them if [he] saw them." And Ronquillo's typewritten report of that conversation states that Boatner told Ronquillo he "could not identify any of the perpetrators of the murder."

At trial, however, Boatner identified Smith and claimed he had been "face to face" with the defendant at the time of the murders. The Court determined that because the testimony was the only evidence linking Smith to the crime, the prosecutors had an obligation to disclose these investigation notes.

> We have observed [in *Agurs*] that evidence impeaching an eyewitness may not be material if the State's other evidence is strong enough to sustain confidence in the verdict. That is not the case here. Boatner's testimony was the *only* evidence linking Smith to the crime. And Boatner's undisclosed statements directly contradict his testimony: * * *. Boatner's undisclosed statements were plainly material.

> The State and the dissent [by Justice Thomas] advance various reasons why the jury might have discounted Boatner's undisclosed statements. They stress, for example, that Boatner made other remarks on the night of the murder indicating that he could identify the first gunman to enter the house, but not the others. That merely leaves us to speculate about which of Boatner's contradictory declarations the jury would have believed. The State also contends that Boatner's statements made five days after the crime can be explained by fear of retaliation. Smith responds that the record contains no evidence of any such fear. Again, the State's argument offers a reason that the jury *could* have disbelieved Boatner's undisclosed statements, but gives us no confidence that it *would* have done so.

2. Brady and Guilty Pleas: United States v. Ruiz

If the prosecutor has materially exculpatory evidence, does Due Process require that it be disclosed before the defendant enters into a guilty plea? Or is the *Brady* right simply a trial right? The question arises in the following procedural context: the defendant pleads guilty, later learns of exculpatory evidence that was suppressed, and moves to vacate his guilty plea as insufficiently knowing and voluntary.

In *United States v. Ruiz*, 536 U.S. 622 (2002), the Court held that during guilty plea negotiations the government is not required to disclose information that could impeach government witnesses, nor information that could be used by the defendant to prove an affirmative defense.

Justice Breyer, writing for a unanimous Court, noted that "impeachment information is special in relation to the *fairness of a trial*, not in respect to whether a plea is *voluntary*." Justice Breyer expressed concern that requiring disclosure of impeachment information during guilty plea negotiations "could seriously interfere with the Government's interest in securing those guilty pleas that are factually justified, desired by defendants, and help to secure the efficient administration of justice." Specifically, early disclosure of impeachment evidence "could disrupt ongoing investigations and expose prospective witnesses to serious harm."

As to required disclosure of impeachment evidence, Justice Breyer concluded that it

> could force the Government to abandon its general practice of not disclosing to a defendant pleading guilty information that would reveal the identities of cooperating informants, undercover investigators, or other prospective witnesses. It could require the Government to devote substantially more resources to trial preparation prior to plea bargaining, thereby depriving the plea-bargaining process of its main resource-saving advantages. Or it could lead the Government instead to abandon its heavy reliance upon plea bargaining in a vast number—90% or more—of federal criminal cases. We cannot say that the Constitution's due process requirement demands so radical a change in the criminal justice process in order to achieve so comparatively small a constitutional benefit.

As to required disclosure of information bearing on an affirmative defense, the Court concluded as follows:

> We do not believe the Constitution here requires provision of this information to the defendant prior to plea bargaining—for most (though not all) of the reasons previously stated. That is to say, in the context of this agreement, the need for this information is more closely related to the *fairness* of a trial than to the *voluntariness* of the plea; the value in terms of the defendant's added awareness of relevant circumstances is ordinarily limited; yet the added burden imposed upon the Government by requiring its provision well in advance of trial (often before trial preparation begins) can be serious, thereby significantly interfering with the administration of the plea bargaining process.

The Court in *Ruiz* recognized the government's duty to disclose information bearing on the defendant's "factual innocence" during guilty plea negotiations, as well as a continuing duty to disclose such information throughout the plea proceedings. Indeed, the government recognized this obligation by including it in the plea agreement in *Ruiz*. *See also Sanchez v. United States*, 50 F.3d 1448 (9th Cir. 1995) (guilty plea vacated because evidence material to innocence was suppressed, noting that otherwise "prosecutors may be tempted to deliberately withhold exculpatory information as part of an attempt to elicit guilty pleas").

What is the test of materiality in a guilty plea context? The court in *Sanchez, supra*, declared that suppressed evidence is material if "there is a reasonable probability that but for the failure to disclose the *Brady* material, the defendant would have refused to plead and would have gone to trial." How is a court to determine this question? Does it rely on the defendant's assertions? On the power of the suppressed evidence? On a comparison between the deal that the defendant received and the sentence that he would have faced if convicted? *See Miller v. Angliker*, 848 F.2d 1312 (2d Cir. 1988) (test of materiality, in the guilty plea context, is an objective one that centers on "the likely persuasiveness of the withheld information").

3. Rule-Based Requirements

Every state has a rule specifically addressing prosecutors' disclosure obligations. For example, Rule 3.8(d) of the Utah Rules of Professional Conduct, drawn directly from the ABA Model Rules, provides:

"The prosecutor in a criminal case shall . . . [m]ake timely disclosure to the defense of all evidence or information known to the prosecutor that tends to negate the guilt of the accused or mitigates the offense, and, in connection with sentencing, disclose to the defense all unprivileged mitigating information known to the prosecutor, except when the prosecutor is relieved of this responsibility by a protective order of the tribunal."

Note that, on its face, the rule's requirements differ from the requirements of the Brady line of cases. In at least one important respect, the rule is less demanding than the case law: Under Brady, a conviction can be overturned if important evidence is withheld, regardless of whether the prosecutor is blameworthy. Even if the evidence is withheld inadvertently or negligently—indeed, even if the prosecutor was unaware of it because the police never provided it to the prosecutor—the constitutional command may be violated.

In at least two other important respects, however, Rule 3.8(d) is more demanding than the constitutional case law. First, Rule 3.8(d) requires the prosecutors to disclose "evidence or information known to the prosecutor that tends to negate the guilt of the accused." The rule does not limit this to evidence or information that is "material" for constitutional purposes. Presumably, there may be exculpatory evidence—*i.e.*, evidence that "tends" to negate the defendant's guilt—that would not be important enough to put a guilty verdict in doubt.

Second, Rule 3.8(d) requires "timely disclosure." This appears to mean that evidence must be provided reasonably soon, so that defendants' lawyers can use it in their investigations, trial preparation, and advice to the defendant regarding such crucial questions as whether to plead guilty.

Disciplinary actions against prosecutors for disclosure violations have been relatively infrequent, as many critics have noted, even though there are many reported cases in which prosecutors failed to disclose evidence that would have been useful to the defense. One reason may be that, in many of the cases, it was not apparent that the prosecutor knew of the evidence and of its significance to the defense. But disciplinary authorities also appeared to be uncertain that the rule meant what it said—that it required timely disclosure of all evidence that tends to negate guilt, and not just whatever evidence must be produced under constitutional decisions and other law.

In 2009, the ABA's ethics committee issued a formal opinion, Opinion 09-454, agreeing with scholars who previously had noted that state rules derived from ABA Model Rule 3.8(d) were more demanding than the *Brady* cases. More recently, the N.Y. City Bar's ethics committee issued an opinion, Opinion 2016-3, interpreting New York's analogue to Rule 3.8(d), and reaching the same conclusion: "While *Brady* has been held to require a prosecutor to disclose only 'material' evidence favorable to the accused, Rule 3.8 on its face is not subject to the same materiality limitation." Opinion 2016-3 also noted that, unlike prosecutors' obligations under *Brady*, Rule 3.8 does not require prosecutors to conduct an investigation to uncover exculpatory information. The Opinion explained that "[i]n this respect, too, [Rule 3.8] is not a codification of disclosure obligations established by law. Rather, in this context the rule is less demanding than applicable legal disclosure obligations." Finally, with regard to the rule's "timeliness" requirement, the Opinion concluded that "once a prosecutor knows of evidence and information that tends to negate the guilt of the accused, or that otherwise falls within the rule's disclosure requirement, the prosecutor ordinarily must disclose it as soon as reasonably practicable." This is so because the "purpose of disclosure ordinarily includes not only facilitating a potential trial defense but also assisting the defense prior to trial."

In recent years, disciplinary authorities have begun initiating disciplinary actions against prosecutors who appear to have violated Rule 3.8(d) as interpreted in the bar opinions. As the next case shows, some state courts, such as the Utah Supreme Court, have agreed with the ABA about the scope of the rule.

Matter of Larsen

2016 UT 26 (2016)

[Larsen, a Utah prosecutor, was charged with violating Rule 3.8(d), which requires the prosecutor to make "timely disclosure" of exculpatory evidence. The disciplinary charge arose out of Larsen's conduct in prosecuting a felony robbery case in 2010. The robbery case turned on eyewitness testimony. Around 10 days before the trial, Larsen showed the eyewitnesses a photo of the defendant. Rule 3.8(d) required Larsen to tell the defense that the eyewitnesses had recently viewed the defendant's photo, because this would cast doubt on the accuracy of any in-court identification. But Larsen did not disclose this before the eyewitnesses testified. One eyewitness denied having seen a photo, and Larsen was silent. He acknowledged having shown the eyewitnesses the defendant's photo only after a second witness testified on cross-examination that she had been shown one. As a defense to a disciplinary charge under Utah's Rule 3.8, Larsen argued, among other things, that his acknowledgement constituted a sufficiently timely disclosure, because it sufficed to satisfy his *Brady* obligation, which requires only that exculpatory evidence be disclosed in time for its effective use.]

The precise timing of Larsen's admission is not clear from the record. But we see no way to characterize the admission he made at trial as a "timely disclosure" under rule 3.8(d).

The timeliness of a prosecutor's disclosure of exculpatory evidence is a matter governed in Utah by our rules of criminal procedure. By rule, a prosecutor must "make all disclosures as soon as practicable following the filing of charges and before the defendant is required to plead." Utah R. Crim. P. 16(a)(5)(b). Our rule also implicitly recognizes that some exculpatory material may not be known before the time for a plea; for such material, the prosecutor "has a continuing duty to make disclosure," and an obligation to do so "as soon as practicable."

The requirement of timely disclosure is important. It is aimed at allowing the "defendant to adequately prepare his defense." And our ethics rule has the same evident focus. Rule 3.8(d) of the Utah Rules of Professional Conduct requires more than just disclosure; it requires "timely disclosure."

Larsen's admission at trial cannot be viewed as a "timely disclosure." He knew before trial that he had shown the defendant's photograph (and no other photographs) to the eyewitnesses of the two robberies. And he failed to disclose that fact "as soon as practicable" thereafter—in advance of trial, at a time necessary to allow "the defendant to adequately prepare his defense."

If the prosecutor's possession of exculpatory evidence is uncovered at trial, a subsequent admission of that fact may be somewhat mitigating at the sanction phase. But the admission is not itself a fulfillment of the rule 3.8(d) duty of disclosure. If that were enough, the rule would be rendered practically toothless, as any savvy prosecutor could avoid an ethics violation by the simple expedient of an after-the-fact admission of a prior failure of disclosure once it is exposed by someone else.

Larsen cites [state and U.S. Supreme Court decisions] for the proposition that there is no violation of the duty to disclose exculpatory material under Brady v. Maryland, unless the prosecution "suppresses information that (1) remains unknown to the defense both before and throughout trial and (2) is material and exculpatory, meaning its disclosure would have created a 'reasonable probability' that 'the result of the proceeding would have been different.' " And because Larsen's act of showing photographs to the eyewitnesses became known during trial, Larsen insists that he also fulfilled his duties under rule 3.8(d).

We see the matter differently. Larsen's argument conflates the *Brady* standard with the prosecutor's ethical duty under rule 3.8(d). But the two standards are distinct. The question under *Brady* is a matter of due process—of whether the prosecution's failure to disclose exculpatory material so undermines our confidence in the verdict that we should order a new trial. If the exculpatory evidence in question is disclosed *during trial*, there may be no prejudice and thus no need for a new trial. But rule 3.8(d)'s focus is different. It is aimed not only at assuring a fair trial—by articulating a standard for a motion for a new one—but also at establishing an ethical duty

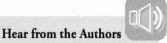

Hear from the Authors

To hear from the authors about prosecutors' disclosure obligations, click here.

that will avoid the problem in the first place. In stating that duty, our rule requires "timely disclosure" by the prosecution. That duty cannot be fulfilled by a prosecutor's mere admission of the existence of exculpatory evidence made *after* a witness first uncovers it.

[The Utah Supreme Court upheld the lower court's six-month suspension of Larsen for violating Rule 3.8(d).]

FYI

Like the Utah court, several other courts have sanctioned prosecutors for withholding evidence helpful to the defense, even if the prosecutor did not violate Brady. *See, e.g., In re Kline*, 113 A.3d 202 (D.C. App. 2015); *In re Disciplinary Action Against Feland*, 2012 ND 174 (N.D. 2012). But several other courts have held that prosecutors cannot be sanctioned under their state's version of Rule 3.8 unless the prosecutor violated due process by failing to disclose *material* exculpatory evidence. *See, e.g., Oklahoma Bar Ass'n v. Ward*, 353 P.3d 509 (Okl. 2015); *In re Petition*, 2019 WL 3978583 (Tenn. Aug. 23, 2019). Most state courts have yet to weigh in. For a discussion of this disagreement, see Bruce A. Green, *Prosecutors' Ethical Duty of Disclosure*, 48 San Diego L. Rev. 57 (2011).

In *Matter of Hudson*, 105 N.E.3d 1089 (Ind. 2018), the court noted the disagreement but did not resolve whether Rule 3.8 was more demanding than *Brady*, because the prosecutor withheld impeachment evidence that was "material." Hudson prosecuted a man who had been charged with molesting his two stepchildren based on the children's statements to the police. Shortly before trial, one of the children told Hudson that he had lied about some of the alleged conduct at his biological father's request. Although Hudson believed the child's recantation, she did not drop the relevant charge – she simply offered no evidence regarding it. Nor did she reveal that the child had been coached to lie, even though both the child and his biological father were trial witnesses and the information was relevant to their credibility. But this was revealed during the defense lawyer's cross-examinations. As a remedy, the trial judge dismissed all the charges. In the subsequent disciplinary proceeding, in addition to finding that Hudson violated Rule 3.8(d), the state supreme court found that she violated Rule 3.8(a) by continuing to prosecute a charge on which there was not probable cause, and Rule 8.4(d), because, given the outcome of the prosecution, her conduct prejudiced the administration of justice. The court suspended Hudson for a minimum of eighteen months.

Hudson is unusual. Disciplinary authorities rarely bring actions against prosecutors even when they violate *Brady* by withholding material exculpatory evidence. Prosecutors' *Brady* violations are regarded as one of the most frequent, and significant, types of prosecutorial misconduct, as well as one of the most frequent causes of wrongful convictions. A federal appellate judge once declared that there was a national "epidemic" of *Brady* violations. But there are few public disciplinary actions against prosecutors, and fewer still for violating disclosure obligations.

Civil lawsuits are not an adequate substitute for discipline. They can almost never be brought successfully against the offending prosecutors themselves, because the Supreme Court has held that prosecutors are absolutely immune from liability under the federal civil rights law when they violate constitutional rights in the course of criminal prosecutions. Under limited circumstances, the case law allows exonerated individuals to sue a locality, or its prosecutor's office, when prosecutors violated *Brady*. But the Supreme Court's decision in *Connick v. Thompson*, 563 U.S. 51 (2011), famously illustrates the challenge that exonerated individuals face in seeking compensation.

The respondent in that case, John Thompson, was tried for murder in New Orleans. At his trial, he decided not to testify in his own defense in order to prevent the prosecutors from cross-examining him based on his prior conviction for armed robbery. He was convicted and sentenced to death. But the armed robbery conviction was later shown to be wrongful. The prosecutors in the armed robbery case withheld evidence proving Thompson's innocence—namely, an item of clothing with the blood of the perpetrator, who had a different blood type from Thompson. Thompson's murder conviction was overturned and he was acquitted on retrial. He then sued the New Orleans district attorney's office and others for violating his civil rights, causing him to be locked up on death row for around two decades. The jury found in his favor and awarded him $14 million, but the Supreme Court, in a 5–4 decision, held that the jury's judgment could not stand, because the New Orleans prosecutors' office did not have a routine practice of withholding *Brady* material–a conclusion that the dissent disputed. The Court also found that the prosecutors' office could not be liable for inadequately training its prosecutors because it could assume that, as lawyers, its prosecutors knew their constitutional obligations (despite evidence to the contrary) by virtue of their professional training and their ethical obligation to comply with their *Brady* obligations, subject to disciplinary sanction if they fail.

The New Orleans district attorney's office has reportedly improved its practices since the late 20th century when it committed Brady violations in Thompson's and others' cases. *See* Ellen Yaroshefsky, *New Orleans Prosecutorial Disclosure in Practice After Connick v. Thompson*, 25 Geo. J. Legal Ethics 913 (2012). For short videos in which Thompson and others discuss his case, click here and here.

F. Post-Conviction Evidence of Innocence

[Question 7-5]

A librarian was prosecuted for murdering a businessman. The case against the librarian rested primarily on the testimony of an eyewitness whose kitchen window overlooked the murder scene. The witness testified that he heard a gunshot, looked out the window, and saw the librarian standing over the victim. Based on this testimony, the librarian was found guilty and sentenced to life imprisonment. Three years later, the police arrested a drug dealer who looked like the librarian. Forensic tests on a gun found in the drug dealer's possession established that it was the same gun that fired the shot that had killed the businessman. The police presented what they learned to the elected prosecutor whose office had successfully prosecuted the librarian. The prosecutor acknowledged that there was a significant likelihood that the librarian had not shot the businessman. But the prosecutor concluded that the evidence of the librarian's innocence was not clear and convincing because the drug dealer may have acquired the gun after the librarian used it or the forensic evidence connecting the gun to the businessman's shooting may be inaccurate. Therefore, the prosecutor decided to take no action.

Is the prosecutor subject to discipline?

- **(A) Yes, because the prosecutor failed to disclose the new exculpatory evidence to the defendant and to conduct further investigation to determine whether the librarian was innocent.**

- **(B) Yes, because the prosecutor did not seek to set aside the librarian's conviction.**

- **(C) No, because there was not clear and convincing evidence that the librarian was wrongly convicted.**

- **(D) No, because a prosecutor has no further obligations in a case once the defendant has been convicted and sentenced.**

In 2006, in the wake of cases in which DNA evidence was used around the country to exonerate convicted defendants, the New York State Bar Association proposed that the ethics rules address prosecutors' obligations after securing a conviction when they learn of new evidence of innocence. The ABA agreed with the state bar's proposal and, in 2008, amended its Model Rule 3.8 to add subsections (g) and (h). Rule 3.8(g) essentially requires prosecutors to disclose significant new exculpatory evidence and to investigate to determine whether there was a wrongful conviction. In part, this codifies the understanding expressed by the United States Supreme Court in *Imbler v. Pachtman*, 424 U.S. 409, 427 n. 25 (1976), which

> **FYI**
>
> By 2019, nineteen states had adopted versions of one or both of these provisions: Alaska, Arizona, California, Colorado, Delaware, Hawaii, Idaho, Illinois, Massachusetts, Michigan, New Mexico, New York, North Carolina, North Dakota, Tennessee, Washington, West Virginia, Wisconsin, and Wyoming.

observed that prosecutors are "bound by the ethics of [their] office to inform the appropriate authority of after-acquired or other information that casts doubt upon the correctness of the conviction." Rule 3.8(h), in turn, calls on prosecutors to seek to remedy wrongful convictions when "clear and convincing evidence" establishes that a convicted defendant in the prosecutor's jurisdiction was innocent.

Some prosecutors recognized that the new provisions codify accepted expectations in light of prosecutors' duty to "seek justice," and that adopting these provisions would help educate prosecutors about their responsibilities and reinforce their duty to rectify, as well as avoid, wrongful convictions. For example, state prosecutors in Wisconsin and Tennessee successfully petitioned their state supreme courts to adopt versions of the rules. Wisconsin's Rule 3.8(g) closely tracks the ABA's version, while that state's version of Rule 3.8(h) is taken verbatim from the ABA model. Wisconsin's Rules 3.8(g) & (h) provide as follows:

> (g)   When a prosecutor knows of new, credible, and material evidence creating a reasonable likelihood that a convicted defendant did not commit an offense of which the defendant was convicted, the prosecutor shall do all of the following:
>
>> (1)   promptly disclose that evidence to an appropriate court or authority; and
>>
>> (2)   if the conviction was obtained in the prosecutor's jurisdiction:
>>
>>> (i)   promptly make reasonable efforts to disclose that evidence to the defendant unless a court authorizes delay; and
>>>
>>> (ii)   make reasonable efforts to undertake an investigation or cause an investigation to be undertaken, to determine whether the defendant was convicted of an offense that the defendant did not commit.
>
> (h)   When a prosecutor knows of clear and convincing evidence establishing that a defendant in the prosecutor's jurisdiction was convicted of an offense that the defendant did not commit, the prosecutor shall seek to remedy the conviction.

Other state prosecutors and various federal U.S. Attorneys' offices opposed the addition of provisions corresponding to Model Rules 3.8(g) & (h), however. Prosecutors have raised various concerns, including that they may have to answer baseless accusations of misconduct by inmates who claim to be innocent. So far, this does not appear to be a problem in the states that have adopted the new provisions, and there is no reported decision sanctioning a prosecutor for violating these rules.

Bruce Green discusses these provisions in *Prosecutors and Professional Regulation*, 25 Geo. J. Legal Ethics 873 (2012). He argues that prosecutors' distrust of the organized bar as an historically pro-defendant regime has fostered now obsolete anti-regulation rhetoric among prosecutors that has prevented further changes to Rule 3.8 over the last twenty years.

NEW YORK CITY BAR, COMMITTEE ON PROFESSIONAL ETHICS

Formal Opinion 2018-2

Prosecutors have many of the same professional obligations as other lawyers, including the duty under Rule 1.1 to conduct their work competently. They also have unique responsibilities as government lawyers to see that justice is done. *See* Rule 3.8 Cmnt. [1]. This includes taking measures to avoid convicting innocent individuals.

The duty to seek justice continues even after a criminal proceeding ends, requiring the prosecutor to take steps to rectify wrongful convictions. In general, if a prosecutor learns new evidence making it likely that a convicted defendant is innocent, the prosecutor must take certain steps: depending on the specific facts and circumstances, the prosecutor must investigate the evidence and disclose the evidence to the court and/or the defendant. This general responsibility is implicit in prosecutors' duty of competence and in their role as ministers of justice, as recognized well before New York's professional conduct rules specifically addressed the issue.

In 2012, the New York judiciary adopted Rule 3.8(c), (d) and (e) of the New York Rules of Professional Conduct (the "Rules") to give expression to prosecutors' minimum post-conviction duties. Rule 3.8(c) [the counterpart to ABA Model Rule 3.8(g)], on which this Opinion focuses, provides:

> When a prosecutor knows of new, credible and material evidence creating a reasonable likelihood that a convicted defendant did not commit an offense of which the defendant was convicted, the prosecutor shall within a reasonable time:
>
> (1) disclose that evidence to an appropriate court or prosecutor's office; or
>
> (2) if the conviction was obtained by that prosecutor's office,
>
> (A) notify the appropriate court and the defendant that the prosecutor's office possesses such evidence unless a court authorizes delay for good cause shown;
>
> (B) disclose that evidence to the defendant unless the disclosure would interfere with an ongoing investigation or endanger the safety of a witness or other person, and a court authorizes delay for good cause shown; and
>
> (C) undertake or make reasonable efforts to cause to be undertaken such further inquiry or investigation as may be necessary to provide a reasonable belief that the conviction should or should not be set aside.

Rule 3.8(d) [the counterpart to ABA Model Rule 3.8(h)], in turn, addresses prosecutors' obligation to seek a remedy upon coming to know of "clear and convincing evidence establishing that a defendant was convicted, in a prosecution by the prosecutor's office, of an offense that the defendant did not commit." Rule 3.8(e) establishes that a prosecutor does not violate Rule 3.8(c) or (d) if the prosecutor made a good-faith, but erroneous, judgment that new evidence did not trigger the obligation. The Rules apply not only to individual prosecutors but also to their offices. Therefore, prosecutors' offices have disclosure and investigative obligations when prosecutors in the office, individually or collectively, learn of new evidence that triggers the obligations of Rule 3.8(c).

In general, the terms of Rules 3.8(c)–(e) are clear, and further useful guidance is provided by the accompanying Comments adopted by the New York State Bar Association, as well as by secondary writings on the New York Rules of Professional Conduct. We write to make the following four points.

First, and most importantly, the Rules governing conduct of prosecutors were adopted solely for purposes of professional discipline. Like other rules, they "state the minimum level of conduct below which no lawyer can fall without being subject to disciplinary action." NY Rules, Scope, para. [6]. These Rules are not meant to state the limit of what prosecutors and their offices can or should do to rectify wrongful convictions. Many prosecutors' offices develop, and train prosecutors regarding, obligations that are considerably more demanding and detailed than the disciplinary rule.

Second, prosecutors have not only a general duty to seek justice but also a professional obligation of competence. See Rule 1.1 (requiring "competent representation"). Rules 3.8(c)–(e) were not meant to establish the full extent of prosecutors' post-conviction duty, as a matter of competence, to investigate and rectify wrongful convictions. In some situations, ignoring new potentially exculpatory evidence will reflect incompetent prosecutorial work, regardless of whether Rule 3.8(c) is triggered. Rule 3.8(c) presupposes that prosecutors receiving new evidence of innocence will make certain threshold determinations, such as whether the evidence is credible and material, and conduct any inquiry necessary to ascertain whether the investigation contemplated by Rule 3.8(c) is needed.

Third, Rule 3.8(c) may be implicated in a variety of ways. New evidence potentially triggering the rule may include new exculpatory evidence of various kinds, such as evidence of an alibi, an account of an eyewitness or accomplice, or physical or forensic evidence such as DNA evidence. But Rule 3.8(c) may also be triggered by new evidence that tends to discredit the proof at trial, such as a recantation, information impeaching a key witness, or new forensic research that casts doubt on the reliability of earlier forensic evidence. Moreover, the rule may be triggered when the defendant pled guilty as well as when the defendant was convicted following a trial, since a guilty plea does not foreclose the possibility that the defendant was in fact innocent. Ultimately, the rule's application depends on a fact-intensive inquiry.

Finally, insofar as state or federal prosecutors have post-conviction obligations under procedural rules, statutes or constitutional case law to disclose or investigate exculpatory information or to rectify wrongful convictions, such legal obligations do not determine prosecutors' duties under Rules 3.8(c) and (d). *See also* NYCBA Formal Op. 2016-3 (2016) (concluding that prosecutor's pre-trial disclosure obligations under Rule 3.8(b) are not coextensive with any obligations under substantive law). Moreover, because the terms of Rule 3.8(c) generally have ordinary, everyday meanings, they were not meant to incorporate legal standards where the same words are used elsewhere in a specialized or restrictive way.

For example, "new" has its everyday meaning in Rule 3.8(c): the evidence was not previously known to the prosecutor or the defense. This is not the same as "newly discovered" evidence for purposes of formal post-conviction proceedings. Prosecutors are familiar with the concept of newly discovered evidence which may justify re-opening criminal proceedings under procedural law. The concept comes with a host of interpretive and limiting meanings. In New York State post-conviction proceedings, a conviction may be vacated based on newly discovered evidence only if, among other criteria, the defendant establishes that the new evidence in question could not have been produced by the defendant at trial, if the defendant exercised due diligence. *See* N.Y. Crim. Pro. Law § 440.10(g). By contrast, "new" evidence under Rule 3.8(c) may include previously unknown evidence that might have been available to the defense at the time of trial if only defense counsel had exercised due diligence.

Likewise, the reference to "evidence" in Rule 3.8(c) is not limited to proof that may be admissible under rules of evidence applicable to judicial proceedings. Exculpatory information is potentially subject to disclosure under the rule regardless of its admissibility under evidence law. This makes practical sense because such information may lead to admissible evidence, provide a basis for an application for executive clemency, or contribute to relieving the convicted defendant of collateral burdens of a conviction.

If the obligation under Rule 3.8(c) is triggered, the prosecutor need not disclose the entire file, but only new evidence that is "new", "material" and "credible". The terms "material" and "credible" do not have special meanings derived from statutes or case law. The term "material" is not intended to incorporate the standard of materiality for review under *Brady v. Maryland*, 373 U.S. 83 (1963), and its progeny, relating to prosecutors' disclosure obligation under the U.S. Constitution. Under case law, previously-undisclosed exculpatory evidence is "material" to a conviction if "the new evidence is sufficient to 'undermine confidence' in the verdict." *See Wearry v. Cain*, 136 S. Ct. 1002, 1006 (2016). In Rule 3.8(c), however, "material" simply means that the new evidence contributes significantly to creating a reasonable likelihood of the convicted defendant's innocence. Likewise, "credible" has its ordinary meaning: To be "credible", evidence must simply be trustworthy or worthy of belief.

The one term in the rule that does not necessarily have its ordinary, everyday meaning is "knows." Rule 3.8(c) is triggered only when a prosecutor "knows of new, credible and material evidence creating a reasonable likelihood that a convicted defendant did not commit an offense of which the defendant was convicted." Knowledge is a defined term in the Rules. A lawyer "knows" a fact when the lawyer has "actual knowledge of the fact in question [which may be] inferred from the circumstances." Rule 1.0(k). Conscious avoidance of the fact in question may also constitute knowledge under the Rules, as under criminal law. Moreover, a prosecutor who does not know of new exculpatory evidence because of a failure to exercise reasonable diligence may have acted incompetently under Rule 1.1. But Rule 3.8(c) does not itself hold a prosecutor responsible for failing to disclose new evidence of which the prosecutor was unaware due to negligence, as distinguished from conscious disregard.

Conclusion

Rule 3.8(c) states a minimum standard of conduct "when a prosecutor knows of new, credible and material evidence creating a reasonable likelihood that a convicted defendant did not commit an offense of which the defendant was convicted." The duty of competence under Rule 1.1 establishes additional duties in the post-conviction context, including, in some cases, a duty to investigate new potentially exculpatory evidence regardless of whether Rule 3.8(c) is triggered. Rule 3.8(c) may be implicated in a variety of ways, including in cases where the defendant pleaded guilty, and its application depends on a fact-intensive inquiry. The terms "new", "credible", "material" and "evidence" have their ordinary, everyday meanings, and were not meant to incorporate legal standards derived from procedural rules, statutes or constitutional decisions. The rule does not apply unless the prosecutor, or the prosecutor's office, has actual knowledge of evidence that triggers the rule or consciously avoids acquiring such knowledge, but a prosecutor who does not know of new exculpatory evidence because of a failure to exercise reasonable diligence may have acted incompetently under Rule 1.1.

II. Ethical Standards for Judges

A. Introduction[1]

When presiding over judicial proceedings, judges are required to be neutral and impartial.[2] To insure an impartial judiciary, judges' extrajudicial conduct and relationships are subject to various bodies of regulation. These include the Constitution's Due Process Clause, federal and state statutes, and codes of judicial ethics. Together, these are intended to promote public confidence in the integrity of the judicial system.

Constitutional Requirements. As interpreted by the Supreme Court and other courts, the Due Process Clause sometimes requires judges to "recuse themselves when they face possible temptations to be biased, even when they exhibit no actual bias against a party or a case."[3] Although the common law rule was that a judge would be "disqualified for direct pecuniary interest and nothing else,"[4] the constitutional rule goes somewhat further. The Due Process Clause requires disqualification where the judge has a direct pecuniary or other interest in the outcome of the case, so that there is a significant incentive for a judge to favor one side.[5] The

---

1   This introduction is adapted from Bruce A. Green, *May Judges Attend Privately Funded Educational Programs? Should Judicial Education Be Privatized?: Questions of Judicial Ethics and Policy,* 29 Fordham Urb. L.J. 941 (2002).

2   *See, e.g., Ward v. Village of Monroeville,* 409 U.S. 57, 62 (1972); *In re Murchison,* 349 U.S. 133, 136 (1955).

3   *Del Vecchio v. Illinois Dep't of Corrections,* 31 F.3d 1363, 1372 (7th Cir. 1994).

4   *See* John P. Frank, *Disqualification of Judges,* 56 Yale L.J. 605, 609, 618–19 (1947).

5   *See, e.g., Aetna Life Ins. Co. v. Lavoie,* 475 U.S. 813 (1986) (decision in case would set legal precedent bearing directly on two pending cases filed by judge as plaintiff); *Ward v. Village of Monroeville,* 409 U.S. 57, 60 (1972) (city mayor could not sit as traffic court judge because responsibility for town finances provided incentive to find against defendants to "maintain the high level of contribution from the mayor's court"); *Mayberry v. Pennsylvania,* 400 U.S. 455, 466 (1971) (judge could not try defendant for contempt of court based on defendant's insults during

constitutional provision does not require recusal, however, where there are other conceivable reasons for a judge to be biased. For example, even though they may offer a "possible temptation" to be biased, "[m]atters of kinship [or] personal bias . . . would generally be matters of legislative discretion."[6] As one court has explained:

> This merely recognizes, at least implicitly, that in the real world, "possible temptations" to be biased abound. Judges are human; like all humans, their outlooks are shaped by their lives' experiences. It would be unrealistic to suppose that judges do not bring to the bench those experiences and attendant biases they may create. A person could find something in the background of most judges which in many cases would lead that person to conclude that the judge has a "possible temptation" to be biased. But not all temptations are created equal. We expect—even demand—that judges rise above these potential biasing influences, and in most cases we presume judges do.
>
> * * *
>
> As the common law recognized, and as experience teaches, the lure of lucre is a particularly strong motivation, and therefore judges ought to be prohibited from presiding over cases in whose outcomes they have a direct financial interest. Of course, the Supreme Court has held that the due process clause requires disqualification for interests besides pecuniary interests. But the constitutional standard the Supreme Court has applied in determining when disqualification is necessary recognizes the same reality the common law recognized: judges are subject to a myriad of biasing influences; judges for the most part are presumptively capable of overcoming those influences and rendering evenhanded justice; and only a strong, direct interest in the outcome of a case is sufficient to overcome that presumption of evenhandedness.[7]

---

previous trial, because defendant's insults were "apt to strike 'at the most vulnerable and human qualities of a judge's temperament' "); *Tumey v. Ohio*, 273 U.S. 510 (1927) (judge in criminal case was paid only if defendant was convicted).

6   *Aetna Life Ins.*, 475 U.S. at 820; *see also Tumey*, 273 U.S. at 523.

7   *Del Vecchio*, 31 F.3d at 1372–73.

Food for Thought

In an opening statement to the 2005 confirmation hearing before the Senate Judiciary Committee, Chief Justice Roberts famously remarked: "Judges are like umpires. Umpires don't make the rules; they apply them. The role of an umpire and a judge is critical. They make sure everybody plays by the rules. But it is a limited role. Nobody ever went to a ball game to see the umpire. . . I will remember that it's my job to call balls and strikes and not to pitch or bat." But does remaining neutral and impartial mean the same thing as being apolitical or without ideology? Lee Epstein, William M. Landes, and Richard A. Posner analyze a large volume of data showing that, overwhelmingly, "[j]ustices appointed by Republican presidents vote more conservatively on average than justices appointed by Democratic ones, with the difference being most pronounced in civil rights cases." As you read this section, consider the difference between how financial or personal biases are treated as compared to political or ideological biases. Does the difference make sense? *See* Lee Epstein, William M. Landes, and Richard A. Posner, *The Behavior of Federal Judges: A Theoretical and Empirical Study of Rational Choice* (Harvard University Press 2013); see also Adam Liptak, *'Politicians in Robes'? Not Exactly, But . . .*, N.Y. Times, Nov, 26, 2012, at A17.

Thus, for the most part, the Constitution leaves questions of judicial disqualification, and judicial ethics generally, to be decided by legislators through the enactment of relevant statutes, by the judiciary through the adoption and interpretation of codes of judicial ethics, and by judges individually.

Statutory Requirements. Various federal and state statutes impose restrictions beyond the constitutional ones.[8] Of course, criminal law forbids judges from seeking or accepting a bribe.[9] Of more frequent relevance are statutes requiring judges to recuse themselves in circumstances where they have, or appear to have, a bias or interest that would influence their decisions. For example, 28 U.S.C. § 455, the federal disqualification statute, which dates back to 1911, requires a judge to disqualify himself in any proceeding where his impartiality might reasonably be questioned. The statute also identifies particular circumstances in which a judge must disqualify himself, including "[w]here he has a personal bias or prejudice concerning a party, or personal knowledge of disputed evidentiary facts concerning the proceeding"; where he worked on the matter while in private practice or as a government employee; and where he or a close family member has a financial interest or other interest or involvement in the controversy. The federal disqualification statute requires a judge to "inform himself about his personal and fiduciary financial interests," 28 U.S.C. § 455(c), in order to decide whether disqualification is required.

Various state and federal laws also require judges to disclose certain financial information. For example, federal law, 5 U.S.C.A., app. 4, §§ 101–111 (West 2001), requires federal judges to file annual financial disclosure forms. These forms identify and describe all gifts of more than a minimal amount received in the prior year (except when received from a relative or, in the case

---

8   *See, e.g.*, 5 U.S.C.A., app. 4, §§ 101–111 (West 2001) (requiring judges to make certain financial disclosures); Mass. Ann. Laws Ch. 268B, § 5 (Law. Co-op 1992) (same).

9   For example, a federal criminal statute makes it a crime for a federal judge to seek or accept compensation in relation to any proceeding, request for a ruling, or other determination or matter involving the United States. 18 U.S.C. § 203(a) (2000).

of food, lodging, or entertainment, as "personal hospitality"), and all reimbursements in more than minimal amounts received in the prior year. Additionally, certain state laws applicable to government officials generally, or to judges in particular, impose further restrictions on state judges.

Codes of Conduct. Finally, judges are regulated by judicial codes of conduct adopted by state and federal judiciaries to govern the conduct of judges. The federal judiciary and most state judiciaries have adopted, with different degrees of variation, a code of conduct drafted by the American Bar Association. The earliest judicial code, the ABA Canons of Judicial Conduct, was drafted by a committee under the direction of Chief Justice Howard Taft and approved by the ABA in 1924. This early code was comprehensively reviewed from 1969 to 1972 by an ABA committee chaired by retired Chief Justice Roger J. Traynor of the California Supreme Court and comprised of thirteen members, including Supreme

For Additional Research

For treatises on judicial ethics, *see* James J. Alfini et al., *Judicial Conduct and Ethics*; Richard E. Flamm, *Judicial Disqualification.*

Court Justice Potter Stewart and five other state or federal judges. The committee produced the Code of Judicial Conduct that was approved by the ABA in August 1972. The Code was substantially amended in 1990 and again in 2007. Most states have judicial commissions, typically comprised of both judges and lawyers, who have authority to investigate violations of the state's judicial code and to discipline judges who are found to have engaged in violations.

B. Performing the Duties of the Judicial Office

Judicial independence and impartiality are dominant principles running through the Codes of Judicial Conduct. Judges must act independently from, and without partiality toward, third parties—be they friends and family, parties and their lawyers, or government officials. Judges must also maintain the appearance of independence and impartiality in order to promote public confidence in the particular judge and the judiciary as a whole, avoiding not only actual impropriety but also even the appearance of impropriety. *See* Rule 1.2.[10]

Some Code provisions express these principles in fairly general terms. For example, Rule 2.4 requires judges to avoid external influences on their conduct: they may not be "swayed by public clamor or fear of criticism," may not "permit family, social, political, financial, or other interests or relationships to influence [their] judicial conduct or judgment," and may not "convey or permit others to convey the impression that any person or organization is in a position to influence" them. Similarly, Rule 1.3 forbids a judge to "abuse the prestige of

---

10   As with the ABA's Model Rules of Professional Conduct, the ABA asserts copyright in the language of the Model Code of Judicial Conduct. Most states have enacted a similar code of judicial conduct (CJC), and the language from these various state codes is in the public domain. Thus, when quoting a particular CJC Rule, we will use the language from a state CJC that matches the ABA's Model Code of Judicial Conduct.

judicial office to advance the personal or economic interests of the judge or others, or allow others to do so."

Food for Thought

Suppose that you serve as an intern or law clerk for a judge. If the judge is pleased with your work, may the judge write a reference letter on judicial letterhead to help you obtain employment with a law firm, or would doing so improperly "abuse the prestige" of the judicial office for the benefit of a third party, namely, you? The Comment to Rule 1.3 clarifies that this use of judicial letterhead is permissible as long as the reference is personal and the judge does not appear to be exerting pressure on the letter's recipient by virtue of the judicial office. Where is the line between a permissible and impermissible letter of reference? And where is the line between other permissible and impermissible uses of judicial letterhead and credentials? May a judge telephone a restaurant and request a reservation for "*Judge* Jones"?

To some extent, the Rule's accompanying Comment illustrates these general prohibitions, and opinions build on them. For example, judges may be disciplined for abusing the prestige of their judicial office to advance private interests when they use their official letterhead or position for personal benefit—*e.g.*, to attempt to persuade the police not to give them speeding tickets or to obtain other favorable treatment by government authorities.

Take Note

May a judge refuse to perform same-sex marriages based on firmly held religious beliefs regarding marriage? According to a number of state ethics opinions and a recent ABA Formal Opinion, the answer is "no," if the judge has discretion to perform marriages and chooses to do so for opposite-sex couples but not for same-sex couples. Such uneven treatment generally calls into question a judge's integrity and impartiality and specifically evinces bias and prejudice. *See* ABA Formal Opinion 485 (Feb. 14, 2019).

[Question 7-6]

A judge presided over a commercial lawsuit in which the parties were bitterly opposed. In the course of discovery, the lawyers on both sides filed motions accusing the opposing party and its lawyers of withholding evidence and other misconduct. After fully familiarizing herself with the lawsuit, the judge concluded that the case was a close one and that the parties would benefit from a settlement rather than continuing to expend thousands of dollars in legal fees. Without telling the parties and their lawyers that she intended to do so, she spoke separately with the lawyers for both parties in an effort to facilitate a settlement. First, she telephoned the plaintiff's lawyer and said that, while she did not intend to intimate anything about how she would rule on future motions, she strongly suggested that the parties try to reach a fair settlement. The judge then telephoned the defendant's lawyer and conveyed exactly the same message. The judge reasonably believed that neither party would gain a procedural, substantive, or tactical advantage as a result of these communications.

come back
to this

Was the judge's conduct proper?

(A) No, because a judge may not confer with lawyers in a pending matter on an ex parte basis other than for scheduling, administrative, or emergency purposes.

(B) No, because the judge did not obtain the parties' consent before communicating with the lawyers on an ex parte basis for settlement purposes.

(C) Yes, because a judge may confer with lawyers in a pending matter on an ex parte basis in an effort to settle a pending matter.

(D) Yes, because the judge reasonably believed that neither party would gain a procedural, substantive, or tactical advantage as a result of the communications.

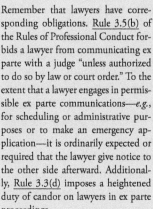

Make the Connection

Remember that lawyers have corresponding obligations. Rule 3.5(b) of the Rules of Professional Conduct forbids a lawyer from communicating ex parte with a judge "unless authorized to do so by law or court order." To the extent that a lawyer engages in permissible ex parte communications—*e.g.*, for scheduling or administrative purposes or to make an emergency application—it is ordinarily expected or required that the lawyer give notice to the other side afterward. Additionally, Rule 3.3(d) imposes a heightened duty of candor on lawyers in ex parte proceedings.

[Question 7-7]

Prior to the trial of a criminal case, a judge heard oral argument regarding whether certain forensic evidence offered by the prosecution was sufficiently reliable to be admitted. At the conclusion of the argument, the judge reserved ruling in order to review the parties' memoranda of law and the authorities they cited. Afterward, still uncertain how to rule, the judge conducted independent online research which led to her discovery of several law review articles that the lawyers had not cited. The articles reached different conclusions regarding the admissibility of the relevant forensic technique, which was a new one. Eager to rule correctly on a novel legal question, the judge sought further guidance. She asked a disinterested scientist at the state university to provide, without compensation, a written opinion regarding the reliability of the forensic evidence in question. The judge notified the prosecutor and defense lawyer before contacting the scientist, and neither objected. After the scientist submitted his written opinion, the judge gave the lawyers an opportunity to submit written responses. However, she denied the defense lawyer's request for an opportunity to question the scientist at a hearing.

Did the judge act properly?

(A) No, because she conducted independent online research and then took the initiative to obtain an opinion from a scientist regarding the reliability of forensic evidence.

(B) No, because she did not provide the lawyers an opportunity to question the scientist at a hearing.

Yes, because she gave the lawyers an opportunity to object in advance to her consultation with the scientist and then to respond to the scientist's written advice.

(D) Yes, because she did not compensate the scientist for providing an opinion.

An important provision of the judicial code promoting judicial fairness is Rule 2.9, governing ex parte communications. In general, Rule 2.9(A) prohibits the judge from communicating with anyone—including, but not limited to, a lawyer or party to a proceeding—"concerning a pending or impending matter" if the communication occurs "outside the presence of the parties or their lawyers." For example, the judge may not communicate about the case with one of the lawyers outside the presence of the other lawyers; nor may the judge talk about the case with a friend. But there are exceptions contained in Rule 2.9(A), including that, in specified circumstances, the judge may engage in "ex parte communication for scheduling, administrative, or emergency purposes, which does not address substantive applications." Also, under specified circumstances, "[a] judge may obtain written advice of a disinterested expert on the law applicable to a proceeding before the judge," talk about the case with another judge (but not *any* other judge), or confer separately with the parties, with their prior consent, in order to promote a settlement. Of course, the judge may consult with court staff—*e.g.*, the judge's law clerks—and with court officials. And the judge may communicate ex parte when authorized by law to do so—for example, when the law allows a party to make an emergency application outside the presence of the opposing party.

Also important is Rule 2.9(C), forbidding the judge from conducting an independent factual investigation or considering facts outside the record other than where the evidence rules allow "judicial notice" of an undisputed fact. This means that a technology-savvy judge must avoid the temptation to go online and seek publicly available information about a case or party. Rule 2.9(D) requires the judge to impose the same restraint on judicial staff.

For Additional Research

For an ethics opinion that elaborates upon the scope of the prohibition against judges conducting independent factual research online or otherwise, see ABA Formal Opinion 478 (Dec. 8, 2017).

Food for Thought

Rule 2.8(B) requires a judge to "be patient, dignified, and courteous" to parties, their lawyers, and others with whom the judge interacts. Bruce A. Green and Rebecca Roiphe criticize the courtesy rule in *Regulating Discourtesy on the Bench: A Study in the Evolution of Judicial Independence*, 64 N.Y.U. Ann. Surv. Am. L. 497 (2009), on the ground that judges should be free to be a bit impatient or discourteous and that, in any event, being human, judges sometimes cannot help it. They argue that judges should be able to bring their full personalities to the task of judging, even at risk of treating parties and lawyers impatiently, particularly in the context of problem-solving courts where judges are not supposed to be the equivalent of umpires, calling balls and strikes, as Chief Justice John Roberts characterized the judge's role in his confirmation hearings. They suggest that the courtesy rule ultimately encroaches on judicial independence: by putting judges at risk of discipline for rudeness, the rule discourages judges from engaging in legitimate judicial techniques.

C. Judicial Disqualification

[Question 7-8]

A judge was recently appointed to the state trial court after practicing law for 20 years. One of his neighbors works at a local manufacturing company. Shortly after taking the bench, the judge chatted with the neighbor at a fundraiser for a local charity. The neighbor was not a close personal friend and was unaware of the judge's appointment to the bench. The neighbor complained about being unfairly denied a promotion, describing in detail how male employees who were less qualified had been promoted instead of her. The neighbor then asked whether the judge might be available to represent her in an employment discrimination action. The judge said he could not do so because he was now a judge, and he was careful not to give the neighbor any advice. The neighbor later retained a lawyer who filed a lawsuit on her behalf. The case was assigned to the judge.

Must the judge disqualify himself in the proceeding?

(A) No, because he did not serve as a lawyer in the matter and had been careful not to give the neighbor any legal advice.

(B) No, because his neighbor was not a close personal friend or relative.

(C) Yes, because he has a personal relationship with the neighbor, who is a party to the proceeding.

(D) Yes, because he gained personal knowledge of disputed facts from talking with his neighbor.

[Question 7-9]

A judge was assigned to preside over a small commercial dispute between a bank and two of its customers. The judge's spouse was a vice president of the bank but was uninvolved in the lawsuit. Reasonably believing that she could fairly preside over the lawsuit, which would be tried before a jury, the judge entered a written order disclosing her spouse's position in the bank and asking the parties and their lawyers to consider waiving her disqualification. The parties' lawyers subsequently advised the judge that they and their clients agreed that she should not be disqualified.

Must the judge disqualify herself in the proceeding?

(A) Yes, because the judge's spouse is an officer of the bank, which is a party to the dispute, and therefore her impartiality might reasonably be questioned.

(B) Yes, because the judge asked the parties and their lawyers to consider waiving her disqualification, rather than leaving it to them to initiate any consideration of the question.

(C) No, because the judge's spouse was not a party to the proceeding, and therefore her disqualification would not be required even if the parties did not waive it.

(D) No, because the parties and their lawyers waived disqualification.

It's Latin to Me

The Code of Judicial Conduct includes a section on Terminology, which defines "de minimis" for purposes of Rule 2.11 to mean "an insignificant interest that could not raise a reasonable question regarding the lawyer's impartiality."

Rule 2.11 addresses judicial disqualification. Rule 2.11(A) requires a judge to "disqualify himself or herself in any proceeding in which the judge's impartiality might reasonably be questioned," and provides a non-exclusive list of circumstances where disqualification is required. These include where:

- The judge "has a personal bias or prejudice concerning a party or a party's lawyer."

- The judge has personal knowledge of facts that are in dispute in the case (*i.e.*, knowledge that comes from outside the judicial proceedings).

- The judge or a family member of the judge is a party to the proceeding, is an officer, director or trustee of a party, or is a lawyer in the proceeding.

- The judge or a family member of the judge, has a "more than a de minimis interest that could be substantially affected by the proceeding."

- The judge or a family member of the judge is "likely to be a material witness in the proceeding."

- The judge previously served as a lawyer in the matter or as a judge in the matter in another court.

In many circumstances, the parties may "waive" a judge's disqualification: Rule 2.11(C) provides that except when the judge's disqualification is based on the judge's "personal bias or prejudice concerning a party or a party's lawyer," the judge may disclose the basis for disqualification and ask the parties and their lawyers to consider, outside the judge's presence, whether to waive disqualification. The judge and his or her staff may not participate in these discussions.

Food for Thought

Should the criminal indictment of a judge automatically result in suspension without pay? Otherwise, wouldn't there be an "appearance of impropriety," as well as the strong potential for a loss of "public confidence"? Should the type of crime make a difference? What if the judge is charged with obstruction of justice in allegedly aiding an undocumented immigrant's evasion of federal immigration authorities? In *In re: Shelley M. Joseph, Sup. Jud. Ct.*, No. OE-140 (Aug. 13, 2019), the Massachusetts Supreme Judicial Court upheld its suspension of a judge under these precise circumstances, but found that she should be paid during the suspension period. Five justices concurred, with the chief justice and one other justice writing separate opinions. In his concurring opinion, Chief Justice Gants explained: "As much as this court respects the usual integrity of prosecutors and grand juries, we cannot delegate to them the decision to suspend a judge without pay through the issuance of an indictment, where any such indictment is based solely on a finding of probable cause and where the process due for returning an indictment is far less than the process due for returning a guilty verdict." What if any other state employee, under similar circumstances, would have been suspended without pay? Does that suggest that the judge in this case received special treatment? If so, was that warranted?

It is important to note that one justice dissented, maintaining that suspending the judge without pay was the only recourse that would preserve public confidence in the judiciary. (Gaziano, J., dissenting) The concurring justices, on the other hand, seemed to believe that the suspension alone was sufficient and necessary to preserve public confidence. What is your view?

Hear from the Authors

To hear from the authors on judicial disqualification, click here.

Among the other specified grounds for disqualification under Rule 2.11 is one directed at elected judges. Rule 2.11(A)(4) provides for disqualification when a party or a party's lawyer contributed more than a designated amount to the judge's campaign. However, few states have adopted this model provision. Consequently, elected judges lack specific guidance about when they must disqualify (or "recuse") themselves when a campaign contributor appears in a case. That is the problem that led to the following decision.

Caperton v. A.T. Massey Coal Co., Inc.

556 U.S. 868 (2009)

JUSTICE KENNEDY delivered the opinion of the Court.

In this case the Supreme Court of Appeals of West Virginia reversed a trial court judgment, which had entered a jury verdict of $50 million. Five justices heard the case, and the vote to reverse was 3 to 2. The question presented is whether the Due Process Clause of the Fourteenth Amendment was violated when one of the justices in the majority denied a recusal motion. The basis for the motion was that the justice had received campaign contributions in an extraordinary amount from, and through the efforts of, the board chairman and principal officer of the corporation found liable for the damages.

Under our precedents there are objective standards that require recusal when "the probability of actual bias on the part of the judge or decisionmaker is too high to be constitutionally tolerable." Applying those precedents, we find that, in all the circumstances of this case, due process requires recusal.

I

In August 2002 a West Virginia jury returned a verdict that found respondents A.T. Massey Coal Co. and its affiliates (hereinafter Massey) liable for fraudulent misrepresentation, conceal-ment, and tortious interference with existing contractual relations. The jury awarded petitioners Hugh Caperton, Harman Development Corp., Harman Mining Corp., and Sovereign Coal Sales (hereinafter Caperton) the sum of $50 million in compensatory and punitive damages.

In June 2004 the state trial court denied Massey's post-trial motions challenging the verdict and the damages award, finding that Massey "intentionally acted in utter disregard of [Caperton's] rights and ultimately destroyed [Caperton's] businesses because, after conducting cost-benefit analyses, [Massey] concluded it was in its financial interest to do so." In March 2005 the trial court denied Massey's motion for judgment as a matter of law.

Don Blankenship is Massey's chairman, chief executive officer, and president. After the verdict but before the appeal, West Virginia held its 2004 judicial elections. Knowing the Supreme Court of Appeals of West Virginia would consider the appeal in the case, Blankenship decided to support an attorney who sought to replace Justice McGraw. Justice McGraw was a candidate for reelection to that court. The attorney who sought to replace him was Brent Benjamin.

See It

Before this Supreme Court ruling, on April 7, 2008, ABC News's *Nightline* presented a report on Don Blankenship and his relationship with judges that you can view here.

In addition to contributing the $1,000 statutory maximum to Benjamin's campaign committee, Blankenship donated almost $2.5 million to "And For The Sake Of The Kids," a political organization formed under 26 U.S.C. § 527. The § 527 organization opposed McGraw and supported Benjamin. Blankenship's donations accounted for more than two-thirds of the total funds it raised. This was not all. Blankenship spent, in addition, just over $500,000 on independent expenditures-for direct mailings and letters soliciting donations as well as television and newspaper advertisements-" 'to support . . . Brent Benjamin.' "

To provide some perspective, Blankenship's $3 million in contributions were more than the total amount spent by all other Benjamin supporters and three times the amount spent by Benjamin's own committee. Caperton contends that Blankenship spent $1 million more than the total amount spent by the campaign committees of both candidates combined.

Benjamin won. He received 382,036 votes (53.3%), and McGraw received 334,301 votes (46.7%).

In October 2005, before Massey filed its petition for appeal in West Virginia's highest court, Caperton moved to disqualify now-Justice Benjamin under the Due Process Clause and the West Virginia Code of Judicial Conduct, based on the conflict caused by Blankenship's campaign involvement. Justice Benjamin denied the motion in April 2006. * * *

In November 2007 that court reversed the $50 million verdict against Massey. The majority opinion [was] authored by then-Chief Justice Davis and joined by Justices Benjamin and Maynard. * * *

Caperton sought rehearing, and the parties moved for disqualification of three of the five justices who decided the appeal. Photos had surfaced of Justice Maynard vacationing with Blankenship in the French Riviera while the case was pending. Justice Maynard granted Caperton's recusal motion. On the other side Justice Starcher granted Massey's recusal motion, apparently based on his public criticism of Blankenship's role in the 2004 elections. In his recusal memorandum Justice Starcher urged Justice Benjamin to recuse himself as well. He noted that "Blankenship's bestowal of his personal wealth, political tactics, and 'friendship' have created a cancer in the affairs of this Court." Justice Benjamin declined Justice Starcher's suggestion and denied Caperton's recusal motion.

* * *

III

Caperton contends that Blankenship's pivotal role in getting Justice Benjamin elected created a constitutionally intolerable probability of actual bias. Though not a bribe or criminal influence, Justice Benjamin would nevertheless feel a debt of gratitude to Blankenship for his extraordinary efforts to get him elected. * * *

Justice Benjamin was careful to address the recusal motions and explain his reasons why, on his view of the controlling standard, disqualification was not in order. In four separate opinions issued during the course of the appeal, he explained why no actual bias had been established. He found no basis for recusal because Caperton failed to provide "objective evidence" or "objective information," but merely "subjective belief" of bias. Nor could anyone "point to any actual conduct or activity on [his] part which could be termed 'improper.' " In other words, based on the facts presented by Caperton, Justice Benjamin conducted a probing search into his actual motives and inclinations; and he found none to be improper. We do not question his subjective findings of impartiality and propriety. Nor do we determine whether there was actual bias.

Following accepted principles of our legal tradition respecting the proper performance of judicial functions, judges often inquire into their subjective motives and purposes in the ordinary course of deciding a case. This does not mean the inquiry is a simple one. "The work of deciding cases goes on every day in hundreds of courts throughout the land. Any judge, one might suppose, would find it easy to describe the process which he had followed a thousand times and more. Nothing could be farther from the truth." B. Cardozo, *The Nature of the Judicial Process* 9 (1921).

The judge inquires into reasons that seem to be leading to a particular result. Precedent and *stare decisis* and the text and purpose of the law and the Constitution; logic and scholarship and experience and common sense; and fairness and disinterest and neutrality are among the factors at work. To bring coherence to the process, and to seek respect for the resulting judgment, judges often explain the reasons for their conclusions and rulings. There are instances when the introspection that often attends this process may reveal that what the judge had assumed to be a proper, controlling factor is not the real one at work. If the judge discovers that some personal bias or improper consideration seems to be the actuating cause of the decision or to be an influence so difficult to dispel that there is a real possibility of undermining neutrality, the judge may think it necessary to consider withdrawing from the case.

The difficulties of inquiring into actual bias, and the fact that the inquiry is often a private one, simply underscore the need for objective rules. Otherwise there may be no adequate protection against a judge who simply misreads or misapprehends the real motives at work in deciding the case. The judge's own inquiry into actual bias, then, is not one that the law can easily superintend or review, though actual bias, if disclosed, no doubt would be grounds for appropriate relief. In lieu of exclusive reliance on that personal inquiry, or on appellate review of the judge's determination respecting actual bias, the Due Process Clause has been implemented by objective standards that do not require proof of actual bias. In defining these standards the Court has asked whether, "under a realistic appraisal of psychological tendencies and human weakness," the interest "poses such a risk of actual bias or prejudgment that the practice must be forbidden if the guarantee of due process is to be adequately implemented."

We turn to the influence at issue in this case. Not every campaign contribution by a litigant or attorney creates a probability of bias that requires a judge's recusal, but this is an exceptional case. We conclude that there is a serious risk of actual bias-based on objective and reasonable perceptions-when a person with a personal stake in a particular case had a significant and disproportionate influence in placing the judge on the case by raising funds or directing the judge's election campaign when the case was pending or imminent. The inquiry centers on the contribution's relative size in comparison to the total amount of money contributed to the campaign, the total amount spent in the election, and the apparent effect such contribution had on the outcome of the election.

Applying this principle, we conclude that Blankenship's campaign efforts had a significant and disproportionate influence in placing Justice Benjamin on the case. Blankenship contributed some $3 million to unseat the incumbent and replace him with Benjamin. His contributions eclipsed the total amount spent by all other Benjamin supporters and exceeded by 300% the amount spent by Benjamin's campaign committee.

* * *

Whether Blankenship's campaign contributions were a necessary and sufficient cause of Benjamin's victory is not the proper inquiry. Much like determining whether a judge is actually biased, proving what ultimately drives the electorate to choose a particular candidate is a difficult endeavor, not likely to lend itself to a certain conclusion. This is particularly true where, as here, there is no procedure for judicial factfinding and the sole trier of fact is the one accused of bias. Due process requires an objective inquiry into whether the contributor's influence on the election under all the circumstances "would offer a possible temptation to the average . . . judge to . . . lead him not to hold the balance nice, clear and true." Blankenship's campaign contributions-in comparison to the total amount contributed to the campaign, as well as the total amount spent in the election-had a significant and disproportionate influence on the electoral outcome. And the risk that Blankenship's influence engendered actual bias is sufficiently substantial that it "must be forbidden if the guarantee of due process is to be adequately implemented."

* * *

IV

Our decision today addresses an extraordinary situation where the Constitution requires recusal. Massey and its *amici* predict that various adverse consequences will follow from recognizing a constitutional violation here—ranging from a flood of recusal motions to unnecessary interference with judicial elections. We disagree. The facts now before us are extreme by any measure. The parties point to no other instance involving judicial campaign contributions that presents a potential for bias comparable to the circumstances in this case.

* * *

One must also take into account the judicial reforms the States have implemented to eliminate even the appearance of partiality. Almost every State-West Virginia included-has adopted the American Bar Association's objective standard: "A judge shall avoid impropriety and the appearance of impropriety." ABA Annotated Model Code of Judicial Conduct, Canon 2 (2004). The ABA Model Code's test for appearance of impropriety is "whether the conduct would create in reasonable minds a perception that the judge's ability to carry out judicial responsibilities with integrity, impartiality and competence is impaired." Canon 2A, Commentary.

* * *

"The Due Process Clause demarks only the outer boundaries of judicial disqualifications. Congress and the states, of course, remain free to impose more rigorous standards for judicial disqualification than those we find mandated here today." Because the codes of judicial conduct provide more protection than due process requires, most disputes over disqualification will be resolved without resort to the Constitution. Application of the constitutional standard implicated in this case will thus be confined to rare instances.

* * *

The judgment of the Supreme Court of Appeals of West Virginia is reversed, and the case is remanded for further proceedings not inconsistent with this opinion.

It is so ordered.

CHIEF JUSTICE ROBERTS, with whom JUSTICE SCALIA, JUSTICE THOMAS, and JUSTICE ALITO join, dissenting.

I, of course, share the majority's sincere concerns about the need to maintain a fair, independent, and impartial judiciary-and one that appears to be such. But I fear that the Court's decision will undermine rather than promote these values.

Until today, we have recognized exactly two situations in which the Federal Due Process Clause requires disqualification of a judge: when the judge has a financial interest in the outcome of the case, and when the judge is trying a defendant for certain criminal contempts. Vaguer notions of bias or the appearance of bias were never a basis for disqualification, either at common law or under our constitutional precedents. Those issues were instead addressed by legislation or court rules.

Today, however, the Court enlists the Due Process Clause to overturn a judge's failure to recuse because of a "probability of bias." Unlike the established grounds for disqualification, a "probability of bias" cannot be defined in any limited way. The Court's new "rule" provides no guidance to judges and litigants about when recusal will be constitutionally required. This will inevitably lead to an increase in allegations that judges are biased, however groundless those charges may be. The end result will do far more to erode public confidence in judicial impartiality than an isolated failure to recuse in a particular case.

* * *

III

A

To its credit, the Court seems to recognize that the inherently boundless nature of its new rule poses a problem. But the majority's only answer is that the present case is an "extreme" one, so there is no need to worry about other cases. The Court repeats this point over and over.

But this is just so much whistling past the graveyard. Claims that have little chance of success are nonetheless frequently filed. The success rate for certiorari petitions before this Court is approximately 1.1%, and yet the previous Term some 8,241 were filed. Every one of the "*Caperton* motions" or appeals or § 1983 actions will claim that the judge is biased, or probably biased, bringing the judge and the judicial system into disrepute. And all future litigants will assert that their case is *really* the most extreme thus far.

Extreme cases often test the bounds of established legal principles. There is a cost to yielding to the desire to correct the extreme case, rather than adhering to the legal principle. That cost has been demonstrated so often that it is captured in a legal aphorism: "Hard cases make bad law."

* * *

Go Online

The respondent, Massey Coal, was the operator of a West Virginia mine where, in 2010, an explosion killed 29 in the United States's worst mine disaster in forty years. Click here for more details.

It is an old cliché, but sometimes the cure is worse than the disease. I am sure there are cases where a "probability of bias" should lead the prudent judge to step aside, but the judge fails to do so. Maybe this is one of them. But I believe that opening the door to recusal claims under the Due Process Clause, for an amorphous "probability of bias," will itself bring our judicial system into undeserved disrepute, and diminish the confidence of the American people in the fairness and integrity of their courts. I hope I am wrong.

I respectfully dissent.

[JUSTICE SCALIA's dissenting opinion is omitted.]

Do you agree with the dissenting Justices' prediction in *Caperton* that elected judges who previously received campaign contributions from a lawyer or party (and who do not disqualify themselves on their own initiative) will be flooded by disqualification motions? Would you predict that if lawyers begin to file frequent *Caperton* motions, the public will become aware of the practice, will perceive that the lawyers are involved in litigation gamesmanship, and will lose respect for the judicial process as a result?

According to *Caperton*, one of the state court justices recused himself "apparently based on his public criticism of Blankenship's role in the 2004 elections." Should he have refrained from making this criticism? Several provisions of the judicial code limit judges' ability to speak off the bench or require their recusal when they have done so. Rule 2.11(A)(5) requires a judge's disqualification when "[t]he judge . . . has made a public statement, other than in a court proceeding, judicial decision, or opinion, that commits or appears to commit the judge to reach a particular result or rule in a particular way in the proceeding or controversy." Rule 2.10 generally forbids a judge from making public statements about a pending or impending case outside the context of the judicial proceedings if the statements might affect the outcome or impair the fairness of the litigation.

Food for Thought

In July 2016, while the presidential campaign was in full swing, Supreme Court Justice Ruth Bader Ginsburg gave a newspaper interview in which she was quoted as saying about the Republican nominee, "I can't imagine what this place would be—I can't imagine what the country would be—with Donald Trump as our president." The Justice was criticized for making this comment. Some noted that Rule 4.1 restricts judges' participation in political activities in order to promote the appearance that judges decide cases solely based on the law and facts, free from political influence and political pressure. Rule 4.1(A)(3) in particular provides that a judge "shall not publicly endorse or oppose a candidate for any public office." Critics acknowledged that Supreme Court Justices are not governed by the Code of Judicial Conduct but suggested that the premises of Rule 4.1 were relevant to the Justices in exercising their judgment. Some also raised concern that, if the election was thrown in doubt and came before the Supreme Court, as in the case of Bush v. Gore, Justice Ginsburg might have to recuse herself. Others defended her, maintaining that all Justices have political preferences, whether or not they are publicly expressed, and that the pretense that the Justices are above politics need not be maintained. After a few days of news coverage, Justice Ginsburg issued a statement acknowledging: "On reflection, my recent remarks in response to press inquiries were ill-advised and I regret making them. Judges should avoid commenting on a candidate for public office. In the future I will be more circumspect."

Another West Virginia justice in *Caperton* recused himself after photos surfaced of him vacationing with Blankenship, the chairman of the appellant company, "in the French Riviera while the case was pending." Was the justice's disqualification ("recusal") required, or was the justice being unduly cautious? Is the risk of judicial partiality diminished because Blankenship was not himself a party but was simply the chairman of a corporate party? Imagine a judge in a small rural community who knows his or her neighbors, especially the community's lawyers, and considers many of them friends. Is it necessary for the judge to be disqualified when a friend or acquaintance is a lawyer or party, because the judge may be partial or have knowledge of the case gained outside the courtroom? Jeremy M. Miller argues in *Judicial Recusal and Disqualification: The Need for a Per Se Rule on Friendship (Not Acquaintance)*, 33 Pepp. L. Rev. 575 (2006) that the existing provisions of the judicial code do not adequately deal with the problems raised by judges' friendships. Recent ABA Formal Opinion 488 maintains that whether a judge's "friendship" with a lawyer or a party should result in disqualification depends on the circumstances. *See* ABA Formal Op. 488 (Sept. 5, 2019).

What about judges using social media? Should judges be disqualified if they have "friended" an attorney or party who appears before them? *Compare* California Judges Ass'n Judicial Ethics Comm. Op. 66 (2010) (opining that judges are prohibited from including in their social media networks lawyers with cases pending before them), *with Law Offices of Herssein & Herssein, P.A. v. United Services Automobile Ass'n*, 271 So.3d 889 (Fla. S. Ct., Nov. 2018), (holding that, standing alone, Facebook "friendship" between a trial judge and an attorney appearing before the judge does not provide sufficient ground for disqualification) *and* Ohio Sup. Ct. Bd. of Comm'rs. on Grievances and Discipline Op. 2010-7 (2010) (judges may include lawyers appearing before them in their online social networks provided the relationship otherwise is consistent with Ohio's Code of Judicial Conduct). *See also* ABA Formal Op. 462 (Feb. 21, 2013) (reaching a conclusion consistent with the Ohio opinion).

Food for Thought

Should there be an exception to the restriction on judicial speech to enable judges to correct public misunderstandings about pending proceedings or to respond to unfair criticism (equivalent to the fair comment provision of Rule 3.6(c) of the Rules of Professional Conduct, which allows litigators to make otherwise impermissible public comments "to protect a client from the substantial undue prejudicial effect of recent publicity")? In 2007, the ABA considered, but rejected, a proposed addition to Rule 2.10 of the judical code to allow a judge to respond "to allegations in the media or elsewhere concerning the judge's conduct in a matter." U.S. District Judge Nancy Gertner argued in favor of the exception in *"Tradeoffs of Candor: Does Judicial Transparency Erode Legitimacy?" Symposium: Remarks of Hon. Nancy Gertner*, 64 N.Y.U. Ann. Surv. Am. L. 449 (2009), based on her experience in a school desegregation case. In response to a newspaper article which erroneously criticized her for denying certification of the lawsuit as a class action, she wrote to the newspaper to explain that she had simply postponed ruling on the motion for class certification pending further discovery and she enclosed a copy of her order. In a divided decision, the court of appeals subsequently disqualified her from continuing to preside in the case, based on what it found to be an impermissible communication with the press. For additional writings on this subject, *see* Nancy Gertner, *To Speak or Not to Speak: Musings on Judicial Silence*, 32 Hofstra L. Rev. 1147 (2004); Mark I. Harrison & Keith Swisher, *When Judges Should Be Seen, Not Heard: Extrajudicial Comments Concerning Pending Cases and the Controversial Self-Defense Exception in the New Code of Judicial Conduct*, 64 N.Y.U. Ann. Surv. Am. L. 559 (2009).

Williams v. Pennsylvania

136 S. Ct. 1899 (2016)

Justice Kennedy delivered the opinion of the Court.

[Terrance Williams was tried for murdering a 56 year old man, Amos Norwood, in Philadephia in 1984. Williams was 18 years old at the time of the murder. The prosecution's principal witness was Williams's friend, Marc Draper, who participated with Williams in beating the victim to death. During the trial, the trial prosecutor sought permission to seek the death penalty, and the elected Philadelphia District Attorney, Ronald Castille, approved in writing, in response to the trial prosecutor's written memo about the case. The jury found Williams guilty and, during the sentencing stage, the prosecutor successfully argued that the death penalty was justified, in part, because Williams had no reason for killing Norwood. Only years later did Williams's lawyers learn from Draper that he had told the prosecutors that Williams was in a sexual relationship with the victim that was the reason for the killing, and also that at the time of the trial, prosecutors had made an undisclosed promise to write to the parole board on Draper's behalf.

Williams brought a succession of post-conviction motions. His fifth habeas petition sought post-conviction relief based on the prosecution's newly discovered failure to disclose helpful information to which he was constitutionally entitled. After conducting a hearing and reviewing the previously undisclosed files of the prosecutor and police, a judge of the Philadelphia Court of Common Pleas stayed Williams's execution and ordered a new sentencing hearing, finding that the prosecution had suppressed material, exculpatory evidence in violation of *Brady*.

When the State appealed the decision to the Pennsylvania Supreme Court, Ronald Castille—the elected prosecutor at the time of the trial—was now Chief Justice. Williams filed a motion asking Chief Justice Castille to recuse himself, but the motion was denied. The state supreme court then unanimously overturned the lower court's order and reinstated the death penalty. Chief Justice Castille authored a concurrence denouncing Williams's lawyers for their "obstructionist anti-death penalty agenda."]

II

A

Williams contends that Chief Justice Castille's decision as district attorney to seek a death sentence against him barred the chief justice from later adjudicating Williams's petition to overturn that sentence. Chief Justice Castille, Williams argues, violated the Due Process Clause of the Fourteenth Amendment by acting as both accuser and judge in his case.

The Court's due process precedents do not set forth a specific test governing recusal when, as here, a judge had prior involvement in a case as a prosecutor. For the reasons explained below, however, the principles on which these precedents rest dictate the rule that must control in the circumstances here. * * *

Due process guarantees "an absence of actual bias" on the part of a judge. In re Murchison, 349 U. S. 133, 136 (1955). Bias is easy to attribute to others and difficult to discern in oneself. To establish an enforceable and workable framework, the Court's precedents apply an objective standard that, in the usual case, avoids having to determine whether actual bias is present. The Court asks not whether a judge harbors an actual, subjective bias, but instead whether, as an objective matter, "the average judge in his position is 'likely' to be neutral, or whether there is an unconstitutional 'potential for bias.' " Of particular relevance to the instant case, the Court has determined that an unconstitutional potential for bias exists when the same person serves as both accuser and adjudicator in a case. This objective risk of bias is reflected in the due process maxim that "no man can be a judge in his own case and no man is permitted to try cases where he has an interest in the outcome."

The due process guarantee that "no man can be a judge in his own case" would have little substance if it did not disqualify a former prosecutor from sitting in judgment of a prosecution in which he or she had made a critical decision. * * *

No attorney is more integral to the accusatory process than a prosecutor who participates in a major adversary decision. When a judge has served as an advocate for the State in the very case the court is now asked to adjudicate, a serious question arises as to whether the judge, even with the most diligent effort, could set aside any personal interest in the outcome. There is, furthermore, a risk that the judge "would be so psychologically wedded" to his or her previous position as a prosecutor that the judge "would consciously or unconsciously avoid the appearance of having erred or changed position." In addition, the judge's "own personal knowledge and impression" of the case, acquired through his or her role in the prosecution, may carry far more weight with the judge than the parties' arguments to the court. * * *

B

This leads to the question whether Chief Justice Castille's authorization to seek the death penalty against Williams amounts to significant, personal involvement in a critical trial decision. The Court now concludes that it was a significant, personal involvement; and, as a result, Chief Justice Castille's failure to recuse from Williams's case presented an unconstitutional risk of bias.

As an initial matter, there can be no doubt that the decision to pursue the death penalty is a critical choice in the adversary process. Indeed, after a defendant is charged with a death-eligible crime, whether to ask a jury to end the defendant's life is one of the most serious discretionary decisions a prosecutor can be called upon to make.

Nor is there any doubt that Chief Justice Castille had a significant role in this decision. Without his express authorization, the Commonwealth would not have been able to pursue a death sentence against Williams. The importance of this decision and the profound consequences it carries make it evident that a responsible prosecutor would deem it to be a most significant exercise of his or her official discretion and professional judgment. * * *

Chief Justice Castille's own comments while running for judicial office refute the Commonwealth's claim that he played a mere ministerial role in capital sentencing decisions. During the chief justice's election campaign, multiple news outlets reported his statement that he "sent 45 people to death rows" as district attorney. Chief Justice Castille's willingness to take personal responsibility for the death sentences obtained during his tenure as district attorney indicate that, in his own view, he played a meaningful role in those sentencing decisions and considered his involvement to be an important duty of his office. * * *

The potential conflict of interest posed by the PCRA court's findings illustrates the utility of statutes and professional codes of conduct that "provide more protection than due process requires." It is important to note that due process "demarks only the outer boundaries of judicial disqualifications." Most questions of recusal are addressed by more stringent and detailed ethical rules, which in many jurisdictions already require disqualification under the circumstances of this case. * * *

The judgment of the Supreme Court of Pennsylvania is vacated, and the case is remanded for further proceedings not inconsistent with this opinion.

It is so ordered.

CHIEF JUSTICE ROBERTS, with whom JUSTICE ALITO joins, dissenting.

* * *

Williams does not assert that Chief Justice Castille had any prior knowledge of the alleged failure of the prosecution to turn over such evidence, and he does not argue that Chief Justice Castille had previously made any decision with respect to that evidence in his role as prosecutor. Even assuming that Chief Justice Castille remembered the contents of the memo almost 30 years later—which is doubtful—the memo could not have given Chief Justice Castille any special "impression" of facts or issues not raised in that memo.

The majority attempts to justify its rule based on the "risk" that a judge "would be so psychologically wedded to his or her previous position as a prosecutor that the judge would consciously or unconsciously avoid the appearance of having erred or changed position." But as a matter of simple logic, nothing about how Chief Justice Castille might rule on Williams's fifth habeas petition would suggest that the judge had erred or changed his position on the distinct question whether to seek the death penalty prior to trial. In sum, there was not such an "objective risk of actual bias," that it was fundamentally unfair for Chief Justice Castille to participate in the decision of an issue having nothing to do with his prior participation in the case.

* * *

[JUSTICE THOMAS's dissenting opinion is omitted.]

Food for Thought

In West Virginia (*Caperton*), there was a process for replacing justices who recused themselves, but that is not true in all jurisdictions, including in Pennsylvania (*Williams v. Pennsylvania*) and the U.S. Supreme Court. Supreme Court Justices, like other federal judges, are governed by 28 U.S.C. § 455(a), which provides "any justice, judge, or magistrate of the United States shall disqualify himself in any proceeding in which his impartiality might reasonably be questioned." In *Liteky v. United States*, 510 U.S. 540, 558 (1994), Justice Kennedy stated: "[U]nder § 455(a), a judge should be disqualified only if it appears that he or she harbors an aversion, hostility or disposition of a kind that a fair-minded person could not set aside when judging the dispute." If a Justice of the U.S. Supreme Court recuses himself or herself, the other eight Justices decide the case. Sometimes, the Justices divide 4–4, with the result that no majority decision is issued and the lower court opinion is affirmed "by an equally divided court." Under these circumstances, should a Justice be more hesitant than a lower-court judge to disqualify himself or herself?

Cheney v. United States District Court for the District of Columbia

541 U.S. 913 (2004)

Memorandum of JUSTICE SCALIA.

I have before me a motion to recuse in these cases consolidated below. The motion is filed on behalf of respondent Sierra Club. The other private respondent, Judicial Watch, Inc., does not join the motion and has publicly stated that it "does not believe the presently-known facts about the hunting trip satisfy the legal standards requiring recusal." (The District Court, a nominal party in this mandamus action, has of course made no appearance.) Since the cases have been consolidated, however, recusal in the one would entail recusal in the other.

I

The decision whether a judge's impartiality can " 'reasonably be questioned' " is to be made in light of the facts as they existed, and not as they were surmised or reported. The facts here were as follows:

For five years or so, I have been going to Louisiana during the Court's long December–January recess, to the duck-hunting camp of a friend whom I met through two hunting companions from Baton Rouge, one a dentist and the other a worker in the field of handicapped rehabilitation. The last three years, I have been accompanied on this trip by a son-in-law who lives near me. Our friend and host, Wallace Carline, has never, as far as I know, had business before this Court. He is not, as some reports have described him, an "energy industry executive" in the sense that summons up boardrooms of ExxonMobil or Con Edison. He runs his own company that provides services and equipment rental to oil rigs in the Gulf of Mexico.

During my December 2002 visit, I learned that Mr. Carline was an admirer of Vice President Cheney. Knowing that the Vice President, with whom I am well acquainted (from our years serving together in the Ford administration), is an enthusiastic duck-hunter, I asked whether Mr. Carline would like to invite him to our next year's hunt. The answer was yes; I conveyed the invitation (with my own warm recommendation) in the spring of 2003 and received an acceptance (subject, of course, to any superseding demands on the Vice President's time) in the summer. The Vice President said that if he did go, I would be welcome to fly down to Louisiana with him. (Because of national security requirements, of course, he must fly in a Government plane.) That invitation was later extended—if space was available—to my son-in-law and to a son who was joining the hunt for the first time; they accepted. The trip was set long before the Court granted certiorari in the present case, and indeed before the petition for certiorari had even been filed. We departed from Andrews Air Force Base at about 10 a.m. on Monday, January 5, flying in a Gulfstream jet owned by the Government. We landed in Patterson, Louisiana, and went by car to a dock where Mr. Carline met us, to take us on the 20-minute boat trip to his hunting camp. We arrived at about 2 pm., the 5 of us joining about 8 other hunters, making about 13 hunters in all; also present during our time there were about 3 members of Mr. Carline's staff, and, of course, the Vice President's staff and security detail. It was not an intimate setting. The group hunted that afternoon and Tuesday and Wednesday mornings; it fished (in two boats) Tuesday afternoon. All meals were in common. Sleeping was in rooms of two or three, except for the Vice President, who had his own quarters. Hunting was in two- or three-man blinds. As it turned out, I never hunted in the same blind with the Vice President. Nor was I alone with him at any time during the trip, except, perhaps, for instances so brief and unintentional that I would not recall them—walking to or from a boat, perhaps, or going to or from dinner. Of course we said not a word about the present case. The Vice President left the camp Wednesday afternoon, about two days after our arrival. I stayed on to hunt (with my son and son-in-law) until late Friday morning, when the three of us returned to Washington on a commercial flight from New Orleans.

II

Let me respond, at the outset, to Sierra Club's suggestion that I should "resolve any doubts in favor of recusal." That might be sound advice if I were sitting on a Court of Appeals. There, my place would be taken by another judge, and the case would proceed normally. On the Supreme Court, however, the consequence is different: The Court proceeds with eight Justices, raising the possibility that, by reason of a tie vote, it will find itself unable to resolve the significant legal issue presented by the case. Thus, as Justices stated in their 1993 Statement of Recusal Policy: "[W]e do not think it would serve the public interest to go beyond the requirements of the statute, and to recuse ourselves, out of an excess of caution, whenever a relative is a partner in the firm before us or acted as a lawyer at an earlier stage. Even one unnecessary recusal impairs the functioning of the Court." Moreover, granting the motion is (insofar as the outcome of the particular case is concerned) effectively the same as casting a vote against the petitioner. The petitioner needs five votes to overturn the judgment below, and it makes no difference whether the needed fifth vote is missing because it has been cast for the other side, or because it has not been cast at all.

Even so, recusal is the course I must take—and will take—when, on the basis of established principles and practices, I have said or done something which requires that course. I have recused for such a reason this very Term. I believe, however, that established principles and practices do not require (and thus do not permit) recusal in the present case.

A

My recusal is required if, by reason of the actions described above, my "impartiality might reasonably be questioned." Why would that result follow from my being in a sizable group of persons, in a hunting camp with the Vice President, where I never hunted with him in the same blind or had other opportunity for private conversation? The only possibility is that it would suggest I am a friend of his. But while friendship is a ground for recusal of a Justice where the personal fortune or the personal freedom of the friend is at issue, it has traditionally *not* been a ground for recusal where *official action* is at issue, no matter how important the official action was to the ambitions or the reputation of the Government officer. A rule that required Members of this Court to remove themselves from cases in which the official actions of friends were at issue would be utterly disabling. Many Justices have reached this Court precisely because they were friends of the incumbent President or other senior officials—and from the earliest days down to modern times Justices have had close personal relationships with the President and other officers of the Executive. John Quincy Adams hosted dinner parties featuring such luminaries as Chief Justice Marshall, Justices Johnson, Story, and Todd, Attorney General Wirt, and Daniel Webster. Justice Harlan and his wife often "stopped in" at the White House to see the Hayes family and pass a Sunday evening in a small group, visiting and singing hymns. Justice Stone tossed around a medicine ball with members of the Hoover administration mornings outside the White House. Justice Douglas was a regular at President Franklin Roosevelt's poker parties; Chief Justice Vinson played poker with President Truman. A no-friends rule would have disqualified much of the Court in *Youngstown Sheet & Tube Co. v. Sawyer*, 343 U.S. 579 (1952), the case that challenged President Truman's seizure of the steel mills. Most of the Justices knew Truman well, and four had been appointed by him. * * *

It is said, however, that this case is different because the federal officer (Vice President Cheney) is actually a *named party.* That is by no means a rarity. At the beginning of the current Term, there were before the Court (excluding habeas actions) no fewer than 83 cases in which high-level federal Executive officers were named in their official capacity—more than 1 in every 10 federal civil cases then pending. That an officer is named has traditionally made no difference to the proposition that friendship is not considered to affect impartiality in official-action suits. Regardless of whom they name, such suits, when the officer is the plaintiff, seek relief not for him personally but for the Government; and, when the officer is the defendant, seek relief not against him personally, but against the Government. That is why federal law provides for *automatic substitution* of the new officer when the originally named officer has been replaced. * * *

To be sure, there could be political consequences from disclosure of the fact (if it be so) that the Vice President favored business interests, and especially a sector of business with which he was formerly connected. But political consequences are not my concern, and the possibility of them does not convert an official suit into a private one. That possibility exists to a greater or lesser degree in virtually all suits involving agency action. To expect judges to take account of political consequences—and to assess the high or low degree of them—is to ask judges to do precisely what they should not do. It seems to me quite wrong (and quite impossible) to make recusal depend upon what degree of political damage a particular case can be expected to inflict.

In sum, I see nothing about this case which takes it out of the category of normal official-action litigation, where my friendship, or the appearance of my friendship, with one of the named officers does not require recusal.

* * *

As the newspaper editorials appended to the motion make clear, I have received a good deal of embarrassing criticism and adverse publicity in connection with the matters at issue here—even to the point of becoming (as the motion cruelly but accurately states) "fodder for late-night comedians." If I could have done so in good conscience, I would have been pleased to demonstrate my integrity, and immediately silence the criticism, by getting off the case. Since I believe there is no basis for recusal, I cannot. The motion is denied.

The code provisions on disqualification potentially put judges in a bit of a bind, because they are not permitted to disqualify themselves simply to avoid criticism. Rule 2.7 requires a judge to "hear and decide matters assigned to the judge, except when disqualification is required by Rule 2.11 or other law." Thus, judges have to get it exactly right: they may not disqualify themselves when disqualification is not required, but they must disqualify themselves when it is. Shouldn't judges have some wiggle room in close cases? As a practical matter, they do because judicial commissions are unlikely to sanction judges who make honest mistakes on close calls.

D. Judges' Extrajudicial Activities

[Question 7-10]

The dean of a nonprofit law school notified a justice of the state high court, who was a graduate of the school, that the law school had voted to award him an honorary doctorate degree. The dean invited the justice to accept the degree at the school's annual fundraising dinner and also invited the justice to give the keynote speech. Reasonably believing that the law school was unlikely to have matters before his court, the justice accepted. Before the dinner, the justice wrote to several of his law school classmates who were successful practitioners, encouraging them to donate to the law school in his honor. The justice gave a speech at the dinner encouraging lawyers to provide pro bono legal services. To commemorate the event, the university gave him a $750 engraved bowl which he reported at the end of the year in his annual public report of compensation, gifts and reimbursements he received.

Which of the following conduct of the justice was improper?

(A) Attending the law school's fundraising event.

(B) Soliciting donations to the law school from practicing lawyers.

(C) Encouraging lawyers to provide pro bono legal services.

(D) Accepting a $750 engraved bowl as a gift.

Judges cannot reasonably be expected to cloister themselves; they have to live in the world. But at the same time, there is a public interest in discouraging judges from activities that might undermine their impartiality. Where should the line be drawn? Robert B. McKay, then Dean of New York University School of Law, observed in *The Judiciary and Nonjudicial Activities*, 35 Law & Contemp. Probs. 9, 12 (1970):

It would be easy, but intellectually lazy, to hold that the sole business of judges is judging, that all else is at least distracting, and that accordingly a judge should avoid all nonjudicial activities that might either be time-consuming or influence his opinion on matters that come before him. The argument proves too much. If a judge is to live in *this* world and not in the isolation of a sequestered juror, he is constantly shaping his views on all kinds of matters that may come before him. The perceptions of a judge are influenced by conversations with family, friends, and colleagues; by his choices among the competing news media; his preferences in recreational activities; and even his tastes in clothes and hair styles (the long and short of it).

Skeptics may well charge overkill at this point, for of course no one suggests that judges cut themselves off from family, friends, and colleagues. But anything short of that impossible dream is unlikely to accomplish the objectives of those who seek immunization of the judiciary from all the opinion-shaping forces that surround them. It is at least arguable—and I for one would so argue—that a judge is likely to be a better dispenser of justice if he is aware of the currents and passions of the time, the developments of technology, and the sweep of events. To judge in the real world a judge must live, breathe, think, and partake of opinions in the real world.

Canon 3 calls upon a judge to "conduct the judge's personal and extrajudicial activities to minimize the risk of conflict with the obligations of judicial office," and brings together rules that are intended to restrict judges' activities that might undermine judicial impartiality without going overboard. Rule 3.1 establishes the general principle: Judges generally may engage in extrajudicial activities, but not those activities that will interfere with the judge's work, lead to frequent disqualification, or appear to undermine the judge's independence, integrity or impartiality. Other rules provide more specific guidance. For example:

- Rule 3.6 forbids a judge from being a member of an organization that invidiously discriminates on the basis of race, sex, gender, religion, national origin, ethnicity or sexual orientation. It also forbids a judge from using the facilities of such an organization (although it allows the judge to attend an isolated event when doing so does not appear to endorse the organization's practices).

- Rule 3.7(A) provides that, subject to the limitation of Rule 3.1, a judge may participate in activities "sponsored by organizations or governmental entities concerned with the law, the legal system, or the administration of justice, and those sponsored by or on behalf of educational, religious, charitable, fraternal, or civic organizations not conducted for profit." The rule provides a non-exclusive list of permissible activities, including assisting such an organization in *planning* relating to fundraising (but not in actually requesting contributions other than from members of the judge's family and other judges whom the judge does not supervise); appearing or speaking at the organization's program; or serving as an officer or director of the organization (as long as the organization does not engage in frequent litigation or have a matter likely to come before the judge). The rule is more liberal in permitting the judge's affiliation with organizations (such as bar associations) engaged in activities involving the law, the legal system or the administration of justice.

- Rule 3.7(B) allows a judge to encourage lawyers to provide pro bono legal services.

- Rule 3.9 forbids a judge from serving as a mediator or arbitrator or performing other judicial functions apart from the judge's official duties, whether or not for pay. (Of course, as part of the judge's official duties, a judge may participate in settlement conferences or attempt to mediate a dispute.)

- Rule 3.12 allows a judge to receive reasonable compensation for extrajudicial activities that are permitted—*e.g.*, for teaching law as an adjunct professor or for writing a book—as long as being compensated does not appear to undermine the judge's independence, integrity, or impartiality.

- Rule 3.13 forbids a judge from accepting "any gifts, loans, bequests, benefits, or other things of value, if acceptance is prohibited by law or would appear to a reasonable person to undermine the judge's independence, integrity or impartiality." The rule specifically permits the judge to accept certain items (in some cases, subject to a reporting requirement). These include "items with little intrinsic value," such as greeting cards; gifts, loans and other things of value from friends, relatives and others whose relationship would require the judge to be disqualified if they appeared before the judge; publications provided by the publisher for the judge's official use; and "ordinary social hospitality."

- Rule 3.14 generally allows the judge to be reimbursed for expenses in connection with permissible extracurricular activities, such as travel costs to speak at a bar association program.

Food for Thought

Is there any aspect of a judge's life that should be completely private and removed from public scrutiny? Consider the case of Texas Judge William Adams who was temporarily suspended from the bench after his daughter uploaded a video to YouTube of a beating she received from him while a teenager. Adams returned to the bench in 2012 after the Texas Commission on Judicial Conduct ruled that he should receive a warning for the conduct. Do you think a judge who hits his child should be professionally disciplined?

E. Seeking Judicial Election

Global Perspective

Many countries use a very different system for selecting judges than the U.S. judicial election or judicial appointment system. In these countries, the judiciary is a career path that one selects immediately after law school. Judges may receive extensive specialized classroom and on-the-job training and may apprentice with more senior judges. For example, in France, immediately after obtaining a law degree from an undergraduate institution, graduates who wish to become judges must take competitive exams for entrance into judicial service. Upon successful completion of the exam, students enter the French National School for the Judiciary (the ENM) where they complete a multi-year program of coursework and internships. After this program, they take another examination and those with the highest scores are the first to select positions from a list of vacancies the Ministry of Justice provides. They begin at the bottom of the hierarchical pyramid and must work their way up to higher courts, with advancement based on seniority and merit. For more information, see John Henry Merryman and Rogelio Perez-Perdomo, *The Civil Law Tradition: An Introduction to the Legal Systems of Europe and Latin America* 34 (3d ed., Stanford Univ. Press 2007); Mary L. Volcansek, *Appointing Judges the European Way*, 34 Fordham Urb. L.J. 363, 369 (2007); *see also* the European Judicial Training Network (EJTN).

Williams v. Florida Bar

575 U.S. 433 (2015)

CHIEF JUSTICE ROBERTS delivered the opinion of the Court, except as to Part II.

Our Founders vested authority to appoint federal judges in the President, with the advice and consent of the Senate, and entrusted those judges to hold their offices during good behavior. The Constitution permits States to make a different choice, and most of them have done so. In 39 States, voters elect trial or appellate judges at the polls. In an effort to preserve public confidence in the integrity of their judiciaries, many of those States prohibit judges and judicial candidates from personally soliciting funds for their campaigns. We must decide whether the First Amendment permits such restrictions on speech.

We hold that it does. Judges are not politicians, even when they come to the bench by way of the ballot. And a State's decision to elect its judiciary does not compel it to treat judicial candidates like campaigners for political office. A State may assure its people that judges will apply the law without fear or favor—and without having personally asked anyone for money. We affirm the judgment of the Florida Supreme Court.

I

A

* * *

Canon 7C(1) governs fundraising in judicial elections. The Canon, which is based on a provision in the American Bar Association's Model Code of Judicial Conduct, provides:

> "A candidate, including an incumbent judge, for a judicial office that is filled by public election between competing candidates shall not personally solicit campaign funds, or solicit attorneys for publicly stated support, but may establish committees of responsible persons to secure and manage the expenditure of funds for the candidate's campaign and to obtain public statements of support for his or her candidacy. Such committees are not prohibited from soliciting campaign contributions and public support from any person or corporation authorized by law."

Florida statutes impose additional restrictions on campaign fundraising in judicial elections. Contributors may not donate more than $1,000 per election to a trial court candidate or more than $3,000 per retention election to a Supreme Court justice. Campaign committee treasurers must file periodic reports disclosing the names of contributors and the amount of each contribution.

Judicial candidates can seek guidance about campaign ethics rules from the Florida Judicial Ethics Advisory Committee. The Committee has interpreted Canon 7 to allow a judicial candidate to serve as treasurer of his own campaign committee, learn the identity of campaign contributors, and send thank you notes to donors.

Like Florida, most other States prohibit judicial candidates from soliciting campaign funds personally, but allow them to raise money through committees. According to the American Bar Association, 30 of the 39 States that elect trial or appellate judges have adopted restrictions similar to Canon 7C(1).

B

Lanell Williams-Yulee, who refers to herself as Yulee, has practiced law in Florida since 1991. In September 2009, she decided to run for a seat on the county court for Hillsborough County, a jurisdiction of about 1.3 million people that includes the city of Tampa. Shortly after filing paperwork to enter the race, Yulee drafted a letter announcing her candidacy. The letter described her experience and desire to "bring fresh ideas and positive solutions to the Judicial bench." The letter then stated:

> "An early contribution of $25, $50, $100, $250, or $500, made payable to 'Lanell Williams-Yulee Campaign for County Judge', will help raise the initial funds needed to launch the campaign and get our message out to the public. I ask for your support [i]n meeting the primary election fund raiser goals. Thank you in advance for your support."

Yulee signed the letter and mailed it to local voters. She also posted the letter on her campaign Web site.

Yulee's bid for the bench did not unfold as she had hoped. She lost the primary to the incumbent judge. Then the Florida Bar filed a complaint against her. As relevant here, the Bar charged her with violating Rule 4-8.2(b) of the Rules Regulating the Florida Bar. That Rule requires judicial candidates to comply with applicable provisions of Florida's Code of Judicial Conduct, including the ban on personal solicitation of campaign funds in Canon 7C(1).

Yulee admitted that she had signed and sent the fundraising letter. But she argued that the Bar could not discipline her for that conduct because the First Amendment protects a judicial candidate's right to solicit campaign funds in an election.

* * *

III

The Florida Bar faces a demanding task in defending Canon 7C(1) against Yulee's First Amendment challenge. We have emphasized that "it is the rare case" in which a State demonstrates that a speech restriction is narrowly tailored to serve a compelling interest.

* * *

A

The Florida Supreme Court adopted Canon 7C(1) to promote the State's interests in "protecting the integrity of the judiciary" and "maintaining the public's confidence in an impartial judiciary." The way the Canon advances those interests is intuitive: Judges, charged with exercising strict neutrality and independence, cannot supplicate campaign donors without diminishing public confidence in judicial integrity. This principle dates back at least eight centuries to *Magna Carta*, which proclaimed, "To no one will we sell, to no one will we refuse or delay, right or justice."

* * *

The vast majority of elected judges in States that allow personal solicitation serve with fairness and honor. But "[e]ven if judges were able to refrain from favoring donors, the mere possibility that judges' decisions may be motivated by the desire to repay campaign contributions is likely to undermine the public's confidence in the judiciary." In the eyes of the public, a judge's personal solicitation could result (even unknowingly) in "a possible temptation . . . which might lead him not to hold the balance nice, clear and true." That risk is especially pronounced because most donors are lawyers and litigants who may appear before the judge they are supporting.

The concept of public confidence in judicial integrity does not easily reduce to precise definition, nor does it lend itself to proof by documentary record. But no one denies that it is genuine and compelling. In short, it is the regrettable but unavoidable appearance that judges who personally ask for money may diminish their integrity that prompted the Supreme Court of

Florida and most other States to sever the direct link between judicial candidates and campaign contributors. As the Supreme Court of Oregon explained, "the spectacle of lawyers or potential litigants directly handing over money to judicial candidates should be avoided if the public is to have faith in the impartiality of its judiciary." Moreover, personal solicitation by a judicial candidate "inevitably places the solicited individuals in a position to fear retaliation if they fail to financially support that candidate." Potential litigants then fear that "the integrity of the judicial system has been compromised, forcing them to search for an attorney in part based upon the criteria of which attorneys have made the obligatory contributions." A State's decision to elect its judges does not require it to tolerate these risks. The Florida Bar's interest is compelling.

* * *

C

* * *

By any measure, *Canon* 7C(1) restricts a narrow slice of speech. A reader of Justice Kennedy's dissent could be forgiven for concluding that the Court has just upheld a latter-day version of the Alien and Sedition Acts, approving "state censorship" that "locks the First Amendment out," imposes a "gag" on candidates, and inflicts "dead weight" on a "silenced" public debate. But in reality, Canon 7C(1) leaves judicial candidates free to discuss any issue with any person at any time. Candidates can write letters, give speeches, and put up billboards. They can contact potential supporters in person, on the phone, or online. They can promote their campaigns on radio, television, or other media. They cannot say, "Please give me money." They can, however, direct their campaign committees to do so. Whatever else may be said of the Canon, it is surely not a "wildly disproportionate restriction upon speech."

* * *

Finally, Yulee contends that Florida can accomplish its compelling interest through the less restrictive means of recusal rules and campaign contribution limits. We disagree. A rule requiring judges to recuse themselves from every case in which a lawyer or litigant made a campaign contribution would disable many jurisdictions. And a flood of postelection recusal motions could "erode public confidence in judicial impartiality" and thereby exacerbate the very appearance problem the State is trying to solve.

* * *

In sum, because Canon 7C(1) is narrowly tailored to serve a compelling government interest, the First Amendment poses no obstacle to its enforcement in this case.

* * *

The desirability of judicial elections is a question that has sparked disagreement for more than 200 years. Hamilton believed that appointing judges to positions with life tenure constituted "the best expedient which can be devised in any government to secure a steady, upright, and impartial administration of the laws." Jefferson thought that making judges "dependent on none but themselves" ran counter to the principle of "a government founded on the public will."

The federal courts reflect the view of Hamilton; most States have sided with Jefferson. Both methods have given our Nation jurists of wisdom and rectitude who have devoted themselves to maintaining "the public's respect . . . and a reserve of public goodwill, without becoming subservient to public opinion."

It is not our place to resolve this enduring debate. Our limited task is to apply the Constitution to the question presented in this case. Judicial candidates have a First Amendment right to speak in support of their campaigns. States have a compelling interest in preserving public confidence in their judiciaries. When the State adopts a narrowly tailored restriction like the one at issue here, those principles do not conflict. A State's decision to elect judges does not compel it to compromise public confidence in their integrity.

[The concurring opinion of Justice Breyer, and the dissenting opinion of Justice Scalia, are omitted.]

JUSTICE KENNEDY, **dissenting.**

* * *

First Amendment protections are both personal and structural. Free speech begins with the right of each person to think and then to express his or her own ideas. Protecting this personal sphere of intellect and conscience, in turn, creates structural safeguards for many of the processes that define a free society. The individual speech here is political speech. The process is a fair election. These realms ought to be the last place, not the first, for the Court to allow unprecedented content-based restrictions on speech.

* * *

JUSTICE ALITO, **dissenting.**

* * *

[T]his rule is about as narrowly tailored as a burlap bag. It applies to all solicitations made in the name of a candidate for judicial office—including, as was the case here, a mass mailing. It even applies to an ad in a newspaper. It applies to requests for contributions in any amount, and it applies even if the person solicited is not a lawyer, has never had any interest at stake in any case in the court in question, and has no prospect of ever having any interest at stake in any litigation in that court. If this rule can be characterized as narrowly tailored, then narrow tailoring has no meaning, and strict scrutiny, which is essential to the protection of free speech, is seriously impaired.

When petitioner sent out a form letter requesting campaign contributions, she was well within her First Amendment rights. The Florida Supreme Court violated the Constitution when it imposed a financial penalty and stained her record with a finding that she had engaged in unethical conduct. I would reverse the judgment of the Florida Supreme Court.

F. Moving from Judging (or Arbitrating) to Private Practice

[Question 7-11]

A judge retired from a state trial court and joined a litigation law firm. The losing party to a lawsuit retained the law firm to represent him on appeal. The lawsuit had briefly been assigned to the judge before he retired from the bench, and he had issued several rulings on discovery motions, but none of his rulings were relevant to the appeal. The former judge assisted in the appeal by reviewing and revising the appellate brief, but he did not include his name on any submissions to the appeals court and did not argue the appeal. The former judge never sought the parties' informed consent to his participation in the appeal.

Is the former judge subject to discipline?

(A) No, because none of his rulings as a judge were relevant to the appeal.

(B) No, because he did not include his name on any submissions to the appeals court and did not argue the appeal.

(C) Yes, because a former judge may never participate in a matter in which he participated personally and substantially as a judge.

(D) Yes, because he did not obtain all parties' informed consent, confirmed in writing, to his participation in the appeal.

[Question 7-12]

A law clerk to a state appellate judge observed all of the oral arguments heard by the judge, including arguments in cases assigned to her co-clerk. One of the appellate lawyers who argued before the judge was particularly impressive. Because the law clerk had not yet secured post-clerkship employment, she wrote the appellate lawyer to ask whether he might be interested in hiring her as an associate. In response, the appellate lawyer arranged an interview with the law clerk and eventually offered her a position as an associate to commence after the completion of her clerkship. The law clerk accepted the offer. They did not discuss the case argued by the appellate lawyer, which was still pending at the time the law clerk received the employment offer. Although the law clerk was privy to discussions about the case, it was assigned to her co-clerk, and she never performed any work on it. The law clerk did not tell the judge about her interactions with the appellate lawyer until after she accepted the job offer.

Is the law clerk subject to discipline?

(A) Yes, because she negotiated for employment with a lawyer for a party in a matter pending before the judge for whom she clerked.

(B) Yes, because she did not notify the judge before negotiating for employment with the appellate lawyer.

(C) **No, because a law clerk is not restricted from negotiating for employment with a lawyer for a party in a matter pending before the judge for whom she is clerking.**

(D) **No, because she did not participate personally and substantially in the matter in which the appellate lawyer was involved.**

Rule 1.12 of the Rules of Professional Conduct

(a)   Except as stated in paragraph (d), a lawyer shall not represent anyone in connection with a matter in which the lawyer participated personally and substantially as a judge or other adjudicative officer or law clerk to such a person or as an arbitrator, mediator or other third-party neutral, unless all parties to the proceeding give informed consent, confirmed in writing.

(b)   A lawyer shall not negotiate for employment with any person who is involved as a party or as lawyer for a party in a matter in which the lawyer is participating personally and substantially as a judge or other adjudicative officer or as an arbitrator, mediator or other third-party neutral. A lawyer serving as a law clerk to a judge or other adjudicative officer may negotiate for employment with a party or lawyer involved in a matter in which the clerk is participating personally and substantially, but only after the lawyer has notified the judge or other adjudicative officer.

(c)   If a lawyer is disqualified by paragraph (a), no lawyer in a firm with which that lawyer is associated may knowingly undertake or continue representation in the matter unless:

(1)   the disqualified lawyer is timely screened from any participation in the matter and is apportioned no part of the fee therefrom; and

(2)   written notice is promptly given to the parties and any appropriate tribunal to enable them to ascertain compliance with the provisions of this rule.

(d)   An arbitrator selected as a partisan of a party in a multimember arbitration panel is not prohibited from subsequently representing that party.

———————————

Rule 1.12 is intended to preserve judges' impartiality by removing the incentive for judges to make determinations with an eye toward future employment. Note that Rule 1.12 applies to judges' law clerks as well as to judges. Rule 1.12(b) does not forbid a law clerk from negotiating future employment with a party or lawyer involved in a matter on which the clerk is working. But it does require a judge's law clerk to notify the judge, who may then decide to take the law clerk off the case.

Rule 1.12 is the only provision of the ABA Model Rules of Professional Conduct that specifically addresses the obligations of lawyers functioning as arbitrators or other third-party neutrals. The ABA Model Code of Judicial Conduct also does not apply to lawyer-arbitrators. That is a subject for other law and standards.

Organizations administering arbitrations may develop and enforce principles of self-governance to avoid appearances of impropriety and, thereby, to promote the confidence of parties and the public in the fairness and neutrality of the arbitration process. For example, the ABA and the American Arbitration Association have approved "The Code of Ethics for Arbitrators in Commercial Disputes," containing various provisions directed at avoiding an appearance of partiality, bias, or other impropriety. Additionally, courts may refuse to confirm arbitrators' awards when the arbitrator was biased. For example, under Section 10(a)(2) of the Federal Arbitration Act, 9 U.S.C. § 10 (1988 & Supp. V 1993), as well as under similar or identical state laws, a court reviewing an arbitration award may vacate the award where there was "evident partiality" on the part of one or more arbitrators. The case law dealing with arbitrators' bias fleshes out the legal standard. In general, what courts expect of arbitrators by way of impartiality is not nearly as stringent as what they expect of judges. For example, it is not uncommon for arbitrators to be selected precisely because of their relationship or familiarity with the parties or the relevant industry.

Global Perspective

The U.S. is not the only country to consider what the rules should be when an individual moves from judging to private practice. For example, this topic is addressed in Rule 7.7 of the Model Code of Professional Conduct of the Federation of Law Societies of Canada. (The FLSC is an "umbrella" group that brings together the provincial and territorial law societies that are responsible for regulating lawyers in Canada. The FLSC promotes the development of national standards, encourages the harmonization of law society rules and procedures, and undertakes national initiatives as directed by its members, among other activities.) Rule 7.7 currently states:

> Rule 7.7 Retired Judges Returning to Practice
>
> A judge who returns to practice after retiring, resigning or being removed from the bench must not, for a period of three years, unless the governing body approves on the basis of exceptional circumstances, appear as a lawyer before the court of which the former judge was a member or before any courts of inferior jurisdiction to that court or before any administrative board or tribunal over which that court exercised an appellate or judicial review jurisdiction in any province in which the judge exercised judicial functions.

In May 2016, the Federation's Standing Committee on the Model Code of Professional Conduct issued a Discussion Paper on Post-Judicial Return to Practice that asked whether the Federation's Model Rules should be amended. The Discussion Paper noted that "issues related to post-judicial return to legal practice are complex and involve a variety of stakeholders and interests. Given the concerns expressed by members of the judiciary and the academic community, the Standing Committee has decided that a review of the Model Code rules is warranted." The Paper identified twelve questions on which the Committee sought input, including: whether a former judge should be eligible for return to practice; whether a former judge should ever appear in court and, if so, under what conditions; and whether the current rules were sufficient to govern marketing of former judges' skills and experience. The Discussion Paper also observed that the "United States and England and Wales take very different approaches to the question of judges returning to practice on retirement; in short, the United States is generally permissive of any activity a former judge may wish to undertake, while England and Wales is absolutely prohibitive."

Test Your Knowledge

To assess your understanding of the material in this Chapter, click here to take a quiz.

CHAPTER 8

What Is the Proper Role of a Lawyer?

Learning Outcomes

At the end of this Chapter, you will understand how to:

- Identify the elements of, and rationale for, the dominant conception of the lawyer's role as a neutral partisan

- Differentiate the neutral partisan role from the historical understanding of lawyers as servants of the public good

- Describe the arguments for and against alternative lawyering models grounded in moral responsibility, feminism, religion, racial justice, LGBTQ rights, and civic responsibility

- Apply each model to lawyering decisions

- Differentiate each model from the neutral partisan role

- Articulate the lawyer's role that you choose for yourself

Topic Outline for Chapter 8

	TOPIC	RELEVANT RULES, STATUTES & REGULATIONS	CHAPTER QUESTIONS
I.	Introduction		
II.	The Dominant Conception of the Neutral Partisan	Preambles to the Canons, Code, and Rules; Rules 1.1, 1.2(b), 1.4, 2.1; TN Op. 96-F-140	8-1 to 8-12
III.	Competing Visions of Professional Morality		
	A. Moral Responsibility		8-13 to 8-16
	B. Feminist		8-17 to 8-19

I.   Introduction

Now that you have learned the basic principles of the law and ethics of lawyering, we return in Chapters 8 and 9 to the questions you will face regarding professionalism, values, and professional roles raised in Chapter 1. Perhaps the most important decision you will have to make is choosing the role you will follow in your own professional life. All of these decisions will have a powerful influence on your ability to make your career a rewarding one. In the *Red State, Blue State* film featured below, Professor David Wilkins of Harvard Law School observes that "[l]awyers who have most successfully found ways to integrate themselves into their jobs and their jobs into themselves are much happier and more likely to be successful than people who feel that those parts of themselves are at war." Moreover, as many commentators with contrasting views argue throughout the Chapter, your decisions will also determine the quality of justice that our society provides.

Today, the dominant understanding of the lawyer's role is that of the neutral partisan, commonly described as the hired gun. This Chapter will explore the justifications for, and criticisms of, the neutral partisan role. It will also describe alternative proposals—the lawyer as civics teacher, moral activist, religious person, feminist, racial justice proponent, and LGBTQ rights advocate. At the end of the Chapter, you will be asked to choose the role of the lawyer with which you most identify.

You should also know that the multiple choice questions in this Chapter will be somewhat different than the doctrinal questions in Chapters 2 through 7. Many of the multiple choice questions will have correct answers. These questions will ask whether you understand the literature and ideas. The last question in the Chapter has no correct answer. It asks for your personal opinion.

II. The Dominant Conception of the Neutral Partisan in Historical and Philosophical Context

We use the term "dominant conception" to describe the neutral partisan role because most lawyers today believe they should pursue that role. Other commentators, such as David Luban, have used the term "standard conception" in the same way.

Read the questions and then find the answers in the text that follows.

[Question 8-1]

The dominant conception of the lawyer's role:

    (A)   Rejects role morality.

    (B)   Requires moral accountability.

    (C)   Requires moral nonaccountability.

    (D)   Views the lawyer primarily as an officer of the court.

[Question 8-2]

Role morality requires lawyers to take actions that are immoral under ordinary morality.

    (A)   True.

    (B)   False.

[Question 8-3]

Which of the following is NOT a justification for the neutral partisan role?

    (A)   The adversary system.

    (B)   The traditional understanding of professionalism.

    (C)   Client autonomy.

    (D)   Democracy and access to law.

[Question 8-4]

According to Professor Sanford Levinson, the dominant conception requires a lawyer to "bleach out" all personal characteristics, including religion, morality, race, gender, and other forms of identity.

    (A)   True.

    (B)   False.

[Question 8-5]

The neutral partisan:

    (A)   Follows her conscience in her lawyering.

    (B)   May choose to incorporate external group identifications.

    (C)   May choose to follow her conscience in her lawyering.

    (D)   Is fungible with other lawyers.

[Question 8-6]

The Preambles to the Canons and the Code emphasize the lawyer's responsibilities to his or her client.

    (A) True.

    (B) False.

[Question 8-7]

The original understanding of the lawyer's role in the United States was that of the European guild.

    (A) True.

    (B) False.

[Question 8-8]

The Rules:

    (A) Require lawyers to be neutral partisans.

    (B) Prohibit lawyers from being neutral partisans.

    (C) Permit lawyers discretion to choose whether to be morally responsible or a neutral partisan.

[Question 8-9]

The Tennessee ethics opinion advises a lawyer opposed to abortion that his ethical obligations require him, in representing a minor seeking judicial consent for an abortion,

    (A) To suggest that she consider talking to her parents.

    (B) To suggest that she consider alternatives to abortion.

    (C) To suggest that she consider the moral pros and cons of her decision.

    (D) None of the above.

[Question 8-10]

The Tennessee ethics opinion is consistent with Rule 2.1.

    (A) True.

    (B) False

[Question 8-11]

The Legal Profession as a Blue State reading argues that the ascendance of the hired gun approach and the decline of lawyers' commitment to the public good results from:

    (A) Increasing business-like behavior by lawyers.

    (B) Law schools' disdain of law practice and legal ethics.

(C) The trend toward greater emphasis on individualism.

(D) The increasing diversity of the legal profession.

[Question 8-12]

The adversary system approach to justice resembles market theory in that it:

(A) Rejects moral relativism.

(B) Distributes justice equally.

(C) Always favors the wealthy.

(D) Assumes that facilitating the pursuit of individual self-interest is best for society.

Go Online

For an entertaining introduction to this section, watch the twenty-five minute film, *"Red State, Blue State: Lawyers, Politics & Moral Counseling,"* available at https://www.fordham.edu/info/23524/publications_and_films. It includes interviews with leading law professors and lawyers, as well as law students and members of the public. It also includes a few selections from the rock super-group R.E.M.

DAVID LUBAN, LAWYERS AND JUSTICE: AN ETHICAL STUDY XX *(1988)*

The theory of role morality takes off from a distinction between universal moral duties that binds us all because we are all moral agents and special duties that go with various roles or "stations in life ." . . . This notion, at the level of general ethical theory, explains how people in certain social roles may be morally required to do things that seem immoral.

[T]he standard conception of the lawyer's role [consists] of (1) a role obligation (the "principle of partisanship") that identifies professionalism with extreme partisan zeal on behalf of the client and (2) the "principle of nonaccountability," which insists that the lawyer bears no moral responsibility for the client's goals or the means.

Lord Brougham

Professor Geoffrey Hazard has described Lord Brougham's famous statement of the advocate's duty as the "classic statement' of the lawyer's role." Geoffrey C. Hazard, Jr., *The Future of Legal Ethics*, 100 Yale L.J. 1239, 1280 (1991).

In 1820, Lord Henry Brougham led the defense of Queen Caroline against King George IV's charges of adultery. Brougham learned "that the King had secretly married a Roman Catholic before assuming the throne and, therefore, was ineligible to rule."[1] If the King's marriage were

---

1   Russell G. Pearce, *Lawyers as America's Governing Class: The Formation and Dissolution of the Original Understanding of the American Lawyer's Role*, 8 U. Chi. Sch. Roundtable 381, 394 (2001).

revealed, turmoil and perhaps even civil war would have resulted. Intent on sending a message to the King and his allies, Brougham claimed he would reveal the King's prior marriage if the matter was not settled in favor of Queen Caroline.

On the floor of the House of Lords, Brougham declared that:

> An advocate, in the discharge of his duty knows but one person in all the world, and that person is his client. To save that client by all means and expedients, and at all hazards to other persons, and among them to himself, is his first and only duty; and in performing this duty he must not regard the alarm, the torments, the destruction he may bring upon others. Separating the duty of a patriot from that of advocate, he must go on, reckless of the consequences: though it should be his unhappy lot to involve his country in confusion.[2]

MONROE H. FREEDMAN & ABBE SMITH, *UNDERSTANDING LAWYERS' ETHICS 13, 15–16, 52–53, 62–63 (5TH ED. 2016)*

Freedman and Smith argue that the neutral partisan role for lawyers is necessary to "maintain a free society in which individual rights are central." The American system promotes human dignity by protecting "the free exercise of individual autonomy." To exercise autonomy, "each person is entitled to know his rights with respect to society and other individuals and to decide whether to assert those rights through the due processes of law." In the American system, the role of the lawyer is key because "[t]he lawyer, by virtue of her training and skills, has a monopoly over access to the legal system and knowledge about the law[,]" and therefore, to provide counseling and advocacy that "are often indispensable . . . to the effective exercise of individual autonomy."

According to Freedman and Smith, if a lawyer were to bring her morality into representing her clients, she would deprive them of their autonomy. They do, however, recognize a few circumstances where a lawyer may properly consider her personal morality: in deciding whether to represent a client, to reasonably limit the scope of representation, and to withdraw without material harm to the client, as well as to withdraw if the lawyer has a conflict because of the repugnance of the client's position or because the client has made factual misrepresentations.

RUSSELL G. PEARCE, *THE JEWISH LAWYER'S QUESTION*

27 Tex. Tech L. Rev. 1259, 1259–70 (1996)

Sanford Levinson has described how the "professional project [of law] . . . 'bleach[es] out' . . . merely contingent aspects of the self, including the residue of particularistic socialization that we refer to as our 'conscience.'" As I have noted elsewhere, "rule of law implies that the quality of lawyering and of justice an individual receives does not depend on the group identity of the

---

2 *Id.*

lawyer or judge." Lawyers are to take a neutral approach to their work, free of external group identifications, including their religion. Under the professional project, lawyers are fungible.

Judge Richard Posner has noted the connection between the adversary system and the market. He asserts that the adversary system "resembles the market in its impersonality, its subordination of distributive considerations. The invisible hand of the market has its counterpart in the aloof disinterest of the judge." Richard A. Posner, *Economic Analysis of Law* 322 (1972). For further consideration of the analogy between the adversary system and the market, see Russell G. Pearce, *Redressing Inequality in the Market for Justice: Why Access to Lawyers Will Never Solve the Problem and Why Rethinking the Role of Judges Will Help,* 73 Fordham L. Rev. 969, 970–72 (2004) and sources collected at n.12 of that article.

The following preambles to the legal profession's ethical codes offer a window into how the organized bar has understood the lawyer's role in society and how that understanding has changed over time.

Preamble, Canons of Professional Ethics (1908)

In America, where the stability of Courts and of all departments of government rests upon the approval of the people, it is peculiarly essential that the system for establishing and dispensing Justice be developed to a high point of efficiency and so maintained that the public shall have absolute confidence in the integrity and impartiality of its administration. The future of the Republic, to a great extent, depends upon our maintenance of Justice pure and unsullied. It cannot be so maintained unless the conduct and the motives of the members of our profession are such as to merit the approval of all just men.

Preamble, Model Code of Professional Responsibility (1970)

The continued existence of a free and democratic society depends upon recognition of the concept that justice is based upon the rule of law grounded in respect for the individual and his capacity through reason for enlightened self-government. Law so grounded makes justice possible, for only through such law does the dignity of the individual attain respect and protection. Without it, individual rights become subject to unrestrained power, respect for the law is destroyed, and rational self-government is impossible. Lawyers, as guardians of the law, play a vital role in the preservation of society. The fulfillment of this role requires an understanding by lawyers of their relationship with and function in our legal system. A consequent obligation of lawyers is to maintain the highest standards of ethical conduct.

Preamble, Rules (1983)

[1] A lawyer, as a member of the legal profession, is a representative of clients, an officer of the legal system and a public citizen having special responsibility for the quality of justice. . . .

[6] As a public citizen, a lawyer should seek improvement of the law, access to the legal system, the administration of justice and the quality of service rendered by the legal profession. As a member of a learned profession, a lawyer should cultivate knowledge of the law beyond its use for clients, employ that knowledge in reform of the law and work to strengthen legal education. In addition, a lawyer should further the public's understanding of and confidence in the rule of law and the justice system because legal institutions in a constitutional democracy depend on popular participation and support to maintain their authority. A lawyer should be mindful of deficiencies in the administration of justice and of the fact that the poor, and sometimes persons who are not poor, cannot afford adequate legal assistance. Therefore, all lawyers should devote professional time and resources and use civic influence to ensure equal access to our system of justice for all those who because of economic or social barriers cannot afford or secure adequate legal counsel. A lawyer should aid the legal profession in pursuing these objectives and should help the bar regulate itself in the public interest.

[7] Many of a lawyer's professional responsibilities are prescribed in the Rules of Professional Conduct, as well as substantive and procedural law. However, a lawyer is also guided by personal conscience and the approbation of professional peers. A lawyer should strive to attain the highest level of skill, to improve the law and the legal profession and to exemplify the legal profession's ideals of public service. . . .

[12] The legal profession's relative autonomy carries with it special responsibilities of self-government. The profession has a responsibility to assure that its regulations are conceived in the public interest and not in furtherance of parochial or self-interested concerns of the bar. Every lawyer is responsible for observance of the Rules of Professional Conduct. A lawyer should also aid in securing their observance by other lawyers. Neglect of these responsibilities compromises the independence of the profession and the public interest which it serves.

[13] Lawyers play a vital role in the preservation of society. . . .

Make the Connection

The next case will look familiar. In Chapter 2, we explored the question of whether the lawyer could ethically seek to withdraw. Review that material. Here we will consider whether he could ethically counsel the client on alternatives to abortion.

BOARD OF PROFESSIONAL RESPONSIBILITY OF THE SUPREME COURT OF TENNESSEE

Formal Ethics Op. 96-F-140, 1996 WL 340719 (1996)

[A lawyer who is morally opposed to abortion is appointed to represent a minor seeking judicial permission for an abortion without the consent of her parents. The lawyer asks for ethical advice on a number of questions, including whether he could] "advise the minor seeking an abortion about alternatives and/or advise her to speak with her parents or legal guardian about the potential abortion[.]"

If the appointed attorney represents only the minor (as we believe), then counsel has a duty to "explain a matter to the extent reasonably necessary to permit the client to make informed decisions regarding the representation." DR 7-101(A)(3). Whether informing the minor about alternatives to abortion and suggesting that she discuss the potential procedure with her parents or legal guardian is ethically appropriate may depend on a case-by-case analysis. If the minor is truly mature and well-informed enough to go forward and make the decision on her own, then counsel's hesitation and advice for the client to consult with others could possibly implicate a lack of zealous representation (a lawyer shall not intentionally fail to seek the client's lawful objectives, or prejudice or damage his client during the course of the professional relationship). Counsel also has a duty of undivided loyalty to his client, and should not allow any other persons or entities to regulate, direct, compromise, control or interfere with his professional judgment. . . . To the extent that counsel strongly recommends that his client discuss the potential abortion with her parents or with other individuals or entities which are known to oppose such a choice, compliance with Canon 5 is called into question.

RUSSELL G. PEARCE, *THE LEGAL PROFESSION AS A BLUE STATE: REFLECTIONS ON PUBLIC PHILOSOPHY, JURISPRUDENCE, AND LEGAL ETHICS*

75 Fordham L. Rev. 1339, 1339–62 (2006)

As a general matter, Blue State voters are less friendly to the promotion of moral values through the public sphere. In contrast to Red State voters, they are more likely to embrace a liberal public philosophy that emphasizes a conception of individual freedom grounded in the "basic principle of human dignity, [that] no person or group has the right deliberately to impose personal ethical values . . . on anyone else."

The dominant—although not exclusive—modern conception of the lawyer as a hired gun tracks this commitment to removing personal ethical values from politics. As Sanford Levinson has observed, the dominant conception requires " 'bleaching' out of [the] merely contingent aspects of the self, including the residue of particularistic socialization that we refer to as our 'conscience.' "

A powerful illustration of the confluence between the conception of the lawyer's role and the Blue State approach to values is a recent decision of the Tennessee Supreme Court's Board of Professional Responsibility. A Catholic lawyer who believed that abortion was murder sought to avoid a court appointment to represent a teenage girl seeking court permission to obtain an abortion without her parents' consent or, in the alternative, to recommend to his client that it would be better for her to seek parental consent and explore alternatives to abortion. Even though a literal reading of the applicable rules would appear to have permitted, though not endorsed, either course of action, the Board found that if the lawyer were to make a recommendation to his client based upon his personal beliefs, or even if he were to withdraw representation, his conduct would improperly create the risk of imposing his values upon the client or upon the legal system. Even in the Red State of Tennessee, the legal profession felt bound to follow a Blue State approach to values.

This approach to values was not always the dominant approach of the legal profession.

I. From Guild to Governing Class

A. The English Guild

In colonial America, the legal profession largely borrowed from the English guild model. Society trusted guilds to rise above self-interest and to police themselves. In turn, the government permitted the guilds autonomy in membership, production, and marketing. In the legal profession, this meant that lawyers would perform their obligations to the legal system with excellence and integrity.

But English lawyers were not the governing class. Although lawyers came from the social class of "gentlemen," possessed of "good behavior, well bred, amiable, [and] high-minded," the task of governing fell to aristocrats and their oldest sons who assumed their place, not their younger sons who might become lawyers.

B. The Original American Understanding

["Beginning with Perry Miller, and continuing through the tremendously influential work of Gordon Wood . . . historians have identified the period following the Revolution as the moment of creation of a uniquely American understanding of lawyers as a necessary governing class in a democracy."] The experience of republican government after the American Revolution shattered the elite's faith in the ability of individuals and majorities to overcome their selfish interests. Observing that legislatures disregarded property and individual rights in expropriating land and in making biased or corrupt decisions, the elite no longer believed that deliberative democracy would result in virtuous government for the benefit of the public good. Instead, they came to fear that unchecked majority rule would result in tyranny of the majority.

They turned instead to a public political philosophy that combined both liberal and republican impulses. Retaining the republican goal of government as promoting the public good, they tended to define that good in liberal terms, such as "security, justice, prosperity and liberty." At the same time, they maintained the republican distrust of commerce and of self-interested factions. They . . . concluded that majority rule would only coincide with the public good, including rule of law and protection of minority rights, so long as an elite governing class provided leadership to the majority. In the view of the framers, professionals, as the sector of society that pursued the public good and not self-interest, were best suited to this role.

Antebellum jurisprudence assigned this vital governing class role to lawyers on account of their virtue and their central role in governance. Virtue inhered in lawyers both in their status as professionals and in the nature of legal practice. Americans transformed the English notion of lawyers as gentlemen by class into a conception of lawyers as gentlemen as a moral badge of their ability to rise above self-interest, whatever their class origin.

As the custodians of the formal and informal institutions of governance, lawyers applied their ability to identify and promote the public good to providing the leadership necessary to ensure that laws would be consistent with the public good and that the majority would respect the rule of law. Within the formal government, lawyers "controlled the judicial branch and dominated the legislature and the executive." Equally important, as representatives of clients and as members of the community, they also served as intermediaries between the formal institutions of government and the people. In "counsel[ing] clients, making arguments in court to judge[s] and jur[ies]," and participating in civic life, they "sought to gain the confidence of and 'to diffuse sound principles among the people.'"

The governing class conception embraced a necessary connection between lawyers' ethics and the public good. Commentators agreed that legal ethics required moral counseling, moral considerations in deciding who to represent, respect for court and colleagues, and personal integrity. Beyond these axioms, the two leading American ethicists disagreed on how to reconcile republican and adversarial obligations. David Hoffman urged lawyers not to pursue a defense or claim that they believed "cannot, or rather ought not, to be sustained," including the Statute of Limitations when based on the "mere efflux of time." In a criminal case "of the deepest dye," where the lawyer believed the client guilty, Hoffman argued that it would be unprofessional to apply "ingenuity . . . beyond securing to them a fair and dispassionate investigation of the facts of their cause." In contrast, George Sharswood urged lawyers to zealously put the prosecution to its proof in order to protect the defendant's liberty interests, even where the crime was heinous. In civil matters too, Sharswood, in contrast to Hoffman, believed that liberty and property rights of defendants required lawyers to defend an "unrighteous claim." Nonetheless, Sharswood limited advocacy of that claim "to assuring the defendant 'a fair trial'" and advised lawyers to refrain from assisting a client in "frustrat[ing] legitimate property rights, such as . . . the 'just demands of creditors.'"

The commitment to the public good in legal ethics, grounded in jurisprudence and public political philosophy, withstood pressures from both inside and outside the legal profession. Throughout the antebellum period, some argued that lawyers were business people. Still others argued for a hired gun perspective. They endorsed Lord Brougham's well-known maxim that "an advocate, in the discharge of his duty, knows but one person in all the world, and that person is his client." Hoffman and Sharswood expressly rejected these approaches.

During the Jacksonian era, prevailing public sentiment rejected the notion that lawyers, or any other elite group, had a superior ability to identify and pursue the public good. As a result of this egalitarian impulse, many states abolished or minimized the qualifications for becoming a lawyer. Rather than accept these critiques, the dominant thinkers in the bar continued to rely on the teaching of natural law jurisprudence and elite political philosophy. Indeed, the Jacksonian era was the time when Hoffman and Sharswood published their legal ethics treatises articulating the governing class approach to the lawyer's role.

II. Redefining and Limiting the Duty to the Public Good

In the period from the Civil War through the 1960s, the duty of lawyers to the public good narrowed both in terms of defining the public good and in terms of lawyers' capacity for pursuing the good. Promoting this redefinition was the shift in the dominant jurisprudence from natural law to empiricism, a shift that reflected the increasing influence of liberalism in the larger society.

A. The Decline of the Public Good in Elite Public Political Philosophy

After the Civil War, the increasing influence of liberalism undermined the republican faith in an organic community that promoted the public good. While liberalism encompassed a variety of particular political prescriptions, its fundamental emphasis was promoting freedom of the individual. At its core, liberalism conceived of the individual as fundamentally self-interested and viewed the role of government as permitting individuals the greatest freedom possible. When individuals maximized freedom, they would also maximize what was best for society through the invisible hand of the market or through the democratic electoral process. As a political philosophy, liberalism did not, at its core, include a conception of the public good independent of individual freedom.

This absence permitted the development of hybrid public political philosophies that combined liberalism with conceptions of the public good that were not apparently inconsistent with the logic of liberalism. . . . Nonetheless, the logic of liberalism made individual freedom primary. As liberalism extended its influence, hybrid approaches like liberal republicanism were less persuasive. First, they were inconsistent with the core of liberalism. The insistence on a public good independent of the pursuit of individual self-interest prevented the maximization of individual freedom. Second, they were unnecessary. Although liberalism may have needed justifications grounded in natural law when it was a less powerful force, as it became dominant it no longer needed external sources of support.

The two most significant changes in public political philosophy that would influence the understanding of the function of lawyers related to knowledge of truth and faith in majority rule. In the antebellum period, access to truth required both virtue and empirical knowledge. Following the Civil War and continuing through the 1960s, empirical knowledge became by far the more dominant way of establishing the truth, at least in elite culture, and the influence of ethics grounded in virtue diminished considerably. Higher education, for example, shifted from a primary emphasis on moral development of the student to a primary—and later almost exclusive—emphasis on empirical knowledge.

As belief in virtue as the source of knowledge declined, the trends in public political philosophy following the Civil War minimized or eliminated surviving republican notions. A more liberal and democratic sense of capacity for self-rule challenged the belief that a particular class in society was qualified to provide elite political leadership. If an elite class was not better able to identify the truth, majority rule shifted from a source of mistrust to grounds for celebration. Indeed, majority rule offered a way, roughly analogous to the market, for self-interested individuals to exercise their political freedom in a way that reconciled their preferences.

Ironically, the increasing influence of liberalism in promoting empiricism and belief in majority rule coincided with a declining commitment to the vision of maximizing economic freedom through laissez-faire economics. By the late nineteenth century, the prevailing conception of natural law enshrined the "ideal that government should not interfere in the natural workings of the market." . . . By undermining the existence of a public good independent of self-interest and embracing deference to majority rule, the emerging dominant liberal approach either permitted government intervention in the name of limiting judicial discretion or encouraged it in order to pursue an empirically justified social good.

B. The Diminishing Role of Lawyers in Jurisprudence

Reflecting these shifts, jurisprudential commentators redefined the role of lawyers in a way so as to minimize—or in some cases eliminate—their role as the governing class. . . . [As a result,] lawyers were no longer central actors. If the majority could be trusted, threats to the rule of law were the exception and not the rule. As virtue became marginal to jurisprudence, so did the need for lawyers as a virtuous leadership class to maintain the public good and rule of law. As the role of lawyers diminished, or disappeared altogether, jurisprudence no longer focused on how the lawyer should combine virtue with empirical knowledge to ascertain the law. Instead, the dominant subject became law as "what the judges say it is."

Lawyers played a supporting role as technicians whose task was to study and anticipate the decisions of judges, a role that required no particular commitment to the public good[.] . . . While judges played the lead role, lawyers who applied scientific methods to legal structures could provide them with beneficial support.

These trends continued through the early 1960s. Empirical approaches to jurisprudence, such as the legal realist, legal process, and positivist perspectives, continued to focus on judges and to minimize the significance of the lawyer's role.

C. Professionalism Both Preserves and Narrows Lawyers' Obligation to the Public Good

With these changes in public political philosophy and jurisprudence, lawyers had to rethink their connection to the public good. Like all professionals, in the late nineteenth century they faced a challenge to their status grounded in the assertion that they were just as self-interested as business people and therefore deserving of no special authority. Resentment of the privileges of professionals in general and lawyers in particular became widespread. Robert Wiebe observed that "[w]ith the exception of bankers, no group late in the nineteenth century stood in lower public repute [than lawyers]."

In the face of this challenge, lawyers turned to the Progressive Era's ideological embrace of professionalism. Professionalism posited "a bargain between the profession and society." Society would permit the profession autonomy in exchange for the promise to use its skills for the good of its clients and the public. Justifying this bargain were two factors. One, the esoteric knowledge of lawyers made it difficult, if not impossible, for lay people to evaluate their services and to regulate them. Two, the altruism of lawyers—the fact that they worked primarily for the public good in contrast to business people who worked for self interest—guaranteed that society could trust lawyers to regulate themselves.

While continuing to find importance in lawyers' commitment to the public good, professionalism nonetheless offered a more circumscribed understanding both of lawyers' capacity and their societal function. Where Hoffman and Sharswood had identified lawyers' innate virtue as the source of their superior ability to identify and pursue the public good, professionalism made the empirically grounded claim that these characteristics derived from lawyers' training and experience. Professionalism also had less confidence in the commitment of the individual lawyer. In contrast to the republican faith in the individual lawyer and the policing power of reputation, the rhetoric of commentators like Brandeis conceded that the standards of the profession had fallen and sought to restore them. Professionalism recognized that lawyers' commitment to the public good could only be guaranteed through self-regulating bar associations that controlled admission to the bar, educated lawyers to their ethical duties, and enforced proper conduct through discipline.

Like the conception of lawyers' capacity for the public good, the conceptions of lawyers' function also narrowed. The antebellum notion that lawyers were a governing class responsible for maintaining the public good and the rule of law gave way to a perspective that defined a more limited scope for the governing class role. Pound's view of lawyers as "social engineers" retained the aspiration that "lawyers [should] lead the people . . . instead of giving up their legitimate hegemony in legislation and politics to engineers and naturalists and economists." But where the antebellum view understood leadership as defining the public good for the people, Pound viewed it as an "adjustment of the relations of men to each other and to society as conforms to the moral sense of the community." Brandeis articulated a similar notion that retained lawyers as a governing class charged with balancing the competing interests of rich and poor in order to maintain a fair and stable social order. At the same time that Brandeis and Pound articulated a narrower, but still robust, conception, Holmes appeared to abandon the governing class project altogether in describing the entire role of lawyers as predicting legal consequences for their clients.

While a view consistent with that of Holmes would ultimately prevail, the bar of his time preferred the governing class vision[.] . . . In 1908, the American Bar Association promulgated the Canons of Ethics, the first national code of ethics for lawyers. The preamble to the Canons stated expressly that "[t]he future of the republic, to a great extent, depend[ed] upon [lawyers'] maintenance of Justice pure and unsullied" through "conduct and the motives [that] merit the approval of all just men." . . . The Canons stated that "The Lawyer's Duty in Its Last Analysis" was "the counter-majoritarian obligation of loyalty to the law and the judicial system despite the contrary urging of any 'client, corporate or individual, however powerful, nor any cause, civil or political, however important . . . .' " At the same time, they urged " 'entire devotion to the interests of the client, warm zeal in the maintenance and defense of his rights and the exertion of his utmost learning and ability.' " The Canons expressly stated that this zealousness did not require the "lawyer to do whatever may enable him to succeed in winning his client's cause." Indeed, the Canons provided that "[t]he responsibility for advising as to questionable transactions, for bringing questionable suits, for urging questionable defenses, is the lawyer's responsibility. He cannot escape it by urging as an excuse that he is only following his client's instructions." The lawyer "must obey his own conscience and not that of the client."

In the period from the early twentieth century through the 1960s, the rhetoric of aspiring to the public good remained consistent, while the understanding of lawyers' function continued to narrow. Toward the end of this period, growing support for the hired gun role led the American Bar Association to restate the profession's commitment to the public good. In 1958, the Joint Conference on Professional Responsibility of the American Bar Association and the Association of American Law Schools . . . declared the "lawyer's role" as a "trusteeship for the integrity of those fundamental processes of government and self-government upon which the successful functioning of our society depends." Erwin Smigel's study of Wall Street lawyers, published in 1964, confirmed that elite lawyers endorsed a similar understanding. The lawyers Smigel interviewed described themselves to be "guardians of the law," urging their clients to adopt "proper and moral legal positions." Although the Joint Conference did describe a narrower obligation to the public good than that of the early twentieth century, Smigel's Wall Street lawyers kept alive the broader construction of Brandeis.

III. The Rise of the Hired Gun

As the influence of liberalism continued inexorably to expand, even this less ambitious commitment of lawyers to the public good would fade. Following the 1960s, while bar leaders retained a rhetoric of professionalism that was necessary to maintain self-regulation, most lawyers abandoned the notion that they had any special obligation to the public good, and, if they acknowledged it at all, they limited it to the margins of practice.

The 1960s represented a watershed in American culture. While proponents of philosophical liberalism, whether identified politically as liberal or conservative, had been dominant in elite culture since the late nineteenth century, certain pre-liberal conceptions, such as the public good, had continued to coexist in a less ambitious form. The 1960s marked the ascendance of purer forms of liberalism that questioned even a rhetorical commitment to the public good.

The dominant trends in jurisprudence reflected those in elite political philosophy. Whether law and economics on the right, liberal jurisprudence in the middle, or critical theory on the left, they either rejected outright the legitimacy of a public good independent of individual freedom or sought to make the concept as thin and private as possible. The rejection of virtue and the acceptance of majoritarianism became so complete that the diminished role lawyers played in earlier jurisprudences, like those of Fuller and of the legal process school, gave way to the dominance of the Holmesian perception that lawyers were mere technicians. Lawyers largely disappeared from jurisprudence altogether as the focus on judges became even more pronounced. . . .

Not surprisingly, consistent with these developments in jurisprudence and public political philosophy, survey data and anecdotal impressions revealed that the hired gun perspective had become dominant among lawyers. If the concept of the public good did not exist, then lawyers could claim no special relationship to it. If all people were self-interested, lawyers could not claim to be above self-interest. If majority rule could be trusted, society did not require lawyers to serve as an elite leadership class.

The hired gun conception rejected an obligation to the public good and privileged individual autonomy. It required lawyers to advocate zealously for their client's self-interest and to disregard their own values in order to avoid interfering with their client's autonomy. Lawyers' role prescribed extreme partisanship on behalf of clients within the bounds of the law and without moral accountability for their actions or those of their clients.

The bar faced a dilemma. According to professionalism, lawyers' commitment to the public good was a precondition to self-regulation. The bar responded in two ways. First, it continued to employ the rhetoric of allegiance to the public good. When it became undeniable that most lawyers were devoting themselves to their own self-interest and that of their clients, bar leaders declared a crisis of professionalism. They implemented commissions and mandatory classes to remind lawyers of their public obligation. Second, the bar redefined legal ethics and the public good to legitimize the hired gun view.

In its ethical codes, the bar minimized the centrality of the public good and expanded the commitment to promote the client's interests. While the 1970 Code of Professional Responsibility echoed the 1908 Canons in proudly declaring that "[l]awyers, as the guardians of the law, play a vital role in the preservation of society," the 1983 Model Rules of Professional Conduct identified the lawyer's first role as "a representative of clients" and only after that "a public citizen having special responsibility for the quality of justice," a less ambitious role than that of a leadership class upon which the very "preservation of society" depended.

Moreover, both the Code and the Rules accommodated the hired gun by elevating the lawyer's duty to the client. The Code directed lawyers to "represent a client zealously" within the bounds of the law and required a lawyer "to seek the lawful objectives of his clients through reasonably available means permitted by law and the disciplinary rules." While this language could have been read to permit lawyers broad discretion, lawyers understood it as a command to serve the client as a hired gun. The Model Rules continued to privilege this vision. Indeed, for the first time in an ethical code, the ABA identified client representation, and not commitment to the public good, as lawyers' primary obligation.

The bar further accommodated the hired gun ideal by shifting responsibility for the public good from the average lawyer to the public interest practitioner. In the 1960s, public interest law emerged as a separate field of practice. It expanded from a few, small groups, such as the NAACP and the ACLU, to include significant numbers of lawyers engaged in a variety of causes. The bar came to embrace public interest work and to identify public interest lawyers as role models. In doing so, the bar located responsibility for the public good in the aptly named public interest bar and discarded it from its historical place in ordinary practice.

The bar also encouraged lawyers to remove any remaining personal obligation they felt to the public good from their everyday work and place it in the limited confines of the new ethical duty of pro bono. Although free legal services for those who could not afford them had long been one part of the larger governing class ideal, the idea of the pro bono duty as a separate ethical obligation arose in the 1970s. In 1970, the Code of Professional Responsibility became the first legal ethics code to articulate a separate, though aspirational, ethical duty to provide pro bono legal services. While the duty remained aspirational, it received greater attention and more detailed consideration in the Model Rules. Commitment to provide a minimum number of pro bono hours, often in conjunction with public interest firms, became a major preoccupation of the bar's professionalism campaign, thereby compartmentalizing the public good into the few hours a lawyer devoted to pro bono and further legitimizing the hired gun approach to representing clients.[3]

III. Competing Visions of Professional Morality

Not surprisingly, as the neutral partisan role became ascendant in the early 1970s, alternative perspectives emerged. We have selected examples from six different approaches to introduce you to the voluminous literature that has developed: moral responsibility, feminist, religious, racial justice, LGBTQ rights, and civics teacher.

We begin with the perspective of moral responsibility. Commentators offer different ways of considering moral responsibility, including the lawyer's personal morality, the morality of the legal system, and the morality of collaborating with clients in promoting social change.

Read the questions and then find the answers in the texts that follow.

A. Moral Responsibility

[Question 8-13]

All of the following fall within David Luban's conception of moral activist lawyering EXCEPT:

    (A) A lawyer should engage in moral counseling on the rightness of client ends and of the public good.

    (B) A lawyer should not assume that the client's ends are preset and inflexible.

    (C) A lawyer is incapable of learning from the client what justice requires.

    (D) A lawyer may have to betray a client.

[Question 8-14]

William Simon's argument that lawyers should promote justice requires all of the following EXCEPT:

    (A) Lawyers should generally consult their personal morality.

    (B) Lawyers should consider unequal access to justice.

    (C) The more reliable procedures and institutions are, the less lawyers need to promote justice in their work.

    (D) Lawyers may properly consider their financial interest.

---

3   Russell G. Pearce, Brian Danitz & Romelia Leach, *Revitalizing the Lawyer-Poet: What Lawyers Can Learn From Rock and Roll*, 14 Widener L.J. 907, 910 (2005).

[Question 8-15]

Rebellious lawyering endorses all of the following EXCEPT:

(A) The primary goal of social change through law reform.

(B) The view that the lawyer-client relationship is a collaborative partnership.

(C) The notion of lay lawyering.

(D) The facilitation of organizing for social change.

[Question 8-16]

Which of the following is true?

(A) Moral activism may be consistent with the Rules.

(B) Promoting justice may be consistent with the Rules.

(C) Cause lawyering may be consistent with the Rules.

(D) All the moral responsibility approaches are inconsistent with the Rules.

(E) All of the moral responsibility approaches may be consistent with the Rules.

DAVID LUBAN, LAWYERS AND JUSTICE: AN ETHICAL STUDY, 173–74 (1988)

It's Greek to Me

phronesis means prudence; practical wisdom. Aristotle considered this the highest of the virtues and the cornerstone of his thesis of the "unity of the virtues."

Luban's argument for "moral activism" applies both to law reform and to everyday practice. Luban describes law reform as "explicitly putting one's phronesis, one's savvy, to work for the commonweal." However, at the same time, Luban recognizes that "client counseling . . . is ultimately more important, because it is available even to lawyers whose humble practices and whose distaste for public life make law reform" unappealing. Accordingly, the moral activist's client counseling will include dialogue regarding "the rightness or wrongness of [the client's] projects, and the possible impact of those projects on 'the people,' in the same matter-of-fact and (one hopes) unmoralistic manner that one discusses the financial aspects of a representation." As a practical matter, then, dialogue between lawyer and client may result in "considerable negotiation about what will and won't be done in the course of a representation; [and] it may eventuate in a lawyer's accepting a case only on condition that it takes a certain shape, or threatening to withdraw from a case if a client insists on pursuing a project that the lawyer finds unworthy." To be clear, Luban posits that counseling does not consist solely of the lawyer sharing her moral wisdom with the client but rather an actual dialogue in the sense that both lawyer and client may "eventually modify her moral stance. If it is a mistake to take the client's ends as preset and inflexible, it is also a mistake to assume that the lawyer is incapable of learning from the client what justice really requires." Luban acknowledges, though, that "the encounter may result in a parting of ways or even a betrayal by the lawyer of a client's projects, if the lawyer persists in the conviction that they are immoral or unjust. Unlike the standard conception of the lawyer's role, moral activism accepts these possibilities without flinching. Without flinching much, at any rate."

WILLIAM H. SIMON, ETHICAL DISCRETION IN LAWYERING

101 Harv. L. Rev. 1083 (1988)

The basic maxim of the approach I propose is this: The lawyer should take those actions that, considering the relevant circumstances of the particular case, seem most likely to promote justice. This 'seek justice' maxim suggests a kind of noncategorical judgment that might be called pragmatist, ad hoc, or dialectical, but that I will call discretionary. 'Discretionary' is not an entirely satisfactory term; I do not mean to invoke its connotations of arbitrariness or nonaccountability, but rather its connotations of flexibility and complexity. Unlike the private norms of the *Code* and *Model Rules*, discretionary norms, as I define them, do not connote standardlessness and nonreviewability. I use the term in what Ronald Dworkin call 'a weak sense' to indicate that the relevant norms 'cannot be applied mechanically but demand the use of judgment.'

There are two dimensions to the judgment that the discretionary approach requires of the lawyer. The first is an assessment of the relative merits of the client's goals and claims and the goals and claims of others whom the lawyer might serve. The second is an effort to confront and resolve the competing factors that bear on the internal merits of the client's goals and claims.

A. Relative Merit

Neither of the dominant approaches adequately confronts a central fact about the legal system: most people are unable to enforce most of their rights most of the time. . . . The legal system cannot be indifferent to the distribution of this resource. . . .

The proper standard requires not only a threshold judgment, but also a relative one. In deciding whether to commit herself to a client's claims and goals, a lawyer should assess their merits in relation to the merits of the claims and goals of others whom she might serve. The criteria the lawyer should employ in making this assessment are suggested by the bases of legal concern about the distribution of services: the extent to which the claims and goals are grounded in the law, the importance of the interests involved, and the extent to which the representation would contribute to the equalization of access to the legal system.

Of course, merit cannot be the only consideration to determine how the lawyer allocates her efforts. The lawyer's financial interests are also necessarily important. But the financial considerations that tacitly determine the distribution of legal services under the dominant approaches are substantially arbitrary in relation to the most basic goals of the legal system—those concerning legal merit. Lawyers can mitigate the tendency of the market to produce an inappropriate distribution of legal services by integrating considerations of relative merit into their decisions about whom to represent and how to do so. In making such judgments, lawyers will have to balance their legitimate financial concerns with their commitment to a just distribution of legal services.

B. Internal Merit

The second aspect of the lawyer's assessment of merit involves an attempt to reconcile the conflicting legal values implicated directly in the client's claim or goal. These conflicts usually arise in the form of the overlapping tensions between substance and procedure, purpose and form, and broad and narrow framing.

1. Substance Versus Procedure—One manifestation of the substance versus procedure tension is the lawyer's sense of the limitations both of her individual judgment of the substantive merits of the dispute on the one hand and of the established procedures for resolving it on the other. We could tell the lawyer to work only to advance claims and goals that she determined were entitled to prevail. The most important objection to this precept is not that the lawyer's decisions about the merits would be controversial—the decisions of judges, juries, and executive officials may also be controversial. Instead, the most important objection is that judges, juries, and executive officials acting within the relevant public procedures are generally able to make more reliable determinations on the merits than the individual lawyer. But the qualification 'generally' is crucial. The lawyer will often have good reason to recognize that the standard procedure is not reliably constructed to respond to the problem at hand, and she will often be in a position to contribute to its improvement.

The basic response of the discretionary approach to the substance-procedure tension is this: the more reliable the relevant procedures and institutions, the less direct responsibility the lawyer need assume for the substantive justice of the resolution; the less reliable the procedures and institutions, the more direct responsibility she need assume for substantive justice.

2. Purpose Versus Form—Part of the substance versus procedure tension could be considered a special variation of the purpose versus form tension. When the lawyer impeaches a witness she knows to be truthful, when she objects to hearsay she knows to be accurate, when she puts the opposing party to proof on a matter the client has no legitimate interest in disputing, she takes advantage of procedural rules designed to promote accurate, efficient decisionmaking in a way that frustrates this purpose. When judges apply rules, we expect them to take account of the purposes underlying the rules. But the judge often lacks sufficient knowledge to determine whether the relevant purposes would be served by applying the rules. The lawyer, however, often does have sufficient knowledge to do so. . . .

Part of the reason for regarding law as legitimate in our culture is that it embodies the purposes adopted by authoritative lawmakers: parties to a contract, legislators enacting a statute, judges pronouncing a common law rule, the people adopting a constitution. . . . The rules cannot be applied sensibly without considering their underlying purposes, but the purposes can only be implemented appropriately by referring to their formal expression as rules.

Now consider a case in which the relevant purpose is less clear and more problematic. The client is a public assistance recipient under the Aid to Families with Dependent Children program. She and her child live, rent-free, in a home owned by her cousin. Under the applicable regulations, the receipt of lodging 'at no cost' is considered 'income in kind' that requires a reduction of about $150 in the welfare grant. The lawyer has to decide whether to recommend that the client make a nominal payment of, say, five dollars to the cousin so that she would no longer be receiving lodging 'at no cost,' and thus avoid the $150 reduction in her grant.

Again, assume that some institutional failure requires that the lawyer take some responsibility for the substantive merits. Upon examination, she is unable to come up with a sense of legislative purpose as clear and coherent as the one involved in the tax case. On the one hand, the benefit reduction seems designed to reflect the lesser needs of people who live rent free, and the fact that the provision could be effectively nullified by the type of financial planning in question suggests that such planning was not contemplated. On the other hand, nothing in the language of the regulation suggests an intention to preclude such planning, although it would have been simple enough to do so by providing for a benefit reduction in cases of low rent payments of the difference between the rent payment and the $150 implicit shelter allowance in the grant. . . .

Suppose that background case law and legislative history suggest that the regulation is in part a compromise between the principle that grants should reflect the lesser needs of people with low rent expense and the competing 'flat grant' principle that need determinations should consider only the basic and easily determinable factors of cash income and family size. The 'flat grant' principle is animated by solicitude for recipient autonomy and privacy as well as administrative efficiency concerns. In addition, the regulations seem to reflect a rough compromise between a half-hearted effort by the federal government (which subsidizes the program) to push the states to raise grant levels generally and efforts by the states to retain flexibility to lower them in some circumstances. In this situation, the lawyer has no clear sense of which course of action would be most consistent with legislative purpose. It is thus proper for her to treat the regulation formally.

Even if the lawyer found stronger indication of a purpose to preclude strategic planning, she might be justified in disregarding it if she thought it problematic. A purpose is problematic to the extent that it endangers fundamental values. The lawyer might decide that the claimant's interest in a minimally adequate income is a value of exceptional legal importance, that the AFDC grant levels provide considerably less than a minimally adequate income, and that the plan in question would move her closer to one. Thus, the lawyer might conclude that a purpose to preclude such a plan should not be assumed without an explicit legislative statement of it. In doing so, she might apply the presumption against a problematic purpose that the Supreme Court seemed to apply in *Kent v. Dulles*, a presumption reflecting both a judgment regarding probable legislative intent and a substantive policy disfavoring certain purposes by requiring more explicit articulation of them.

3. Broad Versus Narrow Framing—This tension arises as ethical issues are defined. If we define an issue narrowly in terms of a small number of characteristics of the parties and their dispute, it will often look different than if we define it to encompass the parties' identities, relationship, and social circumstances. . . .

The broad versus narrow definition tension substantially overlaps the other tensions. For example, in debates that I characterized in terms of substance versus procedure, Monroe Freedman responds to regulatory arguments by hypothesizing situations in which candor and openness may impede the appropriate substantive resolution because of some procedural deficiency. A famous example concerns whether a criminal defense lawyer should cross-examine a prosecution witness who accurately places the defendant near the scene of the crime about her defective vision. In Freedman's scenario, although the testimony is accurate and thus the contemplated impeachment seems irrelevant, the defendant is in fact innocent but lacks an alibi and is the victim of some unlucky circumstantial evidence. So the proper resolution—acquittal—may depend on the willingness to impeach the truthful witness. . . . What Freedman does in these examples is to broaden the frame. The issue initially posed is one of candor about a specific piece of information. He insists that the matter be viewed in the context of the other evidence and in terms of the likely incremental influence of disclosure on the resolution.

The discretionary approach gives individual lawyers substantial responsibility for determining whether broad or narrow framing is appropriate in the particular case. It suggests that the lawyer should frame ethical issues in accordance with three general standards of relevance. First, a consideration is relevant if it is implicated by the most plausible interpretation of the applicable law. Second, a consideration is relevant if it is likely to have a substantial practical influence on the resolution. Equality of resources and of access to information are among the more important factors weighing toward narrow definition under this second standard. Third, knowledge and institutional competence will affect the appropriate framing. More broadly framed issues tend to require more knowledge and more difficult judgments. When the lawyer lacks needed knowledge or competence, narrow framing becomes more appropriate.

C. The Limits of Role and Legality

The discretionary approach is grounded in the lawyer's professional commitments to legal values. It rejects the common tendency to attribute the tensions of legal ethics to a conflict between the demands of legality on the one hand and those of nonlegal, personal or ordinary morality on the other. Although critics of conventional legal ethics discourse often adopt the law versus morality characterization, its strongest influence is to bias discussion in favor of conventional, especially libertarian, responses. Typically the conventional response is portrayed as the 'legal' one; the unconventional response is portrayed as a 'moral' alternative. This rhetoric connotes that the 'legal' option is objective and integral to the professional role, whereas the 'moral' alternative is subjective and peripheral. Even when the rhetoric expresses respect for the 'moral' alternative, it implies that the lawyer who adopts it is on her own and vulnerable both intellectually and practically. The usual effect is to make it psychologically harder for lawyers and law students to argue for the 'moral' alternative. In many such situations, however, both alternatives could readily be portrayed as competing *legal* values.

Almost all lawyers will give weight to clear legislative expression, and many would regard it as dispositive of their obligations. However, a 'natural law lawyer' in the style of, say, Lon Fuller would have to consider whether the decisions of the legislature were so plainly wrong and the values they affronted so fundamental that the lawyer should disregard the decisions. The natural law lawyer cannot divorce 'his duty of fidelity to law' from 'his responsibility for making law what it ought to be.' Such a lawyer believes that a legal system must meet certain normative preconditions to be entitled to respect and compliance, and perhaps even to be considered a system of law. Thus, legal ideals may require that a person repudiate norms that violate such preconditions even when promulgated by otherwise legally authoritative institutions. Such repudiation is the opposite of lawlessness; it moves the system closer to being worthy of respect as lawful.

A lawyer in the welfare case who accepted this natural law theory of legal order would have to consider whether the norm of minimal subsistence income is so fundamental that it amounts to a precondition of legal legitimacy. Such a lawyer might reason that a core value of legality is the autonomy of the individual and that a person who lacked minimal material subsistence would be so dependent and debilitated that she would be incapable of exercising the autonomy that legality aspires to safeguard. In this way, the lawyer might conclude that this value is fundamental and hence that norms that violate it are not entitled to respect. . . .

The discretionary approach does not require that the issues of the relation of institutional and substantive norms and of the lawyer's range of autonomy within the scheme of institutional competence be resolved in any particular way. But how a lawyer resolves these issues will affect how she draws the distinction between professional and private ethics. In some situations, the lawyer will feel that she has a professional obligation to some legally authoritative norm that conflicts with her private, nonlegal commitments. In other situations, she may feel that her private commitment outweighs the professional one. But she will feel such a conflict only when she is reasonably certain that the legal system fails to acknowledge some value to which she is committed or that the system has conclusively rejected such a value. Only at this point is it appropriate to talk of her problem in terms of the limits of 'role morality' or 'role differentiation.' Until then, the problem remains one of the most appropriate performance of her role within the legal system. . . .

Cause Lawyering

One influential manifestation of moral activism has been cause lawyering. Originating in the work of the NAACP and the ACLU, cause lawyering involves the application of legal skills to promote social change. Cause lawyering has come to include a wide range of causes, mostly on the left of the political spectrum but also on the right as well.

Progressive lawyering has critiqued the traditional emphasis of cause lawyering on law reform efforts and has offered an alternative that reconceptualizes the lawyer-client relationship.

Eduardo Capulong, *Client Activism in Progressive Lawyering Theory*

16 Clinical L. Rev., 109, 109–10 (2009)

In contrast to liberal-legalist practice, progressive lawyering rests on the sound assumption that no fundamental social change—be it the eradication of racism, poverty, war, sexism, homophobia or other societal ills—can come about solely through legal reform. Only organized, politicized mass activism from below, aimed at constantly enhancing and enforcing that social change or revolutionizing the entire social and economic order can achieve and maintain such goals. . . .

For many progressive lawyers, in fact, client activism is the primary object of legal advocacy. It is both means and end, powering efforts at reform and fulfilling the promise of democracy—even revolutionary transformation. For these lawyers, the key question driving legal practice is not what will ensure legal victory, but what will motivate, support and further effective activism. Only organized, politicized mass action from below, these lawyers hold—not law reform— produces fundamental, lasting social change. Indeed, this unique objective distinguishes progressive lawyering from liberal-legalist practice, which focuses intently on legal reform, secured by expert litigators, policy analysts and lobbyists.' . . .

Gerald Lopez's 1992 book, Rebellious Lawyering, was perhaps the most influential work to offer a systematic approach in this regard. Criticizing what he termed "regnant" lawyering, he argued for a vision of "teaching self-help and lay lawyering" and of "co-eminent" practitioners of lawyers and clients. The "rebellious lawyer," Lopez argued,

> must know how to work with (not just on behalf of) women, low income people, people of color, gays and lesbians, the disabled, and the elderly. They must know how to collaborate with other professional and lay allies rather than ignoring the help that these other problem-solvers may provide in a given situation. They must understand how to educate those with whom they work, particularly about law and professional lawyering, and, at the same time, they must open themselves up to being educated by all those with whom they come in contact, particularly about the traditions and experiences of life on the bottom and at the margins.

Lopez argued that rebellious lawyers must ground themselves in the communities and lives of the subordinated, continually evaluate legal and nonlegal approaches, know how to strategize, build coalitions and appreciate how all that they do with others requires attention not only to international, national, and regional matters but also to their interplay with seemingly more mundane local affairs. At bottom, the rebellious idea of lawyering demands that lawyers (and those with whom they work) nurture sensibilities and skills compatible with a collective fight for social change.

As Angelo Ancheta summarized in his review essay of Lopez's book:

Lopez's rebellious lawyers . . . are deeply rooted in the communities in which they live and work. They collaborate with other service agencies and with the clients themselves; they try to educate members of the community about their rights; they explore the possibilities of change and continually reexamine their own work in order to help their clients best. Rebellious lawyering thus redefines the lawyer-client relationship as a cooperative partnership in which knowledge and power are shared, rejecting a relationship limited to an active professional working on behalf of the passive, relatively powerless layperson.

Simulations: Morally Responsible Lawyering

In the first three of the following exercises, apply the moral responsibility approaches, and consider whether and how they differ in any way from each other and from the approach of the neutral partisan.

1. A law firm executive committee is deciding whether to represent:

> (a) an alleged perpetrator of the 9/11 attack;

> (b) a Swiss bank accused of hiding accounts from 4 holocaust survivors.

2. You are a lawyer or law firm specializing in ethics issues. The lawyers in two cases discussed in Chapter 4 ask for your advice.

> (a) Frank Armani, David Garrow's lawyer, consults you about whether to disclose the buried bodies. For an approximately 25 minute segment on the case, see *The Criminal Defense Lawyer*, a 1986 episode of the public television program *Ethics on Trial*. A copy should be available from your professor or your law school library. Otherwise, your library may be able to obtain a copy from WETA, Washington, D.C.

> (b) Dale Coventry and Jamie Kunz consult you regarding whether to disclose that their client committed the murder for which Alton Logan was wrongly sentenced to life in prison for murder. You will find helpful background in this approximately 12 minute episode of *60 Minutes*.

3. You are a lawyer representing Client in a deal where "Plan A will yield Client $1.5 million. Plan B will yield Client $2 million but will impose moderate but significant costs on many innocent third parties for which Client will not be legally responsible. Both plans are legal (as in, a good faith interpretation of the law sustains both and will find both reasonable). Client wishes to abide by the law and maximise its profits. What [will you] advise Client to do?" Eli Wald & Russell G. Pearce, *Beyond Cardboard Lawyers in Legal Ethics,* 15 Legal Ethics 125, 135 (2012).

4. The 1000 low-income tenants who live in the city-owned Housing Authority Apartments are finding that the Housing Authority is not making timely repairs, even when

the repairs are quite serious, including mold conditions, leaking water pipes, and nonfunctioning toilets. A group of tenants has asked you, as a legal services lawyer, to represent it. What law reform and rebellious lawyering strategies will you consider? Which will be most effective?

5. You are a member of a bar association committee considering whether to propose an aspirational ethical rule that lawyers are morally responsible for their conduct as lawyers. What is the significance of the rule being aspirational? What would you recommend? Why? How does your approach to the lawyer's role, whether neutral partisan or morally responsible, influence your view?

B. Feminist

The feminist perspective offers a contrast to the neutral partisan role in terms of how to relate to clients, colleagues, and adversaries.

Remember to read the questions first and then find the answers in the readings that follow.

[Question 8-17]

Carrie Menkel-Meadow's approach to feminist lawyering relies primarily upon:

    (A) Women's rights.

    (B) Women's support for individualism.

    (C) Women's understanding of relationships.

    (D) Women's superiority to men.

[Question 8-18]

Under Menkel-Meadow's approach, a man could be a feminist lawyer.

    (A) True.

    (B) False.

[Question 8-19]

Menkel-Meadow suggests that feminist lawyering has implications for:

    (A) The lawyer-client relationship.

    (B) Ethics rules.

    (C) The legal workplace.

    (D) All of the above.

CARRIE MENKEL-MEADOW, *PORTIA IN A DIFFERENT VOICE: SPECULATIONS ON A WOMEN'S LAWYERING PROCESS*

1 Berkeley Women's L.J. 39, 41-60 (1985)

I find persuasive, though not unproblematic, the notion that values, consciousness, attributes, and behavior are gendered, *i.e.*, that some are identified as belonging to women and others to men. The attachment of gender labels is a product of both present empirical research and social process. Thus, we may label the quality of caring a female quality, but note its presence in many men. Further, a man who exhibits many feminine qualities may be per-

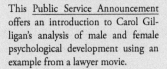

Go Online

This Public Service Announcement offers an introduction to Carol Gilligan's analysis of male and female psychological development using an example from a lawyer movie.

ceived as feminine, *e.g.* "He's too sensitive to be a good trial lawyer," or alternatively, an assertive woman may be met with remarks such as, "She's as sharp as any of the men on the team." Attributing behavior characteristics to a particular gender is problematic, because even as we observe such generalizations to be valid in many cases, we risk perpetuating the conventional stereotypes that prevent us from seeing the qualities as qualities without their gendered context.

Several recent studies and books in psychological development have traced the implications of gender differences in psychological development for personality, moral development, child rearing, and ultimately, the very structure of major social institutions. The common theme that unites this body of work by psychologists such as Chodorow, Dinnerstein, Miller, Schaef, and most recently, Gilligan, is that women experience themselves through connections and relationships to others while men see themselves as separately identified individuals.

In her book, *In a Different Voice: Psychological Theory and Women's Development*, Gilligan observes that much of what has been written about human psychological development has been based on studies of male subjects exclusively. As a consequence, girls and women have either not been described, or they are said to have "failed" to develop on measurement scales based on male norms.

Go Online

Carol Gilligan discusses examples of how female and male students discuss moral issues differently in this video.

An example drawn from Gilligan's work best illustrates the duality of girls' and boys' moral development. In one of the three studies on which her book is based, a group of children are asked to solve Heinz's dilemma, a hypothetical moral reasoning problem used by Kohlberg to rate moral development on his six-stage scale. The dilemma is that Heinz's wife is dying of cancer and requires a drug which the local pharmacist has priced beyond Heinz's means. The question is posed: should Heinz steal the drug?

To illustrate and explain the differences between the ways boys and girls approached this problem, Gilligan quotes from two members of her sample, Jake and Amy. Jake, an eleven-year-old boy, sees the problem as one of "balancing rights," like a judge who must make a decision or a mathematician who must solve an algebraic equation. Life is worth more than property, therefore Heinz should steal the drug. For Amy, an eleven-year-old girl, the problem is different. Like a "bad" law student she "fights the hypo"; she wants to know more facts: Have Heinz and the druggist explored other possibilities, like a loan or credit transaction? Why couldn't Heinz and the druggist simply sit down and talk it out so that the druggist would come to see the importance of Heinz's wife's life? In Gilligan's terms, Jake explores the Heinz dilemma with "the logic of justice" while Amy uses the "ethic of care." Amy scores lower on the Kohlberg scale because she sees the problem rooted in the persons involved rather than in the larger universal issues posed by the dilemma.

In conventional terms Jake would make a good lawyer because he spots the legal issues of excuse and justification, balances the rights, and reaches a decision, while considering implicitly, if not explicitly, the precedential effect of his decision. But as Gilligan argues, and as I develop more fully below, Amy's approach is also plausible and legitimate, both as a style of moral reasoning and as a style of lawyering. Amy seeks to keep the people engaged; she holds the needs of the parties and their relationships constant and hopes to satisfy them all (as in a negotiation), rather than selecting a winner (as in a lawsuit). If one must be hurt, she attempts to find a resolution that will hurt least the one who can least bear the hurt. (Is she engaged in a "deep pocket" policy analysis?) She looks beyond the "immediate lawsuit" to see how the "judgment" will affect the parties. If Heinz steals the drug and goes to jail, who will take care of his wife? Furthermore, Amy is concerned with *how* the dilemma is resolved: the process by which the parties communicate may be crucial to the outcome. (Amy cares as much about procedure as about substance.) And she is being a good lawyer when she inquires whether all of the facts have been discovered and considered.

The point here is not that Amy's method of moral reasoning is better than Jake's, nor that she is a better lawyer than Jake. (Some have read Gilligan to argue that the women's voice is better. I don't read her that way.) The point is that Amy does some things differently from Jake when she resolves this dilemma, and these things have useful analogies to lawyering and may not have been sufficiently credited as useful lawyering skills. Jake and Amy have something to learn from one another.

Thus, although a "choice of rights" conception (life vs. property) of solving human problems may be important, it is not the only or the best way. Responsibilities to self and to others may be equally important in measuring moral, as well as legal decision making, but have thus far been largely ignored. For example, a lawyer who feels responsible for the decisions she makes with her client may be more inclined to think about how those decisions will hurt other people and how the lawyer and client feel about making such decisions. (Amy thinks about Heinz, the druggist, and Heinz's wife at all times in reaching her decision; Jake makes a choice in abstract terms without worrying as much about the people it affects.)

Both Gilligan and Noddings see differences in the ethics men and women derive from their different experiences of the world. Men focus on universal abstract principles like justice, equality and fairness so that their world is safe, predictable and constant. Women solve problems by seeking to understand the context and relationships involved and understand that universal rules may be impossible.

The two different voices Gilligan describes articulate two different developmental processes. To the extent that we all have both of these voices within us and they are not exclusively gender based, a mature person will develop the ability to consider the implications of both an abstract rights analysis and a contextualized responsibilities analysis. For women, this kind of mature emotional and intellectual synthesis may require taking greater account of self and less account of the other; for men, the process may be the reverse. Such an integration will not resolve all issues of personal development.

The basic structure of our legal system is premised on the adversarial model, which involves two advocates who present their cases to a disinterested third party who listens to evidence and argument and declares one party a winner. In this simplified description of the Anglo-American model of litigation, we can identify some of the basic concepts and values which underlie this choice of arrangements: advocacy, persuasion, hierarchy, competition, and binary results (win/lose). As I have argued elsewhere, this conception of the dispute resolution process is applied more broadly than just in the conventional courtroom. The adversarial model affects the way in which lawyers advise their clients ("get as much as you can"), negotiate disputes ("we can really get them on that") and plan transactions ("let's be sure to draft this to your advantage"). All of these activities in lawyering assume competition over the same limited and equally valued items (usually money) and assume that success is measured by maximizing individual gain. Would Gilligan's Amy create a different model?

By returning to Heinz's dilemma we see some hints about what Amy might do. Instead of concluding that a choice must be made between life and property, in resolving the conflict between parties as Jake does, Amy sees no need to hierarchically order the claims. Instead, she tries to account for all the parties' needs, and searches for a way to find a solution that satisfies the needs of both. In her view, Heinz should be able to obtain the drug for his wife and the pharmacist should still receive payment. So Amy suggests a loan, a credit arrangement, or a discussion of other ways to structure the transaction. In short, she won't play by the adversarial rules. She searches outside the system for a way to solve the problem, trying to keep both parties in mind. Her methods substantiate Gilligan's observations that women will try to change the rules to preserve the relationships.

Furthermore, in addition to looking for more substantive solutions to the problem (*i.e.*, not accepting the binary win/lose conception of the problem), Amy also wants to change the process. Amy sees no reason why she must act as a neutral arbiter of a dispute and make a decision based only on the information she has. She "belie[ves] in communication as the mode of conflict resolution and [is convinced] that the solution to the dilemma will follow from its compelling representation. . . ." If the parties talk directly to each other, they will be more likely to appreciate the importance of each other's needs. Thus, she believes direct communication, rather than third party mediated debate, might solve the problem, recognizing that two apparently conflicting positions can both be simultaneously legitimate, and there need not be a single victor.

The notion that women might have more difficulty with full-commitment-to-one-side model of the adversary system is graphically illustrated by Hilary, one of the women lawyers in Gilligan's study. This lawyer finds herself in one of the classic moral dilemmas of the adversary system: she sees that her opponent has failed to make use of a document that is helpful to his case and harmful to hers. In deciding not to tell him about the document because of what she sees as her "professional vulnerability" in the male adversary system, she concludes that "the adversary system of justice impedes not only the supposed search for truth (the conventional criticism), but also *the expression of concern for the person on the other side*." Gilligan describes Hilary's tension between her concept of rights (learned through legal training) and her female ethic of care as a sign of her socialization in the male world of lawyering. Thus, the advocacy model, with its commitment to one-sided advocacy, seems somehow contrary to "apprehending the reality of the other" which lawyers like Hilary experience. Even the continental inquisitorial model, frequently offered as an alternative to the adversarial model, includes most of these elements of the male system—hierarchy, advocacy, competition and binary results.

So what kind of legal system would Amy and Hilary create if left to their own devices? They might look for ways to alter the harshness of win/lose results; they might alter the rules of the game (or make it less like a game); and they might alter the very structures and forms themselves. Thus, in a sense Amy and Hilary's approach can already be found in some of the current alternatives to the adversary model such as mediation. Much of the current interest in alternative dispute resolution is an attempt to modify the harshness of the adversarial process and expand the kinds of solutions available, in order to respond better to the varied needs of the parties. Amy's desire to engage the parties in direct communication with each other is reflected in mediation models where the parties talk directly to each other and forge their own solutions. The work of Gilligan and Noddings, demonstrating an ethic of care and a heightened sense of empathy in women, suggests that women lawyers may be particularly interested in mediation as an alternative to litigation as a method of resolving disputes.

Even within the present adversarial model, Amy and Hilary might, in their concern for others, want to provide for a broader conception of interested parties, permitting participation by those who might be affected by the dispute (an ethic of inclusion). In addition, like judges who increasingly are managing more of the details of their cases, Amy and Hilary might seek a more active role in settlement processes and rely less on court-ordered relief. Amy and Hilary might look for other ways to construct their lawsuits and remedies in much the same way as courts of equity mitigated the harshness of the law courts' very limited array of remedies by expanding the conception of what was possible.

The process and rules of the adversary system itself might look different if there were more female voices in the legal profession. If Amy is less likely than Jake to make assertive, rights-based statements, is she less likely to adapt to the male-created advocacy mode? In my experience as a trial lawyer, I observed that some women had difficulty with the "macho" ethic of the courtroom battle. Even those who did successfully adapt to the male model often confronted a dilemma because women were less likely to be perceived as behaving properly when engaged in according to the stereotypic conception of appropriate trial behavior. The woman who conforms to the female stereotype by being "soft" or "weak" is a bad trial lawyer; but if a woman is "tough" or "strong" in the courtroom, she is seen as acting inappropriately for a woman. Note, however, that this stereotyping is contextual: the same woman acting as a "strong" or "tough" mother with difficult children would be praised for that conduct. Women's strength is approved of with the proviso that it be exerted in appropriately female spheres.

Amy and Hilary might create a different form of advocacy, one resembling a "conversation" with the fact finder, relying on the creation of a relationship with the jury for its effectiveness, rather than on persuasive intimidation. There is some anecdotal evidence that this is happening already. Recently, several women prosecutors described their styles of trial advocacy as the creation of a personal relationship with the jury in which they urge the jurors to examine their own perceptions and values and encourage them to think for themselves, rather than "buying" the arguments of one of the advocates. This is a conception of the relationship between the lawyer and the fact-finder which is based on trust and mutual respect rather than on dramatics, intimidation and power, the male mode in which these women had been trained and which they found unsatisfactory.

In sum, the growing strength of women's voice in the legal profession may change the adversarial system into a more cooperative, less war-like system of communication between disputants in which solutions are mutually agreed upon rather than dictated by an outsider, won by the victor, and imposed upon the loser. Some seeds of change may already be found in existing alternatives to the litigation model, such as mediation.

Does the female voice of relationship, care and connection lead to a different form of law practice? Although the present adversarial system may limit the ways in which concern for others may be expressed toward adversaries, the values of relationship and care may be expressed with one's work partners.

While hierarchy produces efficiency and individual achievement, as lawyers, Amy and Hilary might choose to emphasize other values such as collectivity and interpersonal connection. This attempt to work in a different way not only affects relationships within the working unit, but is also apparent in the work of feminists who seek to demystify law and the legal profession by working with clients on lay advocacy projects or self-representation.

Perhaps the most salient feature of Portia's different voice is in the lawyer-client relationship, where the values of care and responsibility for others seem most directly applicable. Amy and Hilary, with their ability to "take the part of the other and submerge the self," may be able to enter the world of the client, thereby understanding more fully what the client desires and why, without the domination of what the lawyer perceives to be "in the client's best interest." More fully developed sensitivities to empathy and altruism, as reported by Gilligan and Noddings, may enable women lawyers to understand a fuller range of client needs and objectives. As we increasingly become aware that lawyers and clients may not have the same view of the world or what they want from that world, the ability to examine all of the client's perspective becomes even more significant. Where the Jakes of this world may make assumptions about the primacy of economic and efficiency considerations of their cases, the Amys and Hilarys may see a greater number of issues in the social, psychological and moral aspects. Of course, in a fully mature and integrated vision of lawyering all of these aspects of the case would be considered important.

[T]he tendency to personalize and contextualize problems may incline women lawyers to ask for more information on a broader range of subjects and thereby develop a fuller understanding of the context of the client's life. This, in turn, may make women better lawyers, especially in their relationships with clients and in their ability to see the human complexities of some legal problems.

If Amy and Hilary use different considerations in their moral reasoning, would they create different ethical codes for the profession based on their different ways of engaging in moral reasoning? We have some evidence that Hilary would not place the same emphasis on the adversarial model of placing one's own client above the other if the result might be to hurt the other side (as well as to defeat a meritorious claim). Would Amy and Hilary have adopted the original Kutak Commission's proposal to increase the duty of a lawyer to reveal a client's wrongdoing if it caused harm to another? Would Amy and Hilary create rules about relationships between lawyers, based on mutual affiliation in the same profession, and requiring greater candor and fairness in dealing with each other? Would the conflict of interest rules or withdrawal from representation rules be different because of an ethic of care and affiliation that would lead to a different conception of client loyalty? Might a broader conception of the legal problem and its causes lead to less concern about the unauthorized practice of law and more toleration, if not encouragement, of work with other professionals and laypersons to solve those problems?

These are only a few of the available speculations about how our adversarial system might be affected by Portia's different voice.

Simulations: Feminist Lawyering

1. You are representing the defendants in the *Spaulding v. Zimmerman* case described in Chapter 4. Given your knowledge that Spaulding both suffered from an aneurysm and was not aware of that aneurysm, how would you as a feminist lawyer behave differently than the defendants' actual lawyers?

2. Carrie Menkel-Meadow suggests that feminist lawyering could require a rethinking of the ethical rules. You are a member of a committee of your state bar considering revisions of the ethics rules. Provide one or more proposals for a Rules change derived from a feminist lawyering perspective.

C. Religious Lawyering

The religious lawyering movement includes lawyers from all faith perspectives who choose to integrate their religion into their work. Following are Christian, Jewish, and Muslim perspectives.

Remember to read the questions first and then find the answers in the texts that follow.

[Question 8-20]

Professor Joseph Allegretti makes all the following observations regarding approaches to Christian lawyering EXCEPT:

    (A)   Commentators agree that law is a vocation.

    (B)   Some Christian lawyers consider it a religious obligation to follow the Rules.

    (C)   Some Christians believe that a Christian should never become a lawyer.

    (D)   Christian lawyers should consider an ethic of care.

[Question 8-21]

In her work at a large law firm, Professor Azizah al-Hibri found which area of practice most consistent with her values as a Muslim?

    (A)   Litigation.

    (B)   Corporate transactions.

    (C)   Securities regulation.

    (D)   Corporate finance.

[Question 8-22]

According to Professor Russell Pearce, all the streams of Judaism:

    (A)   Agree that a Jew must bring her religion into her work.

    (B)   Agree that a Jew must bring her religion into her work but only to the extent of observing Jewish holidays.

    (C)   Reject the notion that a Jew must bring her religion into her work.

    (D)   Take different positions with regard to the basic principle that a Jew must bring her religion into her work.

[Question 8-23]

Professor Robert Vischer makes all the following arguments EXCEPT:

    (A)   Religious lawyering poses an irrefutable threat to publicly accessible norms, client autonomy, and liberal community.

(B) **Religious lawyers should not be exempted from following Rules they find religiously objectionable.**

(C) **Religious lawyers must respect the client's direction of a matter.**

(D) **Religious lawyers should not be permitted to apply their religious beliefs to decline to represent individuals whom they find religiously objectionable.**

In *Heretics in the Temple of the Law: The Promise and Peril of the Religious Lawyering Movement* 19 J.L. & Religion 427, 427–33 (2004), Robert Vischer observes that communities of lawyers seek to integrate their religious and professional commitments. These include the Catholic Lawyers Guild and Thomas More Society, Christian Legal Society, International Association of Jewish Lawyers and Jurists, and National Association of Muslim Lawyers.

JOSEPH ALLEGRETTI, *CHRIST AND THE CODE: THE DILEMMA OF THE CHRISTIAN ATTORNEY*

34 Cath. Law. 131 (1991)

How is the Christian attorney to render to Christ what is Christ's and to the Code what is the Code's? The word "Code" is used herein as shorthand to signify the basic principles of professional ethics that govern the attorney's work in our legal system.

I. CHRIST AGAINST THE CODE

Let me illustrate with a story. I had been at divinity school only a few weeks when I met another student who was also a lawyer. She told me that she had quit the practice of law because she could not square it with her Christian beliefs. She had grown tired of being a "hired gun" whose job was to help clients avoid their moral obligations. "I couldn't be both a lawyer and a Christian," she told me. She even purported to have Biblical grounds for her view, in 1 Corinthians 6, where Paul expressed his dismay that Christians were bringing lawsuits against each other.

This model bluntly insists that a Christian cannot be a lawyer. Christians are to have as little to do with the structures and institutions of secular society as possible. Between Christ and the Code is a gulf that cannot be bridged. In its more moderate form, this model may motivate those who seek to establish Christian tribunals, divorced from the normal legal process, in which Christians can resolve disputes between themselves through mediation and fraternal correction. This model deserves respect for its single-minded devotion to following Christ. At the same time, however, it risks forgetting that sin resides not just in social structures but also in the human heart, and that God is at work redeeming not only individuals but of all creation. It forgets that Christ came to reconcile all things to God, and that Christians are called to follow Him into the world and make disciples of all nations.

II. CHRIST IN HARMONY WITH THE CODE

According to this view, there is no tension at all between the Gospel and the world. Instead, Christian values are thought to be identical with the highest values of civilization.

As applied to the legal profession, one might call the analogous model "Christ in harmony with the Code." Its adherents see no conflict between their work as lawyers and their lives as Christians. When lawyers act in accordance with the standard paradigm, they not only avoid legal trouble, but they act in a manner that is "fundamentally right." The Code itself embodies a morally appropriate vision of the lawyer's role. Thus, it seems to raise no ethical problem if a lawyer makes an honest witness look like a liar, or reveals only that portion of the truth favorable to the lawyer's client, or defends what he or she knows to be an unjust cause. Under these principles, what the Code says you can do, you can do, and what the Code says you must do, you must do, so to speak. It is this understanding that underlies the model of "Christ in harmony with the Code." There is no tension between Christian values and professional life, because the practice of law serves noble ends, or is noble in and of itself. By fulfilling the lawyer's role in the adversary system, the attorney can be confident that he or she is in fact doing what is "good and right" in the eyes of God.

This interpretation has its own strengths. Initially, it reminds us that the whole world is the arena in which God's kingdom is being realized. It recognizes that God is at work in institutions as well as in individuals. Concurrently, however, it gives rise to a risk that whatever is acceptable to the wider culture will come to be perceived as "God's will." No longer would it be presumed that Christ sits in judgment upon culture. The end result may be that "loyalty to contemporary culture [will have] so far qualified the loyalty to Christ that he [will have] been abandoned in favor of an idol called by [H]is name."

This model presents risks for the Christian lawyer as well. It can lead the attorney to abdicate moral responsibility for his or her actions, which in turn can lead to the collapse of the lawyer's moral universe. It is suspected that society's recognition of this moral abdication results in much of the criticism levied at the legal profession and to the scathing attacks on lawyers as "prostitutes," "mouthpieces," or "hired guns."

III. CHRIST IN TENSION WITH THE CODE

Like the first model, [the third model] admits that human culture is sinful, and to be involved with it leads to sin. Like the second, it insists that our sinful world is sustained and redeemed by a loving God. Christian theologians who favor this model are fond of paradoxical language. They juxtapose law and grace, God's wrath and God's mercy. They describe the individual as simultaneously both saint and sinner. This supposition can be seen variously in the theology of Augustine, Martin Luther and Reinhold Niebuhr. Christians inhabit two worlds, a private realm in which they relate to God as individuals and are bound by the teachings of Christ, and a public realm in which they live and work and must make accommodations to the sinfulness of the human condition. Christ and culture are in conflict, yet each must be obeyed.

This model has its own advantages. It is frank about the moral ambiguities and the interwoven joys and tragedies of everyday life. It captures the central insight of the Reformers—that nothing we can do can make us right with God. That, however, is the whole point. While we were yet sinners, Christ died for us and reconciled us to God. As applied to the legal profession, one might call the analogous model "Christ in tension with the Code." Here, the attorney admits that sometimes he or she does things that a nonlawyer should not do. The attorney admits that "ordinary" morality would sometimes condemn the attorney's actions. The lawyer argues, however, that everyday morality is not applicable to professional life. The attorney's professional obligations give rise to a unique set of concerns. As an agent of the client, the lawyer should be judged solely by the rules of legal ethics embodied in the Code. . . . It becomes easy to "turn aside so many ostensibly difficult moral dilemmas and decisions with the reply: but that is not my concern; my job as a lawyer is not to judge the rights and wrong[s] of the client or the cause; it is to defend as best I can my client's interests."

As in our second model, the appeal to the principles of zealousness and nonaccountability remain. But there is a difference. The individual in the second model has no doubts that a good lawyer can also be a good Christian, while the lawyer in the third model hopes that it is possible to be both, fears that it is not, and knows no way out of the dilemma. The result can be a kind of "moral schizophrenia." The attorney compartmentalizes his or her life. The public and private dimensions of life are separated and the attorney concludes that his or her Christian values apply only to the private.

Such a situation is inherently unstable. Something has to give, and it is no surprise that studies indicate that if a lawyer argues positions that conflict with personal values, over time those values will change. . . .

IV. CHRIST TRANSFORMING THE CODE

In some ways [the fourth model] resembles our third model. It also recognizes that culture is sinful, yet acknowledges that Christians have obligations to culture. Unlike the third model, however, this one claims that the Christian need not be immobilized between the demands of Christ and the demands of culture. The Christian is one under the power of Christ, and Christ is the one who redirects and reinvigorates our world. The Gospel is seen as penetrating all of life, converting both people and institutions.

This model is exemplified in Christian theology in the philosophies of Augustine and John Calvin. It is suggested that this model has a strong Biblical foundation as well. Jesus teaches that the kingdom of God has arrived. "It is presently in our midst, growing like a mustard seed, penetrating all of life. It is here, but it is not yet fully realized." Lawyers who maintain analogous views conform to the model I will call "Christ transforming the Code." Such talk is admittedly imprecise. Critics of Niebuhr have commented at length on the slipperiness of terms like "transformation" and "conversion." Vital questions remain unanswered. What does it mean to say that Christ is at work transforming culture? What counts as evidence? And how would this apply to the work of lawyers?

Despite these difficulties, this model at least recognizes that Christ is the Lord of all, even those in the legal profession, and that Christians are called to serve Him in their private and professional lives. Moreover, this model has the great advantage of rejecting the artificial separation of life into private and public realms, with religion limited to the former. The Christian attorney is to bring his or her values into the workplace, with the hope and trust that these values might revitalize and transform the lawyer's relationships and, ultimately, the profession itself. The lawyer is not a "hired gun," or an "amoral technician," and cannot avoid moral responsibility for his or her actions by resorting to professional rules and roles. The attorney is a "moral agent," whose actions have moral consequences for which the attorney is responsible, not just personally and to others, but ultimately to God.

This model is unfamiliar to most attorneys. Its implications are uncertain. It seems to threaten traditional attorney-client relations. Let me try to advance the discussion by briefly sketching three avenues for reflection. Each is an attempt to realize the goal of a legal profession transformed by the saving power of Christ.

A. The Lawyer's Vocation

First, it is suggested that we need to take a fresh look at the concept of "vocation." A "professional" is what one professes to be, but a vocation is what one is called to be, what God calls one to be. Luther and Calvin were aware that any occupation can be a calling if its primary motive is to serve God and neighbor. In an insightful article, Charles Kammer has argued that the concept of vocation can serve as a check upon the tendency of professionals like doctors and lawyers to prefer their own self-interest to the public good." According to Kammer, a profession that understands itself as a vocation "can escape many of the problems generated by . . . narrow self-interest because it is governed by a higher vision of the purposes the profession is intended to serve.' " As the professional is liberated from self-interest, he or she is set free to serve others. Work becomes an avenue of discipleship to Christ. "Our vocation becomes that of loving our neighbor through our occupation."

Still, several questions come to mind. Does it make sense to talk of a "lawyer's vocation"? In what ways can a lawyer's work be a vehicle of service to God and neighbor? More concretely, how would viewing law as a vocation affect the attorney's relationship to clients, courts, and adversaries? What would be the impact on the standard paradigm of legal ethics and the principles of zealousness and nonaccountability?

B. The Lawyer as Prophet

A second approach would be to focus on the traditional Biblical notions of priest and prophet. Sociologists have been quick to point out that the legal system plays a cultic role in society. It is the mechanism by which society resolves conflicts that threaten the social fabric. It has its own myths and rituals, its own language, its own garb. To the layperson, the legal system can be a mysterious dispenser of blind justice. In the "temple" of the law, the courthouse, lawyers and judges are the priests. Yet we know from the Scripture—from Jeremiah, Ezekiel, and Jesus—that priests can also be prophets. Lawyering can be seen not only as a priestly profession, but as an avenue for prophetic ministry. Generally speaking, a prophet interprets the signs of the time in the light of faith, and speaks God's word for that time and place. The prophet criticizes people and institutions, but not as an outsider. The prophet stands with the sinful as one of the sinful, confronting the terrible majesty of God's justice. At the same time, the prophet holds out a vision of God's mercy and faithfulness, and of the new life possible on the other side of judgment.

The task of the prophet "is to bring to expression the new realities against the more visible area of the old order.' " "The prophet offers an alternative vision of reality based upon God's freedom and God's will for justice." What would it mean to claim a prophetic role for lawyers? What is the alternative perception of reality to which they might point? First and foremost, the acceptance of a prophetic role would mean a new commitment by lawyers to the just distribution of legal services. In today's America, the poor have little access to legal counsel, and the middle-class is finding it increasingly difficult to afford legal assistance. As long as legal representation is a commodity to be purchased like any other, those who can afford lawyers will have them, and those who cannot will be left without the means to assert their legal rights. As the old law school adage goes, a right without a remedy is no right at all. Legal rights without the means to enforce them are a sham.

Although there have been a few notable exceptions, by and large, lawyers in America have served as defenders of wealth, power, and entrenched privilege. An appreciation of their prophetic role would spark a new concern for the weak and poor, those who have little voice in today's system. It would lead lawyers to question the prevailing assumption that pro bono work is a deed of charity rather than a duty of justice. Furthermore, this prophetic role shines new light on the ethical problems that lawyers confront in their daily practice. A heightened sense of social justice, for example, would force attorneys to reexamine their cherished commitment to the standard paradigm. Perhaps unqualified loyalty to the client produces injustice and social harm. Perhaps attorneys should no longer be immune from moral criticism for the ends they achieve or the means they employ. The prophetic dimension raises disturbing questions about the social and personal costs of the principles of zealousness and nonaccountability.

A prophetic role for Christian attorneys would build upon the rich legacy of the Hebrew prophets. Amos, Isaiah, and the others refused to separate worship of God from the duty to help those who could not help themselves. They attacked all who trampled the poor, turned aside the needy, exploited the weak, and corrupted the legal process. Indeed, the plea of Isaiah could almost serve as a credo for the Christian attorney: "Make justice your aim; redress the wronged, hear the orphan's plea, defend the widow." Jeremiah put it succinctly—to know God is to do justice to the poor and needy.

C. An Ethic of Care

Finally, one might follow the lead of Thomas Shaffer, and begin to explore a vision of lawyering which puts less stress on the dictates of position and more on the duty to care. The conventional wisdom too often views lawyers as possessing only two options when they have moral qualms about their client's case. The lawyer must commit to do everything legally possible to win for the client or withdraw from the case. This view of the lawyer-client relationship assumes that lawyers and clients are morally isolated from each other, and do not influence each other. Neither is open to change. Reality is quite to the contrary. An ethic of care recognizes that lawyers and clients are not morally autonomous. They are not islands unto themselves.

As they come together they become mutually dependent. In their dependence each is open to change. Conversion is possible. What Buber called the "I-Thou" relation can emerge. Openness, risk and vulnerability characterize such a relationship. The recognition of an ethic of care would produce an epochal shift in lawyering, away from the amoral provision of technical assistance, towards service to the client as a person. Shaffer writes:

> The broader professional consequences could be revolutionary: Lawyers would have to become morally attentive, attending, that is, to the persons of their clients as much as to the problems clients bring to them. Law students would come to insist on education which trains them in the skills of sincerity, congruence, and acceptance. Every level of the legal enterprise would come again to think of moral development as part of its task, all toward a professional ethic of receiving as well as giving-of unfurling rather than imposing, to use Buber's phrase.

Such an ethic ultimately rests upon the conviction that God is at work in all human relationships, and therefore all things are possible. God is the "invisible third party" in every human encounter. Again, we need to consider the impact of such a view on traditional attorney-client relationships. Would an ethic of care intrude upon client autonomy? How would it inform the attorney's approach to particular ethical duties like confidentiality? Would lawyers who adopted an ethic of care become more or less committed to the principles of zealousness and nonaccountability? Is an ethic of care even possible? Perhaps an attorney can have a relationship of openness and vulnerability with a flesh-and-blood client, but what about the attorney who represents a corporation, a union, or a pension board? An ethic of care is inherently tentative and open-ended. It provides no definitive answers to ethical questions, because only in the give-and-take of the relationship can the morally responsible course of action be discerned. Nevertheless, it deserves further exploration by those who seek an integration of the personal values and professional life of the attorney.

Is it actually an attempt to bring the force of the Gospel message to bear upon the lawyer-client relationship? Here, perhaps, is the seed for a new understanding of the Christian lawyer, a hired gun no longer, but (dare I say it?) a minister to his or her clients.

AZIZAH AL-HIBRI, *ON BEING A MUSLIM CORPORATE LAWYER*

27 Tex. Tech L. Rev. 947 (1996)

Glancing quickly at my recent past, I notice that when I practiced corporate law on Wall Street, I did not assess it from an Islamic vantage point, whatever that might be. Similarly, I do not offer today a religious critique of the subject when I teach it. I teach about the legal aspects of modern business in America; I do not judge these aspects. I take them as I find them. In other words, as an American citizen, I have thoroughly internalized the demand to compartmentalize the religious aspects of my life. I have not failed in being a good citizen.

Yet now that the door of recollection and reflection has been opened on this subject, I look back for the first time at my days as a practitioner with greater compassion and understanding. I recall the first agreement I drafted. I looked at all the precedents and found them lacking. The document related to a big deal and time was of the essence. I therefore felt that drafting a fair agreement that took into account the interests of both parties would get us to the finish line faster. That was of course the first big strategic mistake. The other was to make certain language in the agreement clear and precise.

I was soon reminded that our legal system is based on an adversarial way of doing things. Consequently, I should have looked out solely for the interests of my client and let the other lawyer look after the interest of hers. If she failed to do so adequately, then that only meant that our client had the better lawyers. I also learned that I should have left the ambiguity in the language where such ambiguity worked in favor of my client. I was reminded that these were the rules of the game, but they still did not come to me naturally.

Upon reflection, I now realize that subconsciously I was playing by different rules. As a person of faith I had already internalized my own religious values, which demanded fairness. The Qur'an is replete with statements asking us to deal with others fairly. Some verses refer specifically to commercial contexts. For example, one verse states: "And O my people! give just measure and weight, Nor withhold from the people the things that are their due . . . ." Another enjoins us to "[g]ive just measure, and cause no loss (to others by fraud). And weigh with scales true and upright. And withhold not things justly due to [people], nor do evil in the land, working mischief."

Notice that the last verse mentions commercial injustice in the same passage as doing evil in the land and working mischief. Also, notice that the verse does not permit one to shift the responsibility for achieving justice to others, such as the other person's lawyer. Yes, the firm was not being unethical by professional standards. To the contrary, it would have been remiss if it did not zealously represent the interests of its client. Still, I had problems.

I had difficulty with the common understanding of the concept of zealous representation. I had difficulty with the adversarial system. I had difficulty with common negotiation tactics, starting from those that keep the other side waiting for hours and ending with those that start serious negotiations only when the other side is ready to go to bed. All of these appeared to derive from a worldview based on domination and manipulation which was foreign to my religious beliefs. . . .

I wanted to be in corporate law because I believe in private enterprise. Private enterprise fits nicely with my religious beliefs. The Qur'an recognizes legitimate profit and the fact that people have different levels of wealth. In fact, it discusses business in several places. The Prophet himself, as well as his wife Khadija, were successful business people. What the Qur'an warns against, however, is making a profit by taking unfair advantage of others. It also denounces elevating the profit motive above faith. For this reason, it tells Muslims that it is better for them to pray when it is time for prayer, than to do business. God's "business," it notes, is much more profitable.

Working on Wall Street, it was "business" eighteen to twenty four hours a day. It was the height of market activity, and law firms were leveraging their human resources to the hilt. Driven by the Qur'anic injunction to do my job well, I put in long hours. But my firm and I were not quite on the same page. The firm wanted to maximize its profits, while offering quality services. I wanted to oblige. Yet, I was hampered in my efforts by my ambivalence about the system. I also had no time to do God's "business." There was no time to perform my five daily prayers, even in a corner of my office. It was not possible to fast the month of Ramadan or even celebrate my holidays. How could I when I had to work and bill every working moment of my long days and nights? I couldn't even get sick!

There was, however, one bright spot in my law firm experience. There was one area of the law that (subconsciously) suited my values quite well, that of securities regulation. This area of the law came into existence in order to protect public interest. For this end, full and adequate disclosure (in religious terms, telling the truth) by issuers of securities was required. I therefore launched into this difficult area of the law with a great deal of zest. In fulfilling the injunction of doing my work well, I spent long careful hours conducting due diligence and drafting documents, so that the public interest would be properly protected. I flourished doing that kind of work, I withered doing deals.

In due course, however, I concluded that the world of law firms had something fundamentally wrong with it. It was based on a system of substantive hierarchy or domination (as opposed to a merely formal one). Combined with the principle of maximizing profit to partners (at the top of the hierarchy), the system created a great deal of misery among aspiring lawyers.

The issue of hierarchy is a very significant issue for me as a Muslim feminist. Let me take the time to discuss it. In the story of the fall of Satan, we are told that God asked Satan and the angels to bow to Adam. The angels did, but Satan refused. He objected saying: "I am better than he, [you created] me from fire and [created him] from clay." This Satanic arrogance which led to challenging the Divine Will resulted in God cursing Satan.

The story has become an important symbol of what is wrong with arrogance and hierarchy. Al-Ghazali, a major Muslim jurist from the Tenth Century, states that in Islam, the rich are not better than the poor, nor are the white better than the black. These categories, he argues, are all irrelevant in the eyes of God, but they can imbue a person with a feeling of false power and arrogance, leading him to disobey God and to posit himself or another entity as a false deity. This is why wealth has often been referred to in the Qur'an as a trial or a temptation (as well as a blessing). In another passage, the Qur'an tells the story of two friends. One of them became quite arrogant about his wealth. He told his poor friend: "[I have more wealth] than you, and more honour and power in my following of [people]." God destroyed his wealth overnight.

These kinds of stories are hard to ignore. They are part of one's religious consciousness. Yet, with few exceptions among the old guard, there is increasingly no room for modesty on Wall Street. In fact, arrogance is an important indication of one's stature. A partner for example is less likely to return your greeting than an associate. Indeed, that is one way to tell the two apart. Yet the Prophet encouraged us to greet each other. He also encouraged us to return the greeting with an even better one.

My religious beliefs worked (again subconsciously) to my advantage in academia. There, I could pursue the prophetic injunction that learning is the duty of every Muslim, female and male. So, I tried to keep abreast of all legal developments and do my best toward all my students. Significantly, I was able to do so without being conflicted. I derive great pleasure out of teaching securities regulation and imbuing in my students the ethical values important for a lawyer in this area. I also enjoy teaching corporate law and encouraging my students to take private enterprise seriously. I stay away from teaching negotiating tactics.

I have been uplifted by my school's commitment to diversity. This too springs from my commitment to the principle of fundamental human equality which is another lesson of the story about Satan. Satan thought that being made from fire made him superior to Adam, who was made from clay. His belief was so unshakable that he was willing to risk God's wrath. But there is only one God. Everyone else is God's creature. To forget that is to move away from the true essence of monotheism and fall into Satanic logic. Thus, I celebrate diversity in the classroom by treating it as a very average thing. I treat my students with respect and concern, because they are God's creatures too. I have never consciously tried to place a substantive hierarchal relation between us. The results have been good for all.

Despite the rewards and pleasures of academia, the tension between my faith and profession is not totally eliminated.

I go back to corporate law. In that course, I teach my students about a system of financial organization which is primarily driven by the profit motive. I emphasize to them that a corporation is not a welfare institution. If profitability is down, then serious reexamination should follow. But how do people of faith feel about the fact that profit is the primary driving force in corporate America today? They have mixed feelings.

Clearly, the worship of wealth is idolatry, but the pursuit of wealth need not be synonymous with its worship. Consequently, what is needed is not a rejection of wealth, but a rejection of values that make it possible for a human being to regard wealth as an end in itself. We need to regain a worldview which sees society as an integral whole in which the wealthy have a duty to share part of their resources with the less privileged. We need a system which does not dehumanize workers. But such a refinement in values will require significant changes in the existing legal system itself. It will not, however, require a total rejection of the legal and business status quo.

It is important to note that in seeking such changes, religionists are not alone. Many lawyers and economists have presented humanist secular reasons for the modification of the existing system.

Are there other troublesome points in corporate law? Subconsciously, I am concerned that opening this theological Pandora's box could make it impossible for me to teach a traditional introductory class on corporations.

I turn to this example. I teach about interest and how it works. Am I teaching my students how to engage in *riba* (usury), or is interest a different concept? This issue is not unique to Muslim Americans. It also is familiar to Christians and Jews. Also, since many modern Muslim countries have adopted the same financial and legal structures we have in the United States, what have they done about interest?

On the particular question of interest, debate was heated in Muslim communities for quite a while. Finally, some jurisprudentially acceptable solutions were worked out, which were consistent with the over-all global business and legal structures.

Certain jurists distinguished between the concept of *riba* and the modern concept of interest. Others defined new financial instruments or relations having a similar financial effect as the ones involving an interest-bearing loan. For example, Muhammad Anwar, a Muslim economist, describes many alternative ways which Muslim banks devised in order to do business without falling into *riba*. These include *musharaka*, where the bank is an active partner with the borrower and shares in the profit and loss of his enterprise; *murabaha*, where the bank buys the goods and resells them to the borrower at cost plus an agreed upon profit; and *qard hassanah*, which is a straight forward interest-free loan.

At the same time, other thinkers have found jurisprudential bases for permitting Muslims in the West to become parties to agreements involving interest-bearing instruments. They did so by relying on well-established Islamic principles, such as the principle of necessity. This principle permits a Muslim to even consume pork if that is the only available food. It is founded on express statements in the Qur'an and, more generally, on the fundamental principle of jurisprudence that the Law Giver's intent (*'makasid al-shari'*) in prescribing laws is public interest (the "Public Interest Principle").

For some Muslims, some or all of these solutions remain questionable, for others they are acceptable articulations of Islamic law under existing circumstances. The concept of "existing circumstances" is itself an important concept which is broadly defined. Existing circumstances in Muslim countries are usually understood to include not only the need of the local Islamic monetary system to interact with the global one, but more importantly, a variety of internal conditions within the country itself.

In particular, the Islamic financial system is supposed to be an integral part of an overarching social and political order characterized at minimum by the principles of *takaful* and *shura*. The first principle asserts the collective responsibility of the community in meeting the basic needs of every one of its members. The second principle insures the basic right of every citizen to a democratic government.

The position of a Muslim in a non-Muslim country is complicated by additional or different considerations for various other issues. An American Muslim recognizes the fact that she lives in a society that has in some areas a set of rules that she may disagree with. What should a Muslim do about that? Actually, no more than what any other person (religious or not) is expected to do. If these different rules are patently unfair, discriminatory or otherwise impose a hardship on the person in the exercise of her own religion, then she should try to change these rules. If every possibility of meaningful change is rejected by the majority, then the Muslim is encouraged to move to a community which is more in tune with her values.

Living by one's religious beliefs turns out, however, not to be a problem for the American Muslim. An American Muslim lives in a society which shares the basic principles taught by Islam. It is a society which believes in and practices democratic governance. It is a society which believes in *takaful*, although it has not settled yet the question of whether such social responsibility should be the domain of the government or the private sector. Finally, it is a society which has constitutional guarantees for the freedom of worship. Ideally, a person of faith does not have to leave this country in order to avoid religiously oppressive laws. She only needs to go to court. A Muslim can thus be quite comfortable in this religiously diverse society because she has a place at the table like everyone else and, furthermore, she likes the table manners.

Moreover, all students, Muslim and non-Muslim alike, need to understand the basic financial structure in this country in order to function in the business world successfully. . . . I have no religious problem to teach about how interest works in our society.

From this vantage point, corporate law generally becomes a collection of rules to manage the marketplace in a presumably faith-neutral way. It provides a wide umbrella under which people of faith and secularists can come and do business together. I can thus teach it without being conflicted. . . . Furthermore, had I been teaching a course in international business and finance, I would probably find it interesting to include some lectures on Islamic banking which is now in existence in many parts of the world.

RUSSELL G. PEARCE, *THE JEWISH LAWYER'S QUESTION*

27 Tex. Tech L. Rev. 1259, 1259–70 (1996)

As a lawyer and a teacher of lawyers and law students, my experience has been that Jewish lawyers are even more uncomfortable than Christian lawyers with the possibility that their legal practice might have a religious dimension. Last Spring, for example, I had the opportunity to help lead an Auburn Theological Seminary program for Jewish and Christian lawyers on the role of religion in a lawyer's work. At the first session, the lawyers received text sources and heard talks from a leading Christian theologian and a prominent Rabbi on religious perspectives on professional role. I then separated the lawyers into a Christian group and a Jewish group and asked them to construct a religious concept of the lawyer's professional role. The Christian lawyers debated whether the concepts of vocation and calling applied to their work. Despite explicit guidance from the Rabbinic speaker, the Jewish lawyers ignored the religious implications of their practice. Instead, they focused on how their minority status and the resulting experience of discrimination influenced their approach to lawyering, including their commitment to rule of law and social justice.

When I began to reflect on these differences, I realized that I too for many years had avoided confronting the consequence of my religious belief for my legal work. As a law clerk, associate at a Wall Street firm, legal services lawyer, and general counsel to a governmental civil rights agency, I had only a vague sense of the connection between my Judaism, my pro bono and public interest choices, my integrity, and my treatment of coworkers and adversaries. Despite my belief that Judaism entered all areas of my life, I did not begin to think systematically or in depth about the implications of Judaism for law practice until I became a law professor and I read Joseph Allegretti's and Thomas Shaffer's scholarship on Christian lawyering.

A. The Professional Project's Liberating Appeal to a Religious Minority

The professional project's promise of neutrality affords Jews great comfort because of our minority status and history of discrimination. We are 2.5% of the United States population. In a legal system where the participants acted on their personal affiliations, rather than their duty to the legal system, we would be losers. We would only obtain justice at the majority's sufferance, not as a matter of right.

Equally important to Jewish lawyers is the professional project's promise of equal treatment to all individual lawyers. During the twentieth century, leaders of the bar and members of the public have stereotyped Jewish lawyers as "overly aggressive hired guns," adopting unethical "gutter" tactics, lacking in character, and "Oriental in their fidelity to the minutiae of the subject without regard to any controlling rule or reason." Extensive hiring discrimination against Jewish lawyers was documented as late as the 1960s and stereotypes of Jewish lawyers, both positive and negative, persist today.

While stereotypes and discrimination have coexisted with the professional project, the project offers as an ideal a vision of a profession where individuals are judged solely on their merits, not by virtue of their group identification. The project promised to liberate us from stereotypes and discrimination. Indeed, today, despite the persistence of some stereotypes, this promise seems to have been largely realized. The number of Jewish lawyers significantly exceeds our percentage of the population and many Jewish lawyers are among the profession's elite. Jerold S. Auerbach, the historian who has most thoroughly documented the history of antisemitism in the legal profession, recently noted "the astonishing success story of Jewish lawyers, as they erased the stigma of professional ostracism . . . ."

Auerbach suggests yet another explanation for the attachment of Jewish lawyers to the ideas embodied in the professional project. He suggests that "[e]specially for Jews, American law offered enticing rewards, beyond financial security and professional status." For immigrant Jews, the practice of law was the ultimate opportunity for assimilation as an American. In some sense, lawyers were the definitive "good Americans." They "interpret the traditions and explicate the rules of American society," and serve as the "respected custodians of American culture." Auerbach further asserts that in service of assimilation Jewish lawyers "replaced . . . their own sacred law tradition . . . with the rule of American law."

Each of these perspectives may help explain why on some levels the professional project and its promise of a nonreligious role morality offers attractions to Jewish lawyers beyond those offered majority Christian lawyers.

B. The Availability of Jewish Identities Compatible with Professional Role

Complementing the appeal of the professional project is the ready availability of Jewish identities that interfere little, if at all, with professional role. They offer the Jewish lawyer the opportunity to identify as both a Jew and a good professional.

Although the absolutist version of the professional project excludes all extraprofessional iden-tifications, a more nuanced version permits commitments which do not interfere significantly with the substantive obligations of professional role. Sanford Levinson's use of the example of Sandy Koufax's refusal to pitch in the World Series on Yom Kippur is instructive on this point. If the influence of Koufax's religion was limited to when he pitched and not how he pitched, it only interfered with his professional role to a limited extent. A pitcher who does not pitch on one day when the interests of his team would otherwise require it breaches his professional obligations, but far less so than if his religion required him to depart from professional norms on a day-to-day basis.

A Jewish lawyer could similarly be Jewish in ways which would not disturb the core of pro-fessionalism. One way is nonreligious. In part, this could stem from Jewishness as an ethnic, rather than religious, identification. Louis Brandeis chose to advocate on behalf of Jewish communal interests and economic justice, and Jack Greenberg to advocate for the rights of African-Americans, from commitments derived from a desire not only to end the oppression of Jews but to realize a world where equal justice was available to all. The Jewish lawyers at the Auburn Theological Seminary program I described above similarly attributed the commitment of Jewish lawyers to rule of law and equal justice to their experience of discrimination and not to their religious beliefs.

These ethnic Jewish identifications may influence the causes Jewish lawyers adopt, but do not otherwise influence how a lawyer engages in practice. Ethnicity could of course have broader implications, much the same way some commentators have suggested a feminist style of lawyering. But excluding stereotypes, the only ethnically Jewish approaches to lawyering thus far suggested have been the limited ones described here.

A parallel variety of Jewish religious approaches to lawyering similarly interfere minimally with the professional project. While Helen Neuborne and Joseph Rauh join Brandeis and Greenberg in viewing their lawyering for social justice as the product of their Jewishness, Neuborne and Rauh recognize the Jewish religious content of their commitment. As with Jewish ethnicity, the choice of causes on religious grounds would not interfere with how one practiced law. A similarly limited conception of religious lawyering would involve observing Jewish holy days or other ritual, like Sandy Koufax, "but leaving the internal norms of legal practice untouched."

C. Religious Influences Facilitating the Professional Project

The absence of express religious authority on the lawyer's role and the presence of religious perspectives compatible with the project also facilitate the Jewish lawyer's adherence to the professional project.

While Judaism does have a tradition of great judges who have a duty to develop a full and fair record, it lacks a developed or formal ethic for the specific role of a lawyer. Parties generally represented themselves before a Jewish court. Levinson observes that the opposition of the great medieval Jewish scholar Maimonides to the practice of law resulted from his view that a lawyer was "a legal manipulator, an artful 'arranger' concerned less with absolute fidelity to the law than with crafting ostensibly legal arguments that would enable the client to prevail against an adversary." A seventeenth century rabbi similarly condemned lawyers for "leading to argumentation and strife, deception and the adoption of false argumentation to justify the wicked and defame the righteous." Although Jewish courts have permitted lawyers since the middle ages, only in 1960 did the Israeli rabbinate "formally accept 'practices permitting legal counsel to argue on behalf of either litigant. . . .' "

The Jewish tradition's general hostility to an adversarial role appears to have an ironic result. The tradition offers little specific guidance for the modern lawyer who practices in an adversarial system. Absent a developed or formal code of Jewish legal ethics, a Jewish lawyer may therefore adopt the values of the professional project without confronting any contrary religious authority directly on point to the lawyer's role.

At the same time, two common modern versions of Judaism facilitate observance of the professional project. One version separates the public from the religious. Martin Buber describes how "[m]odern thinking" results in versions of religion where "one participates in religious services without hearing the message commanding him to go out into the world." One manifestation of this trend in Judaism has been "the development of a pure ritualism" which accepts "observance of certain prescribed forms" as the fulfillment of the covenant. The modern versions of Judaism which emphasize "pure ritualism" or other forms which reject the command "to go out into the world" permit the Jewish lawyer to subscribe to the professional project or some limited religiosity compatible with the project.

Another very different version of Judaism identifies the religious with the public. This version involves going "out into the world," but in so doing identifies American values, including the professional project, as being identical with Jewish values. Jerold Auerbach argues that as leaders of the American Jewish community, lawyers such as Louis Brandeis, Felix Frankfurter, and Louis Marshall helped create a "synthesis of Judaism and Americanism." This synthesis "identified Judaism with Americanism, within a common tradition that emphasized the rule of law and the quest for social justice."

II. JUDAISM DEMANDS A PLACE IN PROFESSIONAL PRACTICE

In his essay "The Holy Way: A Word to the Jews and to the Nations," Martin Buber declares the "modern thinking" embodied in professionalism's separation of the religious self from the professional self to be "totally unJewish." In contrast to the professional ideal, "the world of true Judaism is the world of a unified life on earth." Buber observes that "man can do justice to the relation to God that has been given to him only by actualizing God in the world in accordance with his ability and the measure of each day, daily." The separation of work from religion, like the separation of "holiness through works from holiness by grace," is "alien" to Judaism.

In this regard, Buber's observation has roots in traditional Jewish thinking. Godly actions have been a necessary part of being a religious Jew. The portion of the Torah called "The Life of Holiness" enjoins Jews to be holy as God is holy, and requires, among other things, that you leave "the gleanings of your harvest . . . for the poor and the stranger," "love your neighbor as yourself," and treat "the stranger who resides with you . . . as one of your citizens." Similarly, the prophets remind us that faith and prayer alone are not sufficient service to God. The

Prophet Isaiah, for example, told the people that God would not listen to their prayers until they began to "devote yourselves to justice; aid the wronged; uphold the rights of the orphan; and defend the cause of the widow."

The understanding of Judaism as a way of life is common to the diverse strains of modern Jewish thought. According to eminent Reform Jewish theologian Rabbi Leo Baeck, a Jew "directs him [or her] self toward God in such a way that no part of his [or her] life is without this center, without this contact." The great Conservative theologian Rabbi Abraham Joshua Heschel similarly taught that "the meaning of redemption is to reveal the holy that is concealed, to disclose the divine that is suppressed. Every person is called upon to be a redeemer, and redemption takes place every moment, every day." The eminent Orthodox scholar Rabbi Joseph B. Soloveitchik also instructed that the Halakhah "penetrates into every nook and cranny of life. The marketplace, the street, the factory, the house, the meeting place, the banquet hall, all constitute the backdrop for the religious life."

Jewish tradition therefore contains the framework for a version of Jewish lawyering radically different in premise from that underlying the professional project.

III. ANSWERING THE JEWISH QUESTION

Within the Jewish community, I take an expressly pluralist perspective. As a Reform Jew, I respect "the right of individual Jews to make the final decision as to what constitutes Jewish belief and practice for them." In that spirit, and following the teaching that Judaism is a way of life, I offer my own answer-in-progress to the Jewish question. The answer is at once both directly contrary to, and substantially compatible with, the prevailing conception of the lawyer's role. . . .

[T]he Baal Shem Tov reproache[d] his student the Maggid of Mezeritch for reading without "soul." If one can read with soul, one can surely lawyer with "soul." As Abraham Joshua Heschel taught, "[i]t is not enough to do the mitzvah; one must live what he does. . . . When the soul is dull, the mitzvah is a shell." Heschel describes the integration of soul into act as Kavvanah, "direction to God. . . . It is the act of bringing together the scattered forces of the self; the participation of heart and soul, not only of will and mind." Interestingly, Heschel expressly calls for us to bring God into the legal system. He writes that "God will return to us when we shall be willing to let Him into all parts of our lives, including into our courts."

Such a kavvanah of lawyering demands a rejection of the professional project's separation of the professional from the religious self. As a Jewish lawyer, I would direct my heart toward God in every moment of my legal practice. This task requires study and prayer, but it also requires conduct. As Rabbi Leib, son of Sarah, taught, a Jewish lawyer (like all Jews) "should see to it that all his [or her] actions are a Torah."

But how exactly to fulfill this goal is far from clear. As discussed above, this lack of clarity results in part from Jewish tradition's hostility to a lawyer's zealous representation of a client. As a result, those who try to derive a Jewish ethic for a modern lawyer have to look beyond legal ethics to construct explanations of why adversarial legal conduct is appropriate. For example, in two of the few articles discussing Jewish approaches to legal ethics, Rabbis Alfred Cohen and Gordon Tucker examined the extent of a professional's duty of confidentiality when a client poses threat of harm to a nonclient. Both applied the principle that halakhah requires putting the interests of the community above that of the individual. In the application of this principle to the problem of confidentiality, their analysis diverged. Rabbi Tucker argued that the good of the community requires revealing confidences to protect a nonclient from physical or financial harm even though the individual client will suffer detriment. In contrast, while advising consultation with halakhic authority, Rabbi Cohen asserted that "it may be that maintaining professional secrecy is so absolutely integral to the proper function of that profession and the profession so essential to the welfare of society that the halacha would decide that the practitioner must maintain his professional secrets."

In legal ethics, therefore, as in many modern moral questions, the Jewish response is not self-evident. For the Jewish lawyer, legal ethics becomes a subject for Jewish study and reflection. But while recognizing the vital importance of further study, we can find in our tradition foundational principles that on their face not only harmonize with, but require dedication to, the best aspirations of our legal system. Recognizing the risk of oversimplifying our often complicated and sometimes contradictory tradition, I will tentatively suggest two such principles.

One principle is equal justice under law. The Torah's command "[j]ustice, justice, shall you pursue" requires the creation of a just legal system. While the Torah was not speaking of a political system like our own, it does suggest attributes of justice that are applicable today. One such principle is equal justice under law. Decisions should "not favor the poor or show deference to the rich." The "stranger who resides with you shall be to you as one of your citizens." Another such principle is concern for the poor and powerless. Proverbs instructs judges to "open thy mouth for the dumb" and "plead the cause of the poor and needy."

These principles suggest that the conduct of the Jewish lawyer in upholding the rule of law and in serving the poor could be quite consistent with professional ideals. What differentiates this perspective from the simple equation of Jewish and professional values is that its foundation is Jewish values which may overlap with professional values, but will not necessarily do so.

So long as the Jewish lawyer seeks equal justice under law from a religious perspective, she will reject the professional project but not equal justice under law. As I have argued elsewhere, religious lawyering's rejection of the professional project does not necessarily undermine rule of law. Acceptance of personal identity rather than a professionally neutral role suggests a different way to think about realizing the goal. Instead of trying to "bleach out" difference, we should try to "create community" by speaking frankly about how to realize a legal system which results in equal justice given our differences and our similarities. This indeed is very much the task of the Jewish lawyer. As Buber teaches, "holiness is true community with God and true community with human beings, both in one."

ROBERT K. VISCHER, *HERETICS IN THE TEMPLE OF THE LAW: THE PROMISE AND PERIL OF THE RELIGIOUS LAWYERING MOVEMENT*

19 J.L. & Religion 427, 461–88 (2004)

Robert K. Vischer acknowledges that religious lawyering could potentially undermine important elements of our legal system and explains how proponents of religious lawyering could—and should—tailor their approach to respect core values of the legal profession.

First, Vischer argues that religious lawyering could threaten publicly accessible norms if religious lawyers described their views using religious language that was not accessible to lawyers and clients who do not share their religious views. To remedy this problem, Vischer recommends that a religious lawyer "translate her theological convictions into publicly accessible language."

Second, Vischer asserts that religious lawyering threatens client autonomy if a religious lawyer imposes her religious beliefs on her client. Vischer contends that a religious lawyer has the capacity to promote client autonomy so long as she respects her client's autonomous decisions even where they conflict with the lawyer's religious convictions.

Third, Vischer warns that some religious groups may challenge the values of liberal democracy. Vischer argues that religious lawyers should not have "an exemption from any laws or professional regulations that impede on the lawyer's faith. It simply means that the lawyers must be given space to craft their own ethical norms within the wide latitude granted them by the largely vacuous regulatory framework." Vischer further observes that religious lawyers should comply with antidiscrimination norms that are essential to a pluralist democracy. As Vischer asserts, "This is not to say that conservative religious groups will encourage an open embrace of causes like gay rights, but simply that they are more likely to differentiate between stances that diverge from those of the wider profession—e.g., declining to represent causes seeking to advance gay rights—and those that defy the profession—e.g., declining to represent gay individuals." Vischer would exclude from the profession those like Matthew Hale, leader of the white supremacist World Church of the Creator, whose religious beliefs are wholly inconsistent with liberal democracy. Vischer concludes by suggesting that in a pluralist society religious lawyers must either comply with the legal profession's regulatory framework or face the consequences of non-compliance.

Simulations: Religious Lawyering

A. Issues

1. The Bar Association Ethics Committee has been asked to consider whether and when Rule 1.7 requires a lawyer who chooses the religious lawyering perspective to disclose her perspective to her client. What should it decide?

2. Lincoln & Center's executive committee is considering whether to adopt a mandatory pro bono policy for the firm's lawyers. At least one member of the committee has adopted one of the religious lawyering perspectives described above and at least one has adopted the neutral partisan perspective. What considerations would they raise regarding the issue? How would their views differ on the policy question, if at all?

B. Hypothetical[4]

Joan Andrews lives in Tennessee. She is 14 years old and has just learned that she is pregnant. After talking to a counselor at Planned Parenthood, she decides she wants an abortion, but she is afraid to tell her parents. They are very much opposed to abortion and she is scared that they will try to prevent her from getting one. Under Tennessee law, Joan needs court permission to obtain an abortion without her parent's consent.

Scenario One: The Planned Parenthood counselor contacts the court and arranges for Joan to obtain a court appointed lawyer. The court appoints Richard Smith, Esq. to represent her. On the basis of his religious convictions, Richard believes that abortion is murder.

> A. Richard asks the court to relieve him of the appointment. Is it ethical for him to do so? How should the court decide his application?

> B. Assume the court denies his application. Richard now has to decide how to counsel Joan. May he share his personal view of abortion with her? Can he discuss with her the advantages and disadvantages of asking her parents for consent? Can he discuss with her alternatives to abortion, including adoption or keeping the child?

Scenario Two: The Planned Parenthood counselor does not contact the court because the counselor believes the quality of appointed representation is not adequate. Indeed, Planned Parenthood is working with the ACLU on a project to bring in pro bono lawyers from out of state to represent minors in order to develop standards for representing minors seeking abortions. When Joan tells Planned Parenthood she wants a lawyer, the counselor calls the ACLU, which then contacts the New York firm of Lincoln & Center to ask for a pro bono lawyer.

Most lawyers at Lincoln & Center strongly support a woman's right to choose abortion. A small minority believes that abortion is murder. The firm's Pro Bono Committee circulates within the firm its plan to join the ACLU project to represent minors seeking abortions in Tennessee. Two lawyers who strongly oppose abortion respond by asking the Pro Bono Committee not to take part in the project.

> A. How should the Pro Bono Committee decide this issue? Are the ethical rules relevant to its decision? What should a firm do when lawyers in the firm

---

4 Russell G. Pearce and Renata Dias, CLE Program on Religious Lawyering (2012).

have strongly different opinions on controversial issues? Should they take the side of the majority? Should they represent clients on both sides of the issue?

B. The Committee decides to proceed with the ACLU project. The firm assigns associate Amy Adams to represent Joan. Amy believes abortion is murder but has not told anyone at the firm about her views. She knows that a majority of the lawyers at the firm strongly support abortion rights and she is afraid that if she makes her views public she will harm her chances for advancement at the firm. Should she tell the firm she does not want the assignment? If she does, what should the firm do?

D. Racial Justice

An extensive literature discusses the relationship between race and lawyering. David Wilkins analyzes a number of these perspectives with regard to African-American lawyers and explains his own view. Gerald Lopez and Bill Ong Hing describe how their respective experiences as a Mexican-American and an Asian-American have influenced their approaches to lawyering.

Remember to read the questions first and then find the answers in the texts that follow.

Complete the reading before answering the questions.

[Question 8-24]

Anthony Griffin argues that:

    (A)   As an African-American he had an obligation to represent the Klan.

    (B)   As an African-American he had an obligation to refuse to represent the Klan.

    (C)   Being African-American was irrelevant to his decision to represent the Klan.

[Question 8-25]

According to David Wilkins, African-American lawyers:

    (A)   Should place their professional obligations above their racial obligations.

    (B)   Should place their racial obligations above their professional obligations.

    (C)   Should reconcile their professional and racial obligations.

    (D)   Have no legitimate racial obligations.

[Question 8-26]

David Wilkins argues that in the O.J. Simpson trial:

    (A)   Johnnie Cochran appropriately navigated racial and professional obligations.

    (B)   Christopher Darden appropriately navigated racial and professional obligations.

(C) Both Cochran and Darden appropriately navigated racial and professional obligations.

(D) Neither Cochran nor Darden appropriately navigated racial and professional obligations.

[Question 8-27]

Gerald Lopez describes how his experience growing up as a Mexican-American in East L.A. influenced his conception that lawyering should include all of the following EXCEPT:

(A) Seeking community input.

(B) Prioritizing civil rights law reform.

(C) Partnering with nonlawyer problem solvers.

(D) Promoting equitable democracy and equal citizenship.

[Question 8-28]

Bill Ong Hing argues all of the following EXCEPT:

(A) Asian-American lawyers should empathize with underserved members of their community.

(B) Legal education prepares lawyers to pursue the common good.

(C) Asian-American lawyering is not consistent with the dominant understanding of the professional project.

(D) Asian-American lawyers should assist communities of color and other subordinated groups.

DAVID B. WILKINS, *IDENTITIES AND ROLES: RACE, RECOGNITION, AND PROFESSIONAL RESPONSIBILITY*

57 Md. L. Rev. 1502 (1998)

Consider the following cases:

1. Anthony Griffin, a black lawyer affiliated with the ACLU, agrees to defend the Grand Dragon of the Ku Klux Klan. The case involves the State of Texas's attempt to subpoena the Klan's membership list in order to assist a probe into Klan violence against black residents in a newly integrated housing project. The African American head of the Port Arthur branch of the NAACP subsequently fires Griffin from his position as the unpaid general counsel for that organization when Griffin refuses to withdraw from representing the Klan.

[2.] Gil Garcetti assigns Christopher Darden as one of the lead prosecutors in the racially charged Simpson prosecution. During the course of the trial, Darden seeks to bar the defense from questioning Mark Fuhrman about whether he used racial epithets in the past. Subsequently, Johnnie Cochran, the black lead defense lawyer, argues to the predominately black jury that they should acquit his client in part as a means of "sending a message" that police racism and misconduct will not be tolerated.

Each of these high-profile cases has become a part of America's great conversation—or more accurately "angry polemic" on race. At one time or another, each of the major black protagonists—Griffin, the head of the Port Arthur branch of the NAACP, . . . Darden, and Cochran—has been accused of racial "crimes" ranging from "selling out" to "playing the race card." Other equally vociferous combatants retort that one or the other of these attorneys has in fact served the cause of racial justice by upholding the highest standards of professionalism. These high profile cases, therefore, provide useful vehicles for examining the relationship between racial identity and professional role. . . .

Bleached out professionalism is the dominant narrative through which most observers have examined the conduct of [these] attorneys[.] Indeed, most participants in these cases, including virtually all of the black lawyers, have been careful to pay allegiance to bleached out professionalism as a core professional ideal. Thus, Anthony Griffin sometimes claimed that race had "nothing to do" with his decision to represent the Klan, branding as "racist" both "those black folks who told me I should have let a white lawyer take th[e] case" and "Anglos, who regarded me as some kind of oddity because I was a black man who represented the Klan." Similarly, Christopher Darden flatly states that "if I thought I was being assigned to the case primarily because I was black, I would've rejected it." Nevertheless, Darden believes that for many Americans, he "was a black prosecutor, nothing more."

In practice[,] bleached out professionalism has been closely linked to particular normative and empirical claims that are themselves importantly bleached. Specifically, the idea that lawyers should not consider their racial identities when acting in their professional role is closely linked to the understanding that the legal rules and procedures that lawyers interpret and implement are also unaffected by issues of race. The claim that "our constitution"—and indeed justice itself—"is color-blind" is taken by many to be a bedrock principle of our legal order. Lawyers who either explicitly or implicitly call attention to racial issues are frequently viewed as undermining this ideal.

This charge—that a lawyer who interjects race or racism into a legal proceeding has "played the race card" in a manner that undermines "colorblind" justice—is itself formally colorblind, but in practice, color-conscious. The charge is formally colorblind in the sense that it can be leveled against any lawyer regardless of that lawyer's race. . . . When a black lawyer adopts an explicitly race-conscious strategy, however, the charge of "playing the race card" is likely to be closely linked to the related charge of group-based loyalty in violation of the norms of bleached out professionalism. . . . [T]he Simpson case is instructive. When critics accused Johnnie Cochran of "playing the race card," they frequently linked Cochran's explicitly race-conscious lawyering strategy with his identity as an African American.

Finally, the practical link between bleached out professionalism and colorblindness has been strengthened by the implicit empirical claim that the American legal system is in fact largely, if not completely, colorblind. Once again, there is no necessary connection between the normative and the empirical sides of the colorblindness debate. One can subscribe to colorblindness as a normative ideal without also believing that our legal institutions fully, or even largely, live up to this ideal in practice. . . . The practical effect of bleached out professionalism . . . is to push all lawyers in the direction of accepting colorblindness as both a normative ideal and a factual reality in our contemporary culture.

Just as bleached out professionalism provides the dominant narrative through which most Americans have come to understand [these] cases[,] representing race theories have supplied the counternarrative that has helped to give these events much of their saliency. Thus, the country's fascination with Darden and Griffin is fueled in part by the charge, sometimes explicit, often merely implicit, that these two black attorneys have "betrayed" their race—in Darden's case by working on behalf of a "hostile white society to bring a strong black man down," and in Griffin's, by representing an organization that has brutalized and intimidated African-Americans for more than a century. The general perception of Cochran . . . has been similarly influenced by the counternarrative of representing race theories, albeit in the opposite direction. With respect to these lawyers, the charge is that they have represented their racial interests all too well—Cochran by "playing the race card" to free Simpson and Johnson by opposing the death penalty on the basis of his loyalty to his predominately black and Latino constituents—all at the expense of their professional obligations.

The representing race model of lawyering, like the bleached out professionalism it challenges, underscores important goals that are central to our system of justice. . . . For black Americans, however, race continues to pose a substantial obstacle to obtaining anything like equal access to the benefits and protections of the law. Representing race accounts of lawyering, by focusing attention on this disparity and by directing lawyers to identify and to work against race prejudice, arguably help America move closer to its legitimating ideals. . . . It is this feature of the representing race model—its connection to the social justice claims of the entire black community—that provides the strongest justification for transforming a general critique of colorblindness into a repudiation of bleached out professionalism. The claim that blacks who obtain positions of power and influence in American society have an obligation to "give back" to their community is an old and venerable one. . . . The application of this maxim of race-based obligations to lawyers can be traced to Charles Hamilton Houston. In the 1930s, Houston argued that black lawyers should be trained to be social engineers " 'prepared to anticipate, guide and interpret group advancement.' " Over the next twenty years, Houston and his protégé Thurgood Marshall created a new model for achieving social justice through law and the nation's first public interest law firm, the NAACP Legal Defense and Education Fund, with the skill and commitment to put that strategy into action. By calling on black lawyers to pay particular attention to the manner in which their professional activities are likely to affect the interests of the black community as a whole, representing race accounts of lawyering continue this Houstonian tradition.

The benefits of Houston's social engineering model for the justice claims of black Americans in the period leading up to *Brown v. Board of Education* cannot seriously be challenged. Although black lawyers were certainly not the only participants in the civil rights movement—many whites also fought valiantly for the cause of equal rights—the fact that Houston's social engineers were prepared to self-consciously and forthrightly represent their race in the corridors of legal and political power has substantially improved the status of every black American, including those who continue to suffer in poverty and degradation.

Moreover, by dismantling de jure segregation, Houston and Marshall removed a powerful blight on the legal profession's age-old claim that lawyers are connected to justice. It is now common for liberals and conservatives alike to point to the crusade leading up to Brown as definitive proof that the legal profession, notwithstanding all of its connections to power and the status quo, in fact stands on the side of justice for all citizens. As a result, Houston's race-conscious lawyering strategy has ironically become a key element in the defense of the bleached out professional norm that "[l]awyers, as guardians of the law, play a vital role in the preservation of society.". . .

In theory, representing race accounts need not require the level of total commitment to racial issues that Houston sometimes seemed to suggest was required of the black lawyers in his day. For example, none of the theorists cited above suggest that the only appropriate role for black lawyers is the kind of full-time civil rights practice for which Houston prepared his social engineers. Nor must representing race advocates completely reject the moral force of the profession's traditional bleached out norms. Both Houston and Marshall, for example, consistently demonstrated respect for the profession's rules and practices even as they pursued their explicitly race-conscious strategy for social change.

In practice, however, representing race models tend to treat race as the central feature in the lives of black lawyers—a feature that overwhelms other professional commitments. This is clearly true in the popular debate about the obligations of black lawyers. In that debate, racial loyalty is often presented as an "either/or proposition—you're either for us or against us, a race man or a sellout." In such a world, as the popular portrayal of the Darden Dilemma amply demonstrates, when a black lawyer conforms his conduct to the profession's bleached out values, he "risk[s] his status as an authentic black man—and in the race man ideology, to be an authentic black man is to put the black race first."

Academic supporters of representing race models reject this sharp dichotomy. For example, in an important essay, Margaret Russell argues that black lawyers must move beyond the "false dichotomies" of "sellouts" and "race cards" in order to find meaningful ways of representing their clients and their communities.

Nevertheless, a good deal, although by no means all, of the scholarship in this area tends to minimize the importance of a black lawyer's professional obligations relative to those connected to her racial identity. . . . Even Margaret Russell's analysis of Darden and Simpson, although rejecting the popular dichotomy between sellouts and race men, suggests that race is the most important factor in the professional lives of black attorneys. Thus, Russell argues that given pervasive and systematic racism in the American justice system, every case involving a black lawyer "is at some level a 'race case.'"

If bleached out professionalism and representing race theory provide the narrative and counternarrative . . . , personal morality accounts of the lawyer's role constitute a seldom articulated but nevertheless pervasive subtext. For example, in responding to pleas from his NAACP colleagues that he "defer to another lawyer to handle matters involving the Klan," Anthony Griffin repeatedly emphasized his personal commitment to a near-absolutist interpretation of the First Amendment. Similarly, Darden defends his angry exchanges with Johnnie Cochran on the ground that he had "'responsibilities as a human being that were just as important as the responsibilities of being an African American.'" . . . As the statements by Griffin and Darden . . . underscore, one way that black professionals have sought to escape the stark dilemma of the "sellout or race man" trope is to insist that questions such as this are primarily a matter of personal moral commitment.

Finally, as I indicated at the outset, for many blacks, their racial identity carries moral as well as practical significance. As Stephen Carter has observed: "[r]acial solidarity, in the sense of self-love, is the key to our survival in a frustratingly segregated integrated professional world, just as it is the key to our survival in a frustratingly oppressive nation." But even those blacks who view racial identity as an unjust burden that must constantly be challenged have moral reasons for caring about the collective welfare of other blacks. Given the link between individual opportunity and collective advancement, even those blacks who care only about their own moral right to be free from racist constraints ought to recognize a moral responsibility to participate in collective projects to end racist oppression.

It is this complex sense of identity that black Americans bring to their roles as lawyers. None of the three models we have been discussing—bleached out professionalism, representing race theory, or personal morality lawyering—sufficiently accounts for this complexity. . . . Once we view racial identity as relatively rooted and salient in the lives of black Americans—in part as a result of the salience that this identity continues to have in the eyes of those who are not black—neither of these propositions is plausible. Black lawyers, even those who are strongly committed to their roles as lawyers, will have a difficult time "checking" their identities at the door. Christopher Darden is a perfect case in point. Darden repeatedly emphasized that he became a prosecutor in part so that he could "embolden my black brothers and sisters, show them that this was their system as well, that we were making progress." Racial identity, in other words, played a crucial role in shaping Darden's sense of his own professional identity. But, as Darden soon found out, the framing of the intersection of his racial and professional identities was not exclusively, or even primarily, within his control. "[I]nstead," Darden laments, "I was branded an Uncle Tom, a traitor used by The Man." Nor, in Darden's view, were whites able to look beyond "'the pigmentation of my skin.'" Race, in other words, defined the way that others saw him as much or more than it defined his own self image.

Given the saliency of race in our contemporary culture, none of this should be particularly surprising. The claim that lawyers and those with whom they interact can ignore race even if they wanted to requires believing that there is an "essential" core of rationality free from the pervasiveness of racial imagery, or that individuals can "construct" such a self out of existing cultural materials. Neither belief is warranted. Bleached out professionalism does not tell us how to come to terms with this reality.

Representing race theory constitutes one plausible method for filling this void. These theories rightly call attention to the importance of race in the lives of black Americans. By stressing the extent to which race dominates the lives of black lawyers, however, strong representing race accounts tend to undervalue the degree to which the decision to become a lawyer inevitably shapes a black lawyer's moral identity.

The Simpson case is again instructive. As I noted earlier, Margaret Russell divorces her examination of the manner in which race structured the famous exchanges between Christopher Darden and Johnnie Cochran from the legal and ethical merits of the lawyering strategies these two men employed. This way of framing the issue, however, obscures the moral weight of voluntarily assumed professional commitments. Unlike ordinary black citizens, both Darden and Cochran made an express commitment to abide by the rules of legal ethics. Consequently, in order to determine whether Christopher Darden "sold out" the interests of the black community by opposing the introduction of Fuhrman's alleged racism, or whether Johnnie Cochran "played the race card" in urging jurors to "send a message" that police racism and deception would no longer be tolerated, it is necessary to examine the legal and ethical merits of the arguments they employed.

The public—judges, clients, victims—depend upon black lawyers, as they depend upon all lawyers, to honor their professional commitments. Black lawyers, therefore, cannot lightly dismiss professional norms that seek to protect the interests of defendants—particularly black defendants—accused of racially sensitive crimes. Nor should one disregard the professional norms that intend to protect the victims and potential victims—most of whom will also be African American—of black defendants accused of non-violent crimes. Strong versions of representing race ethics run the risk of subordinating all of these individual interests to the greater good of the black community.

Nor is there a credible argument that the legitimate constraining force of these voluntarily assumed professional commitments has been nullified by racism. . . . Indeed, it is precisely because of the racism that pervades American society that black lawyers have an acute interest in being recognized as free and equal moral actors capable of honoring their chosen commitments. As the opportunity critique underscores, the perception that black lawyers consider themselves exempt from ordinary role obligations threatens this status.

Personal morality accounts of the lawyer's role paradoxically reinforce these problems. By emphasizing the importance of lawyers' getting in touch with their own "authentic" moral commitments, personal morality theories validate the element of choice in a black lawyer's moral personality that representing race theories tend to slight. The purpose behind this recognition, however, is to put individuals in touch with the moral commitments that they had before becoming lawyers and to help them learn to recognize circumstances where these commitments modify (or, in extreme cases, trump) what otherwise would be considered binding professional commitments. Once again, this formulation gives too little weight to collectively defined professional values. . . . As I have already indicated, lawyers are more than ordinary citizens; they have been given a monopoly by the state to occupy a position of trust both with respect to the interests of their clients and the public purposes of the legal framework. This status is a part of the moral identity of black lawyers.

The view that moral commitments are the product of individual moral choice underestimates the important role that communal attachments—including attachments that are created without our express consent—play in the development of our moral personalities and in human flourishing more generally. As David Luban argues, "at bottom, moral deliberation takes place within communities—communities that can include friends and families, religious congregations, coworkers, or professional groups." For black lawyers, the black community is an important source of moral community.

Bleached out professionalism, representing race theory, and personal morality lawyering all seek to simplify a black lawyer's moral universe by privileging one set of moral considerations—professionalism, racial solidarity, personal moral reflection—over other arguably relevant considerations. A full understanding of the integration of identity and role must begin by rejecting this kind of simplification. Black lawyers simultaneously inhabit all three of these moral domains: the "professional," representing the legitimate demands that accompany their professional status as lawyers; the "obligation thesis," representing the legitimate moral commitments that black lawyers owe to the African American community; and, for want of a better term, the "personal" universe, representing the inherent right of every black lawyer to pursue her own unique projects and commitments. . . . [In] principle racial obligations are morally justified provided that black lawyers who seek to honor this commitment can do so in a manner consistent with the legitimate constraints imposed by the consumer protection and opportunity critiques. . . . The ethical life of a black attorney involves learning how to evaluate and balance these three moral domains—the professional, the obligation thesis, and the personal—within the confines of our common moral commitments. This is clearly a complex task.

First, it is important to emphasize that the demands of the three moral worlds will not always be in conflict. . . . Second, even in circumstances where two or more of the moral spheres appear to be in conflict, a careful examination of the issues at stake can often reduce, although perhaps not eliminate, the scope of disagreement. Two standard interpretive tools should help black attorneys narrow the range of conflict. [L]awyers should employ the "principle of charity" to define the reasonable scope of each sphere. Under this principle, the lawyer should give professional norms, racial obligations, and personal commitments the best plausible interpretation that is consistent with the fact that each is bounded by the legitimate demands of the others, and ultimately, by common morality. [B]lack lawyers should utilize conventionalist theories of interpretation, which attempt to find coherence in the practices and conventions of a given interpretive community. . . . Third, in the event of a direct conflict—and such conflicts, I believe, are inevitable—black lawyers should choose the course of action that best supports the social purposes of the lawyering role in question. By "social purposes," I mean those aspects of a given lawyer's role that disinterested social actors would describe as necessary to achieve the social function for which the specific legal task at issue is designed to achieve. . . .

Finally, even if black lawyers were scrupulously to follow the method of reasoning I propose, it will still frequently be impossible for them to account for the legitimate demands of each moral sphere in every case. In particular cases, the legitimate moral demands of professionalism, group obligations, and personal commitments will conflict in ways that no overarching decisionmaking criteria can resolve. Black lawyers must develop methods for accounting for this moral residue in future actions.

Let us return to the . . . cases with which we began: the black lawyer who represents the Ku Klux Klan . . . and the Simpson prosecution. The first step in applying the framework I propose is to recharacterize each case in terms of a clash among the lawyer in question's professional, race-related, and personal moral commitments. Thus, Anthony Griffin's decision to represent the Klan is solidly grounded in both a long-standing professional commitment to provide legal representation for even the most repugnant clients and Griffin's strong personal commitment to his colleagues at the ACLU and, more generally, to a robust interpretation of the First Amendment. These professional and personal commitments, however, appear (at least on first blush) to conflict with Griffin's obligation to protect the black community's interest in combating racist oppression, or, at a minimum, not to assist those who victimize blacks from escaping prosecution.

The now infamous Darden-Cochran exchanges highlight additional alignments. As one of the lead prosecutors, Darden had a strong professional obligation to present all reasonable arguments pointing to Simpson's guilt. Moreover, this role-related obligation coincided with Darden's personal belief that Simpson was guilty and, more generally, with his commitment to vigorous law enforcement. In the eyes of many blacks and some whites, however, Darden's efforts to suppress Fuhrman's prior racist statements—and his prosecution of Simpson generally—are emblematic of the manner in which the criminal justice system fails to respect the rights of African Americans. Many of these same blacks and whites viewed Cochran's infamous call for the jury to "send a message" that police racism and incompetence should not be tolerated as speaking directly to this race-related obligation. Like Darden, Cochran's advocacy tracked his personal beliefs, both about Simpson's guilt (*i.e.*, that Simpson was innocent) and about law enforcement generally (*i.e.*, that the police frequently mistreat, and not infrequently attempt to frame, African American defendants). Although these race-based and personal commitments were consistent with Cochran's duty to provide Simpson a zealous defense, many assert that they led him to exceed the legitimate professional boundaries of such a defense by unethically injecting race into the trial.

The first thing to notice about this recharacterization of these three cases is that it demonstrates that adherents of bleached out professionalism exaggerate the danger of allowing lawyers to incorporate their identity into their professional roles. In each of these cases, one important consequence of integrating identity and role is to reinforce, at great personal cost, professional norms. Thus, Anthony Griffin's strong suspicion of state power is rooted in his experience as a black man growing up in the South. This suspicion, in turn, underlies his personal commitment to the ACLU and its strong support of First Amendment rights, which in turn motivates Griffin to uphold one of bleached out professionalism's highest aspirational goals: making legal counsel available to clients with unpopular views. . . . Finally, both Darden and Cochran directly called on their experiences as African American men to support their professional obligation to zealously advocate their respective clients' positions regarding the admission of Fuhrman's prior racist statements. . . .

That being said, all three of these cases also appear to present a classic conflict among the competing demands of race, individual autonomy, and professional role. In order to determine whether there is such a conflict, however, it is necessary to look more closely at the claims that have been made about the content and scope of the obligations emanating from each of these moral domains.

A. Charity and Conventionalism: Narrowing the Gap

As William Kunstler, who for more than four decades was perhaps America's foremost advocate for unpopular clients, once stated when explaining why he would not represent the Klan: "Everyone has a right to a lawyer, that's true. But they don't have a right to me." To note that the professional sphere's demands on Griffin are not as capacious as some have portrayed, however, does not mean that they are unimportant. The rules of professional responsibility urge lawyers not to turn away unpopular clients or causes. . . . As a loyal member of the ACLU, Griffin was committed to defending First Amendment principles regardless of his personal opposition to his client's views. This strongly held personal conviction is crucial to any evaluation of Griffin's actions. Nevertheless, it is important to see that Griffin was not compelled to represent the Klan by the profession's norms. Nor should he have been, given our respect for the very moral autonomy that, in the last analysis, makes me support his decision to represent the Klan in this case.

When faced with a direct conflict between or among the legitimate demands of two or more moral spheres, black lawyers must learn to recognize and give regard to the legitimate social purposes underlying the particular lawyering role in question. . . . Consider, for example, the prosecution's strategy in the Simpson case. Both District Attorney Garcetti and Darden stated repeatedly that race was not an issue in the case. To the extent that these statements were intended to convey the impression that race was irrelevant, they were clearly wrong. Long before Fuhrman's racism or the racial composition of the jury surfaced as issues in the case, the simple fact that a black man was accused of murdering his white (blond, no less) former wife and her handsome white friend ensured that race was likely to play an important role in how people viewed the case. Nevertheless, the prosecution's statements captured an important aspirational norm fundamental to the social purpose of our justice system: that race should not affect the determination of the accused's guilt or innocence. To honor this norm, however, prosecutors are sometimes justified in engaging in race-conscious lawyering strategies.

Viewed from this perspective, Garcetti's decision to prosecute Simpson in Los Angeles County rather than in Santa Monica County and his addition of Darden to the prosecution team support, rather than undermine, the legitimate aspirations of the criminal justice system.

Given the composition of the respective jury pools, a Los Angeles jury would likely include several blacks. A Santa Monica jury would not. In light of the racially charged atmosphere in L.A. at the time of the Simpson trial, and the long history of the demonization of black male sexuality, trying the case before a jury that included at least some blacks arguably made it more likely that the legal system would honor—and just as important, be seen as honoring—its commitment that race should not affect the determination of Simpson's guilt. Similarly, Garcetti's race-conscious decision to add a black prosecutor to the team—particularly one with a history of uncovering and prosecuting police misconduct—plausibly increased the chance that Simpson's allegations of official bias and corruption would receive—and, once again, be perceived as receiving—a fair hearing.

The argument that these race-conscious lawyering strategies support, rather than undermine, the legitimate social purposes of the criminal justice system presumes that those black participants included in the proceeding will honor their legitimate role obligations and will not simply become racial patriots. This does not require that they subscribe to bleached out professionalism.

Similar arguments constrained Darden and Cochran. As I have already indicated, Darden's argument in favor of suppressing Fuhrman's racist statements was expressly color-conscious. Given that he was one of the lead prosecutors on the case, however, Darden was obligated to deploy this color-conscious strategy for the purpose of keeping Fuhrman's statements away from the jury. As a black man, and a strong opponent of racism within the police department, Darden may well have believed that exposing Fuhrman's racism would advance the black community's interests by highlighting the problems with the police that African Americans encounter on a daily basis. Nevertheless, as a prosecutor, Darden had an ethical obligation to make all reasonable arguments in favor of Simpson's guilt. Darden had good grounds under the applicable rules of evidence for seeking to exclude Fuhrman's statements during his initial appearance on the witness stand. To honor the legitimate social purpose that the strength of the State's case should not be affected by the race of the prosecutor, Darden was obligated to present this argument.

One can apply the same analysis to Cochran's "send a message" statement during his closing argument. Once again, Cochran's argument was race-conscious to the extent that it directed the jury's attention to the defense's claim that police racism infected the investigatory process. However, Cochran's argument may not have exceeded the bounds of legitimate advocacy in a criminal case. "Send a message" arguments are a standard part of the trope of both prosecutors and defense lawyers in criminal cases. Although controversial, this rhetorical device arguably is not a call for nullification. Nor did Cochran limit his appeal to black jurors; instead, he emphasized that all Americans have a stake in ensuring that police racism does not taint the trial process. Regardless of whether one finds these arguments convincing, as Simpson's defense lawyer, Cochran was ethically obligated to present all reasonable arguments in favor of his client.

The social purposes underlying criminal defense do not license any and all conduct that might advance the client's cause. Arguments designed to appeal to the racial prejudice of black jurors, for example by suggesting that beating a white man is morally acceptable because of the existence of widespread racism among whites, undermine, rather than support, the legitimate social purposes of criminal defense advocacy. . . . Even in circumstances where a black lawyer feels compelled to violate an express professional command, considerations of social purposes dictate that she do so in a manner that respects the moral force of existing norms.

Let us return to the challenge with which we began. Is it possible to define a role for race-based moral obligations that neither undermines the legitimate rights of consumers nor unduly constrains the opportunities of black lawyers? I submit that we can now answer this question with a qualified "yes."

The analysis I propose offers consumers four interlocking safeguards that their legitimate interests will be protected. First, the model insists that professional obligations carry independent moral weight. Black lawyers, like all lawyers, must take these obligations seriously. Second, all legitimate racial obligations must be derived from, and ultimately be subservient to, common morality. Racial obligations are therefore no excuse for race-based oppression. Third, in cases where there is an unavoidable conflict between a black lawyer's racial obligations and her professional commitments, it is the legitimate social purposes underlying her professional obligations that must eventually carry the day. Racial solidarity, in other words, can never undermine the legitimate (as opposed to the self-interested) demands of professionalism. Fourth, to the extent that a black lawyer finds it impossible to conform to these demands, she must, like Robert Johnson, express her disagreement in ways that ultimately support the moral force of the professional norm.

GERALD P. LOPEZ, *LIVING AND LAWYERING REBELLIOUSLY*

73 Fordham L. Rev. 2041 (2005)

[N]o one ever asked either my brother and other people in the joint or my mother and father or other family members back home what we were facing, what problems we would frame, what help, if any, we received in addressing our problems, and what we thought of our capacity with and through others to do anything to change either my brother's situation or our own. Not one single person ever asked. Even as a wild, sports-crazy, and not-much-reflective-kid, I still said to myself, "How in God's name can they be running a system where the last thing they ever think of doing is asking the people most directly affected, 'What do you think and how can we make it better?' " You didn't have to believe we had all the answers. We certainly didn't think we did. But couldn't you imagine we had something important to share if anyone indeed cared about effectively solving a range of problems obviously implicated? . . .

When officials didn't ask us folks from East L.A., it was principally because they could not imagine that we had anything worth saying. For generations we had been perceived and described as genetically and culturally inferior. We were dumb and lazy Mexicans, messed-up couldn't possibly have within us anything valuable to offer about how best to solve problems or to govern our shared world.

Even at an early age, I knew enough to say, "Hell no!" But I didn't know much else. Driven by some complex mix of emotions and ideas, I'd try to piece together a radically different philosophy about how we should live and work with others. And, in halting ways, I came to understand how much elementally had to change before we could ever be able effectively to solve problems, fully to govern ourselves, and richly to imagine how we might shape the future.

When I launched The Center for Community Problem Solving ("The Center") in September 2003, we decided that our mission would draw upon and reach beyond the work I'd been doing with others throughout my career. The Center would team up with low income, of color, and immigrant communities to solve current legal, social, economic, health, and political problems and to improve our capacity to solve such problems. Along the way, we would strive towards our dream of an accountable and equitable democracy-one where equal citizenship is a concrete everyday reality, not just a vague constitutional promise.

To meet these bold aspirations, The Center puts into action our comprehensive and innovative "rebellious vision of problem solving." Through this vision, we meld street savvy, technical sophistication, and collective ingenuity into a compelling practical force. The power of our rebellious vision lies in extraordinary teamwork-teamwork in fact and not in name only. The Center never works alone. We regularly work with problem solvers of all sorts—including residents, merchants, ministers, organizers, researchers, funders, service providers, artists, teachers, corporate executives, journalists, public officials, doctors, lawyers, bankers, religious leaders, and policymakers. Only by routinely partnering with absolutely anyone who might in any imaginable way contribute can we get to where together we hope to go in the future.

Bill Ong Hing, *The Great Opportunity in Law*

15 UCLA Asian Pacific American Law Journal 30 (2009–2010)

When I was a young law student in the San Francisco Bay Area almost 40 years ago, holding an event this large would have been impossible, because there were probably only a couple dozen Asian American lawyers in northern California law schools. Twenty-five years ago there were only two tenured Asian American law professors in the region, neither of whom identified with Asian American civil rights issues. And it was not until 1983 that an Asian American made partner at a major Bay Area law firm.

[C]onsider these characteristics of the APA community:

- Many face language barriers as more than 1 in 10 Asian households lack anyone over the age of 14 who is able to speak English proficiently.

- Many come from countries with vastly different legal systems and few laws protecting the rights of the individual.

- Many enter as immigrants and are unlikely to know their rights and their responsibilities under the law.

Even if they know their rights, many Asian immigrants fear exercising them because they are concerned it may affect their immigration status and their jobs and families. Their fear stems from lack of confidence in the judicial system. Historically, few legal services programs have served Asian American communities very effectively.

While some segments of the Asian American community are doing well, most ethnic groups within the community have a poverty rate that is at least 50 percent higher than that of white Americans. Southeast Asians face a poverty rate of 25 percent to 50 percent in many refugee communities. Many are unaware that there are agencies in their communities that provide low-cost or free legal services. Those who are aware of such services often do not try to access the services because of language barriers.

The Asian American population has grown at a rapid pace and has become more dispersed with significant communities in areas like Houston, Miami, Atlanta, and Minneapolis, as well as in pockets of Wisconsin, Nebraska, Iowa, and North Carolina. Legal services agencies that assess local legal needs based on demand for services often overlook the needs in Asian immigrant communities since these communities are unlikely to be aware of available services or are hesitant to try to access them.

Is any of this relevant to you? I say a prayer whenever I meet Asian American professionals and students such as you. My prayer is that as Asian Americans, you might empathize with or maybe even understand some of the issues that lower-income members of our communities are facing; and if that's the case, then you might join me and others in the battle for equal justice.

This is also relevant to you because of the set of skills and knowledge you are developing as lawyers. Probably more than anyone in this room, I am skeptical that the legal system is the ultimate answer to the problems most subordinated communities experience. Yet, we skeptics cannot deny the fact that lawyers and the legal system play central roles in the resolution of many, many situations. Community lawyers play an especially central role in this respect because they have community stature and are called upon to resolve conflicts on behalf of community residents. In spite of all the lawyer bashing, lawyers are often viewed as community leaders and continue to enjoy much community respect.

Lawyers also have heightened access to the power structure, including the power to shape both policy and law. Lawyers can win legal rights for underrepresented groups; this gives them the capability of improving the social and economic situations of their clients' lives.

Something very special can happen in the course of legal education. In many respects, lawyers are particularly well qualified for public service. Beyond the argument of the centrality of the legal system, hopefully you have developed or are developing an Aristotelian-like practical wisdom (phronesis): a tolerant and judicious attitude, a unique combination of abstract reasoning ability and empirical keenness, coupled with the necessity of reaching conclusions in real time. With these qualities you are well suited to serve the common good—and especially the aspects of common good that relate to equal justice. As lawyers and part of the community's educated intelligentsia, you have the ability to help transform the legal profession's framework so that it more closely approaches the conditions of justice and civic community. As lawyers, you can take advantage of the opportunities lawyers have to pursue important societal goals on behalf of the underrepresented.

The proposition I advance is that you all have the ability to be good "community" lawyers—even if you can only do it part time. Good community oriented lawyers are humble, not paternalistic. They identify and work with other allies in the community, respect the client's own talents and skills, work in partnership with the client, respect the client's informed judgment on case strategies, strive to demystify the law and procedure for clients, engage in substantial amounts of community education, consider an array of alternative approaches to legal problems, and get to know the community, much like a community anthropologist. . . .

Another argument for community service flows from a vision of moral possibilities of legal practice. Lawyers have a duty to serve as a policy intelligentsia and to promote a culture of respect for and compliance with the purposes of the laws while enabling reasonable interpretations of laws or arguing about their injustices. The philosophical views of Louis Brandeis are relevant here. He believed that lawyers should hold a position of independence between the wealthy and the nonwealthy. . . .

Whether and to what degree the races and ethnicities that comprise our society peacefully coexist depends on factors far beyond any impact lawyering can have on those relationships. We would be foolish not to acknowledge that the work promoting equal justice in our multicultural, increasingly complex community is extremely challenging. But whether or not lawyers have special skills to make positive contributions to this work—and I believe they do—lawyers are well positioned to help shoulder this responsibility. . . .

At the end of the first decade of the new millennium, the work that lawyers do for and with communities of color and other subordinated groups—to strengthen their infrastructures, to make them part of society in a manner that brings them into the country's mainstream institutions, to present their perspectives, and to resolve their conflicts—can strengthen the country. You can be a part of this process. . . .

Simulations: Racial Justice Lawyering

1. The Bar Association Professionalism Committee is considering creating professionalism awards in honor of one or more of the following:

   A. Johnnie Cochran

   B. Christopher Darden

   C. Anthony Griffin

What should the Committee decide? The Committee includes at least one member who chooses the racial justice lawyering perspective and at least one who chooses the neutral partisan conception.

2. The Texas Chapter of Immigrant Youth United for Justice is considering a range of strategies for helping immigrant children who are seeking asylum in the United States. These include filing a lawsuit to establish a right to counsel for the children, creating a

network of legal services groups to provide counsel, civil disobedience actions, marches in support of the children, collaboration with community organizations, and programs to educate the children as to their rights. Leaders of Immigrant Youth United ask Immigration Legal Defense, a lawyer based public interest group, for advice. The leaders meet with staff attorneys, some of whom take a racial justice approach to their work (feel free to choose any of the racial justice perspectives identified in the Chapter) and some of whom are neutral partisan lawyers. What advice should the lawyers provide? How do their role choices influence that advice?

3. Bill Ong Hing has argued that:

> racial harmony is so vital to bettering society . . . that lawyers must elevate the goal of racial harmony above their clients', and their own personal values, and in short, above adherence to the adversary ethic. . . . [In doing so, the ethical rules should require] the lawyer to sit down and discuss with the client the possible negative effects on race relations that the immediate pursuit of certain options may have. Ideally, the lawyer will exercise nonadversarial options first, and as a result, the posture and demeanor of the client's case will be calculated to minimize the threat to race relations. Even if the initial options do not achieve the client's legitimate, nonracial goals, the postponed use of more aggressive options will result in less damage to race relations.[5]

The ethics rules committee of the local bar association is considering whether to amend the ethics rules along these lines. The committee includes at least one lawyer with a neutral partisan perspective and at least one with a racial justice perspective. What should the committee decide?

4. Do White lawyers have an obligation to promote racial justice on account of being White? *See* Russell G. Pearce, *White Lawyering: Rethinking Race, Lawyer Identity, and Rule of Law,* 73 Fordham L. Rev. 2081 (2005). As a law student, what do you think?

E.   LGBTQ[6] Rights

Perhaps the most significant civil rights cause lawyering victory of the past decades has been the achievement of a constitutional right to marry for lesbians and gay men. The lawyer leaders of the movement to achieve freedom to marry have included prominent advocates, such as Evan Wolfson, Mary Bonauto, and Roberta Kaplan. Leonore Carpenter offers a critical perspective and describes how a commitment to LGBTQ rights can shape a variety of lawyering strategies.

Remember to read the questions first and then find the answers in the following text.

---

5   Bill Ong Hing, *In the Interest of Racial Harmony: Revisiting the Lawyer's Duty to Work for the Common Good,* 47 Stanford L. Rev. 901, 904, 919 (1995).

6   *See, e.g., HRC Officially Adopts Use of "LGBTQ" to Reflect Diversity of Own Community* (2016).

[Question 8-29]

Leonore Carpenter argues that LGBTQ justice lawyering currently includes all of the following strategies to determine priorities EXCEPT:

    (A)   Legal expertise.

    (B)   Community voting.

    (C)   Collaboration with community organizations.

    (D)   The needs of individual clients.

[Question 8-30]

In deciding whether to make Freedom to Marry a priority, all of the following describe the actions of LGBT legal advocates EXCEPT:

    (A)   They had ideological disagreements on the merits of freedom to marry.

    (B)   They agreed that freedom to marry should be the top priority.

    (C)   They agreed to pursue freedom to marry so long as the legal strategy did not privilege married couples over other families.

    (D)   Some sought community input.

Lenore Carpenter, *Getting Queer Priorities Straight: How Direct Legal Services Can Democratize Issue Prioritization in the LGBT Rights Movement*

17 U. Penn. J. L. & Social Change 107 (2014)

[I. Priority Setting Models]

A. The Expertise Model of Decision-Making in LGBT Impact Litigation

As in other social justice movements, the expertise of lawyers has been given a position of special prominence in the LGBT rights movement and has contributed heavily to the shaping of litigation priorities within and across agencies. . . . Impact litigators in the LGBT context . . . are informed by a wide variety of sources as to which general issues are most pressing; those sources include the voices of activists and anecdotal, individualized evidence of community need. However, the process by which this cacophony of voices is filtered and transformed into a litigation agenda is frequently almost entirely lawyer-driven. In her 2005 article, *Goodridge in Context*, Mary Bonauto, Civil Rights Project Director at Gay & Lesbian Advocates & Defenders (GLAD) and lead attorney in Goodridge, discusses the process undertaken by GLAD in deciding to fully commit to marriage equality as a litigation priority. In so doing, she provides a rich and fascinating case study of a litigation campaign catalyzed by a broad combination of factors, including cultural shifts, politics, the expressed needs of certain individuals within the community, changes in the legal landscape, and events such as the AIDS crisis. It is clear, however, that although many factors led to Goodridge, it was ultimately the judgment of the GLAD lawyers themselves that led to two important decisions: 1) the decision regarding the triggering of marriage litigation; and 2) the rejection of civil unions as a goal. . . .

Ultimately, . . . GLAD's expertise controlled two critical prioritization questions: the decision to elevate marriage to a top priority; and the question of whether the priority was to be marriage equality, as opposed to a different relationship recognition scheme.

The movement's reliance on lawyer expertise in setting litigation priorities is probably most clearly demonstrated through the existence and continued importance of the LGBT Civil Rights Litigators' Roundtable, a twice-yearly meeting of LGBT rights movement lawyers organized by the four major impact organizations. The purpose of the Roundtable, which first began meeting in the early 1980s, is to coordinate litigation campaigns around LGBT rights, and to collaborate with other LGBT impact litigators regarding litigation strategy and issue prioritization. It is a critical mechanism for agenda-setting within the LGBT rights movement. Nancy Polikoff describes the way in which the Roundtable facilitated the early decision to prioritize same-sex marriage. According to Polikoff, Roundtable participants were not satisfied with the rift represented by the [same-sex marriage] divide. They sought common ground in a position paper designed to capture both the importance of opening marriage to same sex couples and the need to value all families without carving out special status for married couples. Evan Wolfson, then a new Lambda Legal staff attorney, drafted a blueprint for a just policy, entitled Family Bill of Rights. . . .

B. The Democratic Model of Decision-Making in LGBT Impact Litigation

As examples of the democratic model in action, [William] Rubenstein . . . recounts the efforts made by LGBT rights litigators (particularly Lambda Legal and the ACLU) in the late 1980s and early 1990s to obtain some sort of community consensus on the question of whether marriage ought to be a primary litigation goal of the LGBT rights movement. . . . Rubenstein himself identifies that such a proposition carries with it obvious practical problems due to the mind-boggling difficulty inherent in determining who would actually get to vote. In the LGBT context, the questions are numerous and obvious: Who is "gay enough" to be a voting member? How do you reach those people even if you know who "those people" are? . . .

II. HOW LGBT LITIGATORS' PRIORITY-SETTING METHODS ENGENDER CRITIQUE

In Transgender Issues and the Law: The Role of Lawyers in Trans Liberation, transgender rights advocates Gabriel Arkles, Pooja Gehi, and Elana Redfield critique the prominence of "lawyer-only spaces" in the LGBT rights movement and the influence of the perceived expertise of those lawyers in setting priorities for the entire movement. The authors of this piece were, at the time the article was written, all affiliated with the Sylvia Rivera Law Project (SRLP), a legal service organization based in New York City that primarily serves low-income gender-variant people. SRLP's political perspective differs significantly from that of the traditional impact litigation groups; consequently, their article utilizes a distinctly "outsider" perspective and is reflective of SRLP's concentration on the intersectionality of oppression and a preference for the privileging of the voices of the most marginalized community members.

In their article, Arkles, Gehi, and Redfield [hereinafter "the SRLP authors"] present the LGBT Litigators' Roundtable as a prime example of a space in which discussions are considered private and the perspective of non-lawyers is not solicited. The SRLP authors, as recent participants in the Roundtable, critique its dynamics, calling into question not only the narrow and exclusive focus on lawyering, but also the authors' sense that the lawyers present thought their appropriate role to be the dictation of priorities and control of the movement. The SRLP authors specifically critique the Roundtable on a few different aspects of its process. The authors critique the lack of diversity within the participant group itself, noting that not only is the entire event lawyer-driven, but also, "[t]o our knowledge, very few participants have lived in poverty and very few have been openly HIV-positive or disabled. Valuing only privileged voices in planning legal strategy exacerbates the hierarchies and societal power imbalances that we believe movements must dismantle in order to achieve meaningful social change." The SRLP authors also observed a proprietary attitude toward agenda-setting among Roundtable participants, as well as a tendency to avoid or ignore issues that involved intersectional analyses that would have forced consideration of linked issues such as poverty, race, and transphobia. The SRLP authors characterize these dynamics as leading to a "potential for an overly narrow focus and lack of accountability."

Because the SRLP authors speak from subjective personal experience, I feel obligated to corroborate the anecdotal evidence they present, as I am also a former participant in the Roundtable. As first a staff attorney and then the legal director at Equality Advocates Pennsylvania (a small, state-specific LGBT legal organization that focused on the provision of direct legal services), I also had the opportunity to attend several of the Litigators' Roundtable meetings discussed in the SRLP authors' article, and I experienced the event similarly. At the Roundtable, there were usually scores of people in attendance from the four major impact litigation groups, including executive directors, high-ranking project directors, and junior attorneys. In addition, other organizations were invited to send attorneys, so there were generally attorneys in attendance from various other legal advocacy groups. Law professors affiliated with the organizing groups also attended. Despite the invitation having been extended to those not employed by one of the four major impact groups, the agenda was clearly controlled by the organizers. All invitees were solicited for suggestions as to items that ought to be included in the agenda, but the organizers were free to accept or reject any suggestions and to give greater or lesser prominence to suggested topics. At the Roundtable, the most time for discussion was devoted to the work being done by the impact organizations, with the most senior attorneys from those groups leading the discussion. And often, the "discussion" felt more like a presentation, in which the senior attorneys from the impact organizations informed the group about the work being done and the issues being prioritized, and then solicited questions. There was little sense that the impact organizations were actually seeking input into the prioritization of certain issues over others. . . .

The connection between the current priority-setting scheme and the critique is obvious and direct. When LGBT litigators give the impression (whether that impression is accurate, inaccurate as a result of opacity in priority-setting, or inaccurate as a result of misunderstanding) that priorities are set without regard to the expressed needs of the disenfranchised, or even the concerns of other movement lawyers, outsiders will assume that there is no space in the current scheme for a democratic component in the setting of litigation priorities, and further, that there is no desire to locate such a component. . . .

I highlight the marriage debate here, but countless other disagreements within the movement might serve my purpose equally well. The debate regarding the primacy of marriage as a movement priority began decades ago, and has continued to play out, unresolved, ever since. In 1989, Lambda's then-Legal Director Paula Ettelbrick and its then-Executive Director Tom Stoddard engaged in this debate in a highly public manner. They wrote a set of companion essays in the magazine Out/Look, in which Stoddard argued in favor of a marriage priority and Ettelbrick argued against. Their views, expressed on the pages of Out/Look, have become archetypes of the dueling viewpoints of marriage. Stoddard took a pragmatic view, supporting marriage as a priority because it provides a way of accessing otherwise-unreachable legal rights and responsibilities. Ettelbrick, on the other hand, in an essay titled Since When is Marriage a Path to Liberation?, argued that centralizing marriage as a priority would fundamentally alter the nature of an LGBT-rights movement that had previously focused on relationship pluralism and liberation from old, limiting ideas about family structure. In 1993, . . . Nancy Polikoff [argued that a]dvocating lesbian and gay marriage will detract from, even contradict, efforts to unhook economic benefits from marriage and make basic health care and other necessities available to all. It will also require a rhetorical strategy that emphasizes similarities between our relationships and heterosexual marriages, values long-term monogamous coupling above all other relationships, and denies the potential of lesbian and gay marriage to transform the gendered nature of marriage for all people. . . .

[T]here has been little resolution of this fundamental, internal ideological tension within the movement—so little that it is not a stretch to say that the Stoddard and Ettelbrick essays may as well have been written yesterday, last week, or any time between their original publication dates and today. . . .

III. HOW CLOSER CONNECTION TO DIRECT LEGAL SERVICES CAN DEMOCRATIZE ISSUE PRIORITIZATION

In terms of substance, Dean Spade and Craig Willse suggest an alternative to the current substantive issue agenda, stating:

> We envision a broader framework for queer and trans rights, one that makes redistribution a central goal. . . . The most just approach to opposing gender and sexual orientation oppression would be to devote resources first to the struggles of those who experience the greatest impact of that discrimination: people surviving in prisons, people in foster care and juvenile justice, people accessing health care through Medicaid, people working in low-wage jobs or surviving on benefits, people

struggling against immigration policies, people experiencing the intersections of racism and sexual or gender coercion.

Note that, while Willse and Spade's suggestion appears egalitarian in its prioritization scheme, it consciously links those priorities with an overarching political goal that is just as likely not to be shared with the entire community as the system it seeks to replace. Thus, a substantive issue prioritization system that seeks to serve a predetermined political goal does not move us in the direction of democratic goal-setting either. We are left to wonder whether, assuming that we wish to achieve such a goal, we can somehow derive a system of litigation priorities that: 1) is unconstrained in the scope of who is consulted; and 2) does not rely upon an assimilationist, liberationist, or anti-capitalist ideology as its guiding principle.

Douglas NeJaime takes the position that any monolithic approach to priority-setting in the LGBT rights movement is both unhealthy and fundamentally nonrepresentative of a broadly diverse community. He further posits that, given the immense diversity of the LGBT community, it is impossible for any single organization to somehow reflect the entire spectrum of legal needs and ideological positions. Thus, NeJaime advocates for a "polyvocal gay-based advocacy," essentially a pluralistic approach to priority-setting in which different ideological positions are represented by different organizations, some centrist and some more radical. He imagines a playing field on which large impact groups work alongside smaller organizations with different political commitments, and all are respected and able to thrive. . . .

I sympathize with NeJaime's plea for a movement that does not follow the ideological leanings of one particular group and provides representation that spans the demographic and ideological diversity of the LGBT community. However, from a pragmatic standpoint, I have come to believe that pluralistic advocacy cannot be attained without putting in place a mindful, disciplined structure within impact groups to promote such a scheme. I take my lesson from my observations on the marriage issue. In 2003, when NeJaime's piece was published, no state had yet decided the issue of same-sex marriage. The question of whether the movement would begin to fixate on marriage was a growing worry, but not quite a reality. Since the decision in Goodridge, however, all four impact groups have taken on marriage litigation, both at the state and federal level. As each case has been litigated, the marriage issue has become the central focus of public discourse around the place of LGBT citizens in American society. By 2013, as I write this, it feels as though the marriage issue has gone supernova, its immense gravity sucking sexual freedom, antidiscrimination, parenting, the rights of transgender citizens, and pretty much everything else into a kind of black hole out of which no non-marriage issue can seem to escape. . . .

My observations suggest that something a bit different has happened. As a direct legal services staff attorney in 2003 and 2004, I experienced a jarring shift in public attitudes about the marriage question in the immediate wake of Goodridge. Almost as soon as that case was decided, I found myself fielding a growing chorus of demands from enthusiastic Pennsylvania activists who, emboldened by the victory in Massachusetts, wanted my office to litigate marriage in Pennsylvania, and to do so immediately. Oddly, the calls started flowing in despite the fact that marriage had not been either a pragmatic possibility or even a much-discussed aspiration among Pennsylvania's LGBT activists in the years prior. That experience leads me to conclude that issue prioritization can have an echo-chamber-like effect, where impact litigation groups articulate a goal, and articulate it loudly and forcefully, using the kind of "rights" language that carries great moral weight. Rather than feeling coerced, a large contingent of LGBT people instead adopt that goal as their own.

Perhaps instead of a hijacking, the best analogy would be to the protest tactic of the "mic-check," wherein a lead protester makes a speech that is amplified using only the power of human voices. Levitsky might agree with this conclusion, as her article connects the perception of "hijacking" to "the structural fact that legal advocacy organizations . . . have considerably more resources than the grassroots organizations that make up the bulk of the movement" and that "the legal advocacy organizations in this study were able to achieve a high degree of visibility for their actions relative to other organizations in the movement." Gwendolyn Leachman's recent empirical study of mainstream press coverage of LGBT issues suggests that it is in fact objectively true that LGBT-rights litigation has historically received far more press coverage than non-litigation movement tactics.

So what does this mean? I draw the conclusion that we cannot democratize issue prioritization simply by doing so across groups. The impact organizations' influence has simply become too great to be easily resisted by many smaller agencies who, while they might wish to pursue different priorities, may find themselves pressured to either join the bandwagon or risk irrelevance. To continue the analogy of the mic-check, we can, at this point in the movement's development, no more expect effective polyvocal advocacy across organizations than we can expect an audience member to suddenly turn away from a speech that is being mic-checked simply because the person next to her has started saying something else. We must instead ask the impact groups to consider altering their own internal means of selecting priorities to carefully ensure that multiple voices are heard and multiple ideologies represented. . . .

I suggest that LGBT impact litigation organizations can add the missing democratic component to their prioritization schemes by partnering with LGBT direct legal service providers, analyzing those providers' aggregated data for demonstrated community needs, and adjusting their resource allocation to address those demonstrated needs. Unlike other "democratizing" suggestions, an individual's ability to have his or her "vote" counted in such a scheme is dependent solely on his or her ability to locate contact information for a direct service provider and articulate a problem. It is almost completely detached from the community member's access to power or privilege, and does not require that the community member be an activist, an expert, think of themselves as a potential "model" plaintiff, or be a person of means. It also does not lead us into the thicket of a majoritarian "voting" model that would be both silencing of pluralism and impracticable or downright impossible to execute. . . .

In addition to shifting the discussion on marriage away from ideological debate or the sanitized tales of a few model plaintiffs, we might find that the secondary narratives about LGBT life would change dramatically. For example, as the Legal Director of a small Pennsylvania LGBT-rights direct legal services nonprofit, I found that one of the greatest areas of need was name and gender changes for transgender community members. This fact was initially a surprise to my agency, but as we began to systematically provide the service, calls for assistance only continued to grow. What would an impact litigation campaign that was predicated on that recurrent need look like? We might spend a little less time talking and litigating about marriage, and a little more time talking and litigating about the right of each person to determine gender for themselves, and the problems of a system that presupposes a medicalized model of gender and imagines policing of gender as an appropriate activity of the state. My agency also received large numbers of letters from incarcerated transgender women who had been subjected to harassment and sexual assault in prison. What might a national litigation campaign built around that horrendously tragic pile of mail look like? What new coalitions might be formed as a result? What if we aimed for greater geographic diversity, and set up direct service organizations in every state? We might give primacy to the needs of rural same sex couples instead of sacrificing their legal security in the service of an agenda that serves LGBT people living in states most friendly to immediate forward advances in the law.

Simulations: LGBTQ Rights Lawyering

1. You are a staff attorney at Civil Rights Defenders, a public interest law firm. Civil Rights Defenders has decided to represent a transgender high school student. The student's high school segregates gym classes by gender. The student has asked to participate in the gym class that is consistent with the student's gender identity and not the student's assigned gender at birth. The high school has refused to do so. The staff of Civil Rights Defenders meets to consider possible strategies. What are three elements of a strategy that you would recommend? How would a progressive lawyering strategy differ from that of traditional cause lawyering?

2. The staff at a LGBTQ rights law firm is considering two cases. One is to represent a married LGBTQ couple who were refused service at a local restaurant because management objected to their marriage on religious grounds. The other is to represent a trans man who is suing the police because officers who arrested him for a minor violation taunted him "for not being a real man" and subjected him to a car ride that caused him physical harm while sitting handcuffed in the back of the police car. Which case will you represent? How will you make the decision? Draw upon perspectives found in LGBTQ lawyering or in other lawyering models.

F.   Civics Teacher

Today, the original understanding of lawyers as America's governing class has little traction with law students and lawyers who consider this view elitist and anti-democratic. Proponents of the civics teacher approach offer a different way to revive the values of the original understanding without the assumptions that critics find elitist and antidemocratic. Do they succeed?

Remember to read the questions first and then find the answers in the text.

[Question 8-31]

In the 1960s, Erwin Smigel found that big firm lawyers viewed their role as close to that of a:

   (A)   Civics teacher.

   (B)   Neutral partisan.

   (C)   Business person.

   (D)   Judge.

[Question 8-32]

Proponents of the lawyer as civics teacher argue that lawyers are properly civics teachers because they are necessarily more virtuous than nonlawyers.

   (A)   True.

   (B)   False.

[Question 8-33]

Proponents argue that lawyers are civics teachers:

   (A)   Because descriptively they serve that function.

   (B)   Because normatively they should serve that function.

   (C)   Both A and B.

   (D)   Neither A nor B.

[Question 8-34]

A lawyer acting as civics teacher would always:

   (A)   Spy on her client for the government.

   (B)   Be a hired gun because the system requires it.

   (C)   Explain the spirit of the law as well as the letter.

   (D)   Impose her values on the client.

[Question 8-35]

All perspectives on the lawyer as civics teacher require moral counseling.

   (A)   True.

   (B)   False

[Question 8-36]

If clients generally shared the view of Ben W. Heineman, Jr., former Senior Vice-President for Law and Public Affairs for General Electric, they would:

(A) Object to the lawyer as civics teacher.

(B) Welcome the lawyer as civics teacher.

(C) Be indifferent to the lawyer as civics teacher.

Bruce A. Green & Russell G. Pearce, *"Public Service Must Begin At Home": The Lawyer as Civics Teacher in Everyday Practice*

50 Wm. & Mary L. Rev. 1207 (2009)

Fifty years ago, the leading national representatives of the American legal profession, the American Bar Association (ABA), and the Association of American Law Schools (AALS), issued a joint report (the Report) on the nature of lawyers' professional responsibility in the context of the adversary system. Principally authored by legal philosopher Lon Fuller, who co-chaired the joint conference that issued it, the Report's premise was that the legal profession's inherited traditions provided only indirect guidance to lawyers in light of their changing roles, and that a "true sense of professional responsibility" must derive from an understanding of the "special services" that the legal profession "renders to society and the services it might render if its full capacities were realized." A decade later, the Report was quoted throughout the footnotes to the Preamble and Ethical Considerations of the ABA Code of Professional Responsibility, suggesting that the Report captured or influenced understandings that continued at least through the early 1970s.

The conception of the lawyer as civics teacher directly addresses the lawyer's role as client counselor in the daily private practice of law, regardless of whether the matter relates to a transaction or to litigation. It emphasizes that when lawyers counsel clients about their legal rights and obligations, and about how to act within the framework of the law, lawyers invariably teach clients not only about the law and legal institutions, but also, for better or worse, about rights and obligations in a civil society that may not be established by enforceable law—including ideas about fair dealing, respect for others, and, generally, concern for the public good. This conception also addresses aspects of lawyers' work aside from client counseling, because lawyers teach clients by example, especially when lawyers address their own legal obligations in the course of a representation. Adopting and elaborating upon the idea of the lawyer's role as civics teacher, we suggest, would lead lawyers to perform this function more self-consciously and, therefore, more often for the better.

I. The Idea of the Lawyer as Civics Teacher

We would describe lawyers also as potent and omnipresent teachers, particularly on the subject of civic norms and values. In part, our claim is descriptive. In society, lawyers in fact teach their fellow citizens how to understand their rights and responsibilities as members of a community—their obligations to obey the law, aspirations to fulfill the spirit of the law, and responsibilities to the good of their neighbors and the general public. Lawyers teach civics both directly in the course of counseling clients and indirectly by example. They do so through what they say and do, and through their silence and inaction, whether or not they are self-conscious about the role, and, if they are self-conscious, whether they consider this function to be central or incidental to their work. [Lawyers] teach for good or for ill and whether or not they intend to do so.

When lawyers counsel clients about how to act within the law, especially when the meaning of the law is unclear, they explicitly or implicitly teach their clients about civic obligations both under the law and beyond the law. Advising the client to stay comfortably within the law (or to comply with the imperfectly expressed spirit or purpose of the law) teaches one conception of civic obligation. Encouraging the client to exploit legal loopholes or to test legal limits teaches a different conception. Similar lessons are taught by example. When litigators decide how to comply with uncertain discovery and procedural obligations—whether to implement the spirit of the law or to exploit the law's inexactitude—they teach by example, conveying to clients how the lawyer regards her own civic responsibility in addressing legal boundaries.

When transactional lawyers advise clients about what to disclose to those with whom their clients are doing business, independently of legal disclosure obligations, lawyers convey their understandings about mutual obligation among those who engage in commerce within the civic community. Lawyers teach similar lessons by example when clients observe the lawyer's own negotiations and the extent to which the lawyer is candid or unforthcoming.

When a lawyer concludes that the client has only a weak legal claim or defense in litigation, the lawyer's advice (or lack of advice) about whether to proceed in litigation teaches a lesson. The client has a legal right to exploit the proceedings if the claim or defense is not frivolous, and doing so may enable the client to pressure the opposing party to settle on favorable terms. Whether the lawyer encourages this, admonishes that this is not a proper use of the courts or not a proper attitude toward legal rights and obligations, or, indeed, refuses to represent the client in court, teaches the client not only about legal rights but also about the role of the courts and attitudes toward the law and legal institutions. Of course, additional counseling considerations apply where a case raises issues of systemic or distributive justice, such as when a party seeks law reform to promote a broader view of justice, where significant imbalances in power exist between the power of the parties, or where a party's fundamental needs (such as food or shelter) are at stake.

Similar lessons are taught when a lawyer counsels a client whose claim or defense, although legally sound, is inequitable. Two examples are traditionally given. In the first, a debtor client with the financial ability to pay a just debt must decide whether to repay the debt or invoke the statute of limitations to bar the creditor from recovering. In the second, a client who agreed orally to convey property and received money for it, but then received a better offer, might decide whether to convey the property or attempt to defeat a claim for transfer of the property by arguing that a writing was necessary to establish a binding agreement. Whether the lawyer advises the first client to pay the debt or advises the second client to convey the property, as a matter of civic obligation, or instead accepts the representation and invokes the legal defense, teaches the client, for better or worse, about how to regard legally unenforceable agreements made to others in the community. Here, too, questions of systemic or distributive justice may also complicate the counseling challenge.

Although our focus is on everyday private practice, we note also that lawyers unavoidably teach civics by example outside their professional work. When lawyers serve on juries, they make an implicit public statement about the significance of this civic obligation. When they seek to avoid jury service, claiming that they lack the time or suggesting that they know too much to be fair, they teach the opposite lesson, whether or not intentionally.

This means that the lawyer does not rest on the claim that ordinary legal practice plays a significant role in civic life for reasons that are intrinsic to law practice—for example, as may be true, that lawyers promote a just society whenever they advocate for clients within the bounds of the law and that they promote the rule of law whenever they advise clients about the law's limits. The civic teaching role we envision involves a more robust idea of "civics" and a more self-conscious idea of teaching. At a minimum, this includes educating clients about civic obligations that are not legally enforceable and that may be found in the "spirit" of the law. Further, and perhaps even less precisely, our concept includes counseling clients about general concepts (equality, respect for others, fairness, civility) that are not captured by either the law's letter or spirit, but that reflect ideas of civic obligation that influence people's voluntary conduct as an ordinary matter and that may therefore bear on the client's or lawyer's conduct in a legal representation.

Three additional observations: First, we would not limit the lawyer-client conversation about the public good to situations where the clients' proposed conduct is patently antisocial. Lawyers assist clients in making fully informed decisions. This requires consideration of all relevant considerations, not just legal considerations. Considerations of civic obligation are relevant even when it is far from clear which way they point or when they point in conflicting directions.

Second, and relatedly, civic obligations can mean different things to different lawyers and at different moments in history. The nineteenth-century legal elite had a notion of civic obligation that was typically aligned with that of their clients, that gave primacy to property interests, and that was inconsistent in many ways with contemporary notions. Lawyers today may have ideas of civic obligation that are far less closely aligned with their clients' civic intuitions. Thus, we do not suggest that lawyers' civic teachings must have any prescribed content, other than that the "hired gun approach, focusing exclusively on compliance with the "letter of the law," reflects too narrow a view. Generally speaking, as Deborah Rhode has previously observed, the lawyer's role requires counseling about and consideration for "the letter of the law, and . . . core principles of honesty, fairness, and social responsibility."

Finally, it follows from this that our emphasis is on opening up a lawyer-client conversation about civic obligation and the public good. We are not proposing that lawyers demand that the client act in any particular way or that lawyers generally decline or terminate a representation when the client's lawful conduct strikes the lawyer as antisocial, although there may be situations that warrant doing so. Some nineteenth-century writers took that stronger view of lawyers' obligation to integrate civic considerations into their practice, insisting that certain objectives, although lawful, should not be furthered, and certain means, although lawful, should not be employed. Some commentators today take a similar view. We do not do so, in part because we think that discerning obligations of citizenship, beyond maintaining a commitment to compliance with the law, is complicated, and in part because we believe that good "teaching" means having a mutually respectful conversation in which the teacher does not compel adherence to her views.

The Significance of the Concept in Professional and Academic Discourse

The concept of lawyers as civics teachers in everyday law practice offers a different way of thinking about at least four important subjects: the lawyer's commitment to the public good; the lawyer's role in a contemporary democracy; the lawyer's counseling function; and lawyers' relationships with each other.

A. Serving the Public Good

First, the civics teacher concept offers a view of the lawyer's role that is somewhat different from that found in the conventional conversation regarding the lawyer's commitment to the public good. As a general matter, the contemporary conversation does not focus on lawyers' everyday practice. The conversation ordinarily concerns the duties of lawyers to provide pro bono assistance, to defend civil rights and civil liberties. and . . . to promote law reform. To the extent that the conversation about serving the public good touches on everyday practice, it has sought to set boundaries that would prevent lawyers from assisting in client wrongdoing or has identified lawyers as role models in exemplifying obedience to law.

As civics teachers, lawyers have a far broader responsibility for incorporating an understanding of the public good into their practice. Doing so is quotidian, not exceptional. In almost every aspect of practice, whether providing advice, negotiating with an adversary, appearing in court, or in other capacities, lawyers affect how clients and, in many cases, third parties, conceive of their rights and responsibilities. In this work, lawyers have great discretion. They may choose to teach that the only guide to appropriate conduct is maximizing individual conduct within the bounds of the enforceable law-that one's civic responsibility is only to oneself and to respect the law only as a boundary on self-interest. On the other hand, lawyers may choose to teach that appropriate conduct requires taking into account not only one's self-interest but also one's obligations to one's fellows and one's community. Lawyers primarily teach these lessons through their conversations with clients, but they also teach them when they interact with others on a client's behalf.

B. The Lawyer's Role in a Democracy

Second, the concept adds to the broader discussion of the lawyer's role in a democracy. Although this discussion was historically prominent in the United States, today it takes place largely with respect to transitional and developing democracies, where our own bar ascribes to lawyers an important role in promoting and sustaining democratic legal and institutional reform, largely through work outside the everyday representation of private clients. This ascribed democratic role may also include educating the public about its legal rights and how to assert them as well as educating the public about legal obligations and restrictions. The idea of the American lawyer as civics teacher underscores that promoting and sustaining a democracy is not just a job for foreign lawyers and invites us to engage in exchanges with professional colleagues in developing democracies about our comparative roles and challenges.

C. The Lawyer's Counseling Function

The concept also offers a different way of discussing the lawyer's counseling function. The ABA acknowledges the legitimacy of discussing nonlegal considerations with clients, including relevant "moral, economic, social and political factors," and many have argued for the importance of providing "wise counsel," rather than more narrow, technical, and exclusive focus on explaining the meaning and application of the law. But many lawyers feel uncomfortable counseling clients with respect to moral, as distinct from business, considerations out of skepticism about the legitimacy of their own values or out of concern that their values are not shared by the client. The idea of the lawyer as civics teacher suggests a particular class of nonlegal considerations to which the lawyer might refer—namely, those relating to the expectations and obligations of citizenry. In their particulars, civic values may not be universally shared. Nonetheless, ideas of civic obligation and virtue should be regarded as legitimate subjects of discussion and, at the general level as shared values, in a way that other beliefs and ideas may not be.

Although some lawyers are reluctant to discuss these concerns, clients may welcome such guidance. Ben W. Heineman, Jr., General Electric's former senior vice president and general counsel, has explained how he sought in outside counsel both "an outstanding technical lawyer" and "a wise counselor," who could offer "thoughtful insights into all the nonlegal issues—ethical, reputational, and commercial." Heineman similarly understood his own role as general counsel as including "establishing global values and standards beyond what financial and legal rules require; shaping the company's . . . role as a corporate citizen[,] and . . . addressing questions of how to balance the company's private interests with the public interests affected by the corporation's actions."

Discussions about civics may ultimately point clients in the same direction as discussions of morality or other nonlegal considerations, but the discussion will sound different and may resonate with the client in a different way. Both lawyer and client may find it easier to engage in conversation regarding civic responsibility, and both may perceive that lawyers have a stronger claim of expertise when it comes to civic considerations, such as the value of concern for the "spirit" of the law.

D. The Lawyer's Relationship with Professional Colleagues

Finally, the idea that a lawyer should model good citizenship within the context of client representation offers a different way of thinking about relations among lawyers. Within the adversary process, for example, lawyers are in relationships with their counterparts, just as clients are in relationships with their own. Lawyers might think of each other as "opposing counsel" or "adversaries," but they might also think of each other as professional brethren. . . . They might construct uncivil, even hostile relationships. Or they might strive, to the extent possible, to create relationships of civility and mutual trust within which they advocate for their clients zealously and perhaps even more effectively than if they were so-called "hardball litigators."

Thinking about professional relationships as an expression of one's civic understandings provides a different way of thinking about recurring subjects of professional conduct in the adversary process. Among these are whether one comports with civility codes, whether one extends professional courtesy, how one deals with inadvertent disclosures, whether lawyers make and adhere to handshake deals, whether one makes true but intentionally misleading representations, whether one takes an aggressive approach to discovery obligations and other legal and ethical obligations, and the like. Further, the idea of the lawyer as civics teacher may provide a different kind of rationale for resolving these kinds of questions. The preference, where possible, for developing relationships of trust, for treating others fairly, for complying with the spirit of the law, and for negotiation and compromise may serve as a rationale for improving professional relationships when calls for "professionalism" are not sufficiently compelling.

CONCLUSION

At times, lawyers have been asked to serve as societal role models, and particularly as "citizen-lawyers." One aspect of the lawyer's role as citizen-lawyer might be characterized as that of a civics teacher. This conception draws on concepts and discourse going back to the American legal profession's earliest days but finds especially full expression and justification in a Report authored by Lon Fuller a half-century ago. * * * [W]e offer a vision of everyday lawyers who incorporate public service by word and deed into their everyday private law practices, including the manner in which they counsel clients, interact with other lawyers, and regard their own legal obligations. Teaching civics, we suggest, is an unavoidable role for such lawyers. The only question is how well they fulfill it.

Simulations: Civics Teacher Lawyering

1. You are discussing with two law partners how to counsel your client in the following situations. At least one of the law partners follows the civics teacher lawyering perspective and at least one follows the neutral partisan perspective. What decisions do you reach regarding strategy and next steps?

> (a) BigCo has accidentally dumped ToxicTox in Smalltown's water supply. BigCo informs you that a few residents may die soon and a larger number are likely to develop cancer.

> (b) Lincoln Motors is deciding whether to make a design change in the LS Model not required by law this year but required next year. Lincoln Motors informs you that their studies show that the design change would save 100 lives a year but would raise the price of each car $5000.[7]

> (c) Popular Clothing is negotiating a contract with a foreign manufacturer that pays employees 25 cents an hour, forbids union representation, and disregards basic workplace safety standards.[8]

---

7   To read more about the Ford Pinto case, upon which this hypothetical is based, see the contrasting perspectives in David Luban, Lawyers and Justice 210, 214 (1988) (criticizing the lawyers for Ford); Gary T. Schwartz, *The Myth of the Ford Pinto Case*, 43 Rutgers L. Rev. 1013, 1032–33 (1991) (defending Ford's safety record).

8   Amelia J. Uelmen, *Can A Religious Person Be A Big Firm Litigator?*, 26 Fordham Urb. L. J. 1069 (1999).

2. In 2002, soon after 9/11, the President asks you to advise on whether intelligence agents can legally use torture to gain vital national security information from terrorists.[9] What would you advise from the civics teacher perspective? How would that advice compare with advice from the neutral partisan perspective?

IV. Summary

[Question 8-37]

If I had to choose one perspective for my role as lawyer, I would choose:

    (A) **Neutral partisan.**

    (B) **Moral advocate.**

    (C) **Feminist lawyer.**

    (D) **Religious lawyer.**

    (E) **Racial justice lawyer.**

    (F) **LGBTQ rights lawyer.**

    (G) **Civics teacher.**

Test Your Knowledge

To assess your understanding of the material in this Chapter, click here to take a quiz.

---

9   *See, e.g.,* Michael Hatfield, *Professionalizing Moral Deference,* 104 Nw. U. L. Rev. Colloquy 1 (2009); Robert K. Vischer, *Professionalizing Moral Engagement (A Response to Michael Hatfield),* 104 Nw. U. L. Rev. Colloquy 33 (2009); W. Bradley Wendel & Michael Hatfield, *The Effect of Legal Professionalization on Moral Reasoning: A Reply to Professor Vischer and Professor Wendel,* 104 Nw. U. L. Rev. Colloquy 300 (2010).

CHAPTER 9

The Special Privileges and Responsibilities of Lawyers

Learning Outcomes

At the end of Unit I, you will be able to:

- Assess whether standards for bar admission and discipline guarantee that lawyers provide competent representation

- Assess whether restrictions on the unlicensed practice of law protect the public

At the end of Unit II, you will be able to:

- Discuss special obligations of lawyers to the public, including pro bono service and non-discrimination

- Identify the concept of implicit bias and propose solutions through behavioral legal ethics and other tools

- Recognize the unique mental health issues that may face lawyers in their practice

At the end of this Chapter you will be able to:

- Articulate considerations for developing a personally satisfying career in the law

- Describe emerging issues in the regulation of legal services and the future of legal ethics

Topic Outline for Chapter 9

TOPIC	RELEVANT AUTHORITY	CHAPTER QUESTIONS
I. The Professional Privilege		
A. Review of Professionalism & Unauthorized Practice		

This Chapter will explore in detail the privileges and responsibilities that professionalism has traditionally mandated. Today, commentators both inside and outside the legal profession question whether lawyers continue to deserve the exclusive privilege to provide legal services and whether lawyers continue to fulfill their responsibilities to society. The criticism from within the bar has been that law practice has become a business and is no longer a profession; and that as a result lawyers have failed to uphold their responsibilities as stewards of a legal system that provides equal justice under law for people regardless of their income or identity. The criticism from outside the bar has been that lawyers are seeking to preserve their privileges to enrich themselves, and includes the claim that with the knowledge available on the internet nonlawyers have just as much access to legal expertise as lawyers. But even a minority of lawyers have joined in urging some modification of lawyer's privileges to permit limited nonlawyer practice to provide greater access to justice for low and middle income persons or to permit collaborations between lawyers and nonlawyers in order to provide services more effectively and efficiently.

This Chapter will provide you with the tools to make your own decisions regarding these issues. It will ask you to evaluate whether the requirements for admission to the bar justify giving lawyers the exclusive privilege to provide legal services under unauthorized practice laws. It will then revisit the debates regarding allowing nonlawyers to provide some, or all, legal services. Next, the Chapter examines proposals that seek to encourage lawyers to be more responsible for equal justice in the legal system and equal opportunity in the legal profession. The Chapter concludes with considerations about behavioral legal ethics and mental health issues among the legal profession.

Chapter 9 ultimately brings together themes and issues raised throughout the course, in particular the questions about what constitutes the practice of law and who may engage in it raised by the materials in Chapter 2. It ends by returning to the questions with which the course began. How do you understand your life as a lawyer? Will you be entering a business or a profession? Or do you have a different understanding of what it means to practice law?

I.   The Professional Privilege

A.   Review of Professionalism & Unauthorized Practice

Professionalism traditionally rested on a dichotomy between a profession and a business. Traditional lawyer professionalism had three core elements. First, lawyers have expertise in understanding the law that lay people are unable to evaluate. Second, lawyers work to primarily to promote the public good in contrast to business people who work primarily to maximize their self-interest. Third, as a result of the lawyer's inaccessible expertise and commitment to the public good, society permits lawyers greater autonomy to regulate themselves than it permits businesses.

While professionalism provides the basis for lawyers' exclusive privilege to practice law, its broad claims are not necessary to justify the prohibition on nonlawyer practice. These prohibitions require two elements: one, that state licensing is necessary to protect consumers of legal services from unqualified and unethical providers, and two, that the existing procedures for regulating lawyers are both necessary and adequate to protect those consumers.

Review the material in Chapter 1 on Professionalism and Chapter 2 on Competence and Unauthorized Practice of Law.

B.   Do the Standards for Bar Admission and Discipline Guarantee That Lawyers Meet the Standards Necessary to Justify Unauthorized Practice of Law Prohibitions?

This section will ask whether the requirements for admission and procedures for discipline fulfill the consumer protection goals of the unauthorized practice of law statutes. It will examine the contention that consumers can rely on lawyers being more skilled, more ethical, and more easily policed than nonlawyers.

1. Can Consumers Rely on Lawyers to Be Competent?

[Question 9-1]

Law school training ensures that most lawyers are competent providers of legal services.

    (A) True.

    (B) False.

[Question 9-2]

People without law school training are unable to provide competent legal services.

    (A) True.

    (B) False.

[Question 9-3]

Consumer protection requires that legal services providers graduate from law school.

    (A) True.

    (B) False.

[Question 9-4]

The bar exam ensures that lawyers are competent to provide legal services.

    (A) True.

    (B) False.

[Question 9-5]

People who have not passed the bar exam are unable to provide competent legal services.

    (A) True.

    (B) False.

[Question 9-6]

Consumer protection requires that lawyers pass the bar exam.

    (A) True.

    (B) False.

[Question 9-7]

The requirements of law school education and the bar exam together ensure that lawyers can provide competent legal services.

(A) True.

(B) False.

[Question 9-8]

People who have not both graduated from law school and passed the bar exam cannot provide competent legal services.

(A) True.

(B) False.

[Question 9-9]

Consumer protection requires that lawyers both graduate from law school and pass the bar exam.

(A) True.

(B) False.

The following excerpts reflect upon the purpose of legal education and the bar examination components of competent, ethical law practice.

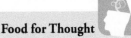

Food for Thought

Would any of your answers be different if you substituted "professionalism" for "consumer protection" in Questions 3, 6, and 9? Why or why not?

POSTING OF MONROE H. FREEDMAN, *ON TEACHING AND TESTING IN LAW SCHOOL, TO LEGAL ETHICS FORUM: THE PURPOSE OF LAW SCHOOL CLASSES?*

Legal Ethics Forum, (Oct. 11, 2006)

I start with the premise that the job of law professors is to train students in the kinds of skills that they need to practice law. These skills include, among others, the following:

- Assimilating facts presented by a client's matter and identifying those that are relevant;

- Identifying potential ways of serving the client's interests, including counseling, drafting, negotiating, and litigating;

- Identifying the legal issues that might be important in serving the client's interests;

- Analyzing the strengths and weaknesses of the client's legal position, including reading and interpreting the language of statutes, contracts, and other legal documents;

- Creating the most effective ways of advancing the strengths and countering the weaknesses in the client's matter, including developing and making persuasive arguments;

- Making judgments about how best to proceed on the client's behalf;

- Determining how to carry out those judgments, through effective counseling, drafting, negotiating, and/or litigation;

- Being able to do the same things on behalf of the other party in the event that that party were your client; and

- Doing all of the above informed by an understanding of the nature of the judicial process, including the practical importance of differing jurisprudential views among judges.

Students tend to think that class discussion, and particularly the colloquies between the professor and students, are a waste of time, because those colloquies don't give them "the rule of the case," the "black-letter law," or "the answer" that they will need to take an exam. As a law professor once said, we should give the students, at the end of the class, "a summary of what the class session has been about," or a "take-away point." I have two objections to this. One is that giving students an end-of-class take-away point encourages them to play video games or do their email during class, secure in the knowledge that nothing they need to know is happening in the class discussions between the professor and other students, and that everything they need to know will come in the last few minutes.

On the contrary, however, the primary purpose of the discussion is the discussion itself, that is, the give and take, the pros and cons, the creative thinking, and the ability to think around and beyond the facts of the case at hand. That is, the entire process of thinking through and arguing out the issues is itself the take-away point. What I believe we should test for in exams, therefore, is not some "right" answer but, rather, the students' ability to do the very kind of analysis that is involved in class discussions, particularly their ability to think through the pros and cons of the issues presented by the cases and statutes, and to exercise their own judgment about them. * * *

SOCIETY OF AMERICAN LAW TEACHERS[1] STATEMENT ON THE BAR EXAM

52 J. Legal Educ. 446 (2002)

* * *

Bar examinations, as currently administered,

- fail to adequately measure professional competence to practice law,

- negatively affect law school curricular development and the law school admission process,

- and are a significant barrier to achieving a more diverse bench and bar.

---

1   [*Ed.'s Note*—The Society of American Law Teachers (SALT) describes itself as "a community of progressive law teachers working for justice, diversity, and academic excellence.".]

Recent efforts in some states to raise the requisite passing scores only serve to aggravate these problems. In response to these and other concerns outlined below, the Society of American Law Teachers (SALT),* the largest membership organization of law teachers in the nation, strongly urges states to consider alternative ways to measure professional competence and license new attorneys.

The current bar exam inaccurately measures professional competence to practice law.

Although the history of the bar examination extends back to the mid-1800s, when law school attendance was not a prerequisite for a law license, the present bar exam format—a 200-question, multiple-choice, multistate exam (the MBE), combined with a set of essay questions on state law—dates only from the early 1970s. In creating the MBE, the National Conference of Bar Examiners was responding to states' desires to find a time-and cost-efficient alternative to administering their own comprehensive essay exams. More recently, some states have adopted a written "performance" test in addition to the MBE, state essay exam questions, and the multiple-choice ethics exam (MPRE).

The stated purpose of the bar examination is to ensure that new lawyers are minimally competent to practice law. There are many reasons why the current bar exam fails to achieve its purpose. First, despite the inclusion of multiple sections, the exam attempts to measure only a few of the many skills new lawyers need in order to competently practice law. A blue-ribbon commission of lawyers, judges, and academics issued a report (the MacCrate Report) detailing the skills and values that competent lawyers should possess. The bar examination does not even attempt to screen for many of the skills identified in the MacCrate Report, including key skills such as the ability to perform legal research, conduct factual investigations, communicate orally, counsel clients, and negotiate. Nor does it attempt to measure other qualities important to the profession, such as empathy for the client, problem-solving skills, the bar applicant's commitment to public service work, or the likelihood that the applicant will work with underserved communities.

* * *

Second, the examination overemphasizes the importance of memorizing legal doctrine. Memorizing legal rules in order to pass the bar examination does not guarantee that what is memorized will actually be retained for any length of time after the exam. Memorization of legal principles so that one can answer multiple-choice questions or spot issues on an essay exam does not mean that one actually understands the law, its intricacies and nuances. In fact, practicing lawyers who rely upon their memory of the law, rather than upon legal research, may be subject to judicial sanctions and malpractice claims. Yet a large part of successfully taking the bar examination depends upon the bar applicant's ability to memorize hundreds of legal rules. The ability to memorize the law in order to pass the bar examination is simply not a measure of one's ability to practice law.

Third, the exam assesses bar applicants' ability to apply the law in artificial ways that are unrelated to the practice of law. In most states, up to one-half of the total bar examination score is based upon the MBE, a multiple-choice test that covers the majority/minority rules in six complex, substantive legal areas. In answering the questions, the examinee must choose the "most correct," or in some cases the "least wrong" of four answers. No practicing lawyer is faced with the need to apply a memorized legal principle to a set of facts she has never seen before and then choose, in 1.8 minutes, the "most correct" of four given answers. No lawyer can competently make decisions without more context for the case and without the opportunity to ask more questions or to clarify issues. Yet if a bar applicant cannot successfully take multiple-choice tests, the applicant may never have the opportunity to practice law.

Fourth, a substantial portion of the examination does not test the law of the administering state. The MBE questions are based upon the majority/minority rules of law that may, or may not, be the same as the law in the administering state. In addition, many states have now adopted the Multistate Essay Examination (MEE), which is also based upon majority rules rather than the administering state's law. In all states, up to one-half of the examination is not based upon the administering state's own laws; in some states, the entire exam requires no knowledge of the particular administering state's governing law. Thus, even if one believes that memorizing the law equates to "knowing" the law, the existing examination does not test how well the applicant knows the law that he or she will actually use in practice.

Fifth, the examination covers a very wide range of substantive areas, thus failing to recognize that today's practitioners are, by and large, specialists not generalists. Although some basic knowledge of a broad range of fields is important, the current examination does not test for basic knowledge, but instead often tests relatively obscure rules of law. In the modern legal world it is virtually impossible, even for the most diligent, skilled, and experienced lawyer, to remain truly current in more than one or two related fields. The examination thus fails to test for competence as it is really reflected in today's market—a market in which lawyers need expertise in their specific area of practice, rather than a broad but shallow knowledge of a wide range of legal rules.

Sixth, most law students take a ten-week bar review course, and some take an additional course on essay writing or on how to take multiple-choice questions, in order to pass the bar examination. These review courses, which may cost as much as $3,000, drill bar applicants on the black letter law and "tricks" to answering bar exam questions. They are not geared toward fostering an in-depth understanding of important legal concepts, nor do they focus on synthesizing rules from various substantive areas. The content of the review courses, and the necessity of taking the courses in order to pass, belie the argument that the bar examination is geared toward testing professional competence or aptitude in any meaningful way.

The current bar exam has a negative impact on law school curricular development and the law school admission process.

In addition to failing to measure professional competence in any meaningful way, the bar examination has a pernicious effect on both law school curricular development and the law school admission process. From the moment they enter law school through graduation, students realize that unless they pass the bar examination, their substantial financial commitment and their years of hard work will be wasted. As a result, many students concentrate on learning primarily what they need to know in order to pass the bar exam, which often translates into high student attendance in courses that address the substantive law tested on the bar examination and reduced participation in clinical courses—the courses designed to introduce students to the skills required for the actual practice of law—and in courses such as environmental law, poverty law, civil rights litigation, law and economics, and race and the law. As a result, the students fail to fully engage in a law school experience that will give them both the practical skills and the jurisprudential perspective that will make them better lawyers.

In addition to being a driving force in the law school curriculum, the bar examination inevitably influences law school admission decisions. Schools want to admit students who will pass the bar exam. A high bar pass rate bodes well for alumni contributions, is perceived to play an important role in *U.S. News and World Report* rankings, brings a sense of satisfaction to the faculty, eases students' fears about their own ability to pass the examination, and makes it easier to attract new students. Since there is some correlation between LSAT scores and bar exam scores, law school admission officers may be overly reliant on LSAT scores in admitting students. As Kristin Booth Glen notes, "If you take students who know how to take a test almost exactly like the bar examination and know how to take it successfully, as the LSAC study tells us is the case with the LSAT, you don't actually have to do much with those students in law school to assure their success on the bar examination." Thus, many schools may overemphasize the value of the LSAT, at the expense of admitting students who will bring a broader perspective into the student body, into law school classes, and ultimately into practice.

Finally, the bar examination has a negative impact on how law schools assess students. Like the bar exam, most law school grades are based upon a one-time make-or-break examination that focuses on only a very few of the many skills that competent lawyers need. If the bar exam assessed a broader range of skills, or assessed skills in various ways, law schools might also adjust their assessment modalities so that they were not all geared toward rewarding just one type of skill or intelligence. In sum, from the admission process through curriculum choices and law school assessment modalities, the bar examination has a far-reaching negative pedagogical effect.

The current bar exam negatively affects states' ability to create a more diverse bench and bar.

In the 1980s and 1990s, many states and federal circuits established commissions on racial and gender equality. After extensive study, many of these commissions concluded that people of color were underrepresented in the legal profession on both the state and the national level, that there is a perception of racial and ethnic bias in the court system, and that there is evidence that the perception is based upon reality. To begin to achieve a more racially and ethnically balanced justice system, many commissions recommended that states take affirmative steps to increase minority representation in the bench and bar.

There are many reasons for states to want a more diverse bench and bar. A diverse bench and bar improves public perceptions about the justice system. It also increases the availability of legal services for underserved segments of our population. Additionally, a more diverse bar is likely to be a more public-minded bar. A University of Michigan study found that, among graduates who enter private practice, "minority alumni tend to do more pro bono work, sit on the boards of more community organizations, and do more mentoring of younger attorneys than white alumni do."

* * *

What are the alternatives?

We cannot hope to exhaust all the possible alternatives to the bar exam in this brief document. But, preliminarily, SALT recommends that states begin to explore one or more of the following alternatives.

1. The diploma privilege. This method of licensure, currently used in Wisconsin, grants a law license to all graduates of the state's ABA-accredited law schools.

2. A practical-skills-teaching term. Using this method of licensure, states could require satisfactory completion of a ten-week teaching term, similar to one phase of the licensing requirements in some Canadian provinces. During the Canadian teaching term, bar applicants must pass two three-hour tests which assess their knowledge of basic principles in ten substantive areas. They also receive training— and must receive a passing grade on assessments—in interviewing, advocacy, legal writing, and legal drafting skills.

3. The public service alternative to the bar exam. States could adopt the pilot project proposed by Kristin Glen, in which bar applicants are given the option of either taking the existing bar exam or working for 350 hours over ten weeks within the court system and satisfactorily completing a variety of assignments in which competence on all of the MacCrate Report skills is evaluated by trained court personnel and law school clinical teachers.

4. Computer-based testing. States also should begin exploring the use of computer-based testing as another potential way to assess a broader range of skills and to measure the skills in ways that better reflect the practice of law.

These alternatives, and others that might be developed, can provide states with options other than the current examination to measure the competence of nascent lawyers. SALT recommends that states begin to study and experiment with these and other alternatives to the existing bar exam so as to ameliorate the pernicious effects of the existing examination structure.

* * *

The bar examination, by testing a narrow range of skills and testing them in a way unrelated to the practice of law, fails to measure in any meaningful way whether those who pass the exam will be competent lawyers. In addition to not measuring what it purports to measure, the examination negatively affects the law school admission process, as well as the curriculum and course content, and impedes the attainment of a more diverse bench and bar. Raising the passing score on the bar examination exacerbates these negative effects. Thus, SALT strongly opposes the move to increase the passing score on the bar examination. Maintaining the status quo is not enough. SALT recommends that states make a concerted, systematic effort to explore better ways of measuring lawyer competency without perpetuating the negative effects elaborated above.

SUZANNE DARROW-KLEINHAUS, *RESPONSE TO THE SOCIETY OF AMERICAN LAW TEACHERS STATEMENT ON THE BAR EXAM*

54 J. Legal Educ. 442 (2004)

In a perfect world there would be no tests, and a test like the bar exam would probably be outlawed instead of required for the practice of law. But not for the reasons the Society of American Law Teachers would have us believe. The bar exam—or any exam—would be unnecessary because we would all be born with superior intellects, abilities, and capacities, and the assessment of individual competencies would be irrelevant. But in our world competence matters, as it does in the case of a lawyer's ability to engage in critical analysis. The bar examination, by testing competency in the most basic and essential analytical skills required for the practice of law, serves a necessary function. * * *

The Bar Exam's Role in Assessing Competency

The bar examination seeks only to test the fundamental skills that should have been learned in law school. SALT faults the bar exam for not addressing the concerns of its Bar Exam Committee, concerns that might well be appropriate for the goals of the profession but not for the goals of the bar exam. It appears to have lost sight of two very important aspects of the bar exam: first, that bar passage is only one of a number of jurisdictionally set criteria candidates must meet before gaining admission to the practice of law, and second, that the bar exam does not purport to test more than the basic analytical skills required for legal practice. Still, the exam has become the most analyzed, criticized, and contested part of the bar admission process. Perhaps that is because it stands as one of the final hurdles to admission; perhaps it is simply because bar exam failures are visible for all to see.

I submit that the bar examination

- seeks to measure the analytical skills required for the practice of law, which requires an understanding of the rules and not just the ability to memorize.

- tests the ability to act and not react under pressure.

- requires a sound mastery of legal principles and basic knowledge of core substance for which tricks or techniques cannot be substituted.

- covers the subjects students should have learned in law school in preparation for the general practice of law.

- neither demands nor requires the sacrifice of skills-based courses for substantive courses.

The bar exam adequately assesses competency in the basic analytical skills required for the practice of law.

The bar exam is designed to see whether the law graduate has mastered the legal skills and general knowledge that a first-year practicing attorney should have. While this means a firm grasp of black letter law, it also means a solid grounding in basic analytical, reading, and writing skills. A candidate must demonstrate mastery of the fundamentals of IRAC (the Issue-Rule-Application-Conclusion structure of legal analysis), must read carefully, and must communicate in the language of the law. * * *

While bar exams vary by jurisdiction, each one tests the candidate's ability to write. * * * The essence of lawyering is communication. Essays afford the bar examiners a basis for evaluating a candidate's ability to communicate knowledge of the substantive law in an organized and articulate way. * * * Bar examiners rely on essays for the same reason that law teachers do: writing a well-constructed legal essay is a learned skill that requires mastery of the law and the nature of logical argument. In working with candidates preparing to retake the bar exam, what I found perhaps most incomprehensible was that after three and sometimes four years of law school, and presumably after reading hundreds of cases, these candidates sounded nothing like lawyers. The language of Holmes, Cardozo, Brennan, and Blackmun had not made the slightest impression on them. In their essays, there was not a scintilla of evidence that they had even attended law school. The "problem" was not in the bar exam questions but in the way they approached and answered the questions. The concept of an issue-based analysis had eluded them; it was absent from their essays and, more important, from their thought process. These are core legal skills. A licensing process that fails to assess the candidate's ability to write, analyze, and reason logically would be not only inadequate but suspect.

The bar exam tests understanding of the rules of law, not simply the ability to memorize.

The bar exam requires one to know the rules of law with precision and specificity; it also requires a solid understanding of those rules. Memorization plays a part, but no more nor less than it does throughout the educational process. We have all had to memorize the elements of the intentional torts, the rule against perpetuities, the types of jurisdiction, and the standard for summary judgment. The same principle applies here. While the process may begin with rote memorization, the end result is knowledge of the material, for the bar exam and for law practice.

If the bar exam were solely a test of memory skills, the students I worked with surely would have passed on their first attempt; they had memorized the rules of law. But because they did not really understand them, they could not recognize a rule when it assumed a different form or appeared in language different from what they had memorized. They needed to know when a particular rule was implicated by the facts. By failing to identify the issue, they failed to recognize when a particular rule was in controversy. Then it did not matter whether they knew the rule or not. They never got to apply it because they did not see the issue.

In working with students in academic difficulty, I have learned that deficiencies in these areas are as typical of poorly performing law students as of those graduates who fail the bar exam. Both groups have the same weaknesses: the inability to identify the legal issues, the failure to separate relevant from irrelevant material, and the absence of a reasoned, organized analysis which demonstrates an understanding of the relevant legal principles. If these deficiencies are not corrected by the time students graduate, it should come as no surprise if they fail the bar exam.

A solid knowledge of the rules of law is required to write bar exam essays and answer objective short-answer questions. Unfortunately, too many candidates walk into the bar exam without truly understanding enough black letter law. A candidate could spend hours studying intentional torts, presumably "know" the elements of a battery, and nevertheless answer questions incorrectly if this knowledge was based solely on memorization without genuine understanding. This is because the bar exam, like a typical law school exam, does not test a candidate's superficial knowledge of the law. * * *

The MBE is meant to weed out those candidates possessing anything less than mastery of the black letter law with a level of detailed sophistication. This is not to say that a candidate must walk into the exam knowing every single rule of law and its fine distinctions. Considering that a candidate can pass the bar exam despite answering almost 80 out of 200 questions incorrectly (depending on the weight accorded the MBE in a particular jurisdiction), it is evident that one need not know every rule to be deemed "minimally competent" to practice law.

Still, SALT objects to the MBE, claiming that these short-answer questions require candidates to apply the law in artificial ways unrelated to the practice of law: "No lawyer can competently make decisions without more context for the case and without the opportunity to ask more questions or to clarify issues" * * * . While this is a true statement, it is not relevant to the bar exam. The point of the exam question is to create a hypothetical universe and test the candidate's knowledge and thought process within that limited universe. The MBE question is crafted to contain all the facts relevant to resolving the issue. There is no need to go outside the question. The ability to read carefully and rely only on the facts presented and the reasonable inferences that can be drawn from them is a critical legal skill—one that the MBE seeks to test.

While it certainly might be improved, the MBE is a means of testing a range of substantive law while keeping the grading process manageable. Multiple-choice tests can be graded objectively, free from the possibility of human inconsistencies. Some candidates actually prefer multiple-choice questions because they find it easier to select the correct answer than to articulate one of their own in an essay.

The bar exam tests the ability to act and not react under pressure.

The bar exam requires a candidate to "think like a lawyer." In law school we teach our students that lawyers act; they do not react. They think deliberately and respond accordingly. The bar exam tests the candidate's ability to "think precisely, to analyze coldly." Bar passage requires that a candidate respond to questions with an orderly thought process. The exam demands that a candidate remain calm under pressure and not panic.

Clearly the bar exam is anxiety-producing, but a certain level of anxiety is a good thing. Anxiety is a very real part of the lawyer's everyday world of deadlines, conferences, and trials. A lawyer cannot afford to lose control because of pressure but must remain focused.

The bar exam requires a mastery of legal principles and core substance; tricks or techniques are no substitute.

When I work with candidates preparing for the bar, especially those who are retaking the exam, I do not teach tricks or strategies for bar passage, unless

- it is a trick to write an issue-based analysis.

- it is a trick to distinguish between legally relevant and irrelevant facts.

- it is a trick to include a solid discussion of the relevant rule of law before applying it to the facts.

- it is a trick to read carefully and thoughtfully and comprehend what you have read.

- it is a trick to organize one's thoughts before writing.

- it is a trick to use language carefully to convey precisely what you mean.

One of the most serious misconceptions about the bar exam is that passing it depends on tricks and techniques. There are no tricks to be learned, only the law, as any retaker will unfortunately be able to tell you. This does not mean, however, that a candidate can afford to be unfamiliar with the exam itself. One must know what to expect.

We tell our students that the key to success is preparation—preparation for class and for exams in law school, preparation for clients and for court in practice. Still, SALT condemns the bar exam because it requires preparation.

Not only do law students prepare for exams by studying from past exams, but practitioners regularly consult previously written complaints, memos, and briefs when drafting new motions. This is especially true of new associates in their first year of practice. Sometimes the only guidance on a project a new associate receives is a file of similar documents showing what the firm expects in terms of format, composition, style, and even specific language. Preparing for the bar exam by working with released exam questions is no different.

Admittedly, bar review courses have come to play a role in the process. But the course will be insufficient for bar passage if the student comes to it without the fundamental skills that should have been acquired in law school. The course simply puts all the rules tested in the jurisdiction in a structured, cohesive package; it does not teach anyone how to analyze a question, write an essay, or think through a problem. It assumes that the candidate learned these skills in law school.

The bar exam tests the subjects students should have learned in law school in preparation for the general practice of law.

The bar exam seeks to test a wide range of substantive law but focuses on the areas important to a beginning lawyer. It tests general topics because most law school graduates become sole or small-firm practitioners and need the basic bread-and-butter knowledge. It tests general subjects and not boutique areas because law students do not graduate as experts in a particular field, although most eventually specialize and practice in one or a few areas. The six subjects tested by the MBE are required courses in virtually every law school; they represent the core substance of a legal education.

Perhaps more important, the bar exam acknowledges our dual system of government and recognizes the lawyer's need to know both federal and state law. Still, the bar exam remains pretty much a creature of the state. Except for the MBE, it is state-specific. Presumably it reflects the interests of the jurisdiction, as determined by that jurisdiction. Different states may test different subjects—a diversity that reflects the complexities of our form of government and, more particularly, state sovereignty in such matters.

The bar exam neither demands nor requires the sacrifice of skills-based courses for substantive courses.

Unfortunately, SALT's assertion that the bar exam has become a "driving force in the law school curriculum" * * * is accurate, at least in some law schools. But the problem is not the exam; it is the schools' misunderstanding of the skills required for bar passage. A school need not design a curriculum around the specific topics tested on the bar exam. Most if not all of the skills that the exam tests are already being taught routinely in law classes—both substantive and practice-based courses. Whether the course is Civil Procedure or Pretrial Litigation, students have to read, think logically about what they have read, and produce a written work product in one form or another. Every course requires legal reasoning. Any distinction between the so-called bar courses and clinical courses is a false one. Students can take both substantive and clinical courses without jeopardizing their bar passage.

SALT contends that concern with bar passage has so influenced law school admission decisions that schools seek "to admit students who will pass the bar exam" at the expense of other criteria, with the effect of reducing the number of students—and graduates—"who will be more likely to serve underserved legal communities * * *. As a member of my school's Admissions Committee, I can say that we look at the sum total of the application package and admit students we believe are capable of learning the law. Our rationale is that if they have the ability to learn the law, they will have the ability to pass the bar exam. This approach rightly places the burden on the institution to fulfill its obligation to the student, instead of the other way around.

Testing What Law School Teaches

Learning to think like a lawyer is the key to passing the bar. The fiction that success on the bar exam depends mainly on proficiency in taking standardized tests such as the LSAT is just that—a myth that does not survive scrutiny. According to a comparison between incoming law students and law graduates from the same law schools, who had virtually identical average LSAT scores, "the highest MBE score earned by the novices was lower than the lowest score earned by any of the graduates. A logical conclusion is that "if general intellectual ability and test-wiseness were the major factors influencing MBE scores, both groups should have had very similar MBE scores." Additional research indicates that MBE scores "are highly correlated with other measures of legal skills and knowledge, such as scores on state essay examinations and law school grades." After controlling for law school quality, test reliability, subject matter and test type, time limits, and the ability to take tests, researchers concluded that "the higher the law school grade point average (LGPA), the greater the likelihood the applicant will pass. No other measured variable really mattered once there was control for LGPA."

Problems with SALT's Suggested Alternatives to the Bar Exam

It would be unwise to abandon the bar exam in favor of any of SALT's suggested alternatives. The proposals either fail to adequately address the need for a uniform measure of minimum competency in the basic analytical skills required for law practice or risk the creation of a legal hierarchy based on the licensing process. Neither the proposed "diploma privilege" nor a licensing measure that relies on public service alternatives would properly serve the interests of the profession as a whole.

First, one goal of an exam that almost every U.S. law school graduate has to pass must be to ensure some measure of uniformity and consistency among test takers who attended widely varying law schools. The requirement of bar passage compensates to some extent for the differences between law schools and individual faculty.

Second, SALT's proposed ten-week practical skills component as a substitute for the bar exam is not only inappropriate but unnecessary. Basic legal education includes assessment of interviewing, advocacy, legal writing, and legal drafting skills. Passing such courses should be sufficient evidence of competency.

Third, SALT's proposal to adopt the teaching-term model of some Canadian provinces would eliminate neither the testing of substantive law nor the need for preparation. The Canadian licensing process relies heavily on both. For example, admission to the bar in British Columbia requires the candidate to complete the ten-week Professional Legal Training Course and pass a two-part qualification examination, which covers substantive law in eight areas and includes multiple-choice, true/false, and short-essay questions. Similarly, Upper Canada requires the candidate to successfully complete an eighteen-week academic phase and pass licensing exams in eight substantive courses before being called to the bar. The Law Society of Upper Canada offers candidates exam-writing tips similar to those provided by the NCBE and such states as New York and New Jersey—for example, "set yourself time deadlines for the exam questions and abide by those deadlines"; "[e]xtraneous information may change a correct answer into an incorrect answer." Apparently there is unanimity not only in what bar examiners expect, but in what bar candidates produce to inspire such advice.

Fourth, the proposal for an alternative licensing system that would rely on a term of public service could create a tiered structure in the profession. Perhaps there are tiers of law schools (as in the *U.S. News and World Report* rankings), but the equality among licensed attorneys is recognized by the general population and the profession. An alternative licensing program could lead to a schism in the profession and create a legal caste system, one caste including those who sat for the bar exam, the other consisting of those who chose public service instead.

While SALT does not specifically advocate oral examinations in place of written ones, it suggests such a move when it faults the bar exam for not testing a candidate's ability to "communicate orally, counsel clients, and negotiate" * * *. Oral exams are problematic for two reasons: first, there is neither time nor resources for a one-on-one dialog with each candidate; and second, the inherent nature of dialog would make such a testing device ineffective and unreliable.

Besides being expensive and impractical, a system based on oral examinations would be inappropriate for evaluation purposes. Oral exams are inherently subjective and generally fail to assess a student's true knowledge. The dynamics of dialog necessarily intrude into the test situation; the questioner may unintentionally give the examinee clues as to the desired response. If you have ever conversed with a student who you thought knew the material and then been astonished by a dreadful final exam, then you know what I mean: there is often a profound difference between an oral presentation and a written one. In oral exchanges the student is as much led by the questioner's subliminal prompts as the questioner is led to fill in gaps in the dialog with her own perception of what the student "intends" to say. The natural prompting that occurs in dialog is entirely absent when the student is left alone to write. Written words stand on their own, and their meaning must be clear without interpretation or question.

VIJAY SEKHON, *OVER-EDUCATION OF AMERICAN LAWYERS: AN ECONOMIC AND ETHICAL ANALYSIS OF THE REQUIREMENTS FOR PRACTICING LAW IN THE UNITED STATES*

14 Geo. Mason L. Rev. 769, 771–788 (2007)

* * * The Law School Prerequisite

* * * [U]ntil 1923, no state required any lawyer to have graduated from law school. Individuals could become lawyers by clerking for a certain period of time and then sitting for the state's bar examination. However, due to lobbying efforts by the ABA during the Great Depression, by 1935, nine states required graduation from an ABA-approved law school in order to sit for the state's bar examination, and twenty-three states had imposed this requirement by 1938. Today, almost all states require graduation from an accredited law school in order to sit for the state bar examination.

* * * [M]andating law school graduation requires a compelling justification due to the significant cost of attending law school. According to John A. Sebert, the average tuition at private law schools in 2003 was $25,584. The average tuition for public law schools was $20,171 for non-residents and $10,820 for residents. Assuming graduation from law school in three years, the average cost of a law degree for a private law student in 2003 was approximately $76,752; for a non-resident public law student, $60,513; and for a resident public law student, $32,460. This great expense requires a compelling justification.

* * * Justifications for the Law School Requirement

There are four main justifications for requiring lawyers to graduate from law school before taking the state bar examination. First, many lawyers and legal scholars contend that law school teaches students to "think like a lawyer." As Benjamin Barton notes, law schools teach lawyers a "specialized bundle of thought processes and heuristics" that allow them to "learn[ ] the operative facts, discern[ ] the law, and apply[ ] one to the other," which they can sell on the market to individuals in need of legal assistance. Law schools, the argument goes, help teach lawyers these skills through the Socratic method, reading cases, writing briefs, writing legal memoranda, and taking law school examinations with hypothetical fact-patterns that require law students to apply an abundance of case law in a particular subject to a new set of facts.

These skills are imperative to effective advocacy in the American legal system. But law school may not be the most efficient and most effective way of teaching lawyers these skills. Law firms, for example, could develop training methods to teach their employees the socially optimal quantity and content of the skills currently taught by law schools. Private markets for courses teaching these skills would develop if these skills were desired by legal employers in the absence of the law school requirement to practicing law. Such courses would more effectively provide the socially optimal quantity and content of these skills due to the market forces certain to be imposed on firms providing such legal education services. In short, it is not obvious that law schools are the cheapest and most effective places to teach prospective attorneys the "specialized bundle of thought processes and heuristics" that are imperative to effective advocacy in the United States.

Second, many argue that law school is needed to teach prospective attorneys the basic legal principles and doctrines of the American legal system. Law schools, through teaching law students the primary legal courses such as constitutional law, torts, contracts, and criminal law as well as more advanced courses, give students a basic understanding of the law that prepares them for their professional responsibilities upon graduation.

But again, law school may not be the most efficient or effective means teaching law. Law students recognize this. Before taking the bar examination, most law students enroll in preparatory courses, such as BarBri and PMBR, in order to learn material tested on the state bar examination and to review material already taught in law school. Also, most law school graduates are not adequately prepared to practice in any particular area, and require substantial additional training in order to effectively represent clients by themselves.

Furthermore, as discussed below, attorneys probably do not need to know the basic legal doctrines in all of the subjects taught in law school in order to be effective advocates. A trans-actional attorney closing an acquisition of a public corporation will be little helped by having memorized the requirements for a prima facie case of conversion of property, and a criminal defense attorney will never be required to know the nuances of the rule against perpetuities. And if law school was eliminated as a requirement to practice law in the United States, attorneys could research the relevant legal doctrines and learn on the job, as most attorneys do when presented with novel or arcane legal issues. In short, it is difficult to argue that the benefits of three years of law school justify its significant economic cost.

Third, many argue that law schools promote legal scholarship, which is a public good that would otherwise be under-produced relative to its socially optimal level. Nevertheless, the fact that legal scholarship is a public good does not promote the argument that such legal scholarship should be provided in law schools. Given the substantial inefficiencies of law school illustrated above, it is not difficult to imagine alternative methods of producing legal scholarship that are more efficient and focused than that currently provided by contemporary American law schools. For example, the government could require licensed attorneys to contribute a fixed sum annually, which would be used to pay full-time legal scholars and sponsor writing competitions tailored towards identified areas of need in legal scholarship. Furthermore, such programs could be supplemented by private donations that are currently provided by law school graduates to their law schools. Finally, it is unlikely that the elimination of the law school requirement will terminate the existence of law schools; legal scholarship would almost certainly continue to be produced by law professors employed by the law schools still in existence following an elimination of the law school requirement to practice law in the United States. In other words, the fact that legal scholarship is a public good does not substantiate requiring graduation from law school as a prerequisite to practicing law.

Fourth, another argument posited in favor of requiring law schools for practicing attorneys is that the grading systems of law schools serve as a signaling mechanism for legal employers to distinguish applicants. The fact that law schools can serve as an effective signal of applicant quality is an insufficient justification to require prospective attorneys to spend tens or even sometimes hundreds of thousands of dollars. Again, it is not difficult to imagine alternative signals for legal employers that are more efficient and focused than that currently provided by contemporary American law schools. For example, SAT and LSAT scores, undergraduate academic records, scored bar examinations tailored to specific areas of law and other examinations developed by the private market for legal employers (as well as tests administered by legal employers themselves) would surely be more efficient and narrowly tailored signaling mechanisms than those currently provided by American law schools. In short, the fact that law schools provide a signal to legal employers is insufficient justification to impose the substantial cost of law school on prospective attorneys.

* * * The Economics of the Law School Requirement

* * * Beyond the weak arguments that support the law school requirement, significant economic and ethical considerations argue against it. * * * The average cost of law school tuition for three years of law school ranges from about $32,460 to $76,752. Assuming for the sake of argument that half of all law students attended private law schools and half attended public law schools as residents, requiring America's approximately one million lawyers to obtain law school degrees would cost over $57 billion at today's prices. This is a steep cost to impose on lawyers and, by extension, consumers of legal services, and it is not clear that it is justified.

That figure does not include the opportunity costs, imposed on lawyers and society, of attending law school. Law students could engage in a multitude of activities rather than attend law school. These activities could include working, vacationing, and performing community service.

Consumers of legal services foot some of the bill for the law school requirement. The cost of law school is a barrier to entry to the legal profession, dissuading many prospective lawyers from becoming attorneys. With fewer lawyers, legal services are more expensive than they would otherwise be. Taken as a whole, these factors once again impose a deadweight loss on society focused upon consumers of legal services.

Finally, * * * American taxpayers also foot the bill of the law school requirement through the enormous sums that taxpayers pay to fund federal and state loan programs, grant programs, and tax breaks that subsidize legal education.

* * * The Ethical Issues Surrounding the Law School Requirement

* * * First, the law school requirement prevents many individuals from lower income families from attending law school and hence becoming lawyers. From a societal standpoint, this is unethical because it unnecessarily prevents members of society from entering a profession based upon happenstance of birth or financial circumstance. Second, the law school requirement deters many prospective public interest attorneys from entering the profession due to the high costs of law school and the low income of public interest lawyers. Third, it does not seem ethical to require individuals to spend three years of their lives studying and paying for law school when it has not been shown that the economic costs of law school are outweighed by its benefits. Such a great cost to an individual, in terms of money and years, requires more justification than has been demonstrated. Finally, law schools discriminate against prospective attorneys who test poorly, which has almost nothing to do with most forms of legal practice. Prohibiting prospective attorneys who test poorly from practicing law is unethical, especially given the fact that there is substantial evidence that law school is inadequately tailored towards teaching law students what they need to know when they enter the legal profession.

Therefore, the two primary justifications for law school prerequisite to becoming a lawyer in the United States, teaching students to "think like a lawyer" and the basic legal doctrines of the American legal system, are open to significant criticism and are insufficient to outweigh the economic and ethical considerations that arise from the requirement.

2. Can Consumers Rely on Lawyers to Be Ethical?

[Question 9-10]

A required law school professional responsibility course ensures that lawyers are ethical providers of legal services.

> (A) True.

> (B) False.

[Question 9-11]

People who have not passed a Professional Responsibility course cannot ethically provide legal services.

> (A) True.

> (B) False.

[Question 9-12]

Consumer protection requires that legal services providers pass a Professional Responsibility course.

(A) True.

(B) False.

[Question 9-13]

The MPRE ensures that most lawyers are ethical providers of legal services.

(A) True.

(B) False.

[Question 9-14]

People who have not passed the MPRE cannot ethically provide legal services.

(A) True.

(B) False.

[Question 9-15]

Consumer protection requires that legal services providers pass the MPRE.

(A) True.

(B) False.

[Question 9-16]

A law graduate who has failed to repay student loans should be admitted to the bar.

(A) True.

(B) False.

[Question 9-17]

A law graduate with a prior conviction for selling marijuana should be admitted to practice law.

(A) True.

(B) False.

[Question 9-18]

A law graduate who served a sentence for manslaughter before beginning law school should be admitted to the bar.

(A) True.

(B) False.

[Question 9-19]

An adulterer should be admitted to the bar.

(A) True.

(B) False.

[Question 9-20]

An alcoholic should be admitted to the bar.

(A) True.

(B) False.

[Question 9-21]

A Nazi should be admitted to the bar.

(A) True.

(B) False.

[Question 9-22]

The character and fitness requirement ensures that lawyers are ethical providers of legal services.

(A) True.

(B) False.

[Question 9-23]

People who do not pass the character and fitness requirement are not ethical providers of legal services.

(A) True.

(B) False.

[Question 9-24]

Consumer protection requires that legal services providers pass a character and fitness test.

(A) True.

(B) False.

[Question 9-25]

Consumer protection requires that legal services providers:

(A) Pass a Professional Responsibility course, the MPRE, and the character and fitness test.

(B) Pass a Professional Responsibility course and the MPRE.

(C) Pass the MPRE and the character and fitness test.

(D) **Pass a Professional Responsibility course and the character and fitness test.**

(E) **None of the above.**

National Conference of Bar Examiners

Read about the purpose of the NCBE Multistate Professional Responsibility Examination and the topics it covers here.

DEBORAH L. RHODE, *MORAL CHARACTER AS A PROFESSIONAL CREDENTIAL*

94 Yale L.J. 491 (1985)

* * *

Those involved in the character certification process have almost uniformly identified its central justification as protecting the public. * * * In response to open-ended questions concerning their objectives in character review, bar examiners generally stressed a need to safeguard the public from the 'morally unfit' lawyer; their goal was both to exclude individuals with 'unsavory characters' or traits 'not appropriate' for practitioners, and to deter those with 'obvious' problems from seeking a license.

More specifically, courts and commentators have traditionally identified two prophylactic objectives for the certification process. The first is shielding clients from potential abuses, such as misrepresentation, misappropriation of funds, or betrayal of confidences. Since the 'technical nature of law' and the attorney's 'peculiar position of trust' place clients in a vulnerable position, individuals whom the state certifies as fit to practice should be worthy of the confidence reposed in them. A second concern involves safeguarding the administration of justice from those who might subvert it through subornation of perjury, misrepresentation, bribery, or the like. * * *

A second, although less frequently articulated, rationale for character screening rests on the bar's own interest in maintaining a professional community and public image. * * *

As the most recent Bar Examiners' Handbook candidly concedes: 'No definition of what constitutes grounds for denial of admission on the basis of faulty character exists. On the whole, judicial attempts to give content to the standard have been infrequent and un-illuminating. * * * More specifically, in *Konigsberg v. State Bar of California*, the Court focused on whether a 'reasonable man could fairly find that there were substantial doubts about [the applicant's] 'honesty, fairness and respect for the rights of others and for the laws of the state and nation.'' Following , a number of courts have applied analogous standards. The difficulty, of course, is that reasonable men can readily disagree about what conduct would raise substantial doubts, a point amply demonstrated by the divergence of views among judges, bar examiners, and law school administrators.

Nor have alternative legislative and judicial formulations added greater determinacy to the character requirement. The most facially precise approach is to catalogue relevant traits such as honesty, candor, trustworthiness, and respect for law. * * * Even greater indeterminacies characterize the most common alternative approach, which is to invoke some broad conclusory definition of virtue. For example, the Oregon Supreme Court demands 'ethically cognizant and mature individuals [able] to withstand . . . temptation[ ].' * * *

Go Online

Should educational debt be a factor in the character and fitness process? Read an article about Robert Bowman, denied admission to the New York bar, here.

At an abstract level, courts and bar committees have similar convictions about what traits are undesirable in candidates for their profession. Conduct evidencing dishonesty, disrespect for law, disregard for financial obligations, or psychological instability triggers serious concern. Yet, at a more concrete level, there is considerable divergence of views as to what prior acts are sufficiently probative to warrant delaying or withholding certification. From a public policy perspective, the justifications for certain of the bar's concerns are less than convincing. * * *

With few exceptions, courts and committees have developed no categorical policies toward particular offenses. Although a few jurisdictions have formally stated or informally determined that certain conduct will not be a matter for concern (*e.g.*, sexual relationships, a single misdemeanor marijuana charge, conduct 'in the nature of horseplay'), most examiners indicated that their decisions would depend on a broad range of factors, including the nature, number, and proximity of offenses, the applicant's age when they were committed, and evidence of rehabilitation. But while agreeing on those common criteria, courts and committees have arrived at quite different conclusions regarding comparable attitudes and activities. * * *

A threshold difficulty in applying character standards stems from the inclusiveness of 'disrespect for law' as a ground for excluding applicants. The conventional view has been that certain illegal acts—regardless of the likelihood of their repetition in a lawyer-client relationship—evidence attitudes toward law that cannot be countenanced among its practitioners; to hold otherwise would demean the profession's reputation and reduce the character requirement to a meaningless pretense. The difficulty, of course, is that this logic licenses inquiry into any illegal activity, no matter how remote or minor, and could justify excluding individuals convicted of any offense that affronted the sensibilities of a particular court or character committee. In fact, bar inquiry frequently extends to juvenile offenses and parking violations, and conduct warranting exclusion has been thought to include traffic convictions and cohabitation.

* * * Decisions concerning drug and alcohol offenses have proven particularly inconsistent. Convictions for marijuana are taken seriously in some jurisdictions and overlooked in others; much may depend on whether the examiner has, as one put it, grown more 'mellow' towards 'kids smoking pot.' * * * Attitudes toward sexual conduct such as cohabitation or homosexuality reflect similar diversity. Some bar examiners do not regard that activity as 'within their purview,' unless it becomes a 'public nuisance' or results in criminal charges. * * *

Other major areas of concern to courts and bar committees have been psychological instability, financial irresponsibility, and radical political involvement, although again attitudes vary widely as to the significance of particular conduct. For example, * * * the bar applications of some jurisdictions make no inquiries as to mental health; others require a psychiatrist's certificate and in some cases an examination for candidates who have a history of treatment. * * *

Financial mismanagement provokes comparable disagreement. Most jurisdictions (73%) make no inquiries concerning debts past due, while others demand detailed information ranging from parking fines to child support obligations. * * * Attitudes toward bankruptcies also varied. Some respondents appeared to assume that applicants who 'don't have a conscience when it comes to paying their own bills . . . may not have a conscience when it comes to their fiduciary responsibilities to their clients.' Discharges to avoid student loans have resulted in denial in some jurisdictions. Yet about a third of all state bar applications made no inquiries in the area, and some examiners, particularly those who handle bankruptcies in private

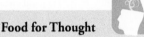

Food for Thought

Later in her article, Professor Rhode argues that the character and fitness evaluations lack predictive value, drain resources needed for professional discipline, and create problems in terms of First Amendment and Due Process values. If you agree with her, how could the bar continue to claim that lawyers have higher moral character than nonlawyers? Does a passing grade on the MPRE provide an alternative? What do you think?

practice, felt that individuals had a right to such remedies. * * * Judicial decisions regarding bankruptcy have yielded equally inconsistent results. For example, applicants who discharged student loans have been admitted or excluded depending on a highly selective assessment of whether 'undue hardship' justified the default. * * *

A third area in which the bar has shown interest is the ideology of its applicants. Religious fanatics, suspected subversives, and 'rabble rousers' have been delayed, deterred, and occasionally excluded under both admission and disciplinary standards. Although existing caselaw constrains states' ability to deny entry solely for political associations, it has done little to curb investigation into political offenses. * * * Denying or delaying admission is typically justified not in terms of the likely risk to the public, but rather by reference to vague generalities about respect for law. Yet in many instances, the appearance of such respect seems to assume greater significance than the values it is designed to reflect. * * *

A final context in which decisionmaking has proven particularly idiosyncratic involves candidates' apparent attitudes toward their prior conduct and committee oversight. Arrogance, 'argumentativeness,' 'rudeness,' 'excessive immatur[ity],' 'lackadaisical' responses, or intimations that a candidate is 'not interested in correcting himself' can significantly color character assessments. * * * The ultimate sin in many jurisdictions is a failure to seem 'up front' with the committee. Nondisclosure, even about relatively trivial matters, may evidence the wrong 'mental attitude,' and 'glib, equivocal responses,' even if technically accurate, may prove more damning than the conduct at issue. * * *

In some, particularly criminal, cases, the applicant's efforts to atone for prior conduct are of equal concern. * * * Yet what evidence will suffice to establish redemption varies considerably. * * *

DECISION OF INQUIRY OF THE COMMITTEE ON CHARACTER AND FITNESS OF THE SUPREME COURT OF ILLINOIS FOR THE THIRD APPELLATE DISTRICT * * * IN THE MATTER OF: THE APPLICATION FOR ADMISSION TO THE BAR OF MATTHEW F. HALE

Decision of Inquiry Panel (1998), *aff'd*, Committee on Character and Fitness of Illinois for the Third Judicial District (1999), *aff'd*, 723 N.E.2d 206 (Ill., 1999).

* * * Introduction

Matthew F. Hale has applied for admission to the Bar of Illinois after having passed its examination conducted in the summer of 1998. * * * [T]he Chairperson of the Third District Committee assigned the application to this Inquiry Panel for further review and examination. * * * In declining to certify the applicant and thereby causing the matter to be referred to a Hearing Panel, we are setting forth our reasons for this decision in some detail.

* * * [T]he Rules of Procedure places the burden on the applicant to prove by clear and convincing evidence that he has the requisite character and fitness for admission to the practice of law. Nonetheless, the denial of a request for admission results in serious adverse consequences for the applicant, as noted by the *United States Supreme Court in Konigsberg v. State Bar of California*, 353 U.S. 252, 257–258 (1957):

The Committee's action prevents him from earning a living by practicing law. This deprivation has grave consequences for a man who has spent years of study and a great deal of money in preparing to be a lawyer.

Additionally, as discussion will demonstrate, the reasons for our decision relate to the applicant's active advocacy of his core beliefs. When an issue of that type is injected into the reasons for denial of certification, "a heavy burden lies" upon the State to demonstrate that "a legitimate state interest" is sought to be protected. *Baird v. Arizona*, 401 U.S. 1, 6–7 (1971). Under these circumstances, the reasons for voting to deny certification should be carefully explained. * * *

Matthew F. Hale is 27 years old, attended undergraduate school at Bradley University in Peoria and received a J.D. degree in 1998 from Southern Illinois University School of Law at Carbondale. By his frank admission he is an avowed racist who, since his teenage days, has been actively involved in promoting white supremacy through organizations and by the distribution of literature. This literature portrays blacks, Jews, and other minorities in an extreme negative light. * * *

Mr. Hale is currently the head of an organization called the World Church of the Creator which is claimed to be a religious organization. His title as head of this church is Pontifex Maximus (Supreme Leader). * * * Mr. Hale has stated that "he would dedicate his life to Creativity," referring to the World Church of the Creator. This religion, according to its founder, Ben Klassen, has as one of its major tenets the hatred of Jews, blacks and other colored people.

Mr. Hale's church admires Adolph Hitler and the National Socialism movement as practiced in Germany, except that it holds Hitler was mistaken in promoting only German nationalism. Instead, his church believes that Hitler's ideas relating to racial superiority should have been applied for the benefit of the entire "white race as opposed to just Germans."

Mr. Hale and his church disavow violence and an intention to seek the forcible overthrow of the United States Government. However, Mr. Hale stated in his interview with us that if his organization would gain power by peaceable means it would call for the deportation of Jews, blacks and others whom his church refers to as "mud races." The United States would then become a country for members of the "white race" only.

[During the] Inquiry Panel's interview[,] * * * Mr. Hale was extremely polite and answered all questions quite candidly. He is intelligent and articulate. He stated that after becoming a lawyer he would continue his activities as leader of his church, including his distribution of racist literature. He also plans to be active on the Internet to promote his church's racist views. * * *

On the issue of moral character, he argued that his frank and open admission of the advocacy of racism shows greater moral character than do lawyers and others who are in fact racist but who utter such thoughts only in privacy.

Mr. Hale was asked whether or not he could take the oath to support the United States Constitution and the Constitution of the State of Illinois in good conscience. * * *

He unhesitatingly answered that he would have no difficulty even though, based on his beliefs, he obviously would be in substantial disagreement with current interpretations of the constitutions. He likened his situation to that of a judge or jury whose duty it is to follow the law even though they may disagree with it.

In connection with the oath, he was shown Article 1, § 20 of the Constitution of the State of Illinois which condemns "communications that portray criminality, depravity or lack of virtue in, or that incite violence, hatred, abuse or hostility toward, a person or group of persons by reason of or by reference to religious, racial, ethnic, national or regional affiliation." In response, Mr. Hale said that to the extent this Illinois constitutional provision limited "communications," it would run afoul of the First Amendment to the Constitution of the United States and therefore would not be binding on him.

Additionally, [Professional Conduct] Rule 8.4(a)(5) * * * was brought to his attention. Mr. Hale was asked if he could abide by that rule if admitted to the Bar. The rule, in part, states that a lawyer shall not engage in conduct that is prejudicial to the administration of justice. In relation thereto, a lawyer shall not engage in adverse discriminatory treatment of litigants, jurors, witnesses, lawyers, and others, based on race, sex, religion, or national origin.

Again, Mr. Hale stated that he would have no problem with following this rule, reaffirming his statements that he would follow the law until such time as he could have it changed by peaceful means. He also said that in a recent employment in Champaign where he worked as a law clerk for a few months, he dealt with black clients and engaged in no acts of racism toward them. The accuracy of this statement was confirmed by independent inquiry.

Analysis Of Moral Character

As noted, the applicant must establish his "good moral character and general fitness to practice law" "by clear and convincing evidence." * * * If these requisites may be established by simply showing an absence of criminal conduct in the past and having one or more persons vouch for one's character, Mr. Hale has established these requisites by clear and convincing evidence?

On the other hand, if the lack of good moral character and general fitness to practice law may be judged on the basis of active advocacy that attempts to incite hatred of members of various groups by vilifying and portraying them as inferior and robbing them of human dignity, Mr. Hale has not established good moral character or general fitness to practice law. As indicated, Mr. Hale's life mission is to bring about peaceable change in the United States in order to deny the equal protection of the laws to all Americans except perhaps those that his church determines to be of the "white race." Under any civilized standards of decency, the incitement of racial hatred for the ultimate purpose of depriving selected groups of their legal rights shows a gross deficiency in moral character, particularly for lawyers who have a special responsibility to uphold the rule of law for all persons.

However, even if the Illinois standards for considering moral character and general fitness to practice law allows the Committee to make a determination in this manner, the question remains as to whether or not denying certification for admission to the Bar is constitutional on that basis.

The Constitutional Analysis

At an earlier time the Committee on Character and Fitness might have desired to disqualify Mr. Hale on the ground that, despite his statements to the contrary, his views make it impossible for him to take the required oath "in good conscience." * * * Moreover, the Membership Manual for his church * * * [states that a church member] "puts loyalty towards his own race above every other loyalty." * * * A reasonable question for the applicant is what happens when that loyalty conflicts with his oath to support the United States and Illinois Constitutions?

Additionally, even though Mr. Hale claimed to be able to abide by the Rules of Professional Conduct relating to non-discriminatory treatment, his activities in this regard arguably cast doubt on these representations. For example, in 1995, only a few weeks before he started law school, he wrote a letter to a woman who apparently had made comments in the Peoria Journal Star on racial issues that were contrary to his. In this letter he referred to "the nigger race" as "inferior in intellectual capacity" and condemned the "misbegotten equality myth" as "garbage" that was "destroying" "our whole country." * * * He also suggested that this woman's rape or murder by a "nigger beast" might enlighten her.

With the applicant capable of such outrageous and intemperate conduct, one might have concluded that he was insincere when he said he could comply with the Rules of Professional Conduct and conscientiously take the oath. However, later cases of the United States Supreme Court suggest that these very real questions about the applicant might be a frail reed upon which to deny certification. *See, e.g., Bond v. Floyd*, 385 U.S. 116 (1966) and *Law Students Research Counsel v. Wadmond*, 401 U.S. 154, 163–164 (1971), which appear to hold that once an oath to support the Constitution is taken, others cannot urge that it was not taken sincerely.

Finally, an applicant cannot be denied admission to the Bar on a ground formerly announced by the Illinois Supreme Court—"that the practice of law is a privilege, not a right."

In Re Anastaplo, 3 Ill.2d 471, 482 (1954). On the contrary, the United States Supreme Court later stated that "the practice of law is not a matter of grace, but of right for one who is qualified by his learning and his moral character." *Baird v. Arizona, supra*, 401 U.S. 1 at 8.

Absolute First Amendment Rights vs. A Balancing Test

The easiest resolution of Mr. Hale's application would be to certify him. This would be in accord with the view that the First Amendment is virtually absolute. By adhering to such a view, line drawing problems and degree questions are avoided, and as the dissenting opinion makes clear, the analysis for reaching a decision can be simple and direct.

Certainly statements found in some Supreme Court opinions, taken in isolation and without regard to the specific facts of the cases, might support this view. For example, in the bar admission case of *Re Stolar*, 401 U.S. 23, 28–29 (1971), it was stated that the State cannot "penalize petitioner solely because he personally. . . 'espouses illegal aims.' "

Nonetheless, on balance, a majority of the Inquiry Panel bas concluded that the constitutional issues involving a case precisely like this one are open, and that the Illinois requirement for moral character and general fitness to practice law precludes the applicant from being certified.

The latest United States Supreme Court decisions relating to bar admissions located by the Inquiry Panel are over 25 years old. In 1971, the year of its most recent cases on this subject, the Court characterized its earlier opinions as containing "confusing formulas, refined reasonings, and puzzling holdings." *Baird v. Arizona*, 401 U.S. 1, (1971).

In that case, the Court, in a 5 to 4 split decision, he'd that "a State may not inquire about a man's views or associations solely for the purpose of withholding a right or benefit because of what he believes." * * * The Court also said in that case:

> While First Amendment issues in this case are difficult and The First Amendment's protection of association prohibits a State from excluding a person from a profession

or punishing him solely because he is a member of a particular political organization or because he holds certain beliefs. * * *

A similar result in another 5 to 4 decision was reached on the same day in 1971 in the case of *Re Stolar*, 401 U.S. (1971).

Neither of those decisions involved individuals who were actively involved in inciting racial hatred and who had dedicated their lives to destroying equal rights under law that all Americans currently enjoy. On the contrary, the applicants in those cases refused to reveal their views. But in this case Matthew Hale has no interest in keeping his views a secret. In a 1997 interview that appears on the Internet, he said that "we have several websites going now. . . . We are . . . , hoping to expand all these operations . . . to give people full knowledge of Creativity. * * * And his * * * autobiography proclaims "that he looks forward to leading Creativity to worldwide White Victory!"

* * *

The Commitment Of The Bar To Fundamental Truths

The balance that the majority chooses requires that a lawyer cannot, as his life's mission, do all in his power to incite racial and religious hatred among the populace so that it will peaceably abolish the rule of law for all persons save those of the "white race." Instead, and by rejecting Matthew Hale's application, let it be said that the Bar and our courts stand committed to these fundamental truths:

- All persons are possessed of individual dignity.

- As a result, every person is to be judged on the basis of his or her own individuality and conduct, not by reference to skin color, race, ethnicity, religion or national origin.

- The enforcement and application of these timeless values to specific cases have, by history and constitutional development, been entrusted to our courts and its officers—the lawyers—a trust that lies at the heart of our system of government.

- Therefore, the guardians of that trust—the judges and lawyers, or one or more of them—cannot have as their mission in life the incitement of racial hatred in order to destroy those values.

Commencing with Jefferson's ringing declaration that all men are created equal, and continuing with the adoption of our Constitution, the Emancipation Proclamation and the Fourteenth Amendment, the moral, ethical and legal struggle for the precious values contained in those writings has been costly, difficult and long. The Bar and our courts, charged with the duty of preserving those values, cannot allow Mr. Hale or any other applicant the use of a law license to attempt their destruction.

Finally, and this is the heart of our analysis, the majority's judgment is that to the extent its decision limits the First Amendment activities of lawyers, the fundamental truths identified above are so basic to the legal profession that, in the context of this case, they must be preferred over the values found in the First Amendment. The relationship of the profession to those truths was eloquently described in *Schware v. Board of Bar Examiners*, 353 U.S. 232, 246 (1957), by the late Justice Felix Frankfurter in a concurring opinion:

> . . . all the interests of man that are comprised under the constitutional guarantees given to "life, liberty and property" are in the professional keeping of lawyers.

The balance of values that we strike leaves Matthew Hale free, as the First Amendment allows, to incite as much racial hatred as he desires and to attempt to carry out his life's mission of depriving those he dislikes of their legal rights. But in our view he cannot do this as an officer of the court.

A preference for antidiscriminatory values over the First Amendment would not be new to Supreme Court decision making. Only five years ago the Court unanimously rejected First Amendment claims that "hate crimes" penalty enhancement statutes were invalid. The * * * Supreme Court had no difficulty in finding the statute constitutional because "hate crimes" are "thought to inflict greater individual and societal harm." * * * Arguably, the rationale in this case for preventing the applicant from becoming an officer of the Court is stronger than it was in the "hate crimes" case.

CONCLUSION

America's chief war crimes prosecutor at Nuremberg, wrote during World War II in *West Virginia Board of Education v. Barnette*, 319 U.S. 624, 638 (1943):

> The very purpose of a Bill of Rights was to withdraw certain subjects from the vicissitudes of political controversy, to place them beyond the reach of majorities and officials and to establish them as legal principles to be applied by the courts. One's right to life, liberty, and property, to free speech, a free press, freedom of worship and assembly, and other fundamental fights may not be submitted to vote; they depend on the outcome of no elections.

> Jackson's statement that the immutable principles of the Bill of Rights are to be "applied by the courts" has significance because "[It]here . . . comes from the [legal] profession the judiciary." *In re Anastaplo*, 3 Ill.2d 471, 479. Mr. Hale's life mission, the destruction of the Bill of Rights, is inherently incompatible with service as a lawyer or judge who is charged with safeguarding those rights.

The quotation from Barnette is important for another reason. Justice Jackson concluded that "fundamental rights may not be submitted to vote." But Mr. Hale wants to do exactly that, and it is a chilling thought indeed, considering that he and his church are admirers of Adolph Hitler, who acquired his absolute power peacefully, "quite legally" and "in a perfectly constitutional manner."

* * *

While Matthew Hale has not yet threatened to exterminate anyone, history tells us that extermination is sometimes not far behind when governmental power is held by persons of his racial views. The Bar of Illinois cannot certify someone as having good moral character and general fitness to practice law who has dedicated his life to inciting racial hatred for the purpose of implementing those views.

Respectfully submitted * * *.

Judge Gregory McClintock, Chairperson of Inquiry Panel Stuart Lefstein, Member of Inquiry Panel

Richard L. Sloane, *Note, Barbarian at the Gates: Revisiting the Case of Matthew F. Hale to Reaffirm That Character and Fitness Evaluations Appropriately Preclude Racists from the Practice of Law*

15 Geo. J. Legal Ethics 397, 425 (2002).

* * * On June 30, 1999, the Illinois Committee on Character and Fitness issued its decision to deny Hale certification to practice law. The next day, Benjamin Smith, a former member of Hale's church, went on a vicious shooting spree. Smith began his rampage in West Rogers Park in Chicago by shooting six Orthodox Jewish men after they had attended an evening synagogue service. He then drove to Skokie, a suburb of Chicago, where he shot and killed former Northwestern University basketball coach Ricky Byrdsong. Later that night, Smith traveled to another Chicago suburb, where he shot at an Asian couple in their car. The following day, Smith injured an African-American man in Springfield, Illinois, and an African-American minister in Decatur, Illinois. Later that night, Smith fired at six Asian students from the University of Illinois, in Urbana, injuring one. The next day, Smith shot at a group of Koreans exiting church in Bloomington, Indiana, killing a 26-year old Korean graduate student named Won-Joon Yoon, who had been studying at Indiana University. In total, Smith shot at twenty minorities. Smith stole a car, which led to a police chase ending with Smith taking his own life. Nine people were wounded in these events, all of them Orthodox Jews or African-Americans.

Following the incident, Hale cited the acts of his character witness Benjamin Smith as "an example of what happens when people at least perceive their freedom of speech is being disrupted." Similarly, following the issuance of the Findings and Conclusions of the Committee and the Smith shooting rampage, Hale was quoted as saying: "If people can't speak, violence automatically results in society."

Even in light of the Smith rampage, Hale has consistently argued that he is opposed to violence. * * *

Global Perspective

One of the ways to regulate lawyers for competence and ethics is to focus on the "middle stage" of regulation, rather than the beginning stage (entry into the profession) or the end stage (discipline). The goal of "middle stage" regulation, which is also called proactive regulation or PMBR, is to prevent problems before they occur, rather than responding afterwards. Illinois has a mandatory PMBR program that requires lawyers who do not carry malpractice insurance to complete an online self-assessment. Colorado has developed voluntary self-assessment forms and other proactive measures such as sending a "tips and resources" letter to Colorado lawyers switch their practice setting from a large firm or government setting to a small firm or solo setting. The ABA approved a PMBR motion at its August 2019 annual meeting. These U.S. developments have been influenced by global developments that include Nova Scotia's commitment to "Triple P" regulation, which is regulation that is *proactive*, principled, and proportionate, and the use of self-assessment forms in Australia and Nova Scotia. See Laurel S. Terry, *The Power of Lawyer Regulators to Increase Client & Public Protection Through Adoption of a Proactive Regulation System*, 20 Lewis & Clark L. Rev. 717 (2016).

C. Who Should Be Permitted to Provide Legal Services?

[Question 9-26]

Who should provide legal services?

    (A) Only lawyers should provide legal services.

    (B) Generally lawyers should provide legal services but independent paralegals should also be allowed to provide simple legal services.

    (C) Anyone should be able to provide legal services but only lawyers should be able to hold use the term "lawyers" to identify themselves.

[Question 9-27]

Should multidisciplinary practice be permitted?

    (A) Yes.

    (B) No.

FYI

An excellent introduction to this section is the portion of the documentary, "The Future Just Happened," on Marcus Arnold and changes in the legal profession. To watch online, click here.

[Question 9-28]

Should lawyers be permitted to share ownership of a law practice with non-lawyers?

    (A) Yes.

    (B) No.

1. Nonlawyer Practice

Marcus Arnold

In his book *Next: The Future Just Happened* (2002), Michael Lewis includes the story of Marcus Arnold, the 15 year old buy who became one of the highest rated legal advisors on the internet. The following description of Marcus Arnold's story, including quotations, is based on a New York Times Magazine article Lewis wrote based on stories from his book. Michael Lewis, *Faking It: The Internet Revolution has Nothing to Do With the NASDAQ*, <u>N.Y. Times Mag., July 15, 2001.</u>

In the early 2000s, AskMe.com emerged as an internet message board. The way the site worked was quite simple—someone posted a question on the site and then another person posted a response. The site ranked responses and identified resident experts based on those ranking. In June 2000, the tenth highest ranked legal expert on AskMe.com was LawGuy1975, aka Justin Anthony Wyrick, Jr., who fielded countless legal questions, often numbering in the hundreds per day, and provided answers to his satisfied "clients." LawGuy1975 was Marcus Arnold, a fifteen-year-old boy. Arnold was not an attorney. He had not yet finished high school.

In general, Marcus Arnold's clients posed simple questions, and Marcus responded with simple, direct answers:

> Q: What amount of money must a person steal or gain through fraud before it is considered a felony in Illinois?
>
> A: In Illinois you must have gained $5,001+ in an illegal fashion in order to constitute fraud. If you need anything else please write back! Sincerely, Justin Anthony Wyrick Jr.
>
> Q: Can a parole officer prevent a parolee from marrying?
>
> A: Hey! Unless the parolee has "no marriage" under the special conditions in which he is released, he can marry. If you have any questions, please write back. Sincerely, Justin Anthony Wyrick Jr.

When Lewis asked Arnold how he knew the answers to these questions, Arnold stated that he " 'just did,' " from watching television and browsing on the Internet. Arnold claimed never to have independently researched the answer to a single question.

Go Online

To view a picture of Marcus Arnold <u>click here</u>.

Eventually, Arnold decided to update his profile on AskMe.com to reflect the fact that was a fifteen-year-old boy. Immediately, other "legal experts" on the site began to send him emails ranging from admonishments to threats and even gave Arnold intentionally low rankings on his legal advice to lower his high-ranking.

Aside from his critics, however, Arnold also received overwhelming support from what might well be called his client base. As Lewis notes, "[a] lot of people seemed to believe that any 15-year-old who had risen so high in the ranks of AskMe.com legal experts must be some kind of wizard. They began to seek him out more than ever before; they wanted his, and only his, advice."

AskMe.com continues to include nonlawyers as legal experts. See www.askmehelpdesk.com.

Two weeks after Arnold admitted he was only fifteen, he was the single-highest ranked legal expert on AskMe.com.

Lewis suggests that Arnold symbolizes the descent of the legal field from a profession to a business that is simply the sum of its parts; one of its parts being information. He writes that, "Once the law became a business, it was on its way to becoming a commodity. Reduce the law to the sum of its information, and, by implication, anyone can supply it." Even a fifteen-year-old boy.

Global Perspective

The 2007 UK Legal Services Act significantly transformed regulation of the UK legal profession. In addition to dramatically changing the structure of the regulatory system and the lawyer discipline system, the 2007 Act allowed the "front-line" regulators to permit alternative business structures (ABS), including those with non-lawyer ownership of law firms that involve passive investment or publicly-traded shares. One of the major justifications was that outside investment would improve access to the legal system by the middle class and others. The Act was sometimes referred to as "Tesco" law with proponents and critics noting that it would allow UK supermarket giant Tesco to have law offices within the supermarket. At the time this edition was written, the UK Solicitors Regulation Authority (SRA), which is the front-line regulator for solicitors in England and Wales, had issued a number of ABS licenses. (You can search for registered ABS entities here). Tesco was not among them, but a number of large entities had received such licenses, including the Cooperative, which is a supermarket and banking chain. (In 2012, the American Bar Association Commission on Ethics 20/20 decided *not* to advance any type of ABS proposal, as did the ABA Commission on the Future of Legal Services.) By 2019, however, several U.S. states, as well as other organizations, were examining the issue of Rule 5.4 and nonlawyer involvement in, or ownership of, law firms. Additional information about the UK ABS situation is found on the Legal Futures blog. In your view, will the ABS structure increase access to justice? What concerns, if any, do you have and how would you address them?

Food for Thought

Should customer satisfaction make a difference? In the Brumbaugh case, Chapter 1, *supra*, the court notes that the allegations of unauthorized practice "did not arise from a complaint by any of Ms. Brumbaugh's customers as to improper advice or unethical conduct—[The action] has been initiated by members of the Florida Bar[.]" Professor Deborah Rhode has observed that "Surveys of federal administrative agencies, consumer regulatory organizations, reported judicial decisions, and bar enforcement committees generally reveal no significant incidence of customer injury from lay practice. So too, the only research on customer satisfaction finds higher approval ratings for nonlawyer specialists than for lawyers." Deborah L. Rhode, *Institutionalizing Ethics*, 44 Case W. Res. L. Rev., 665, 727 (1994).

JOHN S. DZIENKOWSKI & ROBERT J. PERONI, *MULTIDISCIPLINARY PRACTICE AND THE AMERICAN LEGAL PROFESSION: A MARKET APPROACH TO REGULATING THE DELIVERY OF LEGAL SERVICES IN THE TWENTY-FIRST CENTURY*

69 Fordham L. Rev. 83 (2000)

* * *

The American legal profession has * * * embraced the concept that nonlawyers should not become partners or owners in a law firm or other entity delivering legal services for a pecuniary gain. The 1908 Canons of Professional Ethics did not contain any restrictions on nonlawyer ownership of law firms. In 1928, however, the ABA amended the Canons of Professional Ethics to urge that lawyers not create partnerships with members of other professions if any part of the business is to consist of the practice of law. In 1969, the ABA strengthened this ban, making it mandatory in the Model Code of Professional Responsibility. The ABA restated this position in 1983 by adopting Model Rule 5.4(a), which prohibits partnerships between lawyers and nonlawyers.

In 1928, the ABA completed the ban on nonlawyer involvement in the practice of law by adopting Canon 34 of the Canons of Professional Ethics that prohibited any sharing of legal fees with nonlawyers. Canon 35 also prohibited third party interference with the professional independence of the lawyer. The ABA later adopted similar prohibitions in the Model Code and the Model Rules. * * *

In 1982, however, during the drafting of the Model Rules, the Kutak Commission proposed a rule that would have significantly changed the ABA's position on nonlawyer involvement in the practice of law. A proposed model rule on the "Professional Independence of a Firm" provided that a lawyer could be employed by an organization in which nonlawyers held a financial or managerial interest as long as the professional independence of the lawyer was preserved. This rule, however, was completely rejected on the floor of the ABA House of Delegates meeting, and rewritten and replaced with the current version of Model Rule 5.4. Ironically, the 1999 proposals of the ABA Commission on Multidisciplinary Practice came almost "full circle" back to the Kutak position.

In 1988, both the District of Columbia bar and North Dakota bar proposed that their respective versions of Model Rule 5.4 be modified to allow lawyers and nonlawyers to hold ownership interests in a law firm. The District of Columbia bar sought to change the rule in order to allow nonlawyers to contribute to the legal services provided to clients. This proposal was in part a reaction to the non-law divisions of lobbying, real estate, and investment banking that some District of Columbia law firms had begun to develop as subsidiaries. The North Dakota rule sought to allow lawyers and nonlawyers to offer combined services. Ultimately, after much debate and controversy, the District of Columbia rule passed, but the North Dakota rule was withdrawn by the state supreme court.

In reaction to a perceived commercialization of the legal profession that allegedly threatened the ability of lawyers to render independent advice, the ABA began to consider an ethics rule on ancillary business services. Some in the ABA thought that the ABA needed to provide the states with an alternative rule to D.C. Rule 5.4 so that states would have an option when their lawyers pushed for modifying the codes of conduct to accommodate non-legal services. In 1991, the ABA House of Delegates adopted new Model Rule 5.7, "Responsibilities Regarding Law-Related Services." The 1991 version of this rule was very strict as to lawyer involvement in law-related services provided to law firm clients. It required that such services ancillary to the practice of law be provided only to the clients of the law firm, and only by employees of the law firm, not of a subsidiary. Also, the rule required that the lawyer make appropriate disclosure to the client, and required that the law firm not hold itself out to the public as engaging in any non-legal activities. The comments to the rule make clear that the ABA sought to restrict "the ability of law firms to provide ancillary non-legal services through affiliates to non-client customers and clients alike, the rendition of which raises serious ethical and professionalism concerns."

The severe restrictions of the 1991 Model Rule 5.7 were contrary to many practices within state bars regarding the provision of lawyer-owned non-legal services. In many states, lawyers owned title companies that were marketed to the general public as well as to firm clients. Thus, in 1992, the ABA House of Delegates deleted the 1991 version of Rule 5.7. In 1994, the ABA considered a different approach to lawyer provision of ancillary business services and adopted a revised version of Model Rule 5.7. The revised version of Model Rule 5.7 does not address the ethical or professional consequences of lawyers and law firms providing ancillary business services. Instead, it focuses on the client expectations that may arise when ancillary business services are provided by a law firm. Essentially, under revised Model Rule 5.7, a law firm's ancillary business services may or may not be included under the protection of the rules of ethics. To avoid application of the ethics rules, a law firm must provide the services in a manner distinct from the delivery of legal services. Additionally, the client must be informed that the services are not legal services and that the protections of the attorney-client relationship do not apply.

Although the ABA properly identified one key issue in the provision of ancillary business services—whether the attorney-client relationship attaches to those services—the new version of Model Rule 5.7 blatantly ignored all of the concerns that the ABA addressed in 1991. This exhibits the "politics of regulating the bar" within the ABA. Although nothing was done to alleviate the professional concerns in the provision of ancillary business services, the revised rule accommodated the practices throughout the country whereby lawyers provided non-legal services to clients and non-clients for significant profits, in some cases without disclosing the lawyers' ownership interests in the non-law business.

* * * As mentioned above, one major area in which nonlawyers and lawyers in accounting firms have been involved in the delivery of legal services is in the practice of tax law. State unauthorized-practice-of-law statutes and case law must be read in conjunction with the federal system of authorizing lawyers and nonlawyers to practice in certain areas in the federal system. Under the Supremacy Clause, Congress and the Executive Branch can preempt state regulation

of the unauthorized practice of law. Although the federal system has often deferred to the state bar system of lawyer regulation, one major area of federal preemption is federal tax practice. The federal scheme authorized by Congress allows lawyers and certain nonlawyers to practice in the area of federal tax.

In recent years, the Big Five accounting firms, as well as mid-sized accounting firms, have hired thousands of tax lawyers for their growing domestic and international tax planning practices (including well-known partners from major law firms in cities throughout the country). These efforts have been met with great concern and suspicion by state bar authorities and lawyers in general. In fact, several state bars have investigated the activities of the "Big Five" firms for violations of the unauthorized-practice-of-law statutes, but to date no unauthorized-practice-of-law complaints have been successfully maintained against such firms.

The Big Five accounting firms have argued that they are not engaged in the practice of law, but instead are engaged in tax consulting, something somehow different than tax law practice even though it involves interpretation and application of tax law. This argument appears to have no substance. A better argument by the Big Five accounting firms would be that to the extent they are engaged in the practice of tax law, at least at the federal level, the preemption doctrine prevents state bar authorities from successfully maintaining unauthorized-practice actions against them.

Federal law clearly preempts unauthorized-practice-of-law complaints by state bar authorities if and to the extent that the accounting firms' activities fall within the federal scheme of preemption. A federal statute, Treasury Circular 230, and the Tax Court Rules specifically authorize accountants and lawyers to practice in the area of federal taxation. Further, this federal authority does not limit partnerships or associations between lawyers and accountants working in this area. * * *

There is, however, one collateral aspect of tax practice that could involve the unauthorized practice of law. If a nonlawyer or a lawyer in an accounting firm provides tax services about a future transaction, and the client decides to adopt the advice, that client will often need non-tax services to implement the tax plan. Such services may include drafting of a will, transferring title to a property, or drafting the documents for a family limited partnership. Providing these services could arguably constitute the unauthorized practice of law.

There is no doubt that if a nonlawyer or a lawyer practicing in an accounting firm drafted an entire agreement and had the client execute the agreement in the accounting office, this activity would constitute the practice of law and could be enjoined by the state bar under the current ethical rules. A nonlawyer or a lawyer practicing in an accounting firm should, however, be able to propose language for inclusion in a legal document and draft such language without violating the unauthorized-practice-of-law rules. Such language could be provided to a client with the instruction that the client should take the language to an independent lawyer and have the lawyer include it in the legal documents only after review. Furthermore, an accounting firm could also draft an entire document for review by the client's lawyer. Although this comes closer to the practice of law, if the accounting firm sent this draft directly to the client's lawyer, that would arguably still be authorized by federal tax law. For the accounting firm to provide the draft directly to the client raises more serious liability concerns. On a case-by-case basis, it is unlikely that giving the draft to the client would trigger unauthorized-practice-of-law restrictions if the accounting firm makes it clear that the client needs to engage a separate lawyer to review the document before it is executed. There is always a risk, however, that a client could attempt to execute a complete document without review by a lawyer. Thus, an improperly executed will, for example, could be invalid and could subject the accounting firm to liability.

* * * In August of 1998, then ABA President Phillip Anderson appointed a commission to study the concept of multidisciplinary services and what changes, if any, should be made to the ABA Model Rules of Professional Conduct. * * *

The ABA Commission issued its Final Report on June 8, 1999, as part of a submission to the ABA House of Delegates for the August 1999 meeting. The Commission recommended that the ABA House of Delegates amend the Model Rules to permit lawyers to offer legal services through an MDP. The Report ultimately suggested that the ABA not constrain the type of entity that lawyers could use in offering multidisciplinary services. In other words, lawyers could offer legal services through any of the five models, even in the form of a fully integrated MDP. The Commission acknowledged, however, that the delivery of legal services through an MDP could threaten the core values of the legal profession. Thus, if the Commission's recommendations were adopted, MDPs would be required to follow the same rules that law firms followed and would have to certify their compliance with that requirement to the state bar. MDPs controlled by nonlawyers would be subject to an annual state bar audit to determine whether the certification was in fact true. Failure to comply with the certification could result in the firm's disbarment from MDP status. Moreover, nonlawyer controlled MDPs would have to pay the cost of the annual state bar audit. In addition, the Report recommended that the definition of an MDP be expanded to include any entity that employs lawyers for providing legal services. Thus, under the Commission's recommendations, in exchange for permission to deliver legal services through an MDP, all entities hiring lawyers for the performance of quasi-legal services would have to agree to be bound by the lawyer's rules of conduct and to be subject to a state bar audit.

* * * The vigorous debate at the August 1999 ABA meeting led the Commission on Multidisciplinary Practice to withdraw its proposal and to support further study. The ABA House of Delegates adopted a resolution proposed initially by the Florida delegates. * * * In March of 2000, the Commission issued recommendations to the House of Delegates, scaling back its 1999 recommendations to the following:

> 1.   Lawyers should be permitted to share fees and join with nonlawyer professionals in a practice that delivers both legal and nonlegal professional services (Multidisciplinary Practice), provided that the lawyers have the control and authority necessary to assure lawyer independence in the rendering of legal services. "Nonlawyer professionals" means members of recognized professions or other disciplines that are governed by ethical standards.

2.   This Recommendation must be implemented in a manner that protects the public and preserves the core values of the legal profession, including competence, independence of professional judgment, protection of confidential client information, loyalty to the client through the avoidance of conflicts of interest, and pro bono publico obligations.

3.   To protect the public interest, regulatory authorities should enforce existing rules and adopt such additional enforcement procedures as are needed to implement the principles identified in this Recommendation.

4.   This Recommendation does not alter the prohibition on nonlawyers delivering legal services and the obligations of all lawyers to observe the rules of professional conduct. Nor does it authorize passive investment in a Multidisciplinary Practice.

The ABA Commission presented this recommendation to the House of Delegates in July of 2000, and the House of Delegates rejected it. * * *

DZIENKOWSKI & PERONI, *MULTIDISCIPLINARY PRACTICE AND THE AMERICAN LEGAL PROFESSION: A MARKET APPROACH TO REGULATING THE DELIVERY OF LEGAL SERVICES IN THE TWENTY-FIRST CENTURY*

<u>69 Fordham L. Rev. 83, 205–07 (2000)</u>

* * * If the United States is to remain a center of global commerce, the legal profession must accommodate the demand for multidisciplinary services. The state bars now have a unique opportunity to develop a regulatory structure that protects the core values of the legal profession while accommodating consumer demand for integrated services. A decision by the organized bar attempting to reinforce the status quo ultimately will lead to the American legal profession's inability to play a key role in shaping the delivery of multidisciplinary services.

The states should modify their rules of professional conduct as follows. First, Model Rule 5.4 should be modified to allow fee-sharing between lawyers and nonlawyers providing professional services to a client. No pure referral fees should be permitted to nonlawyers. Second, the rules should be amended to permit lawyer participation in the delivery of multidisciplinary services. Although a structure that permitted all models of multidisciplinary services, including the fully integrated MDP, is optimal, such a step may be too radical for many states. Thus, states should strongly consider adopting rules that would permit contractual and joint venture MDPs to exist to offer legal and non-legal services in a coordinated manner. Both contractual and joint venture MDPs would offer experimentation in how conflicts of interest would be handled in the two separate kinds of firms. The organized bar could evolve the rules on conflicts in response to the experience with such arrangements. The contractual and entity joint ventures will afford many of the benefits of multidisciplinary practice with few of the costs.

The optimal approach for allowing lawyer participation in MDPs would involve removing the ban against nonlawyer partners and shareholders in business entities that provide legal services. Lawyers and nonlawyers should be able to form a single entity to offer both legal and non-legal services to clients. The delivery of legal services must conform to the same professional responsibility rules and standards as would apply if a law firm provided the services. The delivery of legal services would need to be controlled by lawyers, although there should be no requirement that lawyers have voting control in the fully integrated, single entity MDP. In order to facilitate lawyer control over legal services, lawyers in a single entity MDP should be organized in a legal department with checks and balances similar to those implemented in a corporate counsel context. There should be no requirement that the nonlawyers in an MDP be only those from a licensed profession because such a requirement is both vague and theoretically indefensible.

The states should also promulgate professional responsibility rules and standards that apply to all MDPs. MDPs should be permitted to litigate in the federal and state courts. Passive investments should be permitted in both law firms and MDPs; if, however, rules governing law firms are not liberalized to allow such passive investment, then the rules for MDPs on this issue must remain consistent with those for law firms. When a client is receiving legal services, a lawyer must supervise all aspects of work falling within the legal umbrella. Nonlawyer partners and managers must agree not to interfere in the delivery of legal services and must also require that all lawyers in the firm follow the rules of professional conduct. Additionally, the profession should implement peer review for law firms and other entities, including MDPs, that are delivering legal services to clients.

The question is not whether MDPs will exist and thrive in the future or whether lawyers in ever greater numbers will choose to work for MDPs. The trends in favor of MDPs are pronounced and unstoppable. Nothing the ABA or the state bars do can change that fact of economic life. The question is whether the ABA and state bars will have any significant role in regulating lawyers who work in MDPs, thereby protecting client interests and ensuring that lawyers' participation in multidisciplinary practice does not undercut the core values of the profession.

* * *

Client protection and protection of the core values of the legal profession should be the primary basis for regulation of MDPs. The rules of professional conduct for lawyers should permit innovation in the professional service marketplace. Unneeded and overbroad regulation, often motivated by economic protectionism, should be discarded. The state bar authorities should design their regulation of MDPs in the manner this Article suggests and thereby protect the public interest without unnecessarily interfering with the operation of market forces in the professional services arena.

ANDREW M. PERLMAN, *TOWARDS THE LAW OF LEGAL SERVICES*

37 Cardozo L. Rev. 49 (2015)

Imagine that someone asks you how legal services are regulated in the United States. You might answer that lawyers need a license in the jurisdictions where they intend to practice, typically after graduating from an ABA-accredited law school and passing the bar examination. You could explain that lawyers are governed by rules of professional conduct and subject to discipline, including disbarment, for failing to comply. You also might mention the growing patchwork of state and federal regulations that govern lawyers' behavior. Each of these answers offers a slightly different perspective on the regulation of legal services, but they share one common feature: they are all about lawyers.

This Article contends that the current lawyer-based regulatory framework should be reimagined if we hope to spur more innovation and expand access to justice. Rather than focusing on the so-called "law of lawyering"—the body of rules and statutes regulating lawyers—this Article suggests that we need to develop a broader "law of legal services" that authorizes, but appropriately regulates, the delivery of more legal and law-related assistance by people who do not have a Juris Doctor (J.D.) degree and do not work alongside lawyers. For example, the Washington Supreme Court recently adopted a framework for allowing specially educated and separately regulated professionals—Limited License Legal Technicians (LLLTs)—to deliver a narrow range of family law services without a traditional law license. Some observers predict that LLLTs will be able to offer assistance at a lower cost than lawyers and improve access to legal services. This type of regulatory reform, which falls outside the law of lawyering, illustrates the growing importance and potential utility of the law of legal services.

* * *

[Other examples of these types of these services currently falling outside the law of lawyering include] automated legal document assembly for consumers, law firms, and corporate counsel; expert systems that address legal issues through a series of branching questions and answers; electronic discovery; legal process outsourcing; legal process insourcing and design; legal project management and process improvement; knowledge management; online dispute resolution; data analytics; and many others.

* * *

Rather than trying to define the practice of law, we should ask a fundamentally different question: should someone without a law degree be "authorized" to provide a particular service, even if it might be the "practice of law"? By focusing attention on whether the provider is competent to deliver a service, we can more effectively achieve what really matters: protecting the public.

Perlman identifies the following "principles for the law of legal services:" (1) competence; (2) free markets and consumer choice; (3) informed consumer choice; (4) accessibility and availability of remedies for incompetence; (5) faith in the justice system and the rule of law; and (6) professional independence and other client-related protections.

RENEE NEWMAN KNAKE, *THE COMMERCIALIZATION OF LEGAL ETHICS*

29 Georgetown Journal of Legal Ethics 715 (2016)

In recent years, some regulators and scholars have called for a more expansive regulatory structure, contemplating legal ethics not only for lawyers but also legal services providers (entities and individuals serving legal needs without the same training and authorization traditionally required of state-licensed attorneys). They argue that the public would best be served under a more expansive consumer-protection focused regime where a diverse array of providers offers legal assistance. Indeed, numerous jurisdictions around the globe have adopted regulatory objectives for this very purpose and, closer to home, the American Bar Association Presidential Commission on the Future of Legal Services as well as some states are contemplating similar expansion of oversight via regulatory objectives. Although to-date an international occurrence in nations like Australia, England, and Wales, we are already seeing movement in the United States as jurisdictions permit individuals without traditional legal training to practice law under limited conditions or debate the adoption of regulatory objectives to expand the reach of professional ethics to legal services providers other than lawyers.

It may very well be that an expanded cadre of legal services providers and lawyer ratings companies can ameliorate the long-standing access to justice issues that perpetuate in the United States and globally. Along with a host of other scholars and commentators on the legal profession, I have argued as much in earlier writings. To be sure, the profession is at a juncture where it must reconsider how to effectively deliver legal representation in the future. We cannot ignore the repeated and penetrating calls for action in this regard. But it is not clear that enlarging the scope of legal ethics to include providers other than lawyers will expand access to justice. Nor does the advent of lawyer ratings websites necessarily accomplish this goal. In other words, we cannot know the impact of their use until we have better assessment and study. In any event, this is not the point—my purpose here is not to speculate on the effect of these newly-flourishing entities, though their impact can and should be evaluated.

Rather, my aim is to provoke consideration about the proliferation of profit-driven legal services providers and lawyer ratings companies in an effort to determine whether and how these entities ought to inform the traditional authorities charged with regulation of the legal profession in the ways they conceptualize and implement lawyer regulation. How should state courts and tribunals as well as bar organizations respond to these emerging forces? Are existing regulations sufficient? Should new regulations be adopted? Do the courts and bar authorities have an obligation to educate members of the profession as well as the public in this regard? Will these new tools for accessing legal services resolve at least a portion of the justice gap? How might these measures be improved in order to better serve the public's legal needs? Should traditional authorities cooperate with new providers and companies to inform and protect the public? Should regulators monitor online ratings and reviews websites as part of ongoing disciplinary enforcement?

The commercialization of legal ethics also presents new sorts of conflicts of interest between the client and lawyer or legal services provider. Does a legal services provider owe duties of confidentiality and loyalty to current, former, and potential clients? If so, how should providers be monitored and disciplined? Or consider how the promise of a favorable review might distort a lawyer's judgment. On the one hand, this may incentivize lawyer fitness and police against malfeasance more effectively than the existing system of internal reporting and professional discipline bodies. On the other hand, maintaining client feedback on various ratings and review websites may become extremely time-consuming for lawyers and expensive for clients to the extent lawyers pass along those costs. Likewise, the pressure to avoid negative reviews might compromise a lawyer's loyalty or confidentiality to the client. Moreover, the measures for a high review ranking by a private company may not parallel the measures for competence, diligence, loyalty, and confidence owed to the client or the obligations of honesty and fairness owed to courts and third parties under traditional professional ethics. And, of course, a risk of manipulation of online ratings and search results is always present.

The commercialization of legal ethics promises to fill long-enduring gaps in access to justice by exponentially expanding the availability of information about how to obtain quality legal representation, as well as the availability of new types of providers. At the same time, lawyers and their regulators should consider how to partner with established and emerging commercial providers in order to best preserve the traditional structure of legal ethics that defines the necessary fitness to practice law. The profession must also engage in meaningful public education about how to accurately assess one's legal needs and to select the best provider to address those needs.

* * *

Approximately two dozen jurisdictions have adopted regulatory objectives over the past decade, including the American Bar Association House of Delegates in February 2016. Australia, Denmark, England, India, Ireland, New Zealand, Scotland, Wales, and several Canadian provinces also either have adopted regulatory objectives or had proposals pending as of 2015.

How might regulatory objectives benefit the regulators of lawyers and legal services, as well as the public?

LAUREL TERRY, STEVE MARK & TAHLIA GORDON, *ADOPTING REGULATORY OBJECTIVES FOR THE LEGAL PROFESSION*

80 Fordham Law Review 2685 (2012)

First, the inclusion of regulatory objectives definitively sets out the purpose of lawyer regulation and its parameters. Regulatory objectives thus serve as a guide to assist those regulating the legal profession and those being regulated. Second, regulatory objectives identify, for those affected by the particular regulation, the purpose of that regulation and why it is enforced. Third, regulatory objectives assist in ensuring that the function and purpose of the particular [regulation] is transparent. Thus, when the regulatory body administering the [regulation] is questioned—for example, about its interpretation of the [regulation]—the regulatory body can point to the regulatory objectives to demonstrate compliance with function and purpose. Fourth, regulatory objectives can help define the parameters of the [regulation] and of public debate about proposed [regulation]. Finally, regulatory objectives may help the legal profession when it is called upon to negotiate with governmental and nongovernmental entities about regulations affecting legal practice.

In February 2016, the American Bar Association House of Delegates passed Resolution 105, adopting a list of ten Model Regulatory Objectives, including public protection, the administration of justice and the rule of law, transparency, affordable and accessible legal services, and diversity/inclusion. The complete list is available on the ABA's website. For more information about the adoption of regulatory objectives by international jurisdictions, *see* Laurel Terry, *Why Your Jurisdiction Should Jump on the Regulatory Objectives Bandwagon*, The Professional Lawyer (2013).

II. Special Responsibilities

In a sense, the entire book explores lawyers' responsibilities flowing from lawyers' special privileges to practice law. In this section, we will examine in more depth the general responsibility for equal justice. In particular, this Section will examine lawyers' responsibilities with regard to equal access to legal assistance, for rich and poor, or depending on identity. We also look at responsibilities lawyers have to address ethical dilemmas not necessarily covered by professional conduct rules—for example recognizing implicit bias and the role of behavioral legal ethics—as well as implications of mental health issues for members of the legal profession.

A. Pro Bono

[Question 9-29]

Should Pro Bono service be mandatory for law students?

    (A) Yes.

    (B) No.

[Question 9-30]

Should Pro Bono service be mandatory for lawyers?

    (A) Yes.

    (B) No.

Rule 6.1 provides that "[a] lawyer should aspire to render at least (50) hours of pro bono publico legal services per year." It further advises that:

the lawyer should:

(a)   provide a substantial majority of the (50) hours of legal services without fee or expectation of fee to:

  (1)   persons of limited means or

  (2)   charitable, religious, civic, community, governmental and educational organizations in matters that are designed primarily to address the needs of persons of limited means; and

(b)   provide any additional services through:

  (1)   delivery of legal services at no fee or substantially reduced fee to individuals, groups or organizations seeking to secure or protect civil rights, civil liberties or public rights, or charitable, religious, civic, community, governmental and educational organizations in matters in furtherance of their organizational purposes, where the payment of standard legal fees would significantly deplete the organization's economic resources or would be otherwise inappropriate;

Go Online

To view the documentary "So Goes A Nation: Lawyers and Low Income Communities," click here.

  (2)   delivery of legal services at a substantially reduced fee to persons of limited means; or

  (3)   participation in activities for improving the law, the legal system or the legal profession.

In addition, a lawyer should voluntarily contribute financial support to organizations that provide legal services to persons of limited means.

In 2012, New York adopted a new rule requiring law students to engage in 50 hours of pro bono work.

DEBORAH L. RHODE, *CULTURES OF COMMITMENT: PRO BONO FOR LAWYERS AND LAW STUDENTS*

67 Fordham L. Rev. 2415 (1999)

Nowhere is the gap between professional ideals and professional practice more apparent than on issues of pro bono responsibility. For decades, bar leaders, ethical codes, and countless commissions and committees have proclaimed that all lawyers have obligations to assist individuals who cannot afford counsel. And for decades, the percentage of lawyers who actually do so has remained dispiritingly small. Recent estimates suggest that most attorneys do not perform significant pro bono work, and that only between ten and twenty percent of those who do are assisting low-income clients. The average for the profession as a whole is less than a half an hour per week. Few lawyers come close to satisfying the American Bar Association's Model Rules, which provide that "[a] lawyer should aspire to render at least [fifty] hours of pro bono publico legal services per year" primarily to "persons of limited means" or to "organizations in matters which are designed primarily to address the needs of [such] persons."

The bar's failure to secure broader participation in pro bono work is all the more disappointing when measured against the extraordinary successes that such work has yielded. Many of the nation's landmark public-interest cases have grown out of lawyers' voluntary contributions. Moreover, particularly over the last decade, growing numbers of attorneys have donated time and talents to less visible but no less critical poverty law programs. For children with disabilities, victims of domestic violence, elderly citizens without medical care, and other low-income clients, these pro bono programs are crucial in meeting basic human needs. For lawyers themselves, such work is similarly important in giving purpose and meaning to their professional lives. Our inability to enlist more attorneys in pro bono service represents a significant lost opportunity for them as well as for the public.

How best to narrow the gap between professional ideals and professional practice has been a matter of considerable controversy. Proposals for mandatory pro bono requirements have come and gone, but mainly gone. The bar generally has resisted mandatory service, although a few jurisdictions require lawyers to accept judicial appointments for limited categories of cases, and one state, Florida, requires lawyers to report their annual pro bono contributions.

This resistance to required contributions, coupled with the limited success of voluntary efforts, has encouraged more pro bono initiatives in law schools. By enlisting students early in their legal careers, these initiatives attempt to inspire an enduring commitment to public service. The hope is that, over time, a greater sense of moral obligation will "trickle up" to practitioners. With that objective, an increasing number of schools have instituted pro bono requirements for students. So too, in 1996, the American Bar Association amended its accreditation standards to call on schools to "encourage . . . students to participate in pro bono activities and provide opportunities for them to do so." These revised ABA standards also encourage schools to address the obligations of faculty to the public, including participation in pro bono activities.

Despite such initiatives, pro bono still occupies a relatively marginal place in legal education. Only about ten percent of schools require any service by students and only a handful impose specific requirements on faculty. At some of these schools, the amounts demanded are quite minimal: less than twenty hours by the time of graduation. Over ninety percent of institutions offer voluntary programs, but their scope and quality varies considerably. About one-third of schools have no law-related pro bono projects or projects involving a few dozen participants. The majority of students have no legal pro bono work as part of their educational experience.

What legal education could or should do to expand such public-service commitments is subject to increasing debate. While law school administrators overwhelmingly support pro bono participation, they are divided about whether current programs are adequate and whether required service is desirable. * * *

* * * The primary rationale for pro bono contributions rests on two premises: first, that access to legal services is a fundamental need, and second, that lawyers have some responsibility to help make those services available. The first claim is widely acknowledged. As the Supreme Court has recognized in other contexts, the right to sue and defend is the right that protects all other rights. Access to the justice system is particularly critical for the poor, who often depend on legal entitlements to meet basic needs such as food, housing, and medical care. Moreover, in a democratic social order, equality before the law is central to the rule of law and to the legitimacy of the state. Social science research confirms what political theorists have long argued: Public confidence in legal processes depends heavily on opportunities for direct participation.

In most circumstances, those opportunities are meaningless without access to legal assistance. Our justice system is designed by and for lawyers, and lay participants who attempt to navigate without counsel are generally at a disadvantage. Those disadvantages are particularly great among the poor, who typically lack the education and experience necessary for effective self-representation. For example, studies of eviction proceedings find that tenants with attorneys usually prevail; tenants without attorneys almost always lose. Inequalities in legal representation compound other social inequalities and undermine our commitments to procedural fairness and social justice. As a New York judicial report noted: "Our justice system cannot proclaim in the bold letters of the law that it is just, but then block access to justice. We cannot promise due process, but raise insurmountable odds for those who seek it."

While most lawyers acknowledge that access to legal assistance is a fundamental interest, they are divided over whether the profession has some special responsibility to help provide that assistance, and if so, whether the responsibility should be mandatory. One contested issue is whether attorneys have obligations to meet fundamental needs that other occupations do not share. According to some lawyers, if equal justice under law is a societal value, society as a whole should bear its cost. The poor have fundamental needs for food and medical care, but we do not require grocers or physicians to donate their help in meeting those needs. Why should lawyers' responsibilities be greater?

One answer is that the legal profession has a monopoly on the provision of essential services. Lawyers have special privileges that entail special obligations. In the United States, attorneys have a much more extensive and exclusive right to provide legal assistance than attorneys in other countries. The American bar has closely guarded those prerogatives and its success in restricting lay competition has helped to price services out of the reach of many consumers. Under these circumstances, it is not unreasonable to expect lawyers to make some pro bono contributions in return for their privileged status. Nor would it be inappropriate to expect comparable contributions from other professionals who have similar monopolies over the provision of critical services.

An alternative justification for imposing special obligations on lawyers stems from their special role in our governance structure. As the New York report explained, much of what lawyers do:

is about providing justice, [which is] . . . nearer to the heart of our way of life . . . than services provided by other professionals. The legal profession serves as indispensable guardians of our lives, liberties and governing principles. . . . Like no other professionals, lawyers are charged with the responsibility for systemic improvement of not only their own profession, but of the law and society itself.

Because lawyers occupy such a central role in our governance system, there is also particular value in exposing them to how that system functions, or fails to function, for the have nots. Pro bono work offers many attorneys their only direct contact with what passes for justice among the poor. To give broad segments of the bar some experience with poverty-related problems and public-interest causes may lay critical foundations for change. Pro bono programs have often launched leading social reform initiatives and strengthened support for government subsidies of legal services.

A final justification for pro bono work involves its benefits to lawyers individually and collectively. Those benefits extend beyond the intrinsic satisfactions that accompany public service. Particularly for young attorneys, such work can provide valuable training, trial experience, and professional contacts. Through pro bono assistance, lawyers can develop capacities to communicate with diverse audiences and build problem-solving skills. Involvement in community groups, charitable organizations, and public-interest activities is a way for attorneys to expand their perspectives, enhance their reputations, and attract paying clients. It is also a way for the bar to improve the public standing of lawyers as a group. In one representative ABA poll, nearly half of nonlawyers believed that providing free legal services would improve the profession's image.

For all these reasons, the vast majority of surveyed lawyers believe that the bar should provide pro bono services. However, as noted earlier, only a minority in fact provide significant assistance and few of their efforts aid low-income clients. The reasons for this shortfall do not involve a lack of need. A wide gap remains between the rhetoric and reality of America's commitment to equal justice. Studies of low-income groups find that over three-quarters of their legal needs remain unmet. Studies cutting across income groups estimate that individuals do not obtain lawyers' help for between thirty to forty percent of their personal legal needs. Moreover, these legal needs studies do not include many collective problems where attorneys' services are often crucial, such as environmental risks or consumer product safety.

The bar's response to inadequate access alternates between confession and avoidance. Some lawyers simply deny the data. Unburdened by factual support, they insist that no worthy cause goes unassisted, thanks to voluntary pro bono efforts, legal-aid programs, and contingent fee representation. A more common approach is to acknowledge the problem of unmet needs but to deny that mandatory pro bono service is the solution. In one representative survey, about sixty percent of California attorneys believed that poor people's access to legal assistance would continue to decline, but an equal number opposed minimum pro bono requirements.

Opponents raise both moral and practical objections. As a matter of principle, some lawyers insist that compulsory charity is a contradiction in terms. From their perspective, requiring service would undermine its moral significance and compromise altruistic commitments.

There are several problems with this claim, beginning with its assumption that pro bono service is "charity." As the preceding discussion suggested, pro bono work is not simply a philanthropic exercise; it is also a professional responsibility. Moreover, in the small number of jurisdictions where courts now appoint lawyers to provide uncompensated representation, no evidence indicates that voluntary assistance has declined as a result. Nor is it self-evident that most lawyers who currently make public-service contributions would cease to do so simply because others were required to join them. As to lawyers who do not volunteer but claim that required service would lack moral value, David Luban has it right: "You can't appeal to the moral significance of a gift you have no intention of giving."

Opponents' other moral objection to mandatory pro bono contributions involves the infringement of lawyers' own rights. From critics' vantage, conscripting attorneys undermines the fundamental rights of due process and just compensation; it is a form of "latent fascism" and "involuntary servitude."

The legal basis for such objections is unconvincing. A well-established line of precedent holds that Thirteenth Amendment prohibitions extend only to physical restraint or a threat of legal confinement. They do not apply if individuals may choose freedom at a price. Since sanctions for refusing pro bono work would not include incarceration, most courts have rejected involuntary servitude challenges.

Leading decisions have also dismissed objections based on the takings clause. Their reasoning is that "the Fifth Amendment does not require that the Government pay for the performance of a public duty [if] it is already owed." As long as the required amount of service is not unreasonable, takings claims generally have failed. * * *

Not only are lawyers' takings and involuntary-servitude objections unpersuasive as a legal matter, they are unconvincing as a moral claim. Requiring the equivalent of an hour a week of uncompensated assistance hardly seems like slavery. * * *

The stronger arguments against pro bono obligations involve pragmatic rather than moral concerns. Many opponents who support such obligations in principle worry that they would prove ineffective in practice. A threshold problem involves defining the services that would satisfy a pro bono requirement. If the definition is broad, and encompasses any charitable work for a nonprofit organization or needy individual, then experience suggests that poor people will not be the major beneficiaries. Most lawyers have targeted their pro bono efforts at friends, relatives, or matters designed to attract or accommodate paying clients. A loosely defined requirement is likely to assist predominately middle-class individuals and organizations such as hospitals, museums, and churches. By contrast, limiting a pro bono requirement to low-income clients who have been given preferred status in the ABA's current rule would exclude many crucial public-interest contributions, such as work for environmental, women's rights, or civil rights organizations. Any compromise effort to permit some but not all charitable groups to qualify for pro bono credit would bump up against charges of political bias.

A related objection to mandatory pro bono requirements is that lawyers who lack expertise or motivation to serve under-represented groups will not provide cost-effective assistance. In opponents' view, having corporate lawyers dabble in poverty cases will provide unduly expensive, often incompetent services. The performance of attorneys required to accept uncompensated appointments in criminal cases does not inspire confidence that unwillingly conscripted practitioners would provide acceptable representation. Critics also worry that some lawyers' inexperience and insensitivity in dealing with low-income clients will compromise the objectives that pro bono requirements seek to advance.

Requiring all attorneys to contribute minimal services of largely unverifiable quality cannot begin to satisfy this nation's unmet legal needs. Worse still, opponents argue, token responses to unequal access may deflect public attention from the fundamental problems that remain and from more productive ways of addressing them. Preferable strategies might include simplification of legal procedures, expanded subsidies for poverty law programs, and elimination of the professional monopoly over routine legal services.

Those arguments have considerable force, but they are not as conclusive as critics often assume.

Moreover, mandatory pro bono programs could address concerns of cost-effectiveness through various strategies. One option is to allow lawyers to buy out of their required service by making a specified financial contribution to a legal-aid program. Another possibility is to give credit for time spent in training. Many voluntary pro bono projects have effectively equipped participants to provide limited poverty-law services through relatively brief educational workshops, coupled with well-designed manuals and accessible backup assistance.

A final objection to pro bono requirements involves the costs of enforcing them. Opponents often worry about the "Burgeoning Bureaucratic Boondoggle" that they assume would be necessary to monitor compliance. Even with a substantial expenditure of resources, it would be extremely difficult to verify the amount of time that practitioners reported for pro bono work or the quality of assistance that they provided.

Supporters of mandatory pro bono programs have responded with low-cost enforcement proposals that would rely heavily on the honor system. In the absence of experience with such proposals, their effectiveness is difficult to assess. There is, however, a strong argument for attempting to impose pro bono requirements even if they cannot be fully enforced. At the very least, such requirements would support lawyers who want to participate in public-interest projects but work in organizations that have failed to provide adequate resources or credit for these efforts. Many of the nation's most profitable law firms and leading corporate employers fall into that category. They could readily afford a greater pro bono commitment and a formal requirement might nudge them in that direction. As to lawyers who have no interest in public-interest work, a rule that allowed financial contributions to substitute for direct service could materially assist underfunded legal-aid organizations.

However the controversy over mandatory pro bono service is resolved, there is ample reason to encourage greater voluntary contributions. Lawyers who want to participate in public-interest work are likely to do so more effectively than those who are fulfilling an irksome obligation. How best to encourage a voluntary commitment to pro bono service demands closer scrutiny.

* * *

The primary justifications for pro bono service by law students parallel the justifications for pro bono service by lawyers. Most leaders in legal education agree that such service is a professional responsibility and that their institutions should prepare future practitioners to assume it.

So too, many law faculties share the enthusiasm for school-based public-service programs that are gaining support among other educators. Such programs share a common premise: that students benefit in unique and valuable ways from community involvement, particularly if it is coordinated with their academic experience. On that assumption, a growing number of secondary schools are requiring community service, and many colleges and graduate schools are expanding support for such service as part of their curricular and extracurricular offerings. Supporters of these requirements believe that public-interest experiences encourage future public service and that they have independent educational value.

Among law students, evidence for the first assertion is thin but consistent. At Tulane, the first school to impose pro bono requirements, two-thirds of graduates reported that participation in public service had increased their willingness to participate in the future, and about three-quarters agreed that they had gained confidence in their ability to represent indigent clients. At other schools, between three-fourths and four-fifths of students who participated in mandatory pro bono programs also indicated that their experience had increased the likelihood that they would engage in similar work as practicing attorneys. * * *

Go Online

New York's mandatory pro bono for law students sparked strong opinions from a number of law professors, including Ben Trachtenberg, David Udell, Erwin Chemerinsky, and Catharine Fisk. Read their op-eds here.

Evidence concerning community-service programs outside of law schools is similarly limited. Surveys of participants generally find an increase in students' reported sense of social responsibility and their willingness to continue working for equal opportunity or helping those in need. But no research has tested those claims by analyzing postgraduate public service. All we know is that youthful involvement in volunteer activity increases the likelihood of adult participation. * * *

From the limited evidence available, the safest generalization seems to be that positive experience with pro bono work as a student will at least increase the likelihood of similar work later in life. * * *

The rationale for pro bono programs in law school does not, however, rest solely on these benefits. Whatever their effects on later public service, such programs have independent educational value. Like other forms of clinical and experiential learning, participation in public service helps bridge the gap between theory and practice, and enriches understanding of how law relates to life. For students as well as beginning lawyers, pro bono work often provides valuable training in interviewing, negotiating, drafting, problem solving, and working with individuals from diverse backgrounds. * * *

So too, pro bono programs can provide other practical benefits to law students and law schools. For many participants, public service offers valuable career information and contacts. Students can get a better sense of their interests and talents, as well as a focus for further coursework and placement efforts. Pro bono experience also may encourage more individuals to press potential employers for information about their public-interest opportunities. Too many students who report interest in such opportunities now lack an adequate basis for comparison.

* * *

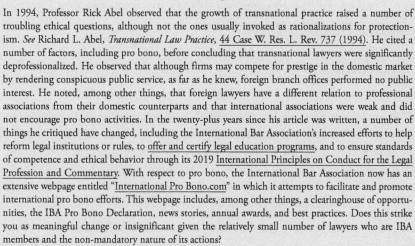

Global Perspective

In 1994, Professor Rick Abel observed that the growth of transnational practice raised a number of troubling ethical questions, although not the ones usually invoked as rationalizations for protectionism. *See* Richard L. Abel, *Transnational Law Practice*, 44 Case W. Res. L. Rev. 737 (1994). He cited a number of factors, including pro bono, before concluding that transnational lawyers were significantly deprofessionalized. He observed that although firms may compete for prestige in the domestic market by rendering conspicuous public service, as far as he knew, foreign branch offices performed no public interest. He noted, among other things, that foreign lawyers have a different relation to professional associations from their domestic counterparts and that international associations were weak and did not encourage pro bono activities. In the twenty-plus years since his article was written, a number of things he critiqued have changed, including the International Bar Association's increased efforts to help reform legal institutions or rules, to offer and certify legal education programs, and to ensure standards of competence and ethical behavior through its 2019 International Principles on Conduct for the Legal Profession and Commentary. With respect to pro bono, the International Bar Association now has an extensive webpage entitled "International Pro Bono.com" in which it attempts to facilitate and promote international pro bono efforts. This webpage includes, among other things, a clearinghouse of opportunities, the IBA Pro Bono Declaration, news stories, annual awards, and best practices. Does this strike you as meaningful change or insignificant given the relatively small number of lawyers who are IBA members and the non-mandatory nature of its actions?

B. Should the Rules Mandate Equal Opportunity?

[Question 9-31]

Should the Rules mandate equal opportunity?

    (a)   **Yes.**

    (b)   **No.**

New York Rule 8.4(g)

A lawyer or law firm shall not:

* * *

(g) unlawfully discriminate in the practice of law, including in hiring, promoting or otherwise determining conditions of employment on the basis of age, race, creed, color, national origin, sex, disability, marital status or sexual orientation. Where there is a tribunal with jurisdiction to hear a complaint, if timely brought, other than a Departmental Disciplinary Committee, a complaint based on unlawful discrimination shall be brought before such tribunal in the first instance. A certified copy of a determination by such a tribunal, which has become final and enforceable and as to which the right to judicial or appellate review has been exhausted, finding that the lawyer has engaged in an unlawful discriminatory practice shall constitute prima facie evidence of professional misconduct in a disciplinary proceeding[.]

AKSHAT TEWARY, *LEGAL ETHICS AS A MEANS TO ADDRESS THE PROBLEM OF ELITE LAW FIRM NON-DIVERSITY*

12 Asian L.J. 1 (2005)

* * *

Several important commentators have recognized the significant lack of diversity in the field of law, and have called for action to resolve it. To address this issue, the ABA created a Task Force on Minorities in the Legal Profession, which issued a set of recommendations and best practices that would improve law firm diversity. In Miles to Go 2000: Progress of Minorities in the Legal Profession, the ABA's Commission on Racial and Ethnic Diversity in the Profession reported numerous disturbing statistics that demonstrate the gravity of the diversity situation.

The field of law is already one of the least integrated professions in the country. In fact, the ABA found that only two professions, the natural sciences and dentistry, feature less diversity than law. For example, whereas African Americans and Hispanics comprised 14.3% of all accountants, 9.7% of physicians, and 9.4% of university professors in 1998, they made up a mere 7.5% of all lawyers. Another report indicates that, in 1996-1997, African Americans received 7.36% of all law degrees granted for that school year, even though they comprised almost 13% of the U.S. population at that time. The case of Asian American representation in the law is somewhat special in that Asian Americans are actually slightly overrepresented, but an analysis of Asian American representation across the professions still suggests a relatively lower presence in the law. The Asian American population according to the U.S. Census 2000 was 4.2% of the national population. According to statistics compiled by the U.S. Department of Education, in 1999-2000, Asian Americans received 10.7% of all professional degrees granted that year, including 18.8% of dentistry degrees, 17.3% of medicine degrees, 20.1% of pharmacy degrees, but only 6.4% of law degrees. Thus, although Asian Americans were overrepresented in virtually every profession, such overrepresentation was smallest in the law.

These statistics are an already troubling disapprobation of commitment to diversity in the legal profession as a whole. Unfortunately, the nation's elite law firms, in particular, suffer even more acutely from non-integration than the legal profession at large. Indeed, the Law School Admissions Council's research confirms that the number of minorities in private practice is disproportionately lower than their number in law schools. According to a survey conducted by David B. Wilkins and G. Mitu Gulati, minorities constitute 17.2% of the lawyers employed by government agencies in the Chicago area. By contrast, they found that minorities make up a mere 3.6% of the large Chicago firms. The disparity is starker at managerial levels: they found that minority lawyers make up 19.5% of supervisors in the government agencies, but only 1.6% of the partners in the elite law firms they had surveyed. Unless one is prepared to assume that the government's lawyers are of a lower caliber, these numbers demonstrate that qualified minority lawyers are "out there," but are underutilized. These statistics are confirmed by more recent research conducted by the National Association for Law Placement (NALP), an organization that surveys the nation's largest law firms annually. The research indicates that, although almost 30% of the country is minority, attorneys of color comprise 15.06% of associate positions and a mere 4.32% of partner positions at major law firms. In fact, 43% of the offices of surveyed firms had no minority partners at all.

It is true that some progress has been made in firm diversity in recent times as compared to years ago. However, there is evidence that this progress can oftentimes be ephemeral; as minorities take one step forward, they seem to take another one back. For example, a 2003 NALP study on associate retention found that 29.6% of male minority associates left within 28 months of starting, as compared to 21.6% of men overall, and 68% of minority males left within 55 months, as compared to 52.3% of men overall. Similarly, 64.4% of female minority associates left within 55 months, as compared to 54.9% of women overall. The ABA confirmed this trend by finding that over 50% of minority associates at law firms leave within three years. There is evidence that minorities suffer such high attrition rates partly because they feel social and professional isolation, and because they are not given quality work assignments. Thus, there is a real risk that, recent gains in hiring notwithstanding, a significant number of minorities at elite firms face difficulty in achieving something more than token advancement. This puts the contrast between the 15.06% figure for minority associates and 4.32% for minority partners, cited above, in startling perspective. These problems are more pronounced for female attorneys of color, who are even less likely than their male counterparts to begin their careers in private practice.

Numerous other commentators have echoed these observations, finding that problems of diversity are especially distressing among elite law firms.

* * *

If one were to accept * * * that elite law firms unconsciously discriminate against minorities, thereby leading to disproportionately fewer minority attorneys working in these firms, a logical conclusion might be that federal employment discrimination law should be utilized to counteract and penalize these practices. However, Title VII has been largely unhelpful in combating non-overt forms of discrimination, both in general and with respect to law firms in particular. There is little reason to believe it could be of much utility to the cause for elite law firm diversity.

Title VII of the Civil Rights Act of 1964 prohibits employment discrimination on the basis of race (and other characteristics). A Title VII case can be brought on the basis of two theories: disparate impact or disparate treatment. Under a disparate treatment claim, the plaintiff seeks to prove that the employer intentionally discriminated against him on the basis of race, color, religion, sex, or national origin. The plaintiff has the burden of ultimately proving this discriminatory intent, although in some cases it can be established inferentially. By contrast, a disparate impact claim is (theoretically) easier to prove since it only requires a plaintiff to show that a facially neutral practice has a disproportionately adverse impact on a protected group (such as a racial group, a religious group, etc.). However, much of the usefulness of this doctrine has been eviscerated by recent cases that have required something akin to proof of discriminatory intent in disparate impact cases.

It has been exceedingly difficult to prove discriminatory intent in cases where employment decisions involve subjective decision-making. * * * [A]side from the usage of (ostensibly) objective signals to screen applicants, law firms make their hiring decisions largely based upon whether the candidate would make a good "fit" for the firm. This is necessarily an amorphous and subjective determination. * * *

Title VII is especially ineffective because it is burdened by what Alan David Freeman has term the "perpetrator perspective." In his view, antidiscrimination law perceives discrimination not as a continuing, psychological process, but rather as an atomistic action or series of actions whereby perpetrators inflict harm upon victims. By focusing solely on inappropriate conduct (malevolent, overt racism), the antidiscrimination regime does little to address the underlying conditions of racial discrimination, such as disparities in money, housing, and in the case of elite law firms, jobs. Freeman would prefer if antidiscrimination law adopted a victim perspective, which would require affirmative efforts to change these discriminatory conditions directly.

The perpetrator perspective is also problematic because it is undergirded by the principle of formal equality. The implication of the formal equality principle is that all people have equal opportunities to succeed in society, regardless of race, and that compensating those few individuals who are discriminated against by blatantly racist acts will ensure that society remains equal. Under this thinking, members of each race are all placed on an even level, and any distributive inequalities that ensue are attributable to merit and worth. * * *

Antidiscrimination law, shackled by the perpetrator perspective, is unable to look beyond the simplistic formal equality doctrine, and is therefore of little use in combating unconscious institutional racism in law firm hiring. Both disparate treatment and disparate impact claims are inherently compensatory and reactionary in that they focus on redressing obvious wrongs and not on effecting positive change.

* * * Not surprisingly, courts have been averse to finding discrimination in the subjective decision-making of firms. The case of Lawrence Mungin serves as an excellent example of antidiscrimination law's inability to correct discriminatory practices at law firms.

Mungin was raised by a single mother in a Queens housing project, and eventually worked his way to Harvard College and Harvard Law School. After working at other firms, Mungin was hired as a lateral by the Washington, D.C. office of Katten, Muchin & Zavis as a senior bankruptcy associate. Mungin claimed that while working at Katten, he was mistreated on a frequent and continual basis. For example, he was excluded from the bankruptcy practice group's meetings even though he was a senior bankruptcy associate. In one instance, the firm called in a white associate from another office to speak with a client about the firm's bankruptcy practice, even though Mungin had had experience dealing with complex bankruptcy transactions at prior firms. Despite being a seventh year associate with extensive experience in bankruptcy, Mungin was consistently given work at a second or third year associate level, and at times at a paralegal level. In fact, Mungin was once called for an important meeting with a client, and was notified that his only role at the meeting would be to carry the overheard projector for a presentation.

Mungin did not receive performance reviews on schedule, but the ones he did receive were generally approbatory. Understandably, Mungin became dissatisfied with his treatment at Katten, and after being passed up for partner, he sued the firm on the basis of Title VII employment discrimination. At the district court level, a jury trial was held, and the jury found that the firm had indeed discriminated against Mungin, and awarded him $1 million in compensatory damages and another $1.5 million in punitive damages. After interpreting the evidence, the jurors admitted that the defense had an extremely weak case, and that they had decided to award punitive damages in order to make sure that it did not discriminate against other attorneys in the way it had against Mungin.

However, two white judges on the D.C. Court of Appeals voted over a single dissent to overturn this decision, holding that no reasonable jury could have found that Mungin had been discriminated against in violation of Title VII. The court held that Mungin had indeed been mistreated, but that this was no different from the kind of mistreatment that some other white associates also experienced. For example, both Mungin and Stuart Soberman, a white bankruptcy associate, had failed to receive raises. Using this reasoning, the court held that the firm had legitimate, nondiscriminatory reasons for its treatment of Mungin, and he could proffer no countervailing evidence to render these reasons to be pretextual. This holding was clearly short-sighted because, given that most firms are likely to be majority-white, the mere fact that some whites were also mistreated says nothing about whether Mungin was or was not mistreated on the basis of race. For instance, Soberman may have been denied a raise for any number of reasons—such as his work ethic, his dedication to the firm, or the quality of his work—but those reasons would probably have no bearing on whether Mungin's failure to receive a raise was discriminatory in nature. This legal sidestepping by the court highlights one of the basic flaws of Title VII burden shifting. Once a defendant has offered any plausible business reason for the mistreatment (*e.g.*, many associates were treated the same way), the onus is on the plaintiff to essentially prove that the defendant's offered reason was not the one that actually applied, which is an exceedingly difficult task unless there is an overt and obvious act of discrimination.

Another interesting part of the Mungin holding has to do with the question of whether Mungin was qualified. Mungin clearly had done complex bankruptcy work at his prior firms, and received good reviews for the work that he did at Katten. However, the work that he received at Katten was at the junior associate level or lower. Eventually, his hourly billing rate was even reduced from $185 to $125. Mungin was overqualified for the work he was doing, and the fact that his hourly rate was reduced should suggest that he was treated unfairly. Interestingly, the judge in the appellate court used this fact to draw the opposite conclusion. In the judge's view, Mungin's former rate of $185 "imperfectly" reflected his capabilities. This point further highlights the vagaries involved in a Title VII analysis, under which evidence can often be interpreted to reach opposite conclusions. Since the plaintiff in Title VII actions bears the ultimate burden of proof, only the most incontrovertible pieces of evidence will suffice to surpass this evidentiary manipulation.

Thus, where there is no "smoking gun" piece of evidence of discriminatory intent, Title VII claims are difficult to prove. In this respect, Title VII suffers from the perpetrator perspective, since only overt and obvious acts of racism end up being actionable. In the context of highly subjective law firm hiring decisions, Title VII's perpetrator perspective precludes its availability as a tool to integrate elite firms.

* * *

In order to improve diversity in elite law firms, principles of legal ethics should be utilized instead of either mere advocacy/exhortation, or the conventional antidiscrimination regime. There are some questions as to whether business organizations need concern themselves with moral or ethical considerations, as long as their actions are legal. However, unlike many other professions, the field of law requires its members to uphold rigid ethical standards in their professional lives. As we have seen, law firm non-diversity can be explained primarily by hiring processes that unfairly disadvantage minorities due to the structural effects of the hiring process and rational economic decisionmaking. In this section I argue that such practices are clearly in contravention of principles of ethical lawyering, and that the ABA and state ethics boards should incorporate these considerations into currently inadequate ethics rules. By doing so, these entities would transform legal ethics into an effecting agent that would impel law firms to act beyond mere tokenism or rhetoric within the realm of firm diversity. Legal ethics could be used to accomplish internally and organically what Title VII and mere exhortation cannot: the integration of elite law firms.

* * *

Typically, state legislatures act in concert with the ABA when it comes to the promulgation of legal ethics rules that bind members of the bar of particular states. Although each state is certainly free to adopt and modify its own state ethics rules, the ABA holds inordinate influence in codifying ethical guidelines and in broaching dialogue on new issues of interest. In 1970, the ABA promulgated the Model Code of Professional Responsibility ("Model Code"), and almost all the states eventually adopted their basic form. The Code comprised of three parts: Canons, Ethical Considerations, and Disciplinary Rules. The Disciplinary Rules were meant to be a basis for disciplinary action, while the Canons and Ethical Considerations were an "inspirational guide to the members of the profession." In the early 1980s, the ABA worked on a new set of model rules that would replace the Model Code's confusing tripartite structure with one with obligatory and discretionary rules, accompanied by explanatory comments. This effort culminated in the Model Rules of Professional Conduct ("Model Rules"), which has been adopted by a majority of the states.

State ethics codes, whether based on the Model Rules or Model Code, barely touch on issues of race in the legal profession in their current form. To the extent that they do, the focus is on acts of discrimination; none address firm diversity. Some state rules of lawyer professional responsibility expressly prohibit discriminatory practices in hiring and in employment. Unlike these state rules, neither the Model Code nor the Model Rules explicitly forbids discrimination in employment by lawyers. Certain commentators have criticized the ABA for not incorporating discrimination into the Model Rules, yet the criticism has gone unheeded. Model Rule 8.4(d) does prohibit "conduct that is prejudicial to the administration of justice." However, the comments to this rule impose burdensome limitations on the applicability of this Rule to the context of discrimination. The knowing manifestation of bias or prejudice by a lawyer, on the basis of race, sex, religion, national origin, disability, age, sexual orientation or socioeconomic status is a violation of 8.4(d) if it occurs "in the course of representing a client" and if "such actions are prejudicial to the administration of justice." It is somewhat unfortunate that the Model Rules did not make a more sweeping prohibition against discrimination in lawyering. Under the comment's current form, it is unlikely that law firm hiring, a purely internal "non-billable" matter, would qualify as being "in the course of representing" a particular client.

In any case, even if the Model Rules adopted a broad prohibition of discrimination (as have states like New York and California), it is unlikely that the rule would be very useful in ameliorating law firm non-diversity for the same reasons that make Title VII ineffective. Indeed, if Title VII, which features a gargantuan amount of caselaw precedent, is poorly suited to address firm diversity, trying to effect change through the hodgepodge of state anti-discrimination ethics rules in their current form smacks of folly. Not surprisingly, there is no case of a firm being disciplined for a lack of diversity under any of the state codes that mirror Model Rule 8.4(d), or any of the stronger state anti-discrimination ethics rules either, and no ethics opinion of any state addresses the issue. Even if the ABA were bold enough to add a disciplinary rule barring discrimination in law firm practice at-large, a case under such a rule would likely suffer the same doomed fate as one under Title VII.

FYI

In August 2016, the ABA House of Delegates successfully adopted an anti-discrimination amendment to the ABA Model Rules. The amendment prohibits lawyers from behavior that is harassing or discriminatory based upon grounds similar to the New York rule excerpted above.

C.   Understanding Implicit Bias

Renwei Chung, *Implicit Bias: The Silent Killer of Diversity in the Legal Profession, Above the Law (2015)*

According to the Sentencing Project, "If current trends continue, one of every three black American males born today can expect to go to prison in his lifetime, as can one of every six Latino males—compared to one of every seventeen white males." Cornell Law School notes, "Race matters in the criminal justice system. Black defendants appear to fare worse than similarly situated white defendants. Why? Implicit bias is one possibility . . . Judges hold implicit racial biases. These biases can influence their judgment."

In other words, justice is not blind. Unconscious racial bias can lead to racial inequality. It is important to be conscious of our hidden biases, but as Stanford Law School points out, "The goal of racial justice efforts should be the alleviation of substantive inequalities, not the eradication of unconscious bias."

Implicit or unconscious bias is a mental shortcut "that fills in gaps in our knowledge with similar data from past experiences and cultural norms." It is a normal part of how we make decisions. Unconscious racial bias pervades our law, education, and politics. It is not always a bad thing, but it often tends to be negative. *National Public Radio* notes, "There are big racial differences in how school discipline is meted out: students of color are much more likely to be suspended or expelled than white students, even when the infractions are the same."

A U.S. Department of Education of Civil Rights 2014 Report revealed that "black students are suspended and expelled at a rate three times greater than white students." The disproportionately high suspension rates start suspiciously early. Although black children make up 18% of preschool enrollment, they account for almost half of the children who receive more than one out-of-school suspension. In addition, the *Washington Post* highlights, "black teens who commit a few crimes go to jail as often as white teens who commit dozens" (*e.g.*, the absurd results from our "war on drugs").

Implicit racial bias is a systemic issue in the recruiting process. According to Marianne Bertrand, an economics professor at my alma mater, The University of Chicago Booth School of Business, "[identical] applicants with white-sounding names are 50 percent more likely to get called for an initial interview than applicants with African-American-sounding names." When it comes to Hollywood, casting directors often say "we just went with the best candidate," but as actress Gabrielle Union points out, "If you're never considered, you never have a chance."

Besides hampering the recruiting process, unconscious racial bias also severely affects a firm's mentorship and culture, which have a direct impact on retention. The Nextions 2014 *Written in Black & White Report* revealed that identical memos written by hypothetical African American and Caucasian persons both named Thomas Meyer had substantially different feedback due to confirmation bias.

Similar to implicit bias, *confirmation bias* is defined as "A mental shortcut—a bias—engaged by the brain that makes one actively seek information, interpretation and memory to only observe and absorb that which affirms established beliefs while missing data that contradicts established beliefs." The report showed how confirmation bias led to the "African American" Thomas Meyer receiving lower scores and worse qualitative comments than the "Caucasian" Thomas Meyer for the exact same memo. The memos were the same, but the results were quite different. How would you account for this disparity?

In their presentation "Implicit Bias in the Legal Profession," Janie Schulman and Stephanie Fong, employment attorneys at Morrison Foerster, point out that that "Awareness of existence of disparities in treatment helps eliminate disparities in decision making."

As referenced by Schulman and Fong, *The Level Playing Field Institute—2007 Corporate Leavers Survey* states that "9.5% of people of color indicated unfairness was the only reason for voluntary departure" and "24.6% of people of color would have stayed at their jobs if they had a more respectful work environment." They argue that a firm's understanding of implicit bias can help protect it against attrition and reduce micro-inequities—"small events which are often ephemeral and hard-to-prove, often unintentional and unrecognized by the perpetrator."

NALP's 2005 report on attrition revealed "that 42% of male associates of color leave their law firms within 28 months. Within 55 months, 78% have left. . . . while minority female attorneys have the highest attrition rate, at 41% within 28 months and 81% within 55 months." In other words, only one in five minority associates last five years at a law firm.

Sometimes bias is understated, sometimes it's rather overt. A new Yale study concluded science professors *widely view* female undergraduates as less competent than male students with the same achievements and skills. As a result, "professors were less likely to offer the women mentoring or a job."

In Joan Williams's study "Double Jeopardy?—Gender Bias Against Women of Color in Science," her team interviewed 60 women of color in the science, technology, engineering and math fields (STEM). In the study, 100% of women of color experienced gender bias. In addition to gender bias, "Women of color also encounter racial and ethnic stereotypes, putting them in 'a double jeopardy.' "

* * *

Judges are not colorblind. Teachers are not colorblind. Our society is not colorblind. To believe you are colorblind is to be naive; to believe the justice system is colorblind is to be clueless. We should all be conscious of our hidden biases. We should be mindful of the legacies we have all inherited. It is important to understand how the media influences us. We are wired for prejudice, but this does not have to be fatal. Practice and training are the best ways, perhaps the only methods, to overcome unconscious racial bias that leads to inequitable decisions and disparate results.

First, we should seek to understand our unconscious racial bias so we can address *substantive inequalities*. Second, law firms must also understand and recognize that unconscious racial bias exists. Third, firms should conduct "Unconscious Bias @ Work Training/Workshops" this year, if they haven't already. A typical one-day course on hidden biases for 50 people costs an average of $2,000 to $6,000. The return on investment on proper training would be tremendous. Willful ignorance of hidden biases coupled with refusal of proper training is a deadly formula for diversity in any profession.

It is evident that unconscious racial bias pervades our law, education, and politics. It is inexcusable for us to permit negative hidden biases to continually operate in our blind spots; they must be brought to light. We must be cognizant and cautious of our automatic behaviors and established beliefs. Our implicit bias is silently killing diversity in our profession. The question is, what are we going to do about it?

D.   The Concept of Behavioral Legal Ethics

JEAN R. STERNLIGHT AND JENNIFER K. ROBBENOLT, *BEHAVIORAL LEGAL ETHICS*

45 Ariz. St. L. J. 1107 (2013)

Unethical decisions are more likely when the decision maker does not see the decision at hand as involving ethical issues or when she believes that any potential ethical challenges can easily be overcome. Each of us tends to believe that we see the world objectively; to see ourselves as more fair, unbiased, competent, and deserving than average; and to be overconfident about our abilities and prospects. This tendency to view the self in positive terms is heightened when the characteristic at issue is socially desirable—as is the case with ethical behavior. Indeed, attorneys tend to believe that their own ethics and their firm's ethical standards are more stringent than those of other attorneys and other firms. These views of the self can lead to an ethical blind spot that impedes our ability to perceive and thoughtfully consider the ethical tensions we inevitably face. If we are objective, fair, and unbiased, then we need not be concerned that we might take unfair advantage of another or unfairly privilege one person or position over another. If we are competent, then we need not question our ability to act or decide appropriately. If we are deserving, then any benefits we receive must be warranted. If we do not realize that our judgments of fairness are influenced by our own interests, then we do not need to be on guard against such conflicts. And if we are overconfident—in our own ethical judgment, or in our ability to fix or otherwise manage ethical problems—then we are unlikely to stop and think carefully about a decision or to revisit that decision later. In addition, people commonly make inaccurate forecasts of their own future emotions and behavior—and, thus, may predict that they will act ethically when this is not necessarily so. It is clear that in the heat of the moment, we respond to a variety of incentives and practical forces. We want to impress (or at least not disappoint) the client by reaching the settlement, getting the contract signed, or winning the case. We want to be seen (and to see ourselves) as competent. Members of a firm don't want to act against the culture of the firm, or put their promotion or job at risk. Decision makers feel pressure to make decisions quickly and efficiently. But when we are predicting our future behavior, we focus on our idealistic self—the self that "places principles and values above practical considerations and seeks to express the person's sense of true self." With this ideal self in mind, abstract ethical considerations, rather than situational pressures, tend to be our focus and we anticipate that we will act ethically. When the time horizon shortens and we are in the moment, our attention shifts to our pragmatic self—the self that is "primarily guided by practical concerns" and is likely to seize opportunity, act impulsively, and focus on the pragmatics of the situation.

* * *

The psychological tendencies that may lead people to behave unethically can be compounded by particular aspects of legal practice. The rules governing professional conduct, the agency relationship between attorney and client, the role of advocate, the demands of practice, the status inherent in the legal profession, and the social environment of the firm or practice area can all influence how lawyers make decisions about issues that implicate ethics. While we recognize that other professions face ethical challenges as well, we think it is helpful to focus on those aspects of law practice that are most likely to influence attorneys.

The regulation of lawyers' professional conduct draws on rules and norms from a variety of sources. Attorneys are, of course, regulated by the rules of professional conduct adopted in their own jurisdiction. These rules typically cover, for example, conflicts of interest, veracity, confidentiality, advertising, billing, trust funds, and sex with clients. Ethical constraints in particular contexts are also sometimes set out in statutes or regulations. For example, statutory provisions governing wiretapping, corporate accountability, and foreign corruption require particular disclosures, proscribe certain behavior, or seek to hold lawyers accountable in other ways. Court rules regarding evidence, discovery, and other matters provide additional regulation. While abundant, the ethical rules governing attorneys leave many gaps, and can be ambiguous and even conflicting. In addition, many of these rules articulate a minimum standard of conduct that must be supplemented with guidance from one's own internal moral code. The frequent opacity of the Model Rules of Professional Conduct is attributable, at least in part, to the potential for intense tension between the duty to diligently represent one's client and duties to opponents, to the public at large, or to the judicial system.

* * *

Resolving such ambiguities is particularly challenging because while laudable values can underlie good behavior, they can also motivate unethical behavior. And, lawyers' expertise at parsing rules, paying attention to exceptions and loopholes, interpreting text, and making arguments on both sides of an issue, while commendable in many ways, can also be problematic in this context. Indeed, psychologists have compared the process of post-hoc moral reasoning to that of lawyering: "moral reasoning is not left free to search for truth but is likely to be hired out like a lawyer by various motives, employed only to seek confirmation of preordained conclusions." This lawyerly approach can contribute to unethical conduct when it comes to ethical rules that specify only minimum standards, that raise conflicting standards and gray areas, that involve discretionary application of underlying moral principles, and that may be supplemented by additional personal morality. All of this is enhanced by the fact that lawyers tend to be more comfortable talking about "rules" and "norms" and less comfortable talking about "morality" or "values." Indeed, law students conclude early on that what matters is not their opinion about a matter but whether they can articulate a credible argument, complicating their inclination to consult their own sense of right and wrong.

* * *

Lawyers may also be affected by the human tendency to be less compliant with rules or authorities that they see as illegitimate. Lawyers in different specialties or communities of practice may encounter different norms or find that particular rules fit the contours of that practice area more or less well.

* * *

For many of the same reasons that we find it difficult to identify ethical challenges in the moment, we also find it difficult to see the ethical implications of our decisions after the fact. Indeed, in one study of lawyer discipline cases, most of the lawyers "were convinced that they had done nothing wrong." And, in many notorious cases—such as the collapse of Enron—the lawyers involved maintain that they acted properly. Once we have engaged in unethical behavior, we feel the need to reconcile that behavior with our otherwise positive views of ourselves, to avoid the distressing feeling known as cognitive dissonance. Thus, we may engage in a post-hoc process of moral disengagement in which we re-characterize what happened so that questionable conduct becomes more permissible. While many people think of ethical decision making as being the product of deliberative ethical reasoning, psychologists have found that ethical decision making tends to be based on relatively intuitive judgments, with moral reasoning occurring after the fact. Once we have made a choice, we are usually able to mobilize reasons to bolster that decision. Given this general human tendency, it is unsurprising that lawyers who face ethical complaints or questions tend to recruit a range of justifications. Conduct that is inconsistent with one's image of oneself as an ethical person can be attributed to situational, rather than dispositional, factors. Attempts may also be made to locate blame elsewhere—on adversaries, on the circumstances, on regulators, on clients, and on judges. The omission bias described above can be invoked to minimize blame of one who did not engage in an affirmative act. Unethical conduct can also be rationalized post-hoc through appeals to different metrics of fairness or to other accepted values—for example, notions of lawyers as zealous advocates or creative interpreters of legal rules, rules protecting client confidences, principles of reciprocity or self-defense, or the need to fight against injustice.

* * *

The common prescriptions for ethical failures are to increase the severity and enforcement of applicable sanctions and to pay greater attention to educating attorneys about the relevant ethical rules. But while some ethical failures are the result of deliberate moral reasoning and cost-benefit analysis that lead to an unethical decision and some ethical failures are due to a lack of knowledge of the relevant rules, a range of evidence suggests that many ethical failures occur unconsciously and unintentionally, even where the attorney has basic knowledge of the relevant ethical rules. Thus, individual attorneys and legal employers should take steps that go beyond these common responses, steps that focus on dealing with ambiguities in rules and standards, ethical issues arising out of the agency relationship, the challenges of the adversarial system, the tolls of law practice, the influence of status and power, issues relating to lawyers' practice in groups, and the difficulties lawyers face in responding to instances in which others fail to act ethically.

To better understand your own potential biases, try taking an implicit bias test offered by Project Implicit (see here, archived at https://perma.cc/HW3D-8Z33) or Understanding Prejudice (see here, archived at https://perma.cc/4RTC-WB4P). The American Bar Association's Diversity and Inclusion 360 Commission also offers tools (see here, archived at https://perma.cc/KNG3-KBXR) along with the National Center for State Courts (see here, archived at https://perma.cc/TU2B-BCSX).

E.   Mental Health and the Legal Profession

JAMES C. GALLAGHER, *DRUGS, ALCOHOL, MENTAL HEALTH, AND THE VERMONT LAWYER*

Vt. Bar J. & L. Dig., Spring 2006, at 5.

* * * [T]he state bars of California, Minnesota, and New Jersey estimate that two-thirds of disciplinary complaints in those states result from substance abuse. A report prepared by the ABA Young Lawyers Division Commission on Impaired Attorneys says "[s]tudies from the Washington State Bar Association found that 21% of lawyers in that state are addicted to alcohol or other drugs as compared to 10% of the general population, based on figures from the National Institute on Alcohol and Drug Abuse. Findings from California and Georgia estimate that 60% to 80% of lawyer discipline cases are the result of addiction. * * *

NEIL GRAFFIN, EMMA JONES, MATHIJS LUCASSEN AND RAJVINDER SAMRA, *THE LEGAL PROFESSION HAS A MENTAL HEALTH PROBLEM—WHICH IS AN ISSUE FOR EVERYONE*

The Conversation, April 18, 2019

Set in a fictional firm in New York, the TV series Suits glamorises the life of lawyers working in a modern corporate firm. One of the main characters, Harvey Specter, dresses impeccably in an expensive designer suit and expects others around him to do the same. The lawyers in the firm are hugely ambitious, work late into the night (we rarely see them away from the office) and demand excellence in everything they do. For these professionals, work is life. This is, we are led to believe, what a lawyer's life could be like.

Suits is a portrayal we are familiar with. Culturally, lawyers are often represented as workaholics and perfectionists, embodying qualities such as meticulous attention to detail, unemotional rationality, and an imperviousness to the distress of others. And so as a society, we often don't think about how legal professionals might be affected by the work that they do.

But lawyers, of course, are not simply hard-nosed workhorses. In fact, the mental health of legal professionals is a growing concern. These concerns were first raised in the 1990s and 2000s in the United States and Australia. In the UK, there is growing literature on the issue, but many of the issues are longstanding.

Recently, UK regulators like the Solicitor's Regulation Authority (SRA) and the Bar Standards Board (BSB) have started to place much more of an emphasis on the well-being of legal practitioners. This may be because it is a growing area of concern, or because professional organisations in general are placing much more of an emphasis on the well-being of their employees than they had been before.

Legal professionals are also reaching out. The charity LawCare, which provides a helpline for legal professionals to discuss issues of well-being, has seen an increase in the number of calls to their service in recent years—an 11% increase from 2016–2017 and a further 5% increase from 2017–2018. And The Open University is currently collaborating with LawCare to produce e-learning resources to support skills to help deal with challenging legal workplaces.

Emotional demands

In our (ongoing) research, undertaken in conjunction with LawCare, we have been conducting focus groups with legal professionals in Belfast, Cardiff, Dublin, Edinburgh and London. They are from a variety of backgrounds—barristers, solicitors, paralegals and chartered legal executives, amongst others.

Participants have disclosed a number of issues which they felt had arisen from their work, including experiencing high levels of stress or witnessing it in others. Our interviewees have been saying that many of the issues facing lawyers appear to be structural, meaning that wider reform may be required to ameliorate some of the problems.

For example, they often speak about the long hours they do, the high billing requirements they have, their large caseloads and the negative effect that these have on them. They also speak of the alienating cultures in which they work and which put them in competition with their colleagues, as well as how cuts to legal aid in the UK have impacted on the service that they can provide.

Many practitioners also speak directly of how the cultures of some legal environments mean that well-being is often not a concern. The focus for many law firms is on fee earning, growth and productivity. Well-being is therefore viewed as irrelevant. For example, practitioners have told us that there is of culture of "you have got to get on with it" when dealing with stressful or emotionally demanding work.

Some have suggested that there is a stigma within the profession with regards to mental health and that highlighting well-being issues could be perceived as a sign of weakness and become a barrier to promotion. Participants have also discussed a traditional lack of investment into supporting the mental health of lawyers.

Legal trauma

Other lawyers have told us about the negative impacts of working with traumatised individuals, hearing traumatic narratives, or working with distressing evidence – for example, material evidence relating to serious crimes or road traffic accidents. Some have discussed the lasting effect that some cases had on them because of their distressing nature.

In a separate study on asylum lawyering, practitioners spoke of working daily with traumatised persons—including victims of persecution, torture, sexual violence or those fleeing from conflict. They spoke of the difficulties of hearing daily traumatic narratives and described difficulties in forgetting specific cases, such as those relating to rape or female genital mutilation (FGM).

Some participants in this research discussed experiencing burn-out from undertaking this emotionally demanding work. So additional mechanisms may be needed to support lawyers who undertake cases of a distressing nature—for example, making free professional counselling available.

Contrary to typical cultural representations of lawyers, such as those typified by Suits, lawyers are not superhuman. Our research—and that of others—has indicated that this as a dangerous assumption to make. Poor well-being within the profession is a real risk. There is a moral duty to care for all professionals—but particularly lawyers, who need to be fit and healthy to look after their clients' interests.

F.   What Does It Mean to Be a Lawyer?

We conclude the course by asking you to reflect on a theme that has been constant throughout the course. Based on what you have learned, do you believe law is a profession, a business, or both? What does it mean to be a profession? A business? Do you understand your career through a different lens, such as a thinking of it as vocation?

[Question 9-32]

Legal practice is a:

    (A)   **Profession.**

    (B)   **Business.**

    (C)   **Vocation.**

    (D)   **Other.**

Index

References are to Pages